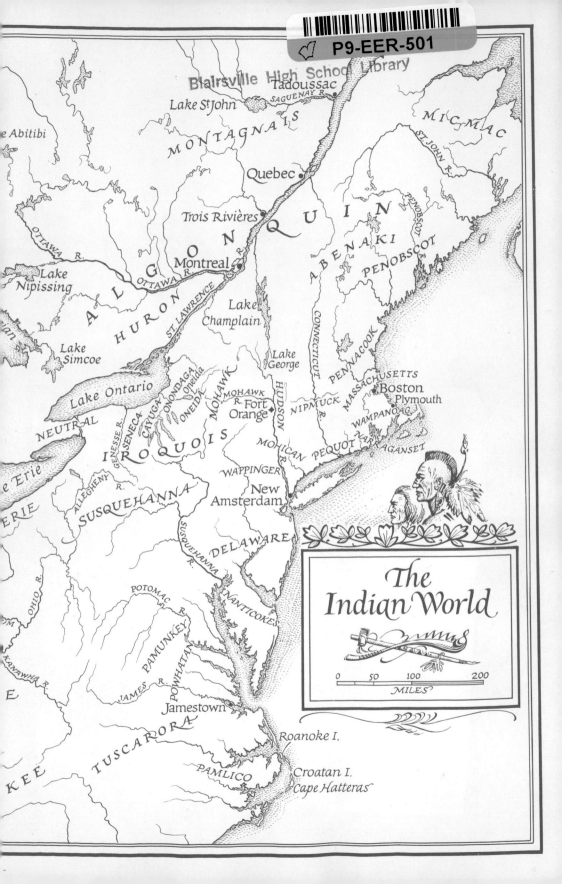

Tadoussac
Lake St John
SAGUENAY R.
MONTAGNAIS
MICMAC
e Abitibi
ST. JOHN R.
Quebec
PENOBSCOT
ALGONQUIN
Trois Rivières
ABENAKI
OTTAWA R.
Lake
Nipissing
OTTAWA R.
Montreal
ST. LAWRENCE
PENOBSCOT
HURON
Lake
Champlain
CONNECTICUT
Lake
Simcoe
Lake George
PENNACOOK
Lake Ontario
ONONDAGA
Oneida
MOHAWK
MOHAWK R.
Fort
Orange
HUDSON
NIPMUCK
MASSACHUSETTS
Boston
Plymouth
NEUTRAL
SENECA
CAYUGA
ONEIDA
WAMPANOAG
GENESSE R.
IROQUOIS
MOHICAN
PEQUOT
NARRAGANSET
e Erie
ALLEGHENY R.
WAPPINGER
SUSQUEHANNA
New
Amsterdam
ERIE
SUSQUEHANNA R.
DELAWARE
OHIO R.
POTOMAC R.
NANTICOKES

The Indian World

0   50   100   200
MILES

KANAWHA R.
PAMUNKEY
JAMES R.
POWHATAN
Jamestown

TUSCARORA
KEE
Roanoke I.
PAMLICO
Croatan I.
Cape Hatteras

DATE DUE

Fac 98-9?			
GAYLORD			PRINTED IN U.S.A.

Books by WALTER D. EDMONDS

ROME HAUL
THE BIG BARN
ERIE WATER
MOSTLY CANALLERS
DRUMS ALONG THE MOHAWK
CHAD HANNA
YOUNG AMES
IN THE HANDS OF THE SENECAS
THE WEDDING JOURNEY
THEY FOUGHT WITH WHAT THEY HAD
THE MUSKET AND THE CROSS

THE MUSKET
AND THE CROSS

The Musket and the Cross

The Struggle of France and England for North America

by WALTER D. EDMONDS

with maps and devices by SAMUEL H. BRYANT

LITTLE, BROWN AND COMPANY · BOSTON · TORONTO

Grateful acknowledgment is made to Ross & Haines, Inc.,
Publishers, for permission to quote passages from *The
Voyages of Pierre Esprit Radisson* by Pierre Esprit Radis-
son, edited by Arthur T. Adams. Copyright 1961 by Ross
& Haines, Inc.

*Published simultaneously in Canada
by Little, Brown & Company (Canada) Limited*

PRINTED IN THE UNITED STATES OF AMERICA

To K
with love
for everything she is

Acknowledgment

*To three friends of long standing
Arthur H. Thornhill, Sr., Gregory Rochlin
and William C. Palmer
each of whom in his own fashion
put me on the way to finishing
this book*

Contents

dealing with the Iroquois menace / Governor Denonville's exchanges with Governor Dongan over English encroachment on the Great Lakes / The unprofitable attack on the Senecas / Dongan's spurring of the Iroquois to side with the English / The Iroquois massacre of the French at Lachine / Frontenac's return to Canada with instructions to capture New York

PART I

The fall of Montreal | The coureurs de bois | Champlain's explorations | The beginnings of the Dutch fur trade | The destruction of the Hurons by the Iroquois | The ordeal of Father Bressani | Father Ragueneau's mission to the Onondagas | Adam Dollard's humiliation of the Iroquois | The exploration of the Great Lakes region by Radisson and Groseilliers | Bishop Laval | The friction between Laval and Governor d'Argenson | The liquor traffic with the Indians | Indian religious beliefs and practices — the Feast of the Dead; the rite of resuscitation | The habitants, seigneurs, and parish priests | Governor d'Avaugour | The earthquake of 1663 | Laval's relations with Governor Mézy | Intendant Dumesnil's investigation of the fur trade | Father Ménard's mission to the upper Great Lakes | Laval and the conversion of the Indians | Mézy's volte-face against Laval | The Marquis de Tracy | Sachem Garakontié's pursuit of peace | Tracy's decision for war with the Mohawks

TWO hundred years ago three British armies came together early in September in front of Montreal to end forever the rule of France in North America. It had been a remarkable campaign, though it was an ironic anticlimax. For the French were already beaten before the armies got under way and had been able to offer no more than token resistance in two brief engagements. The loss of Fort Frontenac at the mouth of Lake Ontario (the present site of Kingston) in 1758 and of Fort Niagara at its head in 1759 had sealed off their posts and garrisons in the west, and the fall of Quebec in the latter year, after Wolfe's brilliant victory, had cut off access to the sea and therefore all hope of reinforcement. Inside the shaky walls of Montreal, which had been built as a defense against Indians but not artillery, Lévis, the French commander, had perhaps twenty-four hundred men; outside, the three armies under Major General Amherst numbered more than seventeen thousand. There was no need for him to haul his cannon, though he did, the nine and a half miles from his landing at Lachine. French Canada had no alternative to unconditional surrender.

Amherst's combined force was the largest, the best-armed, and best-supplied army that till then had offered battle on the American continent, and it was ironic that England and her colonies had managed to produce such an overwhelming force only after their opponent's resources had run out. This was not due to a lack of capacity. In 1754, the population of the British colonies outnumbered that of French Canada 1,162,000 to 55,000. On the face of it, the wonder was that the English had not overrun the French long before. But until 1758 the English had applied their sea power only sporadically; and the colonies were essentially separate governments, with separate and often conflicting interests, lacking a common purpose though menaced by a common danger.

Canada, on the other hand, was a dominion of the French Crown, with a single government, paternalistic in outlook and dictatorial in method. Its spirit was wholly feudal; from the little court of the military governor, through the complete spiritual dominance of the church, to the mass of the people, the peasants or *habitants*, who lived in poverty and accepted unquestioningly the authority of those the king had placed in dominance over them.

[3]

Such a government laid itself open to corruption, and Quebec was rife with it. The fur trade, which was the life stream of the provincial economy, provided fertile ground for endless varieties of graft, which became almost as great an enterprise as the trade itself, and there were periods in which not only petty officialdom but her ministers themselves had bled Canada very nearly white. In the end this corruption played almost as great a role in the downfall of New France as England's naval might or the land campaigns of 1758 and 1759.

But such a government in strong and resolute hands could act with a swiftness and purpose it took England and her stumbling and contentious colonies seventy years to match. Until the final years of warfare there were not many occasions in which, despite the smallness of her population, French Canada did not bring numerical superiority to the field of action. To be sure, most of these actions were small affairs, but that was how the French chose to fight a conflict that they had recognized from the first allowed no compromise: there would never be room for both France and England on the American continent. Partly because of their relative weakness, and partly because in a century and a half they had bred a new species of wilderness man, the *coureur de bois*, or bush loper as the English called him, who as a partisan fighter has had no superior in world history, their policy was to keep the English on the defensive and under pressure by a succession of sharp, murderous thrusts that flickered as unpredictably as wildfire along the frontier.

There have been English and American counterparts of the *coureurs de bois*. Rogers's Rangers became nearly as effective bush fighters, but they were better disciplined, more nearly soldiers; and later the Mountain Men would be a close approximation. But where the English went into the wilderness to conquer it, the Frenchman took it as he found it and made himself part of it with passion — the vast lakes, the network of rivers that enticed him steadily farther westward, the endless shadowy silence of the original forest, the swarms of summer insects that made life hardly bearable, the unremitting winter cold, the deadly polar winds, the iron frosts, and treacherous muskeg north of all; and then the Indians.

Unlike the Englishman or his American successor, who could take an Indian woman when the mood seized him and even in some instances raise her part way to his level, as it seemed to him, by marrying her, the Frenchman lived with the Indian as an equal. He could go whoring through an Indian town with just as much abandon, but when he married he married as an Indian, even though by Christian ritual if that was possible; and not infrequently it was the red-skinned bride who led her white man back with gentle patience to the church. By instinct and the circumstances in which he chose to live, the *coureur de bois* was an Indian. His mind, however, remained a white man's with an emotional acknowledgment of his duty to France.

[4]

So, when called, he could bring bands of Indians who knew no more of France than the taste of brandy or the color of the traders' beads from as far away as Iowa to fight the English on the shore of Lake George or lead them on forays into the Ohio Valley without benefit of white troops to back them in order to bring other wavering tribes into the French line or drive out English traders; but most often his mission was to strike at the English outpost towns or ravage the unprotected settlements.

In these actions he fought like an Indian, but with a feral deadliness that even the Indian could not equal. It was hideous and brutal warfare. To the outer fringe of English settlements it brought terror and agonized desolation that lasted seventy years. What increased the horror was the fact that at no season of the year were the English really safe, for as often as not the French and their Indians would strike out of the midwinter snows. When an Englishman or Dutchman would not dream of leaving his fireside, the French would cross two hundred miles of freezing wilderness to strike and burn and disappear. The English colonists could never quite believe it would happen again; and they were never able to find an effective answer. Now and then a retaliatory raiding party would wipe out a town of French Indians or fight a skirmish with French troops near Montreal, but these were spasmodic efforts at long intervals. They could not contain the raiding French in their own territory. Before their militia mustered, even before the wounds had stopped bleeding, the enemy would have vanished like wolves into the forest, taking with them the scalps and the procession of hapless prisoners, burdened with their own pitiful possessions which now no longer belonged to them. Again and again the "desolate decade" of the opening war was to be repeated until Amherst's campaign in 1760 at last brought peace.

Though, as I have said, this campaign was an anticlimax, it was remarkable for the efficient planning that had gone into it and still more for the discipline with which it was carried through. Amherst's objective was the capture of Montreal, but it was equally important that the French regular troops defending it should not have an opportunity of escaping to the west where, joining with the partisan fighters and the far Indians, they might hold out for years. So he determined to strike at Montreal simultaneously through all three gateways to Canada.

One force, formerly Wolfe's army but now commanded by Brigadier James Murray, 2,450 troops, would move up the St. Lawrence from Quebec. A second of 3,400 men under Brigadier William Haviland was to strike straight north down Lake Champlain and the Richelieu River. But the main blow was to be delivered by Amherst himself down the St. Lawrence from the west with an army of over 10,000.

Murray's army was wholly independent, but Haviland's and Amherst's were supplied through Albany. Haviland was based at Crown Point on

Lake Champlain. Amherst's, however, mustered on the flatland across the Mohawk from Schenectady and then moved by stages up the valley, making the age-old carry into Wood Creek and Oneida Lake and down the rivers to Oswego on the shore of Lake Ontario, which was its jumping-off point. On different dates, Murray on July 15, Amherst on August 10, and Haviland on August 11, the armies set out on their assigned routes, separated from one another by hundreds of miles of wilderness, without possibility of communicating till close to their objective. And yet they came together before Montreal within a space of twenty-four hours. Granted that they had met no resistance along their routes heavy enough to cause any serious delay in their march, this was still an extraordinary performance. Even the enemy were struck with admiration. "Never was seen more beautiful military combinations, or so many troops reunited on the same point and in the same instant," a Lieutenant Bernier wrote home to France shortly after the surrender, ending, however, with Gallic irony, "against a body already expiring."

So, in a bustle of military efficiency, the question that Francis Parkman called the most momentous and far-reaching ever brought to issue on the continent: "Shall France remain here, or shall she not?" was resolved. Bernard De Voto properly took exception to Parkman's statement by quoting Lincoln; but until the Civil War it was true.

The opening move in the long struggle had come nearly a century and a half before Amherst's triumph. It was a small affair, as numbers went: only three Frenchmen were involved, and no English at all. The only English settlement was in Virginia, at Jamestown, and had hardly survived a bitter winter of starvation and disease. Quebec itself was barely a year old, a mere dot of habitation under the shadow of Cape Diamond — three small buildings surrounded by a wooden wall, with a warehouse outside the enclosure. It too had had a bitter winter. Of the twenty-eight men who began it, eight had survived to see the return of ships from France.

Between the St. Lawrence and the James River lay an unbroken wilderness of deep forests, laced by streams and lakes, where no white man had ever walked. The Frenchman who now, in 1609, penetrated it for the first time with two of his own countrymen and a party of Huron and Algonquin Indians was Samuel de Champlain. He had come at the invitation of his Indian allies to make war on their inveterate enemies, the Iroquois.

The French enterprise in Canada had two objectives. One, under supervision of a Breton merchant named Pontgravé, was the development of the fur trade. The second was the colonization and exploration of the new country, which fell to Champlain. In effect, if not in title, he was the governor of New France.

During the summer of 1608 construction of his tiny settlement had absorbed all his energies, but his imagination was on fire with the prospect of finding a passage to the western ocean. Indian descriptions of great lakes to the westward seemed to offer promise of finding the route so many explorers had sought in vain. He was a practical man, but he was a romantic as well: the wilderness lured him like a mistress. And he had also a strain of hardihood not unlike the tough resourcefulness that was to become the hallmark of the *coureur de bois*. Alone of the twenty-eight first settlers, he did not fall ill during the long winter, and when in the spring the ship returned from France to reinforce the survivors, he was impatient to start into the interior.

Any venture to the west. however, had to take account of the Iroquois. Their five separate tribes had once been settled along the St. Lawrence — Jacques Cartier had found Iroquois towns on the sites of Quebec and Montreal in 1535 — but gradually they had been forced out of the country by the more numerous Algonquins and were now living in palisaded towns along the Mohawk and across the Finger Lakes as far as the Genesee River. It was a location of high strategic significance from which they could control the lower Great Lakes, the north-south artery of the Hudson and Lake Champlain, and southward-leading rivers like the Susquehanna and the Allegheny, and hence the Ohio. Moreover in the decade before the French arrival at Quebec they had formed a league which they called the Long House, in symbolic extension of one of their own dwellings, submerging their mutual antagonisms in the face of surrounding enemies. This confederacy was unique among American Indians and gave them a power out of all proportion to their numbers. It enabled them in the following century to destroy their neighbors and dominate all Indian tribes from Lake Huron to the Carolinas and as far west as the Mississippi.

The miserable Montagnais Indians who clustered close to the wooden walls of Quebec that first winter were in constant dread of an Iroquois raid. But the summer before, Champlain had met a young Ottawa chief who, awed by his first experience of firearms, had begged the Frenchman to join him on a war party against the Iroquois. That had been impossible then, but in the following June when Champlain started up the St. Lawrence, he met a band of two hundred Ottawa and Huron warriors who had come to fetch him, and he saw no reason for not going with them on their expedition.

But first the Indians wanted to see the wonders of Quebec, particularly the cannon of which tales had filtered all the way to their homes beyond the Ottawa, so all turned back to survey the strange French buildings and to shout with astonished enthusiasm whenever the cannon were discharged. That night they painted themselves and held a war dance, mak-

[7]

ing the darkness hideous with their yells as they leaped in and out of the firelight, and next day, the twenty-eighth of June, they all set out up the great river, with Champlain and eleven other Frenchmen in a small sailing vessel in the midst of their canoes.

All went smoothly till they reached the mouth of the River of the Iroquois, now called the Richelieu. Here the Indians decided to stop for two days' hunting and fishing, and here Champlain received his first experience of the capricious nature of his allies. A quarrel suddenly rose among them and without warning three quarters of the band jumped into their canoes and paddled off for home.

The rest, sixty men in twenty-four canoes, remained steadfast to their purpose and assured Champlain that he could sail his boat right into the Iroquois country, so they set off again, this time up the Richelieu, a beautiful river in level country "full of forests, vines, and nut trees," Champlain recorded, adding that "up to this time no Christians had been as far as this place except us, and we had a good deal of trouble getting up the river with oars."

On an earlier voyage in 1603, he had been as far up the St. Lawrence as Montreal to look for Cartier's Iroquois town of Hochelaga, which by that time had disappeared; but this was new country, and even through the spare prose of his narrative one can feel Champlain's mounting excitement as they pressed upstream ahead of the Indians; and his disappointment also, when above the small island of St. John the little vessel's way was blocked by rapids. Examination satisfied him that he could neither force them nor, with the few men he had, clear a path to carry his boat around them, and he returned to the foot of the rapids for a council with the Indians. He accused them of bad faith in misinforming him in order to entice him on the expedition, but he told them that as he had given his word, he would go all the way, taking two of his own party with him who had volunteered, and sending the rest back in the boat to Quebec.

So it was that a few days later, with the three Frenchmen riding in separate canoes, the flotilla came through the passage between Grand Island and the western shore, and the lake that was to bear his name broadened before Champlain's eyes. Its beauty captured him, as it has captured visitors ever since. He described the high slopes of the Green Mountains far back from the eastern shore, mistaking their outcroppings of white limestone for snow, which he must have thought strange since the mountains to the west and south had none at all though they were equally high. The forest grew taller than that on the St. Lawrence shore; there were chestnut trees, and quantities of vines "more beautiful than any I have seen in any other place."

They paddled slowly along the western shore, but now they traveled only at night, hauling their canoes from the water before dawn to hide them in the woods. There was no more hunting. They lighted no cooking fires, but lived on sagamité, a meal of parched corn soaked in water. The Indians explained that when they reached the upper part of the lake they would have to make a portage into another lake (Lake George), at the head of which they would leave their canoes and strike overland for the enemy country.

But as it turned out, the carry was not necessary, because on the twenty-ninth of July they met an enemy war party on Lake Champlain itself. They had camped that day somewhere between Crown Point and Ticonderoga, and that evening as they stole over the dark water toward the point on which Fort Ticonderoga was later built they saw a dark mass of the heavier elm bark canoes of the Iroquois coming toward them. The Iroquois sighted them at the same time and both sides started yelling.

But there was no immediate attack and the subsequent procedure was oddly formal and not at all according to Indian warfare as it was later practiced. The Iroquois paddled hastily for shore and chopped down trees to make a circular barricade, while Champlain's party paddled out into the lake and fastened their canoes together with poles tied across the gunwales, to form a single huge raft. They then detached two canoes to parley with the Iroquois to see whether they wanted a fight. The Iroquois replied that they certainly did but preferred to wait for daylight so that they could recognize each other.

There was no thought of sleep on either side. The night was spent in dancing and whooping. From shore the Iroquois hurled taunts of their enemies' feebleness and foretold how they would be exterminated by Iroquois prowess, while Champlain's party yelled back that the Iroquois were going to experience a power of arms such as they had never seen before. When daylight finally came, they urged the Frenchmen, who had put on their armor, to lie hidden on the bottom of their canoes as they paddled ashore.

The Iroquois made no attempt to interfere with the landing, but as soon as it was completed they emerged from their barricade, nearly two hundred men "strong and robust to look at" in a tight formation with three chiefs, recognizable by their taller plumes, marching at their head. Now the Hurons and Algonquins advanced to meet them with Champlain in their midst, but the other two Frenchmen, with a handful of Indians, went into the woods to be able to fire in flank. As the two parties drew near, Champlain's Indians yelled to him to come forward and parted to leave a path. He advanced till he was twenty paces in front and thirty paces from the Iroquois, who had stopped on seeing him, and for a moment Champlain and the three chiefs simply stared at each other; but when the Iroquois began to move, he put his arquebus to his cheek and fired.

Two of the chiefs were killed at the discharge and a warrior fatally wounded. Then as clouds of arrows flew from each party, Champlain put four balls into his arquebus, but before he had finished loading, the gunfire

[9]

from the woods put the Iroquois to flight. In the pursuit, however, he managed to kill several more. So did his Indian allies, and what was even more satisfying to them, they took several prisoners. With one that evening they gave Champlain a demonstration of Indian methods of torture, until at last he was allowed to end the poor wretch's misery with a single shot; but that need not be gone into here.

What made this little battle important was that from Champlain's first shot the Iroquois became implacable enemies of the French. Their enmity was reinforced the following year when Champlain took command of a fight in which a hundred Iroquois had been surprised in their barricaded camp at the mouth of the Richelieu River and all but fifteen killed or captured; and again in 1615 he and a few French arquebusiers accompanied a Huron war party from their country around Georgian Bay across Lake Ontario to attack a palisaded town of the Oneidas. The attack was a failure, but it extended hatred of the French far beyond the Mohawk Valley.

There were to be brief periods in which the Iroquois sought peace, and the French mainly through the efforts of the Jesuits were able to win some over to the church and persuade them to live again in Canada, but by and large they remained utterly hostile, a menace to all French communications to the west, and at one point they succeeded in stopping the fur trade altogether.

Champlain had no conception of the tiger he had roused; and in any case he really had no alternative. The Iroquois were still on the defensive when he met them, and the fur trade had to be supported. The Hurons were the middlemen between the French and the far western and northwestern tribes. By joining them and the Algonquins against the Iroquois, Champlain hoped to cement their loyalty forever to France. No one could have foreseen how quickly the Iroquois were to develop their effectiveness in war, nor the ferocity with which they would wage it, once they had gained access to firearms.

By one of those strange and almost symbolic historical happenstances, hardly more than a month after Champlain's battle a little sailing vessel with a mixed crew of Dutch and English sailed slowly up the Hudson and on the nineteenth of September dropped anchor just off that patch of shore that is the waterfront of Albany today. Henry Hudson also hoped to find a passage to China, but here his hopes ran out. He stayed three days, however, trading with the Indians — not Mohawks but Mohicans, "a loving people" — plying them with aqua vitae and wine and receiving beaver and otter skins and wampum in return.

They had run into hostile Indians farther down the river but here the friendliness of the Mohicans together with the lovely landscape, open in places with natural meadows, "good ground for corn and other garden herbs, with great store of goodly oakes, ewe trees, and trees of sweet wood in great abundance, and great store of slates for houses, and other good stones," made the voyagers feel that this was almost a paradise.

They sent a small boat on up the river on the twenty-first. It returned next day in a shower of rain with a report of rapids and a complete end of navigation. Maybe, too, they saw the mouth of the Mohawk, but there was no reason for them to guess that it would provide the gateway to an inland empire. They were interested only in ship passage to the western sea. So, on the twenty-third, Hudson ordered a start of their return journey.

Though the *Half Moon* had not found China, the Amsterdam merchants who had fitted her out realized that there must be other opportunities of profit where beaver could be had so cheaply. Within a year five small ships were plying the Atlantic to and from the new land; by 1613 there were four ramshackle wooden buildings on Manhattan Island; and the year following, Henry Christiaensen sailed his ship, *Fortune*, up the river to an anchorage off Castle Island, a little below the site of Albany. Here, on the island, on the same spot on which a small French stockade had stood seventy years before, he built a stone fort. It had a palisade, a moat, two cannon, and eleven swivels. He named it Fort Nassau, and he and his companions regarded it as the first permanent Dutch building in the New World.

It stood for only four years, however. A spring flood carried most of it away and the post was moved to the west bank of the river. Then, in 1624, after the West India Company had been granted a monopoly of all Dutch enterprise in North America, the post was finally moved upriver to the site of Albany and named Fort Orange.

The West India Company brought in regular settlers, but it was also determined to push the Indian trade. Most of the Indians who came to Fort Orange and its predecessors had been Mohicans and their affiliated Hudson River tribes. The Mohawks, who were their deadly enemies, had remained aloof. But now Dutch traders, pushing beyond the Mohican boundaries, began to make contact with the Iroquois among the Mohawk towns.

One wonders what they made of each other in those first meetings in the dusky light of a long house. There were no windows. The only light came from the smoke vents in the bark roof. The houses, some of which were over a hundred feet long, were built about a center aisle down which burned a line of fires. On each side were cubicles, raised two to four feet above the earth floor, in which the families sat or slept; and from them the women and children must have watched while the traders spread their packs before the men.

These Dutch were nothing like the quaint and foolish caricatures Washington Irving was to foist on American mythology. They were a hard-bitten, energetic, wholly realistic crew, with about as many compunctions as a flock of crows. A ready market awaited all the goods they carried: iron and steel tools, vermilion, wampum beads (which the Dutch had soon learned to manufacture far more efficiently than the Indians), cottons, and of course brandy and rum. But when they found that the Mohawks would put down twenty beaver for a single musket, they must have realized that this marked a turning point in the Indian trade.

It marked a turning point in the history of North America also, though of this they were not aware. Even if they had been, it would not have concerned them any more than it concerned the Iroquois. To them the Dutchmen were an answer to the fearful French and, being themselves toughly realistic in matters of public interest, in spite of the superstition and mysticism that pervaded all aspects of their emotional life, they were quite ready to buy firearms at any price that would ensure a continuing traffic, and they allowed nothing to affect their good relations with the source of supply. Even when the commandant at Fort Orange, an individual of limited brilliance named Krieckebeeck, joined a Mohican war party against the Mohawks with a view to stimulating trade with the Mohicans, the Mohawks handled the matter with aplomb. They defeated the party, though at the time without guns themselves, killed four of the Dutchmen, including Krieckebeeck, burned three of the bodies, boiled and ate the fourth, and took a few odd Dutch arms and legs home to their villages as edible souvenirs.

The reports of the survivors threw Fort Orange into a panic, and the settlers fled to Manhattan. But the Mohawks made no further hostile gestures; indeed, whatever the reason, they never tasted another Dutchman. They pointed out reasonably enough that they had never attacked the Dutch and said that if, in defending themselves, a few of their arrows had pierced a few Dutchmen, only the latter were to blame. They themselves felt no animus and, as it turned out, neither did Krieckebeeck's successor. But the trade moved slowly until the Mohawks succeeded in driving the Mohicans from the vicinity of Fort Orange. Then it gathered momentum so rapidly that by 1643 Father Vimont, the Jesuit Superior in Quebec, reported that the Mohawks alone had more than three hundred arquebuses.

No Indians ever adapted themselves to the use of firearms more readily than the Iroquois. In the past it had been only their natural ferocity that had enabled them to survive against the superior numbers of their enemies; but now the possession of guns combined with their organizational ability to make them suddenly all but irresistible; and they launched a series of campaigns against their Indian neighbors that were horrifyingly destructive.

Their principal objective was to wrest control of the fur trade from the Hurons who lived east of Lake Huron around the shores of Georgian Bay and had set themselves up as middlemen between the far tribes and the French. The Iroquois beaver grounds were nearly exhausted, and in order to maintain their new-found superiority in arms, as well as to satisfy an awakened appetite for European goods, they needed to divert the flow of western furs into their own hands.

For a few years they continued their old pattern of fierce but scattered raidings along the St. Lawrence and the Ottawa, down which the fur brigades came every summer from the Huron country; but the furs they captured, along with prisoners, were not enough, and by 1645 they decided that the only way to success was elimination of their competition. That the Hurons were of Iroquoian stock (to the French they had always been "the good Iroquois") made no difference. As a tribe, they had to be exterminated.

It took four years. The war was remarkable in Indian history for the relentlessness with which the Iroquois sustained their attack. Instead of sending out a few big war parties at spaced intervals as they used to, they now had parties of varying size continually on their way to and from the enemy country. The Hurons had always counted themselves safe after the deep snow came and seldom posted sentries on their palisades. Now the war whoop might burst from the dark surrounding woods in the frost of a January night. Iroquois parties set out in the fall, built themselves fortified camps, and wintered in the heart of the Huron forests in order to strike when the first March thawing made a long journey over the rotten snow seem impossible. So it was in 1649, when three or four such parties came together to make an army of over a thousand warriors, sacked the two main towns with their Jesuit missions of St. Ignace and St. Louis just south of Georgian Bay, and martyred the Jesuits, Brébeuf and Gabriel Lalemant with almost inconceivably savage torture.

The Hurons by the end of the following year no longer existed as a nation; some were scattered west of the Great Lakes as far as the Mississippi, some had fled to mission villages among the French, and some, taken back as prisoners, had become adopted members of the Iroquois. But the great majority had been killed under the waves of Iroquois assault or had starved to death in their ravaged land or had died on the torture scaffolds inside the palisades of Iroquois towns.

Even before they had finished with the Hurons, the Iroquois turned their attention to the Petuns, or Tobacco Nation, who lived southwest of the Hurons and in peaceful alliance with them. In one short year they, too, were wiped out. Then, without a pause, the Iroquois attacked the Neutrals, so called because they had never allowed themselves to become in-

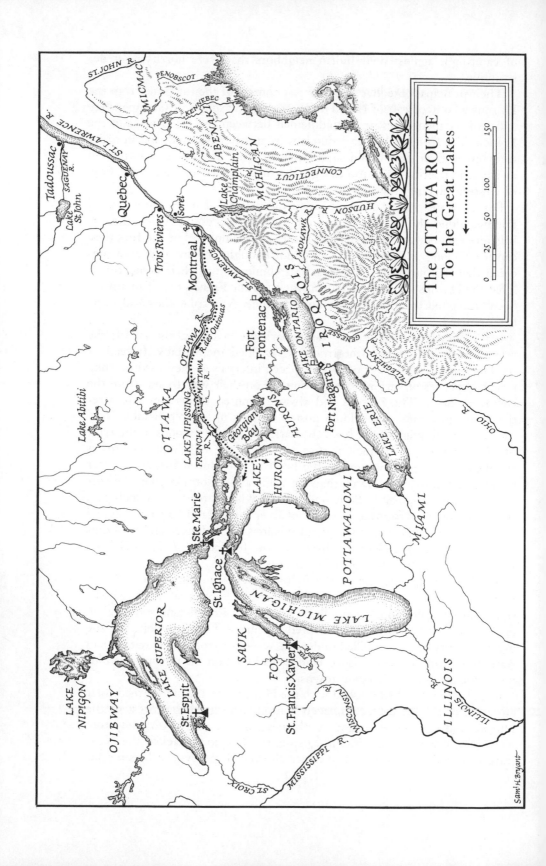

The OTTAWA ROUTE
To the Great Lakes

volved in the Huron-Iroquois struggle. Their country, which straddled the Niagara River and stretched almost the full length of the north shore of Lake Erie, had always been open to the war parties of either side, but no fighting was permitted. So in a Neutral town bands of Iroquois and Hurons might meet to glare at one another across the center passage of the same house while food was being prepared for both sides at the fires separating them.

Now these years of peace were kicked aside. Though the Neutrals were a numerous and powerful people, who long had waged their own bloody war against an Algonquin tribe, the Mascoutens, in Michigan, they could withstand the fury of the Iroquois no better than the Petuns. In the autumn of 1650 and the spring of 1651 their two principal towns were destroyed with terrible slaughter, all the old and the very young being killed on the spot, while lines of prisoners in the hundreds — warriors to be burned and young women for breeding — followed their captors back to the Iroquois towns. The rest of the Neutrals abandoned their villages and cornfields in panic to wander through the wilderness where, being too numerous to find enough game to support them, they starved by thousands.

Yet even the comparative mercy of this fugitive death was denied many of them, for bands of their implacable enemy continued to hunt them down as they would hunt down deer. They covered the whole of Huronia from Lake Ontario and Lake Erie north to the upper reaches of the Ottawa River, from which almost as an afterthought they also drove the Nipissings and Montagnais. The Ottawa was closed to traffic; for four years not a fur went down it to Montreal; and the colony, whose life depended on the trade, was desperate.

But so were the Iroquois, who discovered that they had not only cut the trade line between the French and the western tribes, they had halted the fur trade itself and the far Indians were no longer working the beaver grounds. So, like children striking out in blind fury, they hurled themselves on the Eries.

The Eries, like the Hurons, Petuns, and Neutrals, were also an Iroquois people, but they were far more unified than the other tribes. Their towns along the south shore of Lake Erie were heavily palisaded, and while they had no firearms, their use of poisoned arrows made them almost as effective in battle. The Iroquois found them so formidable that they made peace with the French, and the Onondagas even begged for a French mission colony to be set up in their country.

The year before, in 1654, Father Simon Le Moyne had first visited them at their invitation to explore the possibilities. Now in 1655 Fathers Dablon and Chaumonot came to Onondaga for an extended visit. They admired the setting of the Indian town. It stood on a hill between the forks of Limestone Creek, about two miles south of the present town of Manlius, its one hundred and forty houses placed irregularly among the cornfields. The forests beyond abounded with game, the creeks with fish. The fathers had never met more beautiful country; it was almost a paradise. And one day their hosts took them to see a wonder, a spring of rancid-tasting water about twelve miles to the north. The Onondagas believed that a demon living far underground defiled it; but when the Jesuits tasted it, they found it salt. Here in time would be the saltworks that formed the first great industry of the Syracuse area.

The Fathers were hospitably treated wherever they went, especially by the Christian Hurons, who, though now naturalized Iroquois or slaves, had clung to their religion and greeted the Jesuits with touching warmth. It was encouraging to find such kindness among people who had so lately been the scourge of Canada, even though they were warned that the Mohawks had no intention of giving up their war for long. And they were reminded of the latent savagery of their hosts when a prisoner of the Cat Nation, as the Iroquois called the Eries because of their flat eyes, was brought home for burning. "He was only two hours in torment, because of his youth," reported Dablon, "but he displayed such fortitude that not a tear or cry escaped him from amid the flames." He was ten years old.

The cruelty of the Iroquois to prisoners was a specter that moved step for step with every wilderness traveler. The other tribes practiced torture, but never with the diabolical and obscene imaginativeness employed by the Iroquois.

I know not whether Your Paternity will recognize the letter of a poor cripple, who formerly, when in perfect health, was well known to you. The letter is badly written, and quite soiled, because, in addition to other inconveniences, he who writes it has only one whole finger on his right hand; and it is difficult to avoid staining the paper with the blood which flows from his wounds, not yet healed: he uses arquebus powder for ink, and the earth for a table. He writes it from the country of the Iroquois . . .

Thus the Jesuit, Francesco Bressani, began his first report on his captivity to the Father General of the Order in Europe, a letter that did not leave the Iroquois country, however, until the author himself had been ransomed by some kindly Dutch. At this point he did not mention that there were no whole fingers at all on his left hand, nor that the toes had been twisted from his feet: those details come to light, almost in casual mention, as his modest narrative proceeds with a detachment of statement that gives fresh perspective both to cruelty and man's ability to accept pain.

In many ways Bressani's experience was unique, due as much to the quality of his mind, perhaps, as to Iroquois caprice. As Isaac Jogues had been two years earlier, Bressani was captured with his party on the St. Lawrence by Mohawks while on his way up to the Huron missions in the spring of 1644. Like Jogues, too, he did not die under the tortures that fell to his lot, though his lasted nearly twice as long.

He was taken on the twenty-seventh of April; the date of his letter to the Father General was July 15, and though the Iroquois had decided on the nineteenth of June to spare his life, his wounds still ran and he crouched in the shadow of death. He did not suffer immediate mutilation of his hands as Jogues had on the night after his capture — it was the favorite Iroquois preliminary torment — but he was made to watch while they cut up the body of a Christian Huron, boiled it, and ate it. Then they loaded him with packs he could barely stagger under and drove him barefoot through the snowy April woods, beating him whenever he faltered or failed to understand their orders and mocking him with details of the death they had in store for him.

On the upper Hudson, eighteen days after he had been taken, the party came upon a fishing camp of four hundred Iroquois. It marked the beginning of serious torture. They stripped him naked, and as they led him toward the camp of little huts, he saw for the first time the double line of the gantlet — what Father Jogues had called "the narrow way of Paradise" — men, women, and children, all clamoring with rage or furious laughter, and armed with clubs, iron rods, thorny branches to flog the prisoners past.

Bressani was the first to enter the line, preceded and followed by an Iroquois so that he could not run; but he had hardly taken a step when a young brave confronted him and taking his left hand drove a knife between the third and little finger with such force that the hand was nearly split. He was covered with blood and heavily dazed when he emerged at the far end of the gantlet, and had to be led through the cabins to the torture scaffold in the center of the camp.

This, with the fires burning before it, was the symbol of dread that every forest wanderer carried with him wherever he might travel. "My heart shaked with trembling and fear, which took away my stomach," wrote Pierre Esprit Radisson, who as a youth had been tortured in a Mohawk village and had watched many other captives slowly put to death. The scaffold was a platform of bark raised five or six feet above the ground so that all could watch the prisoner's contortions. Through it rose the posts to which the prisoner was bound with strips of bark, sometimes a single post to which he was tied hand and foot, sometimes two posts, over which his arms were passed and bound by the forearms, which left the rest of his body free "to dance"; and later, as they came to learn more of Christianity, the Iroquois sometimes used a cross. Here the prisoner,

[17]

man or woman, was made to sing; war songs if he was a warrior, or such feeble defiance as a woman might find to utter; but which in any case the torturers, with grave attention to the niceties of pain, tried to reduce to wails of agony, and generally succeeded.

Yet there were many who endured everything without giving way. Such was Bressani, a brilliant and cultivated man like many of his brothers in the Order; he could or would not sing in the Indian fashion, but recited chants from the liturgy, standing in a cold wind that congealed the blood upon his naked body, while the warriors who had captured him, freshly painted and now bedecked in their best finery, feasted on the ground below him and gravely listened. They did not torture him then, but when they had done, they turned him over to the young men who took him down from the scaffold and began the routine of agony that was to continue, in this place and in the Mohawk towns, for nearly six weeks.

By day he was tied on the scaffold, at the whim of every passer-by, though they were too busy with their fishing to spend a great deal of time on him. But when evening came and he had been taken down, the chiefs would pass among the cabins shouting, "Up! assemble yourselves, O young men, and come to caress our prisoners." Then they would all gather in the largest cabin and till midnight all would take a hand in turn in torturing him: piercing his foot with a heated rod, tearing out a nail — the warriors kept their own thumbnails long for the purpose; they would drive them under the sufferer's nail and pry it up so that they could pull it with their teeth, with which they then crushed the bleeding end of the finger, or they would place it in the bowls of their glowing pipes until the end charred and the bleeding stopped. They tore out most of his hair and beard, which was offensive to them. They burned his fingers — the first joint on one night, on the next the second. They burned his body with red-hot irons; they made him walk between the fires on pointed sticks driven in the ground. When they tired, they tied him on the ground, hands and legs outspread in a St. Andrew's cross, and the children came from their corners on the sleeping pads to drop hot coals on his body, or reopened his wounds by scratching them with thorns.

A little after midnight, as a rule, they would tire of the sport and take him outside and leave him in the cold, tied to a stake, without covering, unable to sleep, hardly at times with strength enough to turn his mind to prayer. Then a Huron captive, seeking to ingratiate himself, informed the Mohawks that Bressani was a man of importance among the French, the equivalent of a chief, which overjoyed them. They decided that he was too great a prize to be kept merely for the entertainment of a fishing camp: he should be taken home and there be burned to death and eaten. So the following day, which was the twenty-ninth of his captivity, the war party set out for the Mohawk Valley.

Wounded, nearly naked, half starved, and again loaded down with

[18]

packs, Bressani could barely keep up on the four-day march. Whenever he fell behind, men were sent back to flog him forward. On one occasion he fell into a river and was nearly drowned, but no one would help him. Instead they jeered his feeble efforts to save himself, and that night "they did not omit to burn off one of my nails."

The trail led southwest to strike the Mohawk near present Amsterdam; and the party crossed over to the south bank and struck west, crossing the Schoharie on their way, till they came to the first of the three Mohawk towns. This was Osseruenon, on the site of Auriesville, where Jogues had been tortured with his two lay assistants, Goupil and Couture, and was to suffer martyrdom.

Here again Bressani was led through the gantlet. His hand was split once more, this time between the middle and forefingers. He was beaten so heavily that he fell to the ground, half dead; but that did not stop the blows, which they continued to rain upon his chest and head. They would probably have killed him then and there in their fury had not the chief intervened to order him dragged to the torture scaffold. They brought him to his senses, once he had been bound to his post, by cutting off his left thumb and a joint of the forefinger; and no doubt they would have kept straight on except for the thunderstorm which broke so violently that they were driven to shelter in their houses.

Bressani and the remaining Huron captives were left naked in the rain till evening, when he was taken down and led into a long house. And now for Bressani and his fellow captives began a new rhythm of abuse in which the nights, though shortest of the year, seemed longer and more dreadful than the days. "Oh my God, what nights!" Jogues wrote, and though it added to his agony of heart to see their tortures, it must yet have brought him comfort to have two French companions to turn to in the brief interludes. Bressani was alone, much of the time separated even from the Huron captives. The Mohawks seem to have accepted him as beyond the common run of men, or victims, and they tormented him through these June nights without a moment of rest:

> They forced me to eat filth; burned the rest of my nails, and some fingers; wrung off my toes, and bored one of them with a firebrand; and I know not what they did not to me once, when I feigned to be in a swoon, in order to seem not to perceive something indecent they were doing.

Surfeited with tormenting him there, they sent him and his fellow captives to the second village, Andagoron, where he submitted to similar tortures with the added refinement of being hanged by the feet in chains. For six or seven nights they kept at him; they covered him with coals; they threw hot corn mush on his belly and flanks and called in the dogs to eat, so that their teeth gashed him as they fought for the food; and they inflicted other indignities on him, if that is the proper word, which he refused to describe. "In this manner of living I had become so fetid and horrible that everyone drove me away like a piece of carrion; and they approached me for not other purpose than to torment me . . ."

Yet now and then, even knowing they would be reviled as cowards if they were observed, one Mohawk or another would seize a moment to help him eat. Without such occasional help, in his now fearful predicament, he would have surely died.

> . . . I had not the use of my hands, which were abnormally swollen and putrid; I was thus, of course, still further tormented by hunger, which led me to eat Indian corn raw . . . and made me relish chewing clay, although I could not easily swallow it. I was covered with loathsome vermin and could not get rid of them nor defend myself from them . . .

In his wounds maggots grew; they fell from the stubs of his fingers as he walked about the town. He had an enormous abscess in his thigh which because of his mangled hands he was unable to open; when finally a renegade Huron stabbed it with his knife, it discharged so horribly that the inhabitants of the long house were unable to remain in it and left him alone. And now to please their masters, the Huron captives took to abusing him, except for one thirteen-year-old boy whom the Mohawks put to savage torture in retaliation for his faithfulness, and for Bressani this was almost the hardest cross of all to bear. The boy's sufferings wrung his heart, though he himself was now a walking horror, which even the Mohawks, staring at their own handiwork, could hardly find credible. "I could not have believed," he himself wrote, "that a man was so hard to kill."

It had to come to an end, one way or the other; and on the nineteenth of June the Mohawks met in council to decide his fate. In his own mind Bressani never doubted what it would be, but now, for the first time, he gave way and asked one of the chiefs if, after so long a time, his end by burning might not be changed to some other form of death. To his utter amazement, they voted to spare his life. He was given to an old woman to replace her grandfather and she would have treated him well had not her daughters found his appearance too repulsive to be endured, so finally she sent him to Fort Orange where the Dutch generously ransomed him for about a hundred dollars.

What kept him alive? Ordinarily a captive subjected to torture did not last more than a day, a night, and a climactic hour of the next morning when, again upon the scaffold, his life was offered to Areskoui, the god of war for all Iroquoian Indians. The torture followed a crescendo of mounting fury impossible to stay; the tenacity with which life clung to a human frame was unpredictable. Thus in the Huron town of St. Ignace, the powerful Norman Jesuit, Brébeuf, without once flinching or giving audible acknowledgment of the frightful burning he passed through, lived but four hours, while his companion, Gabriel Lalemant, small and frail and at times unable to repress his agony, endured equally savage torments for seventeen.

They had been doomed on capture to die by burning, and their execution was carried out in an explosion of orgiastic fury. Neither Bressani nor Isaac Jogues was treated with quite the same murderous violence. They became, rather, subjects on which the Mohawks could indulge their preoccupation with experimental cruelty, a phase of torture in which they were adept. They often showed a quick perception of their victim's emotional response, trying continually to breach his religious faith; and the more steadfast he proved, the more they came to fear and hate it. This was especially true when the sufferer was an Indian convert. So Bressani was made to watch the agony of his faithful thirteen-year-old convert in the same way that the Iroquois would make a female prisoner watch her baby being burned alive upon a spit and then offer it to her to eat. This was a spiritual violation beyond any physical torture, which on later occasions reached an apex when they substituted a cross for the usual torture posts to roast a Christian and, in eating his flesh while he could still watch them, performed a monstrous parody of the Communion.

Most of the northeastern tribes practiced cannibalism on their captured enemies, but none quite to the extent of the Iroquois, for whom it had definitely a religious significance. Once when a plague of caterpillars nearly destroyed their cornfields, they thought it was because they had not eaten enough of their captives to appease Areskoui, and the situation was quickly remedied. Human flesh seems to have been distasteful to many Indians, who yet ate it because it was a custom they dared not violate — presumably because they would have been considered dangerous radicals if they had refrained. But some tribes seem to have definitely relished it, the Mohawks in particular, whose name to the New England tribes meant "men eaters." "In a word, they ate the flesh of men with as much appetite as, and with more pleasure than, hunters eat that of a Boar or a Stag."

If he had died under torture, Bressani would certainly have been eaten, for among almost all Indians it was believed that if one ate the flesh of a brave enemy, his courage would enter one. Bressani had impressed the Mohawks not only with his courage but by an inner force which enabled him to turn his mind from the pain being inflicted on him and which allowed him also to subdue even the first impulse of resentment against his tormentors, so that on the contrary, like Jogues, he pitied them; and he found that torture became something he feared more in anticipation than when actually undergoing it.

That the Mohawks sensed this force in him and that it made a deep impression on them is borne out in the narrative: "One evening — while they were burning the ring finger of my right hand for the last time —

instead of singing, as they commanded me, I intoned the Miserere in so awful a voice that I made them afraid; and all listened to me with attention."

Though he attributed his survival to the intervention of the Holy Virgin, Bressani also sought to understand the traits of Iroquois character that finally opened the way to his release. Their cruelty, he thought, with its climax in cannibalism, came from a deep inner insecurity, yet at the same time they considered themselves a master race, born to subjugate the world. To torture and eat their captured enemies was an affirmation of superiority. Superstition governed almost every impulse, and for that reason they feared and hated Christianity, which, once accepted, denied the very fears by which they lived. But as they came to respect Bressani as a man, more and more of them dared show him kindness, not only in helping him to eat, but even brushing live coals from his body as others scattered them upon it. When in the end they decided to let him live, they were probably as surprised as he.

During his long ordeal he had had a recurrent dream of waking to find himself suddenly, miraculously healed. But it did not happen so; though free to wander among the houses and even beyond the palisade, he remained a walking specter, and in his mind he carried the specter, too, of the death he had escaped. In the evenings he could listen to the veeries calling liquidly along the Auries Kill, and at the same time hear the chiefs' voices inside the palisade summoning the young men to another's torture.

But his courage remained. The Dutch put him on a ship for France. In spite of his precarious health, he returned to Canada the following spring and once more started on his journey to the Huron missions, this time reaching his destination. He served there for four more years, escaping the fate of Brébeuf and Lalemant, and twice making the dangerous journey to Quebec.

Bressani, understandably, painted the Iroquois solely from the victim's point of view. He was not concerned with their domestic traits, if indeed he was aware of them at all: their affection for their children, their love of parties, their joy in games. Their mythology, which was often poetic, was sheer idolatry to him. He saw them, as all Frenchmen did, as demons of the wilderness.

Pierre Esprit Radisson was one of the Frenchmen who joined the French mission to the Onondagas. He came with Father Ragueneau a year after its founding in 1656, but his account, though not always accurate, is enlightening on certain details. The original party consisted of five Jesuits, ten soldiers, and some forty artisans and farmers who came in response to the Onondagas' demand for a French colony to be established on the shore of Onondaga Lake. In his early youth Radisson had been captured and adopted by the Mohawks; he had escaped, been recaptured and tortured, and in later years, after his long exploration through the continent, wrote out a catalogue of Iroquois cruelties too awful to be repeated here. He recounted the kindnesses of his adoptive parents, but he also knew the unpredictable violence of the Iroquois character, and he came to Onondaga, as did most of his companions, with profound misgivings that were scarcely allayed by their enthusiastic reception.

They knew that their presence was a condition of peace for Canada, and whatever the terms the Onondagas employed in their invitation, they were themselves actually hostages and, unless they could protect themselves, potential victims of the next outburst of Iroquois fury. Fortunately, the commander of their little squad of soldiers, a tough-minded major named Zachary du Puys, lost no time in raising a stout palisade around the mission. The site was on the east shore, south of the present village of Liverpool; it was the first white settlement in central New York west of the Hudson Valley, and earlier by six years than the founding of Schenectady. Within the log-walled buildings and the palisade that framed them this handful of priests, soldiers, and artisans created a little corner of France, but womanless and wholly isolated; and the sense that they were beleaguered never left them.

This, however, did not deter the Jesuits from their attempts to carry the Faith to the Iroquois. The Order had borne the entire cost of outfitting the expedition, and the Superior in Canada, Father Le Mercier, had himself joined it as its spiritual leader. His first act after establishing the site of the mission was to pay a state visit to the Iroquois capital of Onondaga. As the procession headed by the five black-robed priests with the helmeted du Puys and his ten arquebusiers behind them filed out of the woods along the Indian trail, they were greeted not only by the town's regular inhabitants but by deputations of all the other nations. It was an apparently cordial reception, and the French were feasted to the bursting point, so that Father Le Mercier wrote that if their hosts now murdered them, it would be purely out of fickleness, not treachery.

The others were inclined to agree. Though the Mohawk spokesman had addressed them with unveiled sarcasm and hostility, they felt that the Onondagas, at least, were genuinely friendly. But almost at once, as more and more of the Christian Hurons dared approach them, they began to realize their mistake. The real reason that the Onondagas had demanded a French settlement in their country was that they hoped the refugee Hurons, whom the French had established on the Île d'Orléans below Quebec, might be lured to it. If, the Hurons whispered, the ruse proved to be successful, the Onondagas planned to fall upon the mission and massacre the French to the last man.

[23]

Now they knew that they were living on borrowed time, but they dared not give the least indication that they were aware of it. With quiet heroism the Jesuits decided to proceed with their original plans to use the Onondaga mission mainly as a base from which to send missionaries to the other tribes. Chaumonot, who was the most fluent in the Iroquois tongue and who spoke with the natural eloquence of one of their own orators, set out with Father Ménard to establish a first mission among the Cayugas. Then, leaving Ménard, he went on himself to the Senecas, the most numerous, and powerful, and to him enigmatic of the Five Nations. In the following spring he visited the Oneidas, so that by the summer of 1657 the Jesuits had missions with every nation but the Mohawks.

They could not tell how deep an impression their words made as they spoke with gentle voices in the dusky alleys of the long houses. They found the men inscrutable, but little by little some of the women began to respond and they made converts. This was more encouraging than it would have been in other tribes, for among the Iroquois, women had a unique standing and exerted greater influence than women even among civilized peoples. They had a council of their own which could and frequently did initiate subjects to be considered by the council of chiefs and elders, and the succession to the various chieftainships rested largely in their hands.

But though the missionaries counted each conversion with joy and hope, these came with pitiful slowness; and in the long hours, isolated even from the isolated mission at Onondaga Lake, their lonely situation and the precariousness of their existence must constantly have haunted their thoughts. How much more precarious it was in actuality than they imagined, they had no way of knowing. For the Mohawks were back at war on the St. Lawrence even before the greeting feast had taken place at Onondaga.

They had attacked the Huron settlement on the Île d'Orléans, killing six and taking more than eighty captives whom they paddled openly past Quebec, as if daring the garrison to intervene. They had marauded along the Ottawa and killed Father Garreau on his way up to the Huron mission. Then, in the spring of 1657, a hundred Mohawk warriors had turned up at Quebec to demand more Hurons as slaves. The French had given those who had survived the previous year's attack asylum in a camp just under the town walls, where they could easily have been defended; but the governor, an easily intimidated and incredibly shortsighted man named Charny, turned the Hurons over to the Mohawks with the excuse that in doing so he was saving their lives as well as Quebec itself — an early version of Mr. Chamberlain and Munich.

When news of this deal reached the Onondagas, they went wild with rage, for it made a complete mockery of all their elaborately laid plans, and a party was immediately dispatched to Quebec to demand their rights. Only some fifty Hurons had been left behind by the Mohawks and these, considering themselves abandoned by the French, saw no alternative to submitting to the Onondagas. They were joined on their journey to the enemy country by Father Ragueneau and four or five Frenchmen, among whom was Radisson; and it is from one of the priest's letters that we know what became of the unfortunate Hurons.

On the trip beyond Montreal an Onondaga chief became enamored of a young Christian Huron girl who rejected his advances. At a camp among the Thousand Islands he replied to his fourth rebuff by splitting open her head with his tomahawk. This touched off a minor massacre. Surprisingly the French, though Ragueneau had been warned to expect death by morning, were spared to continue on their way to the mission; but the surviving Hurons were stripped of everything they had and driven on to Onondaga like prisoners of war, some to be burned, the rest to become slaves.

At the mission the desperateness of their situation became daily more evident. The war with the Eries was practically ended; and though the Senecas were still occupied in wiping out the remaining bands of fugitives, the rest of the confederacy had returned to their old game of raiding along the Ottawa and St. Lawrence. They were out in force. In the Mohawk towns only old men remained with the women and children. Their primary objective was to kill Algonquins, but soon they were breaking into French houses and insolently helping themselves to the habitants' possessions. The country around Montreal, particularly, was infested by these marauders. Then three Frenchmen were murdered, and it was reported that a war party of twelve hundred was on its way.

Fortunately for Canada in this crisis, the intimidated Charny had resigned and a resolute soldier named Ailleboust had replaced him as governor. Ailleboust seized twelve Iroquois as hostages. He bluntly refused to give them up to the furious deputations sent to secure their release. His action not only put a damper on the Iroquois looters, it probably also saved the mission at Onondaga, for even the young warriors, who had no respect for treaties as a rule nor the restraining council of the elders, hesitated to murder the French while their own people were held at Quebec.

But it was only a temporary respite for the little colony. Rumors began to come to the Jesuits of a secret council that had determined on liquidation of the mission. Then they were told that the Onondagas intended to make prisoners of them in the spring and by torturing them outside the walls of Montreal gain the release of their own countrymen, after which all the Five Nations would join in attacking the Canadian settlements. As winter closed in, these rumors were finally confirmed by an Onondaga convert. Sometime before spring, he told them, the mission was to be destroyed and everyone in it murdered. It was only because of the hostages in Quebec that the Onondagas had so far stayed their hands.

Panic seized the little colony. Nine of the ten soldiers wanted to desert. But there was no way for them to do so. The Onondagas had put up bark lodges all about the mission and, while they remained friendly enough on the surface, not a move could be made beyond the palisade without their knowledge. Even if it had been possible to elude their vigilance, ice had long since closed the lake and river, and to go afoot would mean a journey through hundreds of miles of frozen wilderness, a prospect which to troops fresh from France was as deadly as the Indian hatchets.

But in the midst of confusion and despair, the Jesuits and du Puys kept their heads and acted coolly. They immediately sent messengers to recall the priests from the outlying missions, a move to which the Onondagas offered no objection, no doubt because it brought all their intended victims together under their own hands.

Meanwhile the Fathers took fresh stock of their resources. Their chief lack was transportation. If the French were to escape successfully, they must all go together, and the eight canoes the mission possessed would carry less than half of them. It was necessary to build two bateaux that would take fifteen men apiece, and the carpenters set about the work in the loft of the main building. Absolute secrecy had to be maintained, for the least whisper of their intentions might have brought on an attack. Radisson, whose quaint account differs in many details from those of others, says that they even built a false floor above the boats and when it was completed took a party of the wildmen, as he called them, through the building to allay any possible suspicion. But the most difficult problem still remained — to get away without the Indians' knowledge.

This the Fathers solved by a stroke of brilliance that can only be described as "Jesuitical." In their dealings with the Hurons and Iroquois they had preached constantly against the superstitions that governed their pagan life. One common to both tribes, which they had found especially revolting, they now proposed without compunction to turn to their own ends. This was called the Eat-all Feast, a mystic affair in which the guests were obliged to eat everything placed before them, no matter how surfeited they might be, in order to cure their host of illness or to ward off his impending death. In March, therefore, the Jesuits instructed a young Frenchman who had been adopted by an Onondaga to tell his foster father that he had dreamed that he would die unless he appeased the evil spirits by giving a great *festin à manger tout*, to which he now invited the Onondagas, setting the twentieth of the month as the date.

This was an invitation that could not be refused, for to an Indian a dream, once it had received utterance, gained independent life of its own that could be ended only by the complete fulfillment of the dream. Not to fulfill an evil dream was in effect to loose an evil spirit on the world, and

[26]

so important did it seem to the Iroquoian character to keep down the demonic population that surrounded them that they would go to any length to put a dream at rest. If, as sometimes happened, someone was injured or even killed in acting out the circumstances of the dream to reduce it to ordinary life and thus deprive it of its evil power, that was a risk to be accepted.

So, in the case of the young Frenchman, it was essential that his dream be enacted, even though his life, which would be saved thereby, might be sacrificed in a day or two in the general massacre. In fact, if there had been a conflict between the date of the feast and that of the projected massacre, it is likely that the latter would have been put off. As it was, no conflict appears to have existed and the Onondagas came thronging to the mission on the appointed day with every determination to exert themselves.

The French, too, had been busy. Out of their store of provisions they had set aside enough to carry them on the journey to Montreal. Everything else had been contributed to the feast. All their remaining pigs had been killed and roasted. There were kettle upon kettle of turkeys or ducks, salted down the fall before; larded pigeons; eels, salmon, carp, and turtle; venison and small game; Indian corn dressed with mincemeat and flour-thickened gravies flavored with bear oil. Never had the Onondagas seen the like before.

The affair was staged outside the mission palisade in an enclosure formed by outbuildings and the Indian lodges and wildly lighted by bonfires and the glare of pine knots. Frenchmen joined the Indians in dancing and pitted themselves against their guests in contests for prizes offered by the Jesuits. It was altogether a wild and bizarre night carried on in an unearthly din of singing, Indian whooping, trumpet calls and the beating of French drums; but as the real business of the meeting began, and the French began bringing the steaming kettles out through the palisade gate, the Onondagas fell silent, settled on the ground in circles, and began to eat.

Hour after hour, while the flaring pine knots were replaced and fresh wood hurled on the fires, the Indians ate, women and men alike; and as they ate, the French came and went through the palisade gate, bearing away empty kettles and returning with new food, so that soon the Onondagas lost count of who was serving them or how many were inside or outside of the palisade. The pace of their gorging slowed. "We see already several postures: the one beats his belly, the other shakes his head, others stop their mouths to keep in what they have eaten."

Meanwhile, with trumpeters and drummers supplying fanfares on cue to cover any telltale noises, the two bateaux and eight canoes were carried from the mission house and down to the lake, where the provisions for the journey were loaded into them. It was now drawing near midnight and had turned bitterly cold. A skim of ice had formed along the shore, but in the darkness the waiting Frenchmen could not tell how far it reached into the lake.

Behind them the mission house and palisade were silhouetted against the glow of the bonfires; and beyond, the drums and trumpets still sounded, but to the anxious listeners by the shore there seemed to be less noise from the feasters. This was indeed the case. Many had long since gone beyond the limit of capacity and were stretched upon the ground asleep or in a gorged and nearly paralytic torpor. Some had simply tipped over from where they sat, their bowls rolling from their hands. The hardy few who still retained consciousness had begun to beg their host to offer them no more; but when he asked them if they wished him to die, they bravely made another try. Only when they also collapsed did the young "dreamer" tell them that they had done enough; and promising to come and wake them in the morning, he and the last of his companions walked quietly out of the enclosure, leaving the inert throng behind them under the first flakes of falling snow.

The two bateaux put off first and with men in the bows to break the ice led the canoes slowly down the lake; but once they reached the outlet they found the river free and from there on made all speed. It was a cold and difficult journey, aside from the terror that quickened every stroke. They had to portage around the falls of the Oswego, cross the eastern end of Lake Ontario, which was always rough in March, thread the maze of the Thousand Islands, and finally run the rapids of the St. Lawrence. But in fourteen days they beached their little fleet at Montreal, after losing only three men out of fifty-three, and on the twenty-third of April the Jesuits reached Quebec to report the failure of their mission.

But if the mission failed, it left the Onondagas in a state of bewilderment and awe. They had waked on the morning after the feast to find the mission gates closed. The snow that had fallen during the night had covered all tracks, and ice had once more closed the channel broken by the fugitives. Obviously the French must still be in the mission house, but when the day passed with no sounds coming from it, the Onondagas began to feel uneasy. Some of the young men climbed the palisade and broke down the mission doors. They found not a soul; the French, with all their possessions, were gone, vanished without a trace into thin air. To the astonished Onondagas it seemed the Black Robes must have medicine more powerful than any they had ever known.

With all pretense of peace ended, the Iroquois once more poured into Canada, their murderous bands roving the Ottawa from end to end and storming through the St. Lawrence Valley to the gates of Quebec. In the summer following the escape of the Onondaga mission, they confronted the new governor, the Vicomte d'Argenson, with his colony's chief problem almost in the moment of his arrival. He was sitting down to dinner on his second evening ashore when an outcry arose beyond the walls and he was told that it must be an Iroquois raid. That was scarcely necessary, for in an instant he could distinguish for himself the war whoops piercing through the screams of the victims.

New as he was to the scene, Argenson at once called for volunteers and bravely sallied to the rescue; but as usual it was too late. The raiders had vanished into the forest, leaving their bloody references behind them. So it was to be through three years of a troubled administration. From Three Rivers to Montreal no farmer dared stay on his land and work his crops alone — though at the latter settlement one exception ought to be recorded. A hardy old man named Jouaneaux, with the tough and independent stubbornness of mind of the French peasant, resenting the time spent in going back and forth between his place and the town, determined to remain. Instead of building himself a hut, he dug out a room of sorts beneath a hollow stump which after dark served as a chimney for his tiny cooking fire. Into this refuge he would creep backward each night like a spider, drawing after him a loose pile of brush to conceal the entrance, and here he remained unsuspected while the Iroquois on silent feet stole forward above him to their morning ambushes nearer town. But there were not many like Jouaneaux, and the governor soon reported that he could not find more than a hundred men among the colonists capable of carrying the fight to the Iroquois.

Not only the life of the colony was at stake, he wrote the Court in Paris; if the Holy Faith itself was to survive in North America, it would be necessary to wage offensive war against the Iroquois, and he asked that regular troops be sent him. When his plea was denied, he turned to the Company of New France, asking for a hundred men of a caliber to join his hundred effectives, a modest force indeed against the twenty-four hundred enemy warriors. But the Company, which had been losing money steadily, especially since the virtual stoppage of the fur trade, refused further investment in the Canadian venture. They wanted their money back and could not have cared less for the fate of the settlers.

At this low point the colony suddenly found itself confronted by a real calamity. In the spring of 1660 a Mohican Indian who had been naturalized by the Iroquois was captured by the Algonquins and brought to Quebec for burning, a fate carried out with all the appropriate agonies. The Jesuits who attended him made no effort to save his life, which they could easily have done: it seemed enough to them to save his soul. Perhaps as one of them wrote afterward they could never feel quite sure about his being on the road to Paradise without seeing him through the fiery ordeal on earth. And possibly there was a practical consideration in this line of reasoning, a converted Iroquois in heaven being a far safer bet than one surviving on earth, whatever the situation of his soul. Be that as it may, they achieved the Mohican's conversion and in doing it so moved him that, before his death, in gratitude he told them that the Iroquois had laid plans for the total destruction of Canada that summer.

Eight hundred of them were even now waiting near Montreal, and they were to be joined by another force of four hundred who had spent the winter up the Ottawa. Together they intended to surprise Quebec, kill the governor, and destroy the town. Then they would sweep back up the river against Three Rivers and Montreal.

The news threw the entire colony into a panic. Possibly Quebec could withstand such an assault, but there seemed no hope for the other towns with their much weaker defenses, unless a miracle should intervene. Strangely, one did, the result of a single young man's romantic idea that amid such gloomy shadows the way to safety could be lighted only by an act of courage.

Adam Dollard, twenty-five years old and only three years in the colony, had for some time dreamed of striking a blow against the Iroquois, and sixteen other young men of Montreal had been inspired to join him and had sworn to meet fate with him, however it might come, for life or death. All but three (the eldest of whom was thirty-one) were in their twenties and came from every walk of life represented in the colony, yet they embarked on the expedition with the same romantic, almost mystical exaltation of spirit as Dollard himself. None of them had done any Indian fighting, none had any real experience of the wilderness; but when some older hands at Montreal begged them to wait till the end of the spring planting that they might also join the party, Dollard refused.

The seventeen young Frenchmen set forth at once on a journey which their inexperience made painfully difficult. They were such inept canoe-ists that it took them almost a week to win past the swift water just above Montreal, and the fact that they managed to fight their way up the spring fury of the Ottawa is almost incredible. But they did, finally reaching the Long Sault.

There was no necessity of struggling farther, for the tumultuous rapids made portaging obligatory to everyone, whether heading up or down stream, and sooner or later the Iroquois were bound to come to them along the shore. Near the foot of the rapids they found an abandoned, half-rotting Indian stockade in which they pitched their camp. Here in a day or two they were joined by forty Christian Hurons under their last great war chief, Annahotaha, and four Algonquins, who had set out from Quebec and Three Rivers to find and fight the Iroquois and who, hearing of Dollard's enterprise, had resolved to join it. The French accepted them as comrades; night and morning the little garrison, now numbering sixty-one, made their devotions together in their separate tongues and, at peace in their own minds, settled down to wait for the enemy. They were not long in coming.

Two days later Huron scouts reported two canoes heading downstream for the rapids. An ambush was hastily set at the landing place, but the French and their allies were so overeager that they fired wildly and some of the Iroquois escaped to carry word back to the main body. This as it turned out was the same one that the Mohican had spoken of as wintering on the Ottawa; they were on their way to their rendezvous with the great war party near Montreal; and the news their returning scouts bore brought them swarming down the river for revenge, two hundred strong.

Dollard's party had barely time to retreat into their palisade before the Iroquois attacked them. They beat them off, and the Iroquois then proposed a truce. When this was refused, the Iroquois withdrew into the woods to build themselves a palisade.

Apparently neither Dollard nor any of his men had given thought to the state of their own defenses, but now the enemy's retreat gave them a chance to repair their palisade and build another inside it. Before the work was finished, however, the Iroquois came at them once more. But again they were driven back. The Hurons and Algonquins fought with unusual coolness and the young Frenchmen were becoming increasingly effective in their fire. They beat off several more attacks during the day; and at each retreat the Iroquois left more dead behind them, until late in the afternoon one of their leading chiefs was killed. Seeing this, the French made a sally, cut off his head, and mounted it on their palisade while the Iroquois raged and howled from the woods.

There was no question now of their leaving. It was bad enough to be thwarted by a handful of men in a fortification little better than a barnyard fence; their honor, after this, could only be restored by the extermination of their enemy, and they sent messengers to the great war party near Montreal to come to their assistance. Meanwhile they sniped at the fort from the woods and mounted sham attacks, keeping the little garrison continually on the alert.

They dared not sleep. Food ran short and the water gave out entirely. Under a covering fire, some of them went to the river, but the small amount of water they were able to bring back was hardly even palliative. By the morning of the fourth day they were like specters of themselves, sleepless, haggard, and weak; but the fire that had brought them to the Long Sault still burned in their hearts.

Not so with their Huron allies. In the Iroquois band were a number of their countrymen who had been adopted and these now shouted to the Hurons in the fort that they had better come over to the Iroquois, for another bigger war party was on its way. At first the Hurons refused to listen, but as evening fell and the woods darkened, the voices became more persuasive, and in little groups they began to disappear over the palisade until only the chief, Annahotaha, and the four Algonquins, who knew they would inevitably be burned if the Iroquois got hold of them, remained with the French.

On the fifth day the war party from Montreal came up the river. Now there were seven hundred warriors to attack the fort and its twenty-two defenders, and the end seemed at hand. Yet for three more days the French fought them off; it was only on the eighth day that, shamed to the point of frenzy, the Iroquois pressed home their attack and finally broke down the flimsy barrier. Even then the French almost drove them out again. Even after Dollard himself was killed they fought on with sword and knife so furiously that the Iroquois gave up all hope of taking any alive and, standing back, poured volley after volley into them until the last man fell.

Though they died, they had saved New France. The Iroquois had no more stomach for war — at least for that year — and they retired to their towns, to mourn the dead and try to forget their humiliation by burning their prisoners — among the bodies in the little fort one Frenchman had been found still living, and the Hurons who had deserted to them were now considered prisoners and paid for their cowardice on the torture scaffolds, except for five who managed to escape and bring back to Montreal an account of Dollard's fight.

Eighty-eight days later the rapids of the Long Sault were witness to a miracle of another sort. Down the river from the north came a large fleet of canoes, laden with beaver and manned by Hurons and Algonquins and also Indians from the western tribes, Ottawas, Chippewas, Beavers, Kiskakons, and even a few Sioux. At their head were two Frenchmen: Pierre Esprit Radisson, of whom we have had glimpses before, now twenty-four years old, and his brother-in-law, Médard Chouart, who called himself Groseilliers, two of the most remarkable in the long gallery of explorers who opened the midcontinent for France and then for nearly a hundred years held it against the growing power of the English.

Two years before, with a party of twenty-nine French and some Hurons and Algonquins, they had come up the Ottawa on a trading venture to the west and at this same spot encountered the Iroquois. The other Frenchmen had lost heart and turned back to Montreal and safety; but Radisson and Groseilliers were not to be deterred. With their Indian allies they had fought their way past and continued a journey that took them through the Straits of Mackinac into Lake Michigan. They pushed on through Green Bay to winter with the Pottawatomies in southern Wisconsin.

Next year they explored Lake Michigan to its head — "the delightsomest lake of the world" — and continued southward to a country where "it never snows or freezes." Everything he saw delighted Radisson — the abundance of game, the rich soil, the tribes of Indians, all of whom treated him civilly. It brought him an exciting vision of what the development of such a country would mean to the people of the Old World, and it grieved him to see they could not discover such an enticing land to live in.

> This I say because the Europeans fight for a rock in the sea against one another, or for a sterile land and horrid country that the people sent here or there by the changement of the air engenders sickness and dies thereof. Contrariwise, these kingdoms are so delicious and under so temperate a climate, plentiful of all things, the earth bringing forth its fruit twice a year, the people live long and lusty and wise in their way.
>
> What conquest would that be at little or no cost, what labyrinth of pleasure should millions of people have, instead that millions complain of misery and poverty?

He saw both what it could mean to France and why it might well never be developed by a government in which entrenched religion and corruption constantly gnawed away the achievement of enterprising men. Indeed, in a few years more, he and his brother-in-law would have their own object lesson. Meanwhile they continued their journeying.

At the end of the second winter, they were somewhere on the south shore of Superior among the Chippewas, but they had made acquaintance with the tribe they wanted most to meet, the Crees "from the Bay of the North Sea," which of course was Hudson Bay. Perhaps recalling then a legend they had heard earlier of a Huron migration from the Great Lakes to Hudson Bay and around Labrador to the St. Lawrence, the seed of an idea for reaching the Cree trade and that of all the northwest by sea was planted in their minds at that time — the idea that was directly responsible for the founding ten years later of the Hudson Bay Company. The Crees fascinated them. They traveled in myriads of tiny canoes, barely large enough for a man, his wife, and a bundle of furs. Radisson reports seeing a war party of three hundred setting forth in three hundred canoes. They were constantly at war with the Sioux, and this determined the two Frenchmen, with the development of the fur trade always in their minds, to make contact with the Sioux in order, if possible, to reconcile the two tribes.

It was probably for this reason as much as any other that toward spring they made an overland journey to the west and so became the first white men to see the upper Mississippi. As the river was already free of ice, they built canoes and paddled upstream for eight days till they reached Prairie Island, above the present city of Red Wing, Minnesota. Here they found a village of refugee Hurons, and Groseilliers, who was suffering from attacks of epilepsy, stayed with them while Radisson went off on a long hunting trip with a band of Indians who may have been Sioux.

The Island Hurons at first refused even to consider a trip down to Canada, so great still was their horror of the Iroquois; but by the time Radisson returned from his hunt, Groseilliers had succeeded in overcoming their fears to a considerable extent and some agreed to join the returning *voyageurs* with their accumulated furs. So also did individuals of other tribes, so that when they were ready to embark in mid-July they numbered five hundred.

It was late in the season to start on such a long journey, but weather and wind favored them across the lakes. Groseilliers's epilepsy had been thrown off, "more by his courage than any good medecine," wrote Radisson, and he attributed the cure to his brother-in-law's having kept active in spite of the fits: "There is nothing comparable to exercise. It is the only remedy for such diseases." So they paddled the full length of the long summer days, and sometimes through the night as well when the wind blew fair, and reached the Ottawa without incident.

There, however, as was to be expected, the Iroquois appeared. But they seemed to lack their usual aggressiveness and after a few skirmishes melted away down the river ahead of the fur brigade. The reason, of course, was the Dollard fight. When Groseilliers and Radisson reached the scene, grisly relics of it still survived. Along the bank at spaced intervals were the bodies of the sixteen Frenchmen and five Indians, tied to stakes where the Iroquois had burned them even though all but three had been already dead and those three nearly so. The little fort with its breached walls was still there, and in its center was a hole in the ground where the French had dug in hope of finding water, but got only a slight muddy oozing through the clay. "It was to be pitied."

Next day the *voyageurs* paddled their laden canoes ashore at Montreal amid universal rejoicing. At Quebec they were greeted with a salute of cannon from the fort and from three ships at anchor, which in a few days would have had to sail for France with holds empty of furs. If Dollard and his party had saved New France from Iroquois destruction, Groseilliers and Radisson by their own enterprise had produced the furs that alone could ensure its continued life.

Yet this was but the first step of their contribution to Canada. During the winter they had discussed whether they should make known their theories about the northern country and decided against doing so. Their ideas rested in large part on what the Crees had told them and therefore they would make no mention of them "for fear that those wildmen should tell us a fib." They must see for themselves how the country lay and what was in it, and determined to set off in the following summer.

But they were twice delayed. The Jesuits had heard rumors about their theories and wanted Groseilliers and Radisson to find a route by which they could bring beaver down from Hudson Bay via the Saguenay River. Whether Groseilliers went with them (Radisson would have no part of the expedition) is not certain; anyway it failed and the Fathers returned to Quebec at the end of July, frustrated, as might have been expected, by the Iroquois. For whatever reason the brothers-in-law were not ready to get started till September, and by then they were having difficulties with the new governor.

This was the Baron Dubois d'Avaugour, a bluff and tactless professional soldier with forty years of service and, according to Parkman, "of a probity which even his enemies confessed." Perhaps the word needs redefining or perhaps the governor, who had arrived on the thirty-first of August, considered it to apply only within the boundaries of his own self-interest. At any rate, he had heard of Radisson and Groseilliers and was determined to get in on their game without delay. They would have his permission to leave, he told them, provided that they took two men of his own choosing with them and turned over half their profits.

Accustomed though they were to graft, the brothers-in-law were outraged. They made the governor "a slight answer and told him for our part we knowed what we were: discoverers before governors: we should be glad to have the honor of his company, but not that of his servants, and that we were both masters and not servants." No one likes to have a dishonest proposal turned down, and the angered Avaugour told them they could not leave without his permission. They then asked the Jesuits to intercede, but the Fathers were still smarting over their own failure to cut in on the fur trade via the Saguenay and in addition would have liked to see the expedition delayed till they could prepare a mission to accompany it. So Radisson and Groseilliers did what might have been expected of them — they took French leave.

They had already made their preparations and at midnight of an early September night they carried their trade goods and provisions out through the gate of Three Rivers, loaded them in their canoe, and pushed off on the St. Lawrence. The sentries on the fort hailed them as they came opposite. "My brother tells his name." Though the governor's prohibition was common knowledge, there was no flurry on the ramparts. Groseilliers and Radisson had become heroes to all Canada, soldiers as well as habitants. "God give you a good voyage," called a sentry. They were good words to carry with one into the western darkness.

The pattern of this journey was the pattern as before, though instead of thirty Frenchmen only one began the voyage with them. Above the Richelieu they picked up seven canoes of Indians who had been waiting for them, mostly Chippewas, and a few Nipissings. Then, about the seventh night, the third Frenchman waked everyone by screaming in a nightmare. He had dreamed that he and the whole party had been taken by the Iroquois. No more evil omen could have occurred near the beginning of a journey; and as the most practical means of voiding it, the Nipissings took him back to Montreal. So once again, except for their Indian companions, Groseilliers and Radisson headed toward the vast midcontinent alone.

They knew now from their own experiences what toll it took emotionally, and before this Radisson had wondered wryly how men could deliberately leave aside the comforts and assurances of normal living — the sight of one's own chimney smoke, the chance to kiss one's wife, or one's neighbor's wife, "with ease and delight" — for the hazards of the long trail . . .

> . . . when victuals are wanting, work whole nights and days, lie down on the bare ground, and not always that happy — the breech in the water, the fear in the buttocks, to have the belly empty, the weariness in the bones, the drowsiness of the body by the bad weather that you are to suffer, having nothing to keep you from such calamity.

On the Ottawa there was the usual trouble with the Iroquois, but they won through without loss by embarking silently after dark while the Iroquois were still busily forting up in the woods opposite, and paddling on for three days and nights without a stop. This left them short of food and they took a brief time out on Lake Nipissing to fish and hunt, but not to camp. They did not feel safe until their canoes floated out of the French River onto the waters of Georgian Bay. "What joy we had to see ourselves!" wrote Radisson. In twenty-two days they had not risked an hour's sleep on land.

But now, for all the hardships that lay ahead, the expedition acquires an almost magic aura. Wherever they moved, whatever they did, they were blazing the trail of history; and at times one can almost believe in Radisson's perception of it. They crossed Lake Huron; then with a twist of the paddle they turned the hinge of the northwest and pointed their canoes for the Sault and so came out on the farthest and greatest of the Great Lakes.

They pressed on along the southern shore, for "the season was far spent, and use we diligence," until nearly at the western end they entered Chequamegon Bay. Here the two men built themselves a "fort," a triangular palisade with a gate at the waterside, while the Chippewas went off to find their wives and families. It became their home post, if so small a place could be called so. But it also became the center of French interest farthest west in the continent.

They did not know that an old Jesuit had already been there early in the summer, in company with a handful of Frenchmen; or if they did hear of them, they did not make any report. By the time they arrived the Jesuit had died more than two hundred miles to the south and his companions had returned to an Ottawa encampment to the east, and by the next year had gone back to Montreal. It is curious that they should have missed each other, for both parties traveled the same routes along the south shore of Superior and the Indians must have been full of news and rumor. It seems most likely that Radisson and Groseilliers, after their brush with the governor, wanted nothing more than to keep their presence unknown. The Jesuits were to follow them to Chequamegon, and it became the first post to draw the far nations into the French trade. The great alliance of western tribes against the Iroquois and English, by which the French were so long to control the whole great western territory, was the work of La Salle, the incomparable one-handed Tonty, Nicholas Perrot, and Duluth, but the seeds were planted by Groseilliers and Radisson, working in Chequamegon from 1661 to 1663.

When their Chippewas returned, bringing a number of young men with them and many of their wives, the brothers-in-law set off with them to the south, taking a substantial load of trade goods, which the young men were glad to carry "for the hope that they had that we should give them a brass ring or an awl or a needle." Their town was on Lake Court Oreille, by the waterside, a hundred cabins without a palisade. Many had never seen a white man. "There is nothing but cries. The women throw themselves backward on the ground, thinking to give us tokens of friendship and welcome." The goods they offered, the gifts they made, were wonders. Everything they did was wonderful. "We were Caesars, being nobody to contradict us."

As winter came on they moved farther into the woods. But before parting company — it was probably late November — they appointed a rendezvous in two and a half months' time, when all should gather to celebrate the Feast of the Dead, and Groseilliers and Radisson would present gifts for peace and union. It proved a heavy winter; the snow lay five or six feet deep and was so fluffy that even though they made oversized snowshoes, six feet in length, they could not travel or hunt and came near starvation.

> Everyone cries out for hunger. The women became barren and dry like wood. You men must eat the cord, being you have no more strength to make use of the bow. Children you must die.

They ate the dogs — even tribes for whom dog flesh was taboo. They ate their own moccasins and deerskins. Finally they ate the beaver skins, the bark of trees, what bones they could find discarded around the villages, ground into a kind of paste. Hundreds died. But the two Frenchmen survived, though "our guts became very straight by our long fasting." And then, to their elation, eight envoys came from the Sioux to establish friendship with the Europeans, each with two wives heavily burdened with a gift of oats.

The brothers-in-law made gifts in return, replied to their speeches in the name of the great and Christian King of France, who, they assured this most warlike and powerful of all the western tribes, would take them under his protection, and they smoked the Sioux tobacco and invited the Sioux to smoke theirs, of which they then threw a handful upon the council fire. It was gunpowder that had been wet but proved, to their own amazement, to have lost not an iota of its potency. The fire flew apart, the lodge was filled with flying embers, and the Sioux were terrified. They were quite willing to believe that the two Frenchmen were demigods and accepted their invitation to the rendezvous, the site for which was now set on the edge of the Sioux country.

In all, eighteen nations came to it and the general council began when the delegates totaled five hundred. While it was in progress, the Sioux arrived "with an incredible pomp," and Radisson's description presents them as vividly as any passage in Parkman.

First the young men and warriors with bows and arrows and shields slung on their shoulders, their faces painted, their hair turned up in a tuft or roll upon the crown, stiffened with a paste of reddish earth and decorated with beads and turquoise. Some wore buffalo horns, some feathers trimmed with swans' down. Their shirts and leggings were of buckskin and their moccasins had two-foot flaps attached to the heels, which dragged behind them when they walked.

Then the elders of the tribe. They were unpainted but wore the same kind of headdress and buffalo robes that reached to the ground. Each carried his calumet and medicine bag. They were men of "great gravity and modesty."

At the end the women, "laden like unto so many mules; their burdens made a greater show than themselves, but I suppose the weight was not equipolent with its bigness." Under the eyes of the surrounding throng the women walked to an appointed spot, "unfolded their bundles and flung there skins whereof their tents are made, so that they had houses in less than half an hour."

Their arrogance, dignity, the aloofness of their bearing, suggest a larger dimension and before he is through with them they have implanted some feeling in Radisson that there is a great west as well as the vast north toward which his imagination and Groseilliers's have been stretching.

> They present us with gifts of castor's skins, assuring us that the mountains were elevated, the valleys risen, the ways very smooth, the bows of trees cut down to go with more ease, and bridges erected over rivers, for not to wet our feet; that the doors of their villages, cottages, of their wives and daughters were open at any time to receive us, being we kept them alive by our merchandises.

To the western tribes the Sioux were as terrible a scourge as the Iroquois were east of the Mississippi, but now they were ready to acknowledge the power of the French and accept the King of France as their master. They were even ready to agree to peace with the Crees, though they warned that they would not wait to defend themselves if the Crees came looking for war, and hinted shrewdly that "the true means to get the victory was to have a thunder." The guns were not forthcoming — not yet, at least — but peace was made with the Crees, and the French had customers who were wild for anything that could help lift them out of their stone age economy and had plenty of the finest beaver with which to pay. "I say that there are no [sic] so good in the whole world."

To cement this new relation, Radisson and Groseilliers were shortly to spend seven weeks among the Prairie Sioux; but before they left, the rendezvous must be brought to an end. The councils over, there were fourteen days of feasting and games, sham battles, and the wild hilarity that were to mark the later rendezvous among the Mountain Men.

From the Sioux country they returned to Chequamegon, built a more adequate fort on the south shore than their first ramshackle effort, and finally set about preparing for the journey on which their hearts had been set from the beginning. Problems had to be solved in finding safe hiding for their huge accumulation of furs and of getting away without the Ottawas and Chippewas following them, and there was a brief interlude with a new tribe that came seeking them from a lake to the northwest — they were probably Assiniboines — but they finally were able to join the Crees with whom they were to travel.

The Crees were overjoyed to see them; they would not permit Groseilliers and Radisson to get out of their canoe but picked the canoe and paddlers bodily from the water and carried them into one of their lodges "like a couple of cocks in a basket." Radisson always liked and admired the Crees. They were the best hunters by far of any nation and scorned to use traps to get their beaver; they were affectionate, completely monogamous, and very modest. He found the women "tender and delicate and takes as much pains as slaves." And unlike all the other nations they would not burn their prisoners, but simply knock them on the head, for cruelty they regarded as indecent.

In their company Radisson and Groseilliers set out from the upper shore of Lake Superior. Some scholars have doubted that they ever reached James Bay — the long southern arm of Hudson Bay — but it is reasonable to believe that they did, probably by way of the Albany River. The circumstantial points of Radisson's narrative offset the ambiguous ones. But whether or not, they learned that summer that the country north and west of Lake Superior and Hudson Bay was a vaster and richer source of beaver than any the French had ever dreamed of; and they were convinced that the cheapest and easiest way to tap it would be by ship, to a post on Hudson Bay. That they never managed to see the bay proper was due to the Crees' jealousy; they did not want their loved Frenchmen to meet and possibly be seduced by these northern people; but they drew maps for Radisson to give him a notion of the shape of the country.

There was an infinite amount still to be learned, but they returned to their fort at Chequamegon with the first picture of the northwest in their minds that had any logic, and with detail enough to furnish staiting gates for the men who were to come after them. No other men in Canada can have had a conception of the North American continent as clear as theirs.

Now they were eager to get home and realize the profits of their trading and of the knowledge they had gained. Though they had served France invaluably as ambassadors, they were practical men; and also like so many men of the woods they were speculators at heart: in their minds the sense of practical reward and their preoccupation with the continental mystery had equal force, if indeed they were not synonymous. But the snows were at hand. They must reconcile themselves to wintering at Chequamegon. Yet the time was not unfruitful. The Sioux continued to pay court with gifts and envoys and, as always, Radisson and Groseilliers kept picking up new information about the vast northwest. They heard about Lake Winnipeg, the stinking lake, and about the people who lived near it and who dared not trade to the south — the Sioux were their informants and undoubtedly a little smug — who were probably the Plains Crees. And of course there were the fanciful stories: of birds with bills as sharp as swords that made war on men; of a river so deep and black it was bottomless and ran always warm — the kind of tale the primitive imagination gives birth to in the confinement of the deep snow and binding frost, as though to warm itself by its own activity. They entranced Radisson, but he adds that "this I cannot tell for truth."

As spring approached they were heartened by visits from the neighboring tribes to promise men and canoes for the journey back to Montreal; and when the time for the gathering came the start presented a sight such as Lake Superior had never seen. In the fur flotilla itself were three hundred and sixty canoes and seven hundred men. Then there were the Crees who had come to say farewell and bring additional furs, four hundred canoes of them. And in addition there were, of course, all the people who had come to see the men off. Radisson does not enumerate them, but says only, "It was a pleasure to see that embarking."

It must have been, for all the young women came into the water "stark naked, their hairs hanging down," to help launch the canoes. Radisson was surprised, for they were not ordinarily so immodest, but they said it was an old custom and thought it a good one.

> They sing aloud and sweetly. They stood in the boats and remained in that posture half a day to encourage us to come and lodge with them again. Therefore, they are not altogether ashamed to show us all, to entice us and animate the men to defend themselves valiantly and come [home] and enjoy them.

This send-off must have tugged at the minds of the paddlers. When they surprised seven Iroquois in one canoe and chased them ashore, they were ready to give up the whole journey then and there, and it took twelve days of hard work on the part of the Frenchmen to persuade them that even if the seven had been scouts for an army, their own fleet was so numerous that the mere sight of it would make the Iroquois turn back.

So once more the flotilla headed east and this time reached its destination — the greatest fur fleet that had ever appeared on the St. Lawrence, so many canoes that they "did almost cover the whole river." As the brothers-in-law looked back at them, "it was a great satisfaction to see so many boats and so many wildmen that never had before commerce with the French. So my brother and I thought we should be welcomed."

They were at Montreal; but they found matters different in Quebec. Avaugour, the governor, had been waiting to get hold of them ever since their clandestine departure; in addition he had been recalled to France. He was on the point of leaving, so their arrival presented him at the last moment with an opportunity of simultaneously venting his spite and feathering his nest. He seized it with enthusiasm.

First he assessed them for four thousand livres (roughly the same as francs) with which, as he claimed, to build a fort at their home town of Three Rivers, adding that if it would make them any happier they would have his permission to put their coat of arms upon it. Then he fined them six thousand livres "for the country," which meant for the government, which meant for himself. Finally he levied the twenty-five percent due the fur monopoly, but which was always distributed by the governor to individuals who could be relied on for a kick-back or, in Radisson's phrase, who would "grease his chops." This last item came to fourteen thousand livres, bringing the total to twenty-four thousand, or forty percent of their profits on two dangerous and arduous years; but as if that were not enough, he sent Groseilliers to jail for having set forth in the first place without his permission. And so, having put his house in order, this man of probity departed.

In New France they had no recourse. They paid, while the Canadian merchants were gloating over the store of furs the brothers-in-law had persuaded the Indians to bring to Montreal, furs of such superior quality that the merchants asked them, "In which country have you been? . . . For we never saw the like." The total value Radisson estimated at something under a million livres, but he may have exaggerated — pardonable enough when he saw others profiting from an enterprise in which they had not had to risk a sou of their own money. And besides the fur, he and Groseilliers had brought a vast new territory within the domain of France. No wonder they felt bitter. As soon as he was freed from jail, Groseilliers sailed for France to seek redress; but, as Radisson said, he might better have stayed at home. He was given fair words enough, but he could get

[41]

no action; and in the end the brothers-in-law were forced to take their great idea to England.

In justice to Avaugour it should be said that his conduct toward Radisson and Groseilliers would not have seemed to him in any way extraordinary or dishonorable. He had had a distinguished career as a soldier before coming to Canada, and not long after his return he was to die under arms while defending a Croatian fortress against the Turks. Fleecing a couple of *coureurs de bois* or milking the fur monopoly was quite within the established pattern. The governor's salary was never adequate, and the position itself was a thankless one. On matters of policy he corresponded with the king's ministers, but his responsibility was to a private company.

Since 1627 the fortunes of Canada had rested in the hands of the Company of New France, a proprietary of one hundred and twenty associates which Cardinal Richelieu had set up with himself at its head and which had been granted the entire St. Lawrence watershed. With this vast grant went also a perpetual monopoly of the fur trade and also a monopoly on all commerce from and into Canada for fifteen years. In return the Company undertook, in those fifteen years, to transport three hundred people a year to the new country, to support them there for three years, and then to settle them on cleared land of their own. The immigrants had to be French and Catholic, and for each settlement at least three priests must be provided.

The intention was idyllic: a society populated only by the pure blood of France and unstained by heresy. That was what they got, but purity of blood and faith were not enough. While the English colonies were admitting men of all races and creeds as the tide brought them, and creating a series of diverse, often contentious communities, jealous of their local interests but filled with vigor and ambition, the line of French along the St. Lawrence remained so thin the wonder is that it survived at all.

The Company of New France was interested in Canada only as a property, not as a colony. Instead of the total of more than four thousand people it had promised to settle by 1643, there were on Avaugour's arrival in 1661 only one thousand Frenchmen in Canada and a total of "less than three thousand souls residing over an extent of eighty leagues" — two hundred miles. Moreover, their lives were strictly limited, on the one side by the monopoly and on the other by the church, neither of which willingly tolerated individuality or enterprise. The new governor, making his first trip up the great valley and its pathetically attenuated line of settlement, at once appreciated this. He had faith in the essential French hardihood when left untrammeled, and though he asked for three hundred soldiers to stand off the Iroquois and twelve hundred artisans and farmers to strengthen the civil population, he also wrote the king's minister, Condé:

> Should the king be unwilling to do either the one or the other, let him leave the people of the country free to act, and grant them authority. I assure your Highness that all will go well, and that they will grow, as all other states have done — provided they be not burdened with useless func- tionaries, such as the petty governors and men of law who are sent out to them every day.

He did not include the church in this category, but he had it in mind for, having said that if the king did not send provisions for the hundred soldiers he had brought with him to garrison Quebec, he added, "I would rather rob the altar than impose on them [the habitants] a burden which they cannot yet bear."

Since 1659 the church in Canada had been presided over by a zealous, hardheaded, and ambitious man, of assertive and arrogant piety named François Xavier de Laval-Montmorency (known more simply from the time he assumed office as Laval), and his purpose was to make it the ruling force in the colonial government. His appointment was the result of a brief struggle for power within the church in New France.

There had been no previous bishop in Canada, and in 1657 the Sulpician Order, which had recently settled four priests at Montreal, proposed one of them, the Abbé Queylus, as a candidate. This brought the Jesuits up in arms. They regarded themselves as the established church in Canada, and so for thirty years they had been, ministering to the French inhabi- tants and carrying the Cross to the Indians. If anyone had a right to nomi- nate a bishop for Quebec, they claimed the right was theirs.

It is not necessary to follow the details of political jockeying. Queylus was at first approved by the French clergy, and apparently also by the prime minister, Cardinal Mazarin. But the Jesuits had too much power at court. Mazarin's approval was withdrawn and the Jesuits were invited to make their own choice. They chose Laval.

At that time the Catholics of France were divided into two parties. The first was strongly nationalistic and believed in the separation of temporal and spiritual powers; the second maintained that the pope, as Christ's representative, to use the word in its equivalent sense, was supreme on earth, and therefore their first allegiance was to Rome. To this view both Laval and the Jesuits subscribed, though the Jesuits carried it a step fur- ther: if the church ruled the world, and the pope ruled the church, then they should rule the pope. To point the moral, Laval was not named bishop of Quebec, he was appointed the pope's vicar apostolic to Canada, thus making clear that he did not hold the see by nomination of the king or the French church but was, rather, solely under the jurisdiction of

Rome. At the same time, however, in order to give him stature in the new land, he was named titular bishop of Petraea, in Arabia.

This was eminently satisfactory from the Jesuits' point of view, for while Laval had been their own choice, they preferred his position to be one from which they could have him recalled if, after trial, they found him impossible to get on with — a procedure that would have been immeasurably more difficult if he had been placed over them as their bishop. But they need not have doubted him. Laval believed passionately in ecclesiastical supremacy, and he arrived at Quebec with an iron determination that he would be a bishop in fact and that under him the church was going to rule in Canada.

Within three months of his arrival he had begun his campaign to make it so. The struggle was to grow increasingly bitter, and he was to experience humiliation and triumph during its course, and at the end of his life see his successor undermine some of his accomplishment, but his devotion throughout to what he conceived his duty under God remained unshaken.

His opening moves seem petty and even frivolous as we read of them today, detailed by Father Jerome Lalemant in the Jesuit *Journals* for 1659 through 1661. They were mainly concerned with matters of precedence: what should be the relative positions of the bishop's and the governor's chairs during mass; whether the governor at midnight mass on Christmas should, like the bishop, be offered incense by the deacon or, as Laval now decreed, by a subordinate thurifer; and as the dispute sharpened, Laval ordered that all priests within the choir should thereafter be given incense before the governor. Again, there rose the question of whether the bishop or the governor, lending their presence to a "minor Action" or catechism, should first receive the applause of the children. So much feeling was engendered over this last issue that the Jesuits decided that "the Children's hands should be kept occupied, so neither the one nor the other should be saluted." The children were given orders to this effect, but two of them, Charles Couillard and Ignace de Repentigny, "instigated and persuaded by their parents, did just the contrary, and saluted Monsieur the Governor first." Laval was infuriated and refused to be appeased even after the two miscreants had been thoroughly whipped the next morning. Though neither boy was to play a prominent role in the future history of Canada, one cannot help feeling that their small smarting backs deserve some sort of memorial, for they were among the very few who ever, for whatever motives, dared stand up to this formidable prelate on his own ground.

Trivial, even petty, as such disputes may seem to us today, they did not seem so to the remote and scattered colony of French along the St. Lawrence. On Quebec all eyes were focused and to it all hearts turned. It was at once the only link they had with France and the fount from which all spiritual and temporal power flowed. No happening was too small to escape notice, and gossip gained dimension out of all proportion to its merit. An open clash, therefore, between the two men who embodied in their persons the authority of the church and the state was a sensational event, as well as deeply disturbing. Laval's insistences on matters of precedence dramatized as nothing else could his determination to win dominion for the church, and he saw to it that something of the sort occurred nearly every month, and sometimes oftener.

His adversary in these opening skirmishes was Argenson, whom we have already met impulsively rushing forth from dinner on his second evening in Quebec to give battle to raiding Iroquois. Moderate in his inclinations, he was also a devout and devoted Catholic, and he had approached his governorship with an almost romantic conception of himself as the defender of the true church in America. Elsewhere on the continent were only what he called the "doctrines of England and Holland" because their colonies nourished as many creeds as there were colonies. To protect New France and strengthen it was to make possible, also, the carrying of true religion to the savages, the implementation of which he regarded as a second part of his task.

Now, suddenly confronted by the hostility of the bishop, he was bewildered and upset. Certainly he was no match for his opponent. When he tried to compromise, Laval became the more intransigent. Thus, on the feast of Corpus Christi . . .

It was the custom to stage a procession around the town in which the Blessed Sacrament was carried from its tabernacle in the Jesuits' church to a series of temporary altars, one of which stood before the fort with the soldiers of the garrison paraded beside it. There were frequent religious processions in Quebec, but the one on Corpus Christi was outstanding. Behind the cross, borne by a Jesuit escorted by two little French boys in surplices, with wreaths of flowers on their heads, walked Indian converts, forty or fifty of them, led by one of the Fathers in surplice and stole; twelve torchbearers representing the twelve trades of the colony — joiner, turner, shoemaker, cooper, locksmith, gunsmith, carpenter, mason, toolmaker, baker, wheelwright, and nailmaker; lay choristers carrying tapers; two lay brothers garbed as angels, in costumes the Ursulines had made, one leading two tiny Indians by the hand, the other bearing a corporal-case and accompanied by two young Indians holding candles; two Jesuits bearing censers; four more, in surplices and carrying silver candlesticks, at the four corners of the canopy, which was carried by three Frenchmen of high rank and a Montagnais chief; secular priests, deacons of the parish church — it made a long procession, but the dominant figure was undoubtedly Laval.

Previously he had sent word to Argenson that this year the soldiers must uncover to the Sacrament or he would pass their altar without offering Communion. Argenson, who was ill and unable, therefore, to take his usual part in the procession, had acquiesced and sent appropriate orders

[45]

to the guard. But now, when the bishop arrived and found them all bare-headed, he demanded that in addition they must kneel, and said that if they refused to do so he would pass on. This not being in their orders, they did refuse, but instead of passing, the procession waited while some-one ran to the governor for instructions.

There is an element of comedy in the episode, and one can hardly doubt that Laval himself relished the suspense he had created — watching with a cold, imperious stare the bewildered and uneasy soldiers, the files of Jesuits, priests, artisans, and Indians behind him waiting tensely, and him-self in his robes the center of it all, almost succeeding with the fierceness of his determination in turning the panorama of the vast river and ageless mountains into a mere backdrop for his act. His long face, which his miter must have made appear still longer, his hooded eyes, his set lips under a nose of a size and arched magnificence that only the blood of France seems able to erect upon the human countenance, could be truly portentous, and one may be sure that he did nothing now to diminish the effect. And yet in his portrait one can see a slight upward quirk at the corners of the disciplined mouth which makes one suspect that the ab-surdities of human nature — though it would be going too far probably to include his own — did not wholly elude him. But now, at length, came the governor's reply: it was the duty of soldiers on guard to remain stand-ing. Without a word Laval turned away, and slowly the procession moved off past the long stone wall of the still unfinished cathedral until all had passed from sight.

Against such arrogations by the bishop, Argenson found himself almost powerless. He could only protest in anger when the bishop refused to let him deliver the blessed bread at the cathedral with a roll of drums as he had always done before, or again when he was removed as an honorary churchwarden. What Laval was practicing against him was not only a sys-tematic belittling of his position, it was a kind of emotional excommunica-tion. As representative of the Crown, Argenson felt bound to uphold the dignity of his office, but against Laval's maneuvers he struck out as in-effectually as a feather in a vacuum; and in point of fact he was to some extent operating in a vacuum, whereas behind his opponent stood all the strength and grandeur of the Roman church and the papacy. The psycho-logical handicap was enormous.

For though the king did appoint the governor, the appointment fol-lowed automatically nomination by the Company of New France, which had no interest in the welfare of the colonists or the problems of their gov-ernor. The Company was concerned only with its own commercial re-turns and those of the fur trade. Even management of the last had been delegated since 1645 to a group of Canadians known as the *Compagnie des Habitants*, who, as long as they turned over the required thousand beaver each year, were allowed a free hand: a monopoly within a monopoly. So assiduously did they develop it to their own profit that a storm of protest swept the colony, reaching even across the Atlantic; and in 1647, by royal decree, a Council of Quebec was created, to consist of the governor, the Superior of the Jesuits (until a bishop for the colony should be appointed), and the governor of Montreal, with elected councilors from the three districts of Quebec, Three Rivers, and Montreal.

The representative aspect of the council was not permanent; in 1663 the right of election was withdrawn and the councilors were appointed, at first by the governor and bishop together, but later solely by authority of the Crown. The various changes in the constitution of the council need not concern us here, nor the change in title first to Supreme Council and then, as its powers were reduced, to Superior Council. Its functions were legislative, but only in minor matters affecting the life of the colony, and administrative, in which capacity its actual power was mainly negative, in that from time to time it might refrain from putting into effect a royal ordinance which in the opinion of the councilors might prove injurious to the colony or to their personal interests; but its chief function was judicial, as a court of appeal in matters both civil and political.

It was to the council as a court that Argenson now carried his perplexities. In a memorial which covered almost every dispute he had had with Laval, he asked for instructions on what the governor's standing should be; what position he should take at various church ceremonies; how he ought to receive incense and from whom; whether the governor should continue to deliver the blessed bread at Easter with a beating of drums as had been customary until the bishop ruled that it should be brought before the service and carried away afterward in order that worship should not be interrupted; whether in purely civil functions the bishop or he as the king's lieutenant should have precedence; and whether the bishop had the right to excommunicate people for civil or political offenses.

In reply the council ruled that the bishop should take second place in civil functions and they denied him the power to excommunicate except for religious offenses, but that was about as far as they cared to go; and it did little to ease the frictions that continued to develop. More and more the governor found himself frustrated and he writes of the "self-will of the Bishop of Petraea, who says that a bishop can do what he likes, and threatens nothing but excommunication."

Argenson's difficulties, in addition to his quarrels with Laval, seemed to be compounding now on every hand. His appeals for troops continued to be ignored. The shrinking of the fur trade under Iroquois harassment had reduced the whole colony to poverty. His salary was inadequate to support him, modest as his way of life was for a governor, and he found himself heavily in debt to the Company. Montreal was a constant irritation: it wanted to be independent of Quebec and also hoped to take over the fur monopoly for itself. It was all too much. He could get no decisions from France, either from the Company or the Court, and at length he asked to be replaced. It was absolutely necessary, he wrote, that the new governor be "a man of some property and some rank, so that he will not be despised for humble birth." It would not have diminished his bitter relief to be leaving had he known that a letter of Laval's had probably carried more weight than his own.

The threats of excommunication which Argenson had complained about were rooted in a problem that had troubled the colony for a long time and shortly was to become a flaming issue between the church and lay authorities of Quebec. This was the liquor traffic with the Indians.

From their first introduction to wine and brandy, and later to rum, the Indians had been fascinated by its hallucinatory effects. "In the end one of them was drunk . . ." Robert Juet, mate of the *Half Moon,* had reported in 1609, "and that was strange to them, for they could not tell how to take it." But the novelty soon wore off, to be replaced by a craving that universally obsessed them. "There is scarcely a Savage, small or great, even among the girls and women, who does not enjoy this intoxication, and who does not take these beverages when they can be had, purely and simply for the sake of being drunk." This was Father Le Jeune in 1637, and he went on to say that they drank without eating, to which fact he attributed the tragic mortality that resulted from the Indians' use of alcohol.

Its effect on them was pathological and devastating. Only a little alcohol could produce drunkenness in an Indian unaccustomed to it. Two hundred years later, when the northwest fur trade had been systematized under the British, and French brandy had given way to trader's rum — which was not rum at all, but concentrated grain spirits known as "high wine" or, to Canadian habitants, as "whiskey blanc" — the traders mixed it in three degrees of strength. The first, for tribes who were new to it, was one part of alcohol diluted by thirty-six of water; for a tribe more accustomed to it, the mixture was one to six, but confirmed addicts would not be satisfied with any thing weaker than one to four. In all cases, however, the results were lethal.

Liquor did more than make them quarrelsome; it literally drove them mad. Men would run wild among the lodges, brandishing guns or tomahawks or flaming torches. Without warning one might shoot his brother, slash his wife, or throw a child into the fire. There was no limit to his capacity for violence, and until he had fallen senseless no one in his path was safe. Women were hardly different. Their habitual modesty evaporated; they would tear off their clothes and, screeching, run as wildly as the men did. Alexander Henry records that one young wife, whom he considered remarkable for her beauty — "she had the handsomest face of all the women on this river" — in a whim of tipsiness stuck the muzzle of his own musket into the mouth of her blindly drunken husband and blew the back out of his head. Except for the fact of her beauty, no one would have thought the incident especially remarkable.

An Indian town to which a supply of liquor had been made available remained a shrieking bedlam till the last drop had been drunk. Nothing that might happen could stop the rest from continuing to drink. Christian Indians succumbed as readily as the rest; in the flash of a moment missionaries would see months of patient work undone. With the return of sobriety came remorse, which was completely sincere, and sometimes so deep as to lead to suicide. The Indians soon realized exactly what liquor did to them, but it made no difference. They were powerless to resist, and the next consignment of brandy or rum inevitably produced a repetition of the same hideous and pitiful routine. In the end whole tribes became debilitated, mere hangers-on of some trading post, listlessly waiting for small handouts of rum, constantly in debt to the trader, doing only the necessary minimum of hunting and trapping, and when no longer inclined even to that, prostituting their wives and daughters to keep themselves supplied with rum and the bare essentials of food and gunpowder. Their pride disintegrated, and with it many of their old skills; to all intents they ceased to be Indians.

This extraordinary susceptibility to the effects of alcohol can be partly explained on physical grounds. Though some Indians made a weak sort of beer out of maple syrup, none of the northern and western tribes had really discovered the secret of fermentation and so had had no opportunity to develop a tolerance for the strong spirits to which the European introduced them. Moreover, many Indians, as we know now, had a very high sugar content in their blood, which, if not actually making them diabetics, was high enough to have felled any white man and, of course, to make the effect of alcohol absolutely lethal. But to account for the compulsion which drove them to alcohol and repeated bouts of senseless violence one must reach deeper than mere physical reaction.

The world of the Indians would have been grim enough if sustaining life in the wilderness had been their only problem. Tribes practicing agriculture to a greater or lesser extent, as did the Iroquoian peoples, were better off in this respect than others who, like the Crees, depended entirely on hunting and fishing; but even the sedentary tribes, as the former were called, were haunted by the specter of starvation when crops or game failed. It was with them even in the midst of plenty, for few Indians had the foresight or self-discipline to provide adequately against periods of want. Their inborn gregariousness also worked against them, and whenever food was abundant the immediate reaction was to hold a feast in which they would often gorge themselves almost to the point of stupefaction, as if in doing so they could blot from their minds even the possibility of hard times to come.

Brandy underlined this natural incontinence. "The Savages have always been gluttons," wrote Le Jeune, "but since the coming of the Europeans they have become such drunkards . . . that they cannot abstain from drinking." There was obviously a parallel between these two compulsions, but drunkenness provided more than an escape into insensibility: it allowed an Indian for a time to flee the awesome hazards and responsibilities he was confronted with by a demonology that haunted every moment of his life, whether waking or sleeping.

Certain deities or spirits were regarded as supreme — such as the benevolent Manabozho of the Algonquins, who restored the world after floods had submerged it and so became in effect the Creator; or the evil, female Ataentsic of the Hurons and Iroquois who, while hunting, fell through a hole in the floor of heaven, though another version has it that her husband cast her through a hole, because she had conceived by inhaling his breath without his knowledge and thus revealed to him her wickedness of heart. However, Ataentsic was saved in her fall by the birds and animals inhabiting the great waters underneath heaven, and they created a world on the back of the tortoise for her to live on. She had a daughter who in turn bore two sons, one good-minded and one bad-minded. The good-minded one killed his brother and then interposed himself between mankind and the malice of his grandmother. He too saved the earth when it had become shriveled and barren by creating the lakes and rivers and therefore, among the Iroquois, was sometimes regarded as the Creator. It is perhaps characteristic that they never thought it worth while to pray to him, since he was friendly anyway, but reserved their sacrifices for the propitiation of the evil grandmother or to gain favor with some other like the war god, Areskoui.

These were what might be called formal deities, and their importance fluctuated with the course of wilderness contingencies. There were others, some maleficent and some good and even charming, like the little people who lived just under the surface of the earth and each spring pushed up the plants and flowers; but they need not be listed here. There was no supreme god. The Great Spirit was an outgrowth of missionary teaching, though in the Indian mind he was less a God in the Christian sense than a mystical force permeating all the complex of forest life. But unlike their pagan gods, the Indian seems to have imagined the Great Spirit always in the shape of man — possibly because of the religious pictures the Jesuits brought now and then, even to the far missions, to show while presenting the concept of a supreme God — whereas the older gods most often manifested themselves in the form of animals or inanimate objects, such as tree stumps or rocks, or in a windstorm or stroke of lightning.

Any object or animal, therefore, which an Indian encountered in the course of even the most ordinary day might suddenly prove to be endowed with supernatural powers, and since more were likely to emanate from evil than benign spirits, the Indian lived in fearful and unending peril. Still more to be dreaded, however, was the invasion of his own body by some spirit or demon in the form of a dream.

The inspiring power of the dream might be a hostile spirit, one in no way associated with the Indian, or it might be the dreamer's own guardian *manitou*, if he were an Algonquin, *okie* to an Iroquoian. An Indian's *okie* was revealed to him at the threshold of manhood when he was sent off by himself, foodless and unarmed, to meditate in solitude. It might take a week or even longer before starvation induced the proper hallucinatory state of mind to make the revelation occur; but almost invariably it did occur, the *okie* generally showing itself in the form of an animal or bird. After that it companioned him through life, and the Indian carried with him, usually in a pouch hung from his neck, the *okie* itself, if it was small enough, or else some fragment of it. It was with him when he slept and often played a helpful role in his dreams.

According to the Hurons, dreams were the language of the soul. They believed that in addition to its natural desires — those that stemmed from previous knowledge or experience — the soul had deep, inborn, and unrealized longings, or *ondinnonks*, which could find expression only in dreams. Quite often the soul, under escort of the *okie*, would be transported to some object far outside its tabernacle in the man's body in order that it might recognize its hidden longing. When the man woke and was able to recount his dream, it was necessary at once to fulfill the expressed desire so that the unsatisfied soul, in resentment, should not turn against the body it inhabited, inducing disease or even death.

The natural desires experienced in dreams were taken less seriously and even turned into a sort of game in which the dreamer asked whomever he met what the object of his dream had been, and if they could not guess, they were obliged to pay a forfeit. But then there were the dreams that came to sick people, and these were not necessarily related to innate desires but were planted by outside spirits or sorcery and involved prophecy or a scene of ritualistic nature.

For instance, a Cayuga chief dreamed one night that he saw ten men dive into a hole in the frozen river near his village and then climb out through another hole downstream. On waking he immediately directed the women of his lodge to prepare a feast, to which he then invited ten of his friends. It was a gay occasion, with much singing and laughter, but in the midst of it he told his guests that he had called them because of a dream and must now test their love for him. He described the dream. Without further discussion or the least hesitation they set out to fulfill it.

[51]

They chopped one hole in the ice and then a second about fifty feet below. Stripping, in spite of the cold, they dived in one after another. Nine managed to find the second hole, but the tenth missed it and was carried on by the current beneath the ice and drowned. Though his loss was lamented, nobody considered that any other course might have been followed.

In the same way, an Indian dreamed that he had given a feast of human flesh. As there were no captives in the village, this presented a serious dilemma, so he asked all the chiefs to come to his house and told them that he had a dream impossible to fulfill, in consequence of which he must himself die. That, he said, would have been of little account if his fate had not also involved that of the whole tribe and, in fact, a universal cataclysm. But his dream was so awful that he could not describe it; they would have to guess. For a long time none could; then one man said that the dream could be of only one thing — a feast of human flesh, and he immediately offered his brother to be cut up for the kettles. The dreamer, however, said that the flesh must be female. So a young girl was picked out and adorned with all sorts of finery and brought to the feast, and as the guests sat round the long house in breathless anticipation, the child, smiling and all unsuspecting, was led to the dreamer, who took her. Then, as he was apparently about to give her deathblow, he stayed his hand and shouted that his dream had already been fulfilled by their willingness to carry out his *ondinnonk* to the very end.

This was an unusual case in which the will was allowed to equal the deed; and there is no other like it recorded in the Jesuit *Relations*. Nor would there be point here in recounting more of these dreams. The pattern is always the same: the fear of disaster if the dream or desire is not fulfilled; the conviction that the soul has been led to it outside the body by either its *okie* or some alien demon; the identification of the dreamer with the dream and therefore the almost abject anxiety with which the rest of the community sought to fulfill the dream and so restore the dreamer to his natural self.

The entire life of an Indian village was thus at the mercy of dreams. The greatest of war captains could not raise a man to follow him if someone had had a dream inimical to the proposed expedition. When a man was seriously ill, the chief men would assemble round his mat to consult with him on possible ceremonies that might effect his cure. Jerome Lalemant has described one of these scenes, in the case of an old Huron dying of blood poisoning from an ulcerated arm:

> The Council is assembled . . . and some persons are deputed to go and learn his desires; these turn upon five or six points, — a number of dogs of a certain shape and color, with which to make a three days' feast; a quantity of flour for the same purpose; some dances; and like performances; but principally upon the ceremony of the "and acwander," a

mating of men with girls, which is made at the end of the feast. He specified that there should be 12 girls, and a thirteenth for himself.

The answer being brought to the council, he was furnished immediately with what could be given at once, and this from the liberality and voluntary contributions of who were present there and heard the matter mentioned — these peoples glorying, on such occasions, in despoiling themselves of the most precious things they have. Afterward, the Captains went through the streets and public places, announcing in a loud voice the desires of the sick man, and exhorting people to satisfy them promptly.

They are not content to go on this errand once, — they repeat it three or four times, using such terms and accents that, indeed, one would think that the welfare of the whole country was at stake. Meanwhile, they take care to note the names of the girls and men who present themselves to carry out the principal desire of the sick man; and in the assembly of the feast these are named aloud, after which follow the congratulations of all those present, and the best pieces, which are carried to the men and women deputed to appear in so wretched characters at the end of the feast; then ensue the thanks of the sick man for the health that has been restored to him, professing himself entirely cured by this remedy . . .

But of course he was not cured, and not long afterward the old man — his name was Taorhenché — died. One cannot help sympathizing with him. At his last feast, according to Lalemant, he said that he died willingly, and that he had only one regret — that of seeing himself deprived of delicious morsels with which he had been all his life honored in the feasts. Lalemant thoroughly disapproved of the old wretch, as he called him, claiming that his soul belonged too much to the flesh to enjoy things of the spirit; but his dislike reached a climax when Taorhenché, just before his death, roused from a long spell of unconsciousness to announce cheerfully to the Jesuit that he had been to the other world and that it contained none of the things the French had said it did. Instead, he had been greeted with the greatest warmth by his family and relatives; they were preparing feasts in his honor; and he had only troubled to return in order to get himself properly outfitted for such distinguished festivities. So he had his whole face painted red, his best clothes all brought to him and laid across his body; "was given his plate and spoon; and thus he died." He had basically offended the Jesuit, who burst forth:

This barbarian passed, in the common opinion of the Savages as one of the most respectable and virtuous men in the whole country; if you asked upon what grounds, they said, "Because he was a peaceable man, who did no harm to anyone, and who greatly delighted in merrymaking and in giving feasts." If the opinion of the Savages is correct, I leave you to imagine of what value all the others are.

One wonders at times how two such disparate minds as Huron and Jesuit ever made contact at all. Brébeuf's stature and unshaken calm could command respect, where Lalemant's relatively smaller height probably allowed the Hurons (who were themselves much bigger than the French) to take him lightly or even tease him as Taorhenché undoubtedly did; but Brébeuf, too, occasionally suffered from the same sense of deep spiritual affront. That they were able to make conversions, many of them truly steadfast, seems nearly the miracle that in their eyes it was. Winter life in a Huron town was a harrowing experience. The gloom of the long houses, the constant smoke that left some people's eyes permanently inflamed, the hunger, the cold, the insipidity of the saltless diet, and the constant danger of an Iroquois invasion — all these preyed on the missionary's nerves, so one can forgive him a moment of pique. One of their number during the bitter winter listed the qualities one had to have: Patience, Courage, Humility, Forbearance, and, of course, Conformity to God's holy will.

This was Paul Ragueneau, and of all the Jesuits who wrote in the *Relations* he is the only one I know of to feel a sympathetic understanding of the Indian in his pagan state.

> Had I to give counsel to those who commence to labor for the conversion of the Savages, I would willingly say a word of advice to them, which experience will, I think, make them acknowledge to be more important than it seems at first sight, namely: that one must be very careful before condemning a thousand things among their customs, which greatly offend minds brought up and nourished in another world. It is easy to call irreligion what is mere stupidity, and to take for diabolical working something that is no more than human; and then, one thinks he is obliged to forbid as impious certain things that are done in all innocence, or, at most, are silly, but not criminal customs . . .
>
> I have no hesitation in saying that we have been too severe on this point . . .

These were unusual words to come from the pen of a Jesuit, but then Ragueneau was an altogether unusual man, as the other members of the mission quickly came to realize. Talented, prudent, and gracious, he had a gift for administration and brought a sense of dignity to the Huron mission that the Fathers had not felt before. "He has not his counterpart here, and I do not know whether he will have in the future," Brébeuf wrote the Father General in Rome, asking that if possible Ragueneau be allowed to remain as Superior of the Huron mission beyond the customary term of three years.

What Ragueneau perceived was that the Huron preoccupation with dreams was neither criminal nor evil nor capricious, as his fellow missionaries generally considered it to be, but was fundamental to the whole fabric of Indian life. The dissociation of the soul, or mind, from the body, and the frequency with which this occurred, was in a way symbolic of the precariousness of Indian life; and this was carried over into the inner life, or one might even call it the integrity, of the soul itself. For they believed profoundly in the duality or divisibility of the soul. When a man died, he had in effect two souls which were, as one Indian described them to Brébeuf, in themselves each material and "reasonable," or of the mind. One of these always separated itself from the body at death, though it lingered near by till final interment took place at the Feast of the Dead, after which it began its long journey west to the land of souls or, as some believed, turned into a turtledove. But the other soul remained with the body, specifically in the bones, thus in a sense preserving the identity of the corpse. The Hurons used the same word, *atisken*, for both the bones and the soul, but the Iroquois made a distinction. To them the word for bone was *esken*, and *atisken*, by which they identified the soul, meant that which lives within the bone; and it was this soul, unless in the meantime it had found new life, that shared the final rite of burial with the body at the Feast of the Dead.

The Feast of the Dead was held among the Hurons and other Iroquoian tribes every ten or twelve years. Among the Iroquois themselves it appears to have occurred in earlier times more or less automatically whenever it became necessary to move a town to a new location. After about ten years an Iroquois town became uninhabitable. The palisades were no longer strong; the cornfields would have lost fertility; and the bark houses, rotting and moldy, would have become infested with vermin. The practical solution was to build entirely new on fresh soil, but before making the move, which to a people with no draft animals was a tremendous undertaking, the bodies and bones of those who had died during habitation in the old town would be brought together from the bark scaffolds on which they had been placed, or the little sheds attached to the long houses to which they were sometimes brought after years of weathering had removed the flesh from the skeleton, and placed in a huge common grave. It was this communal ceremony that finally released the one soul from earthly ties and put to rest the other; and it marked both an end and a renewal of life.

The Hurons, however, do not seem to have tied the feast to any utilitarian circumstance. To them it was purely a religious rite that involved the whole nation (there were four nations in the Huron confederacy) by a spontaneous impulse that seems to have manifested itself every dozen years or so, and of such deep emotional significance that it was hardly ever referred to by its true name. Instead, in discussing their arrangements for holding it, the Hurons used elaborate metaphoric locutions, for even the mention of death would cause pain to the waiting souls surrounding them. The feast which Brébeuf and his fellow missionaries witnessed and described in 1636 was referred to as "the Kettle" and all plans for its organization were carried forward in the terminology of cooking.

That year a rivalry between two factions had resulted in such an irremediable schism in the Bear Nation that two feasts were held; but ordinarily, as had been the case from time immemorial, the entire nation participated. It was perhaps the oldest ritual among the woodland tribes of northern America; one found it everywhere, though the Algonquin versions varied from the Iroquoian. Of the latter, the Hurons' feast was by far the most impressive.

The initial step might be almost adventitious. A chief, sitting in council at Ossossané, the principal town of the Bear Nation, would drop a word intimating that the time drew near when they must think of holding the feast again. There was no way of telling when this first hint would occur — a leaf could fall no more unpredictably; it might be in summer or in early fall, and nothing further might be said about it for weeks. But awareness that it had been said ran like an electric current along the network of trails that threaded the Huron wilderness, until in even the smallest and farthest villages people began to feel the mounting tension, grief, and pity that the prospect of a final parting from the souls of their dead evoked in Indian hearts.

Though grief began with the individual family, it became enlarged and at the same time more poignant as it was merged gradually with that of other mourners until it reached the national climax at the great communal burial pit. For the honor of the dead each step that brought them to it must conform to hallowed traditions that had governed the ceremony beyond man's memory, and the omission of a single detail might bring calamity upon the living.

Time went by as the people waited for the date to be announced. Oblique hints reached them from Ossossané, but nothing sure. Winter came, and they knew then that the Kettle would not boil before spring. Through the lengthening nights they huddled close to the long house fires, while the smoke recoiled from the smoke vents and the driven snow fingered the bark roofs, thinking of the motionless forms on the burial scaffolds in the bitter dark beyond the palisade and listening against the wind for the thin voices of their waiting souls. But meanwhile the council at Ossossané, by oblique and tentative steps, had arrived at a date for the ceremony. As the level of snow sank in the woods and spring came with the faint wind-tossed cries of migratory birds — at times hardly distinguishable from the voices of the dead — preparations for the feast began in all the Huron towns.

The opening of the ritual of the Kettle witnessed by Brébeuf and his companions occurred in the first week of May. Every village, or clan, had selected a leader called the *Aiheonde*, or caretaker of graves, to supervise the preliminary local rites, but the responsibility of preparing the individual dead rested with the family alone. At sunrise of the given day a procession formed among the houses and, led by its *Aiheonde*, moved slowly through the gate of the palisade to the burial place. Here all stopped except for the *Aiheonde* and his assistants, who moved on among the scaffolds and from one after another tore its bark sheath and lowered the bodies to the ground.

Now the wrappings were removed; and while the men watched silently from the verge, the women and girls of each family went forward to claim their dead, uttering shrill, lamenting cries as each was recognized. The corpses were in every stage of decomposition. On some skeletons the merest integument of flesh remained, an almost transparent parchment around the bones. The flesh of others had dried and darkened as it shrank, like that of mummies. The newer dead were still undergoing the corruptive process, too ghastly in most cases to be described. But the women responded to all with equal evidences of affection, stroking the bones and in weeping voices calling out their names, so that the souls would hear them and take comfort.

When the souls had been thus reassured, the women began stripping the bones of the flesh that still covered them, except for those of the more recent dead. Yet even these they tried to make presentable, scraping away the worst areas of putrefaction; "and all this," reported Brébeuf, who had found the stench almost intolerable, "without showing any horror at the corruption." In spite of himself he was profoundly moved by such a demonstration of love, and could not help asking:

> Is not that a noble example to inspire Christians, who ought to have thoughts much more elevated to acts of charity and works of mercy towards their neighbor? After that, who will be afraid of the stench of a Hospital; and who will not take a peculiar pleasure in seeing himself at the feet of a sick man all covered with wounds, in the person of whom he beholds the Son of God?

The cleansed bones were wrapped carefully in deerskins and the bundles adorned with furs. The corrupting bodies were also covered with new beaver robes and placed on litters. Then the flesh that had been removed was burned with the bark sheaths from the scaffolds and the discarded wrappings, and the people, bearing their dead with them, left the burial place for the last time and returned to the village, each family entering its own house.

There they hung the packaged bones from the house framework over their heads and propped the recent corpses up against the sleeping platforms; and as evening fell, the family in the presence of their *atiskens* held their own funeral feast, the older members renewing their memories of the dead and so, by their spoken thoughts, informing the younger

[57]

of the characters of the souls who for the last time were joining them in the house.

The time for the great feast at Ossossané was now drawing near. A day or two before they would need to set out for it, the local *Aiheonde* announced that the village feast would be held in the largest long house. All the souls, the bundles and the bodies on their litters, were carried to the designated house and arranged as they had been in the family lodges. The presents for the feast which each family had brought were strung on poles all along both sides of the house. Then the chief of the village welcomed them in the name of his predecessor whose name he now bore, and during the feast sang the deceased chief's song, in accordance with the request the latter had made on his deathbed; and he and the other chiefs extolled the virtues of the dead around them, much as each family had previously revived memories of its own loved ones at the family feasts; only now the dead were spoken of in their relation to the community. The pattern of grief was entering a new dimension.

At the end of the feast, as they went out carrying their dead with them, the guests in unison uttered a high, plaintive cry, *h-a-éé, h-a-é*, in imitation of the thin voices of the souls, and this completed the preliminary local observances. The climactic ceremony was yet to come, but already people from the most distant villages were on the trails leading to Ossossané.

They walked with mournful slowness, in single file, the *Aiheonde* at their head, covering often less than four miles in the course of a day's march. Every so often, as if moved by a common, spontaneous impulse, all with one voice would utter the cry of souls — *h-a-éé, h-a-é*. It relieved them greatly to do this: otherwise, they explained to the Jesuits, the burdens they bore, although of souls, would become unbearably heavy.

Some of these parties were small; some, according to Brébeuf, numbered three or four hundred. But all followed the same order of march: the *Aiheonde* leading; then the men, painted and feathered, in their finest robes, stalking along the trail in dignified and silent meditation; and lastly the women, carrying the bundles of souls upon their backs, the tumplines pressing against their foreheads with the heaviness of sorrow. So they moved through the damp spring woods, now dark with mist, now revealing hints of green as the meshed sunlight reached through to the forest floor, with only their occasional lament to mark their progress.

When they neared a village along the way, they announced their presence by repeating the cry, *h-a-éé, h-a-é*. All the people in the village would come forth to greet them and exchange gifts, and then the procession would move in through the palisade gate to a long house which had been made ready. Everything was ordered; there was no confusion; each party knew where it would rest. A hush hung over the country, broken only by the plaintive cry as the people moved step by step along the trails; but as they converged on Ossossané, it must have seemed as if the entire forest were alive with souls.

Ossossané was a new town, one of the largest as well as the most important in Huronia, and the largest belonging to the Bear Nation; yet it could not accommodate all the people who came with their souls to the feast in 1636, even though the schism of that year kept away many mourners. So the musty lodges of the old town of Quieuindohan, which Ossossané had replaced, were pressed into service, and the processions of mourners, moving in, hung their souls from the poles overhead as they had in their own villages. In the long house to which Brébeuf was taken with his companions, there were more than a hundred such bundles, "some of which," as he wrote, "smelled a little stronger than musk." Even this additional lodging space, however, was not enough to accommodate all the arriving people, for in addition to the members of the Bear Nation, who had brought their dead, guests had been invited from the three other principal Huron tribes — the Cord, the Rock, and the One-White-House Nations — and various other subsidiary and outside tribes. Bark shelters had to be raised, and soon campfires were gleaming all along the ridge between the two towns.

From the arrival of the first procession until all the mourners and invited guests had assembled, nearly a week had elapsed. During the day there were archery and athletic contests for the younger people, both men and women, and the older people were continually presenting the younger with gifts in the names of the dead; during the evenings they engaged in feasts and councils devoted to oratory in which the past glories of the Hurons were recalled, one suspects for the benefit of the visiting dignitaries from outside tribes as much as for their own people.

A further delay of two days was declared by the master of the feast, Anenkhiondic, the principal war chief, because of the weather, for it was imperative that the ceremony take place under clear sky. But at last the day was settled on. There had been a hint of its arrival the afternoon before when the whole corpses had been carried out of the long houses; and now, about noon, the official word came that the mourners should make ready. Hurriedly, the women took down their bundles of souls and undid the wrappings for a last farewell, caressing the bones and crying over them, combing once more the hair of the skulls that still retained it, and tying little offerings of beads and trinkets in the bundles of their dead children. Then when all the bundles had been closed, each family joined its village procession and in single file, the men ahead, the women following, they set out for the burial pit.

It had been dug in the center of a natural opening in the dense forest of spruce and pine that surrounded Ossossané. It was circular, ten feet deep, and about twenty-seven across. Around the edge of it was a plat-

[59]

form, ten feet high, which Brébeuf described as being "nine to ten brasses in width," which would be fifty feet; but he probably meant the figure to represent the full diameter of the platform's outer circumference, just as in the preceding sentence he had given the diameter of the pit, which would mean that the width of the platform was about twelve feet.

Above the platform was a framework which supported long poles that reached well out over the pit, and beneath it, at the edge of the pit, were scaffolds about six feet high, designed for and now already bearing the swathed bodies of the corrupting dead. Four hundred feet outside the platform and concentric to it posts had been set in the ground to support a circle of poles, nearly three thousand feet in circumference, like a fence to guard the sepulcher, though that was not its purpose. On anyone emerging from the dark woods into the brilliant sunlight of the May noon, the place with its log structures must have made a dramatic impact, entirely apart from its mortuary significance.

As the processions filed slowly into the clearing, they arranged themselves around the edge according to their villages and family groups and placed their bundled dead on the ground in front of them. Next they unfolded the robes and furs they had brought as presents to be buried with the dead or to be given to the living in the name of the dead, and displayed them on the poles of the outer circle of posts, where they were left for two hours in order that guests from outlying tribes should have time enough to admire them and realize the wealth of the country. At the end of this period the gifts were taken down and refolded.

While this putting away was in process, the master of the feast, the war captain Anenkhiondic, and several other selected chiefs had mounted to the platform by various of the many ladders that leaned against the outer edge. Now, at some signal from the platform, previously appointed bearers picked up the bundles of souls, and in the next instant, at another signal, all rushed together to the platform, "running as if to the assault of a town," swarmed up the ladders, and hung the bundles to the poles that reached over the pit. It was a scene of apparent confusion, yet each bearer knew to which section of the poles his bundle should be tied, and in a moment all were back on the ground and rejoining their own parties, and the ladders had been taken away.

Now for two hours they contemplated the souls of their dead, brought together at last above the pit and around its edge, the removal of the ladders being the first symbolic step of their severance from earth; and the grief of the individual mourner was merged with that of the nation. On the platform the master and a few chiefs who stayed with him made brief speeches about the magnificence of the presents to be given in the names of the dead and designating the fortunate recipient of each one.

It was now about five in the afternoon. The time had come for the final preparation of the pit, the lining it with beaver robes — first the bottom and then the sides in such a way that the robes extended a foot or two out over the edge. Only the finest new robes were used. It took forty-eight of them, each made of ten beaver, four hundred and eighty skins in all. These besides the robes needed to cover the whole corpses represented a very heavy expense — the lining alone would have bought two dozen muskets in the Dutch trade, or nearly a hundred a few years later in the French — and then there were the furs and robes attached to the bundles of bones, though not all of them would enter the grave with the souls they had covered.

By this time the sun was low and the shadow of the woods had crept across the meadow almost as far as the pit. The people also began to converge upon it, for on the platform, as the sun neared the treetops, the master had given the order to take down the whole corpses, and each family was anxious to see or help in the lowering of its own dead. There was not room beneath the platform for more than a relative few, however, to watch what was happening, and they surged back and forth in the highest anxiety and excitement, with a babel of voices which "spoke and did not listen." But in the pit ten or twelve appointed men were receiving the bodies without confusion and arranging them in an orderly pattern around the sides. When the last had been put down, three huge copper kettles were placed in the center which, as Brébeuf reported, "could only have been of use for souls"; for one had a hole through it, another had no handle, and the third was of scarcely more value.

This odd little instance of cynicism is hard to reconcile with the extreme emotionalism that characterized the behavior of most participants in the Feast of the Dead; or perhaps one should call it the hard realism of a people who had small resources; but it revealed itself in other ways at the conclusion of the ceremony.

Meanwhile darkness was closing in, the meadow was floored in shadow, and only the bundled souls on their concentric spokes of poles above the pit were left in the sunlight. Some of the packages had been shaped in rude effigies of men, others dangled foxtails, feathers, or small precious furs. In the final moments as the light faded and the shadows flowed over them they recaptured an illusion of life, and all through the clearing there must have been an uneasy sense of the presence of the second souls still waiting for their ultimate release.

That night the mourners spent close to the dead. They lighted fires all about the clearing and slung their kettles, each family as before consorting with its own group and village. There were no further ceremonies, but each visiting chief from an outside tribe was given a present in the name of the master of the feast. Finally the voices quieted and the fires reddened, the waxing moon followed the sun behind the western wall of forest, and dawn and the moment for filling and closing the pit drew near.

Ordinarily this was carried out in a reasonably orderly manner, but at the feast Brébeuf attended an accident disrupted the usual ritual. With the other Jesuits he had retired for the night to their lodging in the old town, planning to return to the burial field by daybreak. But as they started in the morning an unearthly clamor burst out of the woods ahead, and though they ran at their best speed they were only in time to witness the end of the burial.

The platform was aswarm with frantic Indians struggling to empty the packages of souls into the pit as fast as they could, but keeping the robes in which they had been wrapped. What had happened was that just before dawn one bundle, either carelessly tied or fastened with too weak a cord, had tumbled into the pit with a noise that woke the nearer sleepers and they, seeing what had occurred, leaped onto the platform and without waiting for the master's order began scattering the bones of the other souls from their packages. They regarded the mischance as a dreadful omen, for the whole purpose of the feast was united burial, and by throwing the rest of the souls after the first with such promptitude they hoped to mitigate the disaster.

Only a few bundles remained on the poles when Brébeuf ran into the clearing, but he saw enough of what was going on to judge what the rest had been like. It seemed to him that he was looking at nothing less than a picture of hell: the frantic naked workers on the platform, the Indians constantly climbing onto it and others leaping off, the high-pitched wailing, laments, and cries of terror, incomprehensibly wild and barbaric in his ears. But in the pit, with silent efficiency five or six men with poles were leveling the tumbled bones, now inextricably mixed. The pit was nearly full, within about two feet of the top, when the last bundle had been raked into place.

Now the workers turned back over the bones the robes which bordered the edge of the pit, mats and bark were spread over the rest, and then earth, poles, and posts were heaped on top of all; and now watching in the gray light of dawn, Brébeuf realized that silence had fallen on the clearing. Then, with a few women giving the pitch, the song of the dead began to rise from the crouched figures all about him, and soon the whole concourse was singing in voices of indescribable sadness. To Brébeuf they represented "the abyss of despair into which these unhappy souls are forever plunged."

With the end of the song the feast ended, though most of the morning was spent in distributing the robes that had not gone into the grave — a procedure which in some respects has echoes in our own funerary attitudes.

Twenty were given to the master of the feast, to thank the Nations which had taken part therein. The dead distributed a number of them, by the hands of the Captains, to their living friends; some served only for show, and were taken away by those who had exhibited them. The old

[62]

Men and notables of the Country, who had the administration and management of the feast, took possession secretly of a considerable quantity; and the rest were cut in pieces . . . and ostentatiously thrown into the midst of the crowd. However, it is only the rich who lose nothing, or very little, in this feast. The middle classes and the poor bring and leave there whatever they have most valuable, and suffer much, in order not to appear less liberal than the others in this celebration.

Probably throughout the history of human burial men have profited from the love and sense of honor of other people. But, though everything about the feast had seemed an abomination to Brébeuf, who hoped that the economic burden it imposed would lead the Hurons before long to abandon it entirely and who therefore presented it in the most unfavorable light, there can be no doubt whatever of the deep emotional experience it was for the Indians themselves to relive their grief through this renewal of mourning in what they were convinced was the actual presence of the souls of their loved ones, nor of the restoration of spirit with which they returned to their own lives after this last farewell.

The bone souls, covered over in the great pit, were now finally and forever at rest, but the other souls for the most part had their long and difficult journey to the Land of Souls still to make — a journey that for its perils makes one think of "Pilgrim's Progress." At one point the way led between great boulders that continually crashed against each other, so the soul had to be agile, swift, and clearheaded to win through; at another the path crossed a rushing, tumultuous river by a single insecurely fastened tree trunk, and at the far end was a fierce dog which attacked each traveler and tried to hurl him into the torrent. Finally, close to the goal was a bark lodge inhabited by a being named Oscotarach, or "Pierce-head," who drew the brains out of the heads of the dead and kept them — an indispensable step toward immortality, according to Huron belief, though the Algonquins felt that somehow the brains would later be restored.

Having won through, the souls found themselves in villages much like those on earth; living with their own tribe and following their normal pursuits, hunting and fishing, raising corn or curing skins, exactly as they had always done. A few Hurons, like old Taorhenché, whom we met in his last illness and who claimed to have had a good look-around, believed it to be a land in which one could enjoy oneself (as the Algonquins also believed); but for most Hurons it was a sad, gray, sunless place where one spent all one's time repining and complaining, and they did not look forward to arriving there. It seemed far preferable to return to vigorous life on earth and they believed that this could sometimes be accomplished. But before turning to the fortunate few who managed to achieve this return, there is still another category of souls to be considered — those of the very old and the very young, neither strong enough nor resolute enough to attempt the perilous journey.

They leagued in a strange and precarious life of their own, invisible and disembodied, inhabiting villages that the living could not see but whose doors they often heard being closed at night, just as they could often hear the thin, piping voices of the ghostly children driving the birds from their meager fields of corn. Being so feeble and so young they were barely able to raise enough food to sustain their half-life, so if a village happened to catch fire they were quick to enter the ruins before anyone else could and gather up the roasted corn, and often in winter they would steal into the houses of the living to eat the residue from the kettles. Now and then one heard their fingers scratching at the bark doors as they came or left, but their actual presence in the lodge was never sensed by the living, except possibly by someone greatly aged, until in the morning the empty kettles revealed that they had been there. No one regarded this pilfering with anything but pity; no attempt was ever made to shut them out.

Finally there were the infant dead, children who had been dead at birth or died within a month or two. These never shared in the pit burial of the Feast of the Dead, but were given special ceremonies of their own and buried under one of the more used trails in the hope that as some woman passed along it they might be able to creep secretly into her womb, there to regain the gift of life and by this new mother be brought forth into the world a second time.

This attempt to help the infant return to life, relying as it did wholly on chance and the fearful dangers of the biological process (the mystery of generation inspired the Indian mind with dread, and a pregnant woman could bring all sorts of misfortune), was pathetic in the resignation it implied and very different from the Indian practice of resuscitation of their adult dead. It may have been felt that the *atisken* of one so young could not have attained absolute identity, for the bone soul was the vital force in life and though it might share extinguishment in pit burial with the body, it also contained the power to germinate once more into a living human being. It was the bone soul, therefore, by which the Indians were able to accomplish resuscitation or, as they came to think of it after their exposure to Christianity, resurrection of the dead.

Resuscitation was an extremely important factor in the continuity of tribal life. The primitive forest Indian built no monuments to commemorate events or people; he had no literature to remind him of the past. He might paint a pictorial record of a successful raid on a piece of birch bark and keep it in his cabin; or he might strip the bark from a tree in enemy country and on the naked trunk leave a similar record — the number of warriors who had come, the number killed, the prisoners captured, and the scalps taken — in symbols understood throughout the forest world, a sort of lifting of the leg, part in bravado, part as threat. Occasionally he might attempt something more permanent, like the rock painting on the Mohawk near the site of Amsterdam; or the stone crudely shaped like a man, with the head painted red, that Allouez found in the Fox country and destroyed when he learned it was an idol; or the extraordinary pictures on the Mississippi cliffs below the mouth of the Illinois, which Marquette and Joliet were the first white men to see.

But these last were monsters, strange mythological composites and doubly mysterious because one could not see how any man could have clung so high on the sheer wall to paint them and because no one could tell who had been the artist. Marquette's first reaction on sighting them was one of dread, and he wrote that the boldest savages in the party dared not look at them for any length of time.

> They are as large As a calf; they have Horns on their heads like those of deer, a horrible look, red eyes, a beard Like a tiger's, a face somewhat like a man's, a body Covered with scales, and so Long a tail that it winds all around the Body, passing above the head and going back between the legs, ending in a Fish's tail. Green, red, and black are three Colors composing the Picture. Moreover, these 2 monsters are so well painted that we cannot believe any savage is their author . . .

They were still uneasily discussing the paintings when the yellow discharge of the Missouri, muddy and tumultuous, tumbling flood refuse and even whole trees across their course, distracted them.

That the figures must have belonged to some tribal demonology is obvious, for their composite nature sorted with the attributes of other known Indian gods, such as the Algonquin Manabozho, or Great Hare, who was chief of all animals and so might appear in the shape of any one of them, including man, thus in his own person revealing how inextricably and intimately man's life was interwoven with the life of all living things. Manabozho, however, was essentially beneficent; these creatures on the Mississippi cliffs were evil and perhaps even more plainly revealed man's small position in his forest world, where every beast he killed might be a god or demon, to the peril of his soul.

Within this maze of natural and supernatural life the forest Indian found no incentive to perpetuate his physical image for the benefit of future generations. Statues or monuments would obviously have had no meaning for such a complete migrant as the Cree, whose life was patterned to the seasonal movements of game. Yet they would have meant hardly more to the sedentary Huron or Iroquois who, when he abandoned an old town for a new, carried with him only the tools of survival and in a pathetically short time saw everything he had left behind him — the palisades, sagging lodges, and surrounding cornfields — consumed by the returning wilderness. In the long woodland cycle his span of life was only slightly less ephemeral than that of the rabbit he took from his snare, and no more permanent in the impression he left upon it than his own footprint on the way to or from one of his wars.

The fugitive nature of his existence perpetually haunted him. He died as he was born, with no intimation of, or for that matter desire for immortality. He had no convinced belief in future blessedness. Beyond a few furs, he had nothing of tangible wealth to pass on to his descendants. In the end he had only his own soul to turn to for reassurance and a sense of purpose. It was an integral part of the woodland fabric through which it moved, but it also represented the qualities that gave him identity and made him a man. These qualities the Indian sought to preserve and pass on by means of resuscitation.

It was obviously important for the future welfare of the tribe to keep available the attributes of a man who distinguished himself in council or in war; but resuscitation was also performed for purposes of revenge — a man who received the soul of another who had been killed bound himself, automatically, to avenge the murder; or it was used to sustain a widow and her children, the recipient of the dead man's soul assuming immediately the roles of husband and father; or it might be practiced in the heart of the family solely to restore one deeply loved.

Whatever the reason, the responsibility of selecting the one to whom the soul should pass lay with the relatives of the dead, the final decision usually being in the hands of the oldest woman of the family, and the greatest pains were taken to find one whose characteristics resembled as closely as possible those of the soul he was to receive. The details of the ceremony varied from tribe to tribe. There was always a solemn feast to which many guests were invited, to assist and attest the resuscitation, and to which they brought gifts. All stood about the man who was to receive the soul of the dead. Sometimes he lay prone, and at a word all bent down with arms outstretched and made a lifting motion as though raising the soul from its sepulcher and passing it into the living body, all the time calling and exhorting him with the name of the dead man. At this he rose to his feet among them and received their gifts and from that moment became in their eyes actually the man they had honored. Then he would celebrate his resurrection by a solitary dance or song or, if he had received the soul of a celebrated warrior, immediately announce his intention of leading a war party against the enemy.

With the Algonquins the ritual involved the stripping of the soul recipient as he stood among the witnesses and then reclothing him in fine robes presented by the relatives of the deceased and painting his face. Father Jacques Buteux, a frail and devoted man who spent eighteen years among the Montagnais and Attikamegues and dreamed of offering his soul to God from the agony of an Iroquois fire, took part in the resuscitation of a Montagnais chief. When the "captain" had been clothed and painted, the master of ceremony or "herald" explained the meaning of the ritual:

"Let every one remain quiet," he calls out; "open your ears, and close your mouths. What I have to tell you is important. We are here to re-suscitate a dead man, and to bring a great Captain back to life." There-upon, he mentions him, and all his posterity; relates the place and manner of his death, and then, turning toward him who is to succeed him, he raises his voice and says: "There he is, he who is clothed with that fine robe. It is no longer he whom you lately saw, and whose name was Nehap. He has given his name to another savage. His name is Etouait" (that was the name of the deceased). "Look upon him as the true Captain of this tribe. It is he whom you must obey; it is he to whom you must listen, and whom you must honor."

Of course the herald would not have said "another savage." This was Buteux unconsciously revealing the insecurity he felt even among Indians with whom he had lived and worked for years and for whom he had genuine affection. He was not to die in an Iroquois fire; but the Iroquois killed him all the same, while he and a young Frenchman with a Huron convert were making a portage far north of Three Rivers, in the Atti-kamegue country west of Lake St. John. He fell at the first volley, with two balls in his chest and another in his arm, and with the young French-man was immediately dispatched in a frenzy of tomahawking, having only time to utter once the name of his Saviour; then the two bodies were stripped and thrown naked into the river. But in spite of this sub-conscious revelation he, like Paul Ragueneau, with whom he had a close relationship, had a perceptive understanding of the Indian character, and his description of the resuscitation continues with unusual sensitivity to the group's rejoicing, so triumphant that one hears echoes of Easter.

After visiting dignitaries from other tribes had been admonished to take home with them the tidings that once more the great Captain is to lead the Montagnais and had been given gifts to cement their memories, all the people began to sing. First one and then another voice would rise above the rest, calling on the people to rejoice, declaring that the salvation of the tribe had been assured, that the great name of Etouait would now not be forgotten. It is evident that in part the Indians took this resuscitation literally, in part figuratively, for the new Etouait himself in a brief and moving speech pointed out that he could hope to attain the great qualities of the chief whose name he now bore only if the tribe sustained him by their counsel and belief and encouraged him in his own constant striving.

Among the Hurons, as one might expect, resuscitation of a chief was performed in pomp and splendor with the celebration of the most magnifi-cent of all their feasts, the *Atouronta Ochien*, or Singing Feast. "These feasts will often last twenty-four entire hours," wrote Brébeuf; "sometimes there are thirty or forty kettles, and as many as thirty Deer will be eaten." The feast was sometimes given just for the sake of food and song, and sometimes it preceded the departure of a major war party; but when it was tied to the resuscitation of a chief, as many as eight or nine villages would participate, or even the entire nation might be represented. So important was the *Atouronta Ochien* in the life of the Hurons that when they moved to a new town, one lodge was always constructed larger than the rest to house it, often one hundred and fifty feet according to Brébeuf, though Bressani said that some he had seen were nearly twice that length.

The *Atouronta Ochien*, like almost all other Huron feasts, and for that matter the rite of resuscitation also, seems to have had its origin in the fabled resurrection of a Huron hunter by the animals who were his quarry but who, because of his essential goodness, had learned to love and cherish him. He never embarked on a hunt without first making a sacrifice to those he would pursue; he never took an animal at a disadvantage or shot a doe who had a fawn; and when he killed he always left the entrails and a portion of meat as a gift to the predatory birds and beasts — which endeared him especially to the wolves, and above all to the panther, *Ontarraoura*.

One day while hunting far from home he became separated from his companions and was surprised by an enemy war party, who killed him and took his scalp. All day his body lay unseen on the new-fallen red and yellow leaves, but at night the wolves scented blood and came to it through the underbrush; but when they recognized the good hunter, they howled till all the animals of the forest came to mourn. They held a council around the body and decided that such a man must not be allowed to die, so they determined to resuscitate him. Under the direction of the owl and the *Ontarraoura* a medicine was made, so powerful that less than could be contained in an acorn cup was enough to cure any injury or wound, even death. They gave some of it to the hunter, and as he lay on the ground, experiencing the slow return of life, his eyes yet closed and his soul still far out on the trail that leads from life to death, he heard the animals singing. Their words were perfectly comprehensible to him, but their song was like nothing he had ever heard and so beautiful that he could not forget it after his return to his people.

From his experience the Hurons derived their belief in the efficacy of singing feasts to cure the ill, or as an aid in restoring life. The Iroquois from a similar legend, in which through the instrumentality of the wolves the medicine was made available to man, developed a secret order called the Little Water Medicine Society, which still functions with undiminished vigor and offers its services to the sick and injured and plays an important role in preserving their national integrity and pride.

The symbolism that brought a man to life was carried out in the giving of presents. After the relatives had pointed to their choice, discarding his former name and giving him that of their own dead, the visitors came forward.

> . . . each Nation gave its presents, which, according to custom, were differently characterized. Some as they presented their gifts, said: "May these grasp the arm of the deceased, to draw him from the grave." Others said: "May these support his head, lest he fall back again." Another, giving still a new present, would add volubly, that he gave him weapons to repel the Enemies. "And I," a fourth would say, "I make the Earth solid under his feet, so that it may remain immovable during his reign."

With each speech, each a symbolic step back into life, the onlookers exclaimed in unison, "*Ao,*" to mark their approval. At last a collar of wampum was hung around his neck and the bearer of the dead chief's name, taking his place among the other chiefs, became in their eyes actually the man, to be so addressed and spoken of from that time forward.

Thus the name of a great chief never died; his character and deeds were remembered from generation to generation, so that in a sense the living custodian of his name embodied not only the man but a portion of the tribal history. The Iroquois carried this historical aspect much further by formalizing a rite, both moving and eloquent, about the resuscitation of a chief, using it not only to condole with the bereaved, but at the same time to recite the names and classifications of all who had been chiefs in the council at the time the League of the Five Nations had been established. These names, it is true, were still in force, having gained the status of hereditary titles and passed down through the original families, so that in each tribe the men and women used the name and saw its bearer every day as a matter of course. But in reciting the entire list, the people once more were reminded of the source of national strength, just as in Communion a Christian experiences again the sacrifice that is the heart and life of his faith. But the Iroquois were not content merely to recall the circumstances of their origin during the condolence rites; at some point in the ceremony the tribal belts of wampum were brought out and the principal chief, taking them up one by one, explained their significance — the treaties or great events they marked — so that the rebirth of a chief was seen against the panorama of the nation's history.

The Iroquois condolence rites were unique, too, for the fact that they were put into writing, probably in the middle of the eighteenth century, by the Iroquois themselves in the careful calligraphy that had been taught them by the English missionaries. This may account for echoes of the voice of the Biblical psalmist and, in one verse, use of the word "God" almost in the Christian fashion.

> My offspring, now this day we are met together, God has appointed this day. Now, today, we are met together, on account of the solemn event which has befallen you. Now into the earth he has been conveyed to

whom we have been wont to look. Yes, therefore, in tears let us smoke together.

But the imagery of the ceremony and the thought from which it springs are purely Indian and originated, obviously, long before the Iroquois were visited by the first Jesuits or subsequent Anglican or Moravian missionaries. Jean Pierron in the *Relation* for 1669–1670 records attending a condolence ceremony at the Mohawk town of Gandaouagué (Canandaigua), which incidently he almost managed to disrupt. Though he was forced to leave the ceremony, his attacks on Mohawk superstition made a deep impression on the Oneida and Onondaga delegations and even some of the Mohawks, so that he soon found himself making converts.

Pierron was a talented and highly educated man — for years he had taught in Jesuit colleges in France — but he had a gift for talking with the Iroquois in a way they understood, tough, practical, as one man to another, rather than as priest to pagan, though he never forgot or let them forget that he was a priest also. He had invented a game of chance for instructing them in the tenets of Christianity — a kind of religious parcheesi, with the seven sacraments, the three theological virtues, and all the commandments of God and of the church depicted in its course (he was a clever artist) as well as the principal mortal sins, even the venial sins, shown with marks of the horror they should rouse in Christian hearts.

This game is called "from Point to Point," — that is to say, from the point of Earth to the point of Eternity. Our Iroquois name it, "The way to arrive at the place where one lives forever, whether in Paradise or in Hell."

They mastered the game quickly and became so adept that one gathers they generally reached the happier goal and, in the excitement of a new enthusiasm, according to Father Pierron, found other things to talk about than their old myths and fables. But if he was eager to attack their superstitions, he made no attempt to interrupt their singing. "I was not one to disturb their music," he wrote, though he understood not a word of their song nor wished to countenance it. Perhaps the music itself fascinated him, as it had others of his Order. Some of it undoubtedly must have sounded lugubrious to European ears, but much of it was moving, even thrilling to hear, and many Indians had fine voices.

Fathers Pijart and Raymbault, who attended a Nipissing Feast of the Dead in 1642, afterward described an elaborate three-part ballet danced "to the sound of voices and a sort of drum, in such harmonious accord that they rendered all the tones most agreeable in Music." Two thousand Indians of various tribes had come together on the Huron shore from their nomadic wanderings, and the cadence of their chorused voices against the vast panorama of lake and wilderness was something the two Jesuits were not likely to forget.

But of all the northern Indians the Hurons appear to have been the best singers. "Their voices are exceptionally beautiful," Le Mercier reported, "especially the girls." It is possible to understand, therefore, what a shattering impact the *Atouronta Ochien*, with two or three hundred voices in a single long house celebrating the renewal of a great man's soul, must have had upon the man whose body had just become its new tenement. Whether he accepted the rite intellectually as the figurative resuscitation of a man by the adoption of his name or emotionally as the actual transmigration of the soul into himself, he was no longer the person he had been up to that instant in his life. Besides the two souls that had been his at birth, he had now become custodian of a third.

The introduction of alcohol into this hallucinatory world of dreams, demonology, and fractionalized emotions and spiritual beliefs could not have been anything but devastating. With a few drinks of brandy an Indian could release his soul from his body, as occurred in dreams; indeed many Indians described their experience with drink precisely so, recounting their sensations and actions, as far as they could remember, as though they had been looking on from a point of vantage entirely outside themselves. Étienne de Carheil, of the Cayuga mission, wrote that "some drink only to intoxicate themselves, and sing of their intention to do so, and that they are heard to shout: 'I am going to lose my head; I am going to drink of the water that takes away one's wits.' " Carheil took this as a statement of intention merely to get sodden drunk, but actually it seems to me a literal expression of the Indian's experience, as real and fascinating as the disembodiment he experienced in dreams. What they did not at first realize was the violence which their physical being gave vent to once liquor had deprived it of reason, any more than they appreciated the ultimate effect it would have upon them spiritually, for to people so conditioned, threading an endless labyrinth of superstition and fear, the use of alcohol meant literally an unhinging of the mind. When they did begin to comprehend, it was too late.

The drunken Indian, coming to his senses after a murderous debauch, might or might not be aware of having betrayed the whole tradition of his race, but for the more perceptive, especially one who harbored in his body the soul of some greater man, guilt became unbearable and not infrequently resulted in his committing suicide. This is to assume for the Indian a degree of spiritual awareness, something the Jesuits doubtless would have denied by citing the barbarisms, licentiousness, insane cruelties, and what seemed to them perversions of thinking that could have originated only with the devil — just as would the later white men who traded with the Indians for their furs or women and judged them by the degraded standards of Indian life which they themselves had largely brought about.

Alcohol, however, made no religious distinctions. Christian Indians got as drunk as their heathen brothers and suffered an additional guilt from the betrayal of their new faith. They turned to the mission Fathers for help, and the Jesuits in their turn appealed to the governor. Usually he was sympathetic, but in fact there was almost nothing he could do about it. Prohibitory edicts were no more effective than the paper they were published on. In their passion for liquor the Indians who had come with sick repentance to the Father in the morning would in the afternoon sneak off behind his back to ship or trading post, and as long as they had furs they got their brandy. "It is impossible," Vimont wrote in 1644, "to hinder the avarice of some of the French, who in spite of prohibitions and the risk of being punished, still sell brandy and wine to the savages." And three years later Paul Ragueneau reported bluntly, "It becomes a war between liquor and the church."

Laval certainly accepted it as war. He had come to Canada with a deep concern for the Indians and shared the Jesuits' ambition to bring all of them eventually within the Catholic fold. He was profoundly moved by the missionary experience far in the wilderness, thrilled by the hardships it entailed and above all by the occasional exaltation of martyrdom. Perhaps it was his martial inheritance that made him think of the missionary Fathers as actual soldiers of the Cross and there is no reason to doubt the sincerity of his own longing to play a part in this humblest of struggles in the cause of Christ.

If so many benefits received in the past have attached me to your Society [he wrote the General of the Jesuits in Rome], fresh bonds now render those affectionate relations still more binding. In fact, my Reverend Father, I am granted the grace of sharing the labors of your children in that mission of Canada, in that vineyard of the Lord which they have watered with their sweat, and even with their blood. What joy for my heart if I could hope for a like death, a like crown! The Lord no doubt will not grant it to my merits, but I venture to hope it from his mercy. In any case, my fate is a happy one; and the lot assigned me by the Lord is well worthy of envy. What can be more glorious than to devote oneself and to consume oneself entirely for the salvation of souls? Such is the grace that I ask, that I hope for, and that I love.

If he had been stirred by the work of the Jesuits, the impression he made on them from the outset was equally profound. On the very day of his arrival, in June 1659, he baptized a Huron baby and then moving on to the Jesuit hospital gave the last sacraments to a young Huron dying of gangrene. "Thus he gave a noble example to our Savages, who with admiration saw him prostrated upon the earth before a poor carcass, which already smelled of corruption, and which he prepared with his own hands for the holy unctions."

One is irresistibly reminded of Brébeuf's account of the Huron women preparing the putrefied bodies of their dead and his attendant homily: "After that, who will be afraid of the stench of a Hospital; and who will not take a peculiar pleasure in seeing himself at the feet of a sick man all covered with wounds, in the person of whom he beholds the Son of God?"

The spectacle of their bishop lying at the feet of the dying Huron convinced the Jesuits once and for all of Laval's zeal in the missionary cause, and they never doubted the sincerity of his expressed longing to share actively with them the dangers and hardships of their wilderness apostleship.

> He would have done so [wrote Lalemant], could he have divided himself; and the journeys he performed over the snow in his very first winter, to visit his flock — not on horseback or in a carriage, but on snowshoes and over the ice — showed that he would do his part well among the most excellent Missionaries to the Savages, if he could leave the more necessary duties and hasten to those more dangerous. His heart, at least, had flown thither, while he himself remains here, as at the center of all the Missions, to be able to give his attention to, and share his zeal with, all equally.

Laval had the Frenchman's gift of identifying his new country with himself. The extent of it fired his imagination and he embraced it all: from Quebec, along whose steep and narrow streets his thin figure in a wellworn cassock soon became a familiar sight, to the little villages of Three Rivers and Montreal, the farms scattered along the shores of the St. Lawrence, precarious threads of civilization joining the three settlements together, and above all to the endless regions of lake and forest beyond, with their barely tapped supply of unculled souls. Of all this, in its vastness more like an empire than a mere diocese, he was the spiritual proprietor, and he set about its administration with vigor and determination.

During his first months in Quebec, as we have seen, he was preoccupied by his campaign to assert the dignity of his office and the power of the church in colonial affairs; but by the end of November he was ready to come to grips with the brandy question. "Cold and snow Commenced," recorded the author of the Jesuit *Journal* for that year, and sleighs were appearing in the streets when Laval called the Jesuits to a meeting "to decide whether it is a sin to sell liquors, either wine or brandy, to the savages." Needless to say, it was declared a sin, and two further meetings were held early in December to draw up a list of "reserved cases" — that is, of offenders so incorrigible and flagrant in their defiance of the prohibition that the power of restoring them to grace was reserved for the bishop alone.

[73]

This measure proved so effective that within a year Lalemant could report "the almost total suppression of drunkenness among our Savages." The Indians themselves, who had often begged that the brandy trade be stopped, were deeply impressed and sent deputations to the bishop to express their gratitude; and the Hurons betowed a new name on him — *Hariouaouagui* — "the man of the great work."

It is difficult to realize today the shock and horror with which the threat of excommunication was received in a society as simple and devoutly Catholic as that of New France still was. In 1660 life in Canada had not markedly changed in its spiritual aspects from life in the first crude settlement under Champlain and the Recollect Fathers at the foot of Cape Diamond. Champlain and his successor, Montmagny, were imbued with true piety and regarded themselves as instruments for furthering Christianity; it was the duty as well as the honor of the government or, as Champlain put it, of "the Lily of France to protect in Canada the Holy Catholic religion." So also Maisonneuve, the first governor of Montreal, saw himself as the leader of a mission colony whose controlling purpose was to bring the Catholic religion to the savages, not only through the ministration of its Sulpician priests but by the example of its lay colonists, who by their way of life would create once more the atmosphere of the primitive Christian church. Indians were to be encouraged to settle beside the town and so by observation and training to acquire the skills of civilized living.

Probably no town has ever been founded with loftier motives, and for many years the life of its settlers was remarkable for its purity. For more than two decades there was no such thing as a lock on the island of Montreal, whether to a house or even a chest. No one asked for or gave receipts for merchandise delivered. For a long time this was true of the rest of Canada; theft was not unknown, of course, but its occurrence was extremely rare. In fact the rarity of crime of any sort was one of the remarkable features of the first fifty years of Canadian history.

This was partly due to the universal poverty. There was little for anyone to steal. The possessions of the average habitant were meager indeed — tools for the soil; an ax; probably, though not inevitably, a musket; some bedding; a few pots and pans; perhaps, if he were fortunate, a cow — with these and the strength of his own shoulders (except for one presented to Governor Montmagny in 1647, no horses were imported before 1665) he set about the clearing of his land and winning a living from it, something that was seldom possible before the passage of two years.

But a more important factor in the high moral standards of the colony was the character of the people themselves — if we except the *coureur de bois*, who was a law to himself, a thorn to the missionaries, and the despair of the government, which never succeeded in controlling him for long. His allies were the merchants who cared nothing for the colony as such, but were wholly behind the activities of the *coureur de bois* in furthering or violating, as the case might be, the fur monopoly. But the actual colonists, who came to make a home out of the new land, were an unusually homogeneous group. The vast majority — if one may apply such a term to a population that as late as 1646 numbered only two hundred and forty men, women, and children, and by 1663 had increased to barely twenty-five hundred — came from the four northwestern provinces of Normandy, Poitou, Anjou, and Maine. There was a scattering of people from Brittany and the Île de France, but southern and eastern France were not represented at all in New France. Some of the colonists, of course, especially in the early years, turned out to be riffraff, but most of those who became habitants were simple, tough, hard-working artisans and farmers who had been recruited by seigneurs, often returning from Canada to select their prospective tenants in person, and who were willing to leave the arpent or two they had worked as their own in the old country because in the new they could have a farm of one or two hundred — in a few cases of as much as a thousand — arpents without having to put money down in payment. If they did not have the wild adventurousness that carried the *coureur de bois* through half a continent of wilderness, they did have the ambition to cross the ocean in search of a better living and the tenacity to hang on to their new land and develop it in the face of every obstacle.

So too with the seigneurs. They came from the same provinces as their tenants. They were not of the nobility, though some came from established, even distinguished families. Four — the Gardeur brothers, Pierre and Charles, who became *sieurs* of Tilly and Repentigny; Jacques Le Neuf de la Poterie; and Charles Joseph d'Ailleboust, the governor of Montreal — were ennobled by the king in 1666, and nine others received similar patents shortly after. In later years still more were elevated, usually at the request of a governor or intendant who felt he had a debt to pay, if not an ax to grind, so that gradually the Canadian *noblesse* lost significance until, indeed, it was possible for a shopkeeper to achieve it if he had the right amount of money. But the earlier recipients were all leading figures in the colony, and the families they founded were to distinguish themselves in colonial affairs.

There was yet another class of men who stood out because of their professional rather than their social barkground. Louis Hébert, for example, one of the first three to receive a seigneury in Quebec, had been an apothecary with his own shop in Paris; Robert Giffard, who was brilliantly successful in recruiting tenants and developing his grant, was a surgeon; Noël Juchereau was a licentiate in law; Jean Bourdon was a surveyor and engineer, who drew the first map of the colony and moved upward in the public service until appointed attorney general. Men of their sort brought real substance to the crude little society. But the generality

[75]

of seigneurs had little or no education, and none were men of wealth. They were actuated by the same motive of bettering their lot that brought the habitant across the ocean. In the old country they stood no chance of altering their status, but in Canada, once granted land, they expected to live like gentlemen.

Actually the life of the seigneur was not much less rough than that of his tenants. He might have a stone house — if he was able to, he was sure to build one and think of it as his manor — but it was not likely to be a great deal larger or more comfortable than the conventional cabin of logs. The one Hébert built on the heights above Quebec in 1617 or shortly after — the first building to take shape on what was to become the Upper Town — measured thirty-eight feet by nineteen. His first efforts at farming seem equally small, covering less than ten acres. But this, like the house, represented a prodigious feat of labor, for the work was done entirely with hand tools — there was no plow on the farm till the year after his death in 1627, when his widow acquired one. To accomplish even what he did, he and his family had to work on the land together; and this was true of other early seigneurial families.

Their lives were closely bound with those of the habitants, and though the fabric of their little society was drawn on feudal lines, the feudal aspects were more formal than real. The relationship of the seigneur to his tenants was not so much that of a lord as of a land agent. He had received his grant from the Company of New France — or later from the Crown — on condition that he clear the land within a stipulated time, and he held title to his fief by a declaration of faith and homage to the Crown, from which the Company in its turn had received the whole domain. If the property changed hands, the new owner, whether by inheritance or purchase, had to renew the oath of faith and homage to make his title good; and if the land had been sold, one fifth of the price paid for it had to be turned over to the Company or the Crown.

The habitant, who stood at the bottom of this ladder of delegated responsibility for clearing the land and was the instrument which made the creaky system work as well as it did, also held his small acreage under oath of faith and homage, but in his case to the seigneur; and he also suffered a similar penalty for selling, one twelfth of the money he received reverting to the seigneur.

Within this framework of ownership, the habitant's position was unique. The trappings of feudalism which surrounded him were largely meaningless and served mainly to give the seigneur an illusion of nobility. The most serious burden imposed upon him, and the one most often resented, was the *corvée*, his obligation to the seigneur of a certain amount of his labor each year — the number of days being in proportion to the amount of land he held: it rarely came to more than six days, and if he had money, the habitant could get out of it by a small payment in cash. Nor was it actually more onerous than the public labor exacted by New England townships for the upkeep of roads and bridges and, with the additional *corvée* owed to the Crown, served much the same purpose.

The habitant was neither a vassal nor a serf, for he owed the seigneur no military obligation, nor could he be sold with the land, like a serf. As long as he paid his annual rent — never more than two sous per arpent and payable partly in money, partly in produce — the land was his: it could not be taken from him, and he could pass it on to his heirs in any manner he chose.

The seigneur, however, enjoyed various rights which he could when he thought fit exercise over his tenants. These were called *banalités* and were largely carry-overs from the old system of feudal tenure in France. As far as the habitant was concerned, most of them were more a nuisance than a burden. He was supposed to bake his bread in the seigneur's oven and grind his grain at the seigneur's mill; but the former was seldom insisted on, and as for the latter, which in France often imposed a real grievance, only the seigneur could have afforded to build a mill and the rates charged seem to have been seldom, if ever, excessive. More frivolous and calculated to emphasize the difference in class was the obligation of the habitant to deliver every eleventh fish he caught to the seigneur's kitchen, and still more so, the duty to come annually to dance round the seigneurial Maypole.

It is hard to see how the contribution of every eleventh fish could have been enforced, but even if it was, it could not have entailed much hardship, for the St. Lawrence teemed with fish and had a yearly run of eels in numbers almost as unbelievable as the flights of wild pigeons. One fisherman was reported to have taken five thousand in a single day in his weir, and these eels, either fresh or smoked and salted for the winter, were of far better flavor than the ones caught in the old country and, like the pigeons which were also salted or packed in tallow, provided one of the colony's staple foods.

When it came to the celebrating of May Day, the sight of his tenants around his Maypole may have given the seigneur a feeling of proprietary satisfaction, but in a life as bare of even the simple amenities as his was, the early Canadian habitant must have looked forward to this interlude of gaiety and enjoyed it without a thought of its indicating his social inferiority. No doubt he respected the seigneur as the person who supplied some sort of focus for the activities of the seigneurial community, but the seigneur had neither the wealth nor the political power to oppress his tenants, even if he had wanted to, and under the terms by which he held his fief, there was small chance of his attaining either.

He could hunt and fish over his property as much as he pleased but, except for the crops he and his tenants raised, any real wealth that might materialize on his holding was reserved to the Crown: all timber suitable for shipbuilding had to be preserved, and he was obliged to report to the king or his governors "any Mines, Mining-places, and Minerals that might be found throughout the extent of the said Lands." In any case it would have been impossible for him to have developed them without financial assistance from France and it became normal procedure to petition the Crown for aid in any such enterprise.

Fur was the only natural product by which he might conceivably enrich himself, but the fur trade was so politically controlled within the various monopolies that the seigneur had little more scope than the habitant who bartered with a wandering Indian for a pelt or two. The turning over of management of the fur trade by the Company of New France to a group of Canadians in 1645, under terms which among other things involved the importation of twenty new settlers a year and annual payment of a thousand pounds in beaver, merely transferred the monopoly. Even opening the trade to the general public two years later did little to make possible small-scale enterprises by the individual habitant or seigneur. He was permitted to use only products of the country in barter; such furs as he did manage to get hold of had to be carried to the common warehouse and sold at rigidly controlled prices; and in any case the increasing difficulties of the trade because of unceasing Iroquois raids meant that the merchants who could afford to risk capital on hazardous trading parties became fewer and consequently more powerful in their control of the trade. Until 1653 when the Iroquois, about to become preoccupied in their war of extermination against the Eries, temporarily sought peace with the French and for a few short years the traders found the west, with an immense backlog of unsold beaver, opened to them, the only place for restless or ambitious young men of no means was as paddlers or, if they knew an Indian tongue, interpreters to an expedition. But the rewards were not attractive.

Monsieur du Chesne, for instance, was paid twenty écus by the Jesuits for four years' service among the Hurons (the equivalent then of fifteen dollars, though in terms of today's money, of course, considerably more); but obviously the Jesuit Fathers felt that something more was due the young man, so he "was clothed and decently supplied with linen, & sent to 3 rivers as a soldier & Interpreter." It was not until 1663, when the increase of money within the colony began to weaken the monopoly and the renewal of Iroquois raids along the Ottawa and the necessity of sending all the way to the Great Lakes country to find furs made the local trader more important, that the young men of Canada found a wilderness vocation and the real *coureur de bois* was born. So many then were to seek a new life of freedom away from the seigneuries and farms that in 1681 the intendant expressed serious alarm over the effect of their defection on the colony's agriculture.

But before 1663 the people of Canada led a circumscribed life of almost

incredible simplicity, with no outside interests or excitement or real awareness of what was going on beyond their own settlement. There was no
such thing, of course, as a newspaper in the colony; there was not even a
printing press through all the years of French rule. There was nothing
like the New England town meeting to animate minds or provide contact
with the activities of other communities. It was not intended that the Canadian settler should have any such outside contacts. This fact was implicit in the terminology of the seigneurial grant in which the seigneur
was reminded that he held his fief on condition "that he should keep, and
cause his tenants to keep, House and Home thereon."

Two unifying forces governed their lives. One was the specter of death
constantly haunting them from the fringe of the woods in the Satanic
form of the Iroquois. The other was the church and their religion.

Before Laval's arrival in 1659, the religious ministration of Canada, for
the French settler as well as Indian convert, was almost wholly a missionary one. The scarcity of secular priests compelled the colonists to depend
on the missionary Orders, and until the founding of Montreal brought the
Sulpicians to Canada, in 1642, the burden fell entirely on the Jesuits, for
the Recollects, who had left after the brief capture of Quebec by the
British in 1628, did not return until 1670.

The first and for many years the only parish church was built at Quebec in 1633. It stood for seven years before being destroyed by fire. Seven
more years elapsed before the cornerstone was laid for its successor, and
still another ten years went by before it was finally opened in 1657,
though the first mass had been said in the unfinished building on
Christmas Eve in 1650. This was Notre Dame de la Paix, and its construction was a tremendous achievement for the tiny community, for it was a
hundred feet long by thirty wide. Twice enlarged, in 1687 and again in
1745, to an ultimate length of one hundred and ninety feet, it became the
basilica as we know it today; but even in its original form it must have
been an imposing feature of the crown of buildings on the heights. Certainly Laval was impressed by it. "There is here," he wrote,"a cathedral
made of stone; it is large and splendid. The divine service is celebrated in
it according to the ceremony of bishops."

If the first sight of it lifted the heart of a settler visiting from up or
down the river, as indeed it must have, the interior inspired him with awe.
The wealth of ornaments, all of gilt or solid silver; the number of priests
and seminarists constantly in attendance, as well as choirboys; the magnificent music, for on festival days the mass was sung to orchestral ac-
companiment, with organs swelling above the chanting voices – all were
in such contrast to his own experience of religious worship in the tiny
settlement that was his home as to be overpowering.

The chances were that the district he came from had no church at all.
If it had, the church would have been no more than a small wooden build-

ing, crude, with a thatched roof, probably in poor repair, and there would have been no money for even the simplest of sacred vessels. In winter it was heated by fires burning in large open kettles, so that the interior was often as smoke-filled as any Indian lodge. There was no resident priest. Communities were scattered and too small to warrant assigning a priest to a single settlement. A parish might reach for fifty miles along the river — one, in fact, was eighty miles long; and it was seldom that a priest, or a Jesuit who had assumed parochial duties, managed to visit all his parishioners more than three or four times a year.

The hardships and dangers of his calling could hardly be exaggerated. Summer and winter he traveled the St. Lawrence with one lay servant to help paddle his canoe or draw the toboggan on which he carried his portable chapel and a few supplies. The river was the only highway of French settlement and practically every house in Canada stood in sight of it. Each seigneury fronted on the river, however far it might reach inland, and each habitant to whom land was sold received a portion of the river frontage. As time went on and a farm was subdivided among heirs, holdings became mere strips of land, as may still be seen in the fenced ribbons of field and pasture stretching between the river and the Laurentian hills.

In the earlier years, while the population remained small and the marauding Iroquois virtually unchecked, there was mile after empty mile for the priest and his one companion to traverse. They paddled in silence. Their eyes, burning from the reflected glare of the unruffled surface under a brassy sky, unceasingly scanned both the near shore and the distant one, seeking in the behavior of each clump of reeds the direction of the ensuing stroke. The rise of a pair of mallard might be no more than an exhibition of the birds' impulse to flight, but it might also prelude the lashing emergence of canoes amid the high-pitched, unnerving cries of the Iroquois. If the lay paddler owned a gun, there was neither time nor point in using it. The sole hope lay in outstripping the pursuit.

Though the risk of capture by the Iroquois was not then as great, winter brought its own dangers, and the loneliness of the two infinitesimal figures on the white expanse of the river, one attached to the toboggan, was intensified. The cold was an enemy as hostile as the Indian, and now and then snowstorms swept down with such overwhelming force that one could only retreat to a thicket and dig a shelter in which to wait it out. For some the snow proved fatal.

Such a one was Father Anne de Noüe. He had come to Canada twenty years before with a burning desire to convert the savages and had made one trip to the Huron country with Brébeuf; but finding himself incapable of mastering any Indian language, he had dedicated his life to the service of the French and such Indians as lived close enough to towns or forts for him to reach through an interpreter. At the end of January, 1646, in the company of a Huron and two soldiers, he set out from Three

Rivers for the fort at the mouth of the Richelieu, thirty miles as the crow flies across the great wide place in the St. Lawrence called Lac St. Pierre.

They were on snowshoes, for the snow was four feet deep, and the soldiers, who were newly arrived and not accustomed either to such gear or to the bitter cold, made poor progress, so that nightfall found them barely halfway to their destination and stumbling with exhaustion. They went ashore into the thick woods and, digging down into the snow and lighting a fire, bedded down for the night.

But toward two o'clock, Noüe woke to find moonlight flooding the sky, and he resolved at once to push on alone to the fort in order to send back help. He told the others to wait till morning and then follow his tracks, along which they would before long meet the rescue party. He himself was familiar with the route and so confident of reaching the fort before sundown that he left the men his blanket and his flint and steel, and took with him only a piece of bread and a few prunes.

Before dawn, the weather changed. Clouds covered the moon and soon a driving snow set in. His tracks quickly filled behind him. The force of the snow steadily increased until it became so furious that he could not tell when daylight came. Out on the blank whiteness of the river he became confused; he wandered and circled on his tracks but did not see them, and only by luck toward the second night stumbled on the shore; but instead of the south shore for which he had aimed, this was the northern one. He dug himself a little hole in the snow, lined it with spruce branches, and without a fire or covering of any kind he lay down. Somehow, frail and slender as he was, and in his sixtieth year, he survived the night and was able to push on next day. But he was still lost.

Meanwhile the Huron and the two soldiers had finally reached the fort, though it was too late to send out a search party. But next morning groups of the garrison went out to look for the Father. They tramped all day, halooing and firing their muskets without finding a trace of him, and came home discouraged. The day after, however, two Huron converts, in company with a soldier named Baron, set out to sift his trail from under the new snow and, knowing how to find signs of where a man had passed even after so much time, traced him through all his wanderings to his first campsite and eventually back across the St. Lawrence.

In his confusion and fatigue he had missed the fort, though only by a little way, and stumbled on up the Richelieu River. Finally, in a little hollow between two small brooks, they came upon him. Once more he had dug a hole in the snow, and had then knelt in it to pray, and there in that posture the cold had claimed him, frozen in worship, like a statue. They were overcome with awe, and it was a little while before they could summon themselves to pick him up and put him on their sled for the return to the fort.

The Jesuits' accomplishment in Canada fills seventy volumes in which their devotion, self-sacrifice, the hardships they endured, their triumphs in martyrdom are all set down in meticulous detail; but there is little record of the parish priests who, as their number increased, came to serve all the French community. Quite possibly they were too burdened with the griefs and perplexities of their scattered flocks to give as passionate thought as the Jesuits to the cause of furthering the Cross or be as much concerned with their own advancement under Christ.

When a priest and his servant drove the bow of their canoe ashore where a footpath led down from a solitary house, or perhaps from a seigneury like that of St. Denis with only two dwellings, or more rarely a real but small communuity, the same multiplicity of religious duties confronted him. The portable altar had first to be set up against a wall of the single room if there was but the one house, or in the home of the seigneur if the place was a seigneury. But even if the settlers had a church — usually built in cooperation by the seigneur and his tenants, he providing the chancel, they the nave — it would be equally unconsecrated, for it was not believed proper to consecrate a building that was not "solid and durable." Only stone was so regarded, and as late as 1680 only seven parishes had been able to afford walls of stone.

The saying of mass in the little makeshift church was but one of his duties. There were marriages to be solemnized. Sometimes the bride was Indian; quite often she might be no more than a child of twelve or thirteen; or again she would be a young widow with already a brood of her own, for women were not long allowed to remain unclaimed. Not always had the couple contrived to wait for the priest's arrival, but a tardy marriage was better than none at all. The sick had to be ministered to, in which the case the priest was apt to double as physician or surgeon, if he had not come too late; and if he had, there was a burial service to be performed over a grave at the woods' edge for the unshriven dead. Confessions must be heard, with penance meted out and absolution given. He must baptize the babies born since his last visit and, if he could find time, catechize the children who, mingled with the dogs and equally clamorous, had probably come swarming down to greet him at the landing.

There were always children. From the beginning Jesuits and laymen alike had commented on the fruitfulness of women who came to Canada. It was believed that the climate was especially favorable to the female sex for, even with heavy childbearing, they proved long-lived compared with men. They married young and produced eight or eighteen children and, when the husband died, not infrequently added to the total in a second marriage. When a bounty was offered for the production of large families, the reward began for a family of ten, who were paid three hundred livres a year. Any number less than ten, apparently, was regarded as inconsequential.

To these people the arrival of the priest meant for a brief time a restoration of their spiritual life. But also he brought them news of Quebec, of the arrival of ships, of religious occasions, and the activities of governor and council. For most of them he provided their only link with the Old World. Also he served as messenger from one settlement to another, much as in former times in this country the rural mailman performed an unofficial service for the farms along his route. Without the labors of the priest it is hard to see how the attenuated line of settlement could have held together at all. How he himself survived year after year of his arduous rounds is another matter. It became one of the problems of Laval, though at first he was preoccupied with other things, as we have seen. But to the remote settler excommunication would have been a catastrophe beyond even its awesome spiritual implications. No wonder it was so effective in halting the brandy traffic while it remained in force.

It remained in force for twenty months after its first publication in the spring of 1660, and might have remained longer if the Jesuits and priests had been satisfied with it as the sole deterrent penalty. They were not. Nothing but assured and absolute cessation of the brandy trade was acceptable to them, and they seem to have felt that excommunication by itself was not enough. Somewhat on the order of the "overkill" that haunts our own era, they wished to add the penalty of death to the denial of salvation. They succeeded in doing so. By the time Argenson left the governorship and sailed for France in September 1661, the death penalty was in force.

The new governor was the Baron d'Avaugour, who at the end of his own term was to relieve Radisson and Groseilliers of half of their fur profits with such surgical finesse, but on his arrival he was still an unknown quantity in Canada, and there was some anxious speculation among the clergy over what position he would take in the brandy controversy. It became acute, for almost at once he and Laval found themselves at odds.

Laval had made plans for greeting the new governor with all due ceremony, even as to his own robes. He intended to receive him in the lower part of the church, wearing his "rochet and Camail," to offer him holy water, and then conduct him to his proper place, while the "Te Deum" was being chanted. A rochet is merely a narrow surplice-like garment, usually with narrow sleeves, but a camail, or mozzetta, is a short, ornamental cape worn only by higher prelates and is a symbol of jurisdiction, though by a bishop it may not be worn outside of his diocese. If Laval expected to impress on the governor the authority of the church by this reception, he was disappointed, for Avaugour simply did not appear.

Whether from tact or from not wanting to have Argenson's troubles poured over his head during the three weeks that remained before the latter's departure, Avaugour elected to stay not at the Château St. Louis but at a private house. He did go to the Jesuits' church to hear mass on the evening of his arrival, and he later entered their refectory "where, with his suite, he ate a morsel." But he detested ceremony and the next day was off to visit Montreal. On his return, though he did go to the parish church, it was on working days and without fanfare of any sort.

Laval was offended, and as if to rub the matter in, Avaugour made plain his respect for the Jesuits by insisting that their Superior (Jerome Lalemant) take a seat on the council. Evidently he could handle himself in the power struggle which Argenson had found so frustrating. Though he disapproved of the death penalty for selling brandy to the Indians — he thought such interference with the fur trade ruinous and believed that an evil should be accepted when it resulted in greater good — he did not interfere when a test came: two men were shot for the offense and another was publicly flogged.

The people were shaken by these executions, which they had never really believed would be carried out; and also almost everyone had in one way or another some share in the offense. However, the situation did not long remain stationary. In January 1662 a woman was cast into prison for selling brandy to an Indian, and Lalemant, in the kindness of his heart, undertook to plead her cause with the governor. Avaugour, whose temper Colbert was to describe as "bizarre and somewhat impracticable," exploded. If this woman was not to be punished for selling brandy, then no one should be. From that position no amount of pressure could budge him.

The reaction was immediate and violent, not only in unbridled traffic in liquor, among the French settlers themselves as well as to the Indians, but against the church, the bishop, and the Jesuits, many people turning even on their parish priests in open defiance. For the moment the whole fabric of spiritual life in Canada seemed to have collapsed. Laval was torn by rage and despair. His sermons threatening God's retribution went unheeded. Fresh excommunications aroused such fury among the people that he was forced to withdraw them the same day they were uttered.

The ensuing weeks did nothing to better matters. Without the support of the government, Laval now found himself and the church almost helpless. It was a humiliating experience and Avaugour's dissolution of the council in April and his appointment of a new one composed entirely of his own supporters was a fresh aggravation. For the sake of his flock, Indian and French alike, for the sake of the church, for the sake of Canada itself, matters could not be allowed to continue on their present course. He resolved to take his case to the Throne, and on the twelfth of August he sailed for France. It was the first of four round trips across the Atlantic he would make before laying down his duties.

[84]

Meanwhile his absence did little to restore order. The brandy traffic flowed on unchecked; the remonstrances of the clergy were disregarded or mocked. But now strange phenomena appeared in the sky to strike wonder and raise doubts among thoughtful men. "Aerial voices," Lalemant called them, which "were not, after all, mere empty words, since they presaged convulsions that were to make us shudder while making the Earth tremble."

First there were fiery serpents, "intertwined in the form of the Caduceus" and flying through the sky on flaming wings. Then, over Quebec, a great ball of fire was seen, which made the night as bright as day.

This same Meteor appeared over Montreal, but seemed to issue from the Moon's bosom, with a noise like that of Cannon or Thunder; and after travelling three leagues in the air, it finally vanished behind the great mountain whose name the Island bears.

But what seemed to us most extraordinary was the appearance of three Suns. Toward eight o'clock in the morning, on a beautiful day last Winter, a light and almost imperceptible mist arose from our great river, and, when struck by the Sun's first rays, became transparent, — retaining, however, sufficient substance to bear the two images cast upon it by that Luminary. These three Suns were almost in a straight line . . . the real one in the middle, and the others on each side. All three were crowned by a Rainbow, the colors of which were not definitely fixed; it now appeared Iris-hued, and now of a luminous white, as if an exceedingly strong light had been a short distance underneath.

This spectacle was of almost two hours' duration upon its first appearance, on the seventh of January; while on its second, on the 14th of the same month, it did not last so long, but only until, the Rainbow hues gradually fading away, the two Suns at the sides also vanished, leaving the central one, as it were, victorious.

These phenomena, awe-inspiring though they must have been, were later considered to be merely portents of the earthquake soon to follow.

On the fifth of February, 1663, toward half past five in the evening, a loud roaring was heard at the same time throughout the length and breadth of Canada. This noise, which gave one the impression that a house was on fire, made all rush outdoors to escape so unexpected a conflagration; but, instead of smoke and flames, people were much surprised to behold the Walls tottering, and all the stones in motion, as if they had been detached. Roofs seemed to bend down in one direction, and then back again in the other; Bells rang of their own accord; beams, joists, and boards creaked; and the earth leaped up, and made the palisade-stakes dance in a way that would have seemed incredible, had we not witnessed it in different places.

This first shock proved to be the heaviest, though in the next six months shocks occurred that were almost equally severe. For weeks on end the tremors came two or three times a day, but gradually they dwindled in force and frequency and near the middle of August they finally ceased. One of the strange aspects of the earthquake was that almost all the heaviest shocks seemed to be confined to the line of the St. Lawrence. Inland, where the mountains began, returning hunters reported that the noise and the quivering of the ground would go on uninterrupted for hours at a time, but there was nothing of the violence that brought the citizens of Quebec, Three Rivers, and Montreal rushing from their houses.

Two mountains above Three Rivers disappeared wholly into the St. Lawrence, and below Quebec at Bay St. Paul another slid into the water to form a little island. Farther down at Pointe aux Allouettes a long wooded stretch of the shore did the same and turned into an underwater forest, with only the tops of the trees showing above the surface. In other places deep fissures opened in the ground; rivers changed their color, some red, some yellow, while the whole great St. Lawrence from above Montreal to Tadoussac at the mouth of the Saguenay turned the color of milk. At the latter place one day the sky darkened and a heavy shower of what seemed to be ashes crossed the river like a summer thunderstorm. In other places upheavals of the river bed lifted fountains of mud a hundred feet into the air. At Three Rivers one day porpoises were heard crying pitifully in the river; they were white, as if stained by the water. Here during the first shocks the people were convinced that the earth was about to split and swallow them; for days they said it rocked like a great ship in the troughs of the sea.

As was to be expected, people reported strange manifestations in the sky: "fiery phantoms bearing torches in their hands." Everywhere pikes and lances of fire were seen, waving in the air. At Three Rivers, where a long rapid had suddenly been made smooth by the sinking of the rocks into the bottom of the river, "a horrid, shapeless, and monstrous specter was seen crossing from East to West along the edges of the moat constructed for the military defense of the town."

The number and variety of these apparitions were almost unlimited, and the clergy seem to have put as much credence in them as the Indians and habitants who reported them. Father Charles Simon "affirms that he learned, from the very persons to whom they happened, of all the apparitions which he has inserted in his Narrative." Most of all the good Father was impressed by the experience of a certain man "deeply meditating in the presence of God" at half past ten of a night before the second quarter of the moon. He saw the skies divide and for the space of half an hour gazed into the heart of heaven. There an angel stood on a very bright cloud, an arrow in his hand, his arm poised to strike. When the man asked him to withold the blow, the angel asked, "To what purpose a postponement of judgment?" and said, "Look back." Behind the man stood two others whose faces he knew as belonging to "wine-Dealers and retailers of Brandy." Their hands were filled with blood which they threw contemptuously on the ground; he knew that this was none other than the blood of God. So this good man besought the angel not to launch the destroying arrow but to permit him to assume in his person the punishment of all Canadian sinners, for one soul's eternal suffering seemed to him preferable to the exercise of divine wrath. And then, somewhat inconsistently, he finished his account with the statement that "notwithstanding this sentiment of mine, I rejoiced in the knowledge that God would shortly take vengence upon his enemies."

One cannot doubt that nearly all these manifestations were the product of ignorant and simple minds overwhelmed by a massed and massive hysteria, and recorded for the most part by others hardly less simple. Suddenly the populace found themselves confronted by a realization of sin in all its enormity. They had rebelled against the prohibitions of the church; they had defied excommunication; now they remembered the sermons of their absent bishop threatening them with the wrath of God. And here it was.

The more intelligent Jesuits and priests were quick to seize the spiritual opportunity. Dreadful as the earthquake was, they said, it was not catastrophic. God had not sent it as a scourge but in his divine mercy as a means of revealing to them the evil paths in which they had allowed themselves to wander. To reinforce their argument they pointed out that not a life had been lost; in fact not a single house had been demolished in any Christian settlement; beyond the toppling of a few chimneys, they had suffered little damage, though all around them mountains had been swallowed up, forests laid flat, and rivers changed in their courses.

This was further borne out by revelations of the coming earthquake to three women, one a nun of great purity, the others Algonquin girls whose piety and innocence were incontestable. The nun, a few hours before the shocks began, had a vision of four frightful specters holding the four corners of Quebec which they were shaking with demonic glee, "as if bent on working a universal overthrow." This they would have undoubtedly succeeded in doing had not a higher power — "one of venerable Majesty" — interposed, preventing them from harming those it was God's will to frighten, for the sake of their own salvation, but not to destroy.

Of the two Algonquins, the first was a girl of sixteen, suffering from a protracted illness. The revelation to her, also, was visual. She saw herself mounting a great stairway, at the top of which was a beautiful church in whose doors the Virgin appeared with her son and predicted that "the earth would soon be shaken, trees would strike against one another, and rocks would be shattered to the general consternation of the people." She feared it might be an illusion of the Devil's and determined to tell the Father in charge of the Indian church; and that evening, a few minutes before the first shock, she cried out to her family, "It is coming soon, it is coming soon."

Much more circumstantial was the experience of a young Algonquin wife of twenty-six, a Christian, "innocent, simple, and sincere." In the middle of the night before the earthquake she woke suddenly at her husband's side in the darkness, the only person in the cabin to awake. Then in the stillness a voice spoke to her: "Strange things are to happen today; the Earth will tremble." The voice was very clear and perfectly intelligible. It made her fearful, but as it said nothing further, she tried to go to sleep once more. It proved impossible and in the dawn she woke her husband, Joseph Onnetakité, still asleep beside her under the furs, and described what she had heard. He told her somewhat irritably that she was crazy, so she did not pursue the subject. But at about ten that morning, when she entered the woods to gather fagots, the voice spoke to her again, repeating the same words. Very frightened now, because she was alone, she looked all about her. The leaves hung still, it was a serene day without wind, and seeing no one she forced herself to complete her load of fagots, and hurried home. On the way she met her sister, similarly burdened, and told her of the voice. Her sister told their parents when they entered the hut, but the old people, though agreeing that it was remarkable, were not much more impressed than her husband had been. At half past five, however, they began to think otherwise.

> When God speaks, he makes himself heard with distinctness — especially when He speaks with the utterance of Thunders or Earthquakes, which have moved hardened hearts less than our greatest rocks, and have caused greater commotion in men's consciences than in our Forests and on our mountains.

So Lalemant wrote in his *Relation*. There was a genuine revival of religion. People thronged to the churches to receive what they thought would be their last Communion and crowded the confessionals — "Never were Confessions made which came more from the bottom of the heart." It became a time of piety, as in the first days of the colony, of mourning and contrition. People prayed in their homes until midnight; people looked at each other with fresh eyes. "Enmities extinguished," wrote Ragueneau, "disputes laid aside, restorations of offended Charity, kneeling supplications, mutual petitions for pardon," were the immediate effects of the continuing earthquake. And he added, "fear came to all, penalty to none."

This ultimately became apparent to the people as the last tremors ceased in August. Perhaps Avaugour foresaw the impermanence of this spiritual revolution. "On the fifth of February," said his terse report, "we had an Earthquake, which continued during half a quarter of an hour, sufficiently strong to extort from us a good act of contrition." Then he added with what may have been a premonition of the changing course of events in America, "And as these extraordinary events bring Christians completely to their duty, it is probable that they carry terror and fear powerfully into the hearts of others, particularly among that scum of Americans who, to discover the future, are accustomed to sacrifice to the Devil." Whether he meant the British or the Iroquois is immaterial. Very likely he lumped them both together in his mind, for just then he was solidly disgruntled by news he had received from France. "After the above was written, a vessel arrived here, on the 7th July, informing me, by some letters from my friends, that the King's orders relative to this country were changed, and, instead of an aid of two thousand soldiers, that only some women and serveants were coming." Evidently the old soldier was not going to feel too badly about being recalled.

The earthquake was still in progress when, in mid-May, Laval set sail from France on his return voyage. With him on the ship was the new governor, his personal selection, for on Avaugour's recall, Laval had been invited to name his successor. This was Augustin de Saffray, Chevalier de Mézy, a soldier who could claim neither nobility nor wealth, but who was remarkable for his fervid piety. Formerly a Calvinist, he had experienced what was called a "brilliant conversion" and become a zealous Catholic. To Laval and the Jesuits, who also recommended him, this former town major of Caen seemed an ideal man to govern Canada, under the guidance of the church. No one foresaw what changes the command of a vast new country would work in his passionate nature.

However, the appointment of a new governor of his own choosing was only part of Laval's triumph at court. Far more significant was the reversion of Canada to the control of the Crown. By an edict of April 24, 1663, the king divested the Company of New France of all seigneurial rights, revoked concessions on all uncleared lands, and placed all the powers of government in the hands of a Sovereign Council, which was to consist of the governor and the bishop, and of five councilors, an attorney general, and a secretary who would be appointed in concert by the bishop and the governor. Since Mézy already owed his own appointment to the bishop, this apparently placed the latter in the seat of power.

Closer to Laval's heart was Louis's approval of his plan to found a seminary at Quebec for the training of Canadian priests. He hoped in time to see the people of New France served by a truly Canadian clergy; he seems to have been one of the few officials to cross the Atlantic who thought of Canada in a national sense, rather than merely as an appendage of France. This dream of his was never realized. The first native-born priest was ordained in 1665, and shortly thereafter the Seminary began its contribution of priests to the Canadian church, but there were never enough to fulfill the need. Only twenty-three by the turn of the century had been ordained, and at the time of the British conquest the proportion of Canadian- to French-born priests was no more than a third. The population, lacking any general educational system, simply could not provide enough candidates with sufficient ability to qualify for holy orders, and though Laval founded a minor seminary in 1668 to educate boys in the hope that they might go on to training for the priesthood, it produced only a small number.

But the seminary was far more than an institution for the education of priests. It was the very heart and soul of the church in Canada as Laval proceeded to organize it. In a diocese so huge and poor and with so scattered a population, it was impossible to follow the practice of fixed livings for priests as was done in France, where a priest might remain in one parish for the course of his life, and from which he could be removed only for serious reasons. Except for a few about Quebec, there were at first no parishes which could support a priest. He had therefore to draw his living from the seminary, which became the diocesan chapter, and he operated under its discipline.

We have had a glimpse of the fatigues and loneliness of the missionary priest making his rounds. Laval saw the vital importance of creating an institution to which he could annually return for rest and the recruitment of mind and spirit. Moreover, as some parishes made far harsher demands on the priest than others, Laval saw the necessity, to use his own words, of

> . . . reserving to ourselves always, and to the bishops, our successors in the said country, as well as to the said seminary, by our orders and those of the said lords bishops, the power of recalling all the ecclesiastics who may have gone forth as delegates into the parishes and other places, whenever it may be deemed necessary, without their having title or right or particular attachment to a parish, it being our desire, on the contrary, that they should be rightfully removable, and subject to dismissal or displacement at the will of the bishops and of the said seminary, by the orders of the same, and in accordance with the sacred practice of the early ages of the Church . . .

In this way he welded the priests into a group exhibiting remarkable unity, not only responsive to his wishes and ideals, but permitting him, through the regular return of the priests to the spiritual fold from which they had gone forth, to keep in touch with every quarter of his diocese. It increased the power of the church enormously, and therefore Laval's domination of the affairs of the colony. Quebec became the center on which all spiritual matters devolved; priests and gradually their flocks looked to Quebec rather than to France, as the spiritual ties of the church itself were anchored in Rome.

As time went on, the king and his minister, Colbert, not to mention the governors and intendants they sent across the Atlantic, became mistrustful of this system and tried to institute the system of fixed livings. But during his own episcopacy, Laval was able to resist or evade all orders, and even after his resignation of the bishopric, his successor, Saint-Vallier, never quite succeeded in changing the pattern. The stamp of Laval's character remains on the church of Quebec to this day; and, ironically, it has been the character of the church, strong within itself and looking always to the Holy See, that has preserved the national integrity of the Canadian French.

It was his insistence on keeping the church of New France under the jurisdiction of Rome rather than that of the archbishopric of Rouen that accounted for the only disappointment he experienced on this memorable trip to court. He ardently wished to be named bishop of Quebec, feeling that to be so in fact instead of apostolic vicar with a bishopric of name only (that of Petraea) was not only fitting but would strengthen the church's position in dealing with secular officials. But this was to be denied him for eleven more years. Everyone agreed that an episcopal see should be established in Quebec, but the king believed that the bishop should be appointed by himself and rest under jurisdiction of the archbishopric of Rouen, which, being Gallican in inclination, looked first to the Throne. Clement X, who was then pope, refused to agree. He saw the remoteness of the tiny colony and realized that at any time it might fall prey to the British, as it had temporarily been in English possession for three years after the capture of Quebec in 1629 by Admiral Kirke. If the Catholic church in Canada was to survive such an event, it could do so far more readily with ties to the Holy See instead of the Court of France. It was not till 1674 that Louis at last bowed to papal determination and the see of Quebec was established. He nominated Laval for bishop, but Laval received his appointment from Clement.

However, if he could not yet be bishop, he could organize his church and build the seminary, which soon became the chief object of his interest and affection. The main problem was its endowment and support. Laval himself, in keeping with his belief in apostolic poverty, which he practiced with almost fanatical self-discipline throughout his life, had renounced his patrimony on entering the church, and before leaving France in 1659 he disposed of all property in his possession. Otherwise his Montigny inheritance might well have provided for the first expenses in founding the seminary. He came to Canada with an annual pension, or allowance, of a thousand francs contributed from her own funds by the Queen Mother, who had been deeply stirred by the departure of the young and noble prelate for his episcopal duties in the New World, and this sum supplied his personal needs. But as time passed he also received large grants of the most fertile land in the colony. The most important was the seigneury of Beaupré covering forty miles of the St. Lawrence shore from just below Quebec and extending nearly fifteen miles inland. By 1667 it already had more inhabitants than Quebec itself, almost a quarter of the total population of New France, and was by far the richest single holding in all Canada. Some of these grants Laval immediately converted into funds for the initial expenses of the seminary, and in 1680 he was to turn over to it almost every possession he had, including Beaupré, for its endowment. The Seminary remains one of the great Catholic institutions of the hemisphere; from the minor seminary for lay pupils sprang the university that still bears Laval's name.

There remained the support of the priests of the seminary and the parish priests who periodically returned to it. They had no endowment of their own, of course; nor could the secular clergy Laval proposed to create be supported from France as the missionary Orders had been. Contributions for carrying the Cross into the wilderness to the wild savage by men who might and did suffer the most barbarous martyrdom was one thing; paying out money to provide a curé for a Frenchman who had chosen to leave the old country for the new was quite another. The one solution as the bishop saw it was to impose tithes as they had been instituted by Charlemagne long ago to support the church. Under a royal ordinance one thirteenth of every habitant's harvest was to be paid in to the seminary, which in turn would use it to maintain priests and to provide divine services in the parish it was collected from.

The tithes proved unpopular. In the first place they were too high for people who were barely beginning to emerge from poverty; and even when the thirteenth of the harvest was confined to grain harvest only, the people resented having to pay for the services they might receive once a month and toward the support of a priest whom they so seldom saw. Four years later the tithes were reduced to one twenty-sixth of the harvest, but they were still opposed and proved difficult to collect in parishes distant from Quebec, and in addition they did not provide funds adequate for the maintenance of the parish priests — though the number of priests was less than twenty-five for the whole colony. The king was compelled to come to their support, and in 1667 four fifths of the money he allocated to maintenance of his colony was earmarked for the church, and of the latter twenty-eight thousand francs, eight thousand went to the support of the priests. It seemed exorbitant both to the Crown and to the habitant. In France a priest existed comfortably, even well, on two hundred francs a year; but in Canada he seldom got through a year on less than five hun-. dred, and then he would return to the seminary threadbare and exhausted. The French curé lived within the small confines of his parish all his life, but the Canadian, ranging miles of wilderness and river, had to find himself a canoe and keep a man to paddle it; his cassock wore out quickly under his strenuous life and cost him twice what it would have in France to replace, as all other of his supplies cost double. Sometimes the seminary would add a hundred francs to the five hundred allowed him for his year; he seldom returned with any balance in his worn purse. The *coureur de bois* might have comprehended the predicament, but he had small interest in parish priests, and if he had, his voice would not have been listened to on such a subject.

These problems, however, lay in the future when Laval and his chosen governor, Mézy, set sail from France in May of 1663 on what should have been a triumphant voyage home. It turned into a nightmare of near starvation and disease. Repeatedly the ship was driven back by adverse winds; food and water nearly gave out; scurvy appeared among the passengers and crew and Laval was among those stricken, though he was still able to minister spiritually and physically to those worse off than himself. We have had a glimpse of him prostrating himself at the gangrened feet of the dying Huron; nursing his shipmates, if less dramatic, reflected the same deep impulsion to serve the unfortunate and poor, and one cannot doubt that he welcomed his opportunity and took joy in it. They were four months at sea. When at last the ship entered the St. Lawrence, the crew were too badly off to take her beyond Tadoussac at the mouth of the Saguenay. A shallop had to be sent down from Quebec to fetch the governor and the bishop and such other passengers as were well enough to move at once. Laval, however, did not forget the sufferers left behind, and after the shallop had brought them up on its second trip, he found time to visit them repeatedly in the hospital, in spite of new preoccupations.

Though the tremors of the earthquake had now subsided for good, a new upheaval was shaking the Quebec community. Actually its beginnings went back three years before the earthquake, but only now was it coming to a climax.

In 1660 the Company of New France suddenly decided, after years of almost total inaction, that its interests in Canada were not being properly realized, and it sent over a man with powers combining those of judge and intendant to look into affairs for it. He reached Quebec on the third of September.

Jean Péronne Dumesnil, Sieur de Mazé, was an advocate in the Parliament of Paris; he was astute and persevering and thoroughly suited for the task he had been set to. He lost no time in getting to work, and before long he had stirred up a veritable hornet's nest.

As we have seen earlier, in 1645 the Company of New France had turned over its monopoly of the fur trade to a group of Canadians, known as the Company of the Habitants, under terms which called for the importation of twenty settlers a year, the support of the government of the colony, garrisons, and religious establishments, and an annual payment of one thousand pounds of beaver to the Company of New France. The payment was hardly ever made and there seems to have been little interest on the part of the managers of the new company in bringing over colonists. As for their support of the government, garrisons, and church, they were contracting debts which they were unable to pay and barely kept the colony going.

In 1647 the trade had been opened to everyone within the colony, but the increasing scarcity of beaver coupled with Iroquois raiding led to a drop in the take from 250,000 livres to 65,000 in the next eight years. At the same time the cost of administering the management of the colony, as well as the Company's affairs, rose very sharply, and it became necessary in 1653 to release the Company of the Habitants from its payment of a thousand pounds of beaver, and to set aside the annual take at Tadoussac to meet the general charges. Gradually the trade came into the hands of a small group who felt safe in following any policies they saw fit, since some of their number were members of the council. Until Dumesnil began his investigations, they had exercised an absolute monopoly on the fur trade with virtually no regard for the general welfare of the colony and, according to Dumesnil, to their enormous profit.

Now they found themselves at the center of his elaborately worked up charges of fraud and embezzlement. One man over a period of years had had beaver to the value of 300,000 livres pass through his hands without making any accounting. Another, Rouer de Villeray, had earlier been summoned to Paris for an explanation of certain activities, supposed to be criminal; he had returned to Canada with orders to settle his outstanding accounts, which amounted supposedly to 600,000 livres, which Dumesnil pointed out he had not yet done. Others, in his charges, were liable to lesser amounts, but all of them stood at the top of government circles and colonial trade. They were dismayed and outraged.

They refused to accept his judicial authority or answer his charges. He accused the council members of holding their positions illegally; but he was only one man against a group wielding active power — France and the Company of New France were across an ocean — and he got nowhere. But he had made wounds, and threats were made against his life. Then one of his sons was attacked on a Quebec street in daylight and painfully beaten by several men. Young Dumesnil was carried to his father's house, where he died on the last day of August. Apparently the identity of his principal assailant was known, for the Jesuit *Journal* of that date reports, somewhat cryptically, that "he had been killed by a kick from N." — whoever that may have been. Dumesnil himself charged four men with having been participants in the affair, all of them among the group he had been investigating.

Quebec was in a turmoil. Dumesnil was confined to his house by illness at the time. There was talk of mobbing him there, but he was able to persuade enough people that he was in Canada to protect them from those who had been exploiting them to avoid an attack. He next moved, as intendant, to call on the councilors and their allies to pay up their debts to the Company. They ignored him. Matters were at a standstill when in the following spring, as we have seen, Avaugour dissolved the council and appointed a new one of his own choosing.

Probably his action was due partly to the struggle between the council members and Dumesnil, but he also might well have thought this a good opportunity for driving his own wedge into the fur monopoly. That his instincts lay that way, Radisson and Groseilliers were shortly to discover. Certainly he seems to have felt little concern about the payment to the Company of New France of the money justly due it; and as events developed, these debts were never paid at all.

So matters stood when Laval and Mézy came ashore after their long and rigorous voyage. For two months, since the departure of Avaugour in July, Quebec had lived under a vacuum, but the new governor and the bishop wasted no time in filling it by naming the members of the Sovereign Council, the choice of which was theirs to make. The blank commissions had been entrusted to Laval; he himself had selected Mézy; and Mézy knew nothing at all about the affairs of the colony or its inhabitants. He was ready to second any man chosen by Laval, whose conduct on the voyage over had made a deep impression on him.

The men Laval named to the council were all implicated in Dumesnil's charges that besides being demonstrably dishonest they were ignorant and incapable. But in Laval's disputes with the two previous governors, these men had been his supporters — whether from a convinced belief in the justice of his cause and the supremacy of the church or because the maintenance of a situation of near anarchy in the government made possible profitable forays in trade beyond the fringe of law is not easy to say. In any case, the effect was to cut what little ground remained from under Dumesnil's feet.

Bourdon, through whose hands he claimed beaver to the value of 300,000 francs had passed with no accounting, received the principal post, that of attorney general. Villeray became keeper of the seals. One of the other councilors, Jucherau de la Ferté, had also been directly accused by Dumesnil; and, as said, the others were all implicated in his investigations. Now they were in a position to bring themselves to justice if they chose and preside over their own cases.

Their first step was to demand that all Dumesnil's records be turned over to them. He refused to do so and refused to recognize their authority, so in the evening, with an escort of soldiers, Bourdon and Villeray went to his house and took all his papers while the soldiers restrained him by force. The papers were never seen again, as may be readily believed, for they contained all the specifications and material for the trial of Bourdon and Villeray. Dumesnil was then threatened with arrest, but this was not carried through. Instead a plan was made to seize him just before departure of the last ship to France, but being forewarned, he surreptitiously boarded another and made good his escape.

He had had no hope of accomplishing anything once the Company of New France had withdrawn from the administration of the colony. He did make one attempt to find support by turning to an individual who had come across the ocean with Mézy and Laval bearing the title of royal commissioner. This man's name was Gaudais-Dupont, and he came ostensibly to take possession of the colony in the name of the king and also to make a report on prevailing conditions. His instructions were lengthy and precise, and one of the most important directed him

> . . . to see how the establishment of the Council will be made, the selection of the persons to perform its duties, the approval it will meet with the inhabitants, and whether the majority of the honest people among them will be of the opinion that, by means of said Council, they shall be assured against the machinations of the wicked, the latter punished pursuant to the severity of the laws, and wholesome justice be generally established and maintained there amongst them.

Whether Gaudais-Dupont bore these instructions in mind when Dumesnil came to lay his case before him we do not know, but he rejected all of Dumesnil's claims. The reason may have been that he was at this time busily preoccupied with arranging the marriage of his daughter to one Joseph Giffard, whose father, Robert, stood high among the pro-Laval group, and did not want any unpleasantness to come in the way. It was hardly an excuse and when Colbert, having heard what Dumesnil had to say on the latter's return to France, demanded of Gaudais-Dupont why he had mentioned none of these council matters in his own report, Gaudais-Dupont gave only the weakest of replies, and from then on he was regarded by Colbert as not wholly to be trusted. But to establish what was actually occurring in a colony more than three thousand miles across the sea was difficult; as a matter of fact it was something that the king's government never did accomplish.

It is inconceivable that Laval was not aware of the charges pending against the men he appointed to the council with the blind approval of Mézy. Moreover, he knew full well that almost without exception these men were involved in the fur trade and therefore major promoters of the sale of brandy to the Indians, which he himself had so bitterly opposed. In his mind, however, the institution of the church superseded in importance all other human considerations, so the fact that all the men he had selected happened to be at odds with a portion of the secular administration of the colony simply lacked relevance.

Dumesnil read in his action a deliberate attempt to subvert justice for the sake of personal friends, and in addition claimed to believe that with the collusion of the Jesuits Laval had made the voyage to court in the first place for this sole purpose — to remove the Company from power in order to vitiate his, Dumesnil's, authority. There is possibly a degree of truth in this; yet, as we shall see in a moment, Laval was not a man to spare his friend in the face of what he conceived the call of duty. These men might have sinned against the public interest, or even in the sight of God; but that was a matter the church itself was equipped to set right for each individual. And it seems probable that he genuinely questioned the validity of Dumesnil's charges, or at least the extent of them. Without doubt the size of the peculations Dumesnil claimed against Bourdon and Villeray were beyond reason. Of Villeray not much that is good can be said, except that he went on to die the wealthiest man in Canada. His earlier career had been marked, in the kind words of Argenson, by "instability" and Dumesnil claimed that he had been taken out of jail, for a debt of seventy-one francs, to come to Canada as valet to the governor, Lauson. Bourdon, on the other hand, was a different sort and the leading citizen of the colony. He had spent his life in public service as surveyor and map maker. In 1646 he had gone on a dangerous mission to the Mohawks; he had been briefly commandant of Three Rivers, and later of Quebec. The habitants thought so well of him that they elected him the first procurator and syndic of the colony. He had worked on paintings in the cathedral and made numerous, if not excessively large, contributions toward its erection, a gift of twenty livres for the steeple being not the least among them. He had explored the coastline north of the St. Lawrence as far as the 55th degree of latitude, before being turned back by ice. He was indeed a man of parts, active and public-spirited, and beyond question the most intelligent member of the council. It is hard to envisage his embarking on systematic fraud to anything like the extent Dumesnil had claimed. Still, if his hands had been completely clean, one cannot imagine his taking part with such emphasis in the suppression of Dumesnil and his charges, even though he was attorney general. The truth probably was that none of the accused had kept adequate records; most of them were too inexperienced to have done so, or in plain fact too illiterate. Without question they had been lining their own pockets; but it was the enormity of Dumesnil's allegations that threw them into panic, regardless of the degree of their guilt. They had no earthly way of answering his charges or even, probably, of knowing exactly how much they had embezzled.

Conjectures such as these naturally did not trouble Laval. Whatever his own actions, they were not aimed at his personal aggrandizement or profit. The church and his episcopacy were the absorbing forces in his life, together with his love for Canada and the vast inland wilderness it was his charge to Christianize and which he longed to see but never did. Winning the savage souls that roamed it to the Cross stirred his blood, just as it fired the imagination of the young king in Paris or the pious ladies in his court.

He shared the Jesuit dream of some day converting all the wilderness area into a kind of Peaceable Kingdom or "Paraguay," as they called it, after the most successful effort at Christianization in the history of the Order. In that South American country early in the seventeenth century, the Jesuits had gathered cannibal converts into what they called "reductions," communities of sometimes five thousand people, where the converts were instructed not only in religion but in agriculture and various trades — spinning, weaving, building, carving, even in the manufacture of firearms. Each such village was governed by two missionaries, property was communal, and they soon gained a prosperity till then inconceivable to such primitive minds. So, in the heart of the North American continent and on an infinitely greater scale, the Jesuits envisioned a land of simple purity, where the Indians joined in peaceful and useful occupations and the mission Fathers governed them and dispensed the word of God.

This was the dream. But Laval and the Jesuits themselves knew that now and for a long time to come the Cross would have to be carried, often by one man working alone, into the cruel and savage wilderness if the dream was ever to approach fruition. Laval did not hesitate to dispatch men on such missions if he thought they had the gift of winning souls. Not all the Jesuits were so gifted; but of those who were, few ever hesitated to undertake missions even though they knew from experience what it entailed:

> . . . that rich harvest [of souls] is only secured by watering those lands with sweat and blood. I mean that a Missionary destined for this great work must make up his mind to lead a very strange kind of life, and endure unimaginable destitution of all things; to suffer every inclemency of the weather, without mitigation; to bear a thousand impertinences, a thousand taunts, and often, indeed, blows from the Infidel Savages, who are at times instigated by demons, — and all this without human consolation; to be daily in the water or on the snow, without fire; to pass whole months without eating anything but boiled leather, or the moss which grows on rocks; to toil indefatigably, and as if he had a body of bronze; to live without food and to lie with no bed under him; to sleep little and journey much . . .

In writing this Jerome Lalemant was commemorating the departure of René Ménard for the upper Great Lakes. The Superior knew that there was little chance of his ever coming back; so did Ménard himself. "In three or four months," he had written to Lalemant, "you may include me in the Memento for the dead." He was then about to enter his fifty-sixth year; and his body, far from being made of bronze, was slight and frail and worn out from mission service.

Born in Paris, Ménard had entered the Order as a novice in 1624 at the age of nineteen. For the next five years he pursued studies at Paris, La Flèche, Bourges, and Rouen. Then followed two three-year stints of teaching, at Orléans and Moulins. He came to Canada in the summer of 1640 and the following spring with Paul Ragueneau set out for the Huron mission. He served a year there, in one of the more remote posts from Ossossané, then with a companion he lived a year among the Nipissings, after which he returned to the Huron mission and labored there till its destruction by the Iroquois in 1649. For five years after that he was stationed at Three Rivers, where he became Superior in Residence. Then he had gone out with the Iroquois mission at Onondaga, which barely escaped wholesale slaughter, but during his term he was much of the time working alone among the Cayugas. Now after two years he was writing his friend Lalemant from Three Rivers on "this 27th of August, 2 hours after midnight, 1660." In effect it was his way of choosing death, but he knew also that if he did not respond to this duty, "I would experience an endless remorse."

This highly educated and, by the standards of his time, already old man now set his face to one of the most arduous journeys on the continent. He had little to take with him — "I left 3 Rivers with 60 or 80 small beads." He had only a pint of sacramental wine, "which is very little, considering the distance, for a person who has no other consolation in the world." It seemed even less when he reached his destination on the south shore of Lake Superior, for it was a region in which no grapes grew. His altar bread, which he carried in a small box of wood that soon became water-soaked, somehow survived, and he thought that with care it might last till the autumn of 1662; and perhaps it might have, if he had not by then been dead a year.

He left Three Rivers on the twenty-eighth of August with eight Frenchmen, one of them named Jean Guérin, his *donné*, servant or lay companion. One of the others was a surgeon who had a lancet but no medicines, and a third was an armorer or gunsmith; and there were about three hundred Indians, mainly Ottawas, from the upper Great Lakes region.

As far as Lake Huron the journey would be one he knew well, with all its rigors of falls and rapids along the Ottawa, and the near certainty of Iroquois attack. However, such a large force seemed almost sure to win through, and Ménard's heart was high. No Jesuit in Canada was better fitted mentally for the mission before him. He could speak in Huron, Iroquois, and Algonquin with complete fluency. His zeal — "which was full of fire" — impressed his Indian hearers and won converts in such numbers that his Jesuit brothers called him "the fruitful Father." Yet in other respects he embarked on his mission in a state of near destitution. The Indians' decision to permit some French to join them on their return journey was made at the last possible moment, so that Ménard had not had time to get together even clothes for the winter, though he wrote cheerfully that "He who feeds the little birds . . . will take care of his servants." Except for his sixty or eighty beads and a lancet of his own he had nothing at all that would help him in any temporal bargaining with the Indians. But most of all his age and health troubled him, not because he feared death, but because he might be prevented from reaching his goal and serving God's purpose there. "Many wish to frighten me and to turn me aside from my undertaking . . . they adduce my age and the weakness of my constitution." But before leaving the easier route of the St. Lawrence he received comfort and reassurance that buoyed him until his death.

"Between Three Rivers and Montreal, we luckily met Monseigneur the Bishop of Petraea." He does not say where, exactly, or how they met, and one would like to know whether it was an encounter of canoes far out on the water, hands holding gunwales together for a momentary meeting, or whether the parties had made a landing, for the Ottawas' first night camp, perhaps, since they almost never stopped at noon, and the two men walked together along the shore in their worn black cassocks, while the last of sunset tinted the surface of the river, as it would light the lakes and distant rivers Ménard had still to pass. Laval must have been aware of the old priest's inward reservations about himself, for he said, "My Father, every reason seems to retain you here; but God, more powerful than aught else, requires you yonder." In his militant mind no doubt or reservation for an instant could exist in the face of the Divinity's demand. Ménard's confidence was restored, and the words *God requires me yonder!* he carried with him to the end.

There is no need of recounting each stage of the journey up the Ottawa. The Iroquois attacked but did not stop them; but the group of canoes containing the one Ménard had been assigned to became separated from the rest, and throughout the journey he saw no more of his French companions. Whether because of this separation or because he had quickly discovered the Father's utter lack of goods of any value, the leader of these Indians, an Ottawa named Le Brochet (the Pike), proud and with a viciously capricious temper, began to abuse him. At portages he was loaded with packs beyond his strength; at the least excuse he was told to jump into the water and help pull the canoe; or he was sent around minor rapids, compelled to run with all his strength if he was not to be left alone in the woods; he was made to paddle though the Indians knew as well as he that his small strength added nothing to their speed; and with the mean and childish cruelty which so often characterized their aimless persecutions, they tried to deprive him of the comfort of reading his prayers by throwing his breviary into the river.

He cut his foot on a sharp stone, and it became infected and so swollen he could hardly walk. He could get almost no sleep, having no blanket and being compelled to find his bed on the stony shore with the rest of the party, for he dared not leave them for an instant. They stopped only after dark and set out before dawn. Their food was mainly such berries as they snatched time to pick. It was incredible that he survived as far as Lake Huron. But he did; and the small flotilla made its way along the northern shore and through the Sault, and at last Superior lay before the bows of the canoes.

But now a new misfortune fell upon Ménard, literally, in the form of a tree that at their first camping place fell across the canoe he had been traveling in and shattered it beyond hope of repair. He and the three Indians who had shared it with him were left behind at dawn with no promise of rescue. They were given no provisions, though they had nothing of their own. It was not till six days had passed that another flotilla took mercy on them.

In the meantime they had kept themselves alive on any form of food their ingenuity could resurrect from the leavings of previous campers, for the site had been used by travelers along Superior for years. An abandoned, crumbling hut provided the focal point of their researches.

> We remained in this condition . . . living on some offal which we were obliged, in order not to die of hunger, to scrape up with our fingernails around a hut which had been abandoned in this place some time ago. We pounded up the bones which we found there, to make soup of them; we collected the blood of slain animals, with which the ground was soaked; in a word, we made use of everything . . .

At last, in mid-October, the canoes that had picked them up deposited them at their wintering place. The Ottawa encampment was on the shore of Keweenaw Bay, on or near the present site of L'Anse. But Father Ménard was to find little comfort there, for the head man was Le Brochet. He soon resumed his persecutions, driving the old man from his lodge, in which he kept his five wives, and not allowing him to find refuge with any other Indian. The old man was forced to build himself a hut of fir branches, a tiny hovel, hardly bigger than an inverted basket, and the flimsiest kind of defense against the wind and cold. Food early ran short, the fishing fell off desperately. They saved the bones of their catch for making a sort of soup; they made soup, too, out of what they called rock moss, the *tripe-de-roche*, without which northern Indians could not hope to survive severe winters. It made a kind of slime in the kettle, like the gathered tracks of snails, and tasted only slightly of earth, or the uncleaned kettle it had been cooked in. "It is necessary to close one's eyes, when one begins to eat it," another Jesuit wrote later. When they could not find *tripe-de-roche*, they kept alive on bark — oak, whitewood, linden, or birch — pounded and cooked into soup with a few drops of fish oil. When the Indians did net a few fish, he was unable to buy any for himself. They scorned his beads for, being middlemen in the fur trade now that the Hurons had been driven west, they had many of their own and better than the few he had brought.

October 15, the day of his arrival, was the feast of St. Theresa, so he named the great bay for her; but the church he now set out to establish in this bleak corner of the wilderness, he called Notre Dame de Bon Secours. His first visit was to a hovel as wretched as his own. It had been built with spruce and hemlock branches against the rotting trunk of a huge fallen tree, and was so low that he had to enter it on hands and knees, "almost crawling on my stomach." Inside he found a woman and two little children. She had been abandoned by her husband and her daughter, the latter leaving with her two of her children, because, as Ménard presently realized in the green gloom that was almost darkness, both of them were dying. They were two and three years old, she explained, but she could not really find them enough to eat.

When the gentle old missionary began to speak to her about his faith, she was eagerly receptive. Her people, she told him, disapproved of Christian talk, but she liked it very much, for it brought her the first consolation she had had in a long time. She had been expecting his visit, she told him (Indians knew that the Black Robes always sought their first converts among the sick or troubled), and so some time ago she had put aside a gift for him. Here, from a hiding place under the fallen tree, she pulled forth a piece of dried fish, saved against heaven knew what temptation; but he, of course, declined it. Instead, he took his comfort in baptizing the two infants then and there, thus assuring salvation for the first two souls, small though they were, in his new church.

The old woman, whose Indian name was Nahawatkse, proved truly devout; she never failed a day to come and pray with him; and he in turn went frequently to visit her under the fallen tree. It was his only contact with what might be called domestic life, and one can think of him sitting there in his shabby black cassock, his back against the moldering tree trunk, almost invisible in the green smoky dimness of the burrowlike hovel except for his white hair and gentle face. For a while he could take ease there from the labor his conscience drove him to. The two-year-old boy, fascinated by the novelty of his grandmother's new devotions, had learned spontaneously to cross himself each time before he ate, and as the tired old man watched the small hand move to the dirt-seamed forehead in the age-old sign, it seemed to him that he had brought the blessing of God to this poor little family.

This was the beginning of his work. He soon found a young man, whom he baptized as Louys; then Louys's widowed sister and the five children of whom she was the sole support. After instructing them, he baptized the whole family, and they in turn devoted themselves to helping him find food and furs to cover him. Without them it is unlikely that he would have come through the winter. Next he found another widow, childless, and two very ancient men, one totally blind. Around this small nucleus he built his infant church into a congregation of fifty baptized adults, a remarkable achievement for one man, let alone one of his age and infirmities, among a tribe as worldly, arrogant, licentious, and antagonistic as the Ottawa. But he was not satisfied.

"I must push on to the last post," he wrote in March, "the bay of St. Esprit [Chequamegon], 100 leagues from here. There the savages have their rendezvous in early spring, and there we must decide either to leave the country entirely, or to settle permanently in some place where we may hope to grow wheat."

Ménard's letters from Keweenaw Bay make no mention of the wild rice that grew in the marshes all through the region south of Superior; it is probable that there was little or none of it in the starving Ottawa village that winter, and certainly he had never witnessed its harvest. But other Jesuits had.

There is in that country a certain plant, four feet or thereabout in height, which grows in marshy places. A little before it ears, the Savages go in their Canoes and bind the stalks of these plants in clusters, which they separate from one another by as much space as is needed for the passage of a Canoe when they return to gather the grain. Harvest time having come, they guide their Canoes through the little alleys which they have opened across this grain-field, and bending down the clustered masses over their boats, strip them of their grain. As often as a Canoe is full, they go and empty it on the shore into a ditch dug at the water's edge. Then they tread the grain and stir it about long enough to free it entirely of hulls; after which they dry it, and finally put it into bark chests for keeping.

The harvest varied from year to year and was too laborious a process to have made it a practicable staple grain for Frenchmen, who, in any case, had to have their bread, so Ménard was entirely right in wanting to find a place suitable for growing wheat. It seems also from his letters that by then the other Frenchmen in his original party must have come to join him, though when they did so is not made clear in any account of his last year.

Together they left the Ottawa village on the Saturday before Easter and for a while camped with the Ottawa in a better region for game; but game and fish alike soon gave out, and the nine French, in three canoes, paddled on to the west. About the sixth or seventh of May — again the date is not made clear — they arrived at Pointe St. Esprit, where the main body of the Indians, as he said, were camped.

Radisson and Groseilliers had traveled along the south shore of the great lake two years before and were to return to Chequamegon Bay, as we have already seen, late in the fall and after all the Ménard party had gone.

But now, as the Indians gathered at Chequamegon in the middle of May, Ménard began to find the pulse of news, as always happened at these meetings. A Huron who had come from a band of the Tobacco Nation told stories of people dying of starvation; the Iroquois had raided somewhere to the south; Sioux had attacked fourteen Hurons toward the end of May and there had been casualties on both sides; an epidemic of dysentery had carried off a hundred people among the Pottawatomies and a band of Hurons who had wintered among them were terrified into leaving and had made a five days' journey to the north. These were Christian Hurons, originally from Georgian Bay, who had been moving about the western regions since the final Iroquois attack. Ménard's informant said it had taken him eight days to travel overland from where they were to Chequamegon. He said his people were nearly starving.

Three Frenchmen were willing to accompany him back to the tribe to see how matters stood with them and what their plans were, and to see if it was a journey Ménard could make. After they had gone, there was a message that six or seven hundred Algonquins (Ottawas or Chippewas) were on their way to the rendezvous. A Feast of the Dead was announced, and the local Hurons were invited to attend — to Ménard's great satisfaction, for any bit of hospitality toward this outcast people would be an amelioration of their lot. There was much work for his lancet, but he had no cloth for bandages — the Indians were too poor to possess trade goods of that sort. But he started to make new converts, and some of those whom he had already converted arrived from Keweenaw Bay and demonstrated their love and respect. Everyone was hungry. Two Frenchmen, Laflèche and Joliet (not the explorer, Louis, but a man named Adrien) went off to an Indian village to see what they could do to help. Ménard and three Frenchmen remained, a gunshot from the town, with their Christians camped about them.

His letters vibrate with the spring activity of the Indian world. "Private letters," he wrote, "will tell you the remainder." It was his official report to Lalemant, and dated "2nd of June, 1661. From nostre Dame de bon Secours, called Chassahamigon."

Not long afterward, however, he and his companions must have left Chequamegon, for on the second of July he was writing his last letter from Keweenaw Bay, and it was from there that he undertook his final journey. Nothing could dissuade him from making it.

The three young Frenchmen who had gone in search of the starving tribe of Hurons had found them, as they reported, in their "death-agony," mere skeletons, many too weak to move from their lodges or even to stand. Anyone who went to them would die with them of hunger, unless he had strength and skill enough to kill game for himself, and game was short. It would be madness for a man as old as Ménard to visit them, at least before they had a chance to harvest their corn, and of that they had not had strength enough to plant more than a very small and totally insufficient quantity. But it would be equal madness to suppose that a frail old man could make the journey of more than a hundred miles in the first place. It had taken them two weeks to return, and they were men in the full vigor of their strength and traveling hard, taking time only to catch turtles or an occasional catfish after their own provisions had given out. But these poor Hurons were many of them Christians, and Christians who had not seen a priest in twelve years. To attempt to reach them was a duty no true priest could, or would, avoid, though Ménard knew as well as the young men how infinitesimal his chances were of succeeding.

I expect to die on the way: but I am so far on my journey and am so full of health, I shall make every possible effort to reach these nations. The road is composed almost entirely of Swamps, through which it is necessary to pass, sounding the fords, and always in danger of sinking so deep as not to be able to get out. Food is to be had only as one carries it with him, and mosquitoes are frightfully numerous. These are the three great difficulties which make it hard for me to find a companion.

He would not take his own "good companion," his *donné*, Jean Guérin, who begged and begged to go with him. It was important for him to stay, for if Ménard did not return, there was no one else to hold the little church together and bring the consolation of religion to the remaining Frenchmen. Finally, Ménard persuaded the armorer, or blacksmith, Claude David, to go with him. They left early in July with some Hurons from the afflicted village who had come to the Ottawas to trade.

It was the hottest part of the summer. The black flies and mosquitoes, as he had foretold, were almost more than one could bear; when a man knelt to drink from the river, another had to wave a branch of ferns over his head, or he could not stay still long enough to slake his thirst. There was much portaging, and the old man lagged behind. He seems to have traveled in a state bordering on hallucination; for all his doubts of his own capacities, for all the discomforts he labored under, he experienced happiness that bordered on exaltation. He thought of his last days as unremittingly dedicated to this vast west, more than five hundred leagues from home, himself alone among so many savages of so many nations. His mission was a cross from which it was impossible for him to descend.

I know not of what nature are those nails which hold me upon this adorable cross; but the mere thought of anyone's coming to take me away chills me; and I very often wake with a start, thinking that there are no longer any Outaouaks for me, and that my sins consign me again to the same place whence the compassion of my God has, by signal favor, drawn me. I can say with truth that I have had more happiness here in one day, in spite of hunger, cold, and other almost indescribable sufferings, than I have felt in all my previous life in whatever part of the world I may have been.

No other missionary stated better his dedication to his task, and it was fitting that he should end his life there.

The Hurons with whom he and the armorer, David, were traveling were at first good-humored about the length of time it took him to negotiate the endless portages. But as the days passed and their supplies began to run short, they became more and more restive; and finally they made it plain that they could no longer afford to let his pace dictate their own. On the edge of a small lake they put the two Frenchmen ashore, with their small packs, promising that they would press on to the village with all haste and have some young and strong men sent back to fetch them. Then their canoes went on down the lake, dwindling till they were no more than dots to point the smooth V's of their wakes; then they were gone and the wakes themselves crept away along the shores and the two men found themselves gazing at the untouched mirror reflecting only sky and the high wooded banks.

They stayed by the lake for two weeks. Scouting along the shores, they soon found a very small canoe hidden in the underbrush, but they still waited in expectation of returning help. At the end of the two weeks, however, their own provisions had nearly given out. They had started the trip with only a sack of dried sturgeon and a small supply of smoked venison; and they now realized that they must move on or starve where they were. They had only a vague idea of the general direction they were to follow; the Huron village was supposed to be on the upper waters of a Wisconsin river that is now named the Black; the course they followed was little short of being a blind one; and for the old and ailing Jesuit, it seems soon to have become blind in fact.

His faculties were rapidly failing. At the portages he could only stumble on behind Claude David, gradually falling farther behind. The paths, lightly used, were hardly discernible for a man of full eyesight. At one, when Claude David came back to help him on, Ménard had vanished.

For a day the armorer stayed there, searching, shouting, firing his gun along the riverbank. Then he remembered that Ménard had had in his pouch a piece of smoked meat large enough to keep his shrunken body alive for two or three days, and, finding his own strength waning, he decided to push on and somehow find the village and bring back a party large enough to make a proper search.

Unfortunately he missed the Huron settlement and went a full day's journey beyond it. Then he met a party returning to it; they took him with them; and there he tried to describe with gestures and tears and the word or two of Huron he had picked up what had happened. Finally, instead of a party, only one young man could be persuaded to go back with him; but the Indian suddenly became convinced that there were Iroquois in the woods and insisted that they return to the village.

So Ménard was left alone to die on the cross he imagined himself nailed to; perhaps, as one report suggests, stretched upon a boulder, or lying at the waterside. A Huron some time later claimed to have found his bag, but he would not admit having seen his body, for fear of being accused of murdering him — which he may well have done. But the chance is much more likely in the desolate area of wilderness that the old man wandered off, unseeing, unknowing, except for his visions, until he simply fell. It was a death not unlike that of many an Indian.

He was not an explorer-priest like Marquette or Claude Jean Allouez who was to succeed him in his mission and serve twenty-five years among the western tribes, during which he instructed and converted more adults than any other single Jesuit. Like Ménard, he died while engaged in missionary work; and also like Ménard, Marquette died while on a journey, though he was not alone. Both men occupy a larger place in history, but Ménard was the first of his Order to be drawn into the vacuum of the midcontinental wilderness that drew to itself so many hunters, whether of furs or souls; and in single-minded purpose none surpassed him.

Laval would have been returning from one of his pastoral visits when he met Ménard above Three Rivers. He was far more active than any of his immediate successors in making such visits and there can be little doubt that in them he found compensation for the mission work he longed to take part in but which was denied him. He traveled almost as simply as one of his own priests. He did have two habitants, instead of one, to paddle his small bark canoe, but he exposed himself to the same extremes of heat or cold, snow or rain, as they did, and he faced the same possibility of Iroquois attack. According to Claude Dablon, "He had with him merely a wooden crozier, a very simple miter, and only such ornaments as were absolutely necessary for a *golden bishop*, as the authors say when speaking of the first prelates of Christianity." And it is true that Laval sought in the daily routine of his own life to emulate the austerities that governed the lives of those first bearers of the Cross.

He slept on a board bed with the thinnest of ticking for a mattress, and for forty years his hour of rising, summer or winter, was two o'clock. Even during his last years, when his legs had become so weak that they had to be bandaged tightly to enable him to walk, he would not agree to rest longer than three o'clock in the morning. Though he could present an appearance of imposing magnificence in court or at some high festival of the church, he kept but two servants — a gardener, whose services he was forever lending to the poor, and a valet.

The first of his valets was a man named Lemaire who was a lazy good-for-nothing, a liar and a talebearer, who was always complaining of being overworked, and whom Laval had taken from a work gang in Rochelle and brought with him to Canada. From a state of virtual beggarhood, Lemaire now found himself in a sinecure and made the most of it, yet Laval endured his impertinence and neglect for years. "As soon as he entered my room he sat down, and rather than be obliged to pretend not to see him, I turned my seat so as not to see him. . . . We should have left that man at heavy work," he added with a wry bit of humor, "which had in some sort conquered his folly and pride, and it is possible that he had been saved. But he has been entirely ruined in the seminary."

Lemaire, however, was succeeded by a lay brother named Houssart, who was to serve Laval to the end of his days with selfless devotion and who after Laval's death left us an intimate description of his master's domestic life. Laval never allowed himself breakfast, but after two hours of prayer went to the cathedral, opened the doors himself, and then rang the bells for mass, which he said at four-thirty, mainly for workingmen on their way to their jobs. It always gave him pleasure to be with simple people.

For lunch he ate a small piece of meat and a slice of stale bread. His only drink was warm water, flavored with a little wine. At night he had a bowl of soup. He never bought ordinary clothes for himself but went to the Superior of the seminary and, like any priest, asked for them to be given him. Those he had he wore till they were threadbare; in twenty years, Houssart said, he had only two winter cassocks, and one of these was still good when he died.

In 1680, as we have seen, he deeded almost everything he owned to the seminary; what little money came his way after that he gave to the poor and unfortunate; even his bedding went to those in more need of it than he, though one might question whether, after all, this proved much of a blessing to the recipient. Some writers have found it hard to reconcile this austerity and self-denial, almost fanatical in its harshness, with the image of the contentious, overbearing, unrelenting prelate; but there is no need to reconcile them. The same forces in his nature were being manifested, and in either manifestation were wholly in the service, as he saw it, of God.

In this service he drove himself to the end of his life. When he resigned the bishopric to Saint-Vallier, it was because he considered his health too uncertain to allow him to fill wholly the obligations it entailed. Though at the time he wrote that his health was "exceedingly good considering the bad use I make of it," he was in fact suffering repeated attacks of vertigo, an affliction that was particularly embarrassing for one who made much use of canoe travel. Yet for many years afterward, while he continued to perform the duties of the bishop's office during enforced absences of his successor from New France, he continued to make pastoral journeys up and down the river, the last in 1702 to Montreal to administer confirmation, when he was in his seventy-ninth year.

Best of all his duties he seems to have enjoyed his visits to the Indian missions, and of them especially to that of St. Xavier at La Prairie de la Madeleine, near Montreal. It was partly Huron, but many of the inhabitants were from the Iroquois tribes, converted by missionaries like Jogues and Bruyas, Milet and Le Moyne, and brought to St. Xavier so that they might lead Christian lives unharassed by the mockery of pagan relatives. To Laval and the Jesuits these Iroquois, snatched from their villages "of fire and blood," were the most precious fruit of all their labors. The Indians themselves had banned alcohol from their community, and to Laval the sight of those who had so short a time ago been cruel enemies now leading a devout and simple Christian existence was heart-filling. His visits there were an event for him as much as for the Indians.

To the Indians he was a beloved figure, and Claude Dablon, who happened to be in Montreal at the time of one of Laval's visits, has left an account of their preparation for his reception, and of the manner in which they made him welcome. It came in May 1675, the year after Laval had become bishop of Quebec, and for that reason, possibly, he came with what Dablon described as "a retinue." It consisted of a single priest. The customary two habitants paddled the small canoe.

Because the feast of Pentecost was at hand, Laval felt compelled to spend the Sunday on the island of Montreal, especially as many of the French there had not seen him before as their own bishop, but he promised to come to the mission on the Monday following. This gave the Indians time to make their preparations in their own way, after obtaining permission from the principal Jesuit Father to work during the time of the feast. At the shore a few men built a platform, two feet above the water. All the rest disappeared into the woods, men, women, youths, and children, to gather quantities of green boughs. With these they built a sort of arbor, three hundred yards long and reaching from the platform, where the bishop would be greeted, to the door of the chapel. Halfway down this narrow avenue the walls were widened to form a sort of bower, ornamented with ferns and flowers, where a second greeting would be made; and again the walls widened before the chapel doors. Then they went to their houses to put on their best finery.

As the hour of the bishop's arrival neared, they came to the waterside, forming in two groups: the Indians on the right behind Father Frémin, who headed the mission; the French who worked there, or came to services in the little chapel, on the left behind Father Cholenec. Presently, far out on the water they saw the speck of Laval's canoe. Dablon, himself a visitor at the time, as Superior of the Jesuit Mission in Canada, stepped into his own canoe and went out to meet Laval about three quarters of a mile from shore. Both canoes then turned, the Jesuit's following the bishop's; at the same moment both men heard the chapel bell, a small clear sound across the water, and saw the last stragglers hurrying for the riverbank.

When the canoes came within speaking distance, the chief of the Hurons, who had taken a stand on the platform with some of the old men of his nation, shouted in a loud voice: "Bishop, stop thy canoe, and hear what I have to say to thee!" Then, as the canoes drifted, he greeted the bishop in the name of his own people in a typical harangue, praising Laval's virtues and power, and praying that his presence would bring a blessing on all at the mission. Then he invited Laval to come ashore.

As soon as he had landed, Laval robed himself in camail and rochet, donned his miter, and turned to bless the people, all of whom were now on their knees. As soon as he had finished, Father Frémin broke into the "Veni Creator" in Iroquois and all the Indians with one voice, men and women together, took up the chant as he led the way into the green avenue of boughs. Laval fell in behind them, and behind him came the French, taking up the "Veni Creator" in Latin as the Indian voices fell silent. So alternately singing they went as far as the first bower, where the procession halted while an Onondaga chief made the bishop welcome in a speech much like the Huron's.

A third speech of welcome was given at the bower before the church, this time by the foremost catechist, an Iroquois named Paul. At last all entered the chapel, the French and Indian choirs singing together the "Pange Lingua," "Ave Maris Stella," and "Domine Salvum Fac Regem," at the end of which the Indians alone, men and women alternating, sang a second motet, and then Laval gave the benediction.

All this was in the ordinary order of things, as was his going into the Jesuits' house and receiving the Indian men in one room and afterward the women in another. In the morning there were ten adults to baptize, after which he said mass to the chanting of Indian voices and gave Communion. At the end, with Frémin repeating his words in Iroquois, he preached.

Then came the customary feast, with harangues and orations and the presentation of gifts, lasting for hours, but when it was finally over, Laval announced that he now wished to visit every Indian and his family in their own home. They could at first hardly believe that he meant what he said, but when they saw him emerge from the first house and start to enter the second, all the rest hurried home to make what preparations they could to do him honor, spreading woven mats or robes of fur on the dirt floor, improvising a seat of turf if they had no chair to offer him, and then sitting before him while they listened gravely to his interpreted remarks.

It was late in the evening when he came out of the last hut and returned to the chapel to take part in the benediction. A hush hovered over the mission, and the Indians followed him in the twilight on silent feet.

At La Prairie one could at times almost believe in the feasibility of the Jesuits' dream of turning the vast continental wilderness into a "Paraguay," or Christian paradise. The greatest obstacle, as they saw it, was the constant warfare carried into every corner of the Indian world by the unconverted relatives of these same innocent and peaceful people. If the Iroquois could be subdued, not only would the safety of the colony be assured, the progress of the Catholic faith through North America would become triumphant; and Laval undoubtedly stressed this when he appealed to the king and his minister for military aid.

Argenson had asked for it. The king and Colbert would shortly receive another and highly practical recommendation from Avaugour. Writing from Gaspé in August of 1663, on the eve of his departure and apparently without rancor over his recall, the former governor had put down his ideas of what the Crown should do if it wanted to make sure of saving New France. Whatever his notions about personal enrichment at the expense of fur traders may have been, he was an experienced soldier and wrote as one.

He wanted to fortify Quebec, first of all, with two real forts: one on the opposite shore of the St. Lawrence, probably near Lévis, the second at the mouth of the St. Charles. Both of these were key points a century later in Wolfe's campaign.

He also wanted three thousand soldiers sent over, men who not only could fight but were artisans. They were to serve as military for three years and then become settlers. "If this is done, I assert for the third time no power on earth can drive the French from Quebec."

In addition he wanted naval ships permanently on station at Bic to control the lower St. Lawrence, and at the other end of the colony he wanted fortifications on the Richelieu River to control that avenue of Iroquois attack as far as Lake Champlain. These works would be built by his army of artisan soldiers. But then he wanted to go further; he wanted to seize the continent; and he proposed an attack along what was to become the classic route of Lake Champlain and the Hudson.

The first move would be to send the army of three thousand against the Iroquois settlements, "not only to disperse that *canaille*, but to thwart, also, the progress of the heretics, and to open, moreover, in that direction a communication with the sea, which is not subject to be frozen in these regions." This would be assured by "constructing a fort on the same River that the Dutch have built a miserable wooden Redoubt on, which they call Fort Orange." As he saw it, it would be no problem to dispose of the Dutch.

His plan might have worked if it could have been put in train immediately. But it was not. It was far too costly for the king and his minister even to contemplate at that time. Laval's appeal merely for troops to protect the colony from the Iroquois had more effect, and Louis promised that troops would soon follow the bishop to Canada. "We expect next year," Laval wrote the pope, "twelve hundred soldiers." With them was to come the Marquis de Tracy as lieutenant general and the king's viceroy in America. It was not till 1665, however, that he reached Canada; and in his wake came a new governor, for in the two intervening years an explosion had occurred between Laval and Mézy so violent as to compel the latter's recall to France.

The first four months of his governorship had passed in an atmosphere of harmony between church and state that had had no parallel in recent years. Mézy had been entirely cooperative in approving Laval's choices for the Sovereign Council and in supporting him on the unpopular issue of the tithes and especially in his vigorous efforts to enforce the ban on the brandy traffic. But suddenly, at the end of January, 1664, there was a complete reversal of this happy relationship.

Just what triggered Mézy's volte-face is uncertain. Detractors have suggested that it was the council's unwillingness to increase his salary, and this may well have aggravated his feelings, for the governor's salary had never been adequate for the office and Mézy had no means of his own. But his rebellion sprang from more profound and fundamental causes. He had abruptly come to a realization of his true position as governor: the instrument of royal authority — not merely the commandant of an old provincial town, but the king's representative in a land that, however few French it might yet contain, was ten times vaster than the whole of France. Now as the council began to function he saw it, too, for what it was: a tiny assembly of men who were wholly given to the bishop's interest, and the two members who exercised the most control had been the principal figures in Dumesnil's accusations — Bourdon and Villeray. At the same time it dawned on him that he had been used as a pawn, and that the advantage which had been taken of his ignorance of colonial affairs in order to create a council shaped to the bishop's will had put him in a position of betraying the king's trust. For a man of his simple pride and passionate emotions, the position was insupportable; he wasted no time in trying to rectify it.

On the thirteenth of February, a date that could hardly have proved more inauspicious if it had fallen on a Friday instead of Wednesday, he sent Laval a written message by one of the few friends he had in Canada, the major commandant of the fort, announcing that he had ordered Bourdon and Villeray, and a third man, named Ruette d'Auteuil, not to appear at future proceedings of the council, on the ground that they were using their power to promote their own interests. He asked Laval's approval of this dismissal and also his cooperation in calling a general election to name three new members to replace the men he had dismissed.

No suggestion more likely to antagonize Louis XIV, soon to be called the "Golden Monarch" and always thinking of himself in that light, than that of a public election could be conceived; and in making it, anyone less simple than Mézy would have realized that he was ensuring his own defeat. Laval did so at once, and he made his refusal on the sure grounds of conscience, honor, and the loyalty he owed the Crown. Mézy, however, would not or could not turn back. When he received Laval's refusal to cooperate, he had placards made of his declaration and had it posted and proclaimed through the town to the beating of a drum. Laval, in his turn, resorted to the old weapon of the church, threatening to withold the consolations of the sacraments from the governor and even to close the churches against him.

To a man of Mézy's emotional temper, converted as he had been out of the bleak shadow of Calvinism, the church and its rituals were less spiritual restoratives than the actual keys of his being. He was shaken to his soul. Yet he could not relinquish his obligations to the king. In bewilderment and perturbation he turned to the Jesuits for advice and comfort, though he knew that they were completely devoted to Laval. They would not help him, beyond advising him to heed the spiritual admonitions of his confessor, who was himself a Jesuit.

It would be pointless to follow all the moves and countermoves of this dispute through the spring and summer. Mézy replaced Bourdon as attorney general with a Sieur de Chartier; Bourdon protested his dismissal and the appointment before the council; Mézy then proclaimed that he would be allowed to hold no public office of any kind until instructions about the disposal of his case were received from Paris. An election to name a mayor and alderman for Quebec was held, but the men chosen were not acceptable to the bishop and therefore, probably wisely, they declined to serve, so the council decided that instead of a mayor and alderman, the people should be permitted to elect a syndic. The election was held, but again the winner was regarded as favoring the governor, so the priests and Jesuits demanded a new election. It was held, but no voters appeared.

By fall matters were still at a stand-off between the two parties; but now the term of office for council members had expired and a new council must be chosen. The bishop demanded the reappointment of his friends; but Mézy refused and, acting unilaterally, retained only the two most nearly neutral of the old councilors and replaced the other three with men of his own choosing, the crowning insult being that one of these was the son of Dumesnil.

This was too much for Laval; he protested and renewed his threats of closing the churches against the governor. Mézy replied by ordering Bourdon and Villeray banished. They sailed on September 23 on the last ship of the year, but they bore with them the instruments of Mézy's destruction in letters from Laval and the Jesuits detailing the governor's flouting of authority, above all by his appeals to the people.

Meanwhile Mézy had placards made bearing the names of the new council which were nailed up throughout the town to drumbeat — one of them on the door of the cathedral. At that Laval made good his threat and, as Lalemant noted in the Jesuit *Journal* for October 5:

> This caused the Ecclesiastics to consider in their Conscience what they were obliged to do; *de hoc alibi*. Monsieur the governor complained loudly everywhere that he was refused Confession and Absolution; but our answer was that God knew everything.

Enigmatic as this reply sounds, it was fraught with dire meaning to Mézy, who now comprehended that in upholding the king's authority he had jeopardized his own salvation. During the fall months and early winter and through the turn of the year he brooded with increasing despair over the ultimate destination of his soul. He had no spiritual guide to turn to for comfort, and the specters of damnation came increasingly nearer. No resolution of the political impasse between himself and Laval could take place until word returned from Paris.

There his cause stood no chance of winning against Laval's; at no time, though future intendants and governors received instructions to be on guard against Laval's tendency to assume powers that did not belong to him, was Louis willing to come to actual grips with the bishop. His high family name, the reverence with which he was almost universally regarded, and the support he was given by the Jesuits put him out of reach. Mézy, with no wealth or social distinction, was obviously expendable. His immediate recall was ordered, but long before it could reach Quebec he had received another summons.

In March, shortly before Easter, he was stricken by some sort of brain fever. He could not leave his room, but lay on his bed, wracked with fear and haunted by heaven knew what visions. There had been strange phenomena in the skies during the midwinter months, and from early November till January a comet had flashed nightly across the heavens from north to south. Down the steep streets below the Château St. Louis the little town lay hushed in snow. It had been a winter of heavy storms, and even in mid-April the snow still lay six feet deep in the woods.

Now at last the Jesuits took pity on him; penitence overwhelmed him; and at the end Laval himself, perhaps recalling their long voyage together, came on a visit of mutual forgiveness and gave him absolution. On the night of May 5 he died. A brave if not an intelligent man, he had made no real contribution to Canada except, possibly, to provide another triumph for Laval. But the triumph proved illusory. In the new order presently to be established, Laval was never again able to exercise the political power he had enjoyed under Mézy's rule or that of his two predecessors.

The change for Laval and equally for Canada began with the arrival on June 30 of Louis's viceroy and lieutenant general, Alexandre de Prouville, Marquis de Tracy. It was an occasion which all colonists alike had expectantly awaited for more than a year, for the marquis had been commissioned in November 1663. This was Louis's first step in a plan to restore the power and glory of France in her dominions overseas. Besides his lieutenant generalcy, Tracy had also been designated governor general of all French possessions in the western hemisphere, and before coming to Canada he made a long southward circle to South America and the West Indies. In order that he should properly impress his hosts along the route with the intention and power of the king, he had been given four companies of one of France's most famous regiments — Carignan-Salières — two hundred men, with Louis's promise that the remaining sixteen companies would follow him to Canada. His personal bodyguard of twenty-four were permitted to wear the king's own livery, and he had in his train a group of young noblemen.

All this panoply embarked on two vessels, the *Bresé*, one of the largest ships in the French navy, 800 tons, and the *Teron*, only slightly smaller.

They left France on the fourth of February, 1664, stopping at Madeira and the Cape Verde Islands, where they were greeted with great courtesy and honor by the Portuguese officials, and then completed the first leg of their voyage at Cayenne, off the coast of what is now French Guiana. This small island settlement had been taken over by the Dutch, but the Dutch governor surrendered it without demur, and Tracy installed its new French governor, Le Fèbvre de la Barre, in his place.

Everything there being settled to his satisfaction, the governor general now set sail for the French islands, spending time mainly at Martinique and Guadeloupe, where there had been considerable disorder, according to the Jesuit commentator, and where, under Tracy's guidance, religion and justice were firmly established, the people given relief, "and all matters adjusted under the authority of the new Seigneurs, the Honorable Company of the West Indies."

The Company of the West Indies was the Company of New France reincarnated, but on a scale a hundred times vaster. Louis and his minister, Colbert, had set out to invigorate Canada by taking its government into their own hands, but this determination lasted less than two years. Colbert was a believer in the efficiency of great trading companies which in return for the profits of monopoly would assume the tiresome duties of government and defense of the various holdings they were given to exploit. The Company of the West Indies, which was established by royal decree in May 1664, and of which anyone could become a member by subscribing three thousand francs, was given exclusive rights of trade for forty years not only to New France and all land claimed for it in North America, but, as we have just seen, to France's Caribbean islands and all possessions touching on the South Atlantic in Africa as well as South America. It was in all ways a grandiose conception, and of course it worked no better than its more modest predecessor.

There is no point in following its history in detail. The merchants of Canada, finding themselves once more in the shackles of monopolies that covered fur, imports, in fact the whole fabric of commercial existence, vehemently protested to Colbert and set about exercising complete freedom in the fur trade within the boundaries of Canada itself. Something had to give somewhere, and it was the Company, which gave up its fur monopoly in exchange for a duty of one fourth of the beaver and a tenth of the moose hides, plus the full production of the fur station at Tadoussac — which presumably meant the take of all the Indians between the St. Lawrence and Hudson Bay. (A portion of these, however, could be lured to the fur fair at Three Rivers and undoubtedly were.) The Company proved such an inefficient machine so far as its Canadian rights were concerned that by 1674 it was three and a half million livres in debt and was dissolved in consequence by a royal edict of December of that same year.

The Company had hardly been created before it was compelled to relinquish one of the rights granted it in its charter: that of choosing its own governor for the colony, and an intendant. It was very likely the difficulties over Mézy that made Louis decide to keep the power of appointment for himself and thus have officers responsible to the Crown alone. The governorship went to Daniel de Rémy, Sieur de Courcelles, an able and honest man, but with quick passions. The intendant was Jean Baptiste Talon. He was an experienced administrator, a friend and disciple of the minister, Colbert, whose confidence he seems always to have enjoyed, and what was more, he had a continental insight that the administrators of New France until his day notably lacked. Both men received their commissions on the twenty-third of March, 1665, and in a little over two months were at sea.

Meanwhile the hour of Tracy's arrival was drawing near. It had taken months to put the affairs of Martinique and Guadeloupe in order, and it was not till April 25, 1665, that the *Bresé* and *Teron* lifted anchor and set sail for San Domingo. The English on St. Kitts saluted Tracy with "innumerable discharges of cannon" as the two ships sailed past their shores.

He doubled Puerto Rico and made for the Tortugas, but contrary winds drove him into the French port on San Domingo and the governor of Tortugas was forced to come to him there, where he made the oath of faith and homage to the marquis for himself and for the people of the islands.

This was the last of Tracy's duties in the Caribbean, and he now headed north for the Caicos Passage and New France beyond. So many ships had been wrecked in this channel that there was much hesitation aboard about taking such valuable vessels into such dangerous water; but to have rounded the Bahamas would have meant, according to his navigator, adding twelve hundred miles to the voyage and Tracy, who had a schedule to keep, brushed aside the fears of his company, found a new pilot, and brought the ships safely through. One month after leaving San Domingo they were off Cape Ray and entering the Gulf of St. Lawrence.

They crossed the gulf and cast anchor off Percé to take on water and wood. It was now the end of May, a time of blue skies and white clouds sailing from the west above the Gaspé hills, a bright time for men who had been long at sea, and made almost heady by the scent of balsam and spruce blowing on the wind. Then, as they still lay off the shore, occurred the first of several happenings that were to mark this as the brightest and most auspicious year the people of New France had experienced since the founding of Quebec.

Out of the southwest two ships came sailing up to them under the colors of France. They were from La Rochelle; and aboard them were four more companies of the regiment of Carignan-Salières. Tracy's heart was lifted. He had been worrying about the troops. He had two hundred with him, but he knew full well how in the past troops promised had failed to materialize. Here were two hundred more with word that the remainder were supposed to be somewhere behind them. The campaign against the Iroquois, which occupied top priority among his assigned duties, could now certainly be carried through.

After his year and four months at sea and in the subtropical Caribbean, Tracy was suffering from a fever of some kind. He was anxious to be on land and hoped to be able to sail his two ships up the river at least as far as Bic; but the winds were unfavorable and the heavy vessels could not be maneuvered against them. It was decided to return to Percé and have two smaller vessels of shallower draft take them on the final leg of their journey. So more time was lost, though the two ships from La Rochelle had gone ahead with their troops and the word that Tracy was on the river. At last they were under way, still fighting the perverse winds, and finally on the thirtieth of June saw Cape Diamond before them, the foreshore crowded with boats and people, behind them the wooden warehouses and clustered dwellings of the Lower Town and above them the ascending streets and buildings perching steeply toward the gaunt gray stone buildings of the ecclesiastics on the heights, and the wooden sprawling château, and the fort.

Cannon roared from the fort, every bell was pealing, as the viceroy stepped ashore to the shouted welcome of the people. The spectacle was one the like of which Quebec had never seen. As the boats came to the quay from the two ships and unloaded their passengers, a procession was gradually formed and finally set off through the streets of the Lower Town. Heading it was the lieutenant general's bodyguard: twenty-four men in the king's livery, followed by his ten personal servants; then Tracy himself, surrounded by his young noblemen in court attire; and then in a long file the two hundred veteran soldiers of Carignan-Salières. Quebec had greeted the first eight companies on the two ships from La Rochelle on the eighteenth and nineteenth; but this reinforcement was corroborative evidence of the king's interest in his colonists, and for the day the ocean seemed smaller and Old France drawn close to New.

Tracy himself was an impressive man, tall and heavily built, and perhaps even more striking from the jaundiced pallor the fever had left on his face. The climb up the steep streets taxed his strength, but the cheers of the people buoyed every step; he did not pause, and when he came level with the fort and the château and faced the square, he saw across it the cathedral, in the door of which waited the bishop, in pontifical robes, surrounded by his clergy.

Though, like Laval, Tracy could exercise pomp to a degree, he was at heart devout and of simple instincts, and without doubt was deeply moved after his long voyage to come to this door and be offered holy water and at last to feel he had reached home. Laval, who must have wondered what kind of man he would now have to deal with, led Tracy into the choir to a prie-dieu that had been placed there for him; but Tracy declined it and, though near exhaustion, preferred to kneel on the bare stone while the "Te Deum" to the sound of organ and music flowed about him. Watching him, Laval and his priests and the Jesuits must have felt a wave of relief and gratitude that such a man had been sent to rule the colony.

> Never will New France cease to bless our great Monarch for undertaking to restore her to life and rescue her from the fires of the Iroquois. For nearly forty years we have been sighing for this happiness. Our tears have at length crossed the sea, and our plaint has touched the heart of his Majesty, who is about to make a Kingdom of our Barbarous land, and change our forests into towns and our deserts into Provinces.

In this way François le Mercier, who had just succeeded Jerome Lalemant as Jesuit Superior, began his preface to the *Relation* of 1664–1665; and if the words seem almost simple-minded in their optimism, they fairly reflected the universal rise of heart that had taken place among the people of Quebec. Le Mercier himself even believed that it might soon be possible for the Jesuits to realize their great Paraguayan dream. "But our chief complaint was not so much that, groaning under Iroquois cruelty, we could not convert all these regions into a noble French Kingdom, as that we were prevented by Barbarians from turning them into a great Christian Empire." Evidently there was still no doubt in his mind that the first purpose of creating a colony and providing the military means for its protection was actually to promote the power of the church and advance the Cross. But this was not to be.

Louis throughout continued his generosity toward the church, though sometimes sounding almost plaintive in remarks about how much it cost him. He did not fail to treat Laval with respect; but he had become wary of the bishop's influence on the secular arm of government. In the instructions Talon brought with him from France, he was directed to get to the bottom of the imbroglio between Mézy and Laval; but though Mézy's violent acts were catalogued, it was with the cautioning phrase "as they represent" — "they" in this case meaning the bishop and the Jesuits. Then, adding that Courcelles and Tracy had been ordered to act with him on the matter, the king required Talon to "take information, by persons not suspected of partiality, of the truth of the complaints made against him." Only if they were well founded was Mézy to be arrested, tried, and sent back to receive royal justice. When these instructions were issued it was not known in France that Mézy was already dead; and not long after their arrival, the two governors and the intendant concluded that it would not be proper to bring proceedings against the dead man — especially since the Jesuits and Laval had initiated no new steps against him — but in Talon's words they were sure that "his Majesty would not be sorry were his fault buried with his memory."

There were other indications that the royal government, though not denying his worth as a prelate or the holiness of his purpose, would no longer accept Laval's version of what was or was not good for Canada. The drop-off of revenue from furs had for some time been a source of anxiety in France, and among the instructions for Tracy was one from Lyonne, Minister of Marine, concerning the brandy traffic, in which with an amiable cynicism one of Laval's arguments was turned against him. Pointing out that the Jesuits and Monseigneur the Bishop had threatened all engaging in the brandy traffic with excommunication, on the ground that the Indians drinking it always became so drunk that they were likely to fall into mortal sin, Lyonne said that the prohibition was now so strict that no Frenchman dared even to *give* a glass of brandy to a Huron or an Algonquin. This was undoubtedly a praiseworthy principle, but it had proved ruinous to trade, for the Indians merely took their furs to Albany, where the Dutch gladly provided them with brandy. And that was not the whole matter by any means; for in effect this situation was as harmful to religion as to the fur trade.

. . . Having wherewith to gratify their appetites, they allow themselves to be catechised by Dutch ministers, who instruct them in Heresy. The said Bishop of Petrée and the Jesuit Fathers persist in their first opinions, without reflecting that prudence, and even Christian charity inculcate closing the eyes to one evil to avoid a greater, or to reap a good more important than evil.

Laval and the Jesuits were soon to find their position untenable and had to withdraw the threat of excommunication, and within three years Talon succeeded in obtaining a decree from the council permitting unrestricted sale of liquor to the Indians. This became a continuing sorrow for Laval, but there was little he could do about it. Now and then gestures toward prohibition would be made. Traders were forbidden to take brandy into the woods with them, though bartering with liquor remained legal anywhere inside the settlements. But who could imagine a trader's starting into the wilderness without brandy in his stock? And how was he to be stopped from taking it? An attempt was made by issuing trading licenses, and then invoking the death penalty for any man who went into the woods to trade without one; but that did not keep ambitious men from accumulating a canoeload of goods and one day disappearing behind the green curtain of the forest. It was impossible to prevent them even when halfway sincere efforts were made at enforcement; and from 1668 Laval had to live with his defeat on this issue. He found it the more painful because it manifestly killed forever the Jesuits' dream of a North American Paraguay.

But during that summer of 1665 no dark shadow of the future or the past marred the sunshine that bathed all Quebec like a royal dispensation. Tracy had arrived at the end of June. In mid-July another ship arrived, captained by a sailing master most appropriately named Poulet, for it brought eight girls suitable for marriage to woman-hungry settlers. This was another instance of the personal interest of the king; and the eight girls proved forerunners of many young women in the next few years sent over at the king's expense to provide wives for his settlers — from wholesome farm girls for habitants to young ladies of breeding for such officers as elected to stay on as colonists and establish seigneuries.

Besides the eight girls, Poulet's ship had brought twelve horses, the first to come to Canada except for one that had been presented to Governor Montmagny in 1647. The Hurons and Alonquins, seeing them for the first time, were struck open-mouthed with wonder, not so much by their size as by the docility with which these animals, which they were convinced were the native moose of France, obeyed the commands of their handlers. They were even more wonderful than the rolling drums of the regiment of Carignan-Salières.

The drums once more on the nineteenth and again on the twentieth of

August filled the narrow streets with echoes as the final eight companies disembarked from two of the king's ships and made the steep march to the fort. At the head of the first four companies marched the regiment's commander, a veteran grown gray in army service, with his young son at his side. He was Colonel Henri de Chapelas, Sieur de Salières, whose name provided the second half of the regiment's. It must have been an exhilarating experience for a fifteen-year-old boy fresh from France. Everything was strange, the buildings of wood and stone and the steep streets climbing the great rock; the lines of cheering habitants — the men in long vests and wool or leather leggings with blue handkerchiefs worn turbanwise upon their heads as a protection alike against the sun and the mosquitoes, and occasionally a woman in her bright bodice and homespun short gown; and of course the Indians, grave of face, expressionless of eye as they encountered his youthful stare. These would be French Indians, many already converted to Christianity; but at sight of them an image of the savage Iroquois sprang to life in the mind, with all their hideous paraphernalia of the torture scaffolds. So in spite of the drumbeats behind and the solid tread of the marching companies, it was good to come out in the square before the fort and be able to look out and down on the wild land, understanding from this height a little of the river's vastness and the wilderness from which it flowed. But ahead, waiting in the cathedral door to welcome them, were the ecclesiastics; they at least looked as priests and bishops looked in France.

The regiment of Carignan-Salières was composed entirely of veteran troops, as tough and battle-wise as any unit in Louis's professional army of a hundred thousand men, which meant as fine as any body of soldiers in Europe. It was first recruited in Savoy in 1644 by the Prince of Carignan but had afterward been brought into the regular French army. It had fought on the royalist side in the war of the Fronde, the last bloody attempt by the French nobility to oppose the Court with arms. In 1664 it had been sent as part of a force of four thousand troops to the aid of Austria against the Turks and there had taken a key part in the victory of St. Gotthard. On their recall to France they had been allowed barely time to refit before being assigned to Canada, the first French regulars to cross the Atlantic; and now within a year of fighting along the river Raab they were in Quebec, ready as soon as their land legs had been restored to ascend this infinitely greater stream and carry war to the barbarian Iroquois.

They had the air of men who knew their way about, and they impressed the Algonquins and Hurons as much as they did the French, though the Huron chief in welcoming Tracy in a fine harangue found fault with their uniforms. "It is true that the enemy places half his prowess in his fast running, fighting usually entirely naked, and with only his musket in his hand and his hatchet in his belt — either to make it easier for him to win the victory, or to render his flight more unimpeded. When you have defeated him, you will not have captured him — especially as you are embarrassed with clothing ill adapted to running through thickets and the underbrush, unless it is well girt up and secured." All the same, many Hurons and Algonquins volunteered to accompany Tracy once he had mounted his expedition.

They were tough in another way, too, for to the astonishment of the pure little Catholic community, heretics were found among them, sixteen according to Talon's count, but Father Le Mercier claimed there were over twenty. Perhaps the readiness with which the clergy persuaded these tough men to abjure their heresy and return to the Catholic fold had gone a little to the good Father's head. As they set about their task of spiritual regeneration something like the feeling of optimism, almost of gaiety, that had electrified the colony from the day of Tracy's arrival seemed to affect the nuns and priests in a situation that would ordinarily have been considered horrifying: the discovery of so many Huguenots in what till then had been their pure Catholic community. It elated them to think that these soldiers were "to find the road to Paradise by way of Canada."

Only one of them proved really obdurate, but his case was deftly handled by one of the hospital nuns. In the last contingent of troops to reach Quebec aboard the ship which also brought Courcelles and Talon, and on one arriving two days afterward, many of the troops had been taken by a mysterious illness on the way up the river from Tadoussac. By the time they reached Quebec there were a hundred cases, and most of these were brought to the hospital, which was staffed by the Ursulines. They overflowed the sick ward, so the nuns turned their chapel into a hospital too. One of the patients was the obdurate soldier.

Nothing could shake him, neither threats of damnation nor the most gentle pleading. But one of the nuns, named Marie Catherine de St. Augustin, refused to be defeated. She had achieved miraculous success in the treating of some illnesses by making use of the sacred remains of Brébeuf, whose bones with those of his fellow martyr, Gabriel Lalemant, had been disinterred from their first burial place in the Huron country and brought in wrappings of silk to Quebec. She now determined to try their efficacy in this case of sickness of the soul. Grinding an infinitesimal piece of bone to a powder, she stirred it into a drink she had prepared for the soldier and, undoubtedly with shining eyes, watched while he drank it unaware of the unusual ingredient. She was not kept long in suspense for, as Father Le Mercier reported, "Wonderful to relate, the man became a lamb, asked to be instructed, received into his mind and heart the influence of our Faith, and made public abjuration of heresy with such fervor that he himself was astonished." And as was by no means always the case, his bodily health was restored with that of his soul.

It was all part of this wonderful season of restored hope and faith, in which even a gentle nun might feel she was playing a role in the campaign that was to follow in the spring when at last the scourge of the Iroquois would be ended forever. The fervor of the Ursulines was communicated to the soldiers, more than five hundred of whom accepted scapularies of the Holy Virgin which the nuns made for them to wear under their uniforms. The autumn air became bright with the sense that they were to embark on a crusade.

A climactic triumph came when the captain of one of the companies confessed himself a heretic and begged for instruction. He made his abjuration in the presence of the viceroy, the governor, the intendant, and four of the Jesuit Fathers. The ceremony was performed in the cathedral with all possible pomp, the penitent being under the care of Laval himself in pontifical robes and accompanied by all the clergy. This took place on October 8, and by then only the last troops to have arrived, those who had been so sick, remained in Quebec.

The other companies had all been sent up the St. Lawrence under Tracy's order to fortify the Richelieu, which was still generally called the River of the Iroquois. Before the coming of the big snow three forts had been completed: Fort Richelieu at the mouth of the river on the left bank, ascending, which soon came to be known by the name of the captain who had been in charge of building it, Pierre de Sorel; then, about thirty-seven miles above, on the right bank, at the foot of the so-called falls of the Richelieu, Fort St. Louis — though it too assumed the name of its builder, Jacques de Chambly; the third, about seven miles further upstream, with clear passage to the mouth of Lake Champlain and also on the right bank, was named for Ste. Thérèse, and seems to have retained its name.

Colonel de Salières had reserved the building of this fort for himself since it was the one most exposed to Iroquois attack; and so great was the urgency of finishing it before deep winter set in that the old colonel put his own hands to the work and by his example so fired the enthusiasm of his soldiers that the fort was completed on October 15. One wonders whether Salières's young son had gone to the fort with his father or had been left behind in Quebec, as had been the case of a youthful drummer of superior talent whose captain had given him to the Jesuits "with the design that we should do him the charity of making him study." If young Salières had any say in the matter, we should not need to guess; it would have been an exciting place for a boy, especially as the Indians attached to the fort as hunters had begun to bring in unusual numbers of bear and moose. As it was, after falling into some sort of dispute with Tracy, Salières was assigned to winter at Montreal.

In Quebec, as the first week of October ended, Tracy had decided that he should inspect the companies in their respective forts and also the units that had been assigned to Three Rivers and Montreal. He had not been able wholly to shake off his fever, indeed at times his health appeared so feeble that Talon feared Canada would lose him either by death or enforced retirement, but no remonstrance could deter him from what he conceived to be his duty. The war against the Iroquois was his most important assignment, and it was necessary to see that the troops were well quartered and provisioned, so that spring would find them in proper case for the campaign. On the first of the month four companies that were to escort him departed for Three Rivers. It must have been a frustration for the soldiers, because the last ship of the year to arrive in the basin was disembarking no fewer than eighty-two girls and women; there were one hundred and thirty laborers on the ship, too, but men had come to Canada before.

Tracy left on his inspection ten days later, and on the boats that accompanied him Talon sent all additional provisions he could scrape together as well as "some luxuries to charm away the rigors of the winter," a revelation of his intense concern for the people whose welfare had been entrusted to him. He was already enlisted on their side, as against the depredation of the monopolistic and proprietary Company, and in his first official report said so bluntly:

> . . . since the Company's agents have given it to be understood that it would not suffer any freedom of trade, — neither to the French who were in the habit of coming to this country with merchandise from France, nor to the proper inhabitants of Canada, — even so far as to deny them the right of importing on their own account the products of the Kingdom which they make use of, as well for their own support, as in trade with the Indians, which alone will ruin the most considerable of the Inhabitants, to whom agriculture does not afford sufficient inducements to make them remain here with their families, I clearly perceive that the Company, by pushing its power to the extreme it pretends, will doubtless profit by impoverishing the country; and will not only deprive it of the means of self-support, but will become a serious obstacle to its settlement, and that Canada in ten years will be less populous than it is today.

The office of intendant, as it was used in the government of France during the seventeenth and eighteenth centuries, was an outgrowth of the country's transformation from a collective of dukedoms and counties, whose rulers at times exercised more real power than the monarchs to whom they professed allegiance, into a kingdom over which the authority of the Crown was absolute. As fiefs of medieval origin were taken by one process or another into the king's possession and turned into provinces, it was natural to appoint as governors members of the noble families identified with them as the men best fitted by tradition and training to govern.

However, their loyalty to the sovereign more often than not proved open to question; their resentment over the loss of independent authority, with the consequent diminution of their rights and privileges, made them more restless and ready to join any movement to curtail the power of the Crown; and it became necessary for the king's ministers to look in other quarters for men to administer royal policy on provincial levels.

There was at the beginning of the seventeenth century a relatively new class of official, already known as intendant, at work in the French army. In effect he was a combination of commissary general and paymaster, whose integrity presumably could be relied on, and who acted in all things as the king's agent. As the army gradually assumed professional status, the importance of the intendant's office and the responsibilities he carried increased. When he received his first appointment, he was likely to be a young man, of middle class and usually, though not inevitably, with training in the law. His loyalty went naturally to the Crown, from which he had received his elevation to power; he had no private rank to divert his ambition from his career or estates to fall back on if he should be discharged; he was essentially an administrator, trained for his job, the nearest thing to the professional civil servant that had till then existed.

When in 1624 Richelieu became Louis XIII's minister, he began to mine the army for intendants capable of administrating provinces, and the post of intendant grew in stature, though in all matters of precedence at public functions this official ranked below the governor whose duties he actually performed. His role was that of a practical man of business. If he was conscientious, no detail was too insignificant to escape his attention; he supervised and to a large extent controlled the administration of justice, the development of natural resources, the supply and payment of troops, the building of roads and other public works, the encouragement of agriculture. To understand even partially the minutiae of life in the colony that he was supposed to familiarize himself with, one may turn to a sentence in Colbert's instructions to Talon. After pointing out that Louis regarded his Canadian subjects, high and low alike, almost as his own children and therefore wished them, equally with his subjects in the heart of France, to be sensible of "the mildness and happiness of his reign," Talon is urged to encourage them to industry and commerce which alone could bring prosperity to the colony and ease the people's lives.

> And inasmuch as nothing can better contribute thereunto than entering the details of their little affairs and of their household, it will be not mal-à-propos if, after being established, he visit all their settlements, the one after the other, to understand their true state, and afterwards provide as much as possible for the necessities he will have noticed there, so that in performing the duty of a good master of a household, he may expedite for them the means of realizing some profits . . .

Even the upbringing of children became part of his duty, for he was directed to encourage fathers to inspire in their offspring veneration for "things relating to our Religion," and afterward to instill in them "profound love and respect for the Royal person of his Majesty," and thirdly to lead them into industrious habits, "for experience has always unerringly demonstrated, that the idleness of early life is the true source of all disorders that mar it, whilst industry produces a contrary effect among those who avoid sloth at this early season."

Louis XIV had the kind of mind that reveled in details; if he had small imagination, he spent endless time in mastering the insignificant; and one may well imagine him here basking in the light of his own benevolence. But as Talon sailed up the huge river and saw how isolated, poor, and pitifully few were the signs of habitation until Quebec itself came in view, he must have wondered where an intendant could find time and means to accomplish all of the king's intention. The fact that he was to succeed to a remarkable degree is the best measure of his character.

He bore little resemblance to the ordinary conception of what an intendant should look like: a man dressed soberly in black, with a lawyer's cautious eye and the shrewd matter-of-factness of a man of business. Talon dressed like a courtier and wore his hair in long elaborate curls that broke over his shoulders. He loved show, and when he made his march up the hill of Quebec, his appearance and that of his retinue impressed the onlookers as much as Courcelles's had. Mother Juchereau, after commenting on his love of glory (though how she knew it was glory that he loved, after one short glance, is hard to understand), reported that in his train Talon "forgot nothing which could do honor to the king." Judging from a portrait of him painted in the prime of life, his face might have belonged to a painter or a poet; it had in spite of the long arched nose an air of delicacy, fastidiousness; the brows and the lips curved with almost feminine gentleness. But the eyes were strong and humorous and from them gleamed the shrewd intelligence with which he set to work to raise the colony from the edge of failure. Other industrious and capable intendants were to follow him, but only one, François Bigot, was equally intelligent. Bigot, however, was a rogue, whose milking of the colony for his own enrichment during the last years of its defense against the English did almost as much to accomplish the fall of New France as Wolfe's capture of Quebec. But no one ever questioned Talon's integrity, and no one doubted his devotion to Canada from the moment he set about mounting the expedition against the Iroquois.

Word of what was happening in Quebec and along the Richelieu during the late summer and early fall reached the Iroquois with the wildfire swiftness with which important news invariably traversed the wilderness. The arrival of the Carignan regiment in numbers that to them suggested an army was alarming, more so than the building of the three forts which could be regarded as a defensive measure against the Mohawks. Strangely, it was the three western tribes that were most apprehensive, and in December deputations of the Senecas, Cayugas, and Onondagas turned up at Quebec to sue for peace.

They were led by an Onondaga sachem whom the Jesuits considered "the most renowned of all the Savage Captains," including in this rating not only Iroquois but Hurons and Algonquins. His name was Garakontié — "Sun That Advances"; his council name or title was Sagochiendagehté; and if anyone could be said to be so, he was the elder statesman of the whole Iroquois confederacy. He seems to have been unique among his people in favoring the French from the beginning; and the beginning for him had been the first visit to the Onondaga town in 1654 of Father Simon Le Moyne, who more often than any other Jesuit in critical periods risked his life among the Iroquois. Garakontié's first sight of the single black-robed figure walking among the long houses had made a deep impression on him, and the impression deepened as he learned to appreciate the strength of will beneath the priest's calm reserve. Le Moyne's mission on that first encounter was as much ambassadorial as spiritual, and the chief who spoke for all the Iroquois in council could communicate with him as one man to another, not as a man talking to a priest of an alien religion. Their personal bond grew strong, and now when on his mission of peace in 1665 he was informed of Le Moyne's recent death, the grief that came through the apostrophe of his condolence speech was unmistakable.

. . . hearest thou me from the country of the dead, whither thou hast so quickly passed? Thou it was who didst so many times risk thy life on the scaffolds of the Agniehronnons [Mohawks]; who didst go bravely into their very fires, to snatch so many Frenchmen from the flames; who didst carry peace and tranquillity whithersoever thou didst go, and madest so many converts where thou didst dwell. We have seen thee on our council-mats deciding questions of peace and war; our cabins were found too small when thou didst enter them, and our villages themselves were too cramped when thou wast present — so great was the crowd of people attracted by thy words. But I disturb thy rest with this importunate address. So often didst thou teach us that this life of affliction is followed by one of eternal happiness; since, then, thou dost possess that life, what reason have we to mourn thee? But we weep for thee, because in losing thee, we have lost our Father and our Protector.

Garakontié himself had rescued many French from the torture fires of his own tribe and those of the Mohawks; more than twenty-six according to Father Jean de Lamberville, who sat beside his deathbed. By then he had been converted and his baptism in the cathedral by Laval, with Governor Courcelles standing as his godfather, was one of the great events of the Catholic church in Canada, for Garakontié did not waver in his new faith. From the moment of his conversion he had given up the use of brandy and proved one of the rare Indians able to stick to his resolve even when surrounded by repeated orgies of drinking in the Onondaga town.

He was a strong man with the dignified bearing that was natural to an Indian, and when he led his deputation before the viceroy the two men regarded each other with respect. Among the Iroquois with him was an Oneida chief whom they had encountered on the St. Lawrence. The Oneida had come to Canada on an independent prospective mission hoping to pick up a prisoner or a scalp or two before the deep snow made traveling onerous; but he was readily persuaded to turn himself from the warpath and become a member of their peaceful embassy, no doubt because he was curious to see for himself the newly come great men from France. So Garakontié's deputation represented four of the Five Nations, even if the Oneida was attending on a strictly unofficial basis.

The Indians had brought three Frenchmen, among them the Sieur Le Moyne of Montreal, who had been prisoners, and at the outset of his speech Garakontié turned them over to Tracy as evidence of his good faith, pointing out somewhat cannily the good health they were all in, especially Le Moyne "without even one of his nails being torn off or any part of his body being burnt." In return he asked only for the freedom of three prisoners: an Onondaga woman, a child stolen by the Mohicans and brought to the French, and a Huron squaw who had been settled among the Iroquois. These he wished to take back as earnest of the good faith of the French so that he could cement a peace not like that of times past, which "held the French only by the fringe of the coat," but one in which he would "clasp them round the waist." And he concluded with a plea for tolerance toward the Mohawks who, he said, had not realized that the new soldiers had been sent for the extermination of the Five Nations or they would have joined his embassy.

If Tracy was startled by the high-pitched, quavering rise and fall of Garakontié's voice in formal oratory, he continued to be impressed and agreed to every point, except the final plea for the Mohawks, "with all the kindness the other could desire." His confidence in his Indian vis-à-vis was not misplaced. Garakontié continued a strong friend of the French and worked for better relations between them and his own people until 1675, when he died of a bloody flux.

He was taken ill just after Christmas and knew at once that he would die. Father de Lamberville, who never left his bedside, wrote a detailed and touching account of his end. He wished for a burial in the French manner and asked the Father to make him a coffin from four planks which he had kept on hand. He wanted a high cross beside his grave, so that it could be seen from afar and remind people that he had been a Christian and remained true to his faith.

Over the grave the Jesuit exhorted the assembled people to stop their grieving cries and to follow his example of turning Christian if they wanted ever to see him again. "After that, I knelt down and prayed aloud in their tongue for the repose of the soul of the deceased. Then, bending my head over his face, I bade him a last adieu, rejoicing with him that he had so resolutely professed Christianity." And in spite of his admonitions Lamberville found tears falling from his own eyes.

Garakontié had procured peace for the three western nations, but he had not diverted the French from their intention of carrying war to the Mohawks. The original plan called for a campaign in the spring or summer, but now Courcelles, who according to Father Le Mercier had been "breathing nothing but war" from the moment he set foot in Canada, decided that the Mohawks must be given an object lesson before they should have time to sue for peace, and energetically set about preparations for an immediate expedition.

The mere idea of leading a large body of troops — Courcelles proposed to take five hundred men — through what was then believed to be nearly seven hundred miles of wilderness in midwinter seemed preposterous to men who knew what the iron bite of January cold or the white hell of a western blizzard could do to men on the march. It was all right to say that the Iroquois sent out war parties in winter: they knew how to travel, were adept on snowshoes and familiar with the tricks that saved a man from freezing. The first snow had fallen on November 10; now it was deeper, but no one knew when the big storms would come to raise the level of it in the woods to four or five or even six feet. Courcelles, however, was not to be dissuaded; he simply would not listen; he would be at the head of some of the finest troops who had ever carried arms on the continent of Europe and it was absurd to think that they could not do anything an Indian could.

If Tracy entertained any doubts about the wisdom of Courcelles's plans, he made no attempt to interfere, and as a veteran soldier may well have sympathized with Courcelles's ambition to strike a blow on his own before the larger campaign planned for summer. Courcelles's position as governor was completely overshadowed by Tracy's presence as royal viceroy, not only in the colony but in the minds of the English. In a letter protesting French violation of New York territory to attack the Mohawks, the first English governor, Colonel Richard Nicolls, himself a man of distinction and sensibility, wrote: "in all other points I shall be found to entertain y^r Correspondence with mutual Civility & respect, the rather because the

Reputation of y^r honor hath spread itself in all these parts of the world, as well as it is known in Europe. . . ." Tracy was the nearest thing to an international figure that had been seen in the New World; he was by nature a generous man, and if any credit were to be gained in a winter expedition by a subordinate against the Mohawks, he could afford to let the man win it. As a matter of fact it might make the proposed summer campaign unnecessary. But probably no more than Courcelles's could his imagination grasp the effects of the northern winter on shelterless men.

"In all history," declared Le Mercier, "there can scarcely be found a march of more difficulty or greater length than that of this little army." He was not far wrong, though it set the pattern for several others made before the affairs of France and England were settled in North America. "The 9th," begins the Jesuit *Journal* for January 1666, "Monsieur the governor leaves for the war, with about one hundred of the frenchmen of the country." These were probably the first half of his contingent of habitant volunteers, whatever troops he was taking from the Quebec garrison having gone on before. Le Mercier in the *Relation* of 1665–1666 says that he marched out of the town with three hundred troops and two hundred habitants, but Le Mercier was also the author of the *Journal*, which attempted to record events as they occurred, and though most accounts follow the version in the *Relation*, it seems more likely that Courcelles began his bitter march with this small number of volunteers and picked up his regular troops from garrisons along his route.

Be that as it may, they spent the first day in covering the few miles to Sillery. Here in the little mission chapel he and his party knelt before the altar to place the fortunes of their undertaking in the special care of the Archangel St. Michael who was the patron of the mission.

Next morning they were early on their way. It was bitterly cold, and the temperature was soon to approach the low levels that were to make this winter the coldest in thirty years. They followed the St. Lawrence, which had turned into an avenue of glaring ice, swept clean by the northwest wind, and so slippery it was hard to keep one's balance when struck by the harder gusts. On the second day out of Sillery many of the men had frozen noses, ears, knees, and fingers; others in addition to frostbite had suffered severe cuts in falls on the ice; and toward evening men began to succumb entirely to the cold; dropping in their tracks and remaining motionless. They would have died there if others had not returned to drag them like logs of wood to the bivouac.

The camp was off the river in thick woods. Since no one, not even Courcelles, had a tent, the men had followed the usual procedure of digging down in the snow to clear the ground in large circles, lining the edges with evergreen boughs and lighting fires in the middle. They slept sitting up with their backs against the wall of boughs and their legs like wheel spokes pointing to the fire.

It took three more days of painful marching before they stumbled into Cap de la Madeleine just across the mouth of the St. Maurice from Three Rivers. Here the Jesuits had a mission and had built a fort to protect displaced Hurons and Algonquins, and here too since 1649 a French settlement had been growing. There was room enough to care for Courcelles's suffering band; and there were troops of the Carignan regiment both in Cap de la Madeleine and Three Rivers.

At the former place next day Courcelles "gave orders to the troops who are to accompany him." Then he crossed over to Three Rivers where he spent two days organizing his little force, which was augmented by eight regular troops with their four captains and forty-five more habitants. On the eighteenth they were again on their way. But it was now even colder. Men began to fall out of the march on the very first day, with hands, arms, or feet hard frozen, so that until the halfway point to Fort Richelieu was gained they had to be carried back to Three Rivers.

It is just over thirty miles in a straight line across Lac St. Pierre to the mouth of the Richelieu, but as the little army marched, in contact with the river shore, it was probably nearer forty. They had required six days to cover the eighty-odd miles between Sillery and Cap de la Madeleine; it took even longer to march the forty miles to Sorel and they came into the little fort once more carrying or dragging their own frozen.

But nothing could for long stay Courcelles's impatience to find action. He recruited his force with more men from the Carignan companies and seventy habitants from Montreal and pushed on to Fort St. Louis at Chambly where he levied more troops from the companies of Captains Chambly, Petit, and Rogemont. On the twenty-ninth of January he had moved to Fort Ste. Thérèse where, with another contribution from the company of Colonel de Salières, his army was finally brought up to the desired number of three hundred regulars and two hundred habitants. On the thirtieth they left the fort and were soon to come out on the long snowy expanse of Lake Champlain.

The snow was now much deeper: four feet in the open, perhaps six in the woods. The little army, long strung out, followed the western shore with laborious slowness, for the Carignan troops, however tough fighters they might have been in Europe, were finding their snowshoes as difficult as any enemies they had ever had to handle and now made painful discovery of sinews in their legs which they had not known existed. The habitants in their rough blue-hooded surcoats led the van with the seventy from Montreal, who had done Indian fighting and knew the woods as well as any *coureur de bois*, at the front of all. They were invaluable at breaking trail for the stumbling regulars and at night, as before, they made camps in the woods, digging away the snow with their snowshoes and piling a wall as high as could be. Off to the east as they marched they could see the wavering line of the snow-buried Green Mountains. At night the stars came close, the air seemed fairly to crackle with the frost, and minute silvery ice crystals, just visible in the light of the camp fires, floated down from the sky like infinitesimal phantoms. In the distance, but sometimes close, they heard wolves howling; and now and then, as frightening to those who had not heard it before, the portentous hooting of the great horned owl. The habitants always paid close attention to the last, for the cries of owls were the Iroquois's favorite means of calling to each other at night.

They pressed on, making better progress as the troops became more accustomed to their snowshoes. They left Champlain at the point where Fort Ticonderoga was to be built a little less than a hundred years later and not far above the site of Champlain's shore fight with the Iroquois just over half a century before. Crossing the carrying place, they came to the lake the English were to name for the second George but which the French called Lac St. Sacrement. It was white and hushed under its sleeping depths of snow and, after the wide sweep of Lake Champlain, constricted between its mountains in a way that was vaguely menacing.

They marched up the length of it, marveling at the number of islands, some hardly large enough to plant a flagpole on, and came finally to its head where in the future three separate French forces would in turn find defeat, frustration, and a victory that carried shame. Now, however, there was nothing but snow and forest, with here and there the prints of a wild animal or bird, their own clustering figures, and the track beaten by their snowshoes which they could imagine reaching back all the way to the last French outpost of Fort Ste. Thérèse. There was also the chilling realization that the Algonquin guides who were to have led them from this point by an Indian trail direct to the Mohawk towns had never materialized. Yet even that could not shake Courcelles's determination. If they had no guides, they would find their own way; and once more, wearied out and now on reduced rations, they took up their march.

From the head of the lake Indian trails branched southward. One went on a fairly straight line southwest to strike the Hudson at the mouth of the Sacandaga River, followed up that stream to its great bend, and from there went overland toward what is now Johnstown and finally came out on the Mohawk near the town of Fonda. The second curved a little east of south to meet the Hudson at Glens Falls where it forked. One route followed the Hudson down to Albany; the other turned a little west of south and passed west of Saratoga Lake and then of Ballston Lake until it met Fish Creek, which gave the trail its name. There it branched, one path going toward the present site of Amsterdam, the other following the creek down to the Mohawk opposite Schenectady.

The trail by the Sacandaga would have brought Courcelles out on the Mohawk opposite the middle of the three major Mohawk towns, or castles as the Dutch and English called them. But Courcelles chose the other route as far as Glens Falls where, however, he took the Fish Creek trail. Of course, it was not so simple as that, for the habitants at the head of the march continually made false casts while they found their way. Then at Fish Creek, instead of taking the west branch, it seemed best to keep on south as the quickest way of reaching the Mohawk. They did this early on the twentieth of February.

As they came out on the river flatland they saw two isolated Indian cabins which they surrounded. The bark houses contained no warriors, only a few women and children and one or two old men. But one group of soldiers, pressing forward, fell into an ambush. There was a brisk little skirmish in which the French claimed to have killed four Mohawks with a loss of six of their own men, but they seem to have lost at least a dozen soldiers and one officer. The Mohawks, naturally, made larger claims and took off a couple of "heads," more likely scalps, as vouchers and crossed the river with them to the tiny trading post that was already taking the shape of a village.

This was Schenectady, which Arendt Van Curler, the commissary general and cousin of Kiliaen Van Rensselaer, the Great Patroon, had started to build only four years before. Van Curler with fine Dutch enterprise had realized that a trading post at this spot above the lower Mohawk falls and rapids would intercept practically all the Iroquois fur trade so that the profits could be diverted entirely from Fort Orange to his cousin patroon. The post proved the more effective because he himself was liked and respected by the Iroquois; so much so that they came to call all future New York governors by their own pronunciation of his name, *Corlaer;* just as they called French governors *Onontio* (Great Mountain), after their corruption of Montmagny's name.

The commissary of the village (who would have been Van Curler), seeing wet French scalps, could hardly doubt the Mohawks' word and immediately sent dispatches to what had become Fort Albany, for in 1664 the English had taken New Amsterdam from the Dutch and now the province had become New York. After learning from Courcelles what the French mission was, he informed him, according to the French version, that most of the Mohawk warriors were away from their castles making war on a tribe he called the "Wampum-makers" — whoever they might have been — leaving only women and children and old men for Courcelles to attack, something he saw no point in doing. The English, however, reported that the Dutch commissary told Courcelles that all the Oneida warriors had joined the Mohawks and were waiting in the latter's castles to receive the onslaught of the French.

It made no difference, for the French troops were too exhausted to fight anybody. They encamped that night in the open flatland two miles across the river from Schenectady and more miserable than they had been at any time on the entire march, for the temperature had started rising and a thin, penetrating rain began to fall. It fell throughout the night and was heavier when morning, which was Sunday, broke.

The morning, too, brought three English emissaries from Albany. They appeared suddenly at the sodden camp and demanded of "M. Coarsell" what he meant by bringing a body of armed men into the dominions of His Majesty of England without so much as a by-your-leave to the governor, and gave him official confirmation of British possession of the province. This was appalling news; for the Dutch at Fort Orange had presented no problem, beyond the irritating matter of drawing off a portion of the fur trade, and besides they had again and again proved themselves friendly to the French by sheltering escaped prisoners from the Mohawks. But the English were something else entirely. Where they came to trade they also came to settle; and a strong and thriving colony at the very door of New France could be a deadly menace. Even when Courcelles explained that he had no intention of injuring the English and wished only to attack the Mohawks and the three emissaries expressed themselves satisfied and even suggested that he bring his tired men into Schenectady for shelter and refreshment, something near defeatism seems for the first time to have touched him. He declined the invitation on the ground, according to the English commentator's careful phraseology, that "there was not accomodâcon for this soldyers, with whom he had marcht and campt under the blew canopye of the heavens full six weekes, but he prudently foresaw a greater inconvenience if hee brought his weary and halfe starv'd people within smell of a chimney corner," fearing that they could never be induced to leave it. He did accept a present of wine and some provisions and grasped at the opportunity to buy more from the Dutch, and he commended a few of his wounded to their care. Then putting as good a face on his position as he could, late in the afternoon he "made a shew of marching towards the Mohaukes Castles, but with faces about and great sylence and diligance return'd towards Cannada."

In fact this was an understatement. The French were literally on the run. The continuing rain, which was turning the deep snow into a sea of slush, had filled their minds with apprehension amounting to panic that the ice might break in the rivers and the lakes thaw before they could get back to the Richelieu. They moved so quickly that the Mohawks who had come swarming out of their castles at the first rumor of the French retreat could catch up only with the rear guard at Lake George. There was a little skirmishing in which three French were taken prisoner. One, who was wounded too severely to walk, asked to be killed, in which the Mohawks for once speedily obliged him. But there were other Frenchmen here and there along the trail who had died of cold and hunger, and more were to provide souvenirs of Courcelles's foolhardiness all the way to Fort Ste. Thérèse.

Ironically, on the first day of the retreat, the thirty Algonquin guides finally put in an appearance. To Courcelles's icy anger, they explained that they had come by enough brandy at Fort Ste. Thérèse to provide them with a week's debauch, but once sober they had made all haste to overtake the troops. He could not afford to antagonize them, for by their hunting they could partially relieve the shortage of rations. The shortage now became desperate, for a cache of supplies which had been concealed halfway up Champlain was found to have been rifled — not improbably by the Algonquin scouts themselves, though they were now energetically engaged in practicing their new-found virtue. Thirty hunters, however, were not enough to feed five hundred men on the march and the best hope was to push on as rapidly as possible. The vanguard, which included Courcelles, finally reached Fort Ste. Thérèse on the eighth of March, but Courcelles himself kept straight on to Fort St. Louis. As the rest of his little army straggled in and rolls were called, it became apparent that more than sixty soldiers had died of cold and hunger.

Conscious of failure and the extent of the penalty his troops had had to pay for his foolhardiness, Courcelles lashed out at the first scapegoat that occurred to him. He accused Father Albanel, the Jesuit chaplain at Fort St. Louis, who had engaged to provide Indian guides for the expedition, of purposely delaying them. This accusation Albanel was able easily to disprove: it was on the face of it absurd because the Jesuits wished for nothing as much as the subjugation of the Mohawks and Oneidas who had proved consistently the most intractable of the Iroquois tribes. But still smarting with his wounded self-esteem, Courcelles repeated his accusation to Father Frémin in Three Rivers, this time including the whole Order in his charges; and by the time he made his report to Tracy and Talon in Quebec on the seventeenth, he had convinced himself that he had been the victim of a Jesuit plot and declared he would no longer confess to his usual confessor, Father Chastellain, because he was a Jesuit. The Jesuits were naturally disturbed and became more so when they received private information that Courcelles's charges had made a great impression on Talon.

Talon's original instructions had informed him that the Jesuits had assumed authority "transcending the bounds of their profession, which must regard only consciences," and he was warned that one of his principal duties was to preserve "in just equilibrium the temporal authority, which resides in the person of the King and in those who represent him, and the Spiritual, which resides in the Person of the Bishop and the said Jesuits, in such manner always as that the latter be subordinate to the former"; but he showed no inclination to use Courcelles's charges as a lever against the church. Instead he joined Tracy in reassuring Courcelles that his expedition had not at all been a total failure, and the two men so effectively soothed his bruised feelings that two days later, on the feast of St. Joseph, the governor went dutifully off to make his confession to Father Chastellain.

The veteran Tracy had been right about the expedition's not being a waste of effort. Early in May the Senecas sent a deputation renewing last year's plea for peace; then in rapid succession the other tribes followed, the last to come being the Mohawks and a deputation of twenty-four Oneidas. All appeared eager for peace and so sincere in their protestations that Tracy was persuaded to send a deputation of Frenchmen, headed by the Jesuit Thiery de Bechefer, to the Mohawk and Oneida towns to determine on the spot whether any reliance could be placed in the mood of the warriors at large. In their turn the Oneidas agreed to leave hostages from their own party. For the moment Canada seemed nearer genuine peace than at any other time since its founding.

The illusion was short-lived. The French and Oneida delegates were only two days out on their journey when word reached Quebec that a hunting party of officers and men from Fort Ste. Anne had been attacked by Iroquois. Among the three known killed were a captain of one of the Carignan companies and Tracy's nephew, the Sieur de Chasy; and another relative, a cousin named Leroles, was among four men taken captive. Runners were immediately sent out to halt the peace party, and all twenty-four Oneida delegates returned with the French under military guard.

Meanwhile Captain Sorel organized two hundred regular troops and habitants and about a hundred Indians for a flying punitive raid on the Mohawk towns. Their rendezvous was at the same Fort Ste. Anne from which the young men had been hunting. It had been built on the Île La Motte in Lake Champlain, fifteen miles above the outlet, and news of its completion came to Quebec at the same time as word of the Iroquois attack on the twenty-second of July.

Two days later it was decided to release one of the Oneidas from prison, into which all twenty-four had been cast, and send him with a French deputy to the Dutch in Albany who, in Tracy's understanding, had guaranteed the Mohawks' good behavior while peace negotiations were in progress — though on what authority, since they were now under British rule, was not made clear. The deputy was Guillaume Cousture who, as a Jesuit *donné*, had shared captivity and torment with Father Jogues in the Mohawk towns.

He was an able man and known to the Dutch, but his mission, if it could be so called, was almost farcical because of two letters he carried with him from Tracy. In the first, written for Bechefer to deliver, the king's viceroy expressed his satisfaction with the cooperation of the Dutch in securing peace; the second began by urging the Albany commissaries to read the first to see how well disposed he had been, but stated that now he was disillusioned — that while acting on their assurances he had been betrayed and his young men murdered; and he demanded satisfaction from the Dutch, though what kind of satisfaction is nowhere mentioned. At the end he declared that it was his intention, unless he did receive satisfaction, to turn the twenty-three Oneida deputies over to the mercies of his Algonquins.

It was the irrational outburst of an outraged man; but he was shortly to become still more outraged. Meanwhile, however, the Dutch commissaries replied with surprising calmness that if Tracy would read his correspondence he would find that they had never made any guarantee about Mohawk behavior and that the French who would bring back their reply would be able to vouch for their continuing good will.

The Frenchmen, besides Cousture, were the captives from Fort Ste. Anne, and the little party was under a Mohawk escort headed by a famous half-breed chief known in Canada as the Flemish Bastard. On the second day of their return journey they encountered Sorel and his force of three hundred. The sequence of events had taken place with strange rapidity. Sorel was to have followed four or five days behind Cousture; but now Cousture's mission was concluded — he had stayed in Albany only long enough to collect the reply of the commissaries, so briefly in fact that Governor Nicolls, hastening up from New York in order to meet him and send personal messages to Tracy, found him already gone. Though Sorel's men outnumbered the Mohawks under the Flemish Bastard and were in a fine situation to exact a bloody revenge, Sorel himself was impressed by the half-breed's claim that he was coming to make peace, and the swift return of the captives seemed to corroborate him. So, perhaps also aware that it would be suicidal to attack a palisaded Mohawk castle with so few men, he turned about and accompanied the Mohawks as far as Fort Ste. Anne.

When the Flemish Bastard and his Mohawks arrived in Quebec to return their prisoners and sue once more for peace, the town was full of Iroquois from the four other nations, all bent on the same mission. The Cayugas and Senecas alone had sent more than seventy men, some of whom had brought along their women and children. There were the Oneidas in the fort, presently to be released, and a small delegation from the Onondagas. Peace again was in the air, and it seemed that the arrival of the Mohawks might be the clinching act.

Tracy himself was momentarily impressed and a meeting of the delegates of all the five Nations was scheduled on the thirtieth of August in the Jesuits' enclosed garden. The Cayugas and Senecas made gifts of fifty-

[137]

two belts of wampum, and some skeptical Frenchmen became apprehensive that the long-planned attack in force upon the Mohawks might be called off or, to paraphrase the Jesuit chronicler, that His Majesty's arms might be checked by a false hope of peace. The council proved indecisive, at least in the minds of the French, and it may have been to get a closer judgment of Mohawk intentions that Tracy invited the Flemish Bastard and another chief, named Agariata, who claimed to be an official deputy for the tribe, to dinner in the Château St. Louis.

As the meal progressed and the wine flowed, the conversation not unnaturally turned to the unfortunate and irresponsible attack on the hunting party near Fort Ste. Anne and especially on the tragic death of the young Sieur de Chasy. Listening to the talk, his heated eyes glaring from the painted pattern on his face, like a wolf from the thicket, Agariata slowly raised his hand and when he had secured the attention of all the company proclaimed that this hand they were looking at was the one that had burst open the head of that young Frenchman. To his blurred mind such a feat should never be allowed to go unrecognized.

Out of the stunned silence Tracy suddenly made a stark announcement. The Mohawk would never kill a man again. The executioner was summoned. The guards seized the uncomprehending chief and hurried him outdoors, where he was hanged forthwith in the presence of the Flemish Bastard.

There was no further talk of peace, and from that moment preparations for the expedition against the Mohawk castles, which all along had been Tracy's principal assignment in Canada, went forward with all speed. It was now the end of August. By September 6, Tracy had resolved to lead the force in person. This was to be no mere raid, but a little army, consisting of six hundred regulars of the Carignan regiment, six hundred habitants of whom a hundred were "Blue Coats" from Montreal, and a hundred Hurons and Algonquins. They would take with them the accouterments of a real army: the regimental drums, even two small cannon to batter down the gates of the barbarian castles.

As had happened the fall before, the air of Quebec was charged with a sense of impending deeds above the ordinary power of men. The rendezvous for Tracy's army was set for September 28 at Fort Ste. Anne; but his own departure from Quebec with four hundred habitants, volunteers from his own retinue of gentlemen, and Indians took place on the fourteenth, which in Father Le Mercier's excited language was "the day of the Exaltation and triumph of the Cross, for the glory of which the expedition was undertaken." To Le Mercier it seemed indeed a new crusade, and when Tracy asked for the services of Fathers Albanel and Raffeix, "of our own accord we gave six men." And to Mother Mary of the Incarnation, who in her enthusiasm sometimes muddled metaphors, it was evident that instead of storming those palisaded towns with their unending memories of blood and fire, the soldiers were going to lay siege to Paradise, win it and enter in, because they would be fighting for religion and the Faith.

In reality Tracy's army, though aimed solely against the Mohawks, was the opening move in the struggle between England and France which after its desultory and bloody course through three successive "small" wars was to culminate in the seven-year-long struggle we know as the French and Indian War.

PART II

The reluctance of the New England colonies to act against the French / The English and French attitudes toward the Indians / The surrender of New Netherland to the English / The Dutch exploration of the Hudson Valley and Atlantic coast / Peter Minuit's purchase of Manhattan / The early history of New Amsterdam / Admiral Heyn's freebooting exploits / The patroon system / The Van Rensselaers / The tenant rebellion under William Prendergast / Governor Van Twiller's troubles with Jacob Eelkens and English encroachments / The Dutch and English refusal of aid to the Mohicans in their feud with the Mohawks / The establishment of Fort Saybrook / The political, religious, and intellectual ferment in Massachusetts Bay Colony / The settlement of Connecticut / The Fundamental Orders of Connecticut / The Pequot War / Sir Walter Raleigh's attempts to plant colonies in Virginia / The settlement at Jamestown / Captain John Smith's services to the colony / The Starving Time / The blighted efforts of Sir Thomas Gage and Lord De La Warr to aid the colony / Sir Thomas Dale as High Marshal of Virginia / John Rolfe's marriage to Pocahontas / The establishment of representative government under Governor Yeardley / The arrival of the first Negroes / The Good Friday massacre under Opechancanough / The extermination of the tidewater tribes / The Crown colony of Virginia

C OLONEL RICHARD NICOLLS, whose hurried journey up the
Hudson from New York to meet Tracy's messenger, Cousture,
had proved fruitless, was deeply disturbed by the activities of the
French southward from the Richelieu River. He was willing for the moment to accept Tracy's word that their sole purpose was the chastisement
of the Mohawks and in a letter assured him that "I shall constantly attend
the Europœan Interest amidst the heathen in America as becomes a good
Christian"; but this was with the firm proviso that "the bounds and
limitts of these His Majesties of England's dominions be not invaded or
the Peace and safety of his subjects interrupted." The English considered
all territory south of the mouth of Lake Champlain and the Great Lakes
to be theirs; but though one of Nicolls's first acts after taking over possession from the Dutch had been to renew their treaty of friendship with
the Mohawks, the latter were not British subjects and would not be received as such until 1687, though the Iroquois themselves never considered this agreement as an acknowledgment of sovereignty but merely as
an alliance. In 1666, therefore, Nicolls could only object to the invasion
as an infringement of territory.

But from his point of view Courcelles's expedition had been an act of
war, and while as a fellow European he was happy enough that the Dutch
had offered the French food and assistance, he was not deceived by the
latter's protestations of friendship. "I presume," he wrote shortly afterward, "they will not openly profess themselves enemies to us till they have
either vanquisht the Mohawks or made peace with them."

When early in July word reached New York that another French expedition, reported to be seven hundred men, which may or may not have
been Sorel's three hundred (the Iroquois were always prone to exaggerate
a hostile force), Nicolls immediately wrote Governor Winthrop of Connecticut and the Council of Massachusetts suggesting concerted action. "A
speedy force of horse and dragoons not exceeding 150" from Massachusetts with proportional troops from Connecticut joined to what troops he
himself could supply would in his opinion be enough to cut off the French
force and prevent their return to Canada, "and by consequence the rest
of the French will not be able to make any considerable resistance." In
other words, at this early stage, when news of England's declaration of

[143]

war against France had barely reached American shores, he was proposing the invasion and conquest of Canada.

The proposal was utterly chimerical. Its only hope of success would have rested on swift concerted action, which was something the English colonies were almost never able to achieve. Certainly they did not achieve it in this instance. Connecticut, the most enlightened of all the colonies, the first with a written constitution and the only one with a government based firmly on the principle, to borrow the words of Hooker's famous sermon, that "the foundation of authority is laid firstly, in the free consent of the people," and with vivid recollections of its own Pequot war of thirty years before, had no wish to antagonize its own Indians by going to the defense of their inveterate enemies, the Mohawks. Moreover, as Samuel Willis, replying in the name of Governor Winthrop, pointed out, the way to Albany was very difficult for a mounted troop, and it might be a good thing anyway to let "the French and Mohawks try it out awhile." With the French so far away from their own base, if the Dutch could only be prevented from selling them supplies they might be reduced to a weakened condition in which handling them would be no problem. But Mr. Willis made no reference whatever to the idea of invading Canada.

Massachusetts was equally unwilling to take action. It had been an uneasy summer. Men working their fields in the outlying settlements were "forced to stand upon their watch" against the possibility of Indian attack. The local tribes were noticeably restless (Governor Winthrop had been barely able to persuade the Connecticut Mohicans to recall a war party that had set out to join the anti-Mohawk crusade), and there were rumors that hundreds of Indians "unknowne to the English & acquainted with the French" were threading the northern wilderness to join the French on Lake Champlain. Frontier communities in Massachusetts felt they simply could not spare men for forays against Canada (even if, without shipping, it had been possible to get them there) or even against Frenchmen invading what had only recently been Dutch territory and was still inhabited mainly by Dutch. Nobody liked the Dutch anyway.

There were other factors. Ammunition was painfully short in all the New England colonies. The people were suffering from dangerous shortages of food and had been for two years previous, owing to "a general blast uppon the corne besydes great destruction by wormes in many places whiles it was greene," as Winthrop wrote Lord Arlington to explain why the colonies could not have taken action against Canada in 1666.

The worms he referred to were the cutworm and the wireworm, a continuing threat when they were not an actual plague. The opening of the soil in a wilderness area seemed to concentrate them in unbelievable numbers, and often a third, or even half, of a field that had been laboriously cleared from the woods by ax and burning would be devastated before the wheat was four inches high. Nor was wheat the only crop they preyed on. They attacked the young Indian maize and beans and most garden crops with equal voracity. There was nothing to fight them with — no pesticide, no argicultural implements like the moldboard plow or harrow to provide clean tillage, no knowledge of clearing the soil by crop rotation. The Iroquois women sought to protect their plantings with a starlit mystery: slipping from the lodges while the rest of the village slept, speaking no word, making no sound (for a single dog to bark when they left or they returned would break the spell), they would steal down the narrow paths in the dark to the garden plots and, disrobing, each walk naked two or three times around her own planting, dragging her clothes along the ground behind her.

But the New England settler knew nothing of such superstitions. If he had learned of them, he would have rejected them as Satanic, as he regarded the wireworm and cutworm and all other manifestations of the wilderness. For besides the cutworms there were caterpillars that sometimes came crawling from the woods in destructive hordes, and the grasshoppers, as well as the mysterious blast upon the wheat. And above all there were the Indians.

To the mind of the New England settler the wilderness was a hostile and relentless force that had to be destroyed if it was not to destroy him. It had confronted him as he came ashore, still unsteady from the long sea voyage; a few steps brought him to the edge of it; and from that moment it obsessed his waking hours and haunted him while he slept.

He did not have the Frenchman's gift for adapting himself to strange conditions; it would have been utterly impossible for him to cast aside the ethics and constraints of what he considered civilized life as the *coureur de bois* did when he embarked on one of his two- or three-year wilderness voyages and made himself as much at home in woods a thousand miles away as the native Indians did. Unlike the Frenchman, the English settler was temperamentally unable to accept the Indian for what he was, to live his life, to intermarry. He was too race-conscious and as instinctively antagonistic as dog to cat. Like the Jesuits, he considered the Indians as barbarians, but he felt none of the Catholic concern to bring them to Christianity. One suspects that even in that first generation of New England settlers the phrase about "the only good Indian" had already found utterance.

There were exceptions, of course: Thomas Mayhew on Martha's Vineyard and Nantucket, and more impressively John Eliot who after fifteen years spent in mastering the Algonquin dialect and translating the Bible set out on his mission work. Like the Jesuits, he brought his converts into stockaded communities near Christian settlements. After thirty years Eliot could claim fifteen hundred "Praying Indians" in his villages, and the total for the missions on the islands and in Plymouth colony amounted to twenty-five hundred. But these Indians were drawn entirely from tribes or remnants of tribes weak enough to feel dependent on the English. The Narragansetts, Nipmucks, and Mohegans would have none of his teaching. The English had taken their land, as they put it, but they would keep hold of their own gods, and they considered the Christian villages a political device to weaken them numerically and corrupt their way of life. In effect this was true, though Eliot and Mayhew certainly had no such intention. Like the Indians converted to the Catholic faith by the Jesuits, many of the New England Indians were sincere in their reception of Christianity, but many more, it would appear, accepted the English God because their recollection of the extermination of the Pequots still vividly haunted them. In 1637, in one hour seventy-seven Englishmen had killed over seven hundred Pequots in a palisaded town. Only a god of awesome powers could have armed so few against so many, and after that divine demonstration no local Indian dared attack a white man in New England until 1675, when King Philip and his Wampanoags with the Nipmucks and Narragansetts fell upon the English settlements.

West of Massachusetts attempts were made to establish Protestant missions among the Indians. As early as 1641 the Dutch dominie Johannes Megalopensis began making trips out of Fort Orange to the Mohawk towns, but his work was sporadic and notable chiefly for the rescue of Father Jogues. Then in 1711 an Episcopal chapel was built for the Mohawks at the mouth of the Schoharie, with a silver Communion service provided by Queen Anne, a resident minister, and a tiny organ, to whose piping notes they came from their lodges to listen with wonder and a comfortable satisfaction at possessing so marvelous a thing. A succession of clergymen served the chapel, but with diminishing success.

The truth is that the Church of England had little interest in converting the Indians. It was difficult to find clergy willing to endure the discomforts of such a calling for fifty pounds a year when the rector of Trinity or the church in Burlington, New Jersey, was getting a salary of one hundred fifty plus a rent allowance of twenty-six pounds and other perquisites; high pay, indeed, in those early colonial days, though the Reverend William Vesy at Trinity was constantly angling for more — he asked for fifty pounds additional as chaplain for the guard ships of New York Province, though they already had chaplains in Boston and Philadelphia. Protestant efforts to gain converts among the Iroquois — even the devoted work later of the Moravians among the western tribes — proved relatively insignificant; compared with the labors of the Jesuits the results they achieved were negligible.

In part this was due to the greater appeal of Catholic worship for the primitive mind, and in part to the temperament and dedication of the trained Jesuit missionary. The Jesuits rarely allowed a man to go into Indian country until he had mastered the language or given evidence of a capacity to do so; but many Protestants were sent out woefully unprepared for their task. The Reverend William Andrews, for example, second minister to serve Queen Anne's sumptuously appointed chapel for the Mohawks, knew no Iroquois and had to take an interpreter with him. The latter was a Dutchman who proved to have so limited a knowledge of English that Mr. Andrews could understand him no better than he could his parishioners and was compelled to hire a second assistant to translate the Dutchman's translations of the Mohawk, and of course he could only address the Mohawks by a reversal of this procedure. One can imagine his bemused dark congregation hearing the words of their preacher falling from the pulpit, the English assistant just beneath it reuttering them in Dutch to the Dutchman at his side; and then the Dutchman turning stolidly to deliver in their own language words that must by then have carried but the palest tincture of the spirit of the Holy Ghost.

Even so, it worked for a time, for Mr. Andrews's heart was in his mission, and whatever the handicaps of communication, the Mohawks, who were always closest to the English, responded. Though not a well man, Andrews even made a trip to the Oneida castle a hundred miles away, "only a rough Indian path to it: We lay several nights in the woods agoing, and on a bearskin when we came there." But though he baptized nineteen people, most of them were children and several died of some obscure illness after his departure. He was accused of poisoning them and dared not return. And then in his own parish by the Schoharie the people began to lose interest. Here as against the Englishman laboring elsewhere in America, the wilderness undid his work and the young people he had baptized, on their long summers when they left their towns to hunt and fish, one or two families together, in some favorite corner of the mountain forest, slipped back into old habits of thought and returned to the beliefs that grew from the wilderness around them. In six years he resigned and the first Episcopal mission to the Mohawks ended.

This occasioned an outburst from the secretary of the Society for Propagation of the Gospel which goes far toward explaining the ill-success of the Episcopal missionary effort:

It is indeed Matter of great Wonder, that these Wretched People, who have lived joining to the *English* Settlements so many Years, and cannot but observe that the *English*, by Agriculture, raise Provisions out of a small Spot of Ground, to support in Plenty great Numbers of People; whereas they by their Hunting, cannot get a wretched Subsistance out of all their Wilderness of several Hundred Leagues in Extent; should still refuse to till their Ground, or learn any manual Art; should still live a bestial Life, insensible of Shame or Glory. It is true, the *English* have taken from them exceeding large Countries, yet this, far from being a Prejudice, would be a vast Advantage to them, if they would but learn the *English* Language, Arts, and Industry.

The Anglo-Saxon attitude (the italics are the secretary's) toward the American Indian has seldom been more explicitly and cynically stated. The Jesuits, who accepted the Indian for what he was, never made such demands, and even in their dream of a North American Paraguay did not hope for more than his following the simplest of pastoral lives, and for that reason they were far more successful in gaining converts during the first half century of Canadian development. But as England and France encountered each other in the wilderness, first in the seventeenth-century equivalent of a cold war, then in open conflict, both sides began to use their respective churches politically in a kind of religious and military blackmail of the Iroquois.

The latter, however, proved equal to the game and, though often expressing confusion, played the two European nations off against each other for their own profit. "Wee are desired by both parties to turn Christian," Dekanissora, the chief spokesman of the Onondagas, told David Schuyler and Captain Bleeker on the one hand and Paul Lemoine Maricour on the other. He had come into prominence in 1678, three years after the death of Garakontié, and was one of the most eloquent orators ever produced by the Iroquois — "his Person was tall and well made," Cadwallader Colden wrote of him, "and his Features, to my thinking, resembled much the Bustos of *Cicero*." His speech to the French and English suffers from translation by Schuyler into Dutch and then from Schuyler's Dutch into English by Robert Livingston (neither of them a man of any literary gifts), but his ability to state the Indians' case as he regarded the Europeans before him in the council house at Onondaga is not lost:

> You both tell us to be Christians, you both make us madd [confused?], wee know not what side to choose. But I will speak no more of praying or Christianity and take the belts down [one each from the English and the French] and keep them because you are both dear with your goods. I would have accepted of his belt who sold the cheapest pennyworth — would you have me put on a bearskin to goe to church withal a sundays? Wee are sorry we cannot pray, but now wee are come to this conclusion. Those that sells their goods the cheapest whether English or French of them will we have a Minister.

And he added that some of their sachems were already on the way to Albany and others to Canada to obtain price quotations.

However, active competition between the English and the French for the allegiance of the Iroquois had not yet begun when Tracy was mustering his force on the Richelieu and Colonel Nicolls in New York was trying to find reinforcements for the garrison at Albany.

Nicolls had been sent to America on a twofold mission. First, he was to seize the Dutch colony of New Netherland which Charles II, though England and Holland were ostensibly at peace, had presented to his brother James, the Duke of York and Albany, who was named lord proprietor of Manhattan and Long Island and all mainland territory west of the Connecticut and south as far as Delaware. It did not matter that this grant took from Connecticut half of her actual territory as defined in the charter she had received from Charles only two years earlier — not to mention the extension of her boundaries, like those of Massachusetts, to the Pacific. Geographical integrity was a matter of small consequence when a royal gesture was to be made, at least as far as a Stuart king was concerned. Nor could this be ascribed entirely to ignorance on Charles's part. The creation of New Netherland had been a similar violation of the territorial claims of the two English colonies, and one justification for seizing it was that to do so would not constitute an act of war but merely the ejection of a trespassing power.

This cavalier contradiction in land grants became one of Nicolls's problems. His solution, though apparently fair and satisfying to both parties, had to be readjusted twenty years later when it was discovered that his projected western boundary for Connecticut on a line north-northwest from Mamaroneck Creek, instead of keeping at least twenty miles east of the Hudson, actually crossed the river near Peekskill. Even the readjustment to its present course at that time did not produce a final solution or take into account the colony's continental claims, for a century later a bloody little war took place in the upper Susquehanna region of Pennsylvania, the beautiful section of the valley which the Indians called Wyoming, when Connecticut settlers pouring in found themselves at odds with the Pennsylvania claimants.

The settlement of the Connecticut boundary issue, impermanent though it proved to be, had not raised the difficulties that might have been expected. Nicolls had found the governor, the younger John Winthrop, to be a reasonable and capable man with a mind, like his own, of scholarly inclinations, though where he himself turned to the classics, Winthrop's bent was toward science. Winthrop had already cooperated wholeheartedly with him in the seizure of New Amsterdam. He had brought five hundred Connecticut volunteers to join the five hundred regulars under Colonel Nicolls's command, but more important was the active part he played in turning the capture into a bloodless coup.

It was altogether a good performance on the part of both men. Nicolls's instructions left everything to his judgment. He was to use "such force as cannot be avoided for their reduction" if the Dutch resisted, but if they proved reasonable, he was to do everything possible to conciliate them. He had the force in overwhelming measure. Against his thousand muskets the Dutch could pit only those of the one hundred and fifty soldiers of the garrison and perhaps two hundred and fifty more in the hands of civilians, the majority of whom were against making a fight. They considered that they had been neglected by the government at home which, with all its naval power, had spared no ships for their defense. Now in the black hulls of the four stately frigates that had come to anchor below the Narrows on Saturday, the thirtieth of August, there were one hundred and twenty guns against which decaying Fort Amsterdam could present a mere twenty in reply. It was obvious that if he chose to, the English commander could shatter the fort and make a shambles of the little town without putting a man on shore.

Nevertheless, Stuyvesant, the wooden-legged governor of New Netherland, was pugnaciously determined to resist. He kept every able-bodied man at work on strengthening his defenses, and when the first summons to surrender arrived shortly after the frigates anchored, though it promised that there would be no violation of property, he returned it on the ground that it carried no signature. If he indulged in a grim sort of satisfaction as he watched the English emissary depart for the long row back to the Narrows, he had only forty-eight hours for its enjoyment.

On Saturday a detachment from the frigates had taken the blockhouse on Staten Island, evidence of the determination of the English, but thereafter and through Sunday and Monday the ships lay quietly at anchor and no further activities took place ashore. Tuesday, however, was another matter, and quite early in the morning a boat rowed up to Whitehall under a white flag. This time it contained not a uniformed English officer as emissary: it contained no formal emissary at all. The man who came ashore with several companions was Winthrop, and he came as a friend and neighbor to try to persuade Stuyvesant and the burgomasters not only of the hopelessness of their position but of the advantages of accepting citizenship under the Crown of England. Winthrop at that time was fifty-eight; he had open and winning manners; and some of the burgomasters began to find him persuasive, but as far as Stuyvesant was concerned his arguments fell dead. Nicolls, however, had armed Winthrop with a letter addressed not to Stuyvesant but to himself, and this he handed to the Dutch governor before he and his company made their departure.

> As to those particulars you spoke to me, I do assure you that if the Manhadoes be delivered up to his Majesty, I shall not hinder, but any people from the Netherlands may freely come and plant there or thereabouts; and such vessels of their own country may freely come thither, and any of them as freely return home, in vessels of their own country; and this and much more is contained in the privilege of his Majesty's English subjects; and thus much you may, by what means you please, assure the Governor from, Sir, your very affectionate servant,
>
> RICHARD NICOLLS.

Stuyvesant read the letter aloud to the burgomasters, convened with him in the fort — a mistake from his point of view, for they were immediately impressed and wanted it read to the people gathered outside. Knowing that it would have an even greater effect on them, Stuyvesant refused, and when the burgomasters pressed their demand he tore the letter to bits and scattered them over the floor.

Then followed the celebrated scene of the angered burgomasters going out to inform the people; of some of the leading townsmen, headed by Nicholas Bayard, entering the fort and demanding that the letter be handed over to them; and when Stuyvesant walked out on them, collecting the fragments one by one while Bayard at a table painstakingly pieced them together and then wrote out a fair copy. They took it to the crowd outside where its reading was received as favorably as Stuyvesant had feared. Its open and reasonable tone was in marked contrast to the scene that had just taken place, and though the governor was respected for his upright and honest qualities, the people had become tired of his arbitrary ways. There could be small doubt now of where they would stand when the showdown came.

Even so, Stuyvesant did his best to put it off by preparing a brief which argued the validity of the Dutch claim to New Netherland and sending it off down the bay to Nicolls on the following day. Nicolls replied immediately that the question of validity of claims was beyond his jurisdiction; he was merely a soldier with orders to take possession of the colony, and if the town did not surrender on his terms, he would attack it. He added that he would speak with Stuyvesant on Thursday "at the Manhattans," and that he would come with ships and soldiers.

True to his word, on Thursday the frigates came sailing up the bay. People on the tip of Manhattan and Stuyvesant with his soldiers from the fort watched the first two bear toward the Long Island shore near Governor's Island where Nicolls disembarked with three companies and then marched overland toward the little village of Breuckelen to a rendezvous with the companies of Connecticut volunteers a little south of what is now the eastern end of Brooklyn Bridge. Meanwhile the third and fourth frigates, their ports open and guns run out, continued on a course into the North River that would bring them within close range of Fort Amsterdam.

Inside the fort Stuyvesant waited, moody and undecided, his eyes on the oncoming ships, while his gunners stood to their guns with lighted matches. He hardly appeared to listen when someone ventured the statement that to resist under such hopeless odds would be the course not of a soldier but a madman, and the again Dominie Megalopensis asked quietly what use it was to give an order that would mean death for many people when no end could be gained. Stuyvesant answered no one, but the ships passed on and the cannon remained silent. Then he broke away and with a hundred soldiers hurried to meet Nicolls's expected landing. But on his way he was beset by women and children begging him not to resist, and a memorial to the same effect, signed by more than ninety leading townsmen, was thrust into his hand; and suddenly he broke and agreed to the surrender.

So the change from Dutch to British rule was accomplished with no bloodshed, no damage to property, no real interruption to the commercial activities of the little port or the way of life of its citizens. People accepted the change-over with remarkable equanimity, and this proved true throughout the colony except for one brief flare-up of violence between the English garrison and Dutch civilians at Esopus. Perhaps the strongest indication of Nicolls's tact and skill was the friendship that sprang up between him and Stuyvesant.

After the surrender the latter had returned to Holland where the directors of the West India Company, whose own neglect of their responsibilities was the primary cause of the loss of the colony, tried to make him the scapegoat. A flood of testimony from New Amsterdam from sources whose integrity could not be questioned vindicated his conduct, but he found himself nevertheless homesick for the little town from which for seventeen years he had ruled New Netherland, and in October 1667 he petitioned Charles II and the Privy Council for permission to return. As important as this request was his citing of Article 6th of the surrender treaty in which Nicolls had agreed to permit free trade between the colony and its mother country and stipulated that the citizens of each could freely come and go.

Within a month the king in council had granted the petition. Since the needs of the new colony of New York could not be supplied from England its citizens for seven years would be permitted to trade freely with Holland, though with a limit of three ships a year; and "Heere Peter Stuyvesant, late Generall of the New Netherlands" was given permission to return. Whether he crossed in the ship specified in his petition, *The Crost Heart*, I do not know; but it would have been fitting.

Nicolls had taken over his town house, named Whitehall, as the governor's mansion, but Stuyvesant seemed quite content to retire to his farm on the East River about two and a half miles above the wall he had built across the island in 1653, during the first war between England and Holland. He spent time in his neat Dutch garden, but he was often to be seen stumping slowly about the streets of New Amsterdam, which had become New York, and interesting himself in town improvements and affairs, and frequently he would go to dine with Nicolls. It seemed a far cry from the man of forty who in the full vigor of life had come to Manhattan in 1647 in response to a desperate petition from a council chosen by the colonists to confer with the governor in crisis and known as the Eight Men.

Three years earlier the despotic mismanagement of two successive and criminally incompetent governors had brought the colony so low that in describing its situation the Eight Men were writing the literal truth:

Our fields lie fallow and waste; our dwellings and other buildings are burned; not a handful can be either planted or sown this autumn on the deserted places; the crops which God permitted to come forth remain on the fields standing and rotting . . . and we sit amid thousands of barbarians, from whom we find neither peace nor mercy . . .

Again they correctly attributed the immediate situation to one man who had disposed "here of our lives and property according to his will and pleasure, in a manner so arbitrary that a king would not be suffered legally to do." They concluded that the honorable directors had but two alternatives to choose between: either they must send at once a new governor strong enough to bring about a peace with the Indians and allow them at the same time to elect their own magistrates and sheriffs who in turn would be permitted to appoint deputies to sit in council with the governor on matters of public interest, or else they, with their wives and children, must be allowed to return to Holland.

The reaction in Amsterdam was prompt. In May 1645 William Kieft, the governor complained of, was removed from office and Stuyvesant, who had returned to Holland the fall before from Curaçao to recuperate from the loss of his leg, was appointed in his place. The theory perhaps was that if he could fight the Portuguese in South America, he should be able to subdue the small separate Algonquin tribes who, having joined forces after a series of outrages against them, had been inflicting a reign of terror on the Dutch around New Amsterdam and the Long Island towns. But of the colonists' request for a voice in their own government, not a word was vouchsafed nor any action taken, and so many changes of instructions for the new governor and of plans for reinforcement of the colony were made that it was two years before he finally got there. When he arrived it did not take the burghers long to discover that for one autocrat they had received another, the only difference being that the new man was in the main both honorable and honest as well as reasonably efficient in his handling of the colony's affairs. The pattern of colonial government as it had been almost from the beginning was evidently to undergo no material change with Stuyvesant in office, nor would it until its capture by the English put Nicolls in charge.

Early Dutch activity along the Hudson, of which far back we have had a glimpse, was entirely informal and carried forward under the so-called Ordinance of 1614 which granted a group of merchants complete monopoly in an enterprise already in operation for a period of six voyages, but which made no specific territorial claims of any sort. The Netherlands did not yet feel ready to try conclusions with Spain, which had already expressed outrage over the English colony on the James River, and though the Dutch were soon, for a period, to share world naval power with the English, they had as yet no conception of the decline of Spain's strength since the defeat of the Armada. An ordinance with a total absence of place names could hardly, it was believed, incite a war.

Dutch ship captains, however, lost no time in providing place names along the coast. In the summer of 1614 three ships arrived in Manhattan Harbor under the command of Henry Christiaensen, Adrian Block, and Cornelius May. There were then four small rickety buildings on the island, built there the year before by Christiaensen as a base for his fur trading with the surrounding Algonquin tribes. This little cluster of buildings had been discovered in November by an English sloop-of-war which had put in through the Narrows, apparently out of sheer curiosity. Its young commander, Captain Samuel Argall, who was on his way back from attacking the Frence settlement on Mount Desert and had a boatload of prisoners in any case to look after, made no attack but merely told the Dutch that they were trespassing and made them replace their flag with that of England – an act that was promptly corrected as soon as his sails had disappeared down the bay.

But now in 1614 the Dutch felt themselves stronger. Christiaensen, in his ship the *Fortune*, sailed up the Hudson and built Fort Nassau just below the site of Albany where, as we have seen, he inaugurated the fur trade between the Dutch and the Iroquois and cemented the friendship that was to extend to the English. Meanwhile the other two captains set out to explore the coastline. Block sailed up the East River and out along Long Island Sound, up the Connecticut as far as Hartford, and around Cape Cod, continuing up the New England coast presumably as far as Salem Harbor.

While Block was sailing north of it, May explored the south coast of Long Island and then went south down the Jersey shore as far as the mouth of Delaware Bay, whose eastern cape he named after himself; and shortly afterward the Delaware was explored as far north as the site of Philadelphia by another Dutch seaman, named Hendricksen. His vessel was a small yacht called the *Restless*, which had been built on Manhattan during the early summer by Captain Block after his own ship had caught fire and burned beyond hope of repair and which had been used by him for his voyage down the Sound and around the Cape. It was thus the forerunner not only of the Hudson River sloops but of New York's whole great shipbuilding industry of the nineteenth century that turned out the packet ships of the first scheduled trans-Atlantic runs and originated the Clipper.

These early Dutch voyages framed an area whose future commercial development was unrivaled on the Atlantic coast, and the merchants in

Holland who had backed the three voyages and who scented the possibilities of such harbors and inland-reaching rivers now applied for formal recognition of their monopoly. So a grant was made to the New Netherland Company of a monopoly of trade in an area from the mouth of the Delaware, which they called the South River as opposed to the North which after going through various names became the Hudson, to Cape Cod on the east, but limiting their claims to the north (in order to avoid trouble with France) to the 45th parallel, which is the boundary of New York State today.

The charter of the New Netherland Company was to run only three years, so all possible effort was made to realize on their investment, and the principal concentration of activity was on the fur trade up the Hudson. Not only was Fort Nassau completed on Castle (now Van Rensselaer) Island and armed with two cannon, eleven swivels, and a garrison of twelve soldiers; parties began to go west into the woods to seek out fresh tribes to trade with. One of these, consisting apparently of only three men, one of whom was named Kleynties, late in 1614 or early in 1615 went up the Mohawk Valley as far as Canajoharie, looking in on the Mohawk castles along their path, and then found their way overland to the foot of Lake Otsego and so became almost certainly the first white men to see the Susquehanna River.

They called it the New River when with crude drawings they tried to describe its course to a map maker, and they followed it down to its junction with the Chemung, flowing from the west, and down into the Wyoming Valley of Pennsylvania. At this point, as it later became evident to the map maker, the supposed location of certain tribes had to be reconsidered. In reconciling the map he was making "with the rough drafts Communicated, I find that the places of the Sennecas, Gachoos, Capitanisses, and Jottecas ought to be marked down considerably further west into the country."

This seems to be the earliest knowledge the Dutch had of the Senecas. The Gachoos must have been the Cayugas, but what the names of the other two tribes represented is anybody's guess. Kleynties and his two companions then struck overland to the upper Delaware where they were taken prisoners by some Indians. They spent the winter in the Catskills, captives in the Indian village, but were ransomed and returned to Fort Nassau in 1616.

It took bold and resourceful men to make such a journey (and preserve their scalps intact) with what must have been only the most rudimentary knowledge of Algonquin and probably none at all of the Iroquois languages. They were prototypes of the Dutchmen that followed their pioneering among the tribes in constantly increasing numbers — "bosloopers" they were called, the equivalent of the *coureur de bois* but without the latter's bent for continental exploration. But though Fort Nassau was

[155]

surrounded by friendly Mohicans, it was with the Mohawks that the Dutch cemented real relations. The Dutchman's proclivity for confining himself strictly to the business at hand, of arriving at a viable basis of exchange of furs for European goods, without any proselytizing religious riders attached, appealed to the pragmatic Iroquois mind. When the trade entered the public domain for three years following the expiration of the New Netherland charter, more Dutch traders went in small parties among the Iroquois and it was during this time that the exchange of firearms for furs seems to have begun.

Supposedly it was inaugurated in a formal treaty in 1618 between the commandant of Fort Nassau, one Jacob Jacobsen Eelkens (who later defected to the English), and the Mohawks in a council held in the valley of the Normankill. There is no record of this treaty; Colden, for instance, in his *History of the Five Nations*, the earliest formal account of the Iroquois, makes no mention of it though he does say that the Dutch and the Mohawks entered into an alliance in 1609, a manifest impossibility. Moreover, even the Mohawks would have had second thoughts about holding a peace council in open countryside two days' journey into the territory of their deadly enemies, the Mohicans. It seems more likely that the trade in firearms began informally — an Indian with plenty of furs to spend, coveting a Dutchman's snaphance, might make an above-average offer of prime beaver, and the deal was consummated.

Later, as the more practical flintlock superseded other muskets like the snaphance and the dog-lock and became more or less standardized, so did the price — a musket for twenty beaver became the going rate among the Albany traders. At first relatively few guns found their way into the Mohawk country, but by 1643, when the Mohicans had been forced by Mohawk pressure from their lands around Fort Orange, the flow of firearms rapidly increased and, as we have seen, Father Vimont in that year estimated that the Mohawks alone possessed three hundred muskets. The possession of such firepower, especially by a race so warlike, gave the Iroquois an advantage the French were never able wholly to offset and proved to be a vital element in their failure to hold the continent against the English. That the English were aware of how vital to their interest was an armed and powerful Iroquois confederacy is borne out by the treaty they signed, transferring Iroquois friendship with the Dutch to themselves, within a month of the capture of New Amsterdam. The opening clause read:

> Imprimis. It is agreed that the Indian Princes above named and their subjects shall have all such wares and commodities from the English for the future, as heretofore they had from the Dutch.

The Iroquois knew when and how to put first things first, and if for diplomatic reasons the language of the treaty omitted the words for firearms and ammunition, everyone knew what "wares and commodities" actually stood for.

The Dutch trade in firearms received significant impetus from the creation in 1621 of the West India Company, whose principal objective was the management and development of the colony of New Netherland. In conception, however, its scope was imperial, more grandiose even than that of the two companies that had been entrusted with the development of New France. In addition to the government of New Netherland, it was given an absolute monopoly of all Dutch commercial activity and of any settlements that existed or might spring into being on both sides of the Atlantic — in Africa from the Tropic of Cancer to the Cape of Good Hope; in America from Newfoundland to Cape Horn. Within this enormous section of the globe the Company was empowered to appoint governors and other public officials entirely at its own discretion, to make treaties with native races, administer justice, build forts, and fight off invading forces. The only authority withheld was that of declaring war on a European power; this could be done only with the consent of the States General, which guaranteed twenty warships for the Company's defense, the cost to be borne by the Company, provided the latter also maintained at least an equal navy of its own.

In spite of the absolute and dictatorial powers with which it was endowed, the Company's internal structure was much less autocratic than might have been supposed. Government rested in the hands of five separate boards or chambers which represented the five sections of the Netherlands, and while the administration of its affairs was conducted by an executive board of nineteen men, these again represented the five sections of the country, though in proportion to their commercial contribution, Amsterdam for instance supplying nearly half its membership. Moreover the stock was open not only to any and all Dutch buyers but to foreigners as well. Yet, like the French companies, the Dutch West India Company, as we have seen, failed to fulfill its end.

It began operations, however, with considerable vigor. In 1623 Captain Cornelius May was appointed director general, or governor, of the newly created colony and in March sailed from Amsterdam with thirty families who intended to make permanent homes in the New World. Their ship, appropriately named the *New Netherland*, was of impressive size, 260 tons, three times as big as Hudson's *Half Moon*, and much larger than any Dutch vessel that had so far made the Atlantic passage. In spite of her size she followed the customary southern route by way of the Canary Islands and the West Indies and then northerly between the Bahamas on the west and the Bermudas on the east, a long way round but generally kinder to small ships than the northern passage. It was May when she entered New York Harbor and the eyes of the new settlers watched the gateway opening to their new land — what Hudson had called "the handsomest and most pleasant country that man can behold."

Then as the *New Netherland* came up to Manhattan Island they were dismayed to see a French ship anchored in the upper bay. She too had come bringing settlers and seemed prepared to dispute Dutch title to the land, but by coincidence one of the armed yachts used by the fur traders up the Hudson came sailing downriver at this juncture, and the French captain was persuaded to raise anchor and go on his way. The arrival of the yacht, called the *Mackarel,* must also have brought a poignant kind of reassurance to the new arrivals; it was comforting to feel that there were some Dutch already planted in the new land.

Oddly enough, in view of the nationality of the ship that had been turned away, the passengers of the *New Netherland* were themselves French-speaking people and not properly Dutch at all. They were Flemish Protestants of French origin who had come to Holland for refuge from religious persecution by the Spanish; and because they spoke French instead of Flemish, the Dutch called them Walloons, a name derived from Wallus, or Gallus — simply Gaul but to Dutchmen meaning strangers. In 1620 after unsuccessfully applying through the English ambassador for permission to settle in Virginia, fifty or sixty Walloon families petitioned the States General for leave to settle in New Netherland, and permission had been granted. This brought them under the jurisdiction of the newly chartered West India Company, and particularly of its Amsterdam chamber; but as the Company was still in process of organizing, it had taken three years to complete all arrangements for their transportation.

Still more oddly, they were about to go ashore in place of what might well have been an entirely different group of religious refugees who also in 1620 had asked permission to settle in New Netherland. These were English Puritans, who called themselves "Pilgrims," led by their pastor, John Robinson, but they had applied through the New Netherland Company, whose charter had already expired, and their case was referred to the States General. Their petition was rejected.

The States General had already listened more than once to remonstrances of the English ambassador about Dutch activity along the Hudson, which King James considered part of England's American territory, claimed to reach from the southern boundary of what is now Georgia to the Bay of Fundy. The Hudson River, moreover, was more particularly claimed as English on the specious ground that its discoverer was an Englishman. To assist the establishment of a colony of Englishmen there and then grant it Dutch protection was thought to be more than the English would accept.

[158]

Denied access to New Netherland the Pilgrims then turned to the London Company, a stock company which had been granted exclusive right to the settlement and exploitation of America between the 34th and 38th degrees north latitude and received with James's approval permission to make their settlement in Virginia, as this whole territory reaching from southern Georgia to the southern boundary of present Maryland was called. The territory to be administered by the London Company's sister Plymouth Company, which reached from 41 degrees to 45 degrees, that is to say from the Connecticut shoreline east from New Haven to the northern boundary of present Vermont, did not interest them. Actually, they hoped to settle somewhere well up the Delaware River, north of the strict limits of the London Company's jurisdiction, but with the approval of the latter, for to have planted a colony there would have given them a claim on the whole area.

Storms and continual overcast carried them far from their reckoning, and instead of making a landfall at the mouth of the Delaware the *Mayflower* entered Cape Cod Bay. It was already November, too late for any extensive southward exploration if they were to establish themselves before winter; so though by then they realized that they were in territory of the Plymouth Company, they decided to stay where they were and apply for a grant. Meanwhile they set about the building of their small community, administering its affairs under a compact which they had drawn up before landing, in which the will of the people who subscribed to it was made the basis of government, and not the rights of the Crown. It was not a constitution in the sense that the Fundamental Orders of Connecticut was, in which a system of government was created whose powers were defined and limited; the Mayflower Compact was merely an agreement, but it rested on the fundamental truth that authority derives from the consent of the governed.

The Pilgrims, however, must have been little concerned with its philosophic import; they had first to survive and then establish their right to the land. Their application for a grant was approved, but it was made not to them but to the speculative merchant stock company which had put up the funds for their passage. These amounted to seven thousand pounds. Seven years after their landing they bought up the company's stock and by 1633 they had paid off every pound and become wholly independent owners of their own land.

Unlike the Pilgrims, the Walloons were not settled together in one place, for the Dutch West India Company was anxious to make it appear that the whole area claimed as New Netherland was in process of real colonization. Therefore, only eight families were dropped off at Manhattan, and these soon moved over the East River to start farms back from the shore of a deep bay which was soon called Wallabout, a corruption of

Walloon Bay, after its original settlers, and to which subsequent Walloon arrivals were to converge. Two more families, with six unmarried men, were sent some sixty miles up the Fresh River, as the Dutch called the Connecticut, to distinguish it from the salty Hudson, and there began building a fort, actually no more than a redoubt, which they named "Good Hope," the first building on the site of Hartford.

With its remaining passengers the *New Netherland* sailed on up the Hudson. Its ponderous size and the capricious spring airs made it difficult to work the ship upstream, and at the mouth of the Esopus the crew had to lighten her by transferring part of her cargo to some boats found moored there, which had been left by Dutch fur traders the year before. But in due course the *New Netherland* worked her way up as far as Fort Nassau.

Captain May's instructions were either to strengthen the existing Fort Nassau or to build an entirely new one. The original fort on Castle Island had been abandoned because spring floods made it uninhabitable; its successor had been built at the mouth of the Normankill. It was only a rectangular palisade and in May's estimation its position was vulnerable. He cast about for a better site and found what he wanted a few miles upstream on the flatland next to the river, where downtown Albany now stands. Here he staked the outline of a fort, with proper salient angles, and named it Fort Orange.

While artisans and soldiers started work on the walls and trenches under the direction of May's lieutenant, Adrien Jorisz, who had been appointed commandant, the eighteen Walloon families who had been chosen to settle there went to work with spades and hoes turning over their first tiny grain fields. Even to the settlers it must have seemed a woefully small beginning, but word that the Dutch were undertaking a permanent settlement and building a strong fort raced through the wilderness and Indians of many nations thronged to see it, for the Dutch goods were far better than the French and this post promised to be something different from the hit-or-miss trading that had taken place out of Fort Nassau. From their fields the Walloon settlers watched with wonder these strange humans, if they were human beings, in different paint and hairdress, emerging from the woods and heading for the new fort.

> . . . and as soon as they [the settlers] had built hutts of Bark: ye Mahi-kanders or River Indians, ye Maquaes: Oneydes: Onondagas, Cayougas, & Sinnekes with ye Mahawawa or Ottawawaes Indians came & made Covenants of friendship wth ye said Adrien Jorise there Commander Bringing him great Presents of Bever o^r oy^r Peltry & desyred that they might come & have a Constant free Trade with them wch was concluded upon . . .

That was how Catelyn Trico remembered the founding of Fort Orange after the slow trip up the Hudson, but she was eighty-three when she made her deposition and she may have added later recollection to her earlier impressions. One wonders, for instance, whether the Ottawas really sent a deputation then. They and the Iroquois felt toward each other as the rat feels toward the ferret; but Fort Orange stood in what was still Mohican country, and the Mohicans were Algonquins like themselves — though there, too, Algonquin kinship did not necessarily carry friendship with it. But it does not really matter. To a young woman — she was eighteen years old — who had been born in Paris, all Indians must have looked equally strange and fearsome.

There is nothing to indicate whether she was married at the time, but one must suppose so. An eighteen-year-old woman was not allowed to remain long unreproductive; and she and her man would have been classified as a "family" whether there were children yet or not.

Her statement made at eighty-odd is circumstantial, about the arrival in America, the assignment of Walloons to found this colony or that, the working of the ship upriver, the beginning of the settlement. She herself stayed at Fort Orange for three years, during all which time the fur trade was very active, and as she remarked, "ye said Indians were all as quiet as Lambs," a description hard to accept literally if one recalls how Jorisz's second-in-command, the unfortunate Krieckebeeck, got himself and three other Dutchmen killed by Mohawks in 1626 and fractionally eaten. But in 1626, very likely before the Krieckebeeck fiasco, Catelyn Trico had gone down to Manhattan where she was to live for many years before moving on to her final home, a house "in ye Wale Bought" in which, on October 17, 1688, she made her deposition before William Morris, "Justice of ye pece." Just why the deposition was taken is not apparent, perhaps some matter to do with an inheritance or other claim or possibly, for all his rococo punctuation and spelling, William Morris was a man with historical curiosity who wished to record a firsthand account of Dutch beginnings in the country that had become his home.

If by saying that the Indians were "quiet as Lambs" Catelyn meant that they were eager to trade and not overtly hostile, she was recording truth. The Iroquois were still in a power squeeze; it was essential for them to turn their furs into guns and powder. But as they gained power the iron tools the Dutch offered became nearly as important to them, and later cotton goods and oddments that ranged from glass beads to Jews'-harps. They were so eager that in Catelyn Trico's stay at Fort Orange it was hardly necessary for the fur traders to leave the fort. Few had to venture beyond the Mohawk Valley. The Indians would come from anywhere if they could get firearms. The Dutch guns were cheaper than the French, and if the French sold the best grade of gunpowder, as they did, that sold by the Dutch and later the British could at least drive a ball from a musket barrel, and in the close shooting of most wilderness war that was good enough. It may well have been that some representative of the far Indians

[161]

from beyond the Great Lakes found their way to Albany, but if she saw them it is doubtful that Catelyn was stirred by any sense of the vast wilderness areas that drew her Catholic compatriots in the north with almost inexorable force. Behind the few words of her deposition one has a feeling of a young woman a little frightened in a new world but thrilled to find it a free one for people like herself and driven by an instinct to make her home in it.

Fort Orange was still building, but the wheat in the settlers' tiny fields was standing well when Captain May weighed anchor and took the *New Netherland* downriver to complete his final assignment. This was the planting of a fourth settlement on the Delaware, which in the West India Company's overall plan of colonization was to be the seat of government in New Netherland. Why an indeterminate point on the Delaware should have been chosen instead of Manhattan is not very clear. It may have been with the idea that the colony's director general could keep easier watch of English activity in Virginia. The English in New England seemed safely far away beyond the hook of Cape Cod and were not in any case as loyal to the House of Stuart as the colonists along the James River.

Captain May built a small fort on the east bank of the river a little below the present site of Philadelphia and gave it the name of Fort Nassau. The colony was tiny — only two "families," which consisted of two young men and two young women who had been married on the passage over, and six single men. To this minute settlement came May's successor in 1624, William Verhulst, whose term, like May's was for one year. He left no imprint on history, though it was while he held office that the first shipment of livestock to the colony was attempted, and from the point of view of logistics alone this was a remarkable performance.

During 1623 three more ships — the *Eagle*, the *Orange Tree*, and the *Love* — had brought more Walloons to New Netherland, but like the first arrivals they came with no animals and only hand tools. However, reports sent back to the officials of the West India Company about the fertility of the new country and especially its adaptability for "the raising of everything that is produced here" were so glowing that "the aforesaid Lords resolved . . . to provide the place with many necessaries," particularly as they had found a man who was ready (one must assume for a good price) to risk whatever was necessary to carry out the requisite shipment: "To wit; one hundred and three head of cattle; stallions, mares, steers, and cows, for breeding and multiplying, besides hogs and sheep that might be expedient to send thither."

The man willing to risk his capital on this venture was named Pieter Evertsen Hulst, and evidently he was a man not only of bold determination but great ingenuity, with a real knowledge of the care and handling of animals. The stock were to be divided between two ships which were especially reconstructed to accommodate them. Decks were installed to carry the animals; each animal with its own stall stood on a thick layer of sand; each animal had "his respective servant who attended to it and knew its wants." (But one must suppose the meaning here was that each animal was attended by a man who knew how to look after it and probably twelve or twenty more; otherwise the ships would surely have foundered.) Beneath each animal deck, tanks were built to carry three hundred tons of water which could be pumped directly to the animals. Each of the two ships carried enough fodder to last for the first leg of the voyage from Amsterdam to the Canaries. With them sailed a third ship loaded with additional fodder and bedding to last through the second and third legs of the passage; and it also carried six additional families of settlers numbering forty-five persons and, more important, farming implements, plows and carts.

The voyage itself was almost a perfect success. Only two animals died. The rest were disembarked on Governors Island in order to make sure that none strayed off into the wilderness; but they had to be transshipped almost at once to Manhattan because there was not water enough on Governors Island to support the whole herd. On Manhattan twenty of them died, presumably from eating some sort of poisonous weed; but Pieter Hulst could not be held accountable for that. No man since Noah had accomplished an ocean feat to match his.

Whatever vague plans the West India Company might have had for making the tiny settlement on the Delaware the seat of government, they were soon abandoned and Manhattan, as was inevitable, became the center of the colony. The many advantages of its location as an ocean port were already becoming manifest: its unrivaled harbor; its East River entrance to Long Island Sound, and the wide Hudson leading north to the interior and the source of beaver. It was in fact the only secure harbor for ships of any size in the two hundred miles of Atlantic coastline between the mouth of the Delaware and the eastern tip of Long Island. It had its hazards, of course. The sandy beaches of Long Island and the New Jersey shore which looked harmless enough were to claim many a vessel in stormy weather; the sand bars that reached south into the lower bay in ranked lines parallel to the shore of Coney Island left only a relatively narrow deep-water channel, close to Sandy Hook, and as vessels grew in size made pilots obligatory; and then the configuration of the harbor and its two rivers made a complicated tide structure.

A high tide sweeping into the lower bay around Sandy Hook and through the Narrows to reach the tip of Manhattan at any given time took roughly eleven and a half more hours to reach its culminating point where the Mohawk entered the Hudson, at which time the succeeding high tide would be approaching the lower bay. Meanwhile the first tide had been leading a kind of second life in its long journey round the tip of Long Island and up the Sound toward the head of the East River, which it reached one hour after its first manifestation coming up the river from the upper bay had made high tide in Hell Gate. Moreover, the tide funneling in from the head of the Sound was two and a half feet higher than the East River tide, so that in resolving the two levels Hell Gate became a kind of toboggan run of racing waters. It was a bad place for sailing vessels and over the years would fully live up to its name; but it did offer a direct route to New England as well as a back door to Manhattan for Atlantic shipping when violent weather made the Sandy Hook approach too dangerous for sail. With the coming of steam the tidal problems would naturally diminish and the pattern of the harbor with its long reaches of protected navigation through Long Island Sound and up the Hudson to the beginning of the only water-level breach in the Appalachian barrier would give the future port enormous advantages over its rivals in the race for commerce.

Finally there was the little Harlem, itself a salt-water river with tidal currents of its own, but too small to have commercial significance. Its importance lay in linking the East River and the Hudson to complete Manhattan's status as an island. But in 1626 this island held not the slightest intimation of the city that in three hundred years would have covered almost the last vestige of it. When on May 4 of that year Peter Minuit arrived from Amsterdam to succeed William Verhulst as director general and establish the first formal government of New Netherland, it was still a wild, hilly, and heavily wooded piece of land, as much wilderness as any part of the colony. Meat hunters had no need to cross the rivers to find game; its woods held plenty of deer, and even bear. But as Minuit's ships dropped anchor off its southern tip he could see the beginnings of a town and the rising earthwork of fortifications, and however insignificant these may have seemed against the panorama of bay and woods and rivers, they must have looked especially welcome after a voyage that had begun on December 19 the year before, the first three weeks of it shackled by ice in the Zuyder Zee, and then four weary months upon the ocean. This experience may explain why almost the first act of his administration was to buy Manhattan from the Indians.

Even in Holland this purchase was hailed as an event and one finds the deputy of the West India Company, Peter Schagen, reporting on November 4, from the meeting of the Council of Nineteen that ran the Company's affairs, to the States General then in session at the Hague:

High Mighty Sirs:

Here arrived yesterday the ship The Arms of Amsterdam which sailed from New Netherland out of the Mauritius River [Hudson] on September 23; they report that our people there are of good courage and live peaceably. Their women, also, have borne children there, they have bought the island Manhattes from the wild men for the value of sixty guilders, is of 11,000 morgens in extent . . .

The equivalent of sixty guilders in dollars was twenty-four, and whatever inflation would have blown that sum into, it was still a not excessive price for some twenty thousand acres, however rough and forested they might be, so one may pardon the deputy's evident elation, particularly since he could also report that The Arms of Amsterdam had also brought back 7,246 skins of beaver, 178½ otter skins (what about the other half skin?), another lot of 675 otter, 48 mink, a second lot of 33 mink, plus assorted mink and muskrat — enough of a haul, though small in comparison with the annual fur shipments from Canada, to make Minuit's sixty guilders seem like chicken feed, even to a hardfisted Dutchman.

A great deal has been made, over the years, of the tiny price paid for the site of what was to become one of the world's greatest and richest cities, and it makes one wonder a little about the Indians who sold it. They seem to have been satisfied with their bargain, for there never was any subsequent dispute about the amount paid or the area involved — one reason why the Harlem River was important; one can't prevaricate about the boundaries of an island. But exactly who these Indians were is obscure.

The original inhabitants of Manhattan appear to have been relatives of the Lenni Lenape, a group of Algonquin tribes occupying most of New Jersey and eastern Pennsylvania, who were later given the name of a governor of Virginia, and became Delawares. These Manhattan Indians were called Wappingers and they were also related to the Algonquin Mohicans who lived north of them on the Hudson and in western Connecticut. They were indolent, easygoing people, as willing as anyone to make a dollar (or dollar's worth of trade goods) without working for it and ultimately they sold tribal land in the Bronx and Westchester. If any of them were living on Manhattan they cannot have been numerous. Their main settlement was on the site of Yonkers, and there is reason to suppose that Minuit's Indians may not have been Wappingers at all but a tribe camping there briefly on their way to summer ground. They might well have been headed for Long Island to do a little oystering, or dig for clams, or fish for cod in Gardiner's Bay, or even more likely to trade for wampum, for along the shores of that great bay "and the islands therein situate lie the cockles from which wampum is made." (The Dutch commentator would have liked to see the manufacture of wampum turned into an industry, for it was what the Indians all over northeastern America used as currency: he called it "the mine of New Netherland.") Such a journeying tribe, presented with the chance to sell an island that did not belong to them for sixty guilders' worth of trade goods which in turn would be invaluable to them in their coming barter for wampum, could not be expected to exhibit too nice a sense about the validity of land titles. Like much else that has happened in New York during the intervening centuries, the knife probably cut both ways, and in the light of what he saw and what then existed the price Minuit paid was reasonable enough.

The town as it was then hardly forecast the close-stacked towers that like the sprouting of dragons' teeth were to pack the land occupied by the first planned streets. For the engineer and surveyor sent over by the Company to lay out the town of New Amsterdam and design a fort to protect it had brought with him detailed specifications of the town as the Company officials wanted it built. The instructions sound strangely modern.

> With regard to the dwellings of the farmers, we deem it advisable that ten houses be taken in hand first, according to plan A, to wit, Nos. 1, 2, 3, 4, 5, 6, 7, 8, 9, 10, all in accordance with the specifications of model D, and that for each house, including the courtyard and garden, back to the surrounding ditch there be allowed 200 feet, and also 200 feet on the esplanade of the castle, in all 200 feet square . . .

There was to be an avenue twenty-five feet wide exclusive of its ditches, each of which was to be nine feet wide. Crosswise, roadways were to be made twelve feet wide with six-foot ditches. Smaller houses, classified as Model E, were to be built outside the fort. Inside, dormitory buildings were planned to the square foot, "where single persons, such as sailors and others, may be lodged." Roofs of all houses were to be pitched toward street and back yard; there were to be two stories besides a garret. The second story was to be reserved for the uses of the Company, to store supplies or furs or trade goods. The occupying family might use the garret.

It was altogether a remarkable and quite viable plan. The only trouble was that it could not be fitted onto the lower tip of Manhattan and the engineer-surveyor, one Krin Fredericksz, had to follow his own devices. He laid out the outline of the fort and the two main streets the pinched little community was to have — one of them leading northward, which was to become Broadway; the other keeping close to the East River. How much else of the first shape of New Amsterdam was his doing is conjectural. He may have laid out the burial ground and the bouwerie, and he probably began work on the first five company houses, which were deemed of great importance. "The first five of these houses shall be drawn for by the five head farmers, and the remaining houses may be used by the foremen of the commissary, the comforter of the sick, Cryckenbeeck and Fongers." Whether either Cryckenbeeck or Fongers was a foreman or, as a physician, brought comfort to the sick, need not concern us here.

Fredericksz began his work in the summer of 1625, and because of labor shortage he cannot have accomplished a great deal before Minuit's arrival beyond the preliminary work on the fort. Of the town itself little showed. There were those of May's huts that remained, but most of the settlers of 1625, who had had to get themselves quickly sheltered for the winter in the intermissions of working their crops or for the Company, had followed the early practice of the Dutch (and apparently of some New England settlers also) of building the first American equivalent of the sod house.

Those . . . who have no means to build farm houses at first according to their wishes, dig a square pit in the ground, cellar fashion, six or seven feet deep, as long and as broad as they think proper, case the earth inside and round the wall with timber, which they line with the bark of trees or something else to prevent the caving in of the earth; floor this cellar with plank and wainscot it overhead for a ceiling, raise a roof of spars with bark or green sods . . .

These houses were not, of course, an origination of the new continent; in Europe and Ireland peasant houses were often made with floors below the level of the ground, but in America the practice would continue across the country through its extension in Nebraska and in our own time by returning veterans of World War II who, struggling to establish themselves and their new families, first made the concrete cellars for their houses and then roofed and moved into them for one or more years, till money had been found to raise the timbers for the upper stories. Whether all observed the Dutch practice emphasized with such niceness of feeling by Secretary Van Tienhoven in his description I do not know; but he in his report wanted it to be "understood that partitions are run through these cellars which are adapted to the size of the families."

It must have seemed a strange community to Minuit and his fellow passengers, but apparently there was no question that this was the place for the colony's main settlement and seat of government. Across the East River, on Wallabout Bay, there was plenty of room to mark out the town planned by the Company officials. But Manhattan commanded the upper bay and the Hudson down which came the furs from Fort Orange. Fredericksz was right in putting his fort there, and though the farms round Wallabout soon extended into Long Island, and though the East River, both shores of it, remained the important water to shipping through the middle of the nineteenth century, from 1626 the authority of government and of cumulating wealth was vested in Manhattan's narrow island.

*   *   *

New Amsterdam was very slow in growing. Minuit was sufficiently concerned about strengthening it to call back in 1626 the Walloon settlers from around Fort Orange who had been terrified by the Krieckebeeck affair, leaving there only sixteen soldiers to garrison the fort. At the same time he brought back soldiers and settlers alike from both the Connecticut and Delaware Rivers. New Amsterdam therefore in the next three years was to be in effect New Netherland, and the form of government devised for it by the West India Company along the lines of Dutch town governments, with a director general, a council of five, a secretary, and a schout-fiscal or sheriff, was appropriate and seems to have worked effectively enough.

Fortunately no hostile incidents threatened the little settlement during the six years of Minuit's administration. From the start the Dutch had been punctilious about paying the Indians for every bit of land they took over — unlike the English, who moved out into new land when they wished to and appropriated it as their right under the royal claims. But the West India Company was insistent on payment being made, partly no doubt to establish a solid basis for their own claims in America, but partly also out of a genuine concern for what they deemed fair dealing with the Indians, for the stipulation was definitely set down that "everyone should be strict in his dealing with the Indians — no one should give offense to their persons, their womenfolk, or their possessions."

As long as this policy continued, the Dutch had little difficulty with Indians; but already in 1626 there were indications that the period of good feeling might not last forever, at least around Manhattan, for the historian of the day reported that they (the Indians) "were becoming more and more accustomed to the strangers," by which he must have meant that having lost their awe of the white man and his gunpowder they were becoming something of a nuisance. The Reverend Jonas Michaelius, who arrived in 1628, reacted even more strongly to the Indians; he wrote home that they were "stupid as posts, proficient in all wickedness and godlessness . . . thievish and treacherous as they are tall."

It is more than likely that the good divine's judgment may have been warped by his own circumstances, for seven weeks after landing his wife, his faithful and "in every respect amiable yoke-fellow" of sixteen years' standing, had died "not knowing whether she was pregnant" and left him to confront his future in this infant settlement on a new continent "much discommoded" by having to care for three small children.

At that time the whole settlement, including both sides of the East River, numbered no more than two hundred and seventy souls. But already the character of the New York to come was being foreshadowed. Even at this early stage the population was cosmopolitan. In addition to the Dutch and Walloons, some English were beginning to arrive; Portuguese and Spanish transients were found on the waterfront from time to time, and after 1628 a trickle of Huguenots began to appear in New Netherland, forerunners of the emigration that was to result in more than a million people leaving France between 1681 and the end of the century. A minor fraction of these hardheaded, able, and enterprising people came to America to settle in Massachusetts and South Carolina, but the majority chose New York. Wherever they settled, the contribution they made to the development of the colonies of their adoption, especially the commercial development, was significant far beyond their numbers. In New York they concentrated on Manhattan and somewhat later founded a strong French community in New Rochelle.

Strangely enough, many of the English who were to come to New Amsterdam and neighboring Long Island in steadily increasing numbers during the years of Dutch administration to escape the social restrictions and rigid thinking of the Massachusetts colony or of New Haven in Connecticut were themselves descendants of another wave of emigrants from Europe who in the sixteenth century had poured into England — Dutch and Flemish Puritans. They had settled through the eastern counties of England where earlier countrymen of theirs, forced to leave Holland by the flooding of their land, had established themselves in the twelfth century and there developed England's great woolen manufacture which became the staple of her export trade to Europe and especially the Low Countries. Much greater, however, was the second wave of Flemish immigration, which occurred during Elizabeth's reign when Spanish persecution drove more than a hundred thousand people to cross over into England. Many of these immigrants were leaders in their own professions at home; they brought with them all manner of skills in manufacture and agriculture and without question made a major contribution to the sudden rise in the English standard of living that took place at that time.

These Netherland immigrants quickly integrated themselves into English life, often anglicizing their names, so that many family names now accepted as English are really Flemish in origin. It was easy for these people to feel at home, too, for the eastern part of England in which they settled had been the home of Lollardism, the beginning of Protestantism in England, and the temper of thought there was far more liberal and democratic then in the western half of the country, which remained Tory and High Church and was in the Civil War to provide the last stronghold of the Royalist cause while the eastern counties became the major recruiting ground for the Parliamentary armies. Descendants of these Netherland-English were to join themselves to the Puritan migration across the Atlantic. For many the Puritan government of Massachusetts, in which power was kept in the hands of propertied men and the elders of the church, was too confining to leave much hope of realizing one's worldly ambitions. Governor Winthrop and the men around him had no belief in democracy; he himself had made the statement that it was proper that some men must be rich, some poor, some powerful, and some mean and in subjection. Under colonial decree only freemen could vote or hold office as selectmen in the towns. The same held true when, after trying to rule without it, the governor and his associates were compelled to establish the General Court their charter called for. But to be classed as a freeman one had to be an orthodox member of the church, and it was the elders and preachers who decided who was or was not orthodox. Thus a governing clique of wealth and sanctimony was established and it was no trick at all for them to perpetuate themselves in office, or when vacancies were to be filled to find men of their own convictions. As the population began to spread out beyond the first Bay settlements this Puritan elite tried to control the shape of their society by keeping the allotment of free land in their own hands.

Land was still laid out on the system of the town. A man did not live on his own acres, but in the town center, and was assigned here a portion of the meadowland, there a portion of cropland, and so forth; he was not a freeholder, for the land was still part of the town. There were of course advantages in providing mutual support and simplifying defense against the Indians. But it did not suit the temper of men who had been their own masters over generations of farming or in manufacture. Moreover the wealthy kept the better land for their own use and were reluctant to allow the poor to have land of their own for fear that doing so would free them from the necessity of working as servants or cheap laborers or result, as Winthrop put it, in "the neglect of trades."

So men went out of the established communities to found towns of their own — to Rhode Island and the Connecticut Valley as we have earlier seen, and north to the territory that would become Maine and New Hampshire. This outer fringe created the New England frontier. The new communities assumed some of the characteristics of independent thinking that were to mark the frontier all across the continent, and while they still maintained the form of town government, the delegates to the General Court of those founded in Massachusetts did not always share the strict orthodox views of the members from Massachusetts Bay, but it was only when the individual freehold began to penetrate New England in the eighteenth century that Massachusetts began to take shape in the American image.

Many of these dissatisfied colonists who headed south and west found their way to Manhattan and its environs of Long Island, Westchester, and northern New Jersey. It is interesting if not necessarily significant that these various people who undertook the development of what became the greatest American port should have sprung from origins that had so much in common.

*   *   *

In 1628, however, when the Reverend Jonas Michaelius was trying to establish his church and at the same time solve his own domestic problems, indications of the future city and its incredible capacity for growth could hardly have been discernible even to a much less preoccupied man. He could not find a nurse for his children, though he reported that Angola slaves could be bought for a price, but according to him they were "thievish, lazy, and useless trash." Whom he finally found for the job we do not know, any more than we know where he lived. There was no parsonage; the first was to be built for his successor, the Reverend Everardus Bogardus, who arrived in 1633. There was no church building, either. Informal services had first been held in New Amsterdam's one mill, a gristmill powered by a single horse. But Michaelius soon took over a loft in one of the buildings; he had selected Minuit to serve as one of the elders of his church — having the director general on the board must have simplified some of his problems; and he was proud of the fact that a "full fifty" worshipers came to his first administration of the Lord's Supper.

A few were making their first confession of faith; others brought their church certificates; but most of the rest had no certificates to show because, not thinking that a church would be established in so small and crude a settlement, they had left them safe at home in Holland. Apparently they had not considered themselves as permanent settlers. They must have been surprised to see a man over fifty, an old man as age was reckoned then, arrive as their minister.

The other churchgoers who were unable to produce certificates explained that they had been lost in the fire the year before, which Michaelius described as having been "a general conflagration." It had not claimed many houses only because there were so few to claim; but it was the first of the general fires that in the years to come would devastate the developing city and at the same time stimulate it to an extraordinary phoenix growth. At more or less regular intervals there would be five of them in the seventy years that followed the great fire of 1776, during the British occupation — the most disastrous of all being that of 1835 when most of the East River waterfront and countinghouses, six hundred and ninety-three buildings in all, were destroyed in two and a half days with a loss conservatively estimated at seventeen million dollars, an enormous bite from the commercial heart of the city. Yet in a matter of months the buildings had all been replaced, built of "splendid granite, marble, brownstone, and brick," materials that it was hoped would prove more impervious to fire — a hope frustrated when nearly half as many buildings in nearly the same area were razed ten years later by still another.

Early New Amsterdam had shown equal enterprise in repairing its loss, but there was no possibility then of building with stone. The new houses were wooden like the old and with their roofs of thatch or bark were just as inflammable. The only stone building, as one might expect, was the

Company's countinghouse, though some work had been done on facing the bastions of the fort with good "mountain," meaning quarried, stone. The people were less concerned over the permanence of their houses or their style of living than the profits they might realize in what they expected would be their relatively brief sojourn in America. They had come to Manhattan to make money in trade. New Amsterdam was founded, in fact was the only Atlantic coast port to be founded in colonial times, solely for commercial enterprise and its inhabitants never lost sight of their ultimate goal of wealth. Michaelius found them "somewhat rough and loose," but they seem also to have shown respect both for him and his church. One feels that his five years of service there could not have been necessarily all unhappy, though he was glad to return to Holland and refused a second appointment; nor except for a shortage of rations during his first winter could they have been excessively arduous.

He administered the Holy Sacrament four times a year in Dutch, which many of the Walloons could follow well enough, but for the sake of those who could not, as well as for the Huguenots, he conducted the service once a year in French. Occasionally he also preached in French, but always with a written sermon before him, for he found himself incapable of extemporizing in that language. On Sundays, when the Dutch were not using the mill loft, he made it available to the English. The Dutch barred no one from their colony because of his religion — no one, that is, except the Quaker, who was welcome nowhere in America until William Penn founded his own colony — and when the Jesuit Isaac Jogues stopped in New Amsterdam in 1643, after his rescue from the Mohawks, he found men "of various sects and nations" there with eighteen different languages current.

But in that time the population of Manhattan, including the people on the Long Island shore, had grown only to something between four and five hundred. Religious tolerance, though it attracted a great variety of people of differing beliefs, was not sufficient inducement to attract people in any numbers. New Amsterdam remained a busy port, but most of the people were transients, traders, seamen, and longshoremen, an element which still remains. Minuit did what he could to provide facilities that would draw colonists. He tried to start the manufacture of bricks, without much success. He sent crews of men up the Hudson to cut timber to be shipped home for the Dutch navy, and before long there was an over-stock along the East River docks. So he constructed the first sawmill and then, more or less as an advertisement of the colony's capabilities, he decided to build a ship at New Amsterdam which would be larger than any in the Dutch service and at the same time demonstrate the quality and exceptional length of timber obtainable in the Hudson Valley, which made building a ship of such dimensions possible. The idea had been suggested by two shipbuilders, both of them Walloons, and under their instructions work parties were sent upriver as far as Fort Orange, searching out the best trees for beams and spars.

The ship was finished in 1630 and fittingly christened *New Netherland*. Some sources have described her as being 1200 tons, but others called her 800, which seems more likely. In any case she was one of the largest vessels, if not the largest, ever launched on any sea. By comparison the *Bresé*, which was to bring Tracy to Quebec thirty-five years later and was, as we have seen, one of the heaviest warships in Louis XIV's navy, was also 800 tons; and in 1643 Jogues described as "large" vessels three 300-ton ships lying off New Amsterdam for cargoes of wheat. For a community as small and primitive as New Amsterdam to have produced a ship the size of the *New Netherland* was remarkable indeed.

She sailed for Holland and was to make other trans-Atlantic voyages, but to the testy directors of the West India Company the thing most remarkable about her was what it had cost to build her. This became one of the points of contention between them and Minuit which were to lead to his eventual recall. Compounding what in their minds was his extravagance was the money he had sunk in the abortive effort at brickmaking as well as the construction of the mill in which the plank and timbers of the *New Netherland* had been sawed. Though the West India Company had been chartered ostensibly for establishing colonies in the New World, its directors were not, as directors, in the least interested. They regarded colonization as no more than a front for developing the lucrative fur trade and what was expected to be even more profitable, the plundering of Spanish colonial shipping.

The latter proved profitable beyond all imagining. As we have seen, the States General had guaranteed naval support on condition that the West India Company maintain a fleet of its own of at least twenty warships. These were not needed, and certainly were not used when the need finally came, to protect Dutch settlements on the Hudson, Connecticut, and Delaware. But in 1623 the Company had enough warships in service to dispatch a fleet of twenty-six into the South Atlantic under orders to capture San Salvador. This was the chief port and the capital of Portuguese possessions in Brazil, which had fallen under Spanish rule on Philip II's assumption of the Portuguese Crown in 1580 and therefore could be considered fair game.

The venture succeeded mainly because of the fire and enterprise of the second-in-command, a vice admiral named Pieter Pieterzoon Heyn, generally known as Piet Heyn, who was to become as much the embodiment of naval greatness in Dutch annals as Francis Drake was to the English; and in the years between 1624 and 1628 he completed the destruction of Spanish naval power which Drake and Hawkins had begun some forty years before. As a young man captured by the Spanish, he had survived four years in the galleys, which may have given him added incentive for sinking Spaniards.

There was little fighting in the capture of San Salvador, however. The few ships protecting the port were overwhelmed and the town itself surrendered without a struggle. The Dutch fleet then departed for home, except for a squadron sent to capture Angola, where the Company wanted to establish a station for the slave trade. The next year San Salvador was retaken by a combined Spanish–Portuguese expedition, again without any real resistance. But the appetite of the West India Company had been whetted for Spanish plunder, and Heyn, now promoted admiral, was again sent south in 1626.

Next year he sank a Spanish fleet of twenty-six ships and captured most of the merchant convoy it was escorting. This brought in a huge profit, the sugar alone netting $150,000. But in 1628 he capped all his previous exploits by first capturing a fleet from Mexico, laden with the year's produce in dyes and merchandise, and then in intercepting and capturing the entire Silver Fleet, with the year's output of the mines, including eleven vessels carrying Philip II's personal share. This was booty only to be dreamed of, worth more than sixty million dollars in current value — a haul so rich that the West India Company was able to declare a dividend of fifty percent in 1629 and one of twenty-five percent the year following.

But by then Admiral Heyn was dead. At the end of 1628 he had gone into retirement, after refusing to accept any share of the Spanish plunder; but in 1629 he was called back to service to put down the freebooters of Dunkirk who at that time were ravaging the Channel shipping. He succeeded in bringing them to action and smashed their fleet, but early in the engagement he himself was struck by a cannonball. Though he was dead, the Spanish fleet, because of his battles in the South Atlantic and the Caribbean, no longer needed to be reckoned with. The Dutch were so much in the ascendant that when Spain proposed a truce she met a brusque rejection. The war was far too profitable and suddenly too easy to be abandoned. The States General got into the game and in 1630 sent a fleet of sixty ships to Brazil which swept everything before it and seized a large section of the coast above San Salvador. The Dutch navy was now almost on a par with England's. In the Channel actions of 1653 it would give the English about as much as they could handle, and again from 1665 to 1667 under der Ruyter it won as often as it lost and even succeeded in entering the Medway and the Thames.

The reduction of Spain's naval power meant that she would no longer pose a serious threat in North America and that, with the impending elimination of Dutch rule in New Netherland, France and England would have only each other to reckon with in their struggle for the continent.

The fantastic prosperity that resulted from Admiral Heyn's exploits led not only to the dispatch of another force into the South Atlantic after his death but inevitably to the overexpansion of the Company's freebooting operations, and by 1644 it was five million florins in the red. A revolution in Portugal in which in 1640 the Portuguese had thrown off the yoke of Spain further complicated the Company's situation, for it now found itself in possession of vast holdings that in the eyes of the States General belonged to a friendly power. The dilemma was finally compromised by Portugal's paying the Company an indemnity of eight million florins for the restoration of her property. This sum was not enough to balance the Company's accounts; it was still some six million in debt; and twenty years later it was dissolved.

Though these reverses were not foreseeable in 1629, when the Company's affairs were at high tide, the directors were reluctant to squander any of its gains on further transporting of colonists to New Netherland. However, criticism of their failure to do so had been mounting, even to "obtaining some consideration at court," and it was evident that to preserve the Company's charter some solution would have to be found. A group of directors, among whom an astute diamond merchant named Kiliaen Van Rensselaer was the leading spirit, thought they saw a way of establishing colonists at no cost to the Company but very much to their own profit, and therefore in 1629 with the approval of the States General a "Charter of Freedoms and Exemptions" was published.

This was the patroon system, which allowed men of wealth to take possession of immense holdings of land in New Netherland at no more cost to themselves than the bundle of trade goods which would constitute legal purchase from the Indian occupants, provided that within four years they transported to their new acres fifty or more settlers fifteen years of age or older. Needless to say, this privilege was to be open only to directors of the Company, and in the charter almost every contingency had been thought of to protect their investment. "All such shall be acknowledged Patroons of New Netherland."

The patroon must take his land with a frontage of water, sixteen miles if it was coast or one bank of a river, or eight miles on each bank of a river, and "so far into the country as the situation of the occupiers will permit." The charter contained no definition of "situation," so the patroon was free to possess himself of as much land as he saw fit backward from his sixteen miles of river frontage; and this land "would be holden from the Company as a perpetual inheritance," though he was free to dispose of it, *venia testandi*, by testament. On it he would be absolute master. He could exercise justice in his own court, though judgment in excess of fifty guilders might be appealed to the director general and his council in Manhattan. He controlled the use of all streams, fisheries, and game; no trees could be cut, in theory, without his permission; and any deposits of minerals or any pearl fisheries that might be discovered (Kiliaen Van Rensselaer dealt in pearls as well as diamonds) would become the property of the patroon.

To make the starting years of the settlement easier, the patroon and his tenants alike were exempted from payment of any taxes or duties, nor could the Company have claims on the services of any tenant or employee of a patroon except for a possible emergency in building fortifications. The Company moreover agreed to carry over a patroon's tenants and provide provisions at a cost of six stivers (roughly twelve cents) a day, or twice that amount if the passenger wished to eat in the captain's cabin. The tenant was bound completely to the patroon during the term of his contract; if he or any of his relatives tried to leave, the Company would do all in its power to have him returned. The tenant had to buy all supplies from the patroon or his agent; he had to have his wheat ground (like his Canadian counterpart) in the patroon's mill; and he paid in annually as rent a percentage of his crops and the increase of his livestock.

The patroon was supposed to (and usually did) help the tenant establish himself by finding labor (which he could exact from other tenants at no cost) to help build his house and barn and by supplying him with cattle and farm implements. To make the latter easier for the patroon, the Company agreed to transport implements and cattle at no charge; other goods and the tenants' belongings were carried at a charge of five percent of their face value. From the patroons' point of view it was all very well thought out; it made them virtually feudal barons presiding over an agrarian serfdom. The tenants were not truly serfs because they had made a free contract with the patroon, binding themselves for a number of years. But it was at the end of their term that they found freedom of action gone because of an economic vise. They could not sell their land and the improvements they had made except at an insufferable loss to themselves; and to stay they had to sign a contract on the terms of their landlord. The patroon was absolute.

All the Company reserved for itself was the trade in beaver and otter (there were ways of getting round that, too), control over all imports. and Manhattan itself with the stipulation that all produce for export had to stop there for inspection to be bought if needed for the benefit of the town.

* * *

The Charter of Freedoms and Exemptions did not close the door to "such private persons as on their own account" might wish to come to New Netherland as colonists. They would be at liberty, with the approval of the director general and his council, to take possession of as much land as they were able and "shall enjoy the same in full property," but without the privileges, it was made clear, enjoyed by the patroons. This invitation was not enticing enough to lure many individual settlers, and the pattern of landholding in what was to become eastern New York followed largely the patroonship system through, and even after, the Revolution; for, once the English had taken over and corrupt governors like Fletcher and Cornbury had succeeded Colonel Nicolls, enormous tracts of land were handed out to favorites or for a consideration.

In two years following publication of the charter three patroonships were founded but only one survived. The first, on the mouth of the Delaware, was attacked by Indians within a year and all its twenty-eight settlers massacred. A reinforcing group under the sailor and explorer, De Vries, arrived too late, and it too failed, the people being too preoccupied in trading with the murderers of their predecessors to plant adequate crops and De Vries himself spending all his time in search of whales, which also proved an abortive operation. By the end of the year the colonists were forced to return to Holland; the joint patroons dissolved their partnership and induced the Company to buy up their titles on the ground that it had not provided the protection pledged by the charter, which on the face of it seemed true enough.

A second attempt to establish a patroonship was made across the Hudson from Manhattan by Michael Pauw, who planted his small settlement at Hoboken. His grant included the site of Jersey City and later all of Staten Island, but the community did not prosper and within five years Pauw also sold out to the Company.

The third patroonship, however, was to prove an enormous success. It was by many times the largest and in the course of its history was to set the standard for all abuses of land tenure in the state of New York. Kiliaen Van Rensselaer, the founder, wasted no time after the publication of the Charter of Freedoms and Exemptions, in the creation of which he had played a leading part. He knew where he wanted his estate to be and had made up his mind how to develop it. In mid-November he received permission to establish his patroonship; before the end of the month he had written to the then commandant of Fort Orange, Sebastiaen Crol, former Comforter of the Sick, to buy up as much land as he could from the Indians on the Hudson and to have the land surround Fort Orange, which the Company had promised to improve and maintain. Van Rensselaer had no intention of risking his money on an unprotected settlement like the one wiped out on the Delaware, or of putting money into its defense when he could have that service performed by Company funds. Nor did the restrictions of the charter limiting a patroonship to sixteen miles of river-front, or eight miles if both shores were taken, mean anything to him. The tract he acquired was twenty miles long, from Barren Island eleven miles below Fort Orange to the mouth of the Mohawk nine miles above, and twenty-four miles both east and west from the river, or forty-eight miles wide, 960 square miles in all, close to 700,000 acres. Future accretions were to add nearly 300,000 more, so the Manor of Rensselaerswyck, as it came to be called after the English take-over, totaled roughly a million acres.

Kiliaen Van Rensselaer in the development of his estate pursued a double career. As a director of the Company he felt entitled to demand services for his patroonship whenever they proved to his advantage. As the lord of an enormous acreage with interests of his own, he fought the Company tooth and nail. He wanted a monopoly on each last item that came into Rensselaerswyck and he wanted no one else to get a penny's profit on any item that went out of it. For that reason he wanted no trader not under his domination to enter his domain, and since his domain straddled the route to Fort Orange, which was the major post of the Dutch fur trade, he tried to interdict the trade by building a fort on Barren Island on the south boundary of Rensselaerswyck to prevent any ship not bound to his interest from entering his waters, though the charter explicitly reserved free use of all rivers and navigable waters in New Netherland for the Company's ships. In other words he was prepared to control by force of arms the traffic in furs that flowed into Fort Orange, from the Iroquois via the Mohawk Valley and from the Canadian Algonquins via Lake Champlain, in comparison with which the rest of the Dutch fur trade was negligible.

He did send over colonists enough to fulfill the stipulation about colonizing and he was adept at advertising the beauties and natural wealth of the new land on which they might settle, some of his circulars making a keen play toward the Dutchman's appreciation of the table by emphasizing the available fish and game which could be bought for next to nothing from the "Wilden." But those that came found themselves so rigidly under the heel of the patroon's agent and charged such high prices for the goods supplied by his stores (from which alone they could buy) that they at first felt little inducement to take up the laborious work of clearing land and developing farms and tried to better their position by individually trading in beaver, a doubly illegal activity since, though the trade belonged solely to the Company, Van Rensselaer felt that all furs bought within his boundaries should be for his profit only. It was not till the Charter of Freedoms and Exemptions was revised in 1640, among other things opening the fur trade to the individual settler on payment of a ten percent tax on the value of each skin, that any sort of order came out of the traffic. Van Rensselaer then began sending over muskets and gunpowder in quantity as trade goods. That this was in direct contravention of Company policy troubled him not at all. The Indians wanted muskets and powder more than anything else in the world, and as long as they turned their furs over to his agents, muskets they should have.

It took a while to attract people who were in any sort the kind of farmer Van Rensselaer hoped to have as tenants, and the ones that came were reluctant to stake their farms out where he wanted them to settle, along the east bank of the Hudson. The type of feudal land lease with its feudal trappings of sworn allegiance to the proprietor had been abandoned in Holland; it held small lure for an independent farmer in the old country. The people who did come preferred to build their houses close around the fort on the west shore, where the Indians came and where they could horn into the fur trade even if only in a small way. In fact, so many of them built close to walls of the fort that they killed the cannons' field of fire and made it virtually defenseless. Protests from the commandant and even from New Amsterdam had no effect. Van Rensselaer's director himself had built his house there and had no intention of moving away, for the land belonged to the great patroon right to the walls of the fort and had been legally purchased from the Indians. The dispute became so heated that early in his term of office Peter Stuyvesant made a special trip up the Hudson with twenty soldiers. He had the patroon's flag taken down from the director's house, he imprisoned the director, and he laid out the boundaries of a town which he said belonged to the West India Company, and named it Beverwyck. Then he appointed three men as magistrates to hear all cases in civil and criminal law. He did not dare pull down the houses: the Van Rensselaer influence in Holland was too powerful; but it did not much matter. The town he had reclaimed for the Company included the houses of most of the fur traders, and he had planted the municipal seed that eventually grew into Albany.

That was in 1651. Kiliaen Van Rensselaer had been dead for five years. He had never seen his huge American domain, but he had given form to the system of perpetual leasehold that late in the eighteenth century was to be perfected by Stephen Van Rensselaer III and he had set a precedent for the creation of the vast estates that for more than a century preempted the best farming lands of eastern New York. He had also saddled his own estates with the principle of never alienating an inch of land, no matter what the provocation or inducement, which his heirs clung to for two hundred years. It was altogether an iniquitous system, and already before his death he had himself some awareness of the fact that his tenants were holding the small end of the stick; for though at that time his community amounted to no more than thirty houses spaced along the Hudson, his tenants had begun to pay him tribute, and he could see how with a growing population this income would increase. "I would not like my people get too wise," he wrote the then director general, William Kieft, "and figure out their master's profit, especially in matters in which they are themselves somewhat interested."

The income did indeed increase and the Van Rensselaer system of land lease developed steadily to reach the nearest thing to perfection under Stephen III, who had inherited the vast estate on reaching his majority in 1785. It had not diminished an acre since 1630, but the number of its tenants had increased and was to increase far more under his management. He first had all his land surveyed and the unoccupied portions laid out in farms of 120 to 160 acres so that prospective tenants could see the boundaries of the farms they were considering for their home. Like his ancestor the original Kiliaen, he appreciated the importance of advertising and his brochures had glowing descriptions, if not wholly accurate, of the land's fertility. But the real selling line came from his agents, who had received good training, and it was enormously effective.

Pick out a piece of land you like the look of, the prospective tenant would be told. He could settle on it and clear the ground and work it as suited him best. There was no purchase price to pay, nothing to pay for seven years; but then he should come to the land office. He wouldn't have to pay the value of the land, however, even then. Instead he would be granted a durable lease by which he would hold the land perpetually with only an annual rent, which was of course also perpetual and which, according to the size of the farm, amounted to from ten to twenty bushels of "clean winter wheat," four fat hens, and a day's labor with his ox team or horses. There were other points that grew upon the tenant. One was that any taxes on the land would come out of his, not the patroon's, pocket. Another was that whenever the title to the farm changed hands, whether by purchase or inheritance, one quarter of its value belonged to the patroon. A son inheriting could secure his title only by paying one quarter of the value of the land, which had increased through his father's labor. The payment was usually to be made in hard money, something always difficult to come by in backward farming regions, though sometimes it could be worked out by paying in an extra year or two of rent.

The quarter sales gave the proprietor the power to control the quality of his tenants; an undesirable character could be easily excluded. It was the clause that most angered tenants; they had had no inkling of its existence when they first put plow to the land. There never was a written agreement in the preliminary phases, and when they objected they were told that this lease was the only one the patroon had to offer and of course they were under no obligation to accept it.

Stephen III, who before many years was to see his "incomplete sales," as they were also called, bringing in actually millions, was known to his social equals as the "Good Patroon." Living in the large, imposing manor house a little north of what had by then become Albany with his beautiful Schuyler wife, he turned his attention to public affairs, taking part in such state enterprises as the building of the Erie Canal, of which he was one of the original commissioners; he turned some of his great wealth into public charities; and he contributed largely to the establishment of Rensselaer Polytechnic Institute. When he died, a tide of eulogy flowed across his bier. Philip Hone, the New York City diarist, whose gift for the banal cliché was encyclopedic, after pointing out that Stephen had died while enjoying his dinner, proclaimed that he was of "gentlemanly manners, one of 'the Lord's noblemen,' amiable disposition, great benevolence . . ." Another wrote of the "pervading atmosphere of happiness his lifelong goodness created"; and one of his executors commented that "his heart reached well forward into the heart of the republican system."

One wonders exactly what that meant, or how well the others understood the words they used. In all that pertained to his social life, Stephen Van Rensselaer was apparently a generous and humane man; in the administration of his property he showed the underlying and unrelenting shrewdness that had marked the administration of his predecessors, to whom and to God he felt a deep responsibility for his vast estate. Though his admirers often pointed to the churches he helped build and maintain to provide places of worship for his tenants, they did not mention that the ministers were appointed only with his approval and consequently firmly preached the rectitude of manorial privilege and the duty of the tenant under it. He made contributions for studies in agricultural improvement and brought new methods to the attention of his tenants; any improved production was naturally reflected in his rents. But the main evidence of goodness in this "Lord's nobleman" was his leniency toward tenants unable to make up their rent or immediately produce the hard money toward a quarter sale — at his death there were arrears of more than $400,000 which perhaps accounted for the fact that there were fewer demonstrations of resentment on his estate than on any other manors but certainly glossed over the more than $41,000,000 in rents he had exacted in the fifty-four years of his administration, and his will called for the immediate collection of every dollar of these arrears to pay his debts. One must assume that in his own estimation he was a man of good will; but at the end he stood in the image of his ancestor Kiliaen.

Even so he was in many aspects better than his peers along the east side of the Hudson. On Livingston Manor, for example, which neighbored Rensselaerswyck on the south, not only were the annual rents somewhat higher, with two days of labor called for instead of one and numerous stringent stipulations about the methods and rate of developing the farm, but the land was let under a "two-life" lease, which meant that when the second person named as lessee died the property reverted to the proprietor. This was a common practice, not only among the Hudson manors (the Schuylers were somewhat more liberal with a "three-life" lease, though equally unrelenting at its termination), but also on many estates obtained through "patents" of land granted by the state legislature after the Revolution.

Most of the Hudson manors were erected between 1668 and 1697, after the English had taken over, and they followed the Rensselaer pattern of exploitation of their tenantry. It was unique in northern America for its feudal restraints and it did not suit the developing character of free Americans. No one stated its effect better than an itinerant minister, the Reverend John Taylor, who made a trip through upstate New York in 1802: "The Americans can never flourish on leased lands — they have too much enterprise to work for others, or to remain tenants — and where they are under the necessity of living on such lands I find that they are greatly depressed in mind, and losing their animation."

Earlier observers had recognized the evils inherent in the manorial system. In 1732 Cadwallader Colden, whose *History of the Five Indian Nations* was a pioneer in American literature and who was to serve several terms as lieutenant governor of the province, reporting on the lands of New York, described the unfortunate consequences of these immense grants. Population remained relatively small and agricultural development was far behind that of neighboring colonies.

> And every year Young people go from this Province, and Purchase Land in Neighboring Colonies, while much better and every way more convenient lands lie useless to the King and Country. The reason of this is that the Grantees themselves are not, nor never were in a Capacity to improve such large Tracts and other People will not become their Vassals or Tenants for one great reason as peoples (the better sort especially) leaving their native Country, was to avoid the dependence on landlords, and to enjoy lands in fee to descend to their posterity that their children may reap the benefit of their labour and Industry.

He adds that this delayed development was emphasized by the fact that the cost of unimproved land was only a trifle compared with the expense of turning it into farming ground. It cost four and a half pounds (sterling) to clear an acre at the turn of the century, but with the right connections and an unscrupulous governor to accept a bribe a man of wealth could gain control of a huge tract of land for almost nothing. So Colonel William Smith "bought" a tract of fifty miles, east and west, on Long Island, embracing the full width of the island, for fifty dollars handed privately to Governor Fletcher. Fletcher also made vast grants (for varying considerations) to men who were merely speculators and had no plans for immediate development of any sort. Colonel Nicholas Bayard handed him six hundred dollars and received fifty miles of the Schoharie Valley, with no mention of acreage, but granted just "in the lump by miles." A naval captain named John Evans got eight hundred square miles on the west bank of the Hudson for an unnamed sum. Fifty miles of the Mohawk Valley, from the site of Amsterdam to the mouth of West Canada Creek, went to a partnership of five men, William Pinhorn, Major Peter Schuyler, Reverend Godfriedus Dellius, a Major Wessells, and a Captain Banker, each of whom paid him two hundred dollars. The tract was valued at $100,000 and was of course the home country of the Mohawks, but the Indians were persuaded to honor the title on the ground that if the French attacked and the land belonged to Englishmen, the government would be more likely to defend them. When the Mohawks realized how they had been deceived and protested, Schuyler and Wessells withdrew from the partnership. For himself the Reverend Dellius also secured a tract along the east shore of the Hudson above Albany, seventy miles long and twelve wide. It is significant that several of the men named — Smith, Pinhorn, Bayard — were members of the governor's council, as were Frederick Philipse and Stephen Van Cortlandt, whose huge Hudson manors had been erected in 1680 and 1697.

The Earl of Bellomont, a man of curiously liberal temper for his time, especially considering his aristocratic background, and one of the best governors sent out by the Crown, was particularly disturbed about what he called "the extravagant grants" made by his predecessor, and he worked hard to have them annulled. But he succeeded only in three major cases; most of the proprietors carried too much weight in the provincial assembly, and he reported to Whitehall that "if the rest of the extravagant grants shall be broke . . . I believe it must be done by Act of Parliament in England." According to his information "not less than seven million acres have been granted away in 13 grants." Some had only a few settlers, some had none at all. On some, previous settlers had been "wickedly stript of their lands." As New York was the buffer province against the French in Canada, the greed of these few men meant that it was left virtually defenseless against any major invasion. In his mind possibly the most culpable aspect of all was that all these great grants together paid the Crown a quitrent of no more than five pounds a year.

He first proposed that in the future no tract larger than one thousand acres be granted to any single individual, but later raised it to two thousand acres; and these lands and all others should be taxed a quitrent of two shillings sixpence per hundred acres. He asked Whitehall to send him "a good judge or two and a smart active Atturney Generall" to carry through these reforms. (The existing attorney general had found the skinned quarter of a sheep one morning on his doorstep — the usual threat of drawing and quartering, or so he took it — and had lost all enthusiasm for the cause.) But though Whitehall approved Bellomont's suggestions, the requested judges and attorney general never arrived and nothing more was accomplished against the established manors, for in 1701 the earl suddenly died.

The amazing thing about the manorial system is the fact that it was able to endure so long. The idea of the perpetual lease was entirely alien to the temper of northern settlers, and without tenants the manors would have made no profits. The southern plantations could be populated with Negro slaves; but the Negro was not physically or temperamentally adapted for work in the northern woods. The manor lords were able to recruit some settlers abroad: Norwegians, Swedes, some Dutch, and Irish came to Rensselaerswyck; and a percentage were bound to come from New England, for settlers were prohibited by law from crossing the Alleghanies, a measure hopefully designed to keep Indians, and especially the Iroquois, friendly to the English, or at least neutral. The law was only partially effective; in Pennsylvania fur traders first filtered through the passes into Kentucky or the Ohio country, built crude posts, and provided the toehold for future people to clear land and settle. In New York the presence of the Iroquois held back the tide of settlement. Some men decided that the sales talk of the landlords' agents made some sense. It was only after they found themselves caught in the web that they reached the point of open resentment, and finally of violence.

As early as 1711 there was trouble on Livingston Manor, in this case not from Livingston's own tenants but from a group of refugees from the Rhenish Palatinate who had been settled there by the English colonial government with the idea that they might work off the expense of their passage to America, and the cost of supporting them for a year or two, by the manufacture of naval stores — chiefly tar and pitch and turpentine. According to their understanding they had been covenanted forty acres of land for each family but had been told that this would not be forthcoming until they had worked out the money due Queen Anne; and the land they were on and from which the forty acres apiece would come, presumably, was entirely unfit for agriculture, being stony and sandy and good only because it was handy to the pitch pine stands. Robert Livingston had sold it for a thousand dollars and, because he had already built a "brew house" and gristmill there for tenants who had not materialized, had persuaded the then governor, Robert Hunter, to give him the contract for supplying the necessary beer and bread for these poor people. We shall come to their story later. Livingston, in the words of the Earl of Clarendon, was "a man of so ill hands"; in his defense Hunter, essentially a trusting and ingenuous man, replied that "Mr. Livingston was always known, to be a careful, industrious and diligent man, who by these more, than by any other means, hath got a considerable estate"; the two statements did not necessarily cancel each other. We shall meet Mr. Livingston again in this narrative.

Though they did not realize it then, the Palatines were fortunate in being destitute and therefore unable to do much toward improving the land they had been planted on, and still more fortunate in the fact that they were there as laborers on Crown property instead of tenants of the manor. When their claims for the forty acres apiece of good land they thought had been promised them were denied and their protests reached the point of organized demonstrations, and English troops were sent to disarm them of the few firelocks they had been allotted for their defense against the French Indians, they were able to escape to a better farming region, in defiance of the governor's orders, no poorer than when they had arrived. Their protest was not concerned with quarter sales or other manorial abuses of the tenant farmer; in effect it was a statement of the poor man's natural right to hold and improve land of his own on the undeveloped continent and therefore was a first step on the way to revolution as well as being a forerunner of the antirent wars that soon wracked the Hudson manors.

In 1755 and again two years later, tenants on Livingston Manor resisted attempts to evict them or collect unpaid rents. A sheriff was manhandled. Rebellious tenants were seized and jailed, in the case of one lot with no hearing for eighteen months. In each of those years one man was killed, though from the amount of shooting reported by each side one would have expected many more casualties. (Apparently the marksmanship of our agricultural forebears was nowhere near as deadly as tradition has led us to believe.) This resentment with sporadic violence became a continuing pattern. It reached its first serious climax in 1766 when a tenant of Philipse Manor raised an "army" of supposedly more than a thousand armed farmers and for a few bright spring and summer months kept the manor lords and government officials in suspense and dread.

Twelve years before, a young Irishman, named William Prendergast, had come roving down through Dutchess County and near its southern border, south of the town of Pawling, had taken a lease on a farm in Philipsburgh Manor. The place seems to have appealed to him not so much for the quality of its soil as for its proximity to the hilltop farm of a Quaker family whose oldest daughter, then sixteen, had the kind of demure beauty that her sober Quaker dress made only more exciting. It did not take too long to overcome the religious scruples of her family and William embarked enthusiastically on improving his farm and beginning his family.

The first years, of course, went easily. But by 1766, with his third son on the way, William Prendergast had begun to brood over the quarter sale which would take away his farm after he died. But it was not the iniquity of this particular provision that triggered his rage. Two poor crop years had put him behind in his rent and on a trip to Yonkers, made in hope of coming to terms with the manor court which dealt with defaulting tenants, he inadvertently learned that for his manor of 156,000

[185]

acres fat Frederick Philipse paid the Crown a quitrent of four pounds twelve shillings, which was exactly the same rent he himself had to pay Philipse for his small farm. It was the kind of knowledge that had made Kiliaen Van Rensselaer anxious lest his tenants "get too wise," and it infuriated Prendergast.

He began to spend his time moving round among the tenants of Philipsburgh pointing out the monstrous injustice of their situation. Before long he had convinced the farmers not only that the injustice must be righted but that they could do something about it themselves. Men began drilling under his orders. By way of relieving the tedium they pounced on a judge notorious for the severity of his judgments against the tenants, ducked him, and whipped him. Then came the sudden news that two tenants had been seized for nonpayment of their rent and carried off to jail in New York.

Prendergast called out his "army" of now nearly a thousand men. They marched through the lower manors declaring that manor rents were dead; they restored tenants to farms of which they had been dispossessed and drove out the men who had succeeded them. The manor lords in panic raised the old cry of "Leveler" against them (we would say "Communist" today) and called upon the governor for help. But by then Prendergast was marching south, determined to attack the city and free the jailed tenants, and General Gage, commanding there, instead of responding, called all his troops into the fort. One hundred pounds reward was offered for the capture of Prendergast but that was small comfort to Frederick Philipse, whose small counterfeit of a heart must have shivered inside the suety cage that housed it, or to his fellow proprietors.

New York was equally alarmed. But on the first of May, instead of entering the city, Prendergast sent in what he called a "committee" to treat with the governor, Henry Moore, and state their grievances against the landlords. The governor told them that they could free the tenants only by conquering the fort's garrison and showed them the troops standing in ranks before it. It looked too strong a nut for their half-trained bands to crack and they so reported to Prendergast.

New York was saved, but the "army" now turned north and marched through the upper manors, everywhere restoring evicted tenants, emptying jails, and joined by other tenants. For once the sheriffs were powerless to act and the landlords saw their empire about to dissolve; it was an anxious summer.

> . . . The owners of the great Tracts of Land had for several years past harassed the Farmers in their neighborhoods with expensive & ruinous Law Suits. Differences have likewise arose between some of the Landlords & their Tenants. Some of these were committed to jail, others taking advantage of the licentious spirit every where propagated collected in great numbers broke open one of the Jails, set their associates at liberty and threatened the persons and effects of some of the Landlords. On complaint

several of the Riotus Persons are by Proclamation declard Traitors and the 28th Regiment as I am told at the Governor's request is sent to suppress them . . .

Cadwallader Colden, the lieutenant governor, was reporting to Mr. Secretary Conway in Whitehall, and he then made an ironic observation:

> . . . I am far from justifying these Proceedings. I only observe the difference of Sentiment and Zeal in this case and in others where the authority of Parliament was contumed, and the Kings authority was continually insulted, for several months together, by most dangerous Riots, without the least attempt to supress any of them, but rather with public applause.

When the shoe pinched them the great landlords were full of pious zeal to have the government upheld. The Earl of Bellomont had earlier been worried by the extravagant grants because, he believed, in troubled times there was a better chance of making rebellion stick when there were men with great power to lead it. It did not happen so in the Hudson Valley, where only the Schuylers proved strong and capable leaders in the Revolution; but before Prendergast was finally induced to surrender to the 28th Regiment's able commander, Major Browne, British redcoats had run the gantlet of fire between cornfields, a tiny if unsuccessful prelude to Lexington and Concord.

Prendergast was tried in Poughkeepsie before a court that was anything but uninterested: one judge was a Livingston; the attorney general's assistant was married to a Livingston; and naturally there were no tenant farmers on the jury which convicted him of treason — they were all freeholders whose interest was to keep on terms with the great proprietors and who had no sympathy with any disturbance of the peace. Prendergast was sentenced to death and would surely have been executed except for his wife's intercession with the governor. The young Quaker's modesty, beauty, and good sense so impressed him that he stayed the execution till her petition, which she wrote herself, could be presented to the king, and it is pleasant to record that in the end "His Majesty has been gratiously pleased to grant him his Pardon."

Many of Prendergast's followers, some of whom had had pot shots at the redcoats from the cornfields, fought the British again during the Revolution. They thought that when the war was won the manors would be broken and the land turned over to the men who farmed it. But it did not work out that way. Only the estates of landlords who remained loyal to the Crown, like the Philipses and Cortlandts, were confiscated. The northern proprietors, notably the Schuylers, Van Rensselaers, and Livingstons, had backed the patriot cause and at the end of the war they carried great weight in the legislature and courts. It took many more decades to whittle away their power; the end did not come in sight until five years of agitation had swept the manors and there had been another antirent war with bloodshed on both sides.

This one was not at all like Prendergast's brave but spontaneous campaign. For the first time a real attempt was made to organize the tenants, and it was successful enough for them to make themselves felt in politics. This of course brought frantic outcries from the traditionalists of wealth, the friends of manor lords, as has been always the case with the supporters of privilege of whatever degree. "A most outrageous revolt," Philip Hone entered in his diary on December 5, 1839, ". . . of a piece with the vile disorganizing spirit which overspreads the land." And he went on with the almost audible protest that the tenants "have brought themselves to believe that the lands belonged to them . . . and resolved that in a land of liberty there is no liberty for landlords." Also James Fenimore Cooper, whose English-squire mannerisms often roused derision among the citizens of Cooperstown (who loved to regale him with solemn descriptions of impossible feats of marksmanship, which he as solemnly put down to the account of Leatherstocking) came to the defense of Stephen Van Rensselaer IV with the following statement:

> This property is not only invested to his entire satisfaction, as regards conveniences, security, and returns, but also in a way that is connected with some of the best sentiments of his nature.

It strikes an ambiguous note to the modern ear, but it was no doubt a comforting reflection for harried aristocrats, as they considered themselves. There was no question in Cooper's mind, any more than in Van Rensselaer's, that the rights and powers of inherited wealth were as inalienable as the land. When Governor Seward tried to work out a fair compromise between the claims of tenants and landlords, Cooper remarked scornfully on his "gross assumption of having a voice in the matter." This arrogance sprang from the fact that heretofore the great proprietors had been able to control the legislature (tenants were often instructed to vote for assemblymen of the landlord's choice; with the threat of eviction always over them they often did) and to call on sheriffs and even militia if the situation seemed to be getting out of hand. But after 1839 the political climate of the Hudson manors began to change.

The change was the work of a new order of men — amateur and professional reformers who went among the farms. "We had the whole aristocracy of the State to contend with, immense wealth and powerful political influences," reiterating the old argument that the tenant or his forebears had entered freely into a covenant and were where they were of their own or their father's will. The man who so recalled the start of his career in land reform was a physician, Dr. Smith Boughton, a small, rather frail man who like all country doctors of his day traveled endless miles for infinitesimal fees, and he had seen enough of tragedy, small to the proprietor, devastating to the tenant, that eviction caused, and thinking back on his decision to give up his practice and work for land reform, simply remarked that he could not stand idle. He was only one of several doctors who worked to organize the tenants' resistance to the rent. And though an amateur he had a gift for talking with men; one of the first real shocks Stephen Van Rensselaer suffered came from the opinions of several distinguished lawyers secured by Boughton, among them one from the great Daniel Webster who is said to have remarked that if he had time he would tear Rensselaerswyck into shoestrings.

Among the professional performers was an opinionated, violent, and often irrational Irishman named Thomas Devyr who knew how to organize mass meetings and raise men's passions. As a boy he had seen the appalling sufferings under land abuse in Ireland, he had had to flee England for his activities as a Chartist, but in the Van Rensselaer country he found all the material he needed to feed his rage for reform. There were others who also were in the professional category, less spectacular in their methods, but effective. By 1844 they had something like ten thousand armed farmers organized for resistance. Sheriffs could no longer enter the manors safely; at the first word of one's arrival with his deputies, tenants would begin materializing in the darkness, wearing calico costumes, supposed to be of Indian design, and hoods of sheepskin — like the Indians of the Boston Tea Party. Several sheriffs were manhandled, deputies were tarred and feathered, some wounded and some killed. The state beyond the manors was roused by what seemed insurrection; resistance was put down and Boughton and other organizers were arrested. After two trials, the second as prejudiced as any previous tenant trial had ever been, the doctor was condemned to life imprisonment.

But the "Indians" still met everywhere through the manors from the Taconic Mountains to the Schoharie Valley. Francis Parkman witnessed a small meeting in the back-country hamlet of Stephentown and wrote in his journal of 1844 that "the assembly was of the very lowest kind." They were all old men or stupid, they were dirty, one of the leading parties constantly talking but making no sense, "perfuming all near with the stench of filthy, rotten teeth." Another had only a dirty shirt for an upper garment. (The Boston Brahmin who could admire the Sioux, who had their own effluvia, sounds strangely like the white man of the Deep South today.) He evidently neither had nor was inclined to have any understanding of the effect of generations of underprivilege on the human species; but when he speaks of them as "listless and inattentive" one recalls the observation of the young itinerant minister that where men are "under the necessity of living on such lands I find that they are greatly depressed in mind, and losing their animation." But Parkman does finish his entry with the notation that feudal tenure, "so strangely out of place in America, has probably lived its time."

[189]

What Parkman witnessed was a fringe meeting in the poorest country-side. It was far different among the Helderbergs and by 1845 the resistance had grown to a point at which the opponents of feudal tenure in the legislature could begin to act. The first small step came in 1845 when the legislature abolished what was known as the "remedy of distress," which gave the landloard the right to seize all the tenant's possessions until his rent was paid. Even more of a body blow was the taxation of land rents — before then the proprietor's income from leases had been untouched — on the ground that rent received was really interest deriving from a sale.

Then, in 1846, at long last the end of feudal leasehold was finally spelled out. The adherents of the antirenters had gained enough strength to force a resolution through the assembly calling for a constitutional convention. It met during the summer, beginning its session with the reorganization of the judiciary. But finally it got round to land reform.

It declared all agricultural land in New York to be alodial — that is, absolute property of the owner and not subject to rents, services, or feudal acknowledgment of a superior. The convention would not go so far as to invalidate existing leases, but it did prohibit future agricultural leases which involved reservation of rents or services for more than twelve years, and at the same time the courts ruled that the iniquitous quarter sales and other devices to control the alienation of land were illegal. While this did not bring much comfort to tenants suffering under existing leases, it did ensure the ultimate extinction of feudal tenure and the whole manorial system, even though the process was to consume still another thirty years. Nothing like it except the "peculiar institution" of black slavery had existed in America — a skein of evil both for the individual and the state that stretched across almost two centuries and a half, from the time Kiliaen Van Rensselaer and his fellow land-hungry directors in the Amsterdam chamber of the West India Company first dreamed up their Charter of Freedoms and Exemptions.

Though the Company at large could not have foreseen the future evolution of the patroonship, and would not have troubled themselves much about social inequities if they had, they very quickly became concerned over the patroons' assertion of independent powers under the charter, and especially by their open poaching on the fur monopoly. The patroons sought to justify themselves by claiming that the article in the charter reserving the fur trade entirely to the Company applied only to the coastal areas then under Company control and therefore all inland trade was open to the patroons. This was specious reasoning to say the least, and the Company retorted that the primary objective in granting the patroonships was the promotion of agriculture through the colony, which engagement in the fur trade self-evidently precluded. The patroons countered by the charge that the Company had failed to build the adequate forts called for in the charter — which, while undeniably true, was hardly a justification. It was the kind of contentious dispute that goes round in circles — the early Dutch seem to have had a gift for it — and it got nowhere even after it had been referred to the States General. They appointed a special committee who referred the matter back to the executive board of the Company, the Assembly of Nineteen. The dispute was never effectively settled till the Company, bowing to the inevitable, finally opened the trade to the public in 1639. This at least gave them the satisfaction of thwarting a later move of the patroons to have the trade barred to everyone but themselves.

All that came out of it in 1632, however, was that after examining the grants that had been made, the States General decided that they were inordinate and that the patroons had been unwarrantably favored by the director general. They forced the Company to recall him, which was an act of injustice. Minuit had only been following Company policies; the fact that the patroons outranked him left him no other course. He was deeply resentful and, six years later, when the Swedish government decided to found a colony in America and offered him the post of leader, he eagerly accepted it and founded the fortified colony of New Sweden on the west shore of Delaware Bay above the present site of Wilmington.

To succeed him the Company's choice fell on an unlikely character named Wouter (or Walter) Van Twiller. His previous service with the Company had been as a mere warehouse clerk in Amsterdam, and his chief qualification seems to have been his relationship with the Van Rensselaer family; he was a cousin through the marriage of his sister to Johannes, the older son of Kiliaen, and supposedly also Kiliaen's nephew through the marriage of the latter's sister to one Rykert Van Twiller who may have been Wouter's father. Whether or not the latter was true, the importance to the Van Rensselaer patroonship of having a friendly director general in New Amsterdam, and even better one related to the family, needs no underlining.

In his *History of New York . . . by Diedrich Knickerbocker*, Washington Irving caricatured Van Twiller as a sedentary, complacent, dim-witted man of vast obesity — the prototype of all the burghers in that entertaining but misleading work — and so vividly that in spite of Irving's own disclaimers, he remains the typical Dutch settler in the American imagination:

> . . . There are two opposite ways by which some men make a figure in the world: one, by talking faster than they think, and the other, by holding their tongues and not thinking at all. By the first, many a smat-

terer acquires the reputation of a man of quick parts; by the other, many a dunderpate, like the owl, the stupidest of birds, comes to be considered the very type of wisdom. This, by the way, is a casual remark, which I would not, for the universe, have it thought I apply to Governor van Twiller. It is true he was a man shut up within himself, like an oyster, and rarely spoke, except in monosyllables; but then it was allowed he seldom said a foolish thing . . .

Diedrich Knickerbocker went on to describe his physical appearance with equal gusto. "He was exactly five feet six inches in height, and six feet five inches in circumference. His head was a perfect sphere, and of such stupendous dimensions that Dame Nature, with all her sex's ingenuity, would have been puzzled to construct a neck capable of supporting it; wherefore she wisely declined the attempt, and settled it firmly on the top of his backbone, just between the shoulders. . . . His legs were short, but sturdy in proportion to the weight they had to sustain, so that when erect he had not a little the appearance of a beer barrel on skids."

It is all preposterous nonsense, as is Knickerbocker's claim that Van Twiller was the first and best governor of New Amsterdam because nothing untoward happened during his administration. In fact Van Twiller appears to have been a man of considerable shrewdness, if somewhat limited in imagination. He had an eye for good land and a nose for profit, and in partnership with a few cronies he acquired various properties about Manhattan, including islands in the East River, and Nut Island which became known as Governors Island in consequence, and a fine fifteen thousand acres of the best land on Long Island. He conformed to the law by making at least token payments to the Indians, but did not report these real estate transactions to the Company for approval and confirmation of title, an oversight (if such it was) which later helped lead to his removal from office. It was also remarkable how the Company's bouweries, whose management was one of his primary duties, failed to make a profit and were especially unfortunate for the mortality among their cattle, while those belonging to Van Twiller were uniformly successful and showed an exciting annual increase in livestock, which he rented out at good prices to newly arrived settlers and even on occasion to the Company's farms.

If these happy adventures in husbandry and real estate speculations were not on a par with the operations of his Van Rensselaer relatives up the Hudson, they were highly profitable and indicated that Van Twiller was not at all the simpleton of the Knickerbocker legend. In all probability he actually made more money out of them than Rensselaerswyck brought in during the first early years, and his existence in New Amsterdam would have been one of contentment except for two bugbears which would not be exorcised.

The first of these was the successor of Reverend Michaelius, Dominie Everardus Bogardus, who had made the voyage from Holland in Van

Twiller's company. By all accounts he was a passionate man with an uncontrollable temper, a tongue like a rasp, and strong convictions about the morals of other people. With these qualities he combined a love of drink and a capacity for its consumption that rivaled Van Twiller's, which contemporaries have assured us was stupendous. For a while after reaching New Amsterdam they were boon bottle companions, making of any small event warrant for broaching a cask of wine and drinking themselves into a state so nearly riotous that anything could happen and sometimes did. On one occasion as they were leaving the home of their host on the Jersey shore, the latter, thinking it would be in the spirit of the evening, attempted to give them a parting salute with an old swivel mounted on his front lawn, but in his befuddlement the swivel got pointed toward his house instead of over the bay, the discharge set the roof afire, and the house burned to the ground. It is comforting to realize that after such orgies the director did not have to cope with the uncertainties of an internal combustion engine; some of the Company's Negro slaves were always there to row him back to Manhattan.

This mood of mutual good feeling, however, did not endure. Bogardus did not see why he should not be appointed to the director's council, as Michaelius had been, and when it became plain that Van Twiller was never going to appoint him, the minister's joviality turned to spleen. He referred to the director as a child of Satan, he criticized his drinking habits with invective, and he threatened to preach a sermon against him the next time he came to church that would really put the fear of hell in him. Not unnaturally Van Twiller gave up attending church, which compounded his sinfulness in the dominie's eyes. He increased the venom of his accusations, wrote complaints to Holland, and developed such an allergy to director generals that when Van Twiller was succeeded by William Kieft, Bogardus transferred his attacks to the latter with hardly a break.

A less persistent but much more ominous affliction was a series of encroachments by the English on territory claimed by the Dutch. The first occurred only a few days after Van Twiller's arrival in New Amsterdam. He was entertaining David Pieters De Vries — the seafarer and explorer who had brought the second group of colonists to Swanandael on the Delaware — at dinner when a strange ship was reported in the Narrows. As she came sailing up the bay, they saw that she was English. She dropped anchor opposite the fort; a boat was put over and presently rowed ashore. Besides the oarsmen the boat carried one passenger, who asked to be taken to the director general.

The ship, he told Van Twiller, was the *William*, William Trevore master, and had been commissioned by the firm of Cloberry, Morehead and Delabarr to "goe to Hutson's river in New England, within the dominions of the Kingh of England, to trade and trucke away such goodes, as she carryed to the natives of those countries, for beaver skinnes and other skinnes and furrs; the premises hee knoweth to be true, for that he was factor for the said merchants in that voyage."

The bald arrogance of this claim shocked the Dutch. What made it more infuriating was that the man who delivered it was himself a Dutchman. He was Jacob Jacobsen Eelkens, whom we have met earlier as commandant of Fort Orange and who in 1618 supposedly inaugurated the trade in firearms with the Iroquois. He had proved himself resourceful in dealing with all Indian tribes, and he might still have been commanding at Fort Orange if he had not taken it into his head to enrich himself by kidnaping a Connecticut Mohican chief and holding him for the enormous ransom of two hundred yards of wampum. While this act was not in itself a violation of the Company's fur monopoly, it had the effect of virtually halting all fur trading activity east of the Hudson. Eelkens was discharged from the Company service, he defected to the English, and now ten years later he was returning to his old trading ground. The London merchants could hardly have found a more effective man for their purpose, and the Dutch knew it.

Van Twiller demanded to be shown Eelkens's commission; "whereupon this deponent answered, that he was not bound to shewe it, for that he was within the King of Englands dominions," and in turn demanded to be shown the director general's. The confrontation might belong in a comic opera, and De Vries, who considered Van Twiller a deplorable half-wit, has left an amusing if biased account of it. As Eelkens himself reported it:

> . . . And the said Governor replyed, that he had conferred with his counsell, and that hee found it not fittinge, that they should passe up the said river, for that that whole countrye did (as he said) belonge to the Prince of Orange, and not to the Kinge of England. And after the said ship had stayed five dayes before the said forte, this deponente wente to the forte, to speake with the Governor, to see if he would suffer them in a friendly manner to passe up the said river; and hee told the said Governor, if he would not give him his goode will soe to doe, hee would goe upp the said river without it, although it cost him his life. Whereuppon the Governor commanded all the companye of the said shippe to come on shoare. And in the presence of them all, the said Governor commanded, that the Prince of Orange his flagge should be putt upp in the forte, and three peices of ordnance to bee shott off for the honor of the said Prince. And then this deponente commanded the gunner of the said shippe, the William, to goe abord and putt upp the englishe flagge, and to shoote of three peeces of ordnance for the honor of the King of England. And then the said Governor badd this deponente, take heede, that it did not cost him his necke, or his (:the said Governors) . . .

Whereupon Eelkens took his crew back to the *William*, weighed anchor, and set sail upstream for Fort Orange, while Van Twiller watched in speechless rage. According to De Vries he then called all loyal citizens down to the river edge and, ordering a cask of wine to be broached, invited all to drink to the confusion of the English crew and the glory of their own prince and fatherland. De Vries apparently became incensed over the whole show. Why was the *William* not fired on while she was still in range? A few iron beans, he added, would have stopped her fast enough. But since the harm was done, why didn't the director send an armed force after her and compel her to return?

Van Twiller had at his disposal about a hundred soldiers who had made the voyage from Holland with him. They were regulars and represented a formidable army at that time and place; but it took him several days to make up his mind to follow De Vries's advice. The English and Dutch were officially at peace, and under the Company's charter its officers were not at liberty to open hostilities on nationals of another European power without consent of the States General. So it became a question of which man could outbluff the other, and it ended in something like a draw.

Van Twiller sent troops upriver in three small vessels, "a pinnace, a caravel, and a hoy" according to De Vries. They came up to Fort Orange after Eelkens had been trading for about two weeks. He had been refused permission to trade beside the fort, so had set up operations in a large tent some distance below it and had taken in five thousand beaver and used up not quite half his trade goods. Van Twiller's troops, joined by the fort's garrison, did not attack the English but went for the Indians, beating them "with muskets, halfe pykes, swords, and other weapons" until they had decamped.

With no customers Eelkens could do nothing but stand by with his men while the Dutch soldiers tore down his tent and put his trade goods aboard their own small vessels. They did not get hold of his beaver, for like a prudent trader he had bundled the skins aboard the *William* as fast as they came into his hands.

Once more at Fort Amsterdam, he resumed his dispute with Van Twiller. He refused to give up his beaver but finally agreed to let Van Twiller have a "particular of all the skinnes" aboard the ship. In return he demanded and secured a list of the members of Van Twiller's council. Each man apparently considered the other's document criminal evidence and so, honor satisfied, the *William* was at last allowed to leave, taking five thousand skins but with a loss, by Eelkens's reckoning, of some five thousand pounds in trade.

The episode ignited a long series of interchanges between the two governments in Europe, in which old claims and counterclaims were endlessly rehashed. As we have seen, under the Virginia Charter of 1606, England claimed all the Atlantic coast from the 34th to the 45th parallel. But in royal grants to the two original stock companies the London Company was given title to land between the 34th and 41st parallels — from Cape Fear to about ten miles north of Manhattan — while the Plymouth Company received the coast south from the 45th to the 38th parallel. This left the land between the 38th and 41st parallels open to development by both companies, a sort of no man's land the effect of which was emphasized by the stipulation that neither company might begin a settlement within a hundred miles of one already started by the other.

To the Dutch this ambiguous geography seemed an opportunity if not an inducement for settlement and from 1621 on they had steadily refused to accept the English royal claim to the territory, on the ground that settlement and due purchase from the Indians made occupation legal. "Inasmuch," they declared with truth, "as the inhabitants of those countries are freemen, and neither his Brittanic Majesty's, nor your High Mightinesses' subjects, they are free to trade with whomsoever they please," and consequently to sell and convey real estate. (This was the argument, also, of Roger Williams at almost the same time: he wrote a pamphlet in which he denied the right of Englishmen to hold lands under royal grants, contending that the land belonged to the Indians and one could obtain proper title to it only by buying it from them. This was regarded as an attack on the Crown itself and led to Williams's expulsion from Massachusetts and his settlement on Narragansett Bay and the beginning of Providence — and it was in addition, though he did not think of it so, one more step on the road to Revolution.)

England countered this argument of the Dutch by denying "that the Indians were *possessores bonae fidei* of those countries, so as to be able to dispose of them either by sale or donation, their residences being unsettled and uncertain, and only being in common." Nor could it be proved that all the natives using the said territory "had contracted with them [the Dutch] at the pretended sale."

In the end occupation of the land would obviously be the decisive factor and in this respect the advantage already was tilting ominously toward the English. A thousand colonists had accompanied or followed John Winthrop to Massachusetts Bay in 1630, and thereafter arrivals averaged more than two thousand a year for the next decade. New Netherland, however, not only failed to attract settlers, its population during Van Twiller's administration showed a decrease. The Dutch were not colonizers in the sense the English were; they were exploiters, and New Netherland remained a property of the West India Company until the English take-over. The States General so regarded it and despite repeated appeals from New Netherland declined to assume its administration. As a Company property it was therefore under control of the director, who was no more than a Company agent, and his council. But both Van Twiller and his successor, Kieft, either stacked the council with personal cronies or rubber stamps or disregarded it altogether. Representative government, which was finding expression in the House of Burgesses in Virginia and the creation of the General Court of Massachusetts in 1632, was nonexistent in New Netherland.

To the south, Virginia seemed too far away to be a menace, and the beginning of Maryland by the settlement of St. Mary's in 1634 too insignificant to be alarming; but New England was another matter, particularly English encroachment in the Connecticut Valley. As often happened, maneuvering between the European races was closely tied to the intrigues and feuds of the Indian tribes and here, as before, it was the Iroquois who initiated events.

When in 1625 the Mohicans had been driven out of their Hudson River homes about Albany, in the war which had panicked the Walloon settlers of Fort Orange, they had retired to the Housatonic Valley in Connecticut. But in 1628 the insatiable Mohawks started after them again; the Mohicans had to abandon their new home and moved north into Massachusetts but were there turned back by the Nipmucks — in itself a commentary on how their strength had been reduced, for the Nipmucks were never much in war. Then the Mohicans drifted down the Connecticut River and tried to settle below a related Mohican tribe whose clans were centered around the present site of Middletown. Here, however, they found themselves facing the resentment of the Pequots, another related tribe but no friends, who occupied the Thames Valley less than twenty miles away and were then at the zenith of their power. The Mohicans were no match for them and after three defeats were forced to subject themselves and pay tribute. In desperation they appealed to the Dutch, who had professed themselves their friends at Fort Orange, for help.

The Dutch, who have rarely showed much inclination to inhibit profit in the name of friendship, refused. They were perfectly ready and even eager to do business with the Mohicans on a friendly basis, but the bulk of their fur trade was and was bound to remain with the Iroquois, who would have taken violent exception to the equipping of their traditional enemies with firearms. On top of Eelkens's kidnaping of the Mohican chief, this refusal was to bear bloody fruit for the Dutch around New Amsterdam. Meanwhile the Mohicans applied to the English, who also turned them down, and soon found themselves obliged to pay tribute to the Mohawks as well as the Pequots in order to survive.

The Mohawk collection of tribute, mostly in wampum from the lesser tribes in southern New England and around Long Island Sound, was an extraordinary performance. During the summer months older chiefs traveled from one town to another in pairs without warrior escort, confronting the local chief with their arrogant demands, which had been dictated in tribal council at home, and wholly indifferent to the hostile glowering of the local braves. They were covered by the threat of Mohawk retaliation; their mere disappearance on the trail, if there had been another Indian enterprising enough to ambush them for their wampum, or from simple misadventure, would have spelled catastrophe for the Indians of the area. So inevitable and absolute were the consequences of this early form of "protection" that sight of a Mohawk traveling by himself could raise the alarm cry "Mohawk!" and, according to Colden, send a whole village fleeing "like sheep before wolves."

Though the Mohicans's application to the English gained nothing for themselves, it did provide another stimulant to English interest in the Connecticut lands. When in 1633 a trading vessel brought news to Plymouth that the Dutch were buying up large tracts along the river and rebuilding the redoubt called Fort Good Hope, which Minuit had abandoned seven years earlier, the Plymouth colonists reacted instantly. Governor Winslow, accompanied by the former governor, William Bradford, went straight up to Boston to propose that Governor Winthrop join them in establishing an armed trading post close to the Dutch fort. Winthrop, however, declined an active role for his colony, contenting himself by writing a letter in which he reiterated the English claim — the elders of Massachusetts Bay were always more concerned about keeping their own citizens up to scratch than about what might be happening beyond their boundaries.

Disappointed but in no way deterred, Winslow and Bradford hurried back to Plymouth to set about implementing their plan. It would be essential for the English to establish themselves before the Dutch could bring any force against them, so a blockhouse was built and then taken down in sections which were loaded aboard ship — undoubtedly the first prefabricated house to be constructed in America. Under command of Lieutenant William Holmes with a company of seventy men the ship sailed for the Connecticut and worked her way upstream till she raised the squat yellow brick walls of Fort Good Hope. As she came abreast, the Dutch garrison shouted to her to halt, ran out their two tiny cannon, and threatened to open fire; but Holmes ignored them, the ship wore slowly on, and the Dutch, while they continued to shout, "yet they shot not." Five or six miles farther on, near the site of Windsor, the ship dropped anchor. The sections of the blockhouse were taken ashore and assembled and a stockade raised about the finished building. The first English settlement on the Connecticut had been established.

While these events were taking place Van Twiller had replied to Winthrop's letter, expressing the hope that the English and the Dutch could get their boundaries set, "and as good neighbors wee might live in these heathenishe countreyes." There should be no further encroachments on either side, he argued, until the home governments had come to an agreement and anyway, he added rather wistfully, "in this parte of the world are divers heathen lands that are emptye of inhabitants, so that a little parte or portion thereof there needes not any question." But the news of the English blockhouse being built above his fort incensed him, and in 1634 he sent a force of seventy men to drive the English out. However, when they had looked the situation over and found the English determined to remain, these seventy soldiers, like their compatriots in the fort, also "shot not," and returned peaceably to New Amsterdam.

After hearing their report it came to Van Twiller's mind, as should have been evident all along, that the only place to control traffic on the Connecticut was at its mouth. Till then all the Dutch had done was to nail a large signboard decorated with the arms of the States General to a tree on the point running out into the Sound at the river's mouth. Now, Van Twiller decided, they would have to build a fort there; but again he was frustrated. The sloop he sent out with soldiers and artisans found two English ships already at anchor off the point and, without even hailing the strangers, she, too, meekly put about and returned to New Amsterdam.

The English ships had been dispatched to the Connecticut expressly for the purpose of heading off the Dutch and had arrived in November 1635, under command of the son of the governor of Massachusetts Bay, the younger John Winthrop. In 1632 a group of twelve Englishmen, headed by Lord Saye and Sele and Lord Brooke, had been granted a large patent of land along the Sound and on the Connecticut and, hearing rumors of the Dutch activities there, had determined to establish their own control. They had found a good man to head their expedition. John Winthrop at the time was only twenty-nine, but already exhibiting the qualities of energy and tact which, as we have seen, made him so effective in securing the bloodless surrender of New Amsterdam nearly thirty years later.

Winthrop renamed the point, which the Dutch had called Kievit't Hook, Saybrook in honor of the two ranking members of the syndicate, and the fort presently built there took the same name. It was to become the military center of Connecticut, a good deal sooner than anyone had anticipated.

The man left by Winthrop to build it and stay on as its commanding officer after it was finished was Captain Lyon Gardiner, who later gave his name to the great bay and island at the eastern end of Long Island. He had had experience as a military engineer in the Low Countries and was one of several young officers who had seen service there and later emigrated to New England, after the pattern of Miles Standish. Among them were Captains John Mason and John Underhill who were shortly to prove themselves among the greatest Indian fighters of New England. For it was not the Dutch who proved a problem to the English in Connecticut, but the Pequot Indians.

Once Fort Saybrook had been built, Fort Good Hope was isolated, a mere house by a river, of no strategic usefulness whatever. They had been "tricked" out of the Connecticut, the Dutch claimed, and soon the little yellow brick building was surrounded by vigorous English settlements — "a comely city, called Hartford, about a gunshot from Fort Good Hope on the Fresh River, together with divers other towns and hamlets." New Haven was soon to be settled and from New Haven the English would spread to eastern Long Island, founding Southold and Southampton and establishing a codfishery on Gardiner's Island. The main streams of early migration from Massachusetts, however, traced to the Connecticut Valley, where Windsor, Wethersfield, and Hartford were settled by parties from Dorchester, Watertown, and Cambridge (or New Town as it was then called). A fourth group, from Roxbury, settled at Springfield. Within a year, more than eight hundred English were living along the Connecticut and, trespassers or not, their presence made it obvious that in any future boundary negotiations the Dutch claim to the Connecticut was going to carry very little weight.

The new settlers had been induced to move to the valley by the accounts of its fertility and beauty, and of the friendliness of the Indians living there, brought back to Boston by John Oldham. A man with no great affinity for the Puritan system as practiced in Massachusetts, Oldham with a small party had made a trip overland to spy out the country, partly because the area around Massachusetts Bay was becoming so densely settled by the constant arrival of new colonists that men interested in raising livestock were finding it more and more difficult to find sufficient pastureland, and also because many of them, like John Oldham, were becoming restive and increasingly apprehensive of the growing political power of the church. The provision that only church members in good standing should have the right to vote or hold public office gave the clergy an influence over the course of public affairs which even some ministers, recalling the origins of Puritanism and horrified by accounts currently coming out of England of the persecution of all dissenters by Archbishop Laud, had begun to find disturbing.

Another incident a few years before had also alarmed them. At the outset the colonists had tried to govern themselves by periodic meetings of all freemen, who then elected the officers, governor and lieutenant governor, and a board of assistants who acted as advisers. This as a matter of fact followed the pattern of the Charter of the Massachusetts Bay Company (which in a moment of inspiration John Winthrop had brought with him across the Atlantic), but the number of freemen in the colony increased so rapidly that such meetings soon became impractical, and the responsibility of choosing the governor and his lieutenant as well as the enactment of laws was assigned to the assistants. The assistants, as was natural, were the eminent and wealthy, who would have agreed sympathetically with John Winthrop when he declared that in the nature of things some men must be rich and others poor, some wield power and others live in subjection to them; and within a year they had decided that there was no need for yearly election but that members of the board could continue to hold office until rejected by a special vote of the freemen.

It is possible that in Europe, in a community as small as the colony still was in 1631, this autocratic assumption of power might have been successful; but there was something in the long voyage to the American shore and confrontation by the wilderness that worked unforeseen changes in the character of Englishmen and when in 1632 the assistants arbitrarily proposed to levy a tax of sixty pounds on the various settlements in order to build defense works at Cambridge, the citizens of Watertown flatly refused to pay, on the principle that freemen could be taxed only with their own consent.

This put an end to the budding oligarchy. Each town sent two deputies to consult with the board of assistants on the immediate matter of the defense tax; the power of electing the governor and lieutenant governor was reassumed by the freemen; and two years later the system of electing deputies to a General Court was adopted. At first the deputies sat in the same chamber with the assistants, who remained to serve in a judicial capacity and as a governor's council, but in 1644 as the result of a grotesque little lawsuit over a strayed pig the assistants and deputies were separated into two houses.

A pig wandered into the yard of a Captain Keayne in Boston, a man of wealth and some distinction in the community. He had the pig put in a sty with one of his own and advertised it as a stray. Then he killed his own pig. A year later a poor woman named Sherman who had lost her pig heard of the captain's advertisement and came to see if the strayed pig, which mercifully was still alive, was hers. She could not identify it, but for some reason she got it into her head that it must have been her pig that the captain had butchered the year before. He denied it, she accused him of being a thief, and the case was tried before a jury which found the captain innocent. Whereupon he sued her for defamation of character and won his case, with damages of twenty pounds — a sum staggeringly out of proportion for a woman of no means. But the case had captured popular interest as an embodiment of the poor man's struggle against the aristocracy of wealth and when the indomitable Mrs. Sherman took her cause before the General Court she did not lack for backers.

The Court heard testimony and debated the case for a full week before coming to a vote. Then the count showed that the vote had been in favor of Mrs. Sherman, seventeen to fifteen. The deputies' vote was fifteen for her and eight for Keayne; but the assistants had been overwhelmingly on his side, only two out of nine voting for Mrs. Sherman; so in the end she lost by their veto of the deputies' finding. The impossibility of reaching a final decision by this form of joint sitting led after a year to the separation of the Court into two houses, each with the power to veto the other, very much like the form of the Massachusetts General Court of modern times and a pattern which was closely followed by the other colonies.

It was a period of religious and intellectual as well as political ferment in Massachusetts. At Salem, Roger Williams besides giving utterance to his highly unpopular thesis that the land of America was actually the property of the Indians had been preaching religious freedom and the separation of church and state, doctrines that attacked the very roots of the Puritan state as Winthrop, Endicott, and their clerical advisers conceived it; and in 1636 Williams was ordered to take ship for England. Instead he took to the woods, making his way to the village of the Wampanoags where Massasoit gave him shelter through the rest of the winter. Williams was fluent in Algonquin and during his months among the Wampanoags his transparent honesty and sincerity made a deep impression on them and visitors from other tribes. In the spring he was confidentially informed by Winthrop that if he did not return to Massachusetts but settled to the south on Narragansett Bay he would not be further harassed, so he moved on to begin the settlement of what was called the Providence Plantations, which later coalesced with another settlement established by another freethinker to form the colony of Rhode Island, the first English colony spontaneously to guarantee religious liberty to all its citizens.

The second freethinker was Anne Hutchinson, who as an Antinomian believed that man is saved by grace whatever his works on earth, evil or good, and his sins if he was a transgressor are transferred to Christ, so that Christians are freed from observance of the moral law spelled out in the Old Testament. To have such beliefs at all would have been bad enough, but Anne Hutchinson was a highly articulate woman and insisted on setting forth her beliefs in a series of public lectures which not only attracted considerable audiences but brought her a number of followers as well, among them men as distinguished as old John Cotton, the first minister of Boston, and Captain Underhill, soon to gain fame as an Indian fighter. But others like reasonable Winthrop found her disturbing, and her utterances left men like Thomas Dudley, whose bleak conception of Puritanism had room for not even a drop of tolerance, or the violent and psychotic minister, John Wilson, utterly aghast. The church as well as the people of Boston found itself divided; it seemed incredible that such division should result from the speeches of a woman; and her expulsion from the colony, if no worse punishment were visited on her, would surely have followed hard on Roger Williams's, if she had not also won the support of the governor.

This was Henry Vane the younger, son of Sir Henry Vane who was comptroller of the household of Charles I, and a graduate of Oxford. He had emigrated to Massachusetts in 1635 and the following year found himself governor of the colony when, in one of those almost pawky assertions of their independence, the voters turned the perennial John Winthrop out of office and in his place elected Vane. Though still a very young man — he was then only twenty-four — Vane already exhibited the tolerance and breadth of mind that were to distinguish his subsequent career as a statesman in England. In the schism that developed between the followers of Anne Hutchinson, believing in a covenant of grace, and the adherents of Dudley, Wilson, and their kind, who were grimly determined to uphold a covenant of works as the proper way to man's salvation (and their own control of their fellow colonists), Vane sided with Mrs. Hutchinson.

Under his protection she was able to continue her lectures through 1636 into the summer of the following year. However, in the spring of 1637 the Massachusetts voters thought better of their fling with the youthful Vane and restored John Winthrop to the governor's chair. Vane shortly returned to England and Mrs. Hutchinson was ordered to take herself and her followers out of the colony. Some migrated north to found Exeter and Hampton in what became the Crown colony of New Hampshire in 1679, but Mrs. Hutchinson with another group went south, bought Aquidneck Island from the Indians, and formed settlements at Newport and Portsmouth.

It was also in 1636 that the General Court appropriated four hundred pounds to found a college which would open its doors to its first class in 1638, the year John Harvard died and left it his library, half his fortune, and, as it was voted in the next session of the General Court, his name. How much this action was due to the disturbance of mind and conscience provoked by Roger Williams and Anne Hutchinson is hard to say. Perhaps they helped bring the matter to a head somewhat earlier than might otherwise have been the case. But according to the anonymous author of *New England's First Fruits* the creation of a college had been in some men's minds from the start. "After God had carried us safe to New England," he wrote, and they had built themselves houses, planted and reaped their first crop, built churches, and framed their government, "one of the next things we longed for and looked after was to advance learning and perpetuate it to posterity; dreading to leave an illiterate ministry to the churches, when our present ministers shall lie in the dust."

For a community scarce eight years old, with the wilderness still in view from the windows of nearly every house, to have appropriated so large a sum in the first place was remarkable, but still more so was the generosity of private contributions. John Harvard's legacy of seventeen hundred pounds was decisively important, if not as significant as his gift of his library; yet "after him another gave £300; others after them cast in more. . . ."

From 1638 to 1693, the year William and Mary was founded, Harvard was the only institution of higher learning among the English colonies and from the beginning the high standards it set under President Dunster became the model for colleges and universities to come. Students came to the college from as far south as Virginia, some even from abroad. The spirit of looking forward, of pioneering, which has been a moving force in all Harvard's history became evident in its second functioning year when a printing press, the first in North America, began operation in the college yard. Most significant of all was the fact that while many of the Puritan leaders did not believe in separating church and state, in matters of learning they left their teachers free. No oath of allegiance to church or government was exacted of either faculty or students and the corporation of Harvard in its charter from the General Court was made autonomous. It is to the credit of the General Court that in spite of pressure at various times it has never compromised Harvard's academic freedom.

In many ways the foundation of Harvard was the greatest early American event. Though probably few thought that in creating it they were pointing the way to a new society in a new world, one cannot help feeling that there were some who did, for they planted their seed of education at the edge of the wilderness.

It was not surprising, therefore, that in 1636 some men should experience what they themselves termed "a strong bent of their spirits for change." The first contingent to move left Dorchester for Windsor in repetition of an expedition of around a hundred men, women, and children who had set out overland late in October 1635 under Captain John Mason to make sure of beating the Dutch or possibly Plymouth people to occupation of their chosen site. Speed was essential, so they traveled light, taking what they could carry on their backs (they had no horses) and depending for the children's food on the few cows they drove before them — and necessarily on that kind of forced march through the woods the milk would not amount to much. All their winter stores had been shipped on small boats to sail around Cape Cod to the Connecticut and up the latter to the mouth of the Farmington River. There was still color on the leaves when they set out, but winter cold had already begun to clench the land; their campfires at night seemed small, more comforting for light than warmth; women nursing their babies in front of them felt the chill of darkness on their shoulders. It took them fourteen days of hard marching to reach the Connecticut, and many felt that without the leadership of Captain Mason they would never have seen it at all.

There is no record of how they crossed the river, which was running high. More than likely it was the Mohicans who took them over in canoes. They had no way of ferrying the cattle, most of which strayed in the woods to fall prey to wolves or simply die in the hardness of the winter. It had started early. By mid-November the Connecticut froze over. By December in their roughly built cabins the settlers were confronted with near zero cold. The boats which were to have brought their winter stores never reached the Connecticut; they were wrecked, with the loss of several crew. None of the stores were saved, and the people at Windsor faced starvation.

Six men had already gone down to Fort Saybrook to look for news of the provision boats. There they found a small vessel about to sail for Boston and joined her. They themselves suffered shipwreck on the voyage but managed to make shore and finally reached Boston half dead with cold and hunger. Now in early December thirteen more men decided it was time to leave. They struck overland for Boston and managed to get through with the loss of one man drowned in crossing a stream. Meanwhile seventy more men and women with their children saw for themselves the specter of starvation and went down the river to Saybrook, again with the hope of finding the provision boats. Like the preceding party of six they were disappointed, but also like them they found a vessel waiting, a 60-ton bark bound for Boston. She was icebound, so they joined the crew in chopping out a channel to open water; and after unloading the ship to float her over a bar and then reloading her, they too finally reached their old homes. By then it was too late to think of sending aid to Windsor.

Only a few people remained. They had watched three parties leave the settlement with none coming back, no word sent to say they would get help. The winter that closed down was one of the bitterest since the Pilgrim landing, the snow so deep they realized that they were imprisoned. Their scanty wheat had long since gone, they had no bread, their only grain came from what small offerings of Indian corn near-by Mohicans were able to spare. Game was very scarce. The depth of snow made hunting almost impossible. When the snow left they scoured the woods for acorns, from which they had seen the Indians make a kind of flour. They also found groundnuts, which had helped the Pilgrims get through their first winter and were a favorite food among the eastern Indian tribes. The dried whitish vines led down to roots on which tubers grew "as big as Egges, and as good as Potatoes, and 40 on a string and not two

[205]

inches under ground," according to Captain John Smith's description, though it seems doubtful that the hungry settlers of Windsor found many strings as long as that. There is no list of their names. But more than any who were in the valley before them or came later they were the true founders of Connecticut. Not that they regarded themselves as such; they only looked at one another with grim wonder at their own survival.

In June, however, stronger and better organized groups began the westward movement from the Bay towns. Over a hundred men and women and their children, his entire congregation, made up the party that Reverend Thomas Hooker led out of Cambridge, driving their one hundred and sixty cattle before them. They had sold their houses to a congregation newly come from England and they turned their faces west with a sense of finality and a sense, too, of cheerful confidence that marked all of their two weeks' journey to the Connecticut. Mrs. Hooker, too ill to walk, was taken in a litter. They suffered no real hardship except from the swarms of black flies and mosquitoes. As a congregation they seem to have been close-knit; undoubtedly they were inspired by the leadership of their pastor. Hooker was one of the few to have rejected publicly Winthrop's view that in matters of public policy a superior minority was best fitted to rule, and of such minority "the wiser part is always the lesser." On the contrary, Hooker maintained, a general council chosen by all was the proper instrument of government and best designed to protect and further the interests of the people. So almost at the outset were stated the basically opposing views that would later find their great protagonists in Hamilton and Jefferson.

Meanwhile the Dorchester and Watertown groups were also traveling to the Connecticut, the former again marching overland, the latter prudently hiring a ship to carry them and their effects to their projected settlement at Wethersfield. At first the three towns were claimed by Massachusetts (the proprietors of Saybrook also maintained without effect that the three towns should come under their jurisdiction) and affairs were supervised by commissioners. While the settlers were busy with their first crops and building houses and palisades about the towns there was no objection; but at the end of a year they began to feel the mistrust of governments left behind that became a ruling characteristic of the American frontiersman and chose representatives for a General Court of their own.

It was at the opening session of this Court on May 31, 1638, that Hooker delivered his famous sermon in which he maintained that "the foundation of authority is laid, firstly, in the free consent of the people"; that "the choice of public magistrates belongs unto the people by God's own allowance"; and that "those who have the power to appoint officers and magistrates, it is in their power, also, to set the bounds and limitations of the power and place to which they call them." This trinity of principles forms the basis of all democratic government and no one since has stated them more cogently. The delegates at Hartford were deeply impressed and resolved to have a written constitution in which they would be embodied. The result was the Fundamental Orders of Connecticut, adopted at an assembly of all the freemen of the three towns in January 1639, the first constitution creating a government and defining its powers that was ever written. What was more it worked, serving the people well until 1662 when, after the Restoration, the three towns were incorporated with the New Haven settlements under royal charter as the colony of Connecticut. This charter however, was the most liberal granted to an American colony, except that to Rhode Island the following year, and though superseding did little to change the liberal form of government created by the Fundamental Orders.

The General Court sat twice a year, in April and September, months in which traveling conditions could be counted on as reasonably good but coming before the rush of spring planting and after the main harvest. The principal order of business at the April session was the election of public officers for the coming year, most important of whom were the six magistrates from whose number the governor was chosen. He and his council were elected by a majority vote of all the freemen, which under the Fundamental Orders amounted very nearly to universal suffrage. There were no religious restrictions to being a freeman. Any man who had been accepted as a member of his town and taken an oath of allegiance to the commonwealth was automatically considered a freeman. With the election of officials out of the way the Court proceeded to its business of administering the commonwealth. Four delegates from each of the three towns sat with the governor who, if necessary, cast the deciding vote. Being a delegate was anything but a sinecure, for sessions began an hour after sunrise and a man was stiffly fined for being late.

One of the significant things about the Fundamental Orders was the absence of any reference to the Crown; there was not even an allusion to the mother country. This was not because the little federation of towns was disloyal; on the contrary, a man was fined as much as twenty-five pounds for using language derogatory to the king, and until the Revolution Connecticut would remain in many ways the most loyal of all the colonies. But just as crossing the Atlantic worked changes in the way men thought, so leaving the ocean behind them across a hundred miles of wilderness intensified the ordinary man's determination to have his say about the form of government he was going to live under. Here, where he had cleared a piece of land and taken it for his own, building himself a habitation not very much inferior to that built by the wealthier of his fellow settlers, the authority of the parent colony from which he had come seemed now infinitely remote, to say nothing of the authority of the Crown. In the wilderness the only possible source of authority by which a local government could function was the consent of the settlers themselves. So under the Fundamental Orders, except for powers explicitly spelled out for the General Court, authority remained vested in the three towns, a fact annually reasserted by the vote of the freemen.

But if the representative government they had set up was surprisingly liberal for its time, they were still Puritans enough to preserve rigid moral restrictions. Attendance at church both for service and the weekly lecture was compulsory. Profanity even of the mildest sort was inexorably fined. Sexual immorality brought whipping, usually repeated in at least one of the other towns, sometimes at monthly intervals. Anyone caught in adultery faced death. Even to kiss one's wife on the Sabbath made one liable to an hour or so in the stocks. In a way of life in which opportunities for amusement were almost nonexistent such harsh repression must have calloused the human soul. It was, perhaps, as well. In their second year, before they could take time to formulate their government, the Connecticut settlers found themselves confronted by an Indian war.

Till then the Pequots had had little contact with either English or Dutch, having been too preoccupied with their campaigns against their neighbors. The coastal settlements of the English seemed too removed to be a danger to them, and the power of the Dutch was plainly negligible; but now, suddenly, a whole chain of English communities had sprung into being at their back door. They felt themselves hemmed in. If these communities were to grow or, worse still, if English moved into the Thames Valley, they would lose their hunting grounds.

The necessity of great ranges of woods to the Indian was something that the English settler was never able to grasp. An Englishman could support himself and his family on a good deal less than a twentieth of the land an Indian needed for his hunting, and if the Indian was to survive in the way of life that was natural to him the land had to remain wilderness, while the Englishman's driving purpose was to tame it into farmland, and so destroy it. This was the basis of all white and Indian conflict, but the English had given the New England Indians other reasons to fear and mistrust them.

In 1615 an enterprising shipmaster named Thomas Hunt, while loading dried codfish off the Indian village of Patuxet, which John Smith had renamed Plymouth the year before, enticed some twenty Wampanoags aboard on the eve of sailing, kidnaped them, and sold them as slaves to the Spanish at Malaga. According to orthdox Puritan history, half legend and half parable, one of these captives was rescued from slavery by the

Jesuits, who began to educate him. But he managed to escape to England where he spent a year before being returned to his native shore. There in the spirit of returning good for evil he came to the Pilgrims' camp when they were ill and starving and hope had almost flickered out, with the words, "Welcome, Englishmen." They called him Squanto in the books, and whether he had actually seen Spain and England or not, he seems to have shown them how to save their lives by planting corn and leading them to the Indian fishing grounds.

But long before his return, word of the kidnaping had spread among the coastal tribes; more than ten years later settlers hunting lost children or strayed cattle would find people who were still full of the crime or claimed to be relations of the abducted Indians. It laid the basis of a deep mistrust which almost immediately was fortified with fear when a plague, almost certainly it was smallpox, struck the eastern New England tribes from Cape Cod to the Penobscot and all but wiped them out; estimates of those dying varying from fifty to as high as ninety percent. For so terrible a catastrophe some explanation had to be found, and it was finally decided that the epidemic was a retribution for the haphazard murder of two English sailors some time earlier. So, in the minds of many, in addition to gunpowder the English carried the power to let loose a plague.

The English accepted the plague as evidence of God's favor to themselves. The Pilgrims going ashore found at Patuxet only a dead, decaying cluster of Indian huts, the bones of their former occupants lying within them or without, wherever they had fallen. The worst-hit tribes had been the Wampanoag and Massachusett — in the country of the latter a wandering Puritan thought he had come upon a new-found Golgotha, and years afterward Cotton Mather wrote that the woods "were almost cleared of those pernicious creatures to make room for a better growth." This conception of God's favor would have been more convincing had it not been for the fact that the two most powerful tribes in New England, the most warlike and instinctively hostile to arriving white men, had been left untouched. These were the Narragansetts and the Pequots.

One cannot, however, accept the effect of the epidemic as the reason for the Wampanoags' acceptance of the Pilgrims. At any moment during the first two years they could have wiped out the English colony. The friendliness of Squanto and then of Samoset, who brought the Massasoit or chief sachem of the tribe to parley with them is attributable more to generosity than fear; and in 1621 Massasoit, which the English assumed to be his name, made a treaty of peace which he kept until his death in 1660, restraining the more hotheaded of his young men in spite of continuing encroachment by the whites, even when this led to murder.

One of the merchant adventurers who had financed the *Mayflower* expedition, Thomas Weston, decided to break away from the partnership and found a colony of his own. In 1622 he sent out a company of seventy, mostly riffraff from the London streets, who came ashore near Wey-mouth. They were entirely unqualified to plant their own crops or look after themselves in the wilderness and soon went into the Indian villages near by to beg or steal as they saw fit or help themselves to the available squaws. The Indians at first bore with them, gave them enough food to keep them from starving; but as the Londoners became increasingly reck-less and overbearing, Indian friendship turned to resentment and before long two chiefs organized a plot to massacre the whole settlement.

When Massasoit heard of it he sent word to Plymouth of what was in the wind, and Miles Standish, realizing instantly that a massacre of one settlement could easily ignite a spark that would lead to a wiping out of all the English, sent a message to the two chiefs, one of whom bore the interesting name of Peeksnot, asking them to come to see him. They ac-cepted, but as soon as they had entered the stockade he and his soldiers killed them.

This was salutary action with a vengeance, but at the time it worked. The plot to massacre the white men was dropped, and the colony of Londoners soon, to their own relief, returned to England. But for many Indians the double murder was searing confirmation of their mistrust of the white man. That Peeksnot and his companion chief were themselves planning wholesale murder did not in the Indian mind alter the fact that they had accepted an invitation in good faith, only to be fallen on and slaughtered. Yet the very violence of Standish's act achieved his end. Any idea of killing off the English was for the moment abandoned.

One could not expect the English settlers to feel compunction. Their view of the wilderness was one of Satanic menace. They "found the Province fill'd with vast Herds of Salvages, that never saw so much as a *Knife*, or a *Nail*, or a *Board*, or a *Grain* of *Salt*, in all their Days. No better would the Devil have the World provided for," wrote Cotton Mather. The Indian was a creature of the wilderness, no more significant in God's eye or the settlers' than an animal, a conviction simply illustrated by church regulations in Fort Saybrook which provided for a Sabbath guard at the church door, a lookout in the tower, and the bearing of arms to service, though no musket under any pretext was to be fired on a Sun-day, except at an Indian or a wolf.

The Pequots were described by one Puritan chronicler as a stately and warlike people who until the war with them broke out had been guilty of no misdemeanors but were on the contrary just and honorable in their dealings. Their chief sachem and war chief, Sassacus, was an almost leg-endary figure under whose leadership the Pequots, numbering about eight hundred warriors, had become as terrible a scourge to their neighbor tribes as the Mohawks. Even Miantonomo, second sachem of the more numerous Narragansetts, considered him more than human and declared

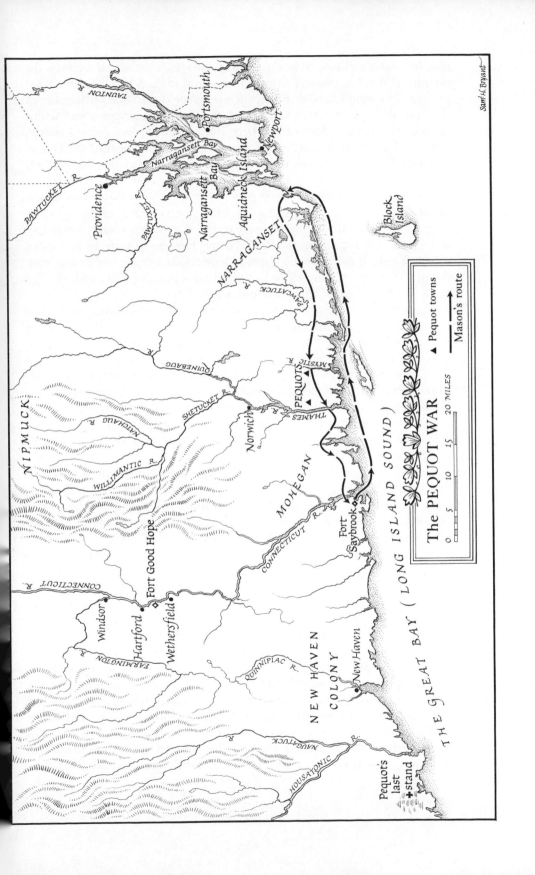

Sam'l H. Bryant

THE PEQUOT WAR

▲ Pequot towns
→ Mason's route

0   5   10   15   20 MILES

TAUNTON R.

Portsmouth

Narragansett Bay

Newport

Aquidneck Island

PAWTUCKET R.

Providence

PAWTUCKET R.

NARRAGANSET

NARRAGANSETT R.

Block
Island

QUINEBAUG R.

PAWCATUCK R.

NIPMUCK

SHETUCKET R.

NATCHAUG R.

WILLIMANTIC R.

Norwich

MYSTIC R.

PEQUOTS ▲
▲

THAMES R.

MOHEGAN

CONNECTICUT R.

Fort
Saybrook ◇

THE GREAT BAY (LONG ISLAND SOUND)

Windsor

Hartford

Fort Good Hope

Wethersfield

FARMINGTON R.

CONNECTICUT R.

NEW HAVEN
COLONY

QUINNIPIAC R.

New Haven

NAUGATUCK R.

HOUSATONIC R.

Pequot's last
stand ✚

that he was unkillable. Their palisaded villages were mostly above the mouths of the Thames and Mystic rivers, and if they had thought it important they could have marched against either the coastal settlements of the English or, in the first year, against the Connecticut towns and wiped them out by sheer weight of numbers. But originally they had no quarrel with the English, their animosity being directed mostly against the Dutch, and actually they were not responsible for the incidents that touched off the war.

The first of these was the killing of two traders with their crew on the lower Connecticut in 1633. The leader of the party was a sea captain from Virginia named John Stone whose flagrant immoralities had caused him to be twice expelled from the Bay Colony. For this voyage he had taken a New England partner, one Captain Norton, and being unfamiliar with the mouth of the Connecticut had hired two Indian guides and allowed them to bring eight of their friends on board.

These Indians were not properly Pequots, under Sassacus's jurisdiction, but members of a disaffected group of the tribe which had splintered off under the leadership of an elderly chief named Totobam. Unlike Uncas, who had led another group from the Pequot towns to settle farther up the Connecticut and who with deadly enmity toward Sassacus now declared himself a Mohegan, Totobam and his people still considered themselves Pequot and though aloof remained on reasonably friendly terms with the parent tribe. But because of their removal Sassacus did not consider himself responsible for what presently happened to the immoral Captain Stone.

He had worked his vessel across the sand bars but darkness overtook him before he had gone only a short way upriver and he anchored in midstream. During that night the Indians murdered him and every white man aboard. The only one to offer any resistance was Captain Norton, who barricaded himself in the galley and fired his musket from the windows. But to maintain a rapid rate of fire he was loading from an open pan of powder and this suddenly exploded in his face, blinding him. The Indians had no trouble breaking in then and killing him. The boat was theirs but then, according to reports that came back to the Pequot towns, it inexplicably blew up.

The incident troubled Sassacus, who without doubt remembered Standish's reaction to what was only intended murder, and he sent an embassy of two to the Bay Colony to ask for a treaty of friendship. By then the English had heard of Stone's fate. They listened somewhat grimly to the ambassadors' disclaimer of responsibility for their own tribe. Not only had the ship blown up, the latter reported, with no profit to any Indian, but of the ten who had taken part in the affray eight had since died of smallpox, and then Totobam, the chief of the tribe to which the murderers belonged, had been taken by the Dutch and put to death. To their

[212]

way of thinking, all impediments to a treaty of peace were thus removed.

The English were inclined to believe their account and agreed to a treaty provided that the two surviving murderers were handed over to them. The Pequot ambassadors accepted this stipulation and gifts were exchanged and the treaty signed. As evidence of their desire for peace they even signed a treaty under English auspices with a party of Narragansetts who had arrived in the colony. Then they went their way and for a time all was quiet. But the two murderers were not handed over.

Early in 1636 report reached Boston of restiveness among the Pequots and there were rumors of sporadic, minor attacks on settlers, which were attributed to them. They were seen constantly in the neighborhood of Fort Saybrook. Then, in July, Captain John Gallup sailed his shallop into the harbor with shocking news. Off Block Island he had come upon John Oldham's pinnace, adrift with Indians on deck, and as he drew near, a canoe put off from the side, heavily loaded, and paddled frantically for the shore.

Gallup, who had only one man and two young boys for crew, dared not board the pinnace with Indians on her deck, so he decided to ram her. The impact and roll terrified the Indians, most of whom jumped overboard to drown. A second ramming sent all but four of the rest overboard where, like their predecessors, they also drowned. As Gallup went aboard her, two more Indians appeared. He made them prisoners and left them bound in the cabin. When they told him there were still two more in the hold, he battened down the hatches.

Oldham had been killed. He was lying on deck. His head and hands and feet had been cut off and arranged beside him, a practice indulged in by many Indians when there was going to be no opportunity for torture, and a large part of his trade goods had already been removed. What remained Gallup put into his own boat. He intended to bring the pinnace back to Boston with her grisly freight, but before taking her in tow, fearing that two Indians together in the cabin would find some way of untying each other, he threw one overboard and took the other into his own shallop. After a few hours, however, the wind turned against him and he was compelled to let the pinnace, with the two Indians still in her hold, go free. What became of them no one knew and probably few cared. But the whole colony was aroused by Oldham's murder.

The Indians of Block Island supposedly were Narragansetts, so Henry Vane, who was governor at the time, sent a deputation to Canonicus, their principal sachem, to demand an explanation. Oldham had been known for his fair dealing with the Indians and had always been received by them with friendship and respect. Canonicus had no explanation to give, except that the murderers had taken refuge among the Pequots. He agreed to send Miantonomo to get them, but instead of bringing in the murderers Miantonomo returned with two boys who had been members of Oldham's crew and the promise that Oldham's trade goods would be given up. It was a good political compromise from the Indian point of view, but in this case it was not enough.

The Bay colonists had been reasonably complacent about the excuses and equivocations in the case of Captain Stone, but after the murder of Oldham it assumed a new importance. Vane chose John Endicott to lead an expedition to Block Island, where he had orders to kill all male Indians but take the women and children prisoners (which meant they would be sold as slaves), to "take Possession of the island," and afterward to sail to the Thames River and demand the murderers of Captain Stone as well as damages of six thousand feet of wampum. If the Pequots did not comply, Endicott was to use force.

The second part of the order seemed hardly realistic, since Endicott had only ninety volunteers, though these included the experienced soldier, Captain Underhill, while Sassacus could command eight hundred warriors. Nevertheless they sailed in three small vessels for Block Island where after a brief skirmish they forced a landing, put the Indians to flight, and burned two villages of wigwams, destroying all the corn they could find. They took no prisoners, their only loot was mats and baskets, but they had reason to feel pleased as they set sail for Fort Saybrook because they had not lost a man.

At the fort Captain Lyon Gardiner was anything but pleased to see them. They would only infuriate the Pequots, he maintained, and then return to Boston leaving the Connecticut settlement at their mercy. His small garrison could give no protection to the river towns; they would have all they could do to hold the fort. However, Endicott would not be deterred and in the end Gardiner contributed a few of his soldiers in a shallop to the expedition in the hope they might be able to lay hold of a supply of Indian corn.

When the flotilla of four little boats sailed into the mouth of the Thames there were Pequots on both shores. They ran along the river edge as the shallops moved upstream shouting questions: had the English come in anger, did they want war, did they want to fight? Approaching darkness made it hard to count their numbers and the English were afraid to risk a landing. They anchored in midstream, lying on their arms, their eyes fixed on the bright points of Indian fires, while the Pequots kept the night alive by calling back and forth to one another, strange birdlike voices, high and mournful. To the listening Englishmen it seemed certain that they were calling for reinforcements, perhaps to attack them where they lay upon the river.

But dawn came with no attack and only a single canoe put out from shore. The spokesman, evidently a man of some importance, asked Endicott the reason for his coming with so many men. Endicott replied with a terse demand for the murderers of Captain Stone and the enormous reparation in wampum. He also wanted some Pequot children as hostages.

With the gift for sliding off a tricky point that marked most Indian negotiations, the Pequot launched into a "real" explanation of Stone's killing. Apparently a Dutch trader had enticed a sachem of the tribe aboard his ship and then killed him. The sachem's son had vowed revenge against the Dutch and killed the next sea captain to come into the river. He could hardly be blamed for a mistake so rooted in filial emotion; it was an accident and involved no enmity toward the English.

This would not do as far as Endicott was concerned. He would have the murderers or he would make war. And anyway he wanted to deal with Sassacus. Sassacus, as it happened, was not there but on Long Island, and the other chiefs were absent, too, though they would return before long. In this impasse it was agreed that the Pequots would draw back from the shore to let the English land. Then the exchanges were resumed, passing back and forth through the lips of Endicott's Indian interpreter, a time-consuming process which might have continued indefinitely if it had not dawned on the English that the Indian women and children, all heavily loaded, had been steadily moving out of the town for hours. Realizing that he had been duped, Endicott halted the negotiations abruptly by declaring war. The Pequots after one ineffective shower of arrows fled and Endicott and his men marched into the empty town, burned wigwams, dug up corn where they could find the caches, and destroyed the crops, "spoiling the country" as Underhill put it. The only Pequot to be killed was a brave discovered hiding in a thicket by Endicott's interpreter, a Massachusett, who later with the bravado of a member of a tribe that has lost standing sent the scalp to Canonicus, the Narragansett — an act that roused the Pequots to fury and in Gardiner's opinion was the spark that exploded the war.

Next day Endicott and his Massachusetts men started home, leaving Gardiner's soldiers to wait a favorable wind. They were to have another skirmish of their own with the Pequots while they were carrying out Gardiner's instructions to get corn. Seeing no Indians about, they had gone to the one field left standing and harvested two baskets of ears, but on their second trip the Pequots jumped them and they were lucky to escape with their pittance of corn and take Gardiner news of the expedition.

Endicott had inflicted enough harm to enrage the Pequots, but not enough to overawe them. His visit also convinced Sassacus that there was not room for both the English and the Indians in his country. He saw too that the most effective way of expelling the English was for the Indian tribes to unite and, swallowing his instinctive antagonism, he determined to make allies of his Narragansett enemies so that both tribes might strike as one when summer came.

*   *   *

The winter of 1636–1637 was almost as hard as the one before it, but the English along the Connecticut did not look forward to the spring. During the time of heavy snow they were left unmolested. Fort Saybrook, however, which lay scarcely twenty miles from the lower Pequot towns, soon found itself in a state of siege. Parties of Indians were continually seen from the palisades. Gardiner had only twenty-four men and women as a garrison, yet fodder had to be brought in for the animals and wheat and corn harvested. Two of the small foraging parties he sent out were ambushed early in the fall. From the first, one man was captured and burned. In the second, two men were killed, ripped open like hogs, their bodies split and the halves left hanging in the trees. A third captive, an old man, was also burned. Gardiner with a fatigue party was himself ambushed while burning brush about the fort to clear his field of fire, and one man, shot through with an arrow, died. Then the Pequots captured a man named Tilly from upriver who had come with a companion to hunt near the fort, and tortured him with every long-drawn agony they could think up. The garrison no longer dared hunt or fish. They were close to starvation rations when Captain John Mason with twenty men and a boatload of provisions came down the river from Windsor.

With this reinforcement of the garrison the Pequots lost interest in their harassment and Mason claimed that during the month he spent at Saybrook he never laid eyes on a hostile Indian. Meanwhile messages had gone from Hartford to Massachusetts criticizing Endicott's expedition and demanding reinforcement for Fort Saybrook. As a result Captain Underhill was dispatched with twenty men from Boston, and on his arrival Mason took his own contingent back upriver to Windsor. Spring was at hand.

Word had also reached Boston of the intention of Sassacus to bring the Narragansetts into the war, and the council at once wrote Roger Williams, whom they had evicted the year before, to try to prevent this red alliance. Williams put aside any resentment he may have felt and immediately headed for Canonicus's town, ". . . scarce acquainting my wife, to ship myself all alone in a poore canow, and to cut through a stormie wind. . . ." No matter what he thought of the Indians' rights, in crisis his white man's blood ruled him. He knew he was risking his life in confronting the Pequot ambassadors, for Canonicus with mordant humor saw fit to lodge them together. "Three dayes and nights my business forced me to lodge and mix with the bloudie Pequot ambassadours, whose hands and arms, methought, reaked with the bloud of my countriemen, murther'd and massacred by them on Connecticut river and from whome I could not but nightly looke for their bloudie knives at my owne throate also." However, he prevailed and with God's help, as he dutifully acknowledged, was able "to break to pieces the Pequots negociation and designe," though the bitter hatred between the two tribes must also have contributed to the Narragansett rejection of the proposed alliance. Canonicus and Miantonomo could think of nothing more to their taste than the sight of the English falling on their traditional foe. They went further. They gave the English permission to cross their territory with an army if it served their purpose to do so, and in the event they even joined the English with a force of four hundred warriors who, however, accompanied the expedition more in the spirit of ticket holders than men of war.

Williams was right enough about the Pequots' "bloudie hands." As the winter snow drained from the woods, bands of Pequots began waylaying settlers on the trails or alone in their fields and followed these ambushes with the customary mutilations or torture. Such incidents were mere forerunners of a raid that struck Wethersfield on the morning of April 23. Two hundred Pequots who had paddled up the Connecticut and lain hidden in a creek the night before fell upon the settlers who were beginning their spring planting. Six men and three women were shot down, two young girls were taken prisoners, and some twenty cattle killed. This may have been the first time the English were made aware of the Indians' delight in killing cows. It may indeed have been the first taste the Indians had of the sport. Something about the sight of a wounded cow, especially one newly freshened, bellowing and gushing blood and bucketing frantically about in the underbrush, udder lashing from side to side and teats spraying milk, appealed immoderately to the Indians' sense of the grotesque and wildly excited them.

Though this was a fearful blow for Wethersfield and left no question of the need to crush the Pequots, what seems to have most concerned the minds of the survivors was the capture of the two girls, the older of whom was only sixteen. Something of a legend began immediately to grow about their fate. Lyon Gardiner saw the flotilla of the war party coming down the river, the paddlers shouting jibes and triumphantly waving the clothes of their white victims, and he could not refrain from firing one round of a cannon at them. The ball tore off the bow of a canoe which, of course, as Mason — who may or may not have been there — recorded, had to be the one "wherein our two Captives were."

At the Pequot town to which they were taken the girls were befriended by an Indian woman, the wife of a war chief named Monotto, and though they were stripped of their clothes they came to no harm, even when the Indians finally were convinced that they did not know the secret of making gunpowder, and were not unkindly treated according to the older girl, who seems to have kept her wits about her, used her eyes, remembered her prayers, and never lost her faith in God as her ultimate rescuer.

However, in this instance she was rescued with the other girl by a Dutch sea captain whose boat had been off Fort Saybrook about the time of the raid, and with the urging of Lyon Gardiner he agreed to try his hand at ransoming the girls. When his first and generous offer was refused he simply took prisoners six of the Pequots who had come aboard to negotiate and held *them* for ransom. The Pequots delivered the girls, virtually naked, and it is said that the Dutch sailors gave them their coats.

It was also claimed that this gallant ransoming was due to Governor Van Twiller's direct intervention. Having heard of the Wethersfield attack and the capture of the two interesting young maidens, he instantly commissioned a ship for the mission and sent it on its way; but though it is not impossible, it does not seem likely. The instantaneous decision which alone could have got the vessel over from New Amsterdam and back in time for the girls to be interviewed before the English punitive force left Fort Saybrook for the Pequot Country is not in character, nor is the expense involved. But the romance of the girls' capture and rescue was captivating and a man like Van Twiller would not unnaturally have enjoyed a claim to gallantry.

The Connecticut settlers realized that the Pequots must be put down at once and that if the other colonies sent no reinforcements they would have to act alone. Accordingly the General Court called for a draft of ninety men from the three towns: forty-two from Hartford, thirty from Windsor, and eighteen from stricken Wethersfield. Captain John Mason was appointed to command this little army, rates of pay were voted, and supplies both of weapons and rations were specified, including a generous quantity of good beer. There was no time for training of any kind; the provisions had to be brought together and, most important, the Mohegans had to be approached. But here there was no difficulty. Uncas was only too eager to act against his former fellow tribesmen; he came to the rendezvous with seventy braves; and though the English entertained some doubts about him, he proved a staunch and faithful ally. Meanwhile Massachusetts and Plymouth were notified of the expedition. Massachusetts promised two hundred men and Plymouth fifty, but none of these were seen until after Mason and his force emerged victorious from the Pequot country.

Mason took his force of one hundred and sixty English and Mohegans down the river in three small vessels. Unfamiliar with the river channel, they often grounded on sand bars and had to work themselves off, a slow and tedious process which the Indians soon tired of, and Uncas asked permission to go ashore with his Mohegans, promising to meet the boats at Saybrook. Mason agreed, though many of his men protested; they were sure that Uncas would not be seen again or, even worse, that he might betray them to the Pequots. Instead Uncas surprised a small Pequot war party, fell on them, killed five, and took one prisoner. When the English reached Fort Saybrook he was already there waiting for them with his prisoner and the heads of the dead Pequots handsomely impaled along the palisades.

When they saw the size of Mason's force and how meagerly they were supplied with arms, both Gardiner and Underhill were aghast. His force, they declared, was entirely unfit to carry out the orders given it by the General Court, which were to sail into the Pequot River and attack the forts. Both said they would not let any of their men join such a foolhardy venture. Mason remained apparently unperturbed by their doubts. During the two days he and his men rested at the fort he interviewed the girl captives and learned that the Pequot town in which they had been held contained sixteen muskets, that the Indians maintained an all-night guard, and that they also had men posted along the river. This led Mason to propose openly what must have been in his mind from the beginning: to go past the Pequot country to Narragansett Bay and then attack the Pequots from the east.

Neither Gardiner nor Underhill considered this any more feasible than the frontal attack, and others took their point of view. Mason went to the troops' chaplain and asked him to pray for divine guidance during the night. At the same time he outlined for Chaplain Stone his own ideas and the reasons for them — one must assume with force and some eloquence, for in the morning the chaplain announced that God approved the captain's plans. No more opposition was raised after that and Underhill, in spite of his previous doubts, asked leave to join the expedition with his nineteen men. When Gardiner granted the request Mason, to what must have been Underhill's dismay, promptly sent twenty of his own men back upriver to reinforce the home garrisons.

So his force was still ninety English and seventy Mohegans when he sailed out of the mouth of the Connecticut on the morning of May 20. They passed the mouth of the Thames well offshore but in full view of Pequot lookouts who yelled in triumph to see them pass, convinced as it turned out that this English force wanted no more than Endicott's to do real battle with them.

It was late on Saturday evening when the flotilla reached Point Judith and turned up into Narragansett Bay. They anchored offshore for the night and as the next day was Sunday stayed where they were all day while Chaplain Stone held services in one ship after the other. It was a day both tense and tranquil and the hours dragged. But after it was over the action through which Mason led them was rapid and without a break.

On Monday morning he went ashore at the first landing place above Point Judith and made his way to Canonicus's town and held a council with Canonicus and Miantonomo, explaining that the need of absolute secrecy had prevented his sending advance notice of the arrival of his army. The Narragansetts again gave permission for the passage of the English through their country but took a cynical view of their chances of success. Tuesday morning Mason heard from a Massachusetts commander, Captain Patrick, that he was at Roger Williams's settlement with forty men and would join Mason as soon as possible. He did not show during Tuesday, so early Wednesday Mason decided to march without him. He left thirteen men on the boats to work them around to the mouth of the Thames where they should lie waiting for his army, and then set off toward the Pequot country.

He now had seventy-seven English and sixty Mohicans. About two hundred Narragansetts had asked to join them, but they kept well in the rear throughout the march. The army made nearly twenty miles before bivouacking, a good performance considering the hot weather, the narrow Indian trails, and the weight of arms and supplies they had to carry. They camped close to a Narragansett fortified town whose inhabitants greeted them with undisguised resentment, no doubt because of their own proximity to the Pequot border. They refused to allow any English inside their palisades, and Mason countered by throwing a guard around the town with orders to shoot any Indian seen trying to leave. In the morning the situation was eased somewhat by the arrival of Miantonomo himself with another one hundred and sixty Narragansetts who had come along to see the show. They insisted on holding a council to predict the fury with which they were going to fight, but no one, probably not even themselves, took them seriously; and as soon as possible Mason gave the order to march.

There were now some five hundred men trailing through the woods, and the chances of discovery as they entered the Pequot country were very much enlarged. The heat continued. Some men, overcome, fell out of the line of march, and when the little army came out on the bank of the Pawcatuck River, Mason called a halt. During the time of rest the men noticed that the ranks of the Narragansetts had thinned considerably. This was a favorite fishing place of the Pequots and many of the Narragansetts had suddenly decided that the march was becoming too dangerous and had returned home. Uncas had already predicted that the Narragansetts would have no stomach for a fight, but he now reiterated his promise that he and his Mohegans would stand by the English, and so it proved.

They marched again in the afternoon. After an hour they came on a cornfield and knew they were getting close to the Pequot towns. At the same time scouts came back to them with the information that the Pequots had two fortified towns about two miles apart. Mason and Underhill discussed the possibility of attacking both simultaneously, but realized that this would be impossible for their small force. They would assault the nearer and beat off any counterattack that might develop from the second.

The march was now resumed under orders of the strictest silence.

Toward night they found a camping place near the Mystic River, a cleft between rock walls that hid them well. Here late at night their Indian spies found them again and reported that the Pequots were evidently still celebrating what they supposed to be the return of an intimidated English army to Boston.

There was a brilliant moon, the night was almost light as day when Mason again gave the order to march. The scouts led them along trails and then halted at the foot of a long grade. The Pequot town, they said, was at the top of the hill; it was surrounded by a circular palisade which had two narrow entrances at opposite sides. Mason and Underhill in a final consultation decided that each with sixteen men would seal a gate while the rest of the English and Mohegans surrounded the palisade.

Once again the little army started, moving up the hill in all possible silence. There was no sound ahead. Evidently after a night of feasting and dancing the Pequots were sleeping the sleep of exhaustion. The palisade came into view, a ring of tree trunks twelve feet high, the tops bound together and with space enough between to fire through. This was a common sort of Indian palisade built with entire disregard of the fact that it could be as useful to the attacker as to the defender. Whoever first seized the perimeter was master of the fight, and now it was nearly within Mason's grasp. A dog barked. A sleepy brave looked out between the trunks and saw muskets and here and there a helmet in the moonlight. The cry of "English! English!" rang through the town; but it was too late. Braves stumbled out of their wigwams, eyes sticky and wits still glazed with sleep, unable for the moment to take in the calamity. Then when they rushed to the two entrances they met Underhill and his men at one and Mason at the other, and at each a galling musket fire. Recoiling they dashed back into the wigwams, and the whole area within the palisade, two acres or more, boiled with confusion. Guns fired into them from all around the palisade. There was no escape hole anywhere.

Mason had hoped to capture the town whole and plunder it for furs and anything else he might find. But when he entered a wigwam the bed mats upheaved and he was barely able to fight his way free from the men who leaped from under them. As he came into the open again he realized that the only way to deal with the situation was to set fire to the town. Dashing into the same wigwam with one soldier as escort he seized a brand from the fire and touched it to the bark sides. It caught instantly; in a moment the fire leaped to another. The bark covering after the long hot days was tinder-dry. A wall of fire swept across the town. To some of the English looking through the palisade it seemed that the air itself was burning. Beneath, there was seething pandemonium.

The Pequots trying to break through or climb the palisade were driven back by English musket fire and Mohegan arrows and often in their panic dashed back into the blazing wigwams for cover, their yells joining the shrieks of the woman and children while Uncas's warriors yelled back in pitiless mockery. The very few who managed to get over the palisade were quickly hunted down. As dawn lit the sky above the tranquil valley mists, the fires began to subside. The voices had been stilled long before. Only the smell of charred human flesh remained to remind the little army of the infernal episode they had taken part in. Seven Pequots were sullen prisoners in the hands of the Mohegans. Seven were said to have escaped, sole survivors of the seven hundred or so who had thronged the town the night before to celebrate the supposed retreat of the English. Sassacus was reported as being still alive, but at one blow Mason had broken his power. To the colonists it was a "sweet sacrifice and they gave praise thereof to God."

The aftermath stretched on for two months more. Mason marched his little army for the Thames where his boats were to be waiting. On the way some braves from the other fort made a halfhearted attempt at a pursuing fight but were beaten off. Two of his men had been killed in the fighting at the fort and sixteen wounded. In these skirmishes a few more had been wounded; but he brought all his people through and as they came out on the river and saw their boats waiting for them their one regret was that their drum had been left behind, forgotten, at their camp-site between the rocks.

Their marching, however, was not yet over. The dilatory Captain Patrick with his forty Massachusetts men had found Mason's flotilla before it sailed from Narragansett Bay and had appropriated one of the boats for themselves. They were now waiting offshore "to rescue" Mason's army as Patrick put it, which was all well enough except that Patrick, who seems to have had an aversion for wilderness marching, refused to disembark. There was a dreary wrangle before Underhill, who owned a share of the boat in question and had a fiery temper to make good his ownership, took possession of it and sailed away with his nineteen men and a part of the wounded. Captain Patrick then was reduced to marching with Mason overland to Saybrook. It must have been a dour journey, for by then Mason had bluntly informed Patrick that he neither wanted his company nor took any pleasure in it.

But like all things it came to an end. They reached the east shore of the Connecticut late Saturday evening, the twenty-eighth of May, just eight days after they had issued from its mouth. In that time they had sailed to Narragansett Bay, and then after two days of palavering with Canonicus had in five days covered more than sixty miles of unfamiliar wilderness and in course of it destroyed seven hundred "salvages." As a military feat it must rate high, and small though the numbers were, its bold conception and the speed and determination of its execution make one think of Jackson or Grant. No wonder that Lyon Gardiner greeted them across the river with a salvo from every "great gun" he had. Mason and his men, however, and even the fiery Underhill recorded a strong sense of having marched under the hand of God. How else account for the near miraculous secrecy with which they reached the fort? The Lord had been pleased to smite their "Enemies in the hinder Parts, and give us their land for an inheritance. . . ."

He had not given it just yet; and the rejoicings gave way to a cold realization that Sassacus was not dead and had still a good portion of his tribe to rally round him. Even the General Court in Boston could see that, and for a change they acted now with quick decisiveness. They raised a force of over one hundred men under the command of Captain Israel Stoughton, who sailed straight for the Pequot country, where he was joined by a large force of much emboldened Narragansetts.

Stoughton succeeded in cutting off a sizable band of Pequots on a point. Some were killed and a large number taken prisoners. Of these, the warriors were taken out to sea and put to death. The prisoners were parceled out among the Narragansetts and the Massachusetts or sent as slaves to Boston. Mason with forty Connecticut men had joined the army on June 28, bringing Uncas and his Mohegans with him, and the combined forces set out in pursuit of Sassacus, who was reported fleeing to the Dutch — a dubious sanctuary one would suppose. However, the English caught up with him before he had a chance to test it.

A Pequot captured by Uncas and his braves was persuaded to betray the location of the Pequot camp, at the foot of a hill near what is now Fairfield. At the approach of the English the Indians fled to the top of the hill and disappeared into a dense swamp. There was a brief skirmish at the edge with casualties on both sides. The swamp was then surrounded, but no one wanted to carry out a general assault in ground where a musket had no advantage over a bow, except for Captain Patrick. He thought the the Pequots were in such a panic that they would fall easy prey. To prove his point he went in with three soldiers but they were instantly set upon, and though they killed five braves they were lucky to come out alive. The place was impossible to burn and everyone was sure that during the night the Indians could break through their ring.

Then an interpreter named Stanton volunteered to go in and parley, with an offer to spare the women and children if the Pequots would surrender. All were sure that the mission would prove suicidal, but Stanton was confident and after a while he came back with two hundred Pequots, old men, women and children, following him. The braves, under Sassacus and Monotto, remained and in the night, after several attempts, they succeeded in breaking the English line and vanished into the mists and shadows of the woods. Sassacus and Monotto made their way to the Mohawk towns, where they sought refuge, but the Mohawks after prolonged deliberation over the political advantage to be gained decided that they had better be killed and their scalps sent with a message of cordiality to the

English on the Connecticut. This accordingly was done, and as if to put the final seal upon the Pequot history the chaplain of Stoughton's victorious force carried a part of each scalp back with him to rejoicing Boston.

The Indians who had surrendered at Fairfield were divided among the soldiers as slaves, the officers claiming the most comely or the strongest of the women as their proper due. Some were handed over to the Narragansetts and Mohegans. Of the Pequots remaining at large little is known except that in the next few years a good many were hunted down by the Narragansetts for scalp bounties and a few bands went to the Abenaki in Maine, with whom in a later generation they exacted a portion of vengeance against the English settlements in Maine, New Hampshire, and northern Massachusetts. But as a nation the Pequots were dead, wiped out in less than three months by less than a quarter of their number. It was a lesson the Indian world of New England would not forget for forty years.

Only a few of the English ever expressed any pity. With most it had been a surgical episode, violent but salutary.

> The very Devotions of those forlorn *Pagans*, to whom the Devil is Leader, are most bloody Penances; and what *Woes* indeed must we expect from such a Devil of a *Moloch*, as relishes no Sacrifices like those of Humane Heart-Blood, and unto whom there is no music like the bitter, dying, doleful Groans, ejaculated by the Roasting Children of Men.

To Cotton Mather, immured in his cruel fantasy of an Invisible World of wilderness and wandering souls, the Pequots had merely had a dose of their own medicine, and it served them right.

The Pequot campaign was a model for the extinction of inconvenient Indians and would be repeated by the English, and after them by Americans, in other wars though never with quite the same stunning finality. It was not, however, the first such war. In 1622 the colony of Virginia declared what was to all effect a series of "open seasons" on Indians of the Powhatan confederacy and after a few years of systematic killing eliminated them completely.

The real settlement of Virginia began in 1607 after two abortive attempts by Sir Walter Raleigh to plant a colony on Roanoke Island in 1585 and 1587. The site was an unhappy choice: living was hard and the surrounding Indians hostile. When Sir Francis Drake, returning with a fleet of more than twenty ships with which he had been raising havoc in the Caribbean, looked in on the first lot of settlers, he found them ill, homesick, and so pitifully eager to be taken home that he made room for all of them in his ships and brought them back to England.

Very soon after their departure Sir Richard Grenville, a cousin of Raleigh's, arrived at the island with stores which would have carried the settlers through the winter. The buildings were still intact and Grenville, who knew nothing of the colony's departure, assumed that the settlers must have been off on some kind of expedition and would in time return. So he put the stores ashore and left fifteen men to guard them.

The unhappy timing of this departure and arrival continued to frustrate Raleigh's plans to the end: the same kind of malevolent misfortune that haunted La Salle, another man with a vision of America, in his confrontation with the wilderness, and eventually accomplished his death, as in a more subtle way it set in motion the events that led to Raleigh's execution. On a less dramatic scale ordinary men entering the forests to hew a living for themselves succumbed to the same unforeseeable and capricious force. Courage, intelligence, determination were not involved. The Indians knew it. It was a vital element in their existence and informed their superstitions.

So now Raleigh, stretching his personal fortune to the utmost, outfitted another colonizing expedition in 1587, the year before the Armada which would monopolize England's attention and all her energies for the next year and a half. In itself this circumstance would have posed a threat to the colony of some one hundred and thirty men and seventeen women, but at the very start of their new American life one still worse befell them. It had been decided that Roanoke was not a good site for them to settle in and they intended going further north into Chesapeake Bay, of whose oyster beds and fisheries the earlier settlers had heard glowing accounts. But their instructions called for them to stop at Roanoke and pick up Grenville's garrison of fifteen men. All the settlers with their governor, John White, who had been artist for the previous expedition and brought home a water-color portfolio of the first accurate studies of North American Indian life, were put ashore. They found that Grenville's men had all been killed and the post looted. Then to their horror they found that the convoy, for what reason no one could conceive, had abandoned them except for one small ship.

Supplies were short from the very outset and by the end of August the situation had become so desperate that John White determined to return to England for reinforcements. The parting was for him especially hard, for a grandchild had been born on August 17 to his daughter, who was the wife of Ananias Dare. The little girl was the first child of English parentage to be born in North America and they named her Virginia. Her birth was a small bright moment in a time of descending gloom.

John White reached England to find the country working at full stretch in every shipyard and foundry to add to the strength of her navy.

No ships could be spared to succor a colony of one hundred and fifty people when the whole of England was confronted with the Spanish menace. Not till two years after the great fleet had been shattered was White able to leave for America.

Then he had to go via a long West Indies voyage at the end of which the master of the ship agreed to stop at Roanoke. When at last he reached the settlement he found it deserted. A growth of grass inside the block-house indicated that it must have been abandoned for some time. Some chests had been dug up and rifled and among the rubble White found torn remnants of some of his own sketches. There was nothing else except, carved deep on a large tree, the word CROATAN.

Before White had returned to England he and the colonists agreed that if for any reason they had to leave the settlement they would carve on a tree the name of the place they were moving to, and if the move was made in peril or under duress they would carve a cross beneath the name. There was no cross.

Croatan was the name both of an island and an Indian tribe and White persuaded the shipmaster to sail there. The outstanding feature of the island is Cape Hatteras; as the ship sailed nearer, it encountered the kind of stormy weather which in mariners' minds became almost a synonym for the cape's name and made its shallow waters a graveyard of ships. The shipmaster lost his nerve and would not be dissuaded from turning about and setting course for England. Neither White nor anyone else found any further trace of the lost colonists, except for a rumor brought sixteen years later to the colonists at Jamestown that the surviving Roanoke settlers on the point of starvation had sought refuge with the Croatans and for a while lived peaceably among them. Then, under one of the shadowy impulses that haunt the Indian mind, all but seven of them had been killed. Of the survivors three were children, one supposedly a girl.

Whether this story had any basis in fact was anybody's guess. Nothing ever turned up to substantiate it. Presumably the young girl was Virginia Dare. She would then have been twenty and the thought of a fair young English girl living as an Indian among Indians had a tragic fascination. Even at the time, she had become a wraith to haunt American mythology; she would remain a legend and become a trademark.

The first permanent colonization of Virginia began when three small ships under Captain Christopher Newport, after a two weeks' exploration of lower Chesapeake Bay, put one hundred and five settlers ashore on an island in the James River. With the Roanoke failures still fresh in mind they began immediately to build a fort and a cluster of thatch-roofed cabins to which they added a warehouse and a church. They named this settlement Jamestown in honor of the king, and it was well that they had

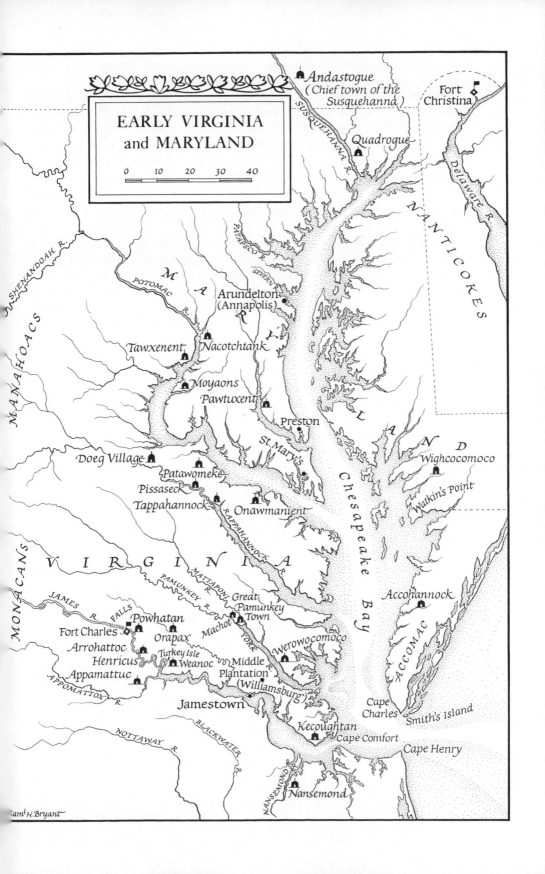

EARLY VIRGINIA
and MARYLAND

0   10   20   30   40

Andastogue
(Chief town of the
Susquehanna)

Fort
Christina

Quadroque

SUSQUEHANNA R.

DELAWARE R.

NANTICOKES

PATAPSCO R.

SHENANDOAH R.

POTOMAC R.

M
A
R
Y
L
A
N
D

SEVERN R.

Arundelton
(Annapolis)

MANAHOACS

Tawxenent   Nacotchtank

Moyaons
Pawtuxent

Preston

St. Mary's

Wighcocomoco

Doeg Village

Patawomeke

Watkin's Point

Pissaseck

Tappahannock   Onawmanient

RAPPAHANNOCK R.

Chesapeake Bay

VIRGINIA

MONACANS

MATTAPONI R.

PAMUNKEY R.

Great
Pamunkey
Town

Accohannock

JAMES R.

FALLS

Powhatan

Fort Charles

Orapax

Machot

Werowocomoco

ACCOMAC

Arrohattoc

Turkey Isle

YORK R.

Henricus

Weanoc

Middle
Plantation
(Williamsburg)

Appamattuc

APPOMATTOX R.

Jamestown

Cape
Charles

Smith's Island

NOTTAWAY R.

BLACKWATER R.

Kecoughtan

Cape Comfort

Cape Henry

NANSEMOND R.

Nansemond

am¹ H. Bryant

begun first on their fort because in two weeks it was strong enough for them to fight off a raid by two hundred Indians.

Selection of the site of Jamestown had been made partly in accordance with and partly in contravention of a remarkably detailed list of instructions for the guidance of the proposed colony's officials. As instructed, they had found a site close to deep water which would make delivery of stores easy; they had settled on a river, but here they had compromised, for the instructions advised them to place their colony as far up as a ship of 50 tons could easily sail, "the further up the better," even if it were a hundred miles, for if they were to "sit down near the entrance" the Spaniards might easily come ashore and sack them as they had the French in Florida. (In the event it was not a Spanish but a Dutch fleet that wrought havoc on the James and then sailed on to recapture briefly New York from the English there.) But if they did light near the river mouth it should be on an island. Well, the Jamestown settlers had an island, but here again they ignored the emphatic warning against "a low or moist place," which Jamestown certainly was, and therefore of course malarial.

They were also warned not to trust the Indians, but at the same time to display friendliness for purely practical reasons. "You must have great care not to offend the naturals, if you can eschew it, and employ some few of your company to trade with them for corn and all other lasting victuals. . . ." It was essential to lay in as many provisions as possible from the Indians before they grasped the fact that the settlement was intended as a permanent plantation. The attack on the fort naturally for a while dispelled any idea of successfully pursuing this mildly fraudulent commerce; and the starvation that resulted, combined with spreading sickness, made it difficult also to observe the penultimate article of their instructions, which was to take care in their reports and letters home to say nothing that might discourage further emigration to Virginia.

They made a strange community. Twenty-nine of the one hundred and five who came ashore were classed as gentlemen, and from their number six were to serve as a council which in turn would elect one of its members governor, or president as he was called in the instructions. But when the ships sailed from England, and through all the one hundred and twenty-nine weary days of the voyage, no one in the expedition knew who the six men were. Their names had been placed in a sealed box not to be opened till they raised the capes of the Chesapeake. What possible purpose lay behind this hocus-pocus is difficult to fathom. There may have been an idea of enhancing Captain Newport's command of the expedition while at sea, which seems unlikely, for Newport was entirely capable of maintaining discipline aboard his ships. If it was done for the purpose of maintaining harmony during the long voyage, on the theory that without knowledge of who their civil officers were to be, factions would be less likely to arise, it proved a mistake. Three months out of Blackwall bitter feeling broke out between Captain John Smith and Edward Maria Wingfield, who accused the captain of plotting mutiny, and Smith spent the rest of the voyage in irons.

He had supporters but not enough. When the king's casket, as the sealed box was called, was opened on the first evening they lay off Cape Henry, the names of Smith and Wingfield were among the six councilors. The other four were Bartholomew Gosnold, the explorer, and second-in-command to Newport during the sea voyage, John Ratcliffe, John Martin, and George Kendall. The council then elected Wingfield president, and with a majority against him Smith was not allowed to sit, though he was freed of his irons. Unable to serve usefully at Jamestown, he joined Newport in a voyage by boat up the James River and so became one of the first group of Englishmen to visit the Indian village named Powhatan, on the site of Richmond. It was not the principal village of the tribe. That, Smith learned, was on the York River about fifteen miles northeast from Jamestown. It was called Werrowocomoco and was the seat of the principal chief, Wahunsonacock, known as the Powhatan. This was the start of Smith's relation with the Powhatans, which was to lead to his genuine if often tricky friendship with Powhatan himself.

Meanwhile life at Jamestown had begun to take form. It was a curious one. In the first place there were no women; they were a hundred and five men living alone. Besides the six members of the council and twenty-nine others who ranked as gentlemen, there were ten artisans, of whom six were carpenters, two bricklayers, one mason, and one blacksmith. There were a tailor and a barber and one sailor, four boys, and a drummer. Twelve were listed as laborers; the remaining thirty-eight seem to have had no calling. And to attend to their spiritual and bodily ills, there were a clergyman and a surgeon. The council decided the priority of work to be done to build the settlement and assigned parties to undertake it. These parties were marched to and from their jobs twice daily, led by the lone drummer, who must have developed considerable self-importance. But the work they did soon lost incentive. It was done at the bidding of the council, who themselves were often uncertain about what the next step should be, and was entirely for the benefit of the community. Even in trading with the Indians what a man bartered for had to be handed over to the council. Life became as cipherless as life aboard a man-of-war — without the discipline to keep men up to scratch. But as sickness and hunger came and men found that idleness got one along as far as work, the place, which was designed at first as a quasi-military trading post, resembled much more a penal colony in which those who were not willing to work were supported by those who were, and soon the same sort of lassitude and depression one would expect in a prison colony tainted life in Jamestown.

It was early apparent that the provisions they had brought would not be adequate, and Captain Newport, the guns of whose ship lying close to shore had furnished some protection, waited only for completion of the fort to set sail for England for fresh supplies. This time, instead of the long route south by the West Indies and Canaries, he followed the great-circle course direct for England, possibly urged by Captain Gosnold who had followed a similar course to Cape Cod five years earlier.

Newport promised to be back in twenty weeks, but to make sure of his voyage he had to take a big proportion of the remaining stocks, and as his sails disappeared down the long reach of the James a profound gloom seized the minds of the settlers. No thought had been given to this inevitable moment of bereavement which afflicts all those left behind on a strange shore. There were no distractions — nothing, however primitive it might have been, to take the place of a pub. All their interest was concentrated on "the common kettle" which as time passed produced no more than "a small Can of Barlie sodden in water to fiue men a day." They did not even have good water, for in the flood tide the James ran salt and in the ebb it was full of mud and slime. Malaria attacked them and all night the well were kept awake by the groans and muttering of the fevered, three or four of whom might die before sunrise, their "bodies being trailed out of their Cabines like Dogges, to be buried."

By October, fifty-one out of the one hundred and five were dead, yet the specter of starvation steadily crept closer. Captain Newport had left behind an estimated fifteen weeks of provisions. Now that the fifteen weeks had run out, it became obvious that the decrease in mouths to feed would not offset the needs of the five weeks still to go — even supposing Newport made good his promise of returning in twenty weeks; and it was to be thirteen weeks more than that before his sails did reappear down the James.

How a community of able-bodied men could have starved in a countryside like that of Tidewater Virginia at that time is hard to understand. Few other places in America were more blessed in game. The woods were alive with deer and rabbits, and wild turkey that often weighed as much as thirty pounds. The marshes teemed with ducks; some of the flocks flying overhead were so long and dense that they cast shadows on the land. In the river there were enormous sturgeon. Yet except for the taking of a few of the latter and shooting ducks in the fall there is little mention of hunting game, certainly none of systematic hunting such as the Indians used in fire drives for deer.

No doubt the Indian attack and the awareness of their own small number made them apprehensive. Probably they were victims also of their own established notions of how things were done in the English way of life. Certainly, except for John Smith, there had been little in their background to prepare them to come to grips with the problem of winning a life from a wilderness. The wheat they planted in the new soil they had cleared by their timber cutting ran all to stalk, six or seven feet high with only rudimentary ears when there was any grain at all. They wasted two more growing seasons before they were willing to believe what the Indians told them: that the virgin lowland soil was too rich for wheat until it had been worked for a couple of years with a coarse crop such as corn. But the Jamestown settlers were not really interested in such prosaic matters. Most of them, and this was true particularly of the gentlemen, did not think of themselves as settlers anyway. They had come primarily to make or mend their fortunes; they were on fire to find gold.

Pie in the sky may be part of the American Dream, but its roots run through the history of all mankind, and the directors of the London Company were not immune. They talked about establishing a permanent colony, but their instructions had resulted in a mere trading post from which they had received no returns other than complaints and endless reports of bickering and factional plotting instead of the gold or pearls they had been counting on. Their minds worked as merchants'; the ships they sent out carrying reinforcements and supplies at a cost of more than two thousand pounds apiece brought back no more than a few skins, a little lumber, from their point of view not even a remote return on the investment. These reinforcement voyages, moreover, were so badly planned and inadequately stocked that they defeated their purpose and in the end aggravated the very condition they were supposed to relieve.

Captain Newport, whose fidelity to the colony was admirable in every way, returned at last on January 8 to find thirty-eight survivors. He brought a large store of provisions, but at the same time he brought one hundred and twenty new settlers and it soon was evident that the provisions would not be adequate to feed the augmented colony, his own ship's crew, and then to stock the ship for its voyage back to England in the spring. Simple logistic facts seem never to have occurred to anyone connected with the development of Jamestown except the settlers themselves. As Captain Smith later pointed out to the directors, though a ship might be stocked with stores worth two thousand pounds when it left London, what finally came to the settlers' hands was hardly worth one hundred pounds. Newport's arrival put off, it did not allay, the problem of starvation.

However, on the same day that Newport arrived from England, John Smith returned from a momentous expedition of his own, walking into Jamestown with an escort of four Powhatan braves. He had been making trips upriver to trade for corn with the Indians, and though he brought back only small amounts, these had been enough to keep the steadily dwindling community from actual starvation, as even his enemy, President Wingfield, conceded. On December 10 he had embarked on another expedition with nine men, taking a pinnace up the James and then the

Chickahominy as far as the pinnace would go. There, leaving seven as a guard, Smith paddled on with two companions, hoping to find new Indian towns which might have corn to spare in trade.

Some miles upstream, hemmed in by dense swamp woods, they were suddenly ambushed by two hundred Powhatans. Smith's companions were killed in the first fire. He himself managed to pistol two braves before being overwhelmed and taken prisoner. He saved his life for the moment by pulling out his pocket compass and showing the Indians the needle and how it pointed always north; they were mystified by it and still more so by the fact that they could see it move and yet not touch it. But the war party was divided, some wanting to kill him at once, some to save him, and it was the war chief, holding the compass in his hand, who decided to take him to the Powhatan.

The war chief was Opechancanough, Powhatan's brother, and whether at this time he was hostile to the English — and his unprovoked attack on three of them would seem to indicate so — he became their inveterate and violent enemy. If now he let Smith live, there is every reason to suppose that he expected to attend his execution before Powhatan.

Smith's account of his next three weeks among the Powhatans and the accounts of other writers of his time carry a sense of history in the making, and they are full also of a kind of wonder that has transferred the whole episode into legend. It was, of course, an entirely typical and normal experience of any person taken captive by American Indians. He was led through one after another of the Powhatan towns, where people were called out to see whether he might be the Englishman who had earlier raided the district and kidnaped several Indians, and fortunately Smith's short stature passed him through every one of these examinations. Though a captive, he apparently kept his eyes and wits about him. The Indian villages had long communal houses, but there were other houses standing apart through the surrounding fields, like the beginnings of suburbia, which was unusual. And he seems not to have suffered the abuses that the Iroquois liked to visit on their captives.

So at last Opechancanough brought him to Werrowocomoco. He was exhibited before the Powhatan, who sat on the far side of the fire with his women painted red behind him and warriors ranked along the walls; the decision was made to kill the captive; stones were placed on the floor before the chief; Smith was dragged to them and made to place his head upon them while an executioner above him raised his club; and then the chief's daughter claimed his life, as any member of the tribe might claim the life of a captive taken in battle. Legend says she threw herself upon the prostrate captain and laid her head on his as though to dare the executioner's blow. And of course she may have done so, for she was a lively girl — her nickname of Pocahontas meant "Frisky" — and like many Indians could easily be carried away by the drama of any scene; but in this one she was in no sort of danger and certainly did not, as Smith supposed, risk her life to save his. It was all in the Indian way of things. What made it memorable were the characters of the four principals.

The simplest and most forthright was Opechancanough who as chief of the numerous Pamunkeys stood next in power to Powhatan himself in the confederacy. In every respect he was the incorrigible Indian. If he was not yet totally committed to the Indians' cause against the white man as with grim frustration he watched his young niece win her claim for the English captain's life, he became so a year later when Smith through personal action defeated his purpose. He was in his late fifties. In his seventies he struck a violent blow against the English. In his nineties he was still fighting them, so frail that he had to be carried to battle, and in the end he was taken and shot — the first of a long line of Indians who tried to protect the integrity of the red man in the face of ruthless white encroachment that did not cease until the surrender of Joseph, the Nez Percé, after his embattled march of a thousand miles in 1877, and nine years later of Geronimo, the Chiricahua Apache.

At any time during the first four years of Jamestown a determined attack in force such as Opechancanough mounted against the much larger settlements in 1622 could have wiped the English off the Virginia shore. The pity was, from the Indian point of view, that it was the wrong brother who ruled the Powhatan confederacy when the first English came.

Powhatan was just as much an Indian, but he was far less Spartan in character and more given to devious solutions. English goods and implements fascinated him, and he saw the value to his tribe of engrossing the English trade. Besides, in spite of his capricious Indian humor, he seems genuinely to have believed in peace and the profitable coexistence between white and red — a delusion born of desire to gain superiority through possession of the white man's tools and guns that spelled the end of many a chief and the history of his tribe. In this context he thought of the English first merely as traders; when he began to realize that they had come as colonizers it was too late.

Most important, he was attracted by Smith's manifest virility and the boldness with which he carried himself; and unlike his brother, in whom these traits roused violent antagonism and foreboding, Powhatan would have had no satisfaction in the splash of English brains upon the execution stone and undoubtedly welcomed his daughter's intervention, for the next day but one he adopted Smith as a member of the tribe, greeted him as his son, and almost in the same breath asked for a grindstone and a couple of cannon. One suspects a frustrated merchant under the robes of the chieftain.

Then there was Matowaka — Pocahontas, "Frisky" — not yet thirteen years old, and highly personable to judge from a portrait painted afterward in London and from the fact that sober John Rolfe fell eagerly in love with her when she was eighteen, married her to replace the wife he had lost on the voyage over, and took her back with him to England. Whether she fell in love with Smith is beside the point; there was never any doubt of her devotion to him and to the Englishmen in their pitiful habitation. In this she was like many other Indian women whose hearts were moved by the situation of these strange people from beyond the sea and who tried to help them; and if she had not risked her life in claiming his, she did risk it two years later when she stole out of Werrowocomoco at night and found her way through the dark and "irksome" January woods to bring Smith and his party warning that a plot was afoot to murder all of them in their outlying quarters while they slept. Again and again she turned up at Jamestown with offerings of corn and game which did much, in the starving time, to keep intact the frail thread of their existence. "Blessed Pocahontas . . ." Smith wrote of her. "She, under God, was the instrument to preserve this colony from death, famine, and utter confusion." But for her intervention and the enterprise of Smith himself the colony at Jamestown, like those at Roanoke, would probably have vanished.

Smith, of course, besides being the near victim, was the central character about whom the other three revolved and would continue to revolve. He had been an adventurer and still was at heart. Every schoolboy used to be familiar with his exploits against the Turks, his individual jousting with three Turkish champions, for each other's head, all of which saw Smith victorious and his opponent headless at the end. Taken in battle, he had been a slave in Constantinople where his mistress took an interest in him that may or may not have been romantic, for after a time she decided not to keep him in her house and sent him to her brother who was Pasha of Nalbrits, beyond the Sea of Azov. Unlike his sister, the brother proved a cruel master, and after killing him with a flail and leaving him underneath the wheat, Smith made his escape through Russia, Poland, and Hungary and finally returned to England when excitement over the projected Virginia colony was approaching a climax.

It made heady reading, however much or little it was based on fact. More interesting in Smith's early life was his choosing, when on an earlier return to England, to spend a long time alone in the woods in a hut he had built for himself, Thoreau-like, dividing his time between hunting and reading — two of his authors being Machiavelli and Marcus Aurelius. That experience perhaps, more than the gaudy exploits in Asia Minor and eastern Europe, prepared him for his role in saving the Jamestown colony. He played it with daring, imagination, determination that had much of the same dogged and unyielding stubbornness that has taken so many Englishmen out in the midday sun, and with another English quality that runs persistently through history from the Elizabethan mariners who fought the Spanish fleets to the defiant Londoners in the blazing ruins of World

War II: the ability to bounce back under adversity. He was, in other words, tough as none of his fellow settlers were and he brought them through their terrible three years almost in spite of themselves.

In June 1607, he had insisted on being tried before a jury on the charge of plotting mutiny, and over the objections of President Wingfield, the originator of the charges, had won a trial and acquittal and a right to take his seat upon the council. However, Wingfield and his adherents remained hostile and, as we have seen, Smith kept out of the settlement as much as possible, making his trips to trade for corn in the Indian villages a pretext, though actually they kept the settlement just above the edge of death.

Even aside from dreadful hunger, Jamestown was an unhappy place. The settlers were torn by mutual suspicion; almost everyone suspected plots against his life or influence. Wingfield was accused of holding out some sherry for his own use, and though he protested it was for use at Communion, almost no one believed him: with so large a proportion sick or idle, minds were preoccupied with fantasies and hallucinations until any reasonableness became impossible.

Wingfield, though an honorable enough man, became thoroughly detested, but when a rumor spread that he planned to desert in one of the small vessels remaining to the colony, they took steps to see that he did not abandon them — at least as their president. He was deposed and Ratcliffe succeeded him.

Ratcliffe proved no better leader. In the first place it soon came to light that he was an impostor whose real name was Sickelmore, though what he had sought to conceal under his pseudonym never came to light. He too bristled with suspicions and also wreathed himself in the importance of his office. When, in an altercation, one of the artisans returned his blows he had the man condemned to death. With the noose virtually around his neck the man suddenly revealed a plot on the part of one of the council, George Kendall, to mutiny. He was taken down and pardoned and George Kendall was tried and condemned but, being one of the gentlemen, was shot, not hanged. In many ways a man's life was safer in an Indian village.

Wingfield returned to England in the spring of 1608 and Ratcliffe, who had been made president in the previous September, held his office for just a year. By that time the settlement was thoroughly fed up with him; he was deposed and Smith chosen in his place. At last some order was to emerge in the small communistic settlement.

As if in celebration of the change of presidents, Captain Newport returned that same September with what was called "The Second Supply"

and seventy new settlers, among whom were the first two Englishwomen to arrive in Jamestown and eight Poles and Germans who had been recruited to begin the manufacture of naval stores and glass. The directors of the London Company had finally realized that if they were to make their plantation in Virginia permanent it would have to find some product it could export. England made no naval stores; all the pitch and tar and turpentine, as well as the spars, for her navy were imported, mainly from Sweden and Russia, a trade which war with France might sever at any time. An adequate supply from her own American dominions would be invaluable. In a hundred and fifty years the pine barrens of North Carolina would prove the greatest producer of tar and turpentine in the British Empire and the belt of virgin white pine in New England would contribute incomparable masts for the British navy. But in Virginia in 1609 export of these stores could never amount to anything but the faintest trickle. As John Smith pointed out, the Company could not expect more from a few miserable colonists whose energies were devoted almost entirely to their own survival and who could find "but here and there a tree fit for the purpose, and want all things else the Russians have."

Though realizing that it was essential to get its plantation on a self-sustaining basis, the London Company still could not give up its dream of a sudden return on its investment. Newport's orders directed him to find a "lumpe of gold" big enough to pay for his voyage, or at the very least a passage to the South Sea. As a result he preempted the services of the one hundred and twenty most able-bodied colonists and made an expedition above the falls of the James, a tedious, frustrating, and wholly unnecessary effort, not without danger. "The people neither used us well nor ill, yet for our security we took one of their petty Kings, and led him bound to conduct us on the way," which can hardly have endeared the English to the inland tribes.

In the end they got no farther than thirty miles and never even reached the Blue Ridge; but they had seen enough to convince them of the truth of what the Indians had told them all along: that there was no sea near at hand, only woods and mountains. And Newport, who had sought to justify his trip with the promise of bringing back two pinnaceloads of corn from Powhatan Village brought back, according to Smith, hardly fourteen bushels. When all members of the settlement should have been out trading for corn or harvesting their own they had been dragooned into this wild goose chase. In the words of one of them:

> To lose that time, spend that victuall that we had, tire and starue our men, having no means to carry victuall, munition, the hurt or sicke, but their own backes: how or by whom they [these orders] were invented I know not.

[236]

Even "more strange" to Anas Todkill, who was one of the men who had undergone the forest drudgery "to perfourme this strange discovery," was the crowning of Powhatan. The directors of the London Company had conceived the notion that the cheapest way to deal with the Indians was to ensure their friendship by bribing their chief with presents which included such items as a basin, a bedstead, bed linen, and a scarlet robe; and to emphasize the idea that they regarded him as a great man, almost on equal terms in his primitive country with his "brother" King James in England, it was determined that he should be crowned — only, since he was a mere Indian, the crown was cheaply made of copper.

Captain Newport had instructions to put it on his head in Jamestown, which in London seemed a simple thing to do. But Powhatan, perhaps because of the reports of the petty king led in bonds along the woodland trails of the upper James, would have none of a proposal which would have made him ripe for a hostage; and he kept Smith, who had gone to Werrowocomoco, waiting for some time for his adverse reply. For Smith, however, there was recompense of a sort for his wait, for Pocahontas entertained him with a dance in which she led twenty-nine other Indian maidens.

Smith's description, in which astonishment mixed equally with enthusiasm, has become the prototype for even more fanciful Indian performances which have plagued American historical romances from that day to this, but there is no reason to doubt its essential accuracy. He and his companions had been seated before a fire in a natural meadow "when suddenly amongst the woods was heard . . . a hydeous noise and shrieking." Thirty young women came racing "naked out of the woods, onely covered behind and before with a few greene leaves, their bodies all painted, some white, some red, some black, some particolour, but all differeing; their leader had a fayre payre of buck's horns on her head, an otter's skin at her girdle, and another at her arm, a quiver of arrowes at her back, a bow and arrowes in her hand . . ." The others, too, bore arms, a sword, a war club, and like Pocahontas all wore deer horns. They ringed the fire for an hour, singing, shouting, brandishing their weapons, "and dauncing with most excellent ill varietie." Then as suddenly as they had come they vanished once more into the woods.

When they appeared again they were in decorous costume and soberly invited the Englishmen to their lodges, which they had no sooner entered "but all these nymphes more tormented us than ever," pressing themselves against the men, clinging to them, and asking over and over in their high voices, "Love you not me? Love you not me?" Whether this was intended as conventional politeness or as invitation, order seems to have been preserved, and shortly a feast was brought in that to the Englishmen must have seemed a feast indeed: "fruit in baskets, fish and flesh in wooden platters; beans and peas there wanted not, nor any salvage dainty their invention could devise . . ."

But for all this hospitality, Powhatan could not be budged from his determination to stay away from Jamestown. So Newport and Smith had to make another journey, with the presents, to Werrowocomoco, Newport with all eagerness to fulfill his orders and Smith entirely skeptical about the value of their mission. Powhatan was skeptical, too. The presents pleased him well enough, especially the scarlet robe, but the old chief, a man described as having enormous dignity, did not understand why he had to kneel to receive a crown, which apparently he did not think much of anyway, and it took all of Smith's and Newport's powers of persuasion backed by a measure of force to get the old man on his knees. But finally it was done and as a gesture of reciprocal good will Powhatan gave Newport his cloak of coonskins to take back to King James.

When Newport sailed once more for England, he took with him the deposed president, Ratcliffe, alias Sickelmore. Wingfield had returned on the voyage before and now, with Gosnold and Martin dead of disease and Kendall executed, of the six original councilors only Smith remained in Virginia. He took over the government of Jamestown with a stern hand. It was necessary. The communistic plan of labor had completely failed; men who refused to work shared equally with those who did and the result was that the settlement of two hundred was being carried by the work of thirty of forty men. Smith gathered all together and bluntly told them that those who did not work would not eat, and it needed only a short period of firm enforcement to bring most of the malingerers round. By the next spring twenty houses had been built and more than thirty acres of ground cultivated and planted; a well had been dug inside the fort that at last gave them dependable sweet water; and a new and better fort was started. But the work was hard and slow for, as Smith said, in a place like Jamestown a plain soldier who could use a pickax was better than five knights, and nearly half the company ranked as gentlemen. "When you send again," he had written the directors of the London Company, "I entreat you send but 30 carpenters, husbandmen, gardeners, fishermen, blacksmiths, masons, and diggers up of trees' roots, well provided," and added that these thirty would be worth more "than 1000 of such as we have."

Meanwhile the problem of finding food obsessed him through the winter months. Game was no answer. They could not kill enough to feed themselves; as he wrote, "Though there be fish in the sea, fowls in the air, and beasts in the woods, their bounds are so large, they so wild, and we so weak and ignorant that we cannot much trouble them." The one possible source was the Indian harvest of corn.

During the first two years the Indians had traded their corn readily. A few blue glass beads or a square of copper as big as a half dollar would get a bushel; in their eagerness to do business the Indians even brought their corn to Jamestown. But in the last summer this had changed. As Smith had feared, Powhatan was becoming more sophisticated; he would not hear of letting the English have corn for beads or copper; he demanded an English house before he would even talk of trade.

Originally Smith had explained the English presence by telling him that they had been driven ashore by the Spanish and would leave when good "father Newport" would be able to take them away. This had won his sympathy. But Newport had now twice returned and instead of taking away the Jamestown people had brought more English who had increased their buildings and strengthened their fort. They were no farmers, how-ever, as every Indian knew who had been to Jamestown, and Powhatan understood as well as Smith the strength of his bargaining position. What he did not understand was the possibility, which continually haunted Smith, of hunger's goading the settlers into outright attacks upon the In-dians. Before that happened, the Indians would have to be persuaded some-how into selling their corn.

He sent off fourteen men at once, including four of the German artisans, to begin building Powhatan's house and then, with twenty-seven men, sailed in a pinnace the longer water route down the James and up the York River. On their first night they stopped at an Indian village whose chief warned them that Powhatan was planning to kill them. Then a blizzard kept them snowbound in the village of the Kecoughtans, near the site of present-day Hampton. It consisted of only eighteen small houses but was an established fishing village and had unusually large cornfields. For a week the Kecoughtans fed and housed them in their lodges, "warm as stoves, al-beit very smoakey." The Kecoughtans were the first Indians the James-town settlers met; they had remained friendly and would continue to be so till the increasing English colony a year later decided that the most practical way of producing tilled land was to appropriate it from the In-dians and easily drove them out.

Ice blocked the York. Leaving the pinnace with a guard, Smith had to break a channel for his barge for half a mile and then went the rest of the way on foot. At Werrowocomoco the atmosphere was cold and ominous; few Indians were visible; the arbor-shaped wigwams stood against the snow-buried landscape in dark silence. Smith appropriated one of the out-lying ones for his use and, sending messages, the English party sat down to wait the coming of Powhatan.

The old chief kept them waiting till the next day, though he had food sent to them; but when he did arrive at the wigwam, the first thing he wanted to know was when they were going to leave; he had not sent them an invitation; and he had no corn to sell them though he knew where there was an available supply — which, however, could be bought only with swords or guns at a value of one good sword per bushel. Smith pointed to the unfinished house among the wigwams and remarked that Powhatan's memory must be short to say he had sent no invitation. The old chief burst into laughter, but he did not change his attitude on trading corn; he wanted real prices, and he wanted to know why Smith and his men always came armed. Seeing them so made the Indians afraid to trade; let them leave their guns aboard the pinnace and come as Powhatans and their needs would be looked after.

There now followed a long sparring match between the two. Smith had no intention of disarming his men. Though he had felt admiration, even liking of a sort, for the old man, whose natural dignity made him at times a kingly figure, his attitude toward Powhatan and all his tribe had become the attitude typical of all American frontiersmen. If it was not as drastic as that of General Sherman taking command in the West in 1867, who said that the more he saw of Indians "the more I am convinced that they all have to be killed, or be maintained as a species of paupers," or even as practical as that of his own contemporary, the Reverend Richard Hakluyt who, in considering their conversion to Christianity, observed that if gentle courses would not serve, then there should be "hammerers and rough masons enow — I mean our old soldiers trained up in the Netherlands — to square and prepare them to our Preacher's hands," he approached them now with every nerve alert for signs of treachery. He did not lose his temper or his sense of humor as he explained that to an Englishman a musket was as much part of his natural dress as a bow and arrows or a tomahawk were to an Indian; and as for their muskets, it was of course obvious that they made the English much superior to the Indians and could have been used against them with grievous effect, yet they had not been. If Powhatan chose to withhold his corn, such a thing as corn should never be allowed to come between them. The English could get along without it, or they could trade for it elsewhere — a covert threat not missed by the old chief, for the only other ready supply would be that of his inveterate enemies, the Siouan tribe of Monacans, above the falls of the James; and the idea of their getting hold of English arms or even possibly some muskets was too much for him. He produced the asked-for corn.

But the hostility remained and no English life was safe in the Indian town. Smith and a companion visiting Powhatan were left suddenly alone in his wigwam and rushing to the door found it ringed with armed braves. Only the fury with which they fell upon the Indians with their swords won their way through. And it was after the corn had been delivered to the English lodging that Pocahontas made her journey through the "irksome woods" at night to warn them of a planned massacre. Smith sent back a message that if Powhatan was coming he would find his welcome well prepared. The Indians did not come and in the morning the English took their corn aboard the pinnace.

Powhatan's corn, however, was nowhere near enough, so Smith, leaving the Germans and two Englishmen to finish the chief's house, went on up-river to the Pamunkey town at the forks of the Pamunkey and Mattapony. Here after an initial welcome the party found themselves surrounded by a vastly superior gathering of warriors and only Smith's prompt action of seizing Opechancanough and holding him at pistol point prevented a general attack. In what was an almost comic parody of the Inca ransom of Atahualpa the Pamunkeys brought out more than three hundred bushels of corn. That they had found themselves unable to withstand a naked confrontation of firearms at close quarters in the open rankled deeply, and Opechancanough had been humiliated before all his tribe, which was something he would not forget.

Yet the Indians made no outright attack. The spies of Powhatan who kept Jamestown under constant surveillance may have been impressed by the building going forward, especially of the second fort; but more likely it was the forcefulness of Smith that intimidated them. It proved a healthier winter than most, but by early summer food was in such short supply that many of the men had to forage for berries and some even took up quarters in the friendlier Indian villages. Then the arrival of a ship captained by young Samuel Argall arrived at Jamestown with news from London — the first event in a train of happenings that reduced the colony to complete confusion and for a time almost spelled its end.

Argall, who had made the swiftest trans-Atlantic crossing on record, reported that the London Company had received a new charter. Two years of experimental colonization had proved its policies inadequate. Fresh ideas and new money were needed if the Virginia project was to continue and the English maintain their foothold in the New World.

In its first incarnation the London Company, like its sister Plymouth Company, had come under the general supervision of a royal council of thirteen men. The royal council had then appointed thirteen members of a second council which was to plant the colony and administer its affairs. The powers granted to this second council over its plantation were wide and absolute. As we have seen, it organized the original expedition and subsequent supply voyages and also appointed a third subsidiary council which was to govern locally in Virginia; but any action taken by either the council in London or that in Virginia was subject to veto by the Crown. The chain of command was too anomalous ever to be effective; action taken by the council in London was hesitant and always inadequate;

and the government of Jamestown was a sheer fiasco till John Smith took power into his own hands.

Under the second charter the Company was reorganized and greatly enlarged. It became a public corporation with 659 private subscribers and 56 of the trade guilds of London as additional subscribers. All members were listed by name and many of them classified by profession or rank; their roster represented to a remarkable degree a cross section of English society. Most numerous were merchants, of whom there were 110; then in order of number followed knights, the inevitable "gentlemen," professional soldiers, and engineers. There were 21 peers, 11 physicians and clergymen. The other 282 came under miscellaneous classifications or were listed merely by name. But besides these the membership of the trade guilds opened the way, possibly for the first time, for people like brewers, greengrocers, masons, and fishmongers to share in a great public enterprise.

Even more significant was the fact that while the original members of the council governing affairs of the London Company received their appointments from the Crown, the officers thereafter were to be chosen and any vacancies filled in annual elections by vote of the full list of the stockholders. The charter also abolished the council in Virginia and substituted a governor with autocratic powers and responsible directly to the London council. This all added up to a colonial administration independent of Parliament and virtually free of royal domination. When in 1620 James I did try to interfere in a Company election, offering alternative candidates of his own choosing, he was rebuffed and the stockholders voted in their own man.

The Company began operations vigorously. Lord De La Warr, who had distinguished himself as a soldier in the Netherlands, was appointed governor of the colony with life tenure. Named with him, as lieutenant governor, was another experienced soldier, Sir Thomas Gates; and Sir George Somers, a veteran sea dog now in his sixties, was named admiral of the fleet which would carry the new colonists to Virginia. These were distinguished appointments and promised well for the future of the colony.

The council in London, however, could not quite bring itself to abandon the old communistic system on which Jamestown had ben founded, though they did liberalize it to some extent. Each emigrant was to receive a share and the Company guaranteed to support him in Virginia for seven years, during which the product of his work belonged to the colony. But at the end of seven years he would receive a grant of land for his share, and if he held additional stock the grant would be proportionately larger.

This prospectus and the promise of support proved attractive to many, especially to people who found living hard in England, and by the spring of 1609 five hundred men, women, and children were ready to emigrate. Lord De La Warr himself had not sufficiently arranged his affairs to feel ready to leave, but he had taken an active interest in assembling the fleet and with such able deputy commanders there seemed no reason for holding the ships, of which there were nine, any longer, for it was known that Jamestown was in stringent need of the supplies they carried. The fleet sailed on June 2, taking the southern route by the Azores. This was in the order of things, for the master of the flagship, *Sea Venture*, was Captain Newport, who might now be said to have almost qualified as an Atlantic packet master. He preferred the roundabout course as promising calmer seas. With him as passengers on the *Sea Venture* were George Somers and Thomas Gates as well as the more important emigrants, among whom might be numbered John Rolfe and his pregnant wife.

The first part of the voyage could not have been more propitious; the account of it by William Strachey, who was to be secretary of the colony, shines with a sense of a sun-filled ocean and uplifted hearts.

> Know that upon Friday late in the evening we brake ground out of the sound of Plymouth, our whole fleet consisting of seven good ships and two pinnaces all of which from the said second of June unto the twenty-third of July kept in friendly consort together, not a whole watch at any time losing sight each of other. Our course, when we came about the height of between 26 and 27 degrees, we declined to the northward and, according to our Governor's instructions, altered the trade and ordinary way used heretofore by Dominica and Nevis in the West Indies and found the wind to this course indeed as friendly as in the judgement of all seamen it is upon a more direct line.

They were by Newport's reckoning not more than eight days from Virginia, but next day the sky blackened, "the clouds gathering this upon us and the wind whistling most unusually," and "at length did beat all the light from Heaven." On the twenty-fifth they were in the grip of a hurricane and within an hour had been forced to cast loose the two pinnaces which till then had been towed astern. All sight of the other vessels had been lost, and for three days and nights there was not a moment in which those aboard the *Sea Venture* did not expect the instant breaking up and foundering of the ship. She came within a hairbreadth of doing so, springing a great leak and "almost having spewed out her oakum" in every joint. Only the courage and resourcefulness of the crewmen and their officers saved them. In parties they crept through the holds, neck deep in water, "master, master's mate, boatswain, quartermaster, coopers, carpenters, and who not, with candles in their hands . . . listening in every place if they could hear the water run. Many a weaping leak was this way found and hastily stopped." But the main leak which "drunk in our greatest seas" could not be found. The pumps, manned night and day, could not keep pace with it.

Three bucket lines were organized and every man aboard labored one hour on and one hour off, "even our Governor and admiral themselves, not refusing their turn." A great wave covered the ship like a garment or a cloud and almost swamped her. They entered the eye of the hurricane and the rain struck them as if "whole rivers did flood the air"; they thought the rain had damped the wind for good, but the wind returned with increased fury. St. Elmo's fire ran on the lashing spars and filled them with new dread for more than half the night. They lightened the ship of everything they could get at, heaving overboard baggage, chests, and all the ship's cannon. They staved in the butts of beer and hogsheads of precious wine, vinegar, cider, and oil, without interruption to the pumping and the endless bailing of the three bucket chains. They were at the end of their endurance — men collapsed all over the ship wherever they had fallen, women voiceless after days and nights of weeping — when toward noon of the third day Sir George Somers, who had taken over the conning of the ship and stood at his post without sleep or food, "discovered and cried land."

Sir Thomas Gates commanded the helm put up and the ship bore in toward shore. The boatswain taking soundings reported thirteen fathom, then seven, then four, and shortly after, about a mile from the beach, the Sea Venture grounded. Where she heeled over in the lee of a point, the water was calm and they were able to get off all the one hundred and fifty men, women, and children who made up passengers and crew, and afterward at their leisure saved a good part of the stores not spoiled by water and all the ship's tackle and most of her ironware. Once again, as during all the fore part of the voyage, they felt God with them, and so indeed it proved to be.

When they first realized on what place they had come ashore, however, dread once more assailed them, for these were the "vexed" Bermudas, subject in mariners' reports to violent storms and, according to the coastal Indians of Virginia and North Carolina, inhabited by a race of remorseless cannibals and haunted by the specters of their victims. (The wreck of the Sea Venture and these legends of island evil were to provide Shakespeare with the atmospheric background of The Tempest.) But the castaways soon found that except for themselves there were no human beings on any of the islands. If there were specters they would have been the ghosts of the vanished cannibals who, in one account, had been overcome by three raiding Spanish ships and transported wholesale into slavery. Far from being "the most dangerous, infortunate, and most forlorn place in the world," the islands were almost an earthly paradise, benign in climate, rich in natural food. Around them the sea teemed with fish, and great marine turtles were easy to take — one of them, according to Sylvester Jourdain, would feed fifty men or give up a bushel of eggs; sea birds also provided an endless supply of eggs and young birds as sweet as squabs; and a vast number of pigs roamed wild, descendants of a shipload of hogs wrecked there nearly a century earlier on their way from Spain to Cuba.

It was the master of this vessel, Juan Bermudez, who had given his name to the islands.

Lovely as they were, there was no thought of settling on them. Sir Thomas Gates had duty waiting for him in Virginia, and once they had scouted the islands and established the routine of their new existence, they turned their energies to building ships in which to finish their journey. To Sir George Somers the native cedar looked promising and he set about building a boat with his own hands, working from morning to night "as duly as any workman doth labor for wages." It proved well; he used it for fishing and taking turtle and transporting hogs killed on other islands. They started work on two vessels, a small ship and a pinnace, using the native cedar and the spars and ironware salvaged from the *Sea Venture*.

It was slow work and meanwhile life flowed on: a man and woman married; a boy was born, and then a girl, daughter to the John Rolfes, whom they named Bermuda. The little girl died before they were ready to embark in the completed vessels which they had aptly named *Deliverance* and *Patience*. They had filled the holds with all the salted pork and fish they could carry and set sail at last on the tenth of May, 1610. Now once more the weather favored them and in just two weeks they had raised the Virginia shore and started up the James.

The six ships and the pinnace that had survived the hurricane, though widely scattered, all reached Jamestown safely. But they were in lamentable condition. Two had lost their mainmasts and all seven had been so wracked and battered by the storm that the supplies they brought were largely spoiled. The three hundred or so people aboard them were exhausted and hungry, many of them seriously ill; they meant three hundred more mouths to feed at a time when the colony was least equipped to do so. When the seven ships reached Jamestown in August there was not food enough on hand to feed the settlers already there. Smith had parties fishing at Point Comfort and oystering in Chesapeake Bay while others moved among the Indian villages trying to trade for corn. More than half of their own last reserve of grain had been eaten or spoiled by an army of rats invading the storehouse in the fort. Small groups of rats had come ashore with each landing of the immigrants and had found the New World hospitable; they had thrived and multiplied until they now infested most of the island.

To Smith and his supporters the arrival of this "Third Supply" was a disaster in still another way. The new arrivals were a much lower order of human than the original settlers who, however impractical and ill suited to the job of building a colony they might have been, had shown considerable spirit. But what was still worse was that John Ratcliffe, the former president of the colony, had returned together with his chief crony, a contentious lawyer and troublemaker named Gabriel Archer. Edward Maria Wingfield, first governor of the colony and Smith's inveterate antagonist, had considered Archer an unmitigated rogue. Smith himself, at the time he had sent Ratcliffe back to England "lest the company should cut his throat," declared that if he and Archer were permitted to return to Jamestown they would promote nothing but trouble. Yet here they were, and so it proved.

Ratcliffe began by demanding that Smith immediately resign the governorship, on the ground that since the Companys reorganization under the new charter Smith's title to office was no longer valid; and in the absence of Lord De La Warr and of his designated lieutenant governor, Sir Thomas Gates, presumably lost in the hurricane, he himself was the ranking officer of the new expedition and therefore the logical man to hold the office. The argument was plausible enough to have won Ratcliffe a considerable faction among the new arrivals; but the old colonists stood solidly behind Smith, who had Ratcliffe arrested for disturbing the peace.

He could not be held indefinitely, however, and a compromise was arrived at: Smith would serve out his term as governor, and Ratcliffe, Archer, and John Martin, who like Ratcliffe had been a member of the original council, would be allowed to take seats on the present council. It was at best a truce; and as it turned out, Smith's tenure was about to terminate in any case.

He had gone on another of his exploring trips, this time upriver beyond the falls of the James to look for a better site for the settlement, and on the way home was caught in an unexplained explosion of gunpowder, badly burned, and temporarily incapacitated. When he reached Jamestown he was literally in the hands of his enemies, who lost no time in getting rid of him. They claimed quite truthfully that he needed medical care which could not possibly be provided in Virginia and bundled him aboard the first ship to sail for England, consigning him to the misery and squalor of an ocean passage. Though he survived, and though he recrossed the Atlantic once more, it was to survey the New England coastline for the Plymouth Company. He never returned to Virginia.

For not quite two and a half years the Jamestown settlement had been kept on its feet, even through intervals of staggering, almost wholly because of the force of John Smith's character; now that it had to get along without him, matters swiftly deteriorated. Ratcliffe did not get the governorship. That went to a veteran colonist and a steady opponent of Smith, George Percy, normally a man of hardihood, but now too ill to have much control over the settlers. Relations with the neighboring Indians became strained; the braves retaliated by killing the settlers' pigs. Ratcliffe, emulating Smith, went off with a party of thirty to trade for grain and with all his men fell victim to a tidy little massacre.

But it was not Indians that came stalking the triangular palisade of the fort at Jamestown; it was cold and hunger and disease. There were not enough huts for all the five hundred settlers; many had to sleep unsheltered, "lying on the bare, cold ground, what weather soever came," as George Percy had written of the miseries of their first winter; but this winter was worse. The food gave out much sooner. They tried to find edible roots and wild plants. They dared not hunt. Indians kept watch from the fringes of the woods; now and then a flurry of arrows came arching into the enclosure. As their strength waned and their bodies became emaciated, the cold bit deeper, and in spite of their fear of Indians they began burning the palisades for warmth. Before long there were more than enough huts to house the living. Starvation drove them to cannibalism, and the living began living off the dead. First it was the body of an Indian slain beyond the palisade; then their own dead. Hallucinations and madness touched almost all who lived. One man burned his Bible. Another, accused of killing his wife in order to live off her body, was burned at the stake. Why the Indians did not storm the fort and wipe them out was a mystery. When spring came there were sixty survivors of the original five hundred, barely able to totter out in the soft May sunshine to meet the little ship and pinnace with Sir Thomas Gates sailing in with his party from Bermuda.

It was a time they could never forget, but they always spoke guardedly of it afterward, referring to it as the Starving Time.

In spite of the supplies brought with them by the Bermuda party, the situation at Jamestown was still close to desperation. There was no livestock left; the settlers had long since eaten all their pigs and chickens — all, that is, that the Indians had not killed. No crops had been planted; much of the palisade had been burned; the cabins had been let go so that much work would be needed to make them habitable again; and the surviving settlers, sick, weak, discouraged almost to the point of shock, had lost the will to struggle on. Gates, Newport, and old Sir George Somers, consulting together, decided that it would be impossible to carry on another year; their only course was to embark all hands on their two small vessels and return to England by the northern route, hoping to pick up enough fish off Newfoundland to sustain them on the final leg of the voyage.

They stripped Jamestown of everything usable that could be transported and on the seventh of June, to the slow beating of a drum, boarded their ships and started dropping down the James. It was an unhappy departure. As if to emphasize it the light breeze died toward evening and, unable to make headway, they anchored for the night off Mulberry Island, only fourteen miles downriver. But in the morning they had scarcely made sail when a ship's boat appeared in the broad reach below and all hands watched as it slowly approached. It brought brave news. Lord De La Warr with three ships heavily supplied and one hundred and fifty new colonists had reached Point Comfort and even now would be on his way upstream.

Without hesitation Gates reversed his course and the two little ships for the second time stood upriver toward Jamestown. Some of the survivors of the Starving Time, who wanted no more of Virginia, protested in dismay. But they were not heeded. The ships were unloaded and when at last De La Warr arrived, the three captains with their men behind them were standing at the fort's gate to welcome him. They knew that he would know that they had abandoned it but had been saved by the news of his coming and were able therefore to stand at their posts only by the mercy of God. Recognizing this, De La Warr himself dropped to his knees before the gate and gave thanks.

Some thanks, however, were also due to him. The arrival of the ships in England in the preceding November, one of which brought John Smith, had made clear the desperate situation the colony might be in, with too many mouths for the food in hand and, since the loss of the *Sea Venture* with, it was assumed, all aboard her, officerless as well. The urgency of his own appearance there as governor was brought home to him and he acted with intelligence and energy. By April he was at sea. His ships were loaded with stores enough to meet the wants of the colonists as well as of their own crews; and the hundred and fifty new recruits making the voyage with him were nearly all mechanics and artisans — as Smith had asked for in his blunt report of 1608. For once the Jamestown colonists would be able to look forward in reasonable confidence to the year ahead; there would be periods of terror and violence, but they would never again be reduced to the desperate straits of the first three years in Virginia.

What De La Warr had not counted on was the total loss of all the livestock belonging to the settlement. Having heard about the huge number of pigs on Bermuda, he determined to import a shipload of them. Sir George Somers, old as he was, "out of his worthy and valiant mind offered himself" to undertake the mission as being of all men the most familiar with the islands. With a small crew he embarked in the little pinnace he had worked so hard to build and on the nineteenth of June dropped down the river. Jamestown never saw him again. He reached the Bermudas safely but died before he could embark on the return voyage — one version says "of a surfeit in eating a pig," so presumably he had had some success. But as soon as he had died, his crew forgot his dying

[248]

command to sail back to Virginia; they had had their bellyful of the wilderness if not of pork; and stocking the pinnace with the pigs at hand, they set sail for England, taking with them the crudely embalmed body of the old knight as a justification.

Though the failure of the pinnace to return with its load of Bermuda pigs was a disappointment, no one starved, for in September the ubiquitous Captain Argall turned up at Jamestown with his ship loaded to bursting with salt fish and Indian corn. He was supposed to have sailed to Bermuda with Sir George Somers, but he reported that a gale had blown his ship north instead, all the way to Cape Cod where he had caught a great many fish, and then cruising homeward he had ventured into Chesapeake Bay and up the Potomac River. There he had met and made friends with the chief of the Potomacs, who had sold him the corn. The food he brought made his explanation acceptable if not wholly believable. Samuel Argall seems to have been instinctively a lone operator and he may well have preferred to go scavenging off on his own to making a Bermuda round trip under an old man's orders.

Shortly after his return Lord De La Warr sent the ships back to England under Newport and with them Sir Thomas Gates to report to the Company on the recent history of the settlement and its needs for the future. Meanwhile he had been busy putting the colony in order, and during the summer a great deal had been accomplished. The palisade, the houses, and the church at Jamestown were all repaired; Gates dispossessed the Indians of Kecoughtan and built two small palisaded redoubts, one on each side of the stream which ran through the place. Though they were hardly more than stockades, he named them Fort Henry and Fort Charles in honor of the king's sons. Kecoughtan was one of the most inviting pieces of land on the whole peninsula — "much corn, and abounding with commodities of fish, fowle, Deere, and fruits." Men posted there needed to draw only half the amount of subsistence stores required by men living at Jamestown. Secretary Strachey considered it the ideal seat for colonial governors. It must have seemed equally bountiful to the Indians.

De La Warr, however, remained in Jamestown through the winter. It was one which, though they had just rations enough, brought a great deal of sickness so that nearly one hundred and fifty died. The governor himself became so ill that it was obvious he could no longer fulfill his duties, and in March of 1611 he sailed for England, leaving George Percy to hold the fort once more until the lieutenant governor should return. At almost the same time Captain Newport sailed from England with a convoy of three ships, loaded with supplies for a full year and with three hundred new immigrants; but instead of Gates, who was not yet ready to return, Sir Thomas Dale was sent out to take over the reins of the colony with the title, since Gates did not want to give up his office, of High Marshal of Virginia.

No better man could have been found to get the colony solidly on its feet. Like so many other Englishmen who came to America in those years, he was a veteran of the Netherlands wars and more than most he bore the stamp of the soldier. Tough-minded, energetic, sensible, ruthless, incorruptible, he ran the colony like a military camp. Regulations were relentlessly enforced; penalties were severe. A man caught pilfering food from the common store would have his ears cut off; a second offense sent him back to England and the galleys. Capital crimes included speaking ill of the king or the Company, trading with Indians, killing cattle or other livestock without permission, even failure to attend the daily services held in the church at ten o'clock and four. Malingerers got short shrift; Dale punished them without mercy, and of course the colony was full of them. They felt as bitterly toward him, and soon there was a plot to depose and murder him. It came to light, however, and the six ringleaders were summarily executed, in ways brutal enough to discourage any future enterprise along those lines.

But Dale was a good deal more than just a driving taskmaster. He realized that the root of the colony's troubles lay in the communistic system that still prevailed. No Englishmen liked to work without a personal incentive, and as mere employees of the absentee London Company they saw no way of bettering their lot. Dale therefore gave every man three acres of his own land, to work as he saw fit, for payment of a minimal tax in corn. This was a first step, if a small one, toward shaping a stable colony and the effect, though also small, was immediate. What a man raised on his three acres, except for the six bushel tax, was for his own benefit; there was less disposition to lie back and depend on other men's work. In 1612 when the London Company had taken out a third charter (mainly for the purpose of annexing the Bermudas) far more liberal in its terms and providing for a much broader participation among its members in colonial management, settlers who had been seven years in Virginia were offered grants of one hundred acres if they chose to remain, with an additional hundred acres if after a term they proved to have managed their land well.

This second step served its purpose as far as men already in Jamestown were concerned; the prospect of having to serve seven years as a servant of the Company to have a right to one hundred acres held small allure for solid yeomen though it might still attract debtors or men on the shady side of the law. In 1616 Dale started offering settlers hundred-acre grants regardless of the seven years of service; and in 1619 at last the transition from a communistic community was completed — any man with the means could purchase land, and the Company offered large grants to men or combines of men who were ready to bring out settlers at their own expense, besides reserving a few great tracts for itself.

This process naturally led to an expansion of settlement beyond the immediate vicinity of Jamestown. Men took land on both banks of the river and Dale, seeing the necessity of some fortified areas, established a new settlement considerably above the junction of the Appomattox with the James on an almost-island in the James with a narrow neck now called Dutch Gap, and named it the City of Henricus. Across the gap he built a palisade, and spaced around the shore of the "island" were five "faire blockhouses." Six hundred and fifty new immigrants had arrived in 1611, raising the total English population to eight hundred, so Dale was able to take more than three hundred men with him to found Henricus. Many of them were German laborers and as a result the town of three streets had "well-framed houses, a handsome church . . . beside store houses, watch houses, and such like." Even while these were building, the foundations for "a more stately church" were laid in brick; it was to be one hundred feet long by fifty wide, an imposing edifice for the time and place. With his stern military qualities Dale combined religiosity; he was a devout churchman and in his leisure moments liked nothing better than taking part in theological discussions.

An air of expansiveness was blowing through the colony; few doubts about its permanence remained; and yet if permanence was to be realized Virginia needed a product for export. A certain amount of cedar and naval stores were sent back every year and some of the manufactured glass, but these were paltry against the colonial expenses. Jamestown was too far south to find a trade in fur and it was obvious to everyone that the hoped-for gold would never materialize. But an answer was at hand.

In 1612 John Rolfe began experimenting in the cultivation of tobacco. The local variety grown by the Powhatans and allied local tribes was an inferior, woody plant. Rolfe, importing seeds from the Caribbean islands, found that they would thrive equally well in the mild Virginia climate and was soon producing a mild, broad-leaved variety of his own, "as sweet and pleasant as any under the sun." A few men were quick to follow his example and in 1615 twenty-three hundred pounds were shipped to England. By 1619 that figure had increased to twenty thousand pounds and the directors of the London Company actively promoted the importation of tobacco in England over the protests of King James who considered the use of it sheer nastiness and urged the Virginia colonists to take up the culture of silk instead. When one considers that an acre could produce five hundred pounds of tobacco which sold for one hundred and twenty-five pounds sterling in London, and that one man by his own labor alone could produce a crop worth two hundred pounds, this was indeed gold in another form, and, appropriately, Virginia tobacco was golden leaved.

John Rolfe made another, almost equally important contribution to the colony two years later by marrying Pocahontas and ensuring peaceful relations with the Indians during this first wave of colonial expansion.

In April 1613, Captain Argall on another of his speculative voyages again sailed up the Potomac and dropped anchor at the mouth of Potomac Creek beside the Indian village of Patawomeke. There seemed to be an unusual amount of activity, but he had no hesitation about going ashore. The Potomacs were still friendly to the English and the chief of the village, a man named Japazaws, was an old acquaintance. An Indian trading fair was in progress; a delegation of Powhatans were attending it, among them Pocahontas, who appeared to have come for the frolic and to act as her father's trading agent.

There had been increasing trouble with the Powhatans, so much so that High Marshal Dale was seriously considering war against them, and it now occurred to Argall that if he could get Pocahontas away in his ship, she would make a useful hostage. He broached the idea to Japazaws, who scented profit for himself, and when Argall promised him "a small copper kettle and some other less valuable toys" the chief agreed to entice her on board. He briefed his wife; and next day accompanying Argall to the shore with Pocahontas and Japazaws, the woman suddenly asked to go aboard the ship. Japazaws indignantly refused her. She then wept, and the chief relenting said she could go if Pocahontas would keep her company. There was no difficulty and presently Pocahontas was safely locked in the gunner's room, Japazaws and his wife were paid off, the anchor raised, and the ship, called *Treasurer*, made sail for Jamestown.

Pocahontas had not seen Jamestown since before Smith left. She was now about eighteen, a comely young woman, and married to a Powhatan warrior named Kocoum. Those of the men who had never seen her had heard of her and her gifts of food, second only to the efforts of Captain Smith in preservation of the settlement; they were curious to see what she looked like, though not as curious as the few veterans of the first years who could remember her leading in her company of Indians with their baskets of corn, after which she would entice some of the young lads "into the market place and make them wheel, falling on their hands and turning their heels upwards," and then follow them herself in joyful cartwheels "all the fort over," naked as a fish, for being still twelve there was no obligation for her to wear the conventional leather apron worn by mature women. In the mind of Secretary Strachey these high spirits indicated a wanton heart; but the play was done in innocence even though she must have noticed the hungry eyes that followed her; and she may well have been reminded of them now as she entered the fort so long afterward.

If she had doubts about her treatment now that Smith was not there, she need not have worried. Dale treated her with courtesy, took her under his own wing up to Henricus, and saw to it that she was converted to Christianity straightaway. Sometime during the year she was baptized and named Rebekah. She had always liked the English because of Smith. It seems reasonable to believe that she was in love with him; but small girl that she was, he regarded her more as a daughter, and she had been satisfied to accept that relationship. Now as she took up her new Christian life her feelings for him must have come flooding back; yet sadly, for somehow she had come to believe that he was dead. The idea may well have been planted in her mind deliberately to further the affair that soon began to develop.

John Rolfe's plantation was not far from Henricus; it was natural for him to encounter Pocahontas, and their meetings soon became more frequent. His baby daughter had died during the winter in the Bermudas; shortly after reaching Jamestown his wife also had died. In his lonely state his eye was taken by the bright, personable, warmhearted young woman and before long he became infatuated by her.

He went through a good deal of agonizing before he made up his mind that he wanted to marry her. This was a rare decision for a man of English blood. Two hundred years later, Daniel Harmon, a fur factor in the northwest, decided to buy a fourteen-year-old half-breed girl to warm his bed during the winter and wrote in his diary for October 10, 1801:

> . . . I have finally concluded to accept of her, as it it customary for all gentlemen who remain, for any length of time, in this part of the world, to have a female companion, with whom they can pass their time more socially and agreeably, than to live a lonely life, as they must do, if single. If we can live in harmony together, my intention now is, to keep her as long as I remain in this uncivilized part of the world; and when I return to my native land, I shall endeavour to place her under the protection of some honest man, with whom she can pass the remainder of her days in this country, much more agreeably, than it would be possible for her to do, were she to be taken down into the civilized world, to the manners, customs and language of which, she would be an entire stranger. Her mother is of the tribe of Snare Indians, whose country lies beyond the Rocky Mountains. The girl is said to have a mild disposition and an even temper, which are qualities very necessary to make an agreeable woman, and an affectionate partner.

Harmon had put off such a liaison for longer than the usual period because of qualms of conscience, in which he was the exception rather than the rule, and he was sincere in planning from the beginning for the little girl's future. If she had belonged to another man, she would have been turned off, with whatever children she might have borne him, when he was done with her as casually as he would have disposed of a dog. Harmon, be it said, after several years found himself under a moral obligation and took her with their children home with him to Vermont where he married her.

But John Rolfe's conscience troubled him from the outset so deeply that he resolved to marry Pocahontas if the high marshal should approve. At the same time he was profoundly disturbed by the fact that such feelings should have been aroused in him by a red Indian. He tried to persuade himself, and also Dale in a letter he presently wrote requesting permission and approval of the match, that his action would be motivated only by his desire to make Pocahontas a good Christian (since she had already been baptized under Dale's sponsorship, this would appear a slight redundancy of pious effort). He claimed that he was "no way led (so far as man's weakness may permit) with the unbridled desire of carnal affection," but impelled to take the step for the good of the plantation, the honor of England, the glory of God, and his own salvation.

It is a curious letter and in the end he had wholly convinced himself:

> Now if the vulgar sort, who square all men's actions by the base rule of their own filthiness, shall tax or taunt me in this my godly labour, let them know it is not any hungry appetite to gorge myself with incontinency; sure, if I would and were so sensually inclined, I might satisfy such desire, though not without a seared conscience. . . . Nor am I in so desperate an estate that I regard not what becometh of me; nor am I out of hope but one day to see my country, nor so void of friends nor mean in birth but there to obtain a match to my great content; nor have I ignorantly passed over my hopes there or regardlessly seek to lose the love of my friends by taking this course. I know them all and have not rashly overslipped any.

Dale saw instantly the advantages that might accrue and gave his wholehearted sanction to the match, and Pocahontas herself was impressed by Rolfe's suit, for he was a leading figure in the colony; and supposing Smith dead, she was not unwilling. Powhatan, informed of the proposed marriage, also was impressed and sent on one of his elderly brothers, Opachisco, to give the bride away. On the fifth of April the wedding took place.

All idea of making war on Powhatan was now dropped; the old chief concluded a firm peace, and friendly trading, abeyant since Smith's departure, was resumed. The neighboring Chicahominies, with whom relations had often been tricky, were so impressed that they came in to cement a peace of their own and offered to become English subjects and even change their tribal name to *Tassantasses*, which was their word for Englishmen. Reassured by these agreements, the settlers soon felt safe enough to drop their former precautions and began to establish themselves in separate unprotected plantations along both banks of the James, and Governor Dale himself felt free to turn his attention to the encroaching French in Nova Scotia, who had begun a small settlement at Port Royal. One would have thought it too far removed from Jamestown to be menacing, but the original Virginia claim of the English was to the 45th degree of latitude, so technically the French were trespassers. Dale sent Captain Argall to get rid of them, which he did with little difficulty, burning the town and loading the inhabitants and some of the livestock aboard his ship; and on his return, as we have seen, he looked in at the mouth of the Hudson to threaten the Dutch on Manhattan.

However much John Rolfe may have protested the absence of carnality in his feelings for Pocahontas, once they were married he fulfilled his obligations as a husband, for in the following year she bore him a son. The boy was destined to become ancestor of several of the most distinguished Virginia families, including the Randolphs, who therefore, whatever the attitude of their descendants, were the product of a form of integration. Rolfe, however, took pride in his alliance and when later in the year Sir Thomas Dale returned to England he sailed also, taking his wife and infant son.

English society received Pocahontas as if she were royalty; she was the dusky princess from Virginia; King James was even supposed to have contemplated censuring Rolfe for marrying royalty without his permission. She was entertained in a whirl of receptions and banquets, had her portrait painted, and met many of the distinguished leaders of social and political life. Subsequent visiting Indian chiefs would also be greeted with acclamation but red America certainly never sent a more effective ambassador than Lady Rebekah, as she was called. The one note of sadness was her meeting with John Smith. She wept, and would not let him call her "Lady Rebekah," saying she was his child and he her father, and told him that until she reached Plymouth she had not known he was still living.

Sharing in her triumph, Rolfe was made secretary of the colony. They sailed in March 1617, but she had picked up smallpox in London and the course of the disease was as quick and fatal as it was for all her race. They took her body off the ship at Gravesend and buried her there.

Powhatan died the following year. When Opechancanough succeeded him as chief of the Powhatan confederacy, the older settlers, or "ancient planters" as they called themselves, felt some alarm because of his long record of outspoken hostility toward the English, and there was talk of the Indians' "slippery designs"; but their fears gradually subsided as the behavior of the Powhatans continued to be friendly. Opechancanough himself became a frequent visitor to the settlements, particular to Henricus. In all, Virginia enjoyed eight years of peace after Pocahontas's marriage to Rolfe, and during them the colony made momentous progress.

The most significant step came in 1619 when, under its newly arrived governor, Sir George Yeardley, representative government was established in Virginia. Yeardley, who was of relatively humble origin, had succeeded Gates as deputy governor and remained in Virginia as acting governor when Dale in 1616 returned to England. But in 1617 Samuel Argall was appointed governor. He was related by marriage to Sir Thomas Smith, who had been treasurer of the London Company from the beginning, and having operated round the outskirts of the colony was now eager for political power and the opportunity to increase his fortune. He proved the most arbitrary governor by far that Virginia had had, administering justice even more harshly than Dale, but where Dale's integrity had never been questioned, Argall was openly accused of unscrupulous operations — "more for love of gain, the root of all evil, than for any true love he bore for this plantation" as one accuser put it. These charges seem to have been reasonably well founded; letters to London forced his recall, and De La Warr was sent out in 1618 to resume active governorship and send Argall home under arrest.

Here again, as in the case of Laval and early leaders of New France, the crossing and recrossing of the Atlantic is astonishing; the months spent in hazardous ocean passages provide a scale against which the seriousness of purpose of these early colonials can be judged and their achievements, which might otherwise seem small, be measured. De La Warr never reached Jamestown. Putting in at St. Michael's in the Azores, he and some of his company were invited ashore and entertained by the Spaniards, and shortly afterward the whole party of thirty fell sick and died. There were many who believed they had been poisoned, but there was no proof and the ship continued to Virginia, where De La Warr's papers came into Argall's hands. He saw no reason to alter his ways, but when word reached him the following year that Yeardley was returning to supersede him, he decided not to wait for possible arrest but packed himself and his wife aboard his own waiting ship and left posthaste for England. Even so, he had not done at all badly for himself, for while on arriving as governor "he had brought only his sword with him," he took home very nearly three thousand pounds — an enormous sum, however it was acquired, when one considers the resources of the little colony. But in a way it was a bargain because Argall was the last Virginia governor to be vested with absolute and arbitrary powers. Yeardley brought with him

[256]

a charter from the Company under which the colony was to establish its own representative government.

This "Great Charter of commission of privileges, orders, and laws" had been the work mainly of two men: Sir Thomas Smyth and Sir Edwin Sandys, who succeeded Smyth as treasurer in 1619. Sandys had studied at Cambridge under Richard Hooker and from him absorbed a tolerance and breadth of view not common among his peers. In the Company he was leader of the so-called "country" party as opposed to the "court" party, to which Smyth subscribed; in Parliament he stood at the head of the liberal party; and in both roles he opposed royal prerogatives and the Stuarts' pretensions to the divine right of kings, which made him anathema to James. A silly quarrel between Sir Thomas Smyth and another member of the "court" party, Lord Rich, over the marriage of Smyth's son to the latter's young sister, produced an upheaval in the Company which placed Sandys and his supporters in control and by doing so ensured that Englishmen in Virginia could live under laws as free as those of Englishmen at home.

The government framed in the Great Charter consisted of the governor, a governor's council originally of six which was called the Council of Estate, and an assembly of twenty-two burgesses who were to represent the freemen of the four "corporations" that comprised the colony: the City of Henricus, Charles City, James City, and Kecoughtan. These in turn were divided into "burroughs" which conformed to the seven "particular plantations" (those granted to important shareholders or reserved for the support of government officials) and four "general plantations" (which were open to settlement by the public). Kecoughtan and Henricus were classified as burroughs and therefore elected two burgesses each. James City was divided into four burroughs, and Charles City into five; but an exception was taken to accepting Martin's "Brandon," apparently on the ground that the terms of its patent were unduly liberal. An offer was made to accept its delegates provided John Martin gave up some of his special privileges, but he seems to have preferred privilege to representation and refused to do so, and after an interminable discussion the two burgesses were not seated. This reduced the number in the first House of Burgesses to twenty. In time in their political function these corporations developed their own local government and came to be known as counties. They had their own courts, which functioned very much as our county courts do today.

At first the burgesses sat with the governor and Council of Estate and their first meeting on July 30, 1619, to approve the charter and begin framing their own laws, took place in the choir of the little church at Jamestown as "the most convenient place we could find to sit in." But this posed an immediate dilemma: the meeting place being a church, should the members remove their hats? Members of Parliament, however, always convened wearing their hats; and after some discussion it was decided that if Parliament sat hatted, the House of Burgesses would sit likewise, church or no.

The session opened properly with a prayer by Mr. Bucke, the minister. The governor sat at the head of the choir with the council on each side of him and the clerk of the General Assembly, John Twine, sitting in front of him with the speaker, John Pory, who was also secretary of the colony, having succeeded John Rolfe in the post. The burgesses sat below them in the choir, and as soon as the prayer was finished were asked to step down into the body of the church and return one by one to take the Oath of Supremacy to the king, which all did, "none staggering under it," and in turn resumed their seats.

This matter taken care of, the speaker, who was barely recovered from a serious illness "and therefore not able to pass through long harangues," reminded them with a briefness that seems to have been appreciated of how and why they had come to meet, and read them the commissions creating both the council and their own assembly. He then passed to a reading of the Great Charter, which done the assembly was ready to get down to the first order of business.

Significantly, this was to appoint committees to consider the provisions of the Great Charter from a Virginian point of view — "not to the end to correct or control anything therein contained, but only in case we should find aught not perfectly squaring with the state of this colony, or any law which did bind or press too hard." Mainly the petitions for alterations sent back to the Company in London concerned the validity of earlier land grants to the ancient planters, the need for tenants for the particular plantations reserved for support of colonial officials, the necessity of having a subtreasurer who could supervise fiscal matters within the colony itself. The burgesses also asked that the Company send workmen of various sorts who could build the university and college projected in the Great Charter.

In the charter a hundred thousand acres were set aside for the support of the university though there was no stipulation about its immediate construction. The "college," however, which was in effect to be a public free school for Virginian boys, was also designed to train young "Infidels in the true Religion, moral virtue and civility"; it was therefore regarded as an important means of furthering peaceful relations between the two races and was to be built without delay. Its endowment would come from a fund-raising campaign throughout England, for which the king had granted a special license, and Captain George Thorpe, "a gentleman of his Majesty's Privy Chamber," was appointed its first superintendent. A final petition requested that Kecoughtan corporation be given an English name.

The burgesses then turned their attention to the forming of burroughs, to establishing boundaries for public and glebe lands, and to guaranteeing that men who had come to Virginia at their own expense before the end of Dale's term should have one hundred acres plus one hundred acres for every Company share of twelve pounds ten shillings they had paid for; and that those brought over at Company cost should have one hundred acres after they had served their time, but should pay a quitrent annually of two shillings on the hundred acres. Settlers arriving after Dale's departure would have fifty acres as their share with a quitrent of one shilling.

The House then gave its attention to the placing of individual plantations and to determining which grants might be illegal; and at last took up the job of framing the laws they were to live under. This body of laws and orders ranged all the way from land grants — to be made in general quarter court, "with equal favors, as near as may be" for all — to such problems as Indians: they were not to be unduly encouraged to fraternize, nor yet should any advances by them be summarily rejected; no more than five or six should be permitted on any hunting expedition or at "the beating of corn"; nor, on pain of death, should any man sell or give them any firearm, powder, or lead. Unlike the Puritan laws, the death penalty does not cast a long shadow over these first Virginia laws. Idleness was inveighed against, and a freeman who ran loose and idle might be given a master whom he must work for, for wages, till he improved his ways. Gambling, drunkenness, and vanity in clothes, called "excess in apparel," were also dealt with; profanity was subject to a five-shilling fine paid to the guilty man's church (if he was a servant he got a public whipping, unless his master wanted to pay the fine for him); sin was disapproved of but to nowhere near the degree of Puritan disapproval. A person guilty of "incontinency or of the commission of any other of the enormous sins" would receive two warnings and then if he (or she) persisted be suspended from the church for a time determined by his minister, and if that did not make him mend his ways he would be excommunicated.

The burgesses themselves were conscious of the rude simplicity of the work they had performed and apologized to the officers of the London Company (from whom approval had to come before their measures could become law) "that in so short a space they could bring their matter to no more perfection." They were still nonprofessionals and it would be some years before the burgesses would convene on a regular schedule. Their work, however, was adequate for the colony's needs, and the laws were administered in the burroughs in meetings where the leading men of the community came together. Some of these same men would sit on the quarter courts, for the governor, though ostensibly he had power to appoint his own choice, had to appoint men who could make the system work. It was from among these same men that the burgesses were chosen. So political power fell naturally into the hands of men who by reason of their large landholdings, wealth, and the number of men in their service wielded the real power in their own communities. It was no democracy, but it was a step toward democracy, and the important thing about it was that the rights and privileges the colonists enjoyed in this form of self-government derived not from the Crown (though it had granted the original London Company charter) but from a public corporation.

By coincidence at this early stage, also in 1619, the first Negroes were brought to Virginia. A Dutch man-of-war which, in the course of raiding in the Caribbean, had picked up twenty Negroes, put in at Jamestown and offered the Negroes for sale. They were bought up and oddly enough accepted as indentured servants and not slaves. Increase in the number of Negroes for many years was slow — the average planter, indeed, much preferred indentured English servants who could be replaced by men or women in full vigor when their term ran out. But by the turn of the century, though there were then only six thousand Negroes in the colony, it had become apparent that black labor was the answer to plantation needs; from that time forward the number of slaves imported increased in bounds, so that by the Revolution almost half Virginia's population was black and slavery with all its side effects of debilitation and ignominy was solidly established at the base of the plantation system and the social life of the South.

Quite another sort of arrival, which occurred the following year, had much more immediate impact on the colony: one hundred and fifty young women, described as "uncorrupt" and thoroughly matroned, were landed at Jamestown "for making of the men feel at home in Virginia." Each girl was entirely free to make her choice — even the less comely found plenty of suitors among the woman-starved settlers — and like the French girls sent to Canada enjoyed a brief but heady foretaste of equality in a world of men which twentieth-century American womanhood takes for granted; and certainly on the part of the settlers no measure taken for their benefit was received with more enthusiasm, even though each man had to put up one hundred and twenty pounds of tobacco to get his girl once she had said yes.

This shipment of young women was an integral part of an overall plan which Sir Edwin Sandys had persuaded the Company stockholders to adopt in order to put the colony on a broader and self-sustaining basis. It was to be completed in five years.

Virginia was no longer to be dependent solely on her tobacco crop. The instructions carried overseas by Sir George Yeardley had emphasized this, and in the laws they passed, the burgesses ordered that each man should have on hand yearly a barrel of corn over and above the needs of himself and his servants, that each year he plant and maintain in growth six mulberry trees, and that he grow hemp, flax, and grapes — to process which Sandys sent vintners from France. More woodsmen from the Baltic were sent out along with sawmill workers to develop a lumber industry, and one hundred and fifty ironworkers who were to build an iron foundry on Falling Creek, the site of Richmond, on which the Company spent more than four thousand pounds.

Cattle, poultry, horses were also on the list, but above all more settlers were needed if the colony was to become strong. The attractions of Virginia, the freedom and benefits to be enjoyed there, were widely publicized, and special grants of land were offered to men or combines of men who brought out two hundred and fifty or more settlers at their own expense. These grants consisted at the least of twelve hundred and fifty acres and came to be known as "hundreds." By all past standards the results were spectacular. In 1619 alone, twelve hundred and sixty-one people emigrated and in the next two years the flow over the Atlantic continued at nearly the same rate. Yet in spite of it disease continued to cut down the population so that in the spring of 1622 it did not amount to quite twelve hundred souls, and of these over a third were struck down in a few hours on March 22, which was Good Friday.

Opechancanough's hatred of the English had not wavered. As he watched the spread of plantations up and down the James, he became more than ever convinced that Indians could not exist in the same country with white men. But he saw weakness in this spreading out of the English. The new plantations were being located at ten-mile intervals, and with the exception of places like Henricus and Jamestown itself, they were without defenses. The English still trusted the peace that had followed Pocahontas's marriage to John Rolfe. While he began slowly to organize the Powhatan tribes for a united attack, he took pains to foster the English trust, and he soon found what he considered an ideal way of doing so through the "college" in which young Indians were to learn Christianity and civility. The superintendent became his stalking horse.

George Thorpe found much to like in Virginia, though he reported that good wine was very hard to come by. But even this lack was compensated for by the settlers' having "found a way to make a good drink from Indian corn" which he considered preferable to good English beer — perhaps this was the prototype of bourbon whiskey. But his consuming interest was his school and the progress being made with some of the Indian boys. He seems to have been an openhearted man and when the elderly chief came round to make his own check on the boys' progress Thorpe was deeply impressed and saw no reason to question his sincerity.

The school was at Dutch Gap in the "city" of Henricus, and Opechancanough became not only a frequent visitor to the school but a familiar figure in the two short streets of the settlement. Thorpe soon came to regard him as a friend and, when the Indian expressed admiration for the English houses, built him a small one for himself in the English pattern. The chief was delighted with it and used it often, taking particular pleasure in locking the door after him and unlocking it when he returned. The idea of a lock, of being able with a little key to prevent the ingress of others, was new to his Indian mind. It may very well have been symbolic too, and when he saw the English settlers watching him with amusement no doubt he had his own inward smile.

He began to visit other plantations and encouraged his braves to do the same, to offer help with some of the plantation chores or guide English hunting parties; but most of his visiting continued to be at Henricus and so receptive did he seem toward the Christianizing of the Indian boys that Thorpe determined to try to convert him. The English gradually became accustomed to this fraternization; they even began to relax the prohibition against giving or selling firearms and powder to the Indians, and frequently entertained Indian guests in their houses. As the report went, both the old chief and his people "for the courtesies of this good gentleman [Mr. Thorpe], did promise such outward love and respect unto him, as nothing could seem more."

Early in 1622 an Indian, Jack-of-the-Feathers, went into the woods to hunt with a planter named Morgan. After a time the Indian returned alone, reporting that Morgan had been ambushed and killed by hostile Indians; but as he was wearing Morgan's hat the latter's servants decided to take him in to Jamestown. The Feather refused to go, tried to escape, was shot, and died on the way down the river. Supposedly this incident triggered Opechancanough's decision to strike a paralyzing blow against the English and drive them forever from his country. But the elaborateness with which he had worked out his points of attack and organized the various tribes suggests much longer planning. The fact that it took place on Good Friday was probably fortuitous.

The "deadly stroake" fell at eight o'clock in the morning. War parties had taken up positions near the major objectives, like the foundry at Falling Creek, Henricus, and Bermuda Hundred; but in smaller places there would be only a handful of braves; and in many individual isolated farms a few Indians had come to spend the night with their white friends and were eating breakfast with them when the hour came and they rose from the table swinging tomahawks and war clubs. The surprise was utter almost everywhere.

. . . for 140 miles up and down the river on both sides, they fell upon the English and basely and barbarously murthered them, not sparing age, nor sex, man, woman, or child . . . so sudden in their cruel execution that few or none discerned the weapon or blow that brought them to destruction.

Henricus, the iron foundry, and Bermuda Hundred were totally destroyed. In the first blazing hour three hundred and fifty people died. Here and there where a settler had time to reach his cabin and his gun, and arm his servants if he had them, the Indians showed no stomach for pressing their attack home but passed on to some unwarned and unsuspecting farm. If it had occurred five years before, at the time Powhatan died, an onslaught of similar weight and ferocity would have wiped out the entire colony. Only Jamestown and Kecoughtan came through relatively unscathed, partly because they had been warned and partly because one of the coastal tribes, whose chief was known to the English for some reason as The Laughing King, changed his mind about joining the attack.

The warning came from a Christianized Indian boy who was spending the night in the house of his godfather, Richard Pace, across the river from the fort. He must have wrestled heavily with his conscience during the night, but before dawn the Christian side of him got the upper hand, and he woke Pace and told him of the imminent attack. Pace rowed over the river; the alarm went out to all neighboring plantations and farms; arms were distributed; and when the Indians came they found the situation much more formidable than they expected.

Even so, if Opechancanough could have driven the attack home, events might have been different; but the Indians were characteristically unable to sustain their momentum. As the pace of killing slowed, they lost their enthusiasm. They had loot in muskets and goods which they wanted to take home, and it is said that they reserved some of the gunpowder to plant in their cornfields so as to have a plentiful crop that fall to use against the English.

The English did not give it time to catch. Sir Francis Wyatt, who had succeeded Yeardley as governor the year before, organized reprisals with utter ruthlessness. Three times a year for the next three years two or more expeditionary forces left Jamestown to march against the Indian towns. Their captains were under oath to accept no bids for peace; Indian men, women, and children were systematically killed, their crops destroyed, their houses burned. When the killing declined, word was quietly passed around that the English were through and it would be safe for this or that tribe to return to its home ground; once it did so it was surrounded and its people exterminated. The greatest single triumph was the wiping out of the Pamunkey town and the killing of a thousand of the tribe.

All tribes of tidewater Virginia came under attack, whether they had taken part in the Good Friday massacre or not. When in 1625 the English felt they had finally cleaned up, there were no Indians left and

Opechancanough had been driven inland. But though he had suffered defeat he had accomplished things he had no inkling of. Higher education in Virginia, with the cleaving of his friend Thorpe's skull, would not be embarked on for seventy years, not till the College of William and Mary was founded in 1693 by a royal charter. It also left a colony woefully weak to be still further weakened by two successive winters of disease. In 1619 there had been over a thousand settlers; but though in the next five years they were joined by four thousand more, in 1624 there were fewer than thirteen hundred survivors. This brought the five-year plan of Sir Edwin Sandys to an end; the stockholders of the London Company were discouraged; the Company itself was split by factions; and in 1624 King James seized the opportunity to end it by annulling its charter.

Virginia then became a Crown colony with a governor and council appointed by the king. But it was allowed to keep its House of Burgesses, and this frame of colonial government became the pattern for all future Crown colonies, of which, in 1755 at the beginning of the French and Indian War, there were eight.

PART III

THE near extermination of the Pequot tribe in 1637 removed an immediate threat to New England but it did not allay the colonists' mistrust of Indian intentions. Seeds of future trouble lay in the deadly rivalry of Miantonomo of the Narragansetts and Uncas of the Mohegans. The latter had sided wholeheartedly with the English against the Pequots, but except for allowing the English army passage through his country, Miantonomo's role had been passive. Before the war he had made an alliance with Massachusetts but he had none with Connecticut, while Uncas had signed a treaty with the Connecticut towns but not with Massachusetts. They now began to play against each other for solid English support in a game in which Uncas proved himself far abler than his enemy.

In 1638 he came to Boston with thirty-odd braves and masses of wampum and, instead of offering an alliance, made a complete submission of himself and his tribe to Governor Winthrop, even agreeing to allow the English to arbitrate any differences that might develop between him and Miantonomo. To counteract this, Miantonomo approached the Connecticut towns and in September signed a joint treaty with Connecticut and the Mohegans. It was impressive on the surface but within two years settlers began to hear rumors of an Indian conspiracy of which Miantonomo was supposed to be the ringleader.

Considering himself equal to the highest English officials, he bore himself haughtily, even when called to Boston to declare his innocence of complicity in the supposed Indian plots; for a long time he refused to come at all unless he could bring his friend Roger Williams as interpreter and adviser; but as Williams had been banned from Massachusetts and was almost equally mistrusted, this was impossible. When Miantonomo finally came, without Williams, he refused to talk when he found that the governor had supplied a Pequot as interpreter, and the meeting was broken off with both sides in a state of exasperation.

Then in 1642 renewed alarms about an Indian plot brought home to the colonies their separation from each other not just geographically but in purpose. The Connecticut towns, which had lain naked to the first Pequot attacks and were still the most vulnerable target for the Narragansetts, wanted to put on another surprise war and wipe out the Narragansetts as they had the Pequots, but with so powerful a tribe they would need the help of Massachusetts. The Massachusetts colonists had no wish to attack a people that had done them no harm; such preventive war would incur God's displeasure. But they did not overlook the fact that if a plot existed it was possible that their own local tribes might be involved, and forcibly disarmed the Massachusetts and Pennacooks.

One of the arguments they used in dissuading Connecticut from waging preventive war on its own hook was that the Indian could not distinguish between colonists; if Connecticut attacked, Massachusetts would be just as much to blame; they were all merely Englishmen in the Indian mind. There should therefore be a means for coordinating the defense and policy of all the New England colonies and from this idea grew the confederation they called "The United Colonies of New England." Under it, Massachusetts, the Connecticut River towns, New Haven, and Plymouth agreed to appoint two commissioners apiece who would meet once a year, but special meetings could be called by any two commissioners whenever they felt it necessary for the public safety.

Domestic government remained entirely in the hands of the individual colonies but in all matters of Indian policy or in dealing with a foreign power the eight federal commissioners would have complete authority. They would coordinate the raising of military forces and allocate the expense to the various colonies on the basis of the number of men in each fit to bear arms, which at that time was calculated as between the ages of sixteen and sixty.

Rhode Island was never considered a fit candidate for membership. Roger Williams was altogether too heretical for Puritan stomachs; his upholding of the Indian as the only natural owner of American soil would alone have been enough to eliminate him and his colony; but he was also too friendly with the Narragansetts. When Rhode Island applied formally for inclusion in the league, in 1644 and 1648, it was summarily refused.

Though not a federation in the strict sense, the league was the forerunner of other movements in this direction, like Benjamin Franklin's Plan of Union formulated at the Albany Congress of 1754, and finally of the Articles of Confederation which, ratified in 1781, gave the thirteen newborn states their first form of federal government. But for forty years it served well enough and after it had ceased to have effective life New Englanders looked back on it with a kind of nostalgia. It had brought their colonies together to a degree and given them a sense of cohesion when the mother country was suffering the disruption of the Rebellion. Whether or not it concerned itself greatly with one of its stated objectives, "propagating the truth and liberties of the Gospel," it did interest itself to some extent in soliciting scholarships for Harvard College. But its primary function and the principal occupation of its eight commissioners was the handling of Indian problems. These confronted them at once, in the deadly enmity between Miantonomo and Uncas.

The destruction of the Pequots had left a power gap among New England tribes which each chief wished and expected to fill — something, however, which could only be accomplished with the consent or at least the neutrality of the English. In the four years since 1638 there had been testing and maneuvering in which Uncas seemed to have the better hand as well as the sympathy of the English. Miantonomo's lukewarmness in the Pequot war as well as the suspicion that he was conspiring against the colonies worked against him; but still more of a handicap was his own character. He could be as devious, tricky, unscrupulous, and cruel as Uncas or any other Indian; but he had the kind of savage innocence that made it wholly impossible for him to play in with the white man as Uncas could, or as Powhatan had done. If he lacked the kind of Roman intensity in his hatred of the whites that distinguished Opechancanough, he was as purely Indian in his thinking. He did not consider himself bound by his treaties either with Massachusetts or Connecticut or the Mohegans since in his own mind he had undertaken them as temporary expedients under a threat of force. Though they were still the most numerous New England tribe, the Narragansetts were now outnumbered by the English, who indeed outnumbered all the tribes of southern New England put together.

This in itself makes it seem unlikely that Miantonomo had any serious conspiracy afoot to annihilate the English — and the memory of what had happened to the Pequots was still vivid — but the situation appears to have aggravated his ambition to become top dog over Uncas, and in 1643 he took measures.

What these were was never entirely clear. Uncas claimed that Miantonomo had bribed a former Pequot sachem, named Sequesson, "adopted" by the Mohegans after the war, to assassinate him, and exhibited a flesh wound on his arm to confirm the accusation. Sequesson's sudden possession of a lot of wampum was adduced as clinching the matter, as was the Pequot's subsequent flight to Narragansett country. Normal Indian procedure would have sent Uncas off on an expedition of revenge; but instead he behaved like a proper civilized Indian and laid the matter before the courts. Hartford passed the case on to Boston where the federation's commissioners were in session.

They sent out a summons for Miantonomo and the accused Pequot and when the Indians appeared, listened skeptically to the Pequot's story. He simply denied attacking Uncas — said Uncas had cut himself deliberately and then bribed him, the supposed assassin, to say that Miantonomo had incited him and also to stage a "flight" to the Narragansetts for protection. It was a pretty good story and not implausible, but listening to it and at the same time watching the expression of disdain on the face of

Miantonomo the commissioners were skeptical, and they became more so when they reexamined the Pequot with Miantonomo excluded and the story began to take on variations. But even though their suspicions of a conspiracy were renewed, there was little they could do, and Miantonomo and the Pequot were told to go their way.

For the latter the way was not long. Someone, presumably Miantonomo, murdered him and whether he had spoken truthfully or lied could never be proved. But Miantonomo reached home breathing vengeance against his enemy, and as if to ensure his taking the warpath Uncas had sent a raiding party of his own to pick up a few Narragansett scalps. It was all too much for Miantonomo, who raised a thousand braves and marched against his enemy.

The expedition turned into an unmitigated disaster. Though outnumbering the Mohegans, the Narragansetts were put to ignominious flight and Miantonomo himself was overtaken on the field by one of Uncas's chiefs who held him humiliatingly at bay until Uncas could be summoned and personally take him captive, by a touch upon his shoulder. In spite of his contempt for the English, Miantonomo was wearing armor which had been given him by a friend and it slowed his flight enough to make his capture easy.

The friend was an eccentric character named Samuel Gorton who had been a follower of sorts of Anne Hutchinson. Gorton had offended the Puritan clergy in about every conceivable way: he maintained the right of laymen to preach the Gospel and said he was a "professor of the mysteries of Christ," and he believed in the power of private inspiration; but he was gifted with immense inconsistencies — he loathed the Quakers though they also believed in private inspiration; he defied the magistrates of Plymouth who wished to try one of his servants for smiling in church. He seems to have been born contentious and there was no room for him in so orthodox a community. He was given a fortnight in which to remove himself and his people from the colony.

So in 1638 he took refuge in Anne Hutchinson's settlement of Portsmouth on Aquidneck, but his theology was no more acceptable there than elsewhere, and he was ordered to leave. He went to Pawtuxet in Providence Plantation which tried to get rid of him finally by ceding Pawtuxet to Massachusetts so that the General Court there could deal with him instead of themselves. However, when summoned to Boston, Gorton merely moved on and persuaded the Narragansetts to sell him a large piece of land at Shawomet on the western shore of Narragansett Bay. Here he made a friend of Miantonomo. The two men may have found a bond in their struggles with the colonial authorities and summonses to Boston; and perhaps — it was not impossible — the rather fuzzy mind of the former London clothier and that of the savage Narragansett wandered the fringes of a similar mystery. Roger Williams, who was a very different caliber of rebel against Puritanism, had been able on occasion to help Miantonomo and had kept his trust; but Samuel Gorton by one act of impulsive kindness managed to seal the Indian's doom.

According to established Indian practice Miantonomo should have been burned. A chief of his stature naturally expected to be tortured with special and attentive refinements. As for Uncas, nothing could satisfy the Indian soul more fully than the spectacle of his personal enemy being destroyed bit by bit. But Uncas denied himself, and it is a measure of his sagacity and the sophistication of his insight into the English way of looking at things that, instead, he turned Miantonomo over to the Connecticut General Court as a violator of treaties with both the English colonies and the Mohegan tribe.

The General Court accepted him as a prisoner and lodged him in jail at Hartford, but the case obviously fell under jurisdiction of the New England confederation, whose commissioners were sitting for the first time in Boston, and it was referred to them. They found the case a knotty one, involving moral scruples, for Miantonomo had at no time attacked the English even though he was suspected of conspiring against them and plotting to make himself "universall Sagomore" of all southern New England. He had broken his treaties with the two colonies, but that hardly called for a death penalty, and his purported plotting to kill Uncas was hardly a crime against the English. But it was apparent from the beginning that to let Miantonomo go free was to put peace in New England in perpetual jeopardy because, with Miantonomo alive, Uncas would never be safe. At the bottom of all their deliberations, which lasted through almost the whole month of September 1643, was their own gnawing dread of a large-scale Indian uprising, and here the most likely tribe to lead it was the Narragansetts: Uncas and his Mohegans, it was felt, were tied too closely to the English interest.

In their perplexity the commissioners turned to a group of leading ministers for guidance. The ministers were not afflicted with the same doubts; it was clear to them that Miantonomo must be put to death. With the concurrence of the church the commissioners now felt able to reach the same decision, which had underlain their deliberations from the start; but they decided that the execution must be purely an Indian affair, that it was proper for Uncas to "put such a false and bloody enemy to death," but that this must be done beyond English jurisdiction and, they also stipulated, "without cruelty or torture."

Uncas was quite ready to assume responsibility for the execution of his enemy and willing to accept the stipulation that Miantonomo should not be tortured. With a party of his braves he took delivery of the prisoner at the door of the jail. Two armed Englishmen went with them as observers for the General Court. In Boston the commissioners had ordered that the execution take place "in the way between Hartford and Windsor (where Onkus have some men dwell)" — that is, on Indian ground. But the legend has long persisted that Uncas took him southeast to the scene of his defeat, on upland ground near Norwich. Such a long march, if not a torture, would provide a testing of the prisoner's stoicism. Neither he nor Uncas betrayed any awareness of what each knew was inevitably to take place, and whether it was at the battle site or "in the way" to Windsor, a brave stalking at Miantonomo's heels, on Uncas's signal, sank a hatchet in the Narragansett's skull.

The whole affair had been an unhappy one. It nagged at the consciences of the commissioners and various leading Puritans, if not of the consulted divines, for some time: the justice of their course is still debated today. It can only be judged in the shadow of a threatened general uprising, which they were convinced was being plotted. There may have been some grounds for their belief, and though Miantonomo never succeeded in organizing a real conspiracy, the possibility certainly had been in his mind. Early in 1642 he sounded out the Algonquin tribes around Manhattan. According to a report to the States General on conditions in New Netherland:

> . . . Miantenimo, principal sachem of Sloop's [Narragansett] Bay, came here with one hundred men, passing through all the Indian villages soliciting them to a general war against the Dutch and English.

The fact that he had had the intention is perhaps some mitigation for the course followed by the commissioners, and at least it served to keep peace, however precariously, for thirty-two years more.

Pessacus, Miantonomo's younger brother, and the old chief, Canonicus, protested that they had sent Uncas a ransom of wampum which he had kept though killing their chief and they offered gifts if the Massachusetts English would stand aside while the Narragansetts took revenge, but their overtures were brusquely rejected. The authorities of Massachusetts, in their fear of an overall conspiracy, had settled on Uncas as their boy, the only man within the Indian world they could even begin to trust; they had promised him aid in the event of a Narragansett attack when they gave him Miantonomo to kill. And while they tried to smooth relations by calling the Narragansetts and Mohegans to air their grievances before the commissioners at their yearly meetings — invitations to which Uncas responded enthusiastically, but the Narragansetts reluctantly if at all — they never left any doubt as to whose side they were on; when in 1645 trouble flared between the tribes, three hundred English soldiers were immediately put into the field.

This was a force the Narragansetts could not cope with. Once more they were forced to negotiate, promising not to make war without permission from the commissioners and agreeing to pay reparations in wampum to defray the cost of the expedition sent against them, as well as an annual tribute thereafter. The fact that a portion of the reparations was handed over to Uncas did nothing to soothe Narragansett pride. Similar threats of force were used to counter sporadic threats to peace as they arose. They continued to be effective as long as the memory of the Pequot extermination remained fresh in Indian minds and to that extent were a justification of the commissioners.

The Dutch in New Amsterdam were not so successful. In 1643 they found themselves confronted with an Indian rising which involved eleven tribes, and for a year the fate of the colony hung in the balance.

In 1638 Wouter Van Twiller had been supplanted as director by William Kieft, a small, wiry, high-tempered man as full of acid as an ant. The only trait he shared with Van Twiller was an instinct for appropriating property. According to some unkind persons, he had on one occasion reserved for his own use a large proportion of funds that had been entrusted to him for ransoming Christian prisoners from the Turks. On the other hand he lacked business acumen and had gone bankrupt after a brief career as a merchant. But he was supposed to be a man of determination, and it was presumably on this account that the Company had appointed him.

For New Amsterdam had fallen into a deplorable condition. The fort was in such a state of disrepair that men no longer troubled to use the gates but walked in through gullies in the walls. Most of the cannon were useless. Public and Company buildings were dilapidated. Only one windmill was in working order. Almost none of the bouweries had tenants; the only prosperous farms were those belonging to Van Twiller.

Inhabiting this run-down settlement was a small population of mixed nationalities, almost wholly illiterate, whose chief occupation was the pursuit of quick money by smuggling, illegal trading with the Indians, and skimming the cream of the Company's fur trade. New Amsterdam was at that time very near to anarchy. Under regulations of the Company there was no death penalty. To be sure, men guilty of serious crimes could be sent back to Holland for trial, but a gallows two months away was not much of a deterrent.

Kieft took energetic measures. He organized a regular watch to police the settlement, erected a gallows, and proclaimed that in the future murderers and homicides would be hanged publicly right on Manhattan Island. He tried to bring order into the fur trade by an edict forbidding all

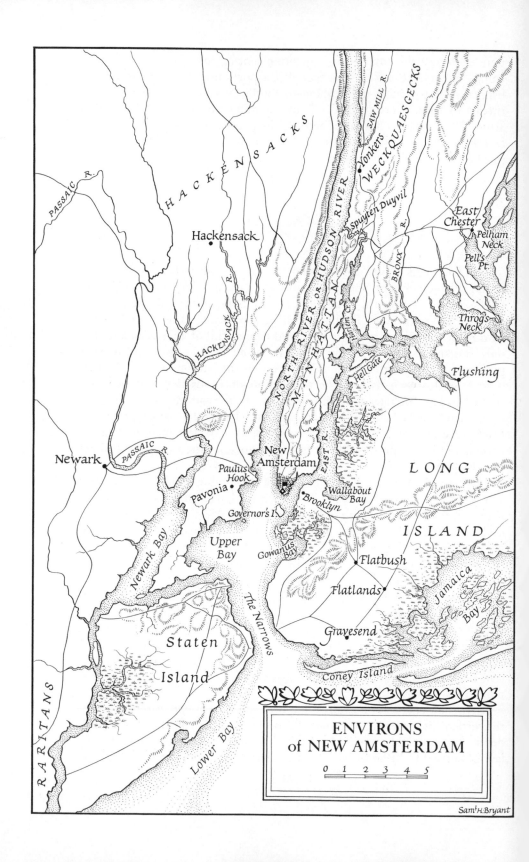

ENVIRONS
of NEW AMSTERDAM

0 1 2 3 4 5

Sam.ᵗH.Bryant

employees of the Company to engage in any phase of it on pain of being fired without salary and forfeiting any claims they might have on the Company. All traders had to obtain licenses; anyone caught without one would have all his goods confiscated. To prevent smuggling and also to keep order along the waterfront he ordered that sailors should be aboard their ships at sundown, and he issued proclamations against drunkenness and brawling.

He seemed to move in a minute whirlwind of righteousness and morality. He had novel ideas of how to put the government of New Netherland on a workable basis. He began by appointing a council. This consisted of one man and himself, with three votes, two of which he himself exercised. The councilor was an intelligent and public-spirited Huguenot physician, named John de la Montagne, but being inevitably outvoted on any difference of opinion he could do little more than make suggestions. Over matters of critical importance Kieft could call on an advisory committee of twelve men elected from the leading citizens; but in the main New Netherland became a dictatorship. Kieft admitted this openly. "I have more power here than the Company; therefore I may do whatever I please."

Meanwhile in Holland the Company, disturbed about the slow growth of the colony, had taken steps to liberalize terms for the individual settler. It gave up its monopoly of the fur trade, opening it to the public but exacting a ten percent tax. It also opened the right to take and cultivate land to everyone, though the small farmer naturally would not enjoy the privileges and exemptions granted wealthy patroons. Foreigners were given equal rights with Dutchmen. Men of small means who were willing to emigrate immediately from Holland were transported with their families at no charge, given a suitable amount of land, livestock, and tools, and helped to build a house and barn, for all of which they were to pay a moderate yearly rent and at the end of six years return the same amount of livestock they had received, keeping the increase for themselves.

These generous terms produced a surprising wave of emigration. Farms and holdings on and around Manhattan more than quadrupled in the next year. The emigrants were of much higher quality than their predecessors and included some men of wealth who came with large parties of settlers at their own expense. One of these was David Pieters De Vries, who had tried with only partial success to nerve Van Twiller to action in the Eelkens episode; before long he was to find himself trying with even less success to restrain Kieft from headlong action. He started a small plantation on Staten Island and then began another, much larger, on the west shore of the Hudson above New Amsterdam which he named Vriesendael. Cornelius Melyn arrived the following year with a shipload of cattle and taking a fancy to Staten Island returned later with a large party of colonists and became a patroon. He and a soldier named Joachim Kuyter, who arrived the same year, became Kieft's articulate opponents.

New farms and bouweries sprang up on Manhattan and a large settlement was begun at Hackensack. Two Virginia tobacco planters started plantations above Turtle Bay and more English — heretics to Puritan eyes — settled on Long Island and along the Westchester shore of the Sound. The Reverend Francis Doughty, who had been dragged from his pulpit and out of his church for saying that the sons of Abraham ought to have been baptized, brought thirty-five families of his congregation with him and was granted a tract of thirteen thousand acres bordering the East River. Anne Hutchinson, whose husband had died, came in 1642 with her family and a few followers to settle at Pelham Neck, which the Dutch called Annie's Hoeck because of her. John Throgmorton started a plantation at Throg's Neck; and Lady Deborah Moody, also widowed, who had left England in search of religious freedom, found herself excommunicated by the elders of the Salem church for rejecting infant baptism and came to New Amsterdam for refuge with a number of her followers. The Dutch considered them "Mennonists" or Anabaptists, but after only slight demur at the introduction of a possibly subversive sect in such number, granted them a patent to a sizable tract at Gravesend. Lady Deborah was well supplied with money and started building a large and unusually substantial house for her own use.

This increase in the population was optimistically regarded in New Amsterdam as an indication that the colony would be able to withstand the growing pressure of the English colonies on either side of them. In 1634 the Calverts had begun the colonization of Maryland. The first settlement at St. Mary's near the mouth of the Potomac was not large but it had been located there, north of Virginia, with the idea of putting a squeeze on the Dutch colony with its small settlements on the Delaware. And the picture north of New Amsterdam had become definitely ominous. When De Vries put his ship in to New Haven in 1638 he found three hundred houses already built although the settlement was not yet a year old. Stemming from New Haven, in 1639 the town of Milford was founded and in the same year Guilford was settled by people coming direct from England, and in the following year Stamford. In 1643 the four towns leagued to form the colony of New Haven, so that the Dutch found themselves with two English colonies virtually on their northern doorstep. But all the time the real threat lay in the growing antagonism of the surrounding Algonquin tribes.

Under Van Twiller's administration relations had been fairly easy; Indians went back and forth to New Amsterdam and the farms near by, sometimes trading, sometimes visiting; but to some Dutch, portents of trouble to come were already visible. With the opening of the fur trade to the public even the licensed traders operated with a view only to their own profit, traveling to the Indian villages or enticing the Indians to their own houses.

> . . . not satisfied with merely taking them into their houses in the customary manner, they attracted them by extraordinary attention, such as admitting them to Table, laying napkins before them, presenting Wine to them, and more of that kind of thing, which they did not receive like Esop's man, but as their due and desert, insomuch that they were not content, but began to hate, when such civilities were not shown them.

Still more dangerous, some people thought, was the practice of taking Indians into domestic employ and using them for housework, "thus exposing them to our entire circumstances."

There were, too, as the farms spread out toward the Indian villages, the inevitable frictions as two societies with no common interests rubbed against each other. It is not to elevate the Indians to call theirs a society, but to show that the Dutch in their practices were nearly on a level. The Indians did not fence their corn patches, nor did the Dutch fence in their cattle or even trouble to have herd boys tend them. The inevitable resulted: the Dutch cattle broke into Indian cornfields and in retaliation the Indians killed Dutch cows and horses, reprisals which, though satisfying Indian ideas of justice and sense of sport, enraged the Dutch farmers who, like wilderness pioneers through all American history, saw no reason to fence their livestock until it became necessary, which meant until they had white neighbors.

But by far the most dangerous element was the Dutch sale (and nonsale) of firearms to the Indians. They were sold to the Mohawks, who were willing to pay twenty beaver for a musket and the equivalent of twelve guilders for a pound of powder, almost without restriction. Settlers at Rensselaerswyck would even part with their own guns for the sake of profit and wait unarmed till the patroon could procure a new consignment from New Amsterdam. But selling guns to any of the Bay or River tribes was prohibited; penalties were severe and getting away with a sale so close to home was virtually impossible. As a result, by 1640, the Mohawks had four hundred muskets but the lower Algonquin tribes, except for a few sold here and there by unscrupulous traders, had none. As the Dutch report stated:

> . . . Four. hundred armed men knew how to make use of advantage, especially against their enemies, dwelling along the River of Canada, against whom they have now achieved many profitable forays where before they had but little advantage; this caused them also to be respected by the surrounding Indians even as far as the Sea coast, who must generally pay them tribute.

And particularly rankling was the fact that at one time it was the Mohawks who had had to pay tribute to the River Indians.

Added to their resentment over this discrimination in favor of their inveterate foe was Kieft's decision to tax them. The restoration of the fort's crumbling walls had proceeded at a snail's pace, mainly due to lack of funds. Kieft therefore developed the ingenious notion of getting the surrounding tribes to contribute to the work on the ground that the fort was as much a protection for them as for the Dutch. The argument was absurd on the face of it, as many of the tribes occupied lands between the fort and the Mohawks; they had not asked for a fort in the first place; and the idea of having to pay tribute to the Dutch on top of that exacted by the Mohawks infuriated them.

By the summer of 1640 the atmosphere had become explosive, and it is extraordinary that the opening incident did not result immediately in war. A group of Company employees on their way to the Delaware settlements decided to provide themselves with fresh pork for their journey by killing some of De Vries's pigs on Staten Island, which they did and proceeded unobserved on their way. As soon as the theft was discovered suspicion fell on the Raritan tribe, whose towns lay just over the Arthur Kill in New Jersey, and Kieft, without waiting to investigate the crime, sent fifty armed men to make an example of the Raritans. The Dutch attacked the first handy village without warning, indiscriminately killed a number of Indians, and burned the lodges and crops. In return the Raritans rallied, swarmed over onto Staten Island, massacred several of De Vries's people, and wiped out the plantation. Now thoroughly aroused, Kieft offered a wampum bounty for every Raritan head brought to him; but perhaps because both sides were too appalled by the mutual burst of violence and because the Raritans must have felt that they had evened the score, there were no further episodes and peace uneasily continued, with lightning in the air, for another year. Then, however, the deliberate murder of a Dutchman by an Indian roused the Dutch blood lust in Kieft as well as a good many other colonists.

The Indian belonged to the Weckquaesgeck tribe whose villages ran along the Sawmill River Valley and he had been getting ready for his act for fifteen years. He had no special animus against Claes Smit, who was a simple wheelwright living quite a way above town on the East River shore near the site of the United Nations building today. Any other white man would have done as well.

In 1626 when he was just a little boy he had come down from his tribe's village to Manhattan Island with his uncle, who had a few beaver skins to trade in at the fort. For a boy it would have been exciting to see the fort and the cannon and the strange soldiers with their muskets, not to mention houses and horses and the people drinking beer, if they had got that far; but they did not. They had reached the edge of a fresh-water pond which the Dutch called Kolk, not far from where the Tombs Prison stands. Some men were at work there, clearing a field of brush, and they looked up and saw the lone Indian with his bundle of beaver and a small boy as his only companion, and there was no one else in sight. They could not resist the temptation of easy money the beaver represented.

They set upon him with their tools, forgetting the little boy, who fled into the brush, from which he watched in horror and helpless rage while the Dutchmen clubbed his uncle until he was dead. He swore then that when he was a man he would exact revenge; and while the Dutch were busy burying the body he stole off through the brush for home.

Claes Smit's house was on the way to New Amsterdam. Smit was alone, and when the Indian entered he saw nothing to be afraid of; and when the Indian asked for something he was eager to oblige. As he turned away to get it — a piece of cloth, a glass of water — the Indian smashed his head open with a hatchet. Whatever else it was, it was a quicker, cleaner end than the Indian's uncle had suffered fifteen years before, and it satisfied the oath of vengeance.

The Weckquaesgeck chief, therefore, saw no reason to give up the Indian merely on Kieft's demand. He pointed out that fifteen years ago an Indian had been killed in cold blood; now a white man had been likewise killed; and in his view the game was even. He forebore to mention, as he might have done, the stolen beaver skins. Most likely he had forgotten them.

But to Kieft it was unthinkable to let an Indian murderer go unpunished. Unless justice was done upon him no Dutchman would be safe, and if the Weckquaesgecks would not give him up, then the whole tribe should be made an example of. That meant war. But he had no money with which to wage it. He knew that the officials of the Company in Holland were against using any kind of violence toward the Indians. The only place he could raise funds would be among the colonists themselves. But after his years of arbitrary rule, he did not see much hope of getting them to hand over the money he wanted. So, though it went sorely against the grain, he issued a summons "for all heads or masters of families" to come to Fort Amsterdam to consider "some important and necessary matters," which as everyone knew meant whether or not to go to war.

The assembled heads of families chose a board of Twelve Men with De Vries as president to sit in consultation with the governor. All twelve were men of substance, very different in caliber from the men with whom once or twice in the past Kieft had thought it politically expedient to augment his council. These had invariably been Company servants whose salaries he paid himself and who therefore were in no position to oppose him even if they had been so inclined. Now that Kieft needed public support, the board of Twelve Men saw an opportunity to whittle away some of his arbitrary powers.

They agreed that the surrender of Smit's murderer should be insisted

[279]

on, but vetoed any idea of immediate attack on the Weckquaesgecks if they continued to shelter him for, as they pointed out, the colony was unprepared for war against any strong Indian tribe. However, if by the following winter the Weckquaesgecks remained obstinate, they should be attacked; but the Twelve Men would consent to this only if the director would agree to a larger council, to consist of not less than five men, four of whom should be elected by the citizens; and these four furthermore should not be employees of the Company.

At the moment, Kieft felt obliged to accept these reforms, and agreed in a grudging manner. But he did nothing about them and before long, finding even the prospect of reform embarrassing, he forgot all about his promises, dismissed the board of Twelve Men, and issued a decree that thereafter no public assemblies would be held in the colony without his permission.

Having reassumed absolute authority Kieft let the year drift away with a series of demands for surrender of the murderer, each of which was rejected with increasing scorn by the Weckquaesgeck chief. But at last, in March of 1642, he decided that he must take action and organized a punitive expedition of eighty men under one Ensign Van Dyck to make a night attack on the main Weckquaesgeck village. No mercy was to be shown, and the brave little army crossed the Harlem abrim with grim resolve. The only trouble was that their Indian guides as they neared the village seemed to lose their way and Ensign Van Dyck, who disliked messing around in the dark, ordered a return march in good order. They recrossed the Harlem in the morning without having pulled a trigger.

But the Weckquaesgecks, coming upon the broad meandering tracks of the Dutch force in the morning, realized with staggering surprise how nearly they had come to extermination and sent immediate promises of delivering up the murderer. This served to keep the Dutch quiet in the immediate future and of course the promise was forgotten.

Meanwhile Kieft became engaged on the one constructive accomplishment of his administration. This was the replacement of the wooden barn-like church with a stone structure of adequate size. It was an expensive undertaking and the problem of raising funds was serious, but the director solved it handily at a wedding breakfast that followed the marriage of Sara Bogardus, daughter of the Reverend Everardus Bogardus, who had been such a valiant pot-companion to Van Twiller. Kieft waited until the gaiety had reached a proper peak — "after the fourth or fifth round of drinking" — and then, announcing the need to raise money for the new church, declared his own subscription for a handsome sum and passed round a paper for pledges and signatures, and all the company, in inebriated emulation, put themselves down for sums that on the morrow looked utterly incredible; but as De Vries reported, "nothing availed to excuse," and Kieft had his funds.

The church was long a-building and some were convinced that a large proportion of the money was used for action against the Indians; but after it was finished visitors to New Amsterdam found it an impressive structure. The only trouble with it was that it was placed within the fort on the exact site Kieft had insisted on, forgetting all other considerations, and as the walls reached a certain height they cut off the south wind from the gristmill, rendering it useless as often as not.

It is possible that the Indian trouble might have died down if Kieft had not decided to make another try at taxing the weaker tribes around Manhattan. This attempt and the fact that the Dutch continued to let their cattle run through Indian plantations kept the Indians in a constant state of irritation. In January 1643 matters came suddenly to a head.

Some Dutchmen in Hackensack had been drinking with one of that tribe and when they got him drunk enough they rolled him, among other things taking away his coat of which he was inordinately proud. De Vries came upon him after he had sobered up enough to make an inventory of his losses; he said he was going back to his lodge to get his bow to shoot a Dutchman, and De Vries could say nothing to dissuade him. So he went on to the settlement to warn the people and they remained on guard that day. But next morning one man went up on his roof to mend the thatch and was shot and killed by an arrow from the woods.

When the news got back to the Hackensack village the chiefs were thoroughly alarmed. They went to De Vries, begging him to intercede with the governor and offering four hundred yards of wampum as compensation for the Dutchman's widow. De Vries took them to Fort Amsterdam, but Kieft would have nothing less than the murderer. They said they could not deliver him; he had fled upriver to the Haverstraws, whose chief, named Pacham, was a leader in the plotting against the Dutch. When Kieft demanded the Hackensack murderer from Pacham, all he got was a derisive refusal.

At this juncture a band of ninety Mohawks, every man armed with a musket, came down the Hudson to gather their annual tribute from Westchester and River tribes. Their appearance started a general panic. More and more Indians fled down the river before them, more than a thousand going ashore at Pavonia to camp along the bank, another group almost as large crossing over to Manhattan and making camp near Corlaer's Hook, and several hundred coming into Vriesendael and asking De Vries to defend them against the Mohawks. He could not interfere between them, as the Dutch were bound by treaty to the Iroquois, but he promised to shelter them as well as he could and himself went over to New Amsterdam to try to persuade Kieft to hold a council with the Mohawks to induce them to withdraw. It seemed to him a heaven-sent opportunity to win back the good will of the surrounding Algonquins.

Others — de la Montagne, Kuyter, Melyn — supported him; but to Kieft the refugee Indians offered an entirely different sort of opportunity. When three hotheaded men named Adriaensen, Damen, and Planck asked permission to lead a punitive force of civilians against the Indians at Corlaer's Hook, he enthusiastically gave them leave to make the attack "and to act with them as they think proper, and time and circumstances will permit." At the same time he organized a force from the garrison to attack the Indians at Pavonia.

It was the twenty-fifth of February, bitter cold, without a trace of wind. By midnight the campfires had burned low, and the bodies of the sleeping Indians huddled under their furs were indistinguishable mounds when the Dutch charged in among them. There was no way to tell which were women or children and which were men even if the Dutch had wanted to do so, which they did not. At both places it was a savage, messy business; the screams of the terrified Indians could be heard by listeners at the fort not only from Corlaer's Hook, which was only a mile away: they carried through the frosty air clear across the river from Pavonia. Eighty men, women, and children were killed there before the rest managed to scramble into their canoes and break away. The toll at Corlaer's Hook was more than forty.

New Amsterdam boiled with jubilation when the victorious parties returned with their bundles of Indian heads. A few, like De Vries, foresaw the trouble to come, but they went unheeded. The blood lust like an infection leaped the East River and a party from a settlement at New Amersfoort attacked the Marechkawiecks at Brooklyn, a strong tribe but always peaceable, killing several and looting two wagonloads of corn from the tribal stores.

The reaction of the Indians was appalling. Eleven of the surrounding tribes took up the hatchet and everywhere outlying houses were burned, their inhabitants killed or carried off for torture. Only a few places proved strong enough to be defensible, like the manor house at Vriesendael where all other buildings except the brewery were burned and all livestock slaughtered, and the house Lady Deborah Moody had built at Gravesend, into which all her colonists packed themselves. Those who could came in to New Amsterdam. Roger Williams, who was waiting there at the time for ship to England, wrote about the panic of the refugees, "the flights and hurries of men, women, and children, and the present removal of all that could for Holland."

A mile beyond the walls of the fort no one was safe. There were people too far away, down the Jersey shore, to try the journey to such safety as the fort afforded; they had to stay where they were, fortifying their cabins as well as they could, with the knowledge that the Raritans were taking up the hatchet. Everywhere the Algonquin warriors began appearing with firearms; muskets bought from unscrupulous independent traders, but mostly taken from the murdered Dutch. New Amsterdam itself no longer felt secure. The deplorable condition of the fort and the garrison which consisted, according to a report, of "50 @ 60 soldiers unprovided with ammunition" meant that the village would be powerless against a concerted attack by the eleven tribes who were calculated to have more than a thousand warriors in the field.

Public opinion now turned against Kieft, who tried to duck all responsibility for the two senseless massacres by putting the blame on Adriaensen as instigator of the whole idea. Afterward he included Damen and Planck. This so incensed the three men that with some followers they broke into the director's room and tried to kill him. They were restrained, but in the course of the scuffle one of their men fired off a pistol at Kieft. The ball went wide and the man himself was instantly shot down, decapitated, and his head then put on public exhibition, after which the people once more began worrying about the Indian problem.

Meanwhile, on rumors that some of the Long Island tribes wanted peace, De Vries with a single companion had gone out to a town at Rockaway where he held a council with the Canarsees while hundreds of warriors sullenly looked on. Almost all Indians respected him as a completely honest man and no other man in New Amsterdam would have dared venture among them or survived for long if he had. After prolonged palavers he persuaded the Canarsee sachem to come to the fort with delegates from the Hackensacks and Tappans and any other tribes who had lost people in the massacres so that the governor could make restitution; and in this way an uneasy peace — uneasy because the Dutch presents were so meager that the Indians remained resentful — lasted through the early summer.

But Pacham, the chief of the Haverstraws, remained unshaken in his resolve to destroy all the whites. He kept working particularly on the Wappingers further up the Hudson until they agreed to join him in attacking Dutch boats coming down from Albany. In August three were set upon; twelve Dutch including a woman were killed, and what seems to have been equally disastrous was the loss of four hundred beaver skins. War was war, but being robbed of profitable merchandise was not to be forgiven and without hesitation New Netherland once more declared war on the Haverstraws and Wappingers. This seems to have been received as general war and the whole countryside blazed again. It was at this time that the English plantations along Long Island Sound were obliterated, largely by the Weckquaesgecks. Among those destroyed was Anne Hutchinson's, and she herself was murdered with all her people except for an eight-year-old granddaughter carried into captivity.

Every man in New Netherland was now serving in the army, if so small a force could be called such, Dutch, Huguenots, and Walloons alike, with fifty English in a separate company. Kieft, finding the situation beyond his powers, once more called on the commonalty and this time it chose a board of Eight Men to advise him. At this point, discouraged by his huge losses and the renewal of the war, De Vries left for Holland, but before boarding ship he predicted to Kieft's face that divine vengeance would strike him down before long for all the deaths and miseries he had so wantonly caused.

The Eight Men, assessing the situation of the colony, decided to report it in detail to the States General instead of the Company and ask immediate help. The picture they drew was desperate: bouweries, plantations, houses burned; cattle killed — what few had been recovered and brought within the settlement would have to be slaughtered without delay because there was not fodder to carry them through the winter; and everywhere people who had been killed lay unburied. The strength of the Indians — now estimated at fifteen hundred warriors — put any thought of plowing and planting wheat completely out of mind. If help did not come promptly the people of New Amsterdam would have to turn to the English in the east for refuge and New Netherland would become an English colony.

When the States General received this report of what they described as "the inconveniences" to which the colonists were exposed, they referred it to the Company's executive Assembly of Nineteen for prompt action. By then it was already April of 1644. It took the Nineteen a month to reply: they felt bad about the situation, but they did not have the money to send help. So the matter rested till October when, just a year after the writing of the report, the States General passed a resolution to look into New Netherland affairs!

The loss of De Vries would have been far more serious than it was — there were other men of courage and integrity in the colony, but few were as farseeing and none held the respect and confidence of the Indians as he did — if affairs had not passed beyond the point where reasonableness and rational argument could have any effect. Only one possible solution remained: to crush once and for all the ability of the Indians to make war; and fortunately a man had arrived in New Netherland with the ability and one suspects the inclination to accomplish the job.

Captain John Underhill, who had shared command with Captain Mason in the liquidation of the Pequots, had found the restrictions of life under a Puritan society year after year a little more than he could stomach. He had had a try at it in the New Hampshire neighborhood to which his fellow Antinomian followers of Anne Hutchinson had migrated from Boston; but there he had found little scope for his pub-haunting instincts any more than his fellow Antinomians found pleasure in his swaggering demeanor; and his own Antinomian convictions were probably founded more in a rebellion against Puritanism than in inner personal belief. He tried living for a term in Stamford, but gave that up also in favor of the freer atmosphere of New Netherland.

But even there it was evident almost from the beginning that John Underhill would not always be an easy man to have around. In an early appearance at New Amsterdam he had turned up at the City Tavern, built by Kieft in 1642 so that visitors would not necessarily expect to be entertained by the director but could wine and dine at their own expense. Underhill arrived in the taproom accompanied by two other Englishmen: one the secretary for the English settlements on Long Island and the other another Plymouth captain, Thomas Willett, whose great-grandson, Marinus Willett, was to be the defender of the Mohawk Valley during the Revolution.

The English party had been sampling freely the alcoholic resources of New Amsterdam for some time before arriving at the City Tavern and had brought along a drummer to beat out the call to arms or any other tattoos or alarums that might seem necessary. Their entry to the taproom naturally created a slight commotion, and when Captain Underhill inquired for the host and was told that he was celebrating his lease of the tavern by giving a dinner for his friends in a private room, Underhill did not wait for an invitation but stormed the door and bursting in on the mixed company, who were seated round a table of fine food and the best wines in New Amsterdam and who included two very pretty and new young brides, instantly in roaring good humor invited himself to the feast.

To the polite, civilized little dinner party where, just before, the women had been singing old-country songs in their bright young voices, the apparition of the flushed captain, complete with clanking sword and now reinforced by his two companions — not to mention the drummer who was playing his part in the riotous nature of the occasion — was a shattering experience and the very idea of admitting such hot-blooded men of war to the party an outrage. Some appreciation of this may have permeated Underhill's mind, for he suggested as a compromise that Gysbert Opdyck, the newest of the bridegrooms, should come out to the tap with him and his friends to celebrate their meeting. Opdyck, not unnaturally opposed to leaving his bride or for that matter good Rhenish wine in favor of beer, declined the proposal and tried to eject Underhill and his companions. It was a mistake.

The English drew their swords and immediately with battle shouts fell upon the pewter and glass lining the taproom shelves and slashed great splinters from the door frames. In the uproar other English came storming to their rescue. Gerritsen, the host, sent for the fiscal and the watch; but Underhill would do no business with anyone less than the director, declaring that he would rather not speak to a fool; and the members of the watch wanted no part in a forcible ejectment of the bloody Englishmen. It was only when the members of the Dutch dinner party slipped away through back doors that Underhill, without feminine eyes to stimulate him further, quieted down and eventually took his leave.

Deplorable as the episode might be, it at once stamped Underhill as a mettlesome and forceful character, even in a community which under pressures of the Indian menace and overcrowding by refugees had become rough and lawless. The situation became so unmanageable that martial law was declared and all able-bodied colonists placed under arms. The "army" thus formed consisted of fifty regular soldiers belonging to the garrison; two hundred settlers of Dutch, Flemish, or Huguenot extraction; and a contingent of fifty Englishmen from Long Island. Underhill was immediately offered command of the latter. He accepted, and though his command was relatively small he proved the leading force in the two expeditions that broke the Indians.

During the winter of 1644 there had been some reason to believe that the tribes might be losing interest in the war. In January de la Montagne, Kieft's lone councilor, with forty volunteers and a handful of English under Lieutenant George Baxter sallied down the bay to Staten Island to attack the Indians supposedly still there and seize any corn they could find. They unearthed caches of nearly five hundred bushels — a welcome addition to New Amsterdam's short supplies — but the Indians themselves had gone; the huts looked long deserted.

Later a second expedition was sent against a supposedly large number of Indians near Greenwich; but the encampment could not be found, if in fact it had existed at all. The only sign of Indians was a tiny group of bark huts, and after killing about twenty warriors the Dutch returned to New Amsterdam. Then sixty-five men under Lieutenant Baxter were sent into the Weckquaesgeck country. Baxter, unlike Ensign Van Dyck, seems not to have been troubled by the dark, for he stayed in the Sawmill Valley until he had discovered all three of the Weckquaesgeck castles. These, too, had been deserted; there was something ominous in their emptiness in the soundless valley, and they were like no Indian castles any of the men had seen. Unlike the usual ramshackle palisade, the defending wall was built of planks five inches thick, closely fitted, heavily braced, nine feet high, and studded with loopholes. In any one of them "thirty Indians could have stood against Two Hundred soldiers," but the arrogant, contentious tribe had vanished. Even when they had gone on almost thirty miles they found nothing more than one or two huts where they killed two or three men more or less haphazardly and brought back a few women and children to be sold as slaves. On the way home they burned two of the castles but left the third standing for possible Dutch use.

This disappearance of the Indians from the immediate neighborhood of

Manhattan Island was mysterious; frightening to some, reassuring to others. Then toward spring the colonists learned that Pennewitz, senior sachem of the Canarsees, was circulating among the tribes with advice to give up all idea of war until Dutch suspicions had been lulled and the Indians would be once more accepted as friends in Dutch houses. Then at a given moment they could attack. It was to be an almost exact replay of Opechancanough's Good Friday massacre along the James in 1622; and as a matter of fact in this same year Opechancanough, again almost on Good Friday, staged another unexpected attack against the westerly Virginia settlements, in which more than three hundred whites were massacred before, for some unexplained reason, the Indians lost heart and drifted back to their own towns.

This was of course coincidence. It would be assuming too much to suppose that any communication existed between the Powhatan and Canarsee tribes however remarkable and swift the passage of news across the Indian wilderness might be. This swiftness of communication applied especially to the Iroquois world, where waterways made natural roads to the centers of the Long House. Along the Atlantic coast, however, the main rivers, running north and south, were barriers more than highways, and contact of the Virginia Indians with northern tribes, inimical or otherwise, led to the western Delawares or Susquehannas, sometimes called the Conestogas, an Iroquoian people as warlike as any Senecas or Mohawks and their deadly enemies.

The Canarsees were thinking on their own and the ancient Pennewitz was merely a more subtle schemer than Pacham of the Haverstraws; but the rumor of what he was up to inflamed the Dutch to a point of near insanity, and a simple incident, based on a false premise, led to a scene which would have been more appropriate to the torture platforms of the Iroquois than the tumble-down fort at New Amsterdam.

In April at Hempstead three pigs belonging to the English settlers were killed and Indians were blamed. It was the custom to turn stock loose upon the so-called Hempstead plains, a tract of nearly seventeen thousand acres of open grassland, as a kind of super common, and admittedly the Indians were continually finding the temptation of strayed animals too much for them. A brave in need of a new powder horn coming on an ox with a fine long pair well beyond sight of the houses would bring him down, hack them off, and leave the carcass. There was also a brisk trade with New Amsterdam in "venison" from Long Island. But in the present instance three hogs had been slaughtered and the presumption was that seven Indians seen in the vicinity must have done the rustling. They were arrested and cast into the cellar of one of the houses while the foreman of the settlement, the Reverend Fordham, reported the arrest to Director Kieft.

Kieft lost no time in dispatching a party of sixteen soldiers, led by Ensign Opdyck and Captain Underhill, who must by then have composed their differences, with orders to bring the malefactors in at once to New Amsterdam. The two officers seem to have taken a liberal view of their orders, for they shot down the first three Indians to emerge from the cellar and then on their return journey threw two of the remaining four overboard and towed them behind their yacht by the neck until they had drowned. The two survivors, however, were delivered to Kieft and cast into cells in the guardhouse where they were kept until Kieft decided that the colony could no longer afford to feed them and turned them over to the soldiers to dispose of as they saw fit.

The soldiers killed them with their "bowelling" knives, weapons with eighteen- to twenty-inch blades which Kieft had had designed especially for hand-to-hand fighting inside Indian huts where sword blades had proved to be too long for efficient work. The first Indian was so savagely set upon that he died at once, but the second took a long time, for the soldiers began skinning him, "beginning at the calves, up the back, over the shoulders and down to the knees" in narrow strips, while he chanted his death song. According to the report, which was undoubtedly biased, Kieft watched the whole proceeding with amusement with his councilor and friends, "laughing heartily, and rubbing his right arm," until at long last the wretched Indian was led to a millstone and decapitated.

The summer passed uneasily, though without serious incident, but by fall the conviction grew that time was running out and that the Indians must be dealt with at once. In November came the first move, against the Canarsees in two of their villages east of Hempstead. Underhill with fourteen Englishmen attacked the smaller village, and eighty Dutch under de la Montagne surrounded the main town called Matsepe. Both places were destroyed. One hundred and twenty braves were killed for only one Dutchman. It was accounted a great success. But rumors persisted of a large concourse of Indians settled somewhere in the neighborhood of Greenwich or Stamford, in search of which the abortive expedition of the preceding January had been undertaken.

John Underhill went along to Stamford to investigate. No one knew the location of the Indian stronghold, though all accepted the fact of its existence. Underhill found that the Indian who had unsuccessfully guided the January expedition was living in Stamford and interviewed him. The Indian said he dared not go alone beyond the outskirts of the settlement. But he reported that there were over five hundred Indians in the town and he swore that given a second chance he would lead the Dutch to it. Underhill accepted his good faith; here was a man with compound motives for making good. He reported to New Amsterdam and was given command of a force of one hundred and fifty men with Ensign Van Dyck as his lieutenant. They sailed for Greenwich as the year was ending, and landed there in a driving blizzard.

The violence of the storm held them in Greenwich that night, but in the morning they started northwest behind their Indian guide, "up over Stony Hills," laboriously breaking trail through the drifts. At eight that night they were still three miles from the spot in which the guide said the Indians had their town. But they decided to wait there for two hours. Underhill did not want to attack till nearly midnight. There were two rivers to be forded, and to wait in soaked clothes in the bitter cold was impossible. The men would have to attack the moment they reached the town.

At ten o'clock they took up the march again. The sky was now clear as polished steel. A full moon, with the deep mantle of snow, turned the night as bright as day. Toward midnight they came into a narrow valley in the hills, a small amphitheater with steeply rising sides, about a hundred yards across, making perfect shelter from the northwest wind. The bark huts were built close together, in three orderly rows, like streets, and in the moonlight the Dutch saw that there had been no surprise. The braves were waiting for them as they made their charge. In a moment the Dutch were taking casualties, one man killed and twelve more wounded on the ground. But the Indians had no avenue of retreat; there were no palisades; their only refuge was the shelter of their huts where their women and children and the old people crouched. In the first few minutes nearly two hundred braves were killed with sword or musket; then with mysterious abruptness the rest had disappeared into the huts. The town lay in front of the soldiers as completely silent in the moonlight as when they had first approached; the only sign of life was an occasional arrow whistling from a hole in the bark wall or from the doorway of a hut. The Dutch, themselves silent, did not feel strong enough to attack the houses, so, "seeing nothing else was to be done," Underhill ordered the town burned.

Almost in moments the first fires leaped from one close-packed house to another and the same sort of firestorm that had swept the Pequot stronghold raged in the narrow valley. For a brief time the Indians tried to escape, but they could not evade the swords and muskets of the Dutch; with dreadful resignation they returned to their blazing huts, "preferring to perish by fire than to die by our hands," according to the Dutch report. "What was most wonderful is, that among this vast collection of Men, Women, and Children, not one was heard to cry or to scream."

If this statement is true the massacre was the most ghastly in the long history of red or white atrocities. It is difficult to credit. According to Indian sources more than five hundred souls died in the flaming huts. Yet it is not impossible. The faculty of the Indian mind that led to mass hysteria may well have seized them here in a mass acceptance of death in the silence with which other creatures of the forest meet their own. A curious fatalism marks the entire episode: the hidden valley; the town without defenses; the huts packed close in the narrow amphitheater whose

[289]

high walls, sheltering from the wind, formed at the same time a perfect trap; the braves waiting in the moonlight, alert and unsurprised; the great fall of snow, shrouding the midnight world and muffling the sounds of march — it is the infernal scene of the Pequot burning all over again, but this time cast in Dante's version of a frozen hell. Eight Indians out of the five hundred, all men and three of them wounded, were said to have escaped.

This dreadful blow ended for some years the Indian appetite for making war. By Dutch reckoning sixteen hundred of them had been killed in the past two years. But the Dutch themselves, and particularly New Amsterdam, had suffered heavy losses. In the spring of 1645 there were probably fewer than one hundred and fifty able-bodied white men on the island. Many had decided to return to Holland; a few had gone up the Hudson to Fort Orange where the near neighborhood of the heavily armed Mohawks kept the Algonquin tribes in check. Men were still hesitant to return to the bouweries across the river or even those on Manhattan at any distance from New Amsterdam. The only outlying communities actively farming were the English settlements at Flushing, Gravesend, and Hempstead. Both sides were therefore more than ready to come to terms.

There were preliminary negotiations with the outer Long Island tribes in May, and in July Kieft and de la Montagne made the trip to Fort Orange to treat with the Mohicans. With these peripheral nations ready for peace the stage was set for signing a treaty with the Westchester, River, and New Jersey tribes, and on the twenty-fifth of August, 1645, sachems of the Hackensacks and Haverstraws, Nyacks, Weckquaesgecks, Sing Sings, Tappans, Connecticut Mohicans, Raritans, Wappinecks, and many others, small tribes and septs of larger tribes, landed on the Manhattan shore from the canoes and joined the leading men of New Amsterdam in a congress within the crumbling walls of the fort. They sat in the open under a clear sky, the tall peaked hats of the Dutch and their doublets of "countrey grey" or sober brown and large, baggy breeches making an odd contrast to the blanketed and feathered, apparently phlegmatic, figures of the Indians confronting them, while at one side a large party of armed Mohawks kept apart, sardonic in the knowledge that without their approval no peace between Indian and white, or Indian and Indian, was worth a muskrat skin.

The treaty was on the whole a good one. No armed Indian would visit a Dutch settlement or bouwerie, and by the same token no white man would visit an Indian village unless by invitation and with an Indian escort. The Indians agreed not to exact revenge for an injury by trying to murder the guilty party but to lodge complaint with Dutch authority which on its side solemnly undertook to see justice done. For the most part, it was to work out well. Only once again would New Amsterdam be invaded by Indians. In 1655 a Dutchman named Van Dyck shot an Indian woman for helping herself to a peach from one of his trees and more than two thousand assorted Algonquins came down the Hudson in a great flotilla and swarmed through the streets. But as every citizen turned out under arms, they satisfied themselves with shooting an arrow through Van Dyck's heart as he stood in his doorway, and then went off to devastate the settlements at Hoboken, Pavonia, and Staten Island. In a day they killed over a hundred people and took more than one hundred and fifty into captivity. But the ill feeling was assuaged as quickly as it had been kindled; the Indians no longer wanted to feed white prisoners and brought them in for gunpowder — all except the Esopus tribe who, hoping for a better deal, hung on to their prisoners, and the then director, Stuyvesant, found himself with two ugly successive little Indian wars on his hands. But for ten years the treaty of 1645 preserved a solid peace.

A footnote to it deserves mention. One of the final articles stipulated that Anne Hutchinson's little granddaughter, who had been taken in the massacre at Annie's Hoeck, should be restored to her own race. The Indians agreed and kept their word; but when they brought her in, white people were dismayed to find that she did not want to be returned. The child, who was then ten, spoke the Algonquin of her adoptive family as fluently as any Indian; she had wholly accepted Indian ways of life and thought; she wished only to remain an Indian. She was one of the first recorded examples, if not perhaps the first, of a phenomenon of early American life which white people, particularly those of English, Dutch, or German stock, found incomprehensible, a violation of their deepest racial belief.

As important as ending the Indian war in the minds of the Eight Men was the removal from power of the man they considered responsible for it and some mitigation of the despotic power of his office. They had been called into consultation mainly to make palatable the taxes Kieft proposed to impose for payment of the war. These were in two parts: one on beaver skins, the other on beer and wines and spirits. The first was bad enough; the second struck home to the very core of a Dutchman's outlook on life; and the Eight Men, five of whom were Dutch, two English, and one German, protested against taxing settlers who had already been bankrupted by war. Instead they argued that traders, who were already making profits of two and three hundred percent on staple foods and general supplies, ought to bear the brunt of taxation. Kieft disagreed and with characteristic perverseness allowed a trader known to have twelve hundred beaver on his ship to sail without paying any taxes whatever. But then he immediately reversed himself and taxed all beaver brought into New Amsterdam port for transshipment to Europe and in addition, over the protests of the burghers, raised the excise on beer and liquors.

In Holland, however, the protests and reports, particularly that of the Eight Men in October 1644, were at last receiving consideration. The universal theme of all complaints was the recall of Kieft. But the Eight Men also asked for greater representation in government: a schout or sheriff and a burgher should be elected by the people in every settlement and they in turn appoint delegates to sit with the director and council on all public matters. The tax roll on colonists, who had lost all their property, amounted to over 16,000 guilders a year. With all the power of government in the hands of a single arbitrary man who "should dispose here of our lives and properties at his will and pleasure" there was little hope of the colony's future. Moreover they warned the directors of the Company to give little credence to a booklet they understood Kieft to have prepared purporting to be a true account of his direction of the war against the Indians. "On that subject it contains as many lies as lines," even though it had been made attractive with water colors of the forests and fauna of New Netherland: a rather livelier, if primitive, version of the "white paper" of our own political apologists.

The weight of evidence was against Kieft and to the Company it was evident that he would have to go. After one false cast they chose Peter Stuyvesant, who had just returned from a term as governor of Curaçao. It was not so much the way Kieft had managed or mismanaged the colony that decided them: it was his declaration that the colony ought "utterly to exterminate all Indians." What troubled them about this, however, was not the inhumanity of the proposal but the high cost of pursuing such a war. The Company had already lost over half a million guilders on New Netherland between 1626 and 1644. A new governor with a pacific policy toward the "wilden" was the obviously practical course to follow; but they refused to consider any suggestion of a more liberal system of government; and Stuyvesant when he arrived — matters of policy and business held him in Amsterdam till 1647 — proved very nearly as dictatorial as Kieft.

One reason that Kieft got into no more trouble with the Indians during the two years before Stuyvesant's arrival was his preoccupation with personal attacks, first by the Reverend Bogardus, and second by two of the Eight Men, Cornelius Melyn and Joachim Kuyter, the German soldier, who declined to step back into the wings after their dismissal as councilors. Both quarrels stemmed from Kieft's position as interim governor; because his power seemed no longer as absolute he was quick to find offense in any criticism and the unconcealed rejoicing of the news of his replacement had done nothing to reduce his natural store of venom.

Kieft's differences with Bogardus were in some sort an inheritance from Van Twiller's regime. Beginning as Van Twiller's boon companion, Bogardus had soon found himself and his church in opposition and had quickly become the director's outstanding public critic, a role he had no intention of relinquishing unless Kieft's policies gave him reason to do so. Kieft, however, was far more dictatorial than Van Twiller had ever been, banishing out of hand people who criticized him, appropriating the property of others on the lightest pretext, exacting fines and imprisonment right and left. When the dominie expostulated, Kieft dismissed him summarily. Before long Bogardus was accusing him of misgovernment from the pulpit with such invective — "vessel of wrath . . . fountain of woe and trouble" — that the director declined to go to church. But then as Bogardus began seriously to impress his congregation Kieft retaliated by having the drummers of the garrison practice outside the church during sermons; and when that failed to silence the dominie's stentorian periods, ordered the cannon on the ramparts of the fort to be fired in salvos. But even cannon could not extinguish Bogardus's fulminations from the pulpit which Kieft now said were being delivered under the influence of liquor, a charge that on occasion may well have been true.

Kieft now retaliated by summoning Bogardus to appear before the court, which meant himself and his councilor; the arraignment of the parson, besides adducing sedition and leading others to traitorous actions, descended almost at once into the sort of personal invective that Bogardus had hurled at the director: the dominie had abused the whole colony and everyone in it, not even sparing his wife and sister, "particularly when you were in good company and tipsy." Worse, he had abused the officers of the colony, had upheld Adriaensen after his attempt to assassinate Kieft, and had in fact behaved so badly that he did not dare to take the sacrament himself.

Bogardus declined to appear. Neither a second summons nor an offer to have the charges arbitrated by four neutral citizens budged him. Most of the people of New Amsterdam were on his side anyway; his performances in the pulpit unquestionably provided the chief entertainment in the colony. So matters stood in stalemate, while charges and countercharges were sent to Holland, until Stuyvesant's arrival.

Kieft's difficulties with Melyn and Kuyter were of a very different sort: There was none of the low burlesque that colored his dispute with Bogardus. They had been the leading spokesmen of the Eight Men and both had strenuously opposed his plan to attack the refugee Algonquins. Their advice had been contemptuously ignored and, in the war that followed, Melyn had lost nearly all his holdings on Staten Island, of which he was commonly regarded as the patroon, and Kuyter's fine farm on the south bank of the Harlem River had been totally destroyed. But they were too high-minded to be motivated only by personal antagonism, however much they detested Kieft. They were convinced that the colony had no hope of surviving unless its form of government was changed: "for it is impossible ever to settle this country until a different system be introduced here." Its fate should never again lie at the mercy of "the whim of one man."

While the one man was still in office there was nothing they could do directly; but immediately after the arrival of Stuyvesant, when Kieft handed over his office and a conventional resolution of thanks for his service was proposed, Melyn and Kuyter refused to assent, saying that they had no reason to feel thankful. They then in their turn proposed that an investigation be made of Kieft's and his council's administration during his whole term as director and the results forwarded to Holland. Stuyvesant, however, rejected their petition. He had no special love for Kieft; he had reported caustically on the low condition of the colony as he found it; but he was acute enough to see that if such an investigation were permitted into his predecessor's record, the same thing might well happen to himself; and he declared that a petition by private citizens to investigate established officers was an act of treason. In the hearings that ensued, therefore, Melyn and Kuyter found themselves accused as malignants and their own conduct in the late war brought under examination. Kieft immediately sprang into the role of prosecutor: he accused them of being sole authors of the report of the Eight Men which had procured his dismissal, claimed that it had been sent to Holland without knowledge of the rest of their committee and, branding their accusations as libelous, demanded that they produce all their correspondence with authorities in Holland. When they complied, the documents proved so damning to Kieft that he dropped this line of prosecution. The two men were now accused of stirring up revolt and even of plotting with the Indians: they were convicted out of hand. Melyn was fined three hundred guilders and banished from the colony for seven years; Kuyter was banished for three and fined one hundred and fifty guilders.

There was no appeal; and they were warned not to think of making one in Holland, Stuyvesant declaring that if he thought there was any chance of their doing so he would hang them.

Kieft was now triumphant and ready to sail with a high heart and the profits of his years in office which were commonly believed to amount to 400,000 guilders. On the sixteenth of August he boarded the ship *Princess*. With him as prisoners went his two enemies; and with him also, as fellow passenger (which he must have relished nearly as much) went Dominie Bogardus, considerably chastened by a summons to appear before the Classis at Amsterdam (the governing body of the church) to explain his behavior, if that was possible, and knowing that his defense would have to be his personal view of recent events in New Amsterdam. There were, of course, other passengers, including Melyn's son and the late fiscal (treasurer) of the colony under Kieft, who may well have watched the low receding skyline of Manhattan with a few wary thoughts of his own.

In a minor way it was a ship of fools, emotionally freighted with avarice, lies, guilt, frustration, passion, jealousies, and rage, and though the captain avoided the familiar southern route by the Azores, the passage was a slow one. Driving in straight from the Atlantic, whether because of bad weather or careless navigation, the *Princess* missed the English Channel and, sailing into the Bristol Channel instead, piled aground on a rocky shoal off the coast of Wales. She broke up rapidly. Eighty-one of the passengers and crew were lost, among them Kieft, Bogardus, the fiscal, and Melyn's son. There is a legend that as the water on deck began to wash about Kieft's knees (as it would have done to the little man sooner than to most of the others) he asked Melyn and Kuyter, who were standing near by, to forgive him. It is, of course, just a legend; it is hard to believe that the weight of his vindictiveness did not carry him directly down with a still unleavened soul.

What is fact, however, is that two of the survivors were Kuyter and Melyn, the one coming ashore clinging to a broken gun carriage, and the other being washed up far along a sandy beach. And as if to emphasize the turn of fate, in the next days men raking the shallows dragged up a chest which proved to belong to Kuyter and contained the papers documenting his and Melyn's charges against Kieft. They served to convince the States General: their fines were remitted, their banishment rescinded, and they were given orders returning their confiscated properties. In addition they were asked to deliver a writ instructing Stuyvesant to appear before the States General to defend his actions. It must have given Melyn peculiar satisfaction to deliver the writ in New Amsterdam and hear it publicly read out in church before a full congregation.

To Stuyvesant, naturally, it was a staggering blow. He was in the midst of a political struggle with the Nine Men who represented the people of New Netherland — or at least those of Manhattan and the neighboring boroughs of Brooklyn, Amersfoort, and Pavonia. This tribunal of nine was in the tradition of local town government in Holland; they were to meet with the governor and council at his request to consider colonial affairs; and three of them each week sat with the council as a civil court; but their representational functions were largely illusory.

In the first place their principal duties were defined in the following order of descending importance: as promoting "the honor of God and the welfare of our dear Fatherland to the best advantage of the Company," and finally "the prosperity of our good citizens." They were to have no private meetings without knowledge and consent of the director, and though they had the right to delay consideration of the director's proposals, they could only meet for this purpose if the director was there to preside over their meeting or had named someone else in his place. The illusion that they were a representational body was promoted by the fact that the citizens of the various boroughs who were eligible to vote were free to elect eighteen "Well-born Men"; but out of these eighteen the selection of nine to serve was made by the director. This was the closest the electorate came to any sort of democratic action, for thereafter the board of Nine Men perpetuated themselves by the curious system of having six of the nine members annually nominate twelve men as possible candidates to succeed themselves, from whom the director was then to name six men to the board; in essence a slow-motion shell game by which, though the original eighteen candidates had been undeniably elected by a free vote of the people, the board was expected to become responsive to the director's will. But before the process had time to take effect, Stuyvesant found himself at loggerheads with his Nine Men.

Again the matter of taxation formed the nub of their dispute. Stuyvesant had to finance his government somehow, and the simplest way seemed to collect thirty thousand guilders in back debts owing to the Company, which was pressing him for the money in any case. This to the Nine Men, some of whom, like the great majority of their fellow colonists, were still struggling to get on their feet after the disastrous Indian troubles, seemed entirely unjust, and compounding their difficulties were the extremely high excise taxes imposed by Stuyvesant, any detected evasion of which was penalized by confiscation of the whole ship's cargo, with the result that New Amsterdam was getting a bad name as a port and trade was badly falling off. It was obvious that colonial policies needed overhauling and the Nine Men, refusing to be cowed, proposed to send over a delegation to Holland to present the States General and the Company with an accurate picture of conditions in New Netherland.

At first Stuyvesant seemed to approve of the idea, but before long it developed that he expected the delegation to be made up entirely of his own supporters and the short term of good feeling came to an abrupt end. The Nine Men insisted that the delegation should represent the people and, though they were willing to let Stuyvesant see their report before sending it, it was not to be presented by the administration. When Stuyvesant refused to let any report go unless coming from him, the Nine Men proposed calling an assembly of all citizens of the colony, but the last thing Stuyvesant wanted was the submission of a political dispute to arbitration by the complete commonality. In answer the Nine Men then organized a surreptitious canvass of all the colonists to record individual opinion and solicit money for the delegation's trip to Holland.

In these moves the leading spirit was a newly appointed member, Adrien Van der Donck, who had lately been treasurer and collector of the Van Rensselaer patroonship. Having indoctrinated himself in the ways of the New World, Van der Donck had come down the Hudson to establish himself in a patroonship of his own. He bought a large tract north of the Spuyten Duyvil from the Weckquaesgecks and began a colony which he called Colendonck but which ultimately took its name from the title of *Jonkeer*, or "Young Lord," which the New Amsterdamers liked to bestow on him. He had unusual gifts for the time and place. Coming from a distinguished family in Holland, he was highly educated and held the degree of Doctor of Laws, and was to prove himself a hard antagonist for Stuyvesant.

In the course of the canvass it was decided that a running record or "journal" should be kept of all interviews and also transactions of the Nine Men in their secret sessions, which of course was strictly forbidden; and Van der Donck was assigned to keep it. When Stuyvesant heard of this "journal" he flew into a passion, declaring that hanging was too easy a punishment for the Nine Men; but he was enraged particularly against Van der Donck because, besides being a member of the board, he also held a seat on Stuyvesant's own council.

Van der Donck was arrested out of hand, his papers seized, and he himself thrown into jail. Stuyvesant appointed a special court to try him for treasonable activities against the government. The court found him guilty and expelled him both from the Nine Men and his seat on the council.

It was at this point that Melyn and Kuyter returned from Holland under protection of the States General and read out in church the latter's condemnation of Stuyvesant's arbitrary actions as well as a summons to the director to return to Holland and defend himself in person. This was altogether too much for Stuyvesant's pride; he refused to go but stated that he would send the provincial secretary, Van Tienhoven, as his attorney to present his case against Kuyter and Melyn. He was sufficiently chastened, however, to keep his hands off Van der Donck and the Nine Men, though he did invoke an earlier law of Kieft's that all legal documents had to be authenticated by the provincial secretary before being offered as evidence "for the purpose of cutting off the conventional mode of proof," and he took the further step of forbidding the acting dominie, Backerus, from reading or allowing to be read by himself or any church officers any documents in any way concerned with politics or colonial government. The dominie was outraged by what he considered an infringement of the privileges of the church, resigned, and took ship for Holland in order to carry the dispute against Stuyvesant in person to the authorities.

In the meantime the Nine Men had worked out a memorial to be presented to the States General asking three things: that the States General take the colonial government out of the hands of the Company and administer it themselves; that they provide for New Amsterdam a "suitable Burgher government"; and that the boundaries of the province should be firmly established through appropriate treaties with pertinent powers. It was a straightforward, dignified document; but to support it they had also prepared a *Vertoogh*, or Remonstrance, an elaborate and at times almost fanciful address to the States General giving the history of New Netherland from the first arrival of white men, describing its geography, its fauna and flora, the habits of its native inhabitants, its innumerable streams of pure running water, and then passing on to a record of events, with detailed accounts of the misdeeds of various governing authorities and the consequent misfortunes of the colony. It was not always just in its criticism of individuals; but the general plaint on which the whole argument rested — for a proper administration with "godly, honorable, and intelligent rulers, who are not indigent and not too covetous," adjectives obviously intended to apply to Van Twiller and Kieft — was entirely justified.

The presentation of these papers, both written by Van der Donck, before the States General roused fresh interest in America and was to stimulate emigration from neighboring countries as well as Holland; and still more of an attraction was the publication six years later of a "Description of New Netherland," again by Van der Donck. It was an engaging elaboration of the first part of the *Vertoogh* with detailed descriptions of the wild animals that roamed its woods and containing among other things a marvelous engraving of some of them, including a beaver and wolf, a wild horse being bitten in the loins by a moose, and an eagle riding the back of a unicorn. It must have roused the ardor of Dutch sportsmen.

Armed with the memorial and *Vertoogh*, Van der Donck embarked for Amsterdam with two other delegates and so, in 1649, three delegations were crossing the Atlantic: first, the Reverend Backerus in solitary indignation — but he was to die shortly in Holland with small accomplishment; then Van Tienhoven, hurried off by Stuyvesant in order to present his case before the representatives of the Nine Men could reach Holland; and lastly Van der Donck and his companions. All made safe voyages; but Van Tienhoven, with the recollection of Kieft's fate fresh before him and possibly not unmindful of his own share in the late director's activities (his signature was affixed to many of the more iniquitous authorizations for Indian slaughter), decided that it would not be wise to follow Kieft's course directly across the Atlantic to the mouth of the Channel. Instead he ordered the shipmaster to sail round the north of Ireland, which would he thought eliminate the chance of confusing the Bristol Channel with the English Channel, and by this roundabout route, though he reached Holland safely, he not only lost his two weeks' advantage in time but arrived after Van der Donck had made his argument before the States General at the Hague.

Van der Donck and his memorial made a strong impression on the States General, who appointed a committee further to consider all the affairs of

New Amsterdam. They were less impressed with Van Tienhoven's argument, which was essentially a blanket denial with the additional statement that if the patroon of Rensselaerswyck had the right to kick anyone he chose off his premises, surely the Director of New Netherland should be able to banish whomever he considered to be detrimental to the public welfare. The committee heard him out, but the report they issued soon after as a provisional order was a humiliating reversal for Stuyvesant. New Amsterdam was to be granted a burgher government with a sheriff, two burghers, and five aldermen; though for the next three years the Nine Men were to continue in office and judge all disputes with liability up to fifty guilders and above that figure with the right of appeal on the part of litigants. And Stuyvesant himself was to be recalled.

It was one thing to order Stuyvesant home, but something else again to get him there. He ignored the summons and the provisional order in toto. In his own opinion all his actions were justified. When he received orders from the Company to stay where he was and pay no attention to the provisional order he thought it right to obey them instead of the States General, against whom he was as enraged as he had been against the Nine Men. His appointment came from the States General, but his salary was paid by the Company, and he took the sensible view that in case of a dispute his allegiance should go to the latter, especially since, unlike some of his predecessors, he lived on his salary and not on graft.

Instead of settling the dispute, therefore, the States General had merely added to the heat. The Nine Men soon issued a new memorial, complaining that while their High Mightinesses had "taken to heart the pitiful and desolate condition of the commonalty here . . . the non-arrival of reform, the neglect of Director Stuyvesant to obey your order . . . and the continuation of affairs in the same sad condition" obliged them to renew their petition. At last, in 1652, after the States General had affirmed their provisional order, the West India Company gave in and granted New Amsterdam a burgher government as prescribed in the provisional order, with the eight officers specified to sit as a municipal court. But the Company refused to recall Stuyvesant as the States General had requested. To do so, they claimed, would be to infringe their privileges, and also, since war with England seemed imminent, it was imperative to have an experienced soldier in command of New Netherland. He was ordered to remain in his post, to fortify New Amsterdam, and if possible to negotiate treaties with neighboring English colonies to fix their common boundaries.

Stuyvesant himself finally realized that there would have to be some compromise. He agreed that there should be a burgher government. Early in 1653 he issued a proclamation incorporating the "City of New Amsterdam" and its government of two burghers and five aldermen, but instead of allowing a free election, he kept their appointment in his own hands and insisted that his own authority in issuing ordinances was not impaired and should be accepted as binding by the "City." The colony would not receive representational government of any sort till 1683 when, under the British governor Thomas Dongan, the first Provincial Assembly was elected.

The Dutch predilection for governing through committees left a colonial governor more or less to his own devices. Responsibility for making a decision could be passed back and forth for inordinate periods; and when a policy finally was arrived at, it was often too late to implement it in New Netherland, the director having taken his own course for good or ill. If the latter, there was nothing left to do but point out the error of his ways. It amounted to government by reprimand, and so it was in the matter of Stuyvesant's treatment of the Quaker, Robert Hodshone.

It is difficult today to comprehend even partly the fear and abhorrence with which the Quakers were regarded in the seventeenth century. We know them today as dedicated and self-contained in their belief; and their conviction that faith flows from personal inspiration or, as they called it, "Inward Light," seems to us entirely reasonable. But it called for absolute separation of church and state, so to the Puritan theocracy it was anathema, and even more so was the Quaker rejection of original sin. They questioned the effectiveness of baptism. To the more fanatic Puritan mind Quaker belief was an assault upon the Bible itself; the Quakers became as much infidels as the aboriginal Indians and as much enemies of society.

Another principle of Quaker faith which roused the public against them was their refusal to bear arms. They seemed, especially to New England citizens, entirely to disregard the Satanic menace of the Indians; and in fact they were to demonstrate during the early years of Pennsylvania that treating Indians on equal terms created peaceable relations. Even when the Pennsylvania frontier was flaming with Indian war the Quaker-dominated legislature in Philadelphia refused to take action until incensed frontiersmen drove cartloads of their mutilated dead into the city streets. The Quaker faculty of disregarding what did not affect them, of simplifying and rationalizing religious belief, and above all denying the state's power to direct spiritual conviction amounted to a violation of tribal taboos and brought on them what amounted to tribal retributions. It is difficult to account in any other way for the savagery with which these, for the most part, mild and gentle people were treated.

Unfortunately a few more zealous members of the sect helped inflame public opinion against them by actions intended to testify to the strength of their faith. They would jeer the governor in the street to manifest their spiritual independence of the state. They would interrupt services.

Two women displayed their enthusiasm by walking stark naked through the streets of Boston. Such performances, whether by sincere zealots or unstable characters with a compulsion to disturb the peace, only roused more violently the visceral loathing of the public at large.

In 1656 two Quaker women turned up in Boston. A group had sailed to the West Indies — part of a missionary wave that in tiny groups threaded their way through much of Europe — and settled in Barbados. From there the two women, Mary Fisher and Anne Austin, left for New England with militant determination to testify to their faith against whatever force Puritan authority could bring against them. John Endicott, that bulwark of the colony who had stirred up the Pequots to fighting pitch, was then governor; but he was absent from Boston. The lieutenant governor, however, took firm charge of the situation. The women were cast into jail, and the literature they had brought with them was burned; they were kept literally under a lid, and just short of starvation, for over a month, until the ship that had brought them from Barbados was ready to return. It seemed an effective handling of a tricky situation — no law had been passed against Quaker preaching — but Endicott, when he returned, was critical: in his opinion the women should have been flogged.

The imperiled commonwealth had been preserved, but no sooner had these two women sailed away than eight more Quakers arrived direct from London. These, too, were thrown into prison; laws were passed providing that all Quakers in future be banished from the colony; and Massachusetts and Plymouth tried to get all four New England colonies to present a united front against these dangerous religious invaders. Rhode Island, under Roger Williams, alone refused to allow civil authority to coerce men's consciences; but the other three passed laws of varying severity, the most rigid being those of Massachusetts, where punishment such as cutting off the ears, piercing the tongue, and finally the death penalty were prescribed for Quakers who persisted in returning after having been banished from the colony. Massachusetts made the law stick, too; in 1659 and 1660 two men and a woman were hanged on Boston Common.

Roger Hodshone was one of those expelled from Massachusetts in 1657. He came ashore at New Amsterdam, supposedly the home of religious toleration, but went on to the English settlement at Hempstead, Long Island. He seems to have been unusually unaggressive in his effort to promote the Quaker cause; he held no meeting, but had talked privately with two or three individuals describing the Society of Friends and its beliefs and purposes before the authorities got wind of him. He was arrested and on principle thrown into jail by the local magistrate, who then went over to New Amsterdam to consult with Stuyvesant.

Stuyvesant's immediate and subsequent reaction toward this unhappy man is almost impossible to rationalize. New Amsterdam was already a cosmopolitan community in complete contrast to Boston. It was the home of men of many nationalities and faiths; as we have seen, the church within the fort was used by different sects in turn on the same Sunday. Yet this lone modest man, who had not yet even attempted to promote his cause in a public meeting of any sort, seems to have fired Stuyvesant with insensate animosity.

A squad of soldiers was sent to Hempstead to fetch him. They hauled him out of jail, destroyed his Bible and his other papers, tied him to a cart's tail, and so brought him over the twenty-odd miles of road to Brooklyn. At the end of the trip he was being half dragged.

In New Amsterdam he was put into an underground cell infested with rats and kept there for days before at last being brought before Stuyvesant and the council. He was allowed no one to defend him; he was not allowed to open his mouth to defend himself; without any sort of hearing he was condemned to two years' hard labor or to pay a fine of six hundred guilders. The fine was manifestly impossible for him to pay, so he was given a wheelbarrow to which he was chained and ordered to load it; one assumes the job would be on the earthworks of the fort, for the embankment and palisade along Wall Street had been completed four years before. The work itself is unimportant. What was important was Hodshone's stamina. He refused to work, protesting that he had harmed no one and committed no crime; and he refused to let his spirit break under the punishment that inexorably followed.

He was flogged at the handles of the barrow until he fell senseless; then returned to his cell for several days and kept on bread and water. Finally Stuyvesant condescended to see him again, but only to tell him that he would continue to be flogged as long as he did not submit. When Hodshone still refused to do so, he was taken back to his prison, hung by the wrists from a beam and flogged and kept for two days without even bread and water, after which he was hung up and flogged again. By then the story of what was happening to him had got about and public sympathy was aroused to the point of outrage. A woman came to minister to Hodshone in his cell. As the protest swelled, the sheriff pointed out that it would take only the payment of Hodshone's fine to set him free. A group promised to raise the necessary money; but now Hodshone refused to let it be paid, and Stuyvesant remained unmoved until finally his own family turned against him. Then, rather in weariness over the whole outrageous affair rather than from any moral change, he consented to Hodshone's release. But the Quaker problem was not yet settled.

The conscience of the people had been roused and in Flushing a man named Henry Townshend held some Quaker meetings in his house. As soon as the news reached New Amsterdam, Stuyvesant ordered him arrested and fined; if he did not pay the fine he was to be flogged and banished from New Netherland. But now something new happened in the history of the New World: the officials of Flushing refused to carry out the director's orders and instead, over their own signatures and those of the leading Dutch and English citizens, amounting to thirty-one in all, issued a statement of their own principles dedicated to upholding the "law of love, peace, and liberty." As this was extended to Turks, Jews, and Egyptians in Holland, so in the Christian faith it should forbid all forms of persecution and hatred, and it was their purpose not to offend anyone of Christian belief whether he be Presbyterian, Independent, Baptist, or Quaker. "Should any of these people come in love among us, therefore, we cannot in conscience lay violent hands on them. We shall give them free ingress and egress to our houses, as God shall persuade our consciences."

As a declaration of conscience in the face of hostile secular authority by a group of simple citizens it was unexampled at that time. The thirty-one men brave enough to put their names to the document knew full well that they were inviting persecution. And so it proved. The town clerk was cast in jail; two justices were dismissed; the sheriff, also a signer, was fined two hundred guilders which he must pay or suffer banishment; and various others received fines. But they made their point in the end. When news of Hodshone's persecution and the utterance of the men of Flushing reached Holland, the members of the Amsterdam Chamber of the Company were unanimous in condemnation of Stuyvesant's conduct. "The consciences of men ought to be free and unshackled, so long as they continue moderate, peaceable, inoffensive, and not hostile to government," they wrote him and reminded him that in Holland the oppressed and persecuted from every country found asylum. The language of their reproof was mild, almost bland, but not in the least ambiguous, and Stuyvesant certainly got the message, for after that he did not try again to quell members of any religious sect.

His behavior throughout this Quaker episode was in the general pattern of resentment against a sect that was basically anti-authoritarian when it came to anything touching their spiritual life; but his savagery is explainable only by fear of something that did not conform to his own conception of his world; it was not far removed from the impulses that formed the Iroquois attitude to torture. Left to himself there is little doubt that he would have persisted in mistreating Hodshone until the man had died or was reduced to something less than human which, in fact, was at once how Stuyvesant and their other enemies regarded the Quakers and provided justification for their abuse of them.

Stuyvesant was not in other respects a brutal man. He was irascible and his temper was as uncompromising as his wooden leg; within two years he had succeeded in alienating all other Dutchmen on Manhattan; but in his treatment of the Indians he proved himself patient and forbearing and managed to win their respect. In coming to terms with Connecticut over their common boundary, he got as good a settlement as could have been expected, even though he did not trust any Dutchmen to negotiate for him but had to rely on Englishmen from Long Island; and in taking forcible possession of New Sweden on the Delaware he treated the Swedish settlers with reasonableness and consideration.

The tranquil valley of the Delaware had been a prize that the Dutch, Swedes, and English in turn had all vied for. The English were first in Delaware Bay — John Smith and Samuel Argall both stopped there (and Verrazano in his voyage along the coast in 1524 for Francis I of France may or may not have seen it even before they did). But the Dutch were the first on the ground. Cornelius Hendricksen sailed the little yacht *Restless* up the river as far as the Schuylkill in 1614, and as we have seen, in 1623 the West India Company decided to establish a trading post on the river, and Cornelius May put up the lightly palisaded Fort Nassau on the east shore at what is now Gloucester Point. He left two Walloon couples as ostensible "colonists"; the other inhabitants were six unmarried men who were to carry on the fur trade.

The first attempt really to colonize the area was the abortive patroonship, started under the direction of De Vries, called Swanendal, a little above Cape Henlopen in 1631. The original contingent of thirty-two settlers was wiped out by Indians as the result of a simple misunderstanding of Dutch purposes and language; the second contingent spent more time in whale hunting than agriculture and more or less starved out, and the project was soon abandoned. After that, Dutch activities were confined mainly to the Indian trade and driving out any English traders who might try to do a little free-lancing in the valley.

Then in 1638 the Swedes arrived. The expedition had been financed by a corporation known as the South Company, in which some of the most distinguished people in Sweden held shares, and was led by Peter Minuit, the former Director of New Netherland whose unjust recall by profit-hungry members of the West India Company still rankled, so that he jumped at the chance of founding a rival colony. After letting Fort Nassau go to pieces, the Dutch had recently rebuilt it on the east bank, so Minuit bought a tract from the Indians on the west bank which extended from near the site of Wilmington almost to the mouth of the Schuylkill. At Wilmington he planted his first settlement around a little palisaded fort he named Christina, for the Swedish queen, and he called the colony New Sweden.

The English in Virginia were alarmed by this planting of a new race

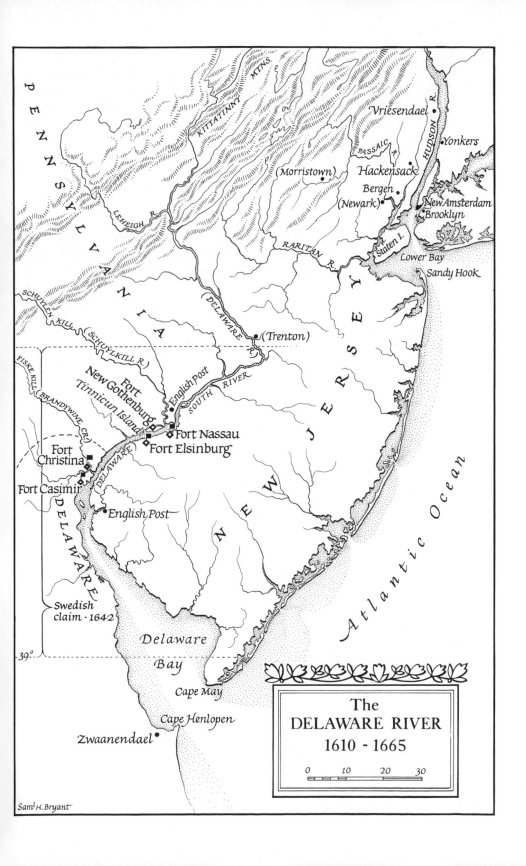

PENNSYLVANIA

KITTATINNY MTNS.

LEHIGH R.

SCHUYLKILL

SCHUYLKILL R.

DELAWARE R.

Vriesendael

Yonkers

PASSAIC R.?

Morristown

Hackensack

Bergen

(Newark)

HUDSON R.

New Amsterdam

Brooklyn

Staten I.

RARITAN R.

Lower Bay

Sandy Hook

NEW JERSEY

(Trenton)

FISKE KILL

BRANDYWINE CR.

Fort
New Gothenburg
Tinnicun Island

English Post

SOUTH RIVER

Fort
Fort Nassau

Fort Elsinburg

Fort
Christina

DELAWARE

Fort Casimir

English Post

DELAWARE

Atlantic Ocean

Swedish
claim · 1642

39°

Delaware

Bay

Cape May

Cape Henlopen

Zwaanendael

Sam. H. Bryant

The
DELAWARE RIVER
1610 - 1665

0   10   20   30

in what, despite the Dutch occupation, they considered English territory: they thought of the Delaware as the boundary between Virginia and New England; and they requested permission from London to remove the Scandinavian intruders by force. Maryland, also, which had been started on Chesapeake Bay by the Calvert family four years before, was alarmed. The Dutch at Fort Nassau naturally protested, and Director Kieft sent a warning to Minuit that if he did not go he would be made to leave.

Minuit, however, was not dismayed. Maryland was still too small to be a source of trouble and the Virginians, after all, had not put out the Dutch. As for Kieft's threats, he disregarded them entirely. In Europe, where the Thirty Years' War was still in progress, Swedish armies were winning notable victories and Dutch sympathies were enlisted in the Swedish cause. It was not likely that the waspish director would try to lead an expedition against the colony of a friendly nation. As for the garrison at Fort Nassau, Minuit soon had his own fort strong enough to stand off any attack they might hope to stage. His colony was well housed and well protected when he set out on the return voyage to Sweden — only to be lost in a Caribbean hurricane. One of the few able early governors in the New World, he had deserved better of his countrymen and of fate than he received.

New Sweden nevertheless persisted. In 1640 a new governor was sent out with fresh recruits, enough to keep the colony in being, but not materially to strengthen it. However, in 1643 Queen Christina became personally interested in the colony's future; a new and much larger contingent of settlers was sent over the Atlantic and at their head a new governor, a former cavalry officer named Johan Printz, who set vigorously about the work of strengthening and expanding the colony.

In the meantime, however, the English had appeared on the scene. They came from New Haven where a Delaware Company had been formed by a group of merchants with a view to muscling in on the fur trade. They established two posts; one was on the east bank at the mouth of the Salem River, but the second, on the west bank, was above Fort Nassau and in a position to intercept Indians coming down with furs. This was an entirely different proposition from that posed by New Sweden. Where profits were menaced the Dutch could take action as swiftly as any other race, and in 1642 Kieft sent out a small company of soldiers to round them up. Oddly enough the Swedes offered to help in removing the English. There was no fighting; the English had no alternative but surrender; and the Dutch sloops carried them back in triumph to New Amsterdam, from which in due course they were shipped back to New Haven.

Another English attempt the following year met with even less success. A ship out of Boston with would-be traders tried to sail up the Delaware but was fired on first by the guns of Fort Christina, then by those of Fort Nassau — which second dose of round shot proved too much for the crew, and she ignominiously turned about.

But the arrival of Johan Printz the following year changed the situation. His expedition was well supplied with armament and fortified by a Lutheran pastor; Lutheran was to be the official religion but the Dutch Reformed Church would be tolerated; by implication New England Congregationalism could not hope to get a foothold, any more than Catholics from Maryland or Anglicans from Virginia could. One may doubt whether Printz labored his mind over such considerations. He was a practical man and a good administrator, and his chief concern was to set up his colony in a way that would allow him to eject any interlopers whatever their religion might be. After casting his military eye over the territory that had become his responsibility, he decided not to strengthen the settlement at Fort Christina but to find a site for a new fort from which he could control all traffic on the river.

When he had explored upstream as far as the site of Trenton, he returned to settle on Tinicum Island, close to the west shore below the mouth of the Schuylkill, and began building an imposing fort out of huge hemlock logs. He named it New Gottenburg and mounted four brass cannon on the walls. Then he built himself a governor's house of some pretension out of hewn white cedar with interior paneling and chimney brick from Sweden. His third major project was a three-cornered redoubt on the east shore called Elsinburg on which he mounted eight cannon. He was now in a position to control absolutely all traffic above Delaware Bay; the Dutch at Nassau were hamstrung if he chose to nick them; and his settlers, strung out along the river from Fort Christina to Tinicum, could work their new farms in real security.

Johan Printz is one of the thoroughly engaging characters in early colonial history; and he seems to have relished his situation in command of the river as much for social enjoyment as for controlling who might or might not proceed on its current. When the cannon of the two forts laid warning shots across the bows of a ship, it had no choice but to strike its colors and heave to while the shipmaster came ashore to learn the governor's pleasure. He might be entertained at dinner or to a glass of wine — most likely to both, for Printz boasted an unusually well stocked cellar for the time and place and enjoyed company and food and drink alike. He made an imposing figure too, for he weighed over four hundred pounds. But a skipper who proved obdurate and took a cannonading before heeding the message of the guns might, as one Englishman did, be forced to wait while the governor worked out the cost of powder and shot that he had expended on the unfortunate vessel and billed the captain for them.

Printz set up the first law court to sit in Pennsylvania, and after he had his forts the way he wanted them, he built a church and school. Under his rule there was an air of freedom in the colony, but it was no democracy. Employees of the company were the governing officials; under them were freemen; and below them were a class of laborers called "malefactors" or "vagabonds" who were little better than slaves and provided labor for the public works. But while he remained governor it was Printz who held the colony firmly in his massive hand.

His relations with the Indians were marked by strict fairness and mutual respect — policies that were to be followed in his turn by William Penn. The Indians, composed of three clans of the Lenni Lenape or Delawares, of which the most important were the Munseys, had not yet come under Iroquois domination and were probably the most powerful single Algonquin tribe; but they seem to have had peaceable inclinations — except for the fortuitous massacre of Swandendal there were no Indian troubles such as those around Manhattan — and their respect for Johan Printz amounted to awe. They had never seen a man built like him; they called him Big Guts. From him and later from Penn they came to rely on the white man's word; and as long as Penn remained in his colony they had reason to do so. But after his going they were to make five separate land treaties with his successors, all five of which were to be broken by the whites, until the Delawares had been forced out of Pennsylvania.

The Dutch were naturally disgruntled over their situation and there were spells of tension in which dire threats were made, which, however, always stopped short of open warfare; and for ten years Printz ruled his domain in relative tranquility. But in 1651 Stuyvesant decided it was time the Dutch regained control of the river; he came with a fleet of eleven ships and sloops and over a hundred soldiers, built a new fort near what is now Newcastle, Delaware, which he named Fort Casimir, and moved the Fort Nassau garrison to it. He had now checkmated Printz as the English had checkmated Fort Good Hope on the Connecticut by building Fort Saybrook at its mouth. But Printz had a thriving colony instead of a solitary post, and he remained unmolested for two years more, when after marrying off his daughter to his temporary successor he sailed for home.

The next year a fleet bringing the new governor from Sweden arrived off Fort Casimir and, finding it for some inexplicable reason entirely out of gunpowder, easily secured its surrender. For Stuyvesant this was too much to tolerate. He decided that Swedish authority on the Delaware would have to be abolished, and in 1655 he mustered an army of seven hundred men and sailed into the river on seven ships. It was a force far too strong for the Swedes to resist. Every fort and post surrendered; the Company officials were sent home; but the colonists were allowed to keep their farms as long as they would swear allegiance to the Netherlands.

The size of Stuyvesant's force was an indication of the regained strength of his colony, though it still lagged far behind those of Massachusetts and

Connecticut. New Amsterdam was once again a bustling and vigorous town, and it began to exhibit a few symptoms of a budding city. That is, in 1655 it suffered its first real estate tax.

> For each morgen (2 acres), 10 stivers yearly.
> For each head of horned cattle, 20 stivers yearly.
> From the rent of houses, the 20th penny.

And no doubt protests were raised with as much anguish as they are today. The first moves toward a regular fire department had also been instituted: stick and clay chimneys were banned within city limits in 1648 (also the use of fowling pieces for shooting partridge) and fire wardens were appointed with the responsibility of regular chimney inspection in case of violation. Every house was assessed the price of one beaver to raise money for the manufacture of two hundred and fifty leather fire buckets; and there was an annual chimney tax of one florin each. The buckets were not delivered till All Saints Day 1658, but it had already become obvious that the costs of city living were proliferating as the freedom of the individual began to decline. In 1652 an ordinance against fast driving was passed and in 1658 the burgomasters took the first steps toward creating a city police — though of course it was still called a "ratel-wackt" or watch. The main difficulty was to find men who would accept the role of the city's finest. Most significant had been the first effort to create a trans-Atlantic mail service.

The usual practice for anyone with mail for Europe was to carry his letter to the waterfront and give it to a random sailor, merchant, or shipmaster, "from which practice result many delays in the delivery of letters and subsequent losses to the writers and their families." To avoid these hazards and ensure that mail should be dispatched on the next ship sailing, the Company in 1652 built a box to receive mail on the outer wall of their warehouse in Amsterdam from which it would be regularly collected and placed in a leather sack for mailing. They urged Stuyvesant to make a similar provision in Manhattan, but it took three years and repeated instructions for him to accept any such frivolous innovation (detractors said because he did not want letters critical of himself to reach Holland any sooner than they had to). But in 1655 the system finally went into effect on a two-way basis.

It was to this lively, pushing town that Stuyvesant triumphantly returned from the Delaware, having as it seemed to him consolidated the Dutch holding in America. Any doubts he may have had about his position and the future of New Amsterdam must have been about the difficulty of finding funds to put the fort into first-rate condition. He was never able to accomplish that; but on his return it would not have seemed so immediately important. He could not have foreseen that in nine years he and his colony would suffer exactly the same fate as New Sweden. But they also were fortunate that in the leader of the conquering English they had a governor as forbearing and tolerant as Richard Nicolls.

The three other members of the royal commission of which Nicolls might be called the chairman were a curious lot. Colonel George Cartwright was a straightforward sort of character, who seems to have taken his duties seriously and acted with as much competence as circumstances allowed, but his whole view of the New World and the New England colonies in particular was colored more by his sufferings from gout than by objective observation. Even with the gout, however, he accepted his assignment by Nicolls to secure the surrender of the Hudson River posts and the allegiance to the English Crown of the great Rensselaer patroonship, and above all to renew the Dutch agreement with the Iroquois, assuring them, as we have seen, that the English would supply them with "all such wares and commodities" — meaning guns and ammunition — as heretofore they had received from the Dutch.

These were vital services and the colonel performed them without a hitch. Fort Orange surrendered peaceably and became Albany; the agent of the Rensselaers was assured that all that needed to be done to retain the great property was to renew the title under England; and the Iroquois contentedly signed a treaty of friendship on the promise of continuing firearms. On his way home down the river Cartwright stopped at the little Dutch post at Esopus to receive its submission and leave a tiny garrison of English soldiers.

The actors in these small, quiet affairs had not the remotest inkling of their significance: that the change from Dutch to English rule meant dropping the keystone into the arch of English colonies against French dominion in the midcontinent; and that also still later the fact that New York was English would expedite and simplify the union of the colonies in their war for independence. Nicolls, however, before long gained an insight into the potentialities of New York as a port and in November 1665 wrote the Duke of York that it was the best of all His Majesty's towns and would in his opinion become the chief port of the continent. "I may without boasting assure Your R. H^s that within five years the staple of America will be drawne hither of which the brethren of Boston are very sensible." It was a boast indeed and many more than five years would be needed to tip the balance, but it was nonetheless prophetic, even if he had a few qualms about his prediction. For he commented that New York was still in such a "meane condition . . . that not one soldier hath to this day since I brought them out of England been in a paire of sheets or upon any sort of bed but Canvass and straw." This may in part, but only in part, account for the very different circumstances attending the English takeover on the Delaware.

The man assigned by Nicolls to lead that expedition was his second commissioner, Sir Robert Carr, an unscrupulous character with the instincts of a freebooter and questionable personal morals — at least later in Boston the report circulated "that he kep't a naughty woman," and his talents at pub-crawling and general and noisy carousings are on the record. On the third of September, 1664, he was given two of the frigates — *Guinney* and *William & Nicolas* — "and all the souldyers which are not in the fort" to take possession of the Delaware settlements, presumably on the same liberal terms observed by Nicolls. And so on the surface Sir Robert tried to make it appear was the case. He took his frigates up the river past Fort Casimir and after three days' parleying with the Swedes and Dutch burghers won their consent to his proposed articles of capitulation which were much the same as those offered to New Amsterdam by Nicolls: all who transferred allegiance to the English king might retain their property; those disaffected might leave any time within six months taking their goods with them; all local officers were to retain their offices for six months or until the king made his wishes known. Two hundred fifty-two freemen of the settlements signed the oath swearing to be "true subject, to the King of Great Brittaine," and to obey all commands as might be received "from his Majestie, His royall Highnesse James Duke of Yorke."

It all looked well enough, except that the Dutch governor, Alexander Hinnoyossa, had holed up in Fort Casimir and refused to surrender. Sir Robert therefore marched his soldiers down the shore and ordered the frigates down the river to within musket shot of the fort, each to fire two broadsides, after which the soldiers were to attack it. The broadsides were so effective that the soldiers had little difficulty in carrying the fort, killing two Dutch and wounding ten in the process. A small affair from a military point of view, but Fort Casimir turned out to be stuffed with valuable goods and the soldiers began looting. Sir Robert, who had stayed on the frigates till the action was over, hurried ashore to take a hand; in fact a principal hand, or in the words of Nicolls' report to the Secretary of State:

> Within the fort a considerable cargo is found and some part plunder'd, but I feare the rest is in hucksters hands, for though Sir Robert stayed aboard the Guinney while Souldy[rs] took the fort, he came early enough to the pillage and says tis his owne, being wonn by the sword. . . .

For the urbane Nicolls to speak so harshly was unusual; he went further, stating that Carr, once he found himself securely in control, confiscated "houses farmes and stocks to whom he doth thinke fitt" — his son and two personal friends among them as well as the former governor's house and farms for himself. Governor Hinnoyossa sought refuge in Maryland. The surviving members of his little garrison Carr sold as slaves in Virginia, and then, his appetite whetted, he began invading houses of the ordinary settlers, helping himself to anything he thought of value. The agreement signed with the Dutch and Swedes proved merely a scrap of paper. Nicolls was incensed and when Sir Robert refused to return to New York he found it necessary to go himself to the Delaware and do what he could in restoration of stolen property. But it took almost five months to extract Sir Robert; even so, he managed to persuade Nicolls to put his son, Lieutenant John Carr, in command of the district, which was now renamed Newcastle.

Because Sir Robert enjoyed Charles II's royal favor he could not be handled roughly; nor indeed would it have been politic, as Nicolls reminded the Secretary of State, even to report his conduct to His Majesty. But it was essential to pry Sir Robert loose from the Delaware if the royal commissioners were to perform the second part of the duty assigned to them, which was to investigate affairs in the New England colonies, with particular reference to Massachusetts, toward which the king felt the most profound distrust. He wanted nothing more than to find an excuse to abrogate the charter which Winthrop, with such forethought, had carried with him out of England, and the commissioners were to check on whether such matters as allowing members of the Church of England, administering justice in the King's name, or liberalizing suffrage to allow non-Congregationalist freemen to vote, as had been agreed to by Massachusetts commissioners sent over to England at the time of his accession, had indeed been carried out. Ostensibly, however, the commissioners had been sent over to hear and referee disputes, such as disputes over colonial boundaries and other jurisdictional differences; but they were empowered to make rulings only if the three lesser commissioners were sitting together, or if one of them were sitting with Nicolls. As Nicolls was fully occupied in setting up a new government for New York, this meant that Sir Robert's five months' fling on the Delaware had severely handicapped the operations of Cartwright and the third commissioner, Samuel Maverick.

Maverick was the only colonial on the commission, and he was something of a character. He was often convivial — Samuel Johnson said he was "loving and courteous" and willingly entertained strangers — but there was a pawky side to him too, and he was easily disgruntled, as if he had been weaned on the wrong end of the pickle. During his tour of New England as a royal commissioner he was for a good deal of the time in a state of disgruntlement. It was not that he did not try to be just in his opinions and reports, but his soul shriveled with dislike of Puritans and all things Puritanical, in particular the theocratic government of Massachusetts. He had come to America well before the Puritans and established himself in a solid little blockhouse on Noddle's Island and it was one of the dark days of his life when John Winthrop's ships sailed into Boston harbor loaded to the gunwales with their Puritan cargo.

By faith he was a Presbyterian, which meant that he was denied the right of suffrage in Massachusetts and therefore was continually at odds with the leaders of the commonwealth. In 1646 with several others he had petitioned the General Court to remove the civil disabilities under which members of the Churches of England and Scotland labored, and threatened to take their case to Parliament if the petition was not heeded. This the officers of the colony regarded not unjustly as a direct attack on the Congregational church and state and, as such, tantamount to treason, and it was the more serious in view of a rising tide of discontent among other disenfranchised members of the colony. The leading signers of the petition were therefore summarily dealt with, fined, cast into prison for six months, and fined again.

The threat of an appeal to Parliament did not carry as much weight as it might have. It was true that by the Massachusetts charter the colony claimed to hold its land as if in East Greenwich near London and was therefore represented in Parliament by members of the county containing it, which meant that it was under the jurisdiction of Parliament rather than the Crown. But Winthrop not long before had stated in public that the first and ruling consideration of the colonial government was the safety of the commonwealth, and to preserve it the colony would be justified in throwing off the yoke of Parliament. This was not too far removed from the statement in the Declaration of Independence of the "Right of the People to alter or abolish" a government hostile to their interests and just powers and to institute a new government "on such principles and organizing its powers in such form as to them shall seem most likely to effect their Safety and Happiness."

Winthrop was hardly thinking of democratic government; the very concept of it would have horrified him. But it was a yeasty utterance and one more reason for the Stuarts, with their conviction of the divine right of kings, to look on Massachusetts with fear and loathing. Fortunately, if one may use Yankee understatement, Charles I was too preoccupied with his difficulties with Parliament to pay attention to what was happening in Massachusetts or any other American colony, and in any case the executioner's ax resolved in 1649 any doubts he may have felt. So from 1649 to 1660 Massachusetts and the other colonies were left free from interference by the home government; first the Commonwealth and then after its failure the Protectorate under Cromwell were absorbed almost entirely in domestic affairs. The only interest showed by either in overseas colonies was the sending of two fleets in turn to the West Indies to bring Barbados, which had recognized Charles II as the ruler of Britain, into line. The first fleet failed to accomplish anything because of a massive onslaught of scurvy; the second, under Admiral William Penn and General Robert Venables, with 50 ships and 2500 drafted soldiers brought Barbados under Parliamentary control and then, after an attack on Hispaniola that turned into a fiasco, made an easy capture of the rich and strategic island of Jamaica.

Charles II on his restoration greeted various commissions and delegates sent to declare allegiance or seek renewal of their charters cordially enough. He welcomed even the Massachusetts commission with a show of warmth which, though it did not deceive them, led them to play up to it by agreeing, as we have seen, to certain stipulations which they had no intention of putting into effect. On the other hand his welcome of the younger Winthrop was perfectly genuine; he recognized him as the son of one of his father's loyal subjects and in consequence the charter granted to Connecticut was unusually liberal and embodied many of the provisions of the Fundamental Orders. It also provided for the incorporation of New Haven within Connecticut; New Haven, it might be added, had taken over a year even to admit the fact of his accession to the Crown. Rhode Island also received a liberal charter. But Charles for all his charm had no intention of leaving his trans-Atlantic colonies to their own devices, and Massachusetts remained the bugbear in his eyes, "a constant receptacle for all mutinous and seditious persons, who flying from our justice as malefactors, or who run from their masters to avoid paying their debts, or who have any other wicked designe as soon as they shall grow to any strength and power." He was not yet ready to start the colony-wide hunt for regicides but he hoped that possibly the commissioners might bag a few "attainted in High Treason" and send them back to England to meet the king's justice.

Originally planning a large commission, he had decided instead to send only one of four men, in large measure due to general Stuart reluctance to spend money — indeed even the smaller commission he referred to as an "extraordinary charge" — and he had chosen the four because three of them were known to him personally and kindly "for affection to our service," and the fourth, Maverick, because he was a colonial; and it seemed well to have a man of local experience serve with the others. If he had any idea that this might disarm suspicion, he was wrong; Massachusetts bluntly retorted that far from being enlightened or unbiased Samuel Maverick had "profest against us."

Some time after being released from prison Maverick had made his way to England, and he had welcomed the Stuart restoration when it came. As a Catholic, Charles II was in sympathy with members of other sects who suffered discrimination in his New England colonies, even Quakers. Maverick, being "strong for the lordly prelatical power" in his own church and that of England, was ready to make himself useful in any procedure against Congregational power in Massachusetts. He had already made himself useful in another field, having co-authored a report on the Dutch settlement in America which covered four points: a statement of Charles II's title to New Netherland which was perfectly logical in English eyes; an account of the Dutch "intrusion" on this royal English domain; a description of the condition of the colony under Dutch management, or rather mismanagement; and a discussion of possible means to bring the colony under English rule and if necessary to forcibly expel the Dutch.

The report was an important factor in Charles's decision to present New Netherland to his brother James and mount the expedition under Nicolls for its capture. To delude the Dutch, Nicolls had first put in to Boston, where the leading magistrates of the colony met the royal commissioners with the utmost coolness. "King" Winthrop, as his detractors called him, and Cotton Mather were dead; but John Endicott, who would be governor till mid-March, 1665, and Richard Bellingham, who succeeded him, were hardheaded men quite ready to prevaricate and obstruct, as was Mather's successor and pastor of the First Church, John Norton, a man of wit and resourcefulness.

The accomplishments of the royal commission were small but not wholly without significance. By January 1665 Cartwright and Maverick were in Massachusetts, their effectiveness limited, as we have seen, by the absence of Sir Robert Carr. They had been met with at least a show of cordiality in both Connecticut and Rhode Island, but in Boston they found the elders of the commonwealth even colder than before and mutual antipathy was fertilized by personal dislike. The commissioners' instructions from Charles called for their meeting with the General Court to pursue such matters as disenfranchisement for religious reason, and "peruse the collection of laws published . . . during the late usurping Government." Perhaps most annoying of all was the order to investigate the colonists' relations with the Indians and if any injustices had been done the latter to see that full reparations be made. Other commission duties, such as a report on education in the colonies and schools both for white and Indian, with the promise of royal support, were dismissed contemptuously by the governors of Massachusetts as mere sops to lull their suspicion, which in effect they probably were; and the commissioners themselves were not much preoccupied with the educational aspects of their investigations — though they did report of Harvard ("at Cambridge they have a wooden colledge") that "this colledge may afford as many schismaticks to yᵉ Church, and yᵉ Corporation as many rebels to yᵉ King, as formerly they have done, if not timely prevented."

They were profoundly suspicious of the motives behind the New England Confederation, which they regarded as an incubator for possible rebellion. The more they probed the greater the resistance they encountered, and the Massachusetts General Court somehow could not manage to be convened; it was not till May that it finally met, and then, as far as the investigating commissioners were concerned, to no useful effect. Necessary documents would be in the towns of their origin; messengers to fetch them met unconscionable delays; it was all very frustrating and "many factious speeches fly up & down." It seemed, as Cartwright acidly reported on February 7, "that the phancy of a commonwealth is yet in some of their braines."

The nub of contention was of course Maverick, to whom the Lord Chancelor, Clarendon, spelled it out frankly from London: "The Governor & Councell there are not at all pleased with y^r Commission . . . they believe all their privileges are to be destroyed"; and added later: "I must tell you they seem most offended and troubled that you, whom they look on as their enemy, should have any authority over them." Cartwright defined their impasse in different terms. "I cannot conceive how it is possible for us to get a good election made for the next General Assembly, seeing none can elect nor be elected but such as are Church members." The situation was about as conducive toward peaceful agreement as if three roosters had inadvertently entered a den of weasels.

In March, however, they still had hopes of making some sort of useful contribution to New England affairs, Maverick writing Nicolls on the sixth:

> Some tyme this weke the p^{r}tended Ppryators to a great parte of the Narragansett cuntrey will meete us there to see if it may be determined who hath most right to it; either they, Conecticott, or Roade Island; all three claiminge a propriety in it.

"The pretended proprietors" referred to were a group of influential men, mainly from Massachusetts, but including some from Connecticut, among them the younger Winthrop, who with a settler on the west shore of Narragansett Bay named Richard Smith and some associates of his in 1659 had bought two huge pieces of land from the Narragansetts and in 1660 had added another big chunk. This combine, which called itself the Atherton Company, was a prototype of the big speculative land companies which after the Revolution were to play dominating roles, for better or worse, in opening the frontier. In the meantime, to complicate things, some young Narragansett braves had been doing a little depredating among the Connecticut settlements and as reparation the commissioners of the New England Confederation ruled that the tribe must pay five hundred and ninety-five fathoms of wampum within four months or lose title to their entire country. Of course such a quantity of wampum was beyond the tribe's capacity to pay; they pleaded for and won a two months' extension, but again failed to make payment; and the gleeful speculators of the Atherton Company now found themselves with a clear title to their land.

To the leaders of Rhode Island these transactions looked like the first steps toward getting control of a section of their own colony; they had always been on friendly terms with the Narragansetts, friction had been less than in any other contact of whites and Indians in New England till that time, but they regarded the Narragansett lands as being within the boundaries of Rhode Island and wanted no muscling in by other colonies for whatever purpose. To further complicate the situation the charters granted in 1662 and 1663 to Connecticut and Rhode Island, with typical Stuart disregard for geographical facts, included the Narragansett lands in the boundaries defined in each charter. This was the situation as it confronted the royal commissioners in 1665.

Their rulings raised a storm in Massachusetts and Connecticut, and indeed they seemed to cement the claim that they were prejudiced against the former colony. First of all they held that the Narragansett country came under the jurisdiction of Rhode Island and should remain so until the king had had opportunity to review the dispute. Then they voided all claims of the Atherton Company and ordered them to quit the country as soon as the Narragansetts had paid three hundred fathoms of wampum, and they declared all grants made by Massachusetts in Rhode Island territory or by the Confederation also void. Their instructions to see that full reparation for any injustices to the Indians be made had been carried out with a vengeance. Connecticut refused to accept the decision as final and for years to come was in a continual struggle with Rhode Island for control of the area. The Narragansetts, who considered the Rhode Islanders as neighbors but in no wise as governors, were naturally puffed up, and infuriated Massachusetts officials were later to claim that the contempt for Massachusetts' authority implicit in the ruling was a factor in the Narragansetts' casting their lot with King Philip in the war beginning ten years later.

It is not surprising that the commissioners on their return to Boston found the atmosphere even more hostile. Writing Nicolls on the nineteenth of April, George Cartwright uneasily intimated the possibility of rebellion. "This day (they say) here is a secret councel & y^t all the ministers within 20 miles are called to it." He thought it essential, even at some risk of leaving New York open to rumored counteraction by the Dutch fleet, that Nicolls should come over to Boston, a trip that should at most consume eighteen days "(7 dayes here & 11 to goe and come in)" in the hope that he "might be prevalent with them because acceptable to them" in contrast to "us 3"; and he added with justice, "our greatest business is to be managed here, and by how much these people are more richer, more proud and factious than the other, by so much more difficulties we shall find and the more stand in need of your help."

When Nicolls felt finally that he could leave New York and come to Boston, it was early May and he arrived the day before the convening of the General Court. It proved almost wholly unresponsive to the commissioners — even Nicolls made no headway. Eleven months later he still saw no way of bringing these fractious colonists to heel: "I dare not presume to find out a way to bring downe the pride of Massachusetts," he wrote Sir Henry Bennet, then secretary of state, and his consolatory hope was that the rise of New York would attract a great proportion of the wealth of shipping then finding its way into Boston Harbor, but though he foresaw the future it was many years in coming.

In Boston meanwhile, Cartwright, Maverick, and Carr remained locked in their fruitless struggle with the General Court and the governor. The latter, Richard Bellingham, was now seventy-four; Samuel Nadorth, a fellow colonist, was to describe him to Secretary Morrice, apropos of a rumor that the king had summoned him to appear at court in London, as decrepit:

. . . yᵉ very truth is, yᵉ Govʳ is an ancient gentleman neare 80 yeares old & is attended with many infirmities of age, often incapacitating him to yᵉ public service of yᵉ country, as stone-cholicks, deafnes &c . . .

and to have compelled him to a trans-Atlantic voyage would have, according to Nadorth, "been extream cruelty." But in any controversy this "pitiful" old man could be tougher than whit-leather, an able abettor of the General Court in defending the commonwealth against royal encroachment, as steadfast in purpose if somewhat less cool-tempered than his predecessor. But there were now few cool tempers on either side, and on the twenty-fourth of May the General Court published a declaration.

The declaration stated that since His Majesty's royal charter (received from Charles I but by implication continuing in force as from the reigning monarch) "under the Great Seale of England" entrusted them with the "maintenance of His Maᵗⁱᵉˢ authority in the governmᵗ of the people of this Colony" and since the official communications from the Crown and Secretary Morrice assured them that the royal commissioners were enjoined from disturbing the governors in their administration of the colony, but sent merely to make inquiries, and since (this with a piousness that deceived nobody) they had done their best to answer all legitimate inquiries though the commissioners had remained unsatisfied and had further given safekeeping to at least one refugee from colonial justice, described as one "John Porter junior, an high offender against God, His Maᵗⁱᵉˢ authority and lawes and the peace of his good subjects here," and since not satisfied with protecting a criminal the commissioners had summoned the "Governor and Company of his Maᵗⁱᵉˢ Colony to answer the complaints of such as claimed injustices done them," and since they apprehended these actions an infringement of their charter, the General

Court "doth therefore in his Maties name and by the authority to us committed by his Royall Charter, Declare to all the people of this Colony, that in observance of our duty to God & His Matie and the trust committed to us by his Maties good subjects in this Colony, wee cannot consent unto or give our approbation of the proceedings of the aforesaid Gentlemen, neither can it consist with our allegiance that we owe to His Matie to countenance any that shall in so high a manner go cross unto Mis Maties direct charge or shall be their abettors or consent thereunto. GOD SAVE THE KING."

The professed allegiance to the king was all well enough, but phrases such as "the trust committed to us by his Majesty's good subjects" struck ominously on the ears of the commissioners. Moreover, the declaration was not only published (by Mr. Oliver Purchas, a deputy of the General Court), it was read at large to the sound of a trumpet in "the Market Place in Boston below the Court House, and at Dock head, and at the cross-way by Captain Breedons." It was in Captain Breedon's house that the royal commissioners had taken lodgings.

The commissioners replied tersely and to the point. They said that the General Court had deliberately misconstrued the letters of introduction and instruction from the king, his chancelor, and the secretary of state as to the purpose of his sending a royal commission and accused the Court of using the authority granted in their royal charter "to oppose that sovraignty which he hath over you" (hardly calming words); and they added rather pompously that "we shall not loose more of our labours upon you, but referr it to His Ma^{tie's} wisdom, who is of power enough to make himself to be obeyed in all his dominions."

They were as good as their word. Nicolls felt compelled to return at once to New York, but Maverick, Cartwright, and Carr packed their chests and moved down east to look into the situation of the towns of Kittery, York, Wells, Scarborough, and Falmouth, which would soon become Portland. A considerable number of colonists there resented the assumption by the General Court of Massachusetts of jurisdiction over their territory and affairs, when they regarded themselves as the Province of Maine. This was the name on the original charter to Sir Ferdinando Gorges who for a time had been a leading spirit in the old Plymouth Company. Now the colonial officers in Boston had renamed it Yorkshire and claimed that it was a part of Massachusetts.

In 1622 Gorges and John Mason had received a grant of all land from the Merrimac River eastward to the Kennebec, and in 1629 Mason had been granted a tract between the Merrimac at the Piscataqua River, which ultimately was to become the Province of New Hampshire and included the towns of Exeter, Hampden, and Portsmouth; it extended north into the interior for sixty miles. Massachusetts' claim rested on the original grant of 1628 to Endicott and five others of all land from three miles south of the Charles River to three miles north of the Merrimac and extending west to the Pacific. In 1644, to underline her claim, Massachusetts had set up a bound-house which, to the prejudiced pen of Maverick, Cartwright, and Carr, was "3 larg miles north of the Merrimacke" and had claimed the whole Mason grant. The settlers here also resented what they called "usurpation" by Massachusetts and asked the commissioners to be taken under government by the Crown. The three commissioners, without Nicolls, did not feel themselves empowered to do this; at best they could only promise to deliver petitions, and a stack of them, further valuable evidence of the disaffection of unruly Massachusetts, went into the chest that traveled with Cartwright, though for some unexplained reason the key to it traveled on the person of Sir Robert Carr.

From the Piscataqua country the three journeyed on into Maine. Here, though the grant reached one hundred and twenty miles inland, the settlements were "all by the sea side," and though each township was five or six miles long, they averaged less than thirty houses, "and those very meane too." The inhabitants were continually irritated by the "contests" between the Gorges interests and those of Massachusetts, as well as weary of "the unjust and partiall actings" of the latter; they complained of being neglected and having no way of handling their own affairs.

The commissioners responded by appointing various men to act as justices of the peace and empowered them to hold sessions, discharging the few who held appointments from the Massachusetts General Court. In their opinion the province would never be "well peopled or well cultivated" unless a proper system of government was instituted under the Crown. But still farther east the cast of the land was bleaker yet.

. . . Upon 3 Rivers, the east of Kennebeck, Shipscot, and Pemaquid, there are 3 plantacôns, the greater hath not over 20 houses, & they are inhabited by the worst of men. They have had hitherto noe governm^t and are made up of such as to avoid paying of debts and being punished have fled thither; for the most part they are fishermen, and share in their wives as they do in their boats.

The only place that caught their admiration was the mouth of the Piscataqua, which provided "an excellent harbour, larg & safe, and 7 or 8 ships in it, and great store of masts." It seemed to them so important strategically that they sent out warrants to the four nearest towns charging them with fortifying the harbor; but this was too much for Massachusetts and the governor and council sent messages to the town officials prohibiting them from obeying the commissioners and wrote the latter accusing them of stirring up the people against constituted authority and concluding rather ominously with the declaration "of our sence of these your irregular proceedings and shall account ourselves bound to provide for the peace of his Maties subjects."

The commissioners immediately characterized this missive as "so full of untruth & in some places wanting grammer construction, that we are unwilling to believe it was pen'd with the knowledge and approbacôn, though in name and by the order (as is said) of the Governor and Councel," and continued their defiance by saying that it was "high time for us to give up treating in privat with those who by sound of trumpet denied that authority which the King had over them." They would not refrain from pursuing their proper course as the king's commissioners. They then spelled out the king's continuing majesty: though he granted powers to make laws by charter, he still had the right to decide which were good and which bad, and to abrogate the latter if he saw fit; and when he gave authority over such of his subjects as lived within their jurisdiction, he did not make them subjects of the Massachusetts government, nor the latter their supreme authority.

They could be ominous themselves: " 'Tis possible that the Charter which you so much idolize may be forfeited"; and they trenchantly continued: "The deserved punishm^t and destruction of some, those who of late made use of the King's authority to oppose his Maties power, and raised armies and fought against his Matie and yet pretended the defence & safety of the King, we think might deter all from broaching or acting according to such illusive and destructive sophismes. Many of your actions . . . give us just grounds to feare that, if you had power, you would try your success the same way."

These were hard words on either side, one suspecting incipient rebellion and the other not far from practicing it. As if to drive home colonial independence, Governor Bellingham sent out warrants to summon a special session of the General Court to consider the proceedings of the royal commissioners in Maine, and this time, in contrast to the earlier session, the Court convened within eleven days. If the commissioners had continued their activities, there would undoubtedly have been trouble and quite possibly open rebellion. Fortunately Cartwright, with his chestful of accusatory documents, sailed for home while Carr and Maverick, though they repaired to Boston, seem to have spent their talents mainly on social pleasures and created no trouble except with the local constabulary by carousing past midnight of a Saturday evening. On the first occasion with their drinking companions they drove the constable away with blows. On a second, with uncharacteristic prudence, they were celebrating in grog the near approach of the Sabbath in a private house across the way when another constable entered to admonish them. On finding they were the people who had beaten his fellow officer with staves he remarked that as for him, if the king himself had been in their company he would have carried him to prison. To Maverick such words were high treason, and he so proclaimed them to Bellingham, demanding justice.

Bellingham for once behaved quietly and firmly; he held the constable for the next sitting of the General Court but refused to take action personally as the alleged charge was too serious for him to judge alone. After a time Maverick virtually withdrew the charge, saying that while the constable had spoken as quoted he believed the words to have been said more in heat than in malice. The case then went to the grand jury, which found merely that the words had been spoken as charged; and the court ordered that the constable be admonished "in solemn manner" by the governor.

But while both sides were willing to compromise the episode, the commission report was emphatic in its criticism of nearly every aspect of Massachusetts' social structure, especially for making church membership the compelling force in politics; for the barbarous treatment of the Quakers ("They have put many Quakers to death . . . they beaten some to jelly"); for falsifying geography in a map made "by direction and guess"; for entertaining the regicides, Goffe and Whalley. Moreover, they "had furnished Cromwell with many instruments out of their Corporation and their Colledge," and they had solicited Cromwell "to be declared a Free State, and many times in their lawes stile themselves this STATE, this COMMON-WEALTH, & now beleive themselves to be so." But they also recognized the strength (in spite of the obvious evils) of this new trans-Atlantic society.

"This Colony which hath engrossed the whole trade of New England . . . Boston is ye cheif towne in it, seated upon a Peninsula in the bottom of a Bay, which is a good harbour and full of fish," but "their houses are generally wooden their streets crooked, with little decency & no uniformity and there are neither dayes, months, seasons of the yeare, churches nor inns are known by their English names." A strange, uncouth, pushing society in which rebellion went hand in hand with overpiousness, but had a vigorous business life:

The comodities of ye Countrey are fish wch is sent into France Spaine and ye Streights, pipe-staves, masts, firr-boards, some pitch and tarr, pork, beif, horses and corne; which they send to Virginia, Barbados &^{c} and take tobacco sugar for payment, which they (after) send for England. There is good store of iron made in this Province. Their way of government is Common-wealth-like; their way of worship is rude and called Congregationall; they are zealous in it, for they persecute all other formes.

The commercial pattern of life in Massachusetts was clearly established by the time they visited it. Now Cartwright had sailed and it was time for Carr and Maverick to leave also, Carr for England and Maverick, because he obviously could not stay comfortably any longer alone in New England, for New York, where the Duke of York made him the grant of a good house. Cartwright had been captured at sea by the Dutch, who put him ashore in Spain, facetiously pointing out that the climate there was beneficent to gout, but keeping his chest and all the papers so laboriously gathered to present a case against Massachusetts — these they confiscated.

When he reached England, war with the Dutch had broken out and the government of Charles II was much too preoccupied to worry its head over Massachusetts. As for the pub-loving Carr, he fell dead the day after he came ashore in England. The commonwealth was left to follow its iniquitous course for several more years relatively undisturbed.

Back in New York after his abortive visit to Boston, Nicolls busied himself with drawing up a code of laws to govern the Duke of York's province. It was the largest territorial grant ever made by an English sovereign to an individual, including not only what is now New York State, but all land between the Connecticut and the Delaware, the whole of Long Island and Martha's Vineyard and Nantucket, and all of Maine beyond the Kennebec. The last was manifestly beyond practicable jurisdiction of a government based on Manhattan; and the two outer islands remained relatively independent; and then the duke further simplified the bounds of the province by making a proprietary grant of what was named the Province of Nova Caesaria, later changed to New Jersey, to two friends, Lord John Berkeley and Sir George Carteret. This gift upset Nicolls, not because he resented any diminution of the territories entrusted to him, but because under the authority given him as governor he had already granted a large patent west and south of Newark Bay to two men, named Ogden and Watson, and some eighty associates, and they had already begun settling their land. But even more serious, in Nicolls's eyes, was the disservice that the duke through his generosity was doing to himself. Nicolls was perfectly aware that the duke knew nothing about the geography of his grant or the potentialities of New York Harbor as a continental port (even though he had already expressed himself on the subject) and it seemed to him vital that not only Manhattan but all surrounding shores of the harbor should remain the duke's property, and he came as near as he ever did to protesting.

He considered the Jersey country the most fertile and the easiest to develop of any of the duke's holding and he did not think that Carteret and Berkeley, if they knew how prejudicial to the duke the loss of this land would prove, would accept it. This was of course a hopeful assumption; its presumed value was a prime attraction to them as well as Nicolls. But he did not give up trying and as late as April 1666 he was urging Secretary Bennet, now Lord Arlington, to induce the royal favorites to accept a grant that would include both banks of the Delaware and extend twenty miles inland. His efforts were unavailing. The proprietors had already sent out Philip Carteret, a cousin of Sir George's, as governor and showed not the least disposition to relinquish or alter their grant. Nor when Philip

Carteret offered to honor the grants made by Nicolls would they agree either to allow these patents to stand or to give the established settlers compensation for the loss of their land.

This was the beginning of a series of complications in land titles in New Jersey that would not be unraveled completely in the course of a hundred years. Further complications developed when, after the Dutch captured New York in 1673 and then again surrendered it to the English in the Treaty of Westminster a year later, British law experts decided that the title to the province had been voided by the Dutch conquest and therefore when the Province of New York was returned to the English it became once more property of the Crown. Charles II solved this by regiving it to his brother, but without taking into consideration any developments since, such as the settlement of the Connecticut boundary, in exactly the original terms. James then restored New Jersey to Carteret and Berkeley. By the time he had done so, however, Lord Berkeley had come to the conclusion that holding property in America was too chancy for his taste and had sold out his share of the province, the land bordering the east bank of the Delaware, to two Quakers named Byllinge and Fenwick. This was one of the significant points in early New Jersey history, for it brought the rich Delaware Valley to the attention of the English Quakers and resulted in William Penn's bringing his "Holy Experiment" to Pennsylvania.

Through some vagary of Stuart thinking, when Charles II restored New Jersey to Carteret and Berkeley and found that Berkeley had already sold out his half of the province for a thousand pounds in cash, he decided that Carteret should still have only half, so he split the province up the middle, letting Carteret have the eastern half, a solution that only added further to the muddled cat's-cradle of land titles. The western half Charles ignored entirely. So two Jerseys came into existence, West and East, each with its own government and a mutual boundary continually in dispute. However, in 1702, under Queen Anne, the proprietors were made to cede their rights in the colony and it became a royal province, annexed to New York to the extent that the two provinces shared a governor (and probably the least effectual that either colony ever enjoyed, a strange transvestite named Edward Hyde Cornbury, who in addition to his proclivity to appearing in female dress had the most acquisitive instincts and stickiest fingers of almost any official in early colonial history). The two colonies, however, maintained their own assemblies.

Unlike New York, New Jersey had representational government from its inception. The "Concessions and Agreements of the Proprietors of New Jersey" under which the colony's political and social guidelines were established was the most liberal grant of its kind by colonial proprietors in America. It provided for a governor, to sit with council, and also for an assembly to be elected by the people; it guaranteed religious liberty and promised generous terms for buying land. These provisions immediately attracted emigrants from New England in search of a freer environment in which to pursue their lives, among them a large group from New Haven who had no desire to be governed by the Connecticut General Court and its Fundamental Orders and thought they saw in New Jersey's liberal outlines a haven in which to continue unmolested the practice of their particular and repressive brand of Puritanism. Their settlement on the Passaic River was the genesis of the city of Newark, a small historic episode not without an incongruity of its own.

The New Jersey assembly met for the first time in 1668, but adjourned almost immediately in a state of uproar. The freedoms promised by the Concessions seem to have led the delegates into unwarranted expectations. When they found that their legislation was to be subject to veto by the governor and council, they demanded that the assembly and the council sit in joint session, as had originally been the practice in Massachusetts Bay, which would have given them the majority vote, and when this was peremptorily refused they refused to sit further by themselves. Three years later the towns elected an independent but illegal assembly and this, though it was put down by the proprietors, forced the return of the governor to England, and it was not until 1675 that a proper assembly was seated and orderly government began to function.

However, during this disturbed period the settlers had gained a point of their own. From the beginning the proprietors had expected quitrents to be paid for all land taken. This the settlers refused to do; they organized opposition through their town meetings and short of a military expedition they could not be coerced. The Carterets bowed to the inevitable and quitrents were not collected in New Jersey.

The conversion of New York from a Dutch to an English colony went much more smoothly. Partly this was due to the Duke of York's having made the adamantine ruling in his instructions to Richard Nicolls that, though every consideration was to be given the Dutch already there, no representative assemblage of the people was to be permitted; partly, too, it was due to the five hundred veteran troops Nicolls had under his command, most of whom he kept with him on Manhattan; but mainly it was due to the tact, kindliness, and intelligence of Nicolls himself and the fact that he liked New York, however dim his view of the conveniences of the little town may have been.

He seems to have taken genuine satisfaction in drawing up what came to be called "the Duke's Laws" himself. Liberal on the surface, the effect of this code, which Nicolls modeled on those of New England, listing his laws alphabetically, was completely autocratic. There was no representation of the people, no elective provincial officials. All were appointed by the governor and all taxes levied by him. If trial by jury was assured, land could be held only by the duke's license. But at the same time the patroons and large landholders were confirmed in their estates; no effort was made to make English the first language of the colony; and while the Church of England was established, it lived amicably side by side and shared the place of worship of the Dutch Reformed Church. Moreover, for a year local officials were allowed to serve under their Dutch titles; only afterward did the schout become the sheriff and the burgomasters aldermen.

When his code had been approved by the duke, Nicolls summoned deputies from all the towns to read it to them. Many, especially men from Long Island, were dumbfounded when they realized that they had been brought under what seemed to them despotic rule — only the great landowners were complacent — and in the end this taxation without representation was to create serious trouble. But for the four years of Nicolls's governorship a harmony prevailed that was remembered as one of the golden periods in the history of the colony.

He enjoyed sport as much as he enjoyed philosophical discussion and started a race course on Hempstead and the first race meeting to be organized north of Virginia. To it he contributed a cup which is still raced for. His spontaneous good feeling toward his fellow men made him universally liked; he even made the Indians his friends, as Maverick wrote to Lord Arlington: "And as to the severall Nations of the Indyans, they were never brought into such peaceable posture & faire correspondence, as by his means they are now." Generous and openhanded, he was nearly unique among early colonial governors in making no effort to feather his own nest; in fact he almost impoverished himself trying to meet the payrolls of his soldiers out of his own pocket, for the duke, like other Stuarts, had no inclination to spending money of his own if he could find a loyal servant to do it for him. Nor did he send over promised ships of supplies.

> The whole trade, both inwards & outwards is lost for want of shipping; but the charge of foure Garrisons with all their fortifications and supplies falls upon me. I most humbly therefore beseech your R. H^s to dispatch a speedy supply hither before we fall into extremities.

To Lord Arlington, whom he begged to stir up action, Nicolls wrote more pointedly of his own situation. "For myselfe I am utterly ruin'd in my small estate and creditt, &, which is worse, without very great supplyes I shall not bee able to secure an honest defence of His Maties interest, should we be attacked by a forain force." None of his pleas availed; the colony remained as helpless after his departure as when he captured it and, as we shall see, fell without a struggle to a Dutch fleet under Admiral Evertsen in 1672.

The garrisons Nicolls had to maintain, besides that at Fort James on Manhattan, were at Fort Albany and Esopus on the Hudson, and Newcastle on the Delaware. In late summer of 1665, alarmed by the attitude of the French, he visited the two Hudson River forts, where he relieved the commandant, putting Captain John Baker in his place with instructions to keep strict watch to the north and at the same time do everything in his power to maintain friendly relations with the Dutch. Finding also that one of Baker's soldiers had some education, he licensed him as the first English schoolmaster of Albany. He also renewed English relations with the Mohawks: they were New York's only actual defense against the French.

Dropping down the river to Esopus, he gave the English commandant there the same good advice he had given Baker, but Captain Brodhead and his garrison were soon at odds with the settlers — probably lack of pay had much to do with it: occupation troops without money are apt to help themselves to what they want — and the only real hostility between Dutch and English during Nicolls's term of office broke into the open there.

Like many another traveler, before and since, he fell under the spell of the Hudson Valley, and while at Esopus he bought large tracts from the Indians — apparently hoping to offset the loss of New Jersey. To attract settlers, he wrote a prospectus describing the easy terms under which land could be taken up under the Duke's Laws and extolling the fertility of the Hudson River country. He must have appreciated the irony of having to have it printed by the press at Harvard College, so thoroughly vilified by his fellow commissioners; it was still the only printing press in the English colonies.

He made only one other trip up the Hudson, in the summer of 1668, when he took his successor, Francis Lovelace, north on an inspection of Albany; after he sailed for England in August of that year he never returned to New York or visited the New World again. He spent the last four years of his life in England, dividing his time between the court in London and his home at Ampthill. He was only forty-seven when he died in the naval battle of Sole Bay, during the third Dutch war. He had never married.

The duke's neglect of his American province had not been due to the customary Stuart parsimony and heartless exploitation of a servant's loyalty. England's energies were absorbed in its second war with Holland, which had broken out in 1665 and involved some of the heaviest naval encounters in the country's history. In the opening battle of Lowestoft on June 2, in which the Duke of York himself held a command, there were over one hundred line-of-battle ships and twenty thousand men on each side. The English won and drove the Dutch ships back into their own ports, but the Dutch effort had been an astonishing one, for during that summer of 1665 the plague was raging through their cities.

Yet they rallied from their defeat and in 1666 under their great admiral De Ruyter they sent another fleet of one hundred line-of-battle ships to attack the English, who were led by Monk and Prince Rupert. In two days of fighting off the North Foreland the English were driven into their ports after very heavy losses and De Ruyter, pursuing closely, burned part of the fleet in Chatham. There was great fear that the Dutch would sail up the Thames and capture London; and they might have done so, for in that summer the city was staggering under its own visitation from the plague.

But as the Dutch had the year before, the English rallied, rebuilt their fleet, and once more under Monk's command sailed forth to engage the Dutch under De Ruyter and Tromp — names with stirring echoes in the early engagements of the Pacific war in World War II. This time it was the Dutch who broke, and though De Ruyter managed to save most of his force by escaping through the shallow waters of the Zeeland sands where the English dared not follow, the English for a time ravaged the Dutch coast. Yet in the following June the Dutch were once more ascendant; they sailed into the Medway, burned Sheerness, and for a time blockaded the Thames, the greatest humiliation ever suffered by the British navy.

There was scarcely ever a war in which the ebb and flow of fortune ran faster or more fiercely, and in 1667 the English people had had enough. The two countries along with France and Denmark made peace in the Treaties of Breda, in which Holland formally resigned all claim to her North American colony in return for Surinam, and the English Navigation Acts of 1651 prohibiting the importation into England of any goods not carried in English bottoms, which had been a direct cause of the first war with Holland in 1652, were relaxed slightly to permit Dutch ships to bring goods originating in the Rhineland into English ports.

The Navigation Acts also applied to commerce with the colonies — all goods from whatever country entering the colonies had to be carried in English ships, as did all exports from the colonies. "Applied" is the correct word, because the colonials observed these laws only when it suited their purpose, and in their early evasions one sees the birth of the American inclination to disregard or openly break any law that interferes with business and profits.

This disregard of law when it does not suit us, moral as well as civil law, threads the entire fabric of our history. It has plagued the South in racial ways; the North in financial ways; and all rural America in all sorts of petty discrimination. It was one of the considerations that troubled members of the Constitutional Convention of 1787; it is a gray presence that stalks the chambers of state legislatures all across the country and even the national Congress today. Jefferson's statement that a little revolution is good for democracy and that the tree of liberty should be refreshed at times with the blood of patriots and tyrants is rooted partly in this same notion that laws are to be obeyed or disobeyed depending on their "goodness" or the lack of it, a distinction which under certain stresses the rank-and-file American has always felt entitled to make entirely on his own. There have been times when this ambivalent point of view has been exercised for the moral welfare of the country, as in the antislavery conflict and Abolitionist defiance of the Fugitive Slave Law, or to liquidate an impossible situation like Prohibition. But these internal acts of disobedience were carried forward on a national scale. In their opposition to the Navigation Acts the early colonials were animated by personal interest only; and they felt that they could disobey Parliamentary or royal edicts with impunity, shielded as they were by the width of the Atlantic.

Much more irritating were the Trade Acts that accompanied the Navigation Laws. According to these, the entire output of certain commodities could be exported only to the mother country: masts and spars from New England, naval stores and tobacco from Virginia and Maryland, rice and indigo from South Carolina and later Georgia, iron, furs, and hides from the colonies at large, were all engrossed for the English market. In some instances this amounted to giving one or other of the colonies a monopoly in England against imports from other countries; in the case of one or two commodities, particularly indigo, the Crown partially subsidized production; but the colonists resented the fact that prices for their crops were set by English merchants. Moreover, goods under consignment to other countries had to pass through the hands of English merchants who therefore reaped a profit that to the American shipper seemed unearned and unjust. Further regulations, instituted for the protection of British industrial interests, prohibited, for example, the export of woolen goods manufactured anywhere among the colonies, or even the sale of them between the colonies themselves; and in time such prohibitions were extended to various young industries, almost invariably at the behest of and for the protection of its counterpart in England.

Since enforcement of these restrictions would have required a virtual army of officials, very little was done to curtail local manufacturing enterprises throughout the colonies; intercolonial trade flourished and, until the English took possession of New Netherland, New Amsterdam served as a port where colonials could obtain European goods in exchange for their own products. Boston merchants simply disregarded the Trade Acts and Navigation Laws as it suited them, and ships from France and Spain as well as Holland put in there to trade directly.

The Navigation Laws, in addition, stimulated shipbuilding in New Eng-

[329]

land; colonial ships classed as British vessels under the laws and merchants saw no reason for not shipping goods in ships of their own instead of paying freight to British shipowners. This budding colonial maritime activity was not confined to carrying goods between colonial ports and those of the mother country. Respectable merchants in the northern colonies often outfitted ships for long speculative voyages which, during the various wars that embroiled Britain with Holland, France, or Spain, could be reasonably called privateering but at other times amounted to simple piracy, mostly against shipping originating in the Caribbean but sometimes reaching as far as the coast of Africa. It was not unnatural that in due course some of the latter should get into the lucrative slave trade and so, selling their cargoes in the West Indies, load their holds with sugar which would be processed into rum in their home ports, the second step in the triangular trade of rum, slaves, and sugar that founded some of New England's largest fortunes. However, colonial slavers were not confined to New England and New York. There were instances of southern plantation magnates who, motivated by the same frugal instincts that made Yankee merchants build ships for themselves, sent their own ships to pick up slaves. The landing of a cargo of four or five hundred ungainly, frightened, primitive black men and women on the James River shore must have contrasted grotesquely with the image of gracious life exemplified by Westover, though William Byrd would not have found the two irreconcilable.

Whatever the consequences of the Navigation Acts in America, they had the effect of making England's merchant marine the greatest in the world. Before 1651 more than three quarters of her ocean trade had been carried in Dutch ships. Now in relatively few years the picture changed, and Holland was never to regain her maritime supremacy, though her navy for one more time would find itself locked in battle with the English.

This third Dutch war was the result of some typically Stuart double dealing. After making peace with the Dutch in the Treaties of Breda in 1667, England joined Holland and Sweden in the Triple Alliance, designed to curb the power of Louis XIV. But in 1670 Charles, going behind the back of Parliament, agreed with Louis to make war on Holland and Spain. The clinching provision, as far as Charles was concerned, was Louis's guarantee of 200,000 pounds a year for the duration of the war and the promise of six thousand soldiers if Charles found himself with a revolution on his hands.

The war opened on May 28, 1672, with the battle of Sole Bay (now more generally called Southwold Bay) in which the Dutch and English were savagely engaged while the French navy elected for themselves the role of spectators. The English suffered heavy losses but it was the Dutch fleet which retired. In the following month Louis's army in overwhelming force crossed the Rhine. The Dutch states had kept their navy at strength but had virtually disbanded their army. The French had everything their own way; town after town fell into their hands with no more than token resistance, and national panic seized the Dutch. They turned on the man they considered responsible.

John De Witt had become grand pensionary, or prime minister, of the Netherlands in 1653 at the age of twenty-eight, three years after the death of William II. His taking office was a milestone in a long power struggle between the House of Orange and the wealthy merchants of the States of Holland and, to some extent, of Zeeland. The official governing instrument of the United Netherlands was the States General, but this had often proved itself, as we have seen in at least one instance, incapable of coming to a prompt decision or at times any decision at all. The States of Holland, the governing body of the province, in which members of the great merchant and banking houses of the city of Amsterdam were dominant, became the controlling force in many matters of national policy. The rich burghers who held seats in it formed in effect an oligarchy and were extremely jealous of the House of Orange. They regarded themselves, as often happens with a group of entrenched wealth, as the upholders of republican rights. The leading figure in their resistance to William II's attempt to secure a unified government for the Netherlands and one which in his opinion would serve more impartially the general interests of all the provinces was Jacob De Witt, the father of John.

In 1648 the States of Holland had forced through a treaty of peace with Spain, mainly for the benefit of Amsterdam's commercial interests, by which the independence of the United Provinces was recognized. William, who had succeeded to his father's titles of Stadholder and Captain General too late to prevent the signing, believed that the war should be continued until the Spanish Netherlands also had been freed. When therefore the States of Holland began disbanding all regiments for whose pay they were responsible, with the backing of the army, he seized Jacob De Witt and five other leading members and cast them into prison. Though he failed to take the City of Amsterdam with troops, the States of Holland capitulated and William II became ruler of the Netherlands and entered at once into negotiations with Louis XIV against Spain. But before any of his plans could be implemented he died of smallpox, leaving behind him a power vacuum, and for eight days not even an heir.

His posthumous son, born on November 14, 1650, was for years to play the role of a hidden child, keeping in the background, always conscious of being among enemies, controlling every action, watchful, constantly suspicious, but unvarying in his determination to succeed eventually to his father's place. Confronting him from the very beginning of his life and equally inexorable in his suspicion and dislike of the House of Orange was the young grand pensionary. De Witt worked tirelessly to promote peace with England and did much to restore prosperity after the ending of the first war in 1654; but remembering his father's imprisonment, he was hostile to the army and set about disbanding the regiments, resisting even the suggestion of maintaining cadres.

This was the situation of the Netherlands when the French army invaded in 1672. Finding himself helpless to defend the country, De Witt looked on submission as the only practicable course. But at this the country rose against him and in their dismay and terror turned to William, now a man of twenty-two, to save the country. De Witt was forced to resign the title to which he had been three times reelected. His brother, Cornelius, who had worked closely with him, was thrown into prison and tortured, and it was while John was visiting him there that an infuriated mob broke in and was allowed without interference to kill the two brothers by literally tearing them limb from limb and in the established Dutch tradition of violence hanging the sectioned bodies from lampposts outside the prison walls.

The deprivations of his upbringing had tempered the soul of William; incredibly, though he had no forces capable of standing against Louis's, he rallied the Dutch people, persuaded them to open the dikes and so prevent French occupation of large sections of the country. Meanwhile the States General had voted him the titles of Stadholder, Captain General, and Admiral for life. He proved equal to the country's trust. At sea De Ruyter was able to stand off the combined French and English fleets. England soon tired of what was in the people's estimation really only Charles's war and in 1674 made peace in the Treaty of Westminster, while William found allies in Spain, Sweden, and Denmark for prosecuting his war with France. The French evacuated Dutch territory in 1674 and three years later began negotiating for peace, a procedure hastened by William's marriage to Princess Mary, the daughter of James, Duke of York. This marriage resulted in his sharing the throne of England and was to make him the most effective as well as relentless foe of Louis XIV.

One of the stipulations of the Treaty of Westminster was that all territories captured during the war should be restored; and so New York, which had been taken by a Dutch fleet in August 1673, became once more an English colony.

The Dutch capture of New York had been as easy as the earlier capture of New Amsterdam by Nicolls. For one thing, the Dutch arrived in overwhelming force with nineteen ships and sixteen hundred men under Admiral Cornelius Evertsen, while opposing them there were fewer than eighty soldiers in the garrison of Fort James. The governor, Francis Lovelace, was absent in Connecticut, busy with arrangements for setting up a postal service between New York and Boston, a project that had become his major preoccupation. There had been word in March that a Dutch fleet was heading north from the Caribbean for the Chesapeake and would probably continue on to New York, but Lovelace only half believed it. He did agree to accept enlistments of one hundred and thirty men and the garrisons up the Hudson were milked to bring the strength in Fort James up to three hundred and thirty; but after time had passed with no further news of the Dutch, all but eighty of the soldiers were sent back to their posts of origin; and in July Lovelace had set out for Connecticut to work out details for expediting the mail with Governor Winthrop. He had already urged Winthrop to "discourse with some of the most able woodmen, to make out the best and most facile way for a post."

The start of service had been announced in January of that year, for the wagon road from Broadway to Harlem, long talked about and sporadically worked at, had finally been finished or at least been made passable at the end of 1672. This was the first leg of the route for what was announced as the monthly post rider, described as "active, stout, and indefatigable." He made a sensation in Harlem when he stopped for beer. And he had need to be indefatigable and still more to observe the fidelity he had sworn, for the rest of the way took him along Indian trails and over tricky fords and, as though these duties were not arduous enough, he was expected to blaze trees along the more obscure parts of his route for the benefit of less knowledgeable travelers and also to detect and secure the arrest of fugitive soldiers and servants. He did not have a change of horses until he got to Hartford.

Though Lovelace was a man of very ordinary attainments, the creation of a regular colonial postal service was a conception of the first magnitude and it is no wonder that he allowed it to obsess him and to keep him away from his post in New York for long periods. He was at New Haven when he received news of the arrival of the Dutch warships in New York Bay, and he was plainly shocked and filled with a sense of guilt not to have been on hand to meet them. He tried to put the best face on it in a hasty letter to Winthrop:

> At newhaven I receiued an unwellcome news of the Dutch approach before New York, I call it unwellcome in regard I was not in the place. They appeared at first wth ten sayle afterwards with seauenteen. Yesterday about five or Six of the Clock they stormed it, a hot dispute it seems it was, how the success I canôt as yet learne, they I understand have breakefasted on all my Sheepe and Cattell on Staten Island. I am hastening as fast as I can to make on, and I doubt not to give a good account of it. Yo^r Gentlemen have formed a post from Mr. Richbells to you . . .

Even then, guiltily conscious as he was of his inadequate measures for the protection of the province, the postal service was at the forefront of his mind. The rest of his letter to Winthrop was all fantasy. There had been no storming of the fort nor anything that could approximate "a hot dispute." Fort James was in even poorer state than it had been under Van Twiller and Kieft. In a statement signed by four noncommissioned officers and eighteen privates shortly after the event, its lamentable condition was spelled out:

> Wee whose names are under written are ready to mak oath y^t when the dvsh floet cam to New York we had in the ffort Jeams bvt fovr spvnges & Ramers [that of all] the gvns in the ffort we covld [not get] bvt six to beare vpon the [Enemy when] they were fired for want of [platforms] all the men upon the bastion covld not bring them to beare Againe or else the Carridge brooke and their was neither Bed nor Koyn plank spad Hand spick or any materiall to help defend vs . . .

Admiral Evertsen, who had lain to off Staten Island on July 29 and 30 (no doubt when his crews had the opportunity to breakfast on Lovelace's sheep and cattle), had been thoroughly briefed on the condition of the fort by Dutch colonists, and on the thirty-first he brought his ships up the bay, formed them in a half moon before the fort, and fired a single broadside, which apparently did no damage beyond removing the head of an overeager soldier brandishing his sword upon the ramparts. The fort managed to reply with four guns. Under cover of the smoke two hundred (some said five hundred) soldiers were put ashore. Captain John Manning, the sheriff, who in Lovelace's absence was in command of the fort, decided to surrender. He had powder for less than four hours' musket fire; the warrants he had sent out to officers of the Long Island militia had proved fruitless for similar reasons. Indeed, Cornet Elias Doughty of Jamaica closed his acknowledgment with a request for Manning's protection:

> . . . soe I hunble desier your worship to send hvs povdar and shott for whee are vnprovided and vnable to defend ovur selves if whe should meet with an enemy Nothing els bvt my prayers to the Lord to give yov wisdom and a valiant arm to Maneg and defend his Maties interest and ovur ovne lives from the enimy that shall upose them.

Manning could have accomplished nothing by a few hours of fighting. Evertsen had orders to destroy the town if he met resistance; and as it was, the take-over was as peaceable and painless under the new Dutch governor, a tough no-nonsense infantry captain named Anthony Colve, as it had been under the English. Towns and districts reverted to their old Dutch names or acquired brand-new ones. Officials once more became schouts, and schepens and other weights and measures similarly reverted. Colve's main interests were in strengthening the fort, which he set about with great vigor, tearing down all houses and outbuildings in its vicinity, and levying special taxes on beaver and Indian trade goods, lead, powder, and muskets, and what to many seemed worst of all, five percent on wines and all spirituous liquors. Taxes, however, were not enough to pay for the kind of wholesale renovation Colve had in mind and which, from rumors issuing from New England, had become imperative. For the New England Confederacy, to which the English communities in eastern Long Island had appealed for rescue, was said to be planning an attack on New Orange itself. To raise more money for the fort, Colve began confiscating the properties of French and English citizens, except those owned by members of other colonies, and particularly those belonging to agents or friends of the Duke of York. Among these Lovelace was the most seriously injured, for with a prescient eye for the town's future growth he had been speculating in real estate. Besides the big farm on Staten Island he had acquired houses and plots of farmland all over Manhattan, a good many of which he had not yet finished paying for. When, therefore, Colve confiscated them Lovelace found himself heavily in debt, and on his return to New Orange his creditors had him arrested.

He had, of course, no means for paying, and after keeping him in apprehension for some weeks, Colve finally allowed him to slip aboard a ship for Holland. He himself poured all his energies into completing the fort. By spring of 1674 its works were in good order and mounted one hundred and ninety cannon. For the first time in the colony's history it was in condition not only to stand off a naval attack but one from land as well. But the Treaty of Westminster left its strength untested. In October the new English governor, Major Edmund Andros, arrived and the colony once more changed hands.

New York was to remain English till the end of the Revolution, but that fact did nothing to help poor Lovelace, who found himself as much out of favor in London as in America. His properties in and around New York were reconfiscated by the Duke of York to repay money he claimed to be due him, and Lovelace died shortly afterward, his affairs still in chaos.

When Richard Nicolls sought to prevent the Duke of York from presenting his friends Carteret and Berkeley with the whole of New Jersey, and instead suggested to Lord Arlington that they be persuaded to accept twenty-mile belts on each side of the Delaware River, he knew that the one on the west bank fell within the boundaries of the grant of Maryland, but he added that that need not be considered, "well knowing that my Lord Baltimore can never make good his pretences within twenty miles of any part of the River by the lines mentioned in his patent."

Though Carteret and Berkeley were not interested in exchanging New Jersey for the Delaware, Nicolls proved to be right in his estimate of Maryland's future growth. The west bank of the lower Delaware was at first included in the grant to William Penn but later it became a separate colony with the boundary of Maryland fixed from ten to thirty-five miles west of the river and bay.

The story of Maryland, curiously enough, began on the southern peninsula of Newfoundland where in 1623 George Calvert, soon to become the first Lord Baltimore, feeling an inclination, as he put it, "to further . . . the enlarging of your Majesty's empire" in the New World, had established a small plantation which he named Avalon. It eked out a precarious four years; then in 1627 Lord Baltimore came out himself, bringing his wife and children with him. A house of some pretension for that time and place had already been built for him, but he found Newfoundland not at all as it had been represented.

In 1615 a Captain Richard Whitbourne had been assigned by the admiralty to straighten out disorders and controversies in the Newfoundland fishing fleet and had spent some of his time ashore. After his return to England in 1622 he had published a "Discourse" on Newfoundland in which his impressions of the island in June played a prominent part. He described it as a land of sunshine, carpeted with strawberries along the edges of the woodlands, filled with singing birds, wild game none of which was harmful to men, an idyllic island indeed. He had even seen a mermaid in the harbor of St. Johns. His description was so alluring that King James ordered it distributed throughout England with the hope that it would encourage men to settle there.

George Calvert was one who took the lure; but he quickly learned that it was not always June in Newfoundland. For nearly six months life there stood still. Men were bound by the intolerable cold, occupied only with the work of trying to keep their houses warm. No farming could be done; no fish came from the sea. Calvert described it as "a sad fare of winter upon all this land" and wrote Charles I, who had succeeded his father on the throne, that his pecuniary losses were more than he could carry and that he proposed to move his family and his followers to some place in Virginia. Charles replied sympathetically, urging him to come back to England, but before the royal letter reached Newfoundland, Calvert had sailed south, and on October 1, 1629, he reached Jamestown; but the Virginians did not welcome him.

George Calvert was the son of a wealthy Yorkshire farmer who by devoted service had gained the favor of the Crown. Though he did not profess Catholicism till 1624, he had probably been secretly a Catholic for some time and had supported the project of the Spanish marriage for Charles I. In doing so he had lost the confidence of Parliament; and the marriage and the treaty with Spain, proposed to go with it, proved a fiasco.

It was the beginning of his loss of interest in a public career in England and his turning to thoughts of America, with the pervading objective of founding a colony in which Catholics would be free to worship without fear of molestation.

The Virginians had as little use for a Papist as a Puritan. In their eyes, besides being a Papist, Calvert was a favorite of the king and had served on a commission, of which the hated Samuel Argall was also a member, appointed by King James to examine affairs in Virginia. This commission was the first step taken in the process of rescinding the charter of the Virginia Company and transforming Virginia itself into a Crown colony. The Virginians wanted no part of George Calvert and they got rid of him by the simple means of asking him to take the oath of supremacy (which declared the king to be the supreme authority in ecclesiastical matters throughout all English dominions), which of course, as a Catholic, Calvert refused to do. Whereupon he was told to leave the colony forthwith.

But the Virginians were not content merely to get rid of him; they sent the colonial secretary, William Claiborne, after him to keep him under observation and if possible to frustrate any designs he might have of acquiring property within the boundaries of Virginia. Claiborne was successful in defeating Calvert in his first choice of the land lying between the south side of the James and Albemarle Sound in what in due course was to become North Carolina. Enough interested parties with schemes of their own involving the Carolinas joined their objections to Claiborne's to have the charter already granted Lord Baltimore withdrawn. But Charles was determined to deal generously with his friend and suggested instead the desirability of inserting a buffer colony between the Potomac and Delaware rivers to prevent further Dutch expansion southward. He offered it to Baltimore, who accepted. Ironically, from Virginia's and Secretary Claiborne's point of view this second grant was infinitely more valuable than the one that had been Calvert's first objective.

However, while the charter of Maryland was still being drawn up, George Calvert died. Charles immediately confirmed the grant to his oldest son, Cecilius, the second Baron Baltimore, two months later. In November 1633, the first expedition set out for the new colony, three hundred and twenty strong, headed by Cecilius Calvert's younger brothers, Leonard, who was the first governor, and George, in two ships, the *Ark* and the *Dove*. In February they raised Point Comfort, stopping only to restock their stores, and then passed on up Chesapeake Bay to the mouth of the Potomac and briefly up that to the St. Mary's River. After celebrating the first mass held in English America on March 25, 1664, they began to build their settlement, mindful of the sufferings of Jamestown, on high ground above the river.

The site was that of a small Algonquin village with considerable cultivated ground around it (the large proportion of the land already under Indian cultivation was to make the settlement of Maryland much less of a problem than in other colonies), and the Indians were quite willing to sell. They had in fact for some time been considering a move southwestward. The great tribe to the north of them was the Susquehanna, an Iroquoian people who dominated Indian life through the length of the Susquehanna country to the northern Pennsylvania border and eastward to parts of Delaware. Though blood kin of the Five Nations they were their bitterest enemies, and though they were a single tribe, not a confederation of several, they fought the Iroquois to a standstill and early in the century came close to destroying the Mohawks, who were saved only by the acquisition of Dutch muskets. As the fortunes of war fluctuated, the Susquehannas, known as Minquas to the Delaware tribes, a name corrupted in Pennsylvania to Mingoes, at times pressed down the great valley, to the apprehension of the small Algonquin tribes in the lower stretches; and it was in one of these periods of unease that the Calverts and their followers came ashore.

As in this first instance, they were punctilious in their dealings with all Indians. When the Susquehannas put in an appearance the new settlers established peaceable relations with them. Maryland did not have to face the threats of instant massacre that had so continually confronted the Jamestown settlers. Maryland, in fact, had no real Indian troubles until the Susquehannas were finally defeated by the Iroquois and driven from their home ranges on the upper Susquehanna and came down to the Potomac. Then they began raiding, and after the Marylanders had made a peace treaty with the deadly Senecas, the Susquehannas turned hostile; but even then they attacked mainly Virginia frontiersmen. It was this situation that furnished the spark that in 1675 touched off Bacon's Rebellion.

The only war that troubled Maryland during the first two decades of its existence was with Virginia, mainly as personified by William Claiborne. Hurrying back from England, once it was apparent that the Calverts would get their charter, he had with the backing of the colony set out at once to establish a Virginia trading post on Kent Island high up in Chesapeake Bay. But to lend more weight to his and Virginia's claim to what they still considered part of their grant — when the charter of the Virginia Company had been rescinded the Crown had specifically stated that this was not to infringe the territorial rights of the colony, a point subsequently affirmed by King Charles — Claiborne stocked Kent Island with cattle and brought in farmers to turn it into a bona fide Virginia settlement which he could claim to have established before the Maryland charter actually had been issued. The Privy Council, considering a petition from Virginia, had decided that the Baltimores should not be disturbed in their grant; but now Claiborne - who had been informed that if he continued his Indian trading, he must do so under a Maryland license — refused to admit Baltimore's sovereignty.

It would be pointless to sort through all the claims, counterclaims, petitions, and messages that crossed and recrossed the Atlantic over this bitter issue between the two colonies, inflamed still more by the peculiar clause in the Maryland charter which gave that colony sovereignty over *both* banks of the Potomac and soon led to open hostilities between the oystermen of the respective colonies that have continued sporadically to this day. Only a Stuart could have thought of anything so bizarre, even though motivated only by kindness toward a friend. Nor would there be much point in following the encounters between small ships belonging either to Claiborne or the Baltimores, with bloodshed on both sides. The struggle continued until 1644 when Claiborne, joining forces with a Puritan captain named Ingle, who claimed to be operating under a commission from Parliament, captured both Kent Island and St. Mary's and drove Leonard Calvert into, of all places, Virginia. But in 1646, with the powerful backing of Sir William Berkeley, who had returned to Virginia as governor the year before, Leonard was able to drive Claiborne and Ingle out of the colony and reassert his authority. He did not have long to enjoy his success, however, in half a year he was dead.

His death left Cecilius Calvert, in England, with the problem of finding a successor. He was in much perplexity as to the course he ought to follow. Though his sympathies had always been strongly royalist, the tides of the second Civil War were running against the Crown; 1648 was the year of Preston, of the final fruitless negotiations with Charles, of Pride's Purge, and the conveyance of the king under guard from Hurst Castle to Windsor. The trial and execution would come the next year, though the mass of English people almost certainly had not the least comprehension of the possibility of such things coming to pass. But it was obvious that the times were becoming steadily more precarious for those of Catholic faith and to Cecilius it seemed evident that he should conduct his colonial affairs in a way that would meet Parliamentary approval in order to ensure the continued toleration of the Catholics in Maryland. The man he chose, therefore, to succeed his brother was a Protestant of liberal outlook and a strong upholder of Parliament, Sir William Stone. He then turned his attention to drawing up an act to give Catholics formal guarantee of their right to worship.

It was obvious that this could not be overtly accomplished in a single colony surrounded by Protestant neighbors; the suspicion and fear of Papists then was as pathologically consuming as the fear of Communists is in our own time. Cecilius Calvert's solution was the celebrated Toleration Act which was passed by the Maryland Assembly in April 1649 and under which it was "ordered and enacted that noe person or persons whatsoever within this Province . . . professing to believe in Jesus Christ, shall from henceforth be any waies troubled, molested or discountenanced for or in respect to his or her religion."

This was a noble statement, and the act went further in furnishing protection to various sects from vilification because of their beliefs: "That whatsoever person shall henceforth . . . declare, call, or denominate any person or persons whatsoever, inhabiting, residing, traffiqueing, or commerceing within this Province . . . an heretic, Scismatick, Idolator, Puritan, Independent, Presbiterian, popish priest, Iesuit, Iesuited papist, Lutheran, Calvenist, Anabaptist, Brownist, Antinomian, Barronist, Roundhead, Sep'atist, or any other name or term in reproachful manner relating to matter of Religion" shall for each offense pay a fine of ten shillings.

Yet the act did not acknowledge anyone who did not believe in the Trinity a professed Christian. Whoever "shall deny the holy Trinity, the ffather sonne and holy Ghost, or the godhead of any of the said three persons of the Trinity . . . or shall use or utter any reproachful speeches, words or language concerning the said Holy Trinity . . . shall be punished with death," and his land and property would be forfeited to the Lord Proprietor and his heirs. Sects of every kind, peculiar or not, could find haven in Maryland; but it was no place for a Unitarian.

The charter of Maryland provided for a proprietary colony, giving the lord proprietor the widest kind of power. In the life of the colony he took in fact the place of the Crown. Ordinances issued by him or laws passed by the assembly with his approval needed no further authority, and the governor, who served in the colony in his place with a council to advise him, controlled practically all activities of the colony. Besides heading the civil administration, he served as lord chancellor, presided as chief magistrate, and as lord lieutenant commanded the militia. About the only power he lacked was the approval of any act passed by the assembly repealing one formerly approved by the lord proprietor. By appointing his brother and later other members of the family to the governorship (except for the brief period of the Protectorate and again for twenty-seven years following the Revolution of 1688 that brought William and Mary to the throne, when Maryland was made a Crown colony) the Baltimore proprietors kept affairs of their province in tight control. In fact they were so independent of the Crown that by stipulation of their charter no taxes could be levied in Maryland by the government of England.

The framework was purely feudal, yet as the colony developed it became surprisingly liberal and democratic. This was due mainly to the common sense and sensibility of Cecilius Calvert. An instance in point was the assembly, which the charter expressly called for. As defined it was to be an assembly of the freemen of the colony; and at its first meeting all freemen who felt like coming attended, sitting in camera with the governor and his council; as had been the case in Massachusetts and Virginia;

but before long it was found so unwieldy that the idea of having all free-men attend was abandoned; the colony was divided into hundreds and one representative from each hundred was elected. After 1650 the assembly broke away from the council, sitting separately as a lower house.

The first session, however, proved fruitful and significant. The combined assembly and council sitting with the governor produced a body of laws for the government of the colony and sent it to the proprietor for his approval. This he refused to give, on the ground that the charter vested in the proprietor the right to originate legislation. Though his position was unarguable, the assembly stubbornly insisted that they should be allowed to make their own laws; and in the end Cecilius Calvert conceded, and then went further by agreeing that, because of the length of time required by two Atlantic crossings, all laws passed by the assembly would be considered valid until vetoed by him. But at the same time he reserved to himself the right to vote any previous law without limit of time.

Though this involved an inherent threat to the assembly's freedom of action, in practice the system worked out well. The assembly fixed and paid the salaries of all colonial officials except the governor and members of his council, who held their appointments from the proprietor. Justice was administered on lower levels by the county courts, which handled minor civil cases and criminal cases which did not call for the death penalty. Major criminal cases, cases in equity, or admiralty cases were tried before the provincial court. Theoretically decisions of the provincial court could be appealed to the governor's council; but since the justices of the former were all members of the council, the appeal meant little more than a replay of the case before the same justices in different robes.

Below these were the courts of the manors, which Cecilius expected to be an enticement to emigration. In 1636 he had decreed that every holding of two thousand acres or more should be designated a manor, whose proprietor would then exercise the customary manorial powers over his tenants. Later, in 1641, he declared further that every settler who brought over with him twenty well-armed men (the type and quality of weapons were specified in detail, even to the quantity of ball and lead and powder) should be granted a manor of his own.

The manors were self-contained properties with their own government, and justice in each was administered on two levels in separate courts. "Court leet," the lower, heard cases between tenants, complaints which the lord's steward was empowered to settle, and took care of casual male-factors such as poachers, thieves, and dishonest peddlers, and also all matters (except capital crime) concerned with the indentured servants. But it also had an additional function: the administration of community activity, in which it operated like a small assembly of all free tenants or, as John Fiske has pointed out, very much like the New England town meeting.

The "court baron" convened to settle differences between the manor

[341]

lord and his tenants and again was attended by all the freemen. Before it were heard cases dealing with transfer of property, boundary disputes, escheats (the reversion to the lord of land left by a tenant who had no heirs or made no provision for its inheritance), and actions for trespass or debt. Together the two courts, within a feudal framework, provided a practical and surprisingly democratic rural government. They might have endured much longer except for the introduction of black slavery. Maryland's staple crop, like Virginia's, was tobacco and plantation owners soon found it far more profitable to keep their acreage in their own hands and cultivate it with slave labor than to lease the land in farm lots to tenants.

In form Maryland's manorial system resembled the Canadian seigneury or the Hudson patroonship, but in both of the latter the element of self-government was almost totally lacking; in neither did one find the aggressive furtherance of life and business among the ordinary inhabitants that existed in Maryland. If its population did not grow as rapidly as the Calverts had hoped, and would be a long time approaching that of its bigger neighbor, Virginia, the colony never had to undergo the ordeals of famine and disease that had wracked Virginia's early years. The land was healthy as well as one of the loveliest in the American scene. In spite of the political struggles that took control from the proprietor and again restored it to his hands, the colony prospered. For that, probably the chief reason was Cecilius's decision that he should remain in England where he acted in effect as Maryland's supreme agent, giving it an authoritative voice at court, before Parliament, and in the City of London such as no other colony enjoyed.

He never saw America, but at his death in 1675 Maryland was still a Catholic asylum as his father and he had planned it to be. However, Catholics never emigrated to it in the numbers he had counted on. Even as late as 1750 there were probably no more than five thousand in the colony — possibly six thousand if one allows for those who did not acknowledge themselves. But until the turn of the century Catholics held virtually all the higher offices, which came through the authority of the proprietor. In the 1660s, for example, when Catholics amounted to only one twelfth of the population, Governor Charles Calvert's council was not only made up wholly of Catholics: it contained an uncle, two cousins, the husband of a female cousin, and the uncle's best friend.

To the rank and file such nepotism and, as it seemed, religious favoritism were hard to swallow. The Toleration Act which allowed Catholics to survive had also brought in a flood of Protestant settlers, a small proportion of them of the Church of England (though they outnumbered the Catholics two to one), but the rest, amounting to over three fourths of the total population, were Puritans. A few were refugees from the harsh theocratic climate of New England. For the most part, however, they had emigrated directly from England itself. But in one curious instance, involving more than a thousand people, an entire community had transplanted themselves from Virginia.

The first Puritans in Virginia had arrived in 1611 with Sir Thomas Dale. Their original settlements south of the James gradually concentrated along the Nansemond River. There seems to have been little prejudice against them among their fellow colonists of the Church of England, and except for losing their first minister, Alexander Whitaker, who was unfortunately drowned in the James, they prospered, faring rather better than other settlements up the James when Opechancanough launched his massacre in 1622. In 1641, however, they seem to have run short of ministers (there was always a tendency in Virginia to be short of men of the church, whether Anglican or Puritan; or perhaps it was a reluctance of men in comfortable English pastorates to pack up for an ocean voyage and the prospect of rigorous living at the end of it), and the Nansemond Puritans appealed to Boston to send them some ministers.

Three men responded — two from Braintree and Watertown in Massachusetts, the third from New Haven — and deciding to join forces they took passage together in the same ship, sailing from Narragansett Bay in December 1642. It was not to be an auspicious voyage. Their ship struck Hell Gate at its boisterous worst and went to the bottom; and though, unlike the holy Whitaker, they did not drown, they received but a glum reception from the Dutch authorities in New Amsterdam and very little help in being put on their way. However, after a time they did find a ship to take them on to Virginia and they finally reached the James eleven weeks after leaving Rhode Island.

Unfortunately for their mission, there had arrived in Virginia in the preceding year a new governor with an inborn hostility toward all things Puritan. This was Sir William Berkeley, completely cavalier in his thinking, who liked things his own way and who, once he had achieved it, displayed an iron aversion to change. All in all, he was to be governor of Virginia for twenty-seven years, with an eight-year interruption of his power under the Commonwealth, when governors were elected by the assembly or burgesses.

An act had passed the assembly in 1631 prescribing conformity throughout the colony to the canons of the Church of England; but no one had ever taken it very seriously and the then governor, Sir John Harvey, had been personally well disposed toward Puritans. But now under Berkeley's eye the assembly passed a new act of conformity with real teeth in it; all ministers living in the colony must be of the Church of England and "not otherwise be admitted to teach or preach publicly or privately;" and the governor and council were enjoined to see to it that all reported dissenters be immediately ejected from the colony. Empowered by this act Berkeley lost no time in moving against the three Puritan divines. Two, after a few weeks of frequent and rather hectic preaching, obeyed; the third, William Thompson of Braintree, managed to keep on with his work through the summer of 1643, but in the end he too was compelled to get out, and the Puritans were once more left without spiritual leadership.

Then in the following spring, 1644, and again on the eve of Good Friday, Opechancanough staged his final uprising of the Powhatan. Again some three hundred Virginia colonists, mostly in the western area of settlement, were slaughtered before the relentless old warrior was finally captured and brought to Jamestown, from which he was to be sent as a curiosity to England — a fate he was spared by being ignominiously murdered by one of his guards. But the massacre served to inflame anti-Puritan sentiment still further, the Anglicans with Berkeley at their head proclaiming the massacre was a divine retribution against the colonists for harboring dissenters. The Puritans, naturally, saw the matter in a different light: to them it was a retribution all right, but one meted out for the expulsion of men of God. At this point Berkeley was obliged to return to England for business reasons. During the year he stayed away the controversy simmered on, but after his return in 1645 pressures against the Puritan community were renewed.

The atmosphere by 1648 had become so inflamed that several elders had to flee to Maryland. There the newly appointed governor, Sir William Stone, himself a Protestant, welcomed them kindly and shortly after, under pressure from Cecilius Calvert to find more settlers, invited the Virginia Puritans to move to Maryland. Three hundred came in 1649, though with considerable reservations. The Toleration Act promised them complete spiritual freedom, but this was an unheard-of action by any government controlled by Catholics. It was hard to overcome the old visceral alarm over what to many seemed to be a move into a nest of Papists. For a while the rest clung to their Virginia homes.

In 1649, however, the news of Charles I's execution crossed the Atlantic, and by fall Cavalier immigrants were pouring into Virginia. The execution was declared an act of treason; to uphold it in any way was punishable by death; and Charles II was declared the true and rightful ruler of England. Under these conditions Catholic Maryland began to look a great deal better to the Puritans and in a few months all of them had made the move. They bought land along the Severn — it belonged to some Susquehannas, or so at least they claimed — and named their new settlement Providence. Unlike the land around St. Mary's which had been under Indian cultivation, this was wooded country, so the Virginia Puritans had their pioneering to do all over again.

In accepting Maryland's hospitality they had believed they would be able to maintain themselves as a completely autonomous community; they were convinced that with the Puritan revolution in England the colony would be taken away from the Calverts and therefore cease to be Catholic. For this reason they held aloof from participation in the colonial government, refusing to elect the two members they were entitled to send to the assembly. On Governor Stone's urgent pleading they relented in 1650 and elected two members, but though one was immediately chosen speaker, they repented in the following year and again refused to elect assemblymen. And then, in the year after that, it began to look as if they were going to have things fall their way.

A Parliamentary commission of four men had arrived in Virginia in 1652 in a heavily armed frigate to demand that Berkeley's government make submission to the Commonwealth; and after protracted wrangling the Virginians, who had begun negotiations with every intention of defying Parliament, decided, especially in view of the naval artillery anchored in the James, that it would be more politic to give in. Berkeley therefore resigned his governorship and retired to his plantation, and one of the commissioners, Richard Bennett, was named by the burgesses to succeed him. In other respects there were no changes in the government of the colony.

The instructions issued to the commission had been originally directed solely against Virginia, but at the last moment two of the commissioners had persuaded Parliament, whose members had small knowledge of colonial geography and not much interest in it, that their authority should also extend to "the plantations within Chesepeake Bay." One of these commissioners was Richard Bennett who had been one of the Puritan elders evicted by Berkeley from the Nansemond settlement and now found himself governor in Berkeley's place. The second was none other than the ineluctable William Claiborne, now armed with authority from Parliament as well as with the cannon of the frigate that bore him up the bay for a final showdown with the province that had twice driven him out.

Strangely enough he did not try to further his personal interests, not even to regaining Kent Island, but instead was content to demand that the governor and council acknowledge fealty to the present English Commonwealth, which Governor Stone agreed to readily enough. But Stone would not accept the further stipulation that writs and warrants should no longer be issued in the name of the proprietor but in that of the Parliament. For this he was deposed and a provisional government set up to replace him.

However, after two months' reflection Stone gave in and notified Claiborne that he was willing to issue writs in the name of Parliament, whereupon he was immediately restored to office. But now the tide of events was running faster in England than could easily be followed in America. Cromwell threw out the Rump Parliament, and when the news reached

Maryland, Stone naturally began issuing writs once more in the name of Baltimore. This was a bitter disappointment for the Puritans along the Severn. They began making trouble for the governor and, when Bennett and Claiborne returned in the summer of 1654, joined forces with them to turn Stone out of office and replace him with one William Fuller and a new council of their own choosing, who then issued writs for the election of a new assembly.

These writs, with the Puritans now acting the role of the ungrateful dog, specified that Catholics could neither vote nor be elected burgesses. The resulting assembly was therefore Puritanical from every angle and celebrated its assumption of powers by passing a new "Toleration Act" which guaranteed religious liberty to all, except where popery and prelacy were concerned, which ruled out the Church of England as well as the Catholic and, on paper at least, reduced Maryland to a purely Congregational state.

Meanwhile in England the adroit Cecilius had reestablished the validity of his title. Cromwell, as Lord Protector, considered himself responsible for upholding contracts and patents issued by his royal predecessors; and besides, he liked to see a colony well managed, as Maryland had been before the Puritan upheaval. Cecilius therefore now ordered Stone to resume his office and bring the Puritans into line. But this, as Stone fully realized, meant fighting.

The biggest force he could muster amounted to one hundred and thirty men and with these he marched against the Puritans on the Severn. There he met the Puritan array of one hundred and seventy-five under William Fuller, who had deployed his force along the riverbank with two armed merchant ships anchored behind them. There was a dirty little fight and Stone and his army were completely beaten; he himself was wounded and taken prisoner along with several of his leading officers. Fuller held a drumhead court-martial and sentenced nine to death, including Stone. Four were executed immediately, but then cooler tempers prevailed and the rest, Stone among them, were pardoned.

The Puritans, in Virginia as well as in Maryland, were confident that this defeat would spell the end of the Calvert proprietorship. A mission, led by Bennett of Virgina, went to London in an effort to have Calvert's charter abrogated, but then soon found that he had Cromwell's solid support. It was obvious that the Puritan government of Maryland would have to give way; but here Cecilius Calvert once more displayed his calm good sense by promising amnesty for all who had stood against his proprietorship, not only in the recent crisis but from the colony's beginning. In 1658 he appointed a new governor, Josias Fendall, and sent him across the Atlantic accompanied by his brother, Philip Calvert, as a secretary of the colony.

Virginia at last had to accept the validity of his charter and withdrew her claims, and in addition recompensed Claiborne for the loss of his property on Kent Island; and except for the oystermen the two colonies settled down as peaceable neighbors. The Puritans along the Severn in 1660 made one last attempt to wrest the province from the proprietor; but in this case they were foiled by the accession of Charles II to the throne. Again Cecilius refused to take vengeance on his enemies, and thereafter except for the period from 1688 to 1715 when Maryland was a royal province, the Calverts remained undisturbed in their proprietorship, their most serious problem being the encroachment of William Penn on their eastern and nothern borders.

With the passage of years the character of Maryland changed and became more complex. The Catholics still controlled the choicest land along the great bay; the Puritans were concentrated along the Severn; after the turn of the century a wave of German immigration, sucked in perhaps by the much larger immigration into Pennsylvania, settled in the western part of Maryland. Many of them were ironworkers, with the result that at the time of the final war with the French, Maryland was the second largest producer of iron among the colonies. These people had come with a passionate desire to find personal liberty; they were suspicious of entrenched authority and in later years were often in opposition to the proprietor and the upper house of the assembly. In some measure their attitude was responsible for the fact that Maryland, like Delaware, took almost no part in the fighting against the French and Indians.

Maryland's greatest contribution, imperfect though it was, was her Act of Toleration and the demonstration that Protestants and Catholics not only could live together in one province but could actively share together in its government. In the wave of anti-Catholic feeling that swept the English people everywhere during the great war against Louis XIV, which we called Queen Anne's, the Catholics in Maryland were viciously discriminated against in a variety of ways including being disenfranchised — permanently as it proved; for when in 1715 the Calverts, now become Protestants, regained their proprietorship, they were no longer concerned with religious freedom, and the discriminatory statutes against the Catholics were allowed to stand on the books. But the demonstration had been made and, with the examples of Rhode Island and Pennsylvania, furnished a bright light in the confused and largely violent course of the English colonial experience.

Sir William Berkeley, who had stepped down from his office as Virginia's governor in 1652, spent the eight years of colonial rule under the Commonwealth on his plantation at Green Spring just above Jamestown. Here in his manor house, four stories high, with a double tier of dormers in the great roof and with a private jail for petty malefactors that would in time also house his political enemies — not to mention a greenhouse where he grew oranges and other exotics, and an icehouse the ice from which cooled the innumerable fiery toasts to the royal Stuarts elbowed up by himself and his visitors, of whom there were many — he waited for the end of the Cromwell Protectorate. It must have irked him sore to sit idly at Green Spring while three successive Puritan governors presided at Jamestown. They did not make any drastic changes in the government, but they did succeed in materially broadening the elective franchise. He himself, while governor, had not been wholly unmindful of the difficulties of poorer planters, and one of his most popular actions had been the elimination of the poll tax. He had in fact been a popular governor, if we except the Puritans; but to his mind there could be no possible parallel between the act of a Cavalier and that of a Roundhead governor.

He was a complex man: forceful, aristocratic, brave, loyal to his friends, well educated (he had been to Oxford and even boasted literary pretensions, having written a play which had been published just before he came to Virginia), arbitrary and often cantankerous (Samuel Pepys found him "frowardy"); he was narrow-minded, if not actually bigoted, and a firm believer in the appurtenances and privileges of rank and power and ready to exert them for his own profit; but he suited the cavaliers who had poured into Virginia after the execution of King Charles. They shared his feelings toward monarchy so strongly that within ten months of the news of Richard Cromwell's resigning the Protectorate, they had put Sir William — Samuel Mathews having tactfully died just at this critical turning of events — once more in the governor's chair.

However, in spite of the tide of royalist enthusiasm that impelled them, the members of the assembly had not lost sight of their own inherent rights as English freemen. They stipulated that until acceptable instructions came from England all writs and warrants should be issued in the assembly's name; and they further made Berkeley's election as governor conditional on his calling an assembly at least every two years and not dissolving it without majority consent.

Berkeley offered no objection, but the eight years of waiting at Green Spring had changed and hardened him, narrowing what tolerance he had and intensifying his distrust of the common people. Receipt of his royal commission from the king in October 1660 may have seemed to him to supersede the terms on which he had accepted office from the assembly. As it turned out, the first assembly he called in 1661 reflected the popular enthusiasm for the monarchy; its members were mainly well-to-do and shared the governor's views about royal prerogatives and class privilege. With the council, which consisted of the wealthiest planters and his own cronies, he had as governor a legislative frame that from his point of view could hardly have been more ideal, and in spite of the conditions under which he had accepted office, he had no intention of allowing the situation to change. He achieved his purpose by simply adjourning the assembly each year and refusing to issue writs for a new election. In this way he kept his House of favorable Burgesses in being until 1676 and then only called for a new election when his hand was forced.

So for fifteen years Virginia was controlled by what amounted to an oligarchy under whose complacent sway petty officials were allowed to practice extortion and embezzlement and enrich themselves at the expense of the public just about as they pleased. This gnawing corruption was conveniently ignored by Berkeley and his friends, some of whom were not above indulging themselves indirectly in the profits. Indeed, Berkeley confessed to a friend that as he grew older his ambition waned, but not his cupidity.

Meanwhile hard times had come upon Virginia. In 1660 the price of tobacco began to toboggan, and by 1667 it was to sink to a rock-bottom price of half a cent a pound on James River jetties. In a community whose prosperity depended on a single staple, this amounted to catastrophe and fell with special cruelty upon the poorer planters who depended on their small harvest of tobacco to carry them through the year to come.

The two principal causes were overproduction and the Navigation Law passed in 1660 and enforced under Charles II far more stringently than under the Commonwealth. To his credit Berkeley tried to do something about both, but he was unsuccessful. In 1662 he urged Maryland to join Virginia in prohibiting the planting of tobacco for one year. Maryland, however, would not go along; Virginia naturally was not willing to sacrifice herself, so planting continued at the usual rate. And in 1661 Berkeley went to London, and though his main purpose was to resist an attempt by the old London Company to regain its charter to Virginia, he also made a plea for a softening of the Navigation Law, the effects of which bore particularly heavily on a one-crop colony like Virginia.

New England, where farmers were nearly self-sufficient and a fishing industry was developing, found the yoke less desperate, though it complained loud enough. So too New York where the patroonships were separate principalities and again produced much of what they needed to sustain life, and again New Jersey. Maryland had a second staple in wheat. But the Virginian, whose sole crop of importance was tobacco, which could only be shipped in English ships which in turn brought only English goods in which to trade, found himself in a bind, especially the man lately arrived and short of money who could find no rich bottomland and staked out his small acreage along a ridge. Before 1660 he had been able to sell the lower-grade tobacco he grew there to Dutch ships; for Dutchmen then as now were not as fastidious about tobacco as the English. But the Dutch ships were now kept out and the poorer tobacco accumulated in sheds and barns. Even the small planter on the fringe of tidewater who could raise a few hogsheads of the better grade felt the pinch; on the one hand the London merchants, enjoying their absolute monopoly, forced down the price of tobacco while on the other they raised the prices on the goods they shipped into Virginia on the ground that it cost more to run an English ship crewed by Englishmen than it did one of any other nationality. To add grue to the gruel of the small planter or simple artisan, the taxes made necessary by the enlarged number of government officials (Charles was recklessly liberal in rewarding applicants with colonial posts whatever their qualifications) were levied largely on the men of lesser means. The wealthiest planters, members of the governor's council, paid none at all.

Other things alarmed the people above the tideland plantations. In 1673 news came that the king (with the Stuart disregard of former grants or geographical integrity that is perhaps their best demonstration of a divine right) had made a thirty-one-year grant of the whole province of Virginia to two friends, the Earl of Arlington and Lord Culpepper. There was no intention on the part of the new proprietors to dispossess anyone, but the fact remained that under their grant the administration of the government at Jamestown would be entirely in their hands, all lands in escheat would be theirs automatically, no matter who had bought them since, and they would also own all the revenues.

The House of Burgesses immediately sent a commission to London to protest; and King Charles, seemingly nonplused that people could be so upset merely because he had made a gift of a portion of his own dominions to two honorable noblemen, promised to settle the matter to the satisfaction of everyone; but before the machinery for doing this could be put in operation, the temper of the Virginians reached the boiling point. Meetings to protest taxes were held in churches and in the open fields. Only loyalty to the Crown, religious faith in divine mercy, and "affection for the government," as one man wrote Berkeley, stood between Jamestown and outright rebellion. It is to be doubted that by 1673 there was much affection left; all the small landowners needed was a man to organize and lead them.

The owners of plantations along the James, complacent and secure in their rich acreage, were little aware of what was taking place in the hilly wilderness west of their boundaries. This was the creation of the first real frontier society. The emigration from Massachusetts into Connecticut in 1636 had also created a frontier, but it differed in being rather the transplantation of a society in being, which carried with it its own system of government and almost immediately established its General Court. But the frontier in Virginia was the frontier as it was to move steadily west across the continent during the next two hundred years, a taking up of land by men who came individually into it because they had not the capital to buy richer land which, if not already worked by wealthy owners, was held by them or by speculators who could scent the great prospective tobacco fortunes once labor became available.

The men of the frontier then were poor men living for themselves. Sometimes men would come to help a new arrival raise his cabin, but mostly men worked alone helped by their wives or children large enough to be useful. All, however, shared a growing resentment of the established society to the east, where the money was, which owned the power of government and set a head tax that fell equally on the poor frontiersmen and themselves. This tax, one might say, was almost the only thing the frontier and tidewater had in common.

There was, however, a dubious connection between the moneyed "East" as it was soon to become and the outer fringe of the frontier where fur traders worked from their trading posts and forts, many of which had been financed by rich James River men like William Byrd. These traders threaded the paths to the Indian towns still farther west or hunted to sustain the post, prototypes of the long hunters or, in the case of literature, of Cooper's Leatherstocking. They were largely a law to themselves; their life was free, they both liked and hated the wilderness, but they understood it; the established society east of them, except for the merchants they dealt with, hardly knew of their existence, and they felt they owed that society nothing.

Behind the traders operated a group of men who seem to have been peculiar to the Virginia frontier, cattle raisers who grazed their stock through the open woods and in marshes and natural meadows. They were as independent of the settlements they had left behind as the traders, and through the summer followed their herds where fodder took them. But in the fall they rounded up the cattle to be sold and drove them east into tidewater.

It was the settlers who came to cultivate the land and build homes who really shaped the frontier. They hungered for security as well as freedom, and like nearly all men they hoped to get rich, though very few ever did. Work was endless and desperately hard; they cleared the woods and wrestled with the virgin soil with the most primitive tools; pigs were turned loose in the woods to forage for acorns, and the family cow, if there was one, wandered at will; if everything went well, a man would be ready in the next summer after his arrival to put in his first tobacco crop. He readied the best piece of land he had on his place for it. He started the plants in a seedbed in March; in May they had to be transplanted to the waiting field, and all summer he and his family were busy keeping it hoed. The crop represented the family money; it bought them sugar, tea, cloth, nails, tools, and above all gunpowder and lead. Unless it found a sale, they spent the next year scrabbling on the edge of misery.

Life remained primitive here longer than it did, for instance, in New England. The church was slow to reach them — all Virginia suffered from a dearth of ministers — and courts nearly as slow. Schools were rarities; the first college, William and Mary, was not founded till 1693. There was no printing press and consequently no newspaper, and William Berkeley is supposed to have thanked God for the fact.

With power and wealth remaining in the grip of established society in the east, these pioneer settlers were conscious not only of the inferiority of their living standards but of the fact that eastern planters and merchants considered them inferior as people. In the first settlements rich and poor had worked together and no man was looked down upon because he had less education; but now people in the east spoke of the frontier settlers with more or less contempt as "buckskins." The mistrust and antagonism which here found root was to color the whole frontier experience. Out of it grew a phenomenon of the south, not exemplified by the settlers we have been talking about, who came from hardy English yeoman stock or solid middle-class artisan or merchant levels, but from the indentured servants or outright criminals that made up almost the entire early labor force of Virginia.

Not all transported criminals at that time were guilty of crime as it would be considered today. The gallows rather than the scales was the instrument of justice in England and persons guilty even of the pettiest crimes — a woman stealing a piece of meat, for instance, if it was worth more than a shilling — might find themselves on the grim road to Tyburn. Or an Oxford student caught stealing a book from his college library. But as the labor vacuum developed in Virginia, English judges found transportation a solution for what had been a manifest imbalance of justice, and more and more people were deported to be servants for periods varying according to the degree of the crime. Among those so transported were also prisoners of war. After the battle of Dunbar, Cromwell shipped one hundred and fifty Scottish soldiers to New England, and the next year some fifteen hundred captives from the battle of Worcester were sent to Virginia. Such men, though they arrived impoverished, were as much Cavaliers as those who came at their own expense, and when they had worked out their terms of service many were able to take their place in colonial society on equal footing with the earlier settlers, more than one even rising to the House of Burgesses.

But with this superior class of imported labor were included the habitual petty culprit, dissolute women, the sweepings of the London streets. As servants they were nearly useless. When finally they had served their terms or earlier had run away, their freedom did nothing to redeem them.

Increasing use of Negro labor gradually forced them toward the frontier, most of them moving southward toward North Carolina where justice was still in a rudimentary state, the climate kind to people without ambition or diligence, and the forest stocked with fruit and game. Here they lived in shabby communities, looked down on even by Negroes and Indians and, because of being white, unwilling to do what they considered menial work done elsewhere by dark-skinned people, except to avoid actual starvation. Colonel William Byrd, admittedly viewing them from what one might call his plantation saddle, reported their way of life at first hand:

> Surely there is no place in the World where the Inhabitants live with less Labour than in N Carolina. It approaches nearer to the Description of Lubberland than any other, by the greater felicity of the Climate, the easiness of raising Provisions, and the Slothfulness of the People. Indian corn is of so great increase, that a little Pains will Subsist a very large Family with Bread, and then they may have meat without any Pains at all, by the Help of the Low Grounds, and the great Variety of Mast that grows upon the High-land. The Men, for their parts, just like the Indians impose all the Work upon the poor Women. They make their Wives rise out of their Beds early in the Morning, at the same time that they lye and Snore, till the Sun has run one third of his course, and disperst all the unwholesome Damps. Then, after Stretching and Yawning for half an Hour, they light their Pipes, and, under the Protection of a cloud of Smoak, venture out into the open Air; tho' if it happens to be never so little cold, they quickly return Shivering into the Chimney corner. When the weather is mild, they stand leaning with both their arms upon the corn-field fence, and gravely consider whether they had best go and take a Small Heat at the Hough; but generally find reasons to put it off till another time. Thus they loiter away their Lives, like Solomon's Sluggard, with their arms across, and at the Winding up of the Year Scarcely have Bread to Eat . . .

They would not take discipline and their greatest fear was that when the boundary was surveyed between North Carolina and Virginia they would find themselves back in the Old Dominion where justice was sterner. Byrd reports an instance in which a magistrate who was holding court in the local tavern sentenced a man brought before him to a turn in the stocks. So outraged was the community at having one of their number brought to justice that it was the unfortunate magistrate who occupied the stocks.

As North Carolina developed and government became more orthodox, these poor whites were gradually forced westward and southward from Tennessee to the Gulf Coast, but they did not lose their identity or their conviction of their own racial superiority: it was indeed the principal fantasy which allowed them to accept themselves as human. Narrow, bigoted, shiftless, cruel, qualities passed down to their descendants, we can see their pictures in the news stories of our own time.

This illusion of superiority has led to the massive fantasy that colors the southern air to this day: that the origins of the "first families" of the Virginia establishment were aristocratic or even noble. They were, of course, nothing of the sort. The planters and merchants who earned fortunes along the James came from middle-class stock, just as did the Puritans in New England. The aristocrats who came in the early starving times had been unable to make a living in Virginia; they had all starved, died of disease, been killed by Indians, or returned thankfully to England. The founders of the first families were the sons of merchants or yeoman farmers and had the intelligence and enterprise to succeed in their new environment. But as they rose above their neighbors in wealth they instinctively began to think of themselves in aristocratic terms; they called their first frame houses "manors," and they jealously reached for and protected the perquisites of wealth. Today the illusion is a dreamy attribute of the South's self-history; in 1675 it was a major cause of antagonism between the planters and merchants and the struggling citizens of the frontier. A year later, resentment flamed into open rebellion.

As so often happened, it was trouble with the Indians that struck the first spark, but at the root of the Indian trouble was a war between two Indian nations entirely apart from the white colonists.

All along the Susquehanna River from the southern boundary of New York to the head of Chesapeake Bay were the towns of the Susquehanna tribes, loosely related and of Iroquoian stock. They were not confederated, as were the nations of the Iroquois Long House, but they proved to be the most formidable adversaries the Iroquois ever had to handle. For at least seventy-five years they had been making sporadic war on the Iroquois, attacking first one nation and then another. Between 1650 and 1660, according to Jesuit missionaries, they attacked the Mohawks with such furious persistence that for a time the latter, who were also fighting a war with the Mohicans, despaired of surviving. What saved them was the increasing number of firearms they received from the Dutch.

After 1660 the Susquehannas, whom the French called Andastes, turned their attention to the four western nations, and were attacked in turn themselves. But whether on the defensive or the offensive, for the next ten years they more than held their own. In 1662 a war party of eight hundred warriors of the Senecas, Cayugas, and Onondagas set off down the Susquehanna determined to take and sack the principal town of their enemies, Andastogué.

When they came upon it, far from their own country, near the present site of Columbia, they saw that it was impregnable. It had a massive double palisade, the river face of which was right on the river's edge, and two bastions armed with small cannon acquired from the Swedes. Always pragmatic, the Iroquois, according to Father Lalemant's account of the expedition, ". . . abandoned their projected assault, and, after some light skirmishes, resorted to their customary subtlety, in order to gain by trickery what they could not accomplish by force. Making overtures for a parley, they offered to enter the besieged town to the number of twenty-five, partly to treat for peace, as they declared, and partly to buy provisions for their return journey."

But the Susquehannas were subtle, too. The instant they had closed the gates behind the "ambassadors" they fell upon and bound them. Then, building scaffolds high above the palisades, they burned the twenty-five men in full view of the raging but helpless war party, shouting down that this was but a foretaste of what would happen when their own braves attacked the Long House. The Iroquois returned so chastened that Lalemant thanked God for the Andastes, since for the first time he could make a little headway toward a few conversions. He did still better that fall as an epidemic of smallpox swept the Senecas and humbled them still more.

For the next few years the Susquehannas almost always had the upper hand in the raiding, on one side or the other. Then they themselves fell under the scourge of smallpox, and the tide of war turned against them until in 1670 they were ready to suggest making peace. But the Iroquois would have none of it, and in 1674–1675 they crushed the upper tribes, the remnants of whom came piling down the Susquehanna and tried to establish themselves on the fringe of the Maryland settlements. They had had a treaty of friendship with the Marylanders almost from the colony's inception and it seemed to them a natural place for refuge, but almost at once friction began to develop, and this intensified to the verge of violence when bands of harassing Senecas came down the river hunting them; for, adhering to the standing policy of maintaining friendly relations with all Indians, Maryland had signed a peace treaty with the Senecas also.

This action, which to them seemed an arrant betrayal, deeply angered the Susquehannas, who had now come to ground along the upper Potomac. No overt violence broke out immediately, but there were ugly incidents, and as always happened with Indians and English living close to each other, pigs and cattle began to disappear. This was all the more natural as their location brought them into contact with the cattle herdsmen, whose stock customarily ran loose. The incident that touched off war, however, was not the work of the Susquehannas but of some members of the remnant of one of the Powhatan tribes. These, like other surviving fragments, had been given little reservations on what had been the borders of the colony but which had now become islands in the expanding white frontier. The tribe in question, called Doegs, were settled near the site of Fredericksburg, and some of their men one night made off with a number of pigs. A settler organized a pursuit in which two or three of the Indians were shot. Some days later, wandering herdsmen found another herdsman lying wounded in the doorway of his hut. Just as he died he managed to say that the Indians who had killed him were Doegs.

The militia turned out under their commander, Colonel George Mason, who divided them into two parties. One drove the Doegs from their village and in the pursuit killed eleven. The other party encountered a band of Indians and began shooting without asking who they were. Fourteen of the Indians had been killed when a chief found Mason and told him that they were Susquehannas and therefore friends, and with an eye to using all the possibilities he also tried to pin the herdsman's murder on the Senecas. Mason halted the little battle, but now the Susquehannas' blood was up and presently isolated murders began occurring all along the border.

Maryland called to Virginia for help and sent a company of militia under Major Thomas Truman to the Susquehannas' stronghold — an old blockhouse they had taken over and repaired on the north shore of the river — where the Virginia militia were to join them.

When the Virginians, commanded by Colonel John Washington, the great-grandfather of George, forded the river, they found the Maryland soldiers in front of the blockhouse, surrounding five Indians who had come out to parley. From them Washington demanded an explanation of the murders that had occurred. The Susquehannas denied all knowledge of them and said they must be the work of Senecas. But Washington produced evidence of Susquehanna guilt that was valid enough — members of the tribe captured in Virginia wearing the clothes of dead Virginians. Then Truman said that on a plantation not far away there were the bodies of nine Susquehannas who had been shot during an attack and suggested that the envoys be taken to view the remains. Washington agreed and the Marylanders marched off with the five Indians and then, still in sight of the Virginians and the other Indians in the blockhouse, put them all to death.

From that moment the sporadic raiding became open warfare. Bands of Indians swarmed all over the border, falling on isolated cabins and killing hapless settlers and their wives and children. Ten, twenty, forty people would be murdered in a day. The militia under Washington were totally unable to cover the frontier. From raiding isolated cabins the Indians began to move in on the small outer plantations. In seventeen days sixty of these were burned to the ground.

Settlers and planters called to Jamestown for help, and as pressures mounted, Berkeley convened the Long Assembly for what was to prove its final session in March 1676. A little army of five hundred men was mustered; they were almost ready to march when Berkeley suddenly disbanded them and announced that he had decided to repair the forts in existence and build new ones to provide a chain which would protect the colony.

Berkeley was motivated by his interest in the Indian trade (and according to detractors by the opportunities this policy would give his cronies to embezzle money tagged for the forts), and he also feared that such an expedition would result in a general uprising by the Indians like the one King Philip even then had brought against New England, hair-raising accounts of which had been filtering through to Virginia. So, in the end, to all intents he did nothing, and it became evident to the settlers at the head of the James and York Rivers that if they were to be saved it would have to be by their own efforts. Fortunately at this crucial moment they found a man to lead them.

Francis Bacon was young, mercurial in temper, tall, handsome in an almost swarthy way, and apparently gifted with what was rare for those days in men of wealth, something like a social conscience. He had only arrived in the colony as lately as 1674, but he had quickly established himself, buying plantation land at Curle's Neck, forty miles above Jamestown, and settling there with his young and lovely wife. He himself was then only twenty-seven, but he had had considerably more education than the run of his compeers, having spent some time at Cambridge and studied law at Gray's Inn, and afterward had toured the continent before coming to Virginia.

Almost at once he was made a member of the council, partly because of the influence of another Francis Bacon, a cousin of his father's, who had been fifteen years in the colony, but in due measure also because of his attainments. The majority of people took to him immediately, but others soon found him unduly critical of the way the governor's clique was managing the colony; his way of speaking was to some "prevalent logical" and hard to take, especially from a young man so recently arrived. But he found men who felt as he did, most prominently two leading citizens of Jamestown, William Drummond and Richard Lawrence, who listened to his ideas on tax reform, broadening the franchise, and finding a way to ending the special privileges the governor extended to his personal friends.

Soon after establishing himself at Curle's Neck, Bacon had bought a second plantation near Fort Charles at the falls of the James in what would now be the outskirts of Richmond. In May 1676 the Indians raided it and killed his overseer, and Bacon promptly left his plantation at Curle's Neck to join a meeting of planters, settlers, and traders at Fort Charles, called in an effort to find a way of putting down the Indians. It was a heated gathering, and Bacon's own blood was thoroughly roused. It was proposed to raise an army and when the question was put of who should lead it there was a general shout of Bacon's name. If he had any hesitation about accepting the command, it was quickly allayed by the urging of Colonel Byrd and a few other wealthy planters who had lost their control of the fur trade when Berkeley had restricted it to five of his friends; they were delighted at the prospect of a social upheaval during which the "peevish and brittle" old tyrant might be unseated.

To avoid that, however, though his army was at the pitch of enthusiasm and ready to march at once, Bacon sent a courier to Jamestown "beseeching a commission to go against those Indians at their own charge," as the chronicler of the day phrased it (he signed himself only T.M., but was probably Thomas Mathews, a burgess from Stafford County). Berkeley was evasive, and the commission "which his Honor so often promised" did not come.

To go without it was tantamount to rebellion, but people were daily being killed and with his three hundred men chafing to be gone, Bacon finally started his march. Berkeley in a rage issued a proclamation denouncing all members of the expedition as rebels unless they immediately returned. When this caught up with the marchers and was read out to them, a good many defected. How many is hard to say. The chronicler reports that only fifty-seven decided to proceed with Bacon; but in the light of the action that followed, it seems likely that there were more.

The number of defectors is not the only puzzling element in this episode. For instead of marching north to the Susquehanna blockhouse on the Potomac, Bacon and his followers seem to have headed southwest till "they came nigh a fort of friendly Indians, on the other side a branch of the James River." This apparently was Occaneechee Island in the Roanoke near what is now the southern boundary of Virginia. Presumably Bacon's force headed for it on rumors that the Susquehannas had retreated there.

The Occaneechee tribe had developed a monopoly of the fur trade in their region and had never given trouble. When Bacon's force appeared on the far side of the water from their palisade they made no motion to come out in welcome, but when Bacon asked for provisions to take them home, they replied in a friendly way, promising to bring some over next day. But next day they put it off till the following one. When evening began to fall and still no Indians or food had put in an appearance the English, tempers drawn fine with real hunger, waded shoulder-deep across the stretch of river to the foot of the palisade and again, offering payment, asked for food. While the palaver was in progress a single shot sounded from the wooded shore they had just left, killing one of their men. It was natural to assume that the Occaneechees had summoned other Indians, perhaps the Susquehannas themselves, to attack their rear.

They became instantly beserk and, as the chronicler succinctly re-

[358]

ported, "Hereupon they fired the palisades, stormed and burnt the fort and cabins, and (with the loss of three English) slew one hundred and fifty Indians."

On his return to tidewater, Bacon found himself at once a rebel and a hero. To the small plantation owners, especially those on the frontier, it did not matter that the massacred tribe had done the English no harm; Indians were for extermination and Bacon had delivered them a mortal stroke. His rebel status was soon resolved. When Berkeley in outraged indignation set out up the James with mounted troopers to arrest him, he had gone only a short way before reports of uproar and near revolt behind him in the York peninsula forced him to return. It was now plain that the only way for him to avoid outright war was to dissolve the Long Assembly and issue writs for an election.

Under the Long Assembly the franchise had been severely limited by property qualifications, but in this election the voters more or less restored themselves to universal suffrage and the burgesses consequently were of a far more liberal turn than their predecessors. Among them, elected from Henrico County, was Bacon.

When he came downriver for the opening of the assembly with twenty or thirty followers, his sloop was stopped by a ship with cannon and all were ordered to come on board, where Major Hone, the high sheriff, arrested them. Bacon's followers were taken off to jail in irons, but he himself was brought before the governor. To everyone's surprise Berkeley, perhaps sobered by the way the election had gone against him, received his rebel prisoner with uncommon civility.

"Mr. Bacon, have you forgot to be a gentleman?" "No, may it please your Honor," answered Mr. Bacon; then replied the Governor, "I'll take your parole," and gave him his liberty.

Bacon took up quarters in the house of Richard Lawrence, where his elderly cousin, the other Francis, joined him and, persuading him of the advisability of coming to terms with Berkeley, wrote out a brief retraction with a request for pardon, and informed the governor that Bacon would read it before the assembly. When, therefore, it had convened next day, after a statement by Berkeley that if Indians had killed "my grandfather and grandmother, my father and mother and all my friends, yet if they had come to treat of peace, yet they ought to have gone in peace" — apparently an allusion to the killing of the Susquehanna envoys — he stood up again and said, "If there be joy in the presence of the angels over one sinner that repenteth, there is joy now, for we have a penitent sinner come before us. Call Mr. Bacon." And when Bacon, on one knee, had read the retraction written for him by his cousin, the old governor uplifted his voice, repeating three times over: "God forgive you, I forgive you," and in addition agreed, one gathers only on his own account, not troubling God with lesser malefactors, also to pardon Bacon's companions who had lain all the while in irons.

Though still on parole, Bacon was free to take his old seat on the council. In fact Berkeley used it as a device to keep him from the burgesses while at the same time he insisted on two other councilors sitting with the burgesses, as had been customary in the sessions of the Long Assembly, "to assist in the debates." He got his way, but the burgesses went manfully to their work of reform. They restored universal suffrage; they limited the sheriff's term to one year, dealt with matters such as self-perpetuating vestries and trade monopolies; and they passed an act abolishing the immunity of council members from taxation, which must have been a bitter pill for the governor and his favorites to swallow.

They also took up the Indian problem which the pro-Berkeley councilors had been insisting should be the only order of business for the present session. Naming quotas for each county, they voted to raise an army of a thousand men, provided the funds to arm and supply them, and chose Bacon as their commander. But that was more than the old governor would stand for; he refused irately to grant a commission to a rebel.

While matters stood at this impasse, a cry went round the little town one morning that "Bacon is fled, Bacon is fled." Hearing from his cousin that there were designs against his life, he had slipped his parole. In three days he had raised the countryside, and expresses reached Jamestown warning of his approach with four hundred men, and four days later at two o'clock in the afternoon he entered the town and drew up his men on the green "not a flight shot from the end of the state house." Then with his left arm linked in the arm of a companion, Bacon strode toward the state house while the old governor went out to meet him.

As a confrontation it was almost *opéra bouffe*. Berkeley stopped on the steps. "We saw from the window the Governor open his breast, and Bacon strutting betwixt his two files, with his left arm on Kenbow, flinging his right arm every way, both like men distracted." But no violence was done by either, though there was no visible opposition to Bacon.

The governor turned toward his living quarters at the end of the state house, followed by the members of his council, Bacon tailing the procession "with outrageous postures of his head, arms, body, and legs, often tossing his hand from his sword to his hat, and after him came a detachment of fusiliers (muskets not being there in use), who with their locks bent presented their fusils at a window of the Assembly chamber filled with faces, repeating in menacing voices, 'We will have it, we will have it,' meaning Bacon's commission."

Whether Bacon's demeanor was as antic as described may be doubted. T.M., if he was the son of Mathews, was a Puritan and would not have found the actions of a Cavalier gentleman with an instinct for hyperbole much to his taste. He even himself had doubts, it seems, for he admits that later a friend, who had stood near, repeated the words exchanged by the two men when Berkeley bared his breast.

> "Here! shoot me. 'Fore God, fair mark! shoot!" [said the old man] often rehearsing the same, without any other words; whereto Mr. Bacon answered: "No, may it please your Honor, we will not hurt a hair of your head, nor of any other man's; we are come for a commission to save our lives from the Indians, which you have so often promised, and now we will have it before we go."

But he was under enormous strain and at another point in the proceedings was said to have cried out that he would kill the "Governor, Council, Assembly, and all, and then I'll sheathe my sword in my own heart's blood." One cannot have it both ways; but it is certain that Bacon made his determination plain, for the assembly drew up his commission and the governor signed it.

Now that he finally had his commission, Bacon lost no time in heading for the Susquehannas. He soon demonstrated that he could move his little army, and in less than four weeks the unfortunate Susquehannas were not only beaten, they were all but wiped out of existence. But before he could move on against other tribes, events behind him caused Bacon to turn back to Jamestown.

Berkeley was by no means reconciled. He had been humiliated but not humbled, and once Bacon was safely away on his campaign, Berkeley, declaring him to be another Cromwell, proclaimed him and all who followed him rebels. He called out the militia of Middlesex and Gloucester Counties, twelve hundred in number, and "proposed to them to follow and suppress that rebel Bacon; whereupon a murmuring arose before his face, 'Bacon, Bacon, Bacon,' and all walked out of the field, muttering as they went, 'Bacon, Bacon, Bacon,' leaving the governor and those who came with him to themselves, who being thus abandoned wafted over Chesapeake Bay thirty miles to Accomac."

Accomac, Virginia's Eastern Shore, was perhaps the most royalist corner of the New World and Berkeley was immensely popular there not only as being the representative of King Charles but in his own right. He quickly raised a force of almost a thousand men and sailed back to Jamestown. Taking possession of the town without any opposition, he proceeded to throw up an earthwork across the narrow neck of land connecting the peninsula and mainland.

Meanwhile Bacon was marching back to meet him. He paused briefly at Green Spring, using Berkeley's house for his headquarters, and addressed his soldiers in a ringing speech in the manner if not with the magic of Prince Hal before Harfleur. Berkeley's supporters were no match for Bacon's Indian fighters when the latter charged them; they turned and fled, and Berkeley, embarking just in time, wafted once more across the bay to Accomac.

Bacon was now in control of virtually all Virginia except its eastern shore. He had earlier issued a manifesto explaining his reasons for the course he had adopted. William Drummond, his principal adviser, had urged him to expel Berkeley from office and appoint another governor. But Bacon had demurred and chose instead to present his case, pointing out that he and his followers had molested no one, interfered with no magistrates, and acted only to protect the people of Virginia from Indian depredations. The men really to blame were the governor and his friends, "those juggling parasites whose tottering fortunes have been repaired at the public charge," and he catalogued their misdemeanors in a list reminiscent of the indictment of George III in the Declaration of Independence. At the end he listed the "parasites" by name.

After issuing this document, which one supposes he hoped would come to the eyes of the king and plead the cause of his subjects in Virginia, Bacon called a meeting of the leading men of the colony at Middle Plantation, which was to be the site of Williamsburg, in an effort to get pledges of support against the governor. Almost unanimously they agreed not to give aid to Berkeley if he should again attack, but many were hesitant about taking the offensive against him, and still less did they like the idea of fighting him if the king, as seemed only too likely, were to send regular troops from England to his support. Bacon had already accepted that issue in his own mind and was ready to retreat into the wilderness and "oppose them till they should propose or accept to treat of an accommodation," a desperate expedient which, as the chronicler observed, "we who lived comfortably could not have undergone." The meeting continued into the night under the wild light of torches; it might have lasted till dawn had not a rumor of fresh Indian violence reminded them of the primary reason of their actions. With emphatic statements that what they were doing should not in any way be construed as treason, the majority of those present signed.

Now, with Jamestown once more in his grasp, Bacon made up his mind to burn it in order that "the rogues should no more harbour there," and it was reported that so high did feeling run that Lawrence and Drummond, as an example to carry the rest, each set fire to his own house, described as being the two finest in the town. Nothing was left. Even the church and state house lay in ashes when they marched away.

There was now no turning back, though Bacon must have known that he had very little chance of final success. It was scarcely likely that, with England's experience under the Roundheads fresh before him, Charles II would allow a governor of his to be overthrown. All Bacon could hope for was to cement enough men to his cause to enable him to hold out until a fair presentation of the people's grievances could be heard in London.

He halted his army at Green Spring again and drew up an oath of fidelity to himself, which many swore to voluntarily but others had to be forced to take. He began to use harsh measures, also, for those who opposed him, putting them in jail and appropriating their property. But his army had begun to shrink and his luck was running out. In a last brief expedition he could find no Indians. Word came that a regiment of regular troops was on its way from England. When he took his army into Gloucester County in October he was a sick man.

He had picked up malaria in Jamestown and on his subsequent marches against the Indians he "had not had a dry day." It was a peculiarity of that summer in Virginia which no one could explain that while there was continual rain in the woods the plantation country had had a season so dry that it "stinted" the Indian corn. At the house of a friend he was forced to take to his bed, and on October 26 he died of a flux.

A few of his closest companions under the direction of Richard Lawrence buried his body with the utmost secrecy, and then staged a mock burial with a coffin loaded with stones in a solitary little churchyard in the open country. They were determined Berkeley should never find his body to hang it in chains.

With Bacon's death his rebellion, which had lasted less than five months, fell to pieces. Many made their submission to Berkeley, who had been quick to bounce back into power. He instituted a relentless manhunt for Bacon's chief lieutenants, and when they fell into his hands he showed no mercy. Miles Bland, who had been captured before Berkeley's abortive expedition from Accomac, was hanged even though it was common knowledge that his pardon from the king was on its way from England. Indeed, it was said that Berkeley watched Bland swing with the pardon in his pocket. When William Drummond was brought in, Berkeley said, "Mr. Drummond! you are very welcome; I am more glad to see you than any man in Virginia. Mr. Drummond, you shall be hanged in half an hour." And as soon as council of war could meet to sentence him and a gibbet be built, he was turned off. And so it went till Charles II, listening to an account of the old man's insensate behavior, exclaimed, "That old fool has hang'd more people in that naked Country than I have done for the Murther of my Father." When three royal commissioners arrived in January 1677 with a regiment of soldiers, there was no more hanging to be done; but Berkeley was summoned home and the people celebrated his departure with gunshot and bonfire.

After Bacon died it was hard to assess what had really been accomplished by his rebellion. There had been some reforms, and no succeeding governor ever had the nerve to build an oligarchical machine like the one with which Berkeley had ruled Virginia. The immediate Indian threat had been done away with. But the Navigation Laws remained in force, and the price of tobacco still stayed down. Bacon's effort had been a fierce but lonely one. The plain people cherished their memory of him, but he had had relatively few followers among the wealthier planters and still fewer friends. Only one of those closest to him survived old Berkeley's hanging spree. That was Richard Lawrence. According to the chronicler, T.M.:

> The last account of Mr. Lawrence was from an uppermost plantation, whence he and four others, desperadoes, with horses, pistols, etc., marched away in a snow ankle-deep, who were thought to have cast themselves into a branch of some river, rather than be treated like Drummond.

The Indian war in New England, reports of which had so raised Sir William Berkeley's apprehensions, was unique in having been touched off by the murder of an Indian by Indians. Though not the longest — it began in June of 1675 and was ended sixteen months later — it was by all odds the bloodiest, most grinding. It mounted the fiercest battle ever fought on New England soil, caused the greatest loss in property, and put a dark squeeze on the Puritan soul that finally had to find release in the persecution of the Salem witches. The causes underlying it lay partly in the Indians' diminishing share of New England lands, partly in their growing awareness of their own inferior status compared with the white man's, and partly in the mind of one chieftain who found the mingling of white and Indian ways within himself as incompatible as alcohol and diabetic tendencies were in the body of the average Indian.

His Indian name was Metacom, but the English called him Philip, as they called his older brother, Wamsutta, Alexander. The English had given them these English names as evidence of good feeling; it was of course another assertion in reverse of the Indian's racial inferiority. Whether the two young men took it so is debatable, but Philip, at least, displayed throughout his life a highly sensitive personal vanity. The two brothers were of the Wampanoag tribe which almost from the first had befriended the Pilgrims, and their father was Osamequin, whose title of Massasoit the English had always mistaken for his name. In 1660 Massasoit died and the title passed to Wamsutta, or Alexander — since the war that followed became celebrated as King Philip's War, it makes sense from here on to call these two young men by the names the English gave them.

After Massasoit's death the mood of the Wampanoags underwent a change. On visits to the white settlements their manners were presumptuous and short; before long, rumors sifted into Plymouth of a plot against the colony and Alexander was summoned to Duxbury for questioning.

He came with some reluctance but he succeeded in persuading his questioners that his tribe had no fell intentions against the English. The magistrates dismissed him and he made his way to Marshfield. There, while staying in an English household, he fell ill and became worse so rapidly that he had to cut short his visit and have himself taken back to his town at Mount Hope on the upper shore of Narragansett Bay where, shortly after reaching it, he died. Whatever it was he died of, pneumonia or some form of influenza, he had contracted it while staying with English people, and the course of the disease was so rapid that it raised ugly suspicions in the minds of the Wampanoags, who spread the rumor everywhere that he had been poisoned.

Whether or not Philip, who now succeeded his brother, believed this, it was useful propaganda, though it is doubtful that at the beginning of his rule he had any firm ideas about a war against the English. By tradition the far more powerful Narragansetts were still the principal enemy of the Wampanoags; by tradition the tribe was still friendly to the English, and Philip continued his visits among the white settlements.

Like Powhatan he was attracted by English things and his mind divided between his Indian heritage and his wish to play a role on the English scene, and in the beginning he was received kindly enough. As an opponent of the Narragansetts and their southern relatives the Niantics, he was valuable to the colonies. But there were small incidents that he must have found galling. The sale of horses and boats to Indians was forbidden by law, ostensibly to preserve the "peace" of the colonists, but one suspects that white men on foot did not like to see an Indian above them; and when Philip, three years after becoming sachem, requested permission to buy a horse, he was refused; but then, in a way italicizing the law, the colony made him a present of one. With the Indian love of fine apparel he was also running up debts with tailors which he could settle only by selling tribal land.

The sale of Indian lands lay at the root of the growing hostility between the Wampanoags and the Plymouth settlers. By and large these transactions were carried forward more equitably in New England than in other English colonies. The Puritans for the most part were meticulous in defining boundaries and tried reasonably hard to be certain that the Indians understood the property contained in the deed of conveyance. But the Indians never seemed quite able to comprehend that in signing away their title to the land they were giving up all use of it. Forest land especially had been free for them to hunt in, though it is true that even here various clans or various tribes kept within tacitly understood boundaries in their hunting. But as the white farms increased, the woodland shrank; and as the new settlers pushed closer to established Indian communities, their cattle began raiding the Indian cornfields and there was constant friction.

As he observed these slow, inexorable encroachments and the gradual

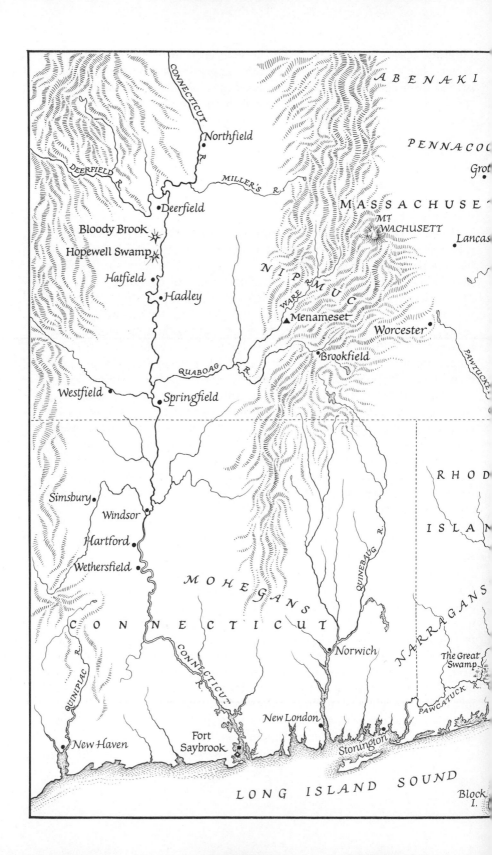

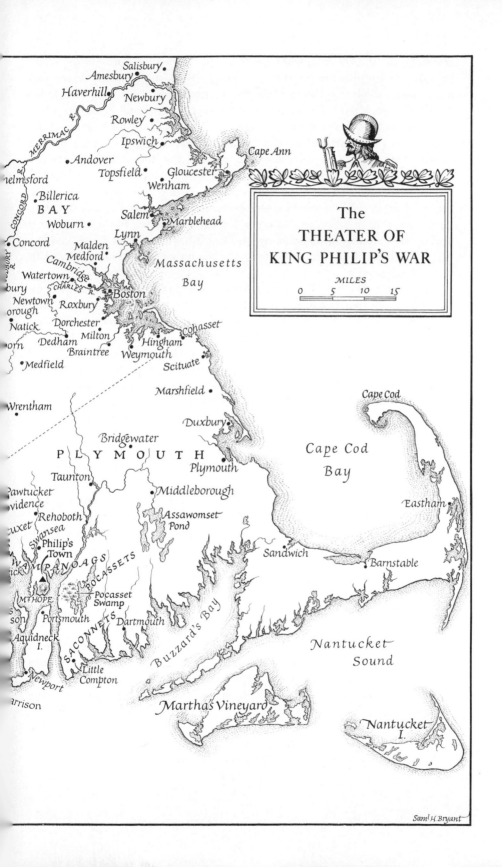

Salisbury

Amesbury

Haverhill

Newbury

MERRIMAC R.

Rowley

Ipswich

Cape Ann

Andover

helmsford

Topsfield

Gloucester

Wenham

Billerica

CONCORD

BAY

Woburn

Salem

Marblehead

Massachusetts

Lynn

Bay

Concord

Malden

Medford

Cambridge

Watertown

CHARLES R.

bury

Boston

Newtown

orough

Roxbury

Natick

Dorchester

Milton

Cohasset

orn

Dedham

Hingham

Medfield

Braintree

Weymouth

Scituate

Wrentham

Marshfield

Cape Cod

Duxbury

Bridgewater

Cape Cod

PLYMOUTH

Bay

Plymouth

Taunton

awtucket

Middleborough

vidence

Assawomset

Eastham

uxet

Rehoboth

Pond

Swansea

Philip's

Town

Sandwich

WA MPANOAGS

Barnstable

ick

POCASSETS

MT HOPE

Pocasset

son

Swamp

Portsmouth

Dartmouth

Buzzard's Bay

Nantucket

Aquidneck

SACONNETS

Sound

I.

Newport

Little

Compton

rrison

Martha's Vineyard

Nantucket

I.

The
THEATER OF
KING PHILIP'S WAR

MILES

0   5   10   15

Sam.l H. Bryant

shrinking of land the Wampanoags could call their own and saw the numbers of the English constantly increasing, Philip stayed away more and more from the Plymouth and Massachusetts settlements and brooded in his own town at Mount Hope, nursing his resentment and pride. In 1666, however, he made an effort to win approval of the English by warning the officials on Long Island that the Niantic chief, Ninigret, a man with a knack of stirring up trouble, intended to cross the Sound to exact tribute from their Indians. What he really hoped to gain from this is dubious — it may have been that he expected to play a leading role against the Niantics, and presumably their kin, the Narragansetts, with English backing. And from this ambition it was but a logical step to see himself playing a leading role among Indians against the English. In any case he lacked the capacity Uncas displayed of playing the games of both white and red to his own advantage.

However it may have been, from 1666 onward rumors of Indian plots on one side or another began reaching Plymouth and Boston with increasing frequency. In 1667 Philip was summoned before the Plymouth General Court to explain reports that he had plotted with the French to attack English settlements. He blamed the rumor on the Niantic, Ninigret, and denied any complicity with the French. For lack of evidence he was let go. But from this time onward the English were suspicious of him.

In 1669 it was the Narragansetts and Niantics toward whom the rumors pointed, but again, after examination at Newport, Ninigret and Pessacus, one of the important sachems of the Narragensetts, were released, again from lack of solid evidence. But in 1671 an Englishman from Swansea, a small new settlement four miles above Mount Hope on an arm of the bay, while visiting the Indian town saw Narragansetts there, busy at work repairing Wampanoag muskets. Report was quickly sent to Plymouth and relayed as quickly to Boston, and soon all New England was in alarm.

The authorities lost no time in calling Philip to an accounting in Taunton, a village fifteen miles from Swansea on the road to Plymouth. Philip came promptly, but with an escort. He had no arguments when confronted with the harsh facts of the Swansea man's report, admitted its truth, and agreed to surrender the Wampanoags' muskets, and as evidence of good faith he and his followers handed over their own. But no other guns were forthcoming during the rest of that summer.

In September the commissioners of the New England Confederation came together in Plymouth and Philip was summoned to appear before them. The evidence gathered against him was overwhelming and once more he had to humble himself. He signed a new treaty pledging the Wampanoags to peace, and agreed to pay a fine of one hundred pounds. He also was made to declare submission of himself and his tribe as subjects both of the English Crown and the government of Plymouth.

These successive humiliations brought home to Philip the debasement of his tribe and his own ignominious standing as their leader, and in brooding over them during the next three years he hatched the idea of one great devastating blow against the English in which the major New England tribes would be united. The Wampanoags would be at the heart of the plan, joined by the much more numerous Nipmucks of central Massachusetts and of course the Narragansetts, the most powerful of all, who had become increasingly restive and arrogant since the business of the Atherton Company, its huge speculative purchases of their territory, and the decision of the three royal commissioners more or less in their favor.

How much negotiating he had done, how far his plans had matured before hostilities began, there is no way of knowing. Probably not very far, for the beginning of the war was haphazardly fought by the Indians and there was no concerted action by the three tribes. The conspiracy lacked the sweep and weight of the one woven later by Pontiac, but that there was a conspiracy of some sort was proved to the satisfaction of all New Englanders early in June of 1675, during the trial and execution of three Wampanoags for the murder in the preceding January.

At the very end of 1674 an Indian named Sassamon had come to Plymouth and warned Governor Josiah Winslow that Philip and the Wampanoags were engaged in a far-ranging conspiracy against the English. Sassamon was a Christian convert who had received some education at Harvard, who could read and write fluently, and who often taught and preached to Christian Indians at Natick. But he had also for a period served Philip as a secretary and courier, and there were some English who considered him a tricky fellow who was not to be trusted. Perhaps for these reasons Winslow had not been overimpressed. But Sassamon was deadly serious and left the governor with the observation that his life would be in danger should news of his warning become public property.

Somehow the news did leak out; Philip heard of it and came straight to Plymouth to make angry denials; and only a few days after that, Sassamon's hat and musket were discovered by some Indians on the ice of Assawompsett Pond near his home in Middleborough. Cutting a hole in the ice, the Indians found his body. His head was badly battered and his neck broken. There seemed little reason to doubt that he had been murdered.

For a time the murder remained a mystery. Then an Indian came forward who, standing on a nearby hill, had with a curious detachment watched the killing taking place. He offered to identify the three murderers, and did so. He also agreed to testify at their trial. The three Indians were found and brought to Plymouth and early in June they were tried before a jury containing Indians as well as white men. The evidence of the solitary witness was enough to convince even the Indian members of the jury; the three accused men were convicted and on June 8 they were taken out and hanged.

The hanging became a macabre affair. The two older Indians, one of whom was known to be a counselor of Philip's, were turned off efficiently enough, but when the young man was swung up the rope broke. In his panic, and possibly hoping to be pardoned, he then confessed the guilt of the two older men but professed himself merely a looker-on. It did him no good, for in a moment he too was swinging beside the others. But to the onlookers his confession damned Philip utterly. They now had no doubt that he was as guilty of the murder as the men they had just hanged.

To die by hanging was to the Indian mind a violation of the soul. The Wampanoag town of Mount Hope swarmed with seething braves and as the word spread of what had been done at Plymouth a kind of shock settled on the smaller close neighbors, the Pocassets and Sakonnets, to whom Philip was now sending envoys urging them to join in the war against the English. Meanwhile braves in war paint were reported among these lower tribes and also at Mount Hope. Accumulating evidence indicated that an outbreak of violence might come at any moment and it was plain that for that first time in thirty-seven years New England was on the brink of a real Indian war.

There was still some hope that it might be confined to Plymouth Colony. Governor Winslow had asked Governor Leverett of Massachusetts for cooperation and in answer Leverett, in session with his council, determined to send out three missions, to the Narragansetts, the Nipmucks, and the Wampanoags. The mission to the Narragansetts was joined in Providence by Roger Williams, now in his seventies. They had planned to meet the Narragansett sachems at Wickford, where one Richard Smith ran a trading post but the Indians insisted that the English come to them. The meeting went smoothly enough and the Narragansetts said they had no intention at all of joining Philip, though the grudging manner with which they made these statements left some reservations in the minds of the commissioners.

The mission to the Nipmuck villages that lay across central Massachusetts between the frontier towns of Dunstable, Lancaster, Marlboro, and Mendon and the Connecticut Valley also received promises that the Nipmucks would not join Philip's war. But the Nipmucks were the wildest and most backward of the three tribes, and though the members of the mission were encouraged, they too came home with doubt.

When the three men of the mission to the Wampanoags rode into Swansea on their way to Mount Hope, their first horrified glimpse of the town showed them that they had come too late. Along the road which threaded the widely spaced houses they found the bodies of nine men, burned, scalped, and mutilated with all the varieties of Indian triumph. On the day before, June 24, the Wampanoags had begun their war.

Yet this first attack was nothing like the fell stroke Philip had dreamed about. For days before, the braves on Mount Hope had been nerving themselves for war. Continually, passing whites had heard the sound of Indian drums and the shrill cries of warriors. There were other ominous indications of the attack to come. On the eleventh of June the women and children of Mount Hope were seen being taken across the bay for sanctuary in the Narragansett country. Bands of braves in paint appeared more and more frequently in the neighborhood of the smaller outlying hamlets such as the one next below Swansea, and another at Mattapoisett. The people below Swansea abandoned their houses and came up to the village, and the people of Swansea itself who lived nearest the Indians gradually clustered in two garrison houses — Miles's at Swansea and Bourne's at Mattapoisett. The abandoned houses were too much to be resisted and on the eighteenth the Wampanoags began breaking in and looting.

As soon as news of these developments reached Winslow he ordered seventy men to march immediately to Swansea. One hundred and forty more were to follow them next day. When they marched into the garrison houses, the villagers began to breathe easier; their houses were almost sure to be destroyed, but at least it seemed as if their lives had been saved. But on the twenty-fourth the Indians began sporadic attacks on parties who had incautiously exposed themselves. Eleven men were killed that day, including three of the Miles garrison house sentries after dark.

Even before the three men who had set out on their fruitless mission to the Wampanoags returned to Boston, Massachusetts had begun mustering her militia. The first troops started out for Swansea — a company of one hundred men under Captain Henchman, accompanied by a troop of horse — on June 26. They were hardly under way when urgent messages to hurry arrived. The female sachem of the Pocassets was said to be about to join Philip and there was great fear that the two tribes together would break out of the Mount Hood peninsula.

At the end of June, three hundred troops had come together at Swansea and on the thirtieth they marched down the neck and on into the Mount Hood peninsula. They found nothing but the abandoned wigwams of the Indian town. No sign of life at all showed anywhere. Even the canoes had disappeared. Philip had escaped and with his warriors, though the English had yet to discover him, was hiding in a tangled swamp in the Pocasset country. The obvious course would have been to concentrate the troops of both colonies for the pursuit of Philip, or at least to pen him in his boggy lair; and this indeed was vehemently urged by Benjamin Church, who was soon to distinguish himself as an Indian fighter and in the end was the man who finally hunted Philip down. But his advice was not heeded and the troops were withdrawn to Swansea and placed on patrol duty which for the most part proved ineffective.

Meanwhile Philip was mounting attacks where he could, and smaller outlying communities like Dartmouth were wiped out. Rehoboth and

Taunton were attacked soon after Swansea and in mid-July an assault on the Massachusetts frontier village of Mendon by Nipmucks ominously forecast the spreading of the war. In Boston, however, the main preoccupation was still with the Narragansetts, and early in July a second mission was dispatched, led by Captain Edward Hutchinson, who had also led the first one. This time he was instructed to call on the Massachusetts troops already at Swansea as a means of lending weight to his negotiations. Therefore, when they might have been used to confine Philip on his swamp, one company was at Wickford in support of the Hutchinson mission while all the rest waited in reserve just below Providence.

At first the Narragansetts were reluctant to come at all, but finally the sachems appeared at Wickford with a large escorting company of warriors. For several days the meeting was a stand-off. Hutchinson's position was made difficult by the arrival of Captain Waite Winthrop from Connecticut with instructions from his government to do everything possible to appease the Narragansetts. This of course served to undercut the effectiveness of Hutchinson's show of force; but for the moment Connecticut was in desperate need of time as she was under threat of attack from the west.

This was another instance of Stuart disregard of agreements and geography. Sir Edmund Andros, who had succeeded Lovelace as governor of New York the year before, carried with him instructions, in disregard of the boundary settlement between Connecticut and New York engineered by Nicolls in 1664, to reassert the Duke of York's rights under his original patent from his brother by annexing all Connecticut land west of the Connecticut River. Accordingly in the spring of 1675 Andros had written Governor Winthrop laying claim to this half of Connecticut and as bona fides enclosing copies of his commission and of the original patent. It was of course an unthinkable claim; Hartford itself would no longer be in Connecticut, and Winthrop simply did not answer.

The outbreak of Philip's war seemed to Andros entirely auspicious and in July he sailed in two armed sloops for Saybrook with the idea of capturing the fort, which was supposed to be lightly garrisoned. The Connecticut settlers had already proved that control of the mouth of the river meant control of the whole valley.

But when he arrived off the fort he found that in addition to the small garrison the fort was occupied by two companies of militia under Captain Thomas Bull. The latter was not to be daunted and raised the king's ensign on the fort's flagstaff, and Andros, unwilling to fire on the flag, after a ceremonial call on Captain Bull reboarded his sloop and returned to New York.

This episode, incidentally, showed the satisfaction with which the other, royalist colonies were observing events in Puritan New England. She was left without aid either from her sister colonies or from King Charles, though he could afford to send ships and troops to Virginia to quell Bacon's rebellion.

But Connecticut authorities remained unwilling to commit troops to the eastern frontier when New York threatened their colony from the rear. In any case, though they did not yet know it, their western militia would soon be needed for the defense of the upper settlements along the Connecticut. Waite Winthrop was recalled from Wickford, but before the orders arrived, the Narragansett sachems, with the unexpectedness that often marked Indian bargaining, agreed to sign a treaty with the English, promising to keep peace with the colonies and to use the Wampanoags as enemies, and handing over four hostages as evidence of good faith. It was significant, however, that the chiefs who signed the treaty were not the leading sachems of the tribe, but lesser functionaries.

The treaty with the Narragansetts was signed on July 15 and the Massachusetts troops began their march back to Swansea. In four days they had reassembled there and were ready to join the Plymouth militia in attacking the Wampanoags still supposedly in the Pocasset swamp. They plunged into it with great resolution but soon found themselves frustrated. None were really experienced in Indian fighting; the Pequot war had occurred nearly two generations ago and in any case had not developed fighting such as this war was beginning to. Then it had been a matter of guns against arrows and spears, of overwhelming Indians penned in a palisade, and afterward of running down small bands of miserable fugitives. Now it was war in the woods, and even though the English army had Christian Indians aiding them as scouts (the Christian Indians were to exhibit the greatest loyalty throughout the war, even after many of them were put away in concentration camps), the men found it impossible to get at the enemy, especially in this densely wooded swamp where one's eyes had to trace one's footing as often as to search the woods and underbrush ahead. In a whole day of skirmishing they took only a single prisoner. They knew the Indians were there about them, they found and razed their shelter huts, they took casualties and had no way of knowing what they administered in exchange, and by dark both officers and men had had their bellyful. It was enough of a job to extricate the army and bivouac on the bay shore.

The officers now held a council to consider future policy and it was decided to build a fort on the bay side of the swamp and garrison it and another small fort on Mount Hope and then to maintain a sort of flying squadron as an instrument to contain the Indians in their present situation, cutting off supplies whenever possible. The rest of the army was to return home except for the Massachusetts troop of horse, which went to Mendon. These dispositions were thought sufficient to hold the Wampanoags in check for the summer, while the soldiers who had returned could lend a hand with the summer crops.

The troops started back near the end of July. Captain Henchman and his soldiers were busy building the forts, and the "flying squadron" under Captain Cudworth, one hundred and twelve strong, acting on a suggestion of Governor Winslow's, were making a roundabout visit by boat to the scene of Dartmouth, thus leaving the back door to the Pocasset swamp unguarded. On the night of the twenty-ninth, Philip and his Wampanoag warriors, accompanied by the Pocasset tribe, broke from the swamp, crossed the Taunton River, and headed at top speed toward central Massachusetts. They kept up their forced march through the night and all next day, hoping to get over the open country around Rehoboth without being seen, but they were spotted by some men from Taunton who scattered to spread the alarm. Strenuous efforts were made to cut the Indians off, but Philip had too long a start, and the interception became a pursuit.

The English caught up on the thirty-first and after a short fight the Indians fled into a near-by swamp. Here the English were joined by the fort-building Captain Henchman who had been alerted on the thirtieth but had taken two days to bring his men round by water to Providence and march the remaining twelve miles to the scene of battle. There is little doubt that the combined force of English was strong enough to have overcome Philip's exhausted Indians, but Henchman decided to put off fighting till the next day, and when he finally did attack, the Indians weren't there. They had stolen off during the night. Philip was on his way to join the Nipmucks. It was chilling news.

The Nipmucks were in an incendiary mood, stimulated by the taste of blood at Mendon, but the Boston authorities were determined to make one more effort to negotiate peace The presence of a number of Christian or, as the settlers called them, Praying Indians among the Nipmuck villages raised some faint hope that such a mission might succeed, and Captain Edward Hutchinson, who had just successfully dealt with the Narragansetts, was appointed to lead it.

For escort he was given some twenty troopers under Captain Thomas Wheeler of Concord, and as guides they had three Praying Indians, Sampson and Joseph Petuhanit and George Memecho. The whole party started from Cambridge on the twenty-eighth of July, spending the first night out in Sudbury. Four days later they approached their destination, Brookfield, the newest and most lonely of the outpost settlements of Massachusetts, perched on a hilltop right in the heart of the Nipmuck country. One trail, known as the Bay Path, connected it with civilization — Springfield lay thirty miles farther to the west; Marlborough, the next most western of the towns behind it was thirty miles to the east; Boston was sixty miles away — but the narrowness of the path along which for most of the way men must ride or march in single file made the distance seem longer.

Hutchinson found the people in the little village extraordinarily confident about the friendliness of their Nipmuck neighbors. There had never been any trouble before and the settlers did not see why there should be any now just because King Philip had started a war over in Plymouth Colony. No doubt the very nakedness of their situation was responsible for this delusion, for without it life on their remote hilltop would have been too frightening to bear. Hutchinson and his companions, however, soon enough began to have doubts.

The Nipmucks were said to be encamped about ten miles west of the settlement, so Hutchinson sent four men to find the camp and invite the sachems to a parley. When they reached the camp they found the Nipmucks in a hostile and excited mood, but after much persuasion they got the chiefs to agree to meet the English next morning. The Nipmucks chose a spot for the meeting a few miles west of the settlement and named the hour.

Next morning Hutchinson set out for it with his troop, to which three of the men of Brookfield attached themselves. When they reached the rendezvous they found no Indians. There was no sound of an approaching party and for a while they debated their next move. The three Indian guides were emphatic that it was not safe to go farther, but the three men of Brookfield were importunate in urging Hutchinson to go on to the camp, and in the end they persuaded him to do so, and the party took the trail again.

It became steadily rougher and more narrow. The woods closed in. Four or five miles beyond the spot where they had expected to meet the Indians they found themselves threading their way between a swamp on one side and a steep hill on the other. It was an ideal place for an ambush.

The first burst of musket fire hit them without warning from both sides. Almost immediately after, a volley poured into them from the rear. Eight men were shot from their saddles in that first fire, including all three of the men from Brookfield. Hutchinson and Captain Wheeler were badly wounded, and for a few moments the troop, strung out along the trail on their frantically plunging horses, milled in utter confusion. They could not ride into the swamp. Retreat along the path was cut off. The one chance was to charge uphill.

Miraculously they broke through. Wheeler had two horses shot from under him and with a ball through his body was unable to mount a third till his son, himself with a shattered arm, came to help him. Once past the Indians, they set out on the eight- or nine-mile race back to Brookfield. They dared not use the trail, and if it had not been for their Indian guides, who knew an alternate route, they would never have got there; the Nipmucks would have found and made an end of them.

When they pounded into Brookfield, exhausted and harrowed, the wounded barely able to keep in their saddles, there was just time to warn the people. Between eighty and ninety men, women, and children crowded into the largest and strongest house; together with the seventeen survivors of Hutchinson's party they must have jammed the building almost to the point of suffocation. It was a confused and terrifying moment. Men and unwounded troopers took posts at windows or loopholes; water had to be carried to the loft against the possibility of fire arrows; and the wounded, who had had no attention since the ambush, had to be cared for.

They were not yet properly organized when the first outlying houses burst into flame and the yelling of the Indians, improbable and shrill, swept toward them. Wheeler, too seriously wounded to move, had turned over command to Lieutenant Simon Davis, also of Concord, and at the same time he picked Ephraim Curtis of Sudbury and Henry Young of Concord to ride to Marlborough for help. The men made the attempt but were turned back and were lucky to regain the house. Between two and three hundred Nipmucks were swarming through the settlement, most of them concentrating on the garrison house, which was lapped by an incessant uproar of firing, Indian yelling, the screams and bellows of the wounded livestock, and the roar of burning houses.

The Nipmucks pressed their attack through the afternoon with undiminished fury. They seemed to have inexhaustible supplies of lead and gunpowder. But the musket fire of the garrison managed to keep them at a distance. They tried fire arrows, but the men in the loft were able to douse the started fires. When they built a fire against the side of the house the English broke through the wall to put it out; and a later effort was drenched by a providential cloudburst.

Meanwhile, after a second unsuccessful attempt to get through the swarming Indians, Ephraim Curtis a third time, after dark, crept out of the house on hands and knees, and succeeded finally in getting beyond the Indian lines. From there he had to find his way in darkness for thirty miles along the Bay Path. When he reached Marlborough the alarm was already out — some people headed for Brookfield had come near enough to hear the uproar of battle and returned pell-mell to Marlborough — and the only available body of troops had been alerted.

This was a company of forty-six troopers under the command of Major Simon Willard and Captain James Parker. They had been running a patrol between Marlborough, Lancaster, and Groton and were found a little beyond Lancaster. Major Willard, then over seventy, abandoned his patrol and started at top speed for Brookfield.

The troop arrived in the outskirts of the village in the evening of August 4, the second day of the siege. The blackened ruins of the houses were grim to see but ahead, beyond the center of the settlement, the bedlam of musket fire and Indian screeching showed that they had come in time. The Nipmucks were so absorbed in their attack that they failed to hear the warning shots of their sentries, and the troops were able to ride right through them to the garrison house, which they entered immediately.

The Nipmucks continued to attack through the night but on the morning of the fifth they apparently became convinced that it would cost them too much to carry the garrison house; suddenly they were gone and silence so profound settled over the scene that men almost hesitated to venture forth into it. Brookfield as a community had ceased to exist in those sixty hectic hours. The people lingered for a few days trying to make up their minds what to do, but in the end all decided to return to the east.

Willard and part of his troop remained until October, for it was thought best to keep most of the wounded where they were until they recovered. Edward Hutchinson, however, was removed to Marlborough, where he died on the nineteenth of August. He was the eldest son of Anne Hutchinson, the female preacher who had created such a furor in Boston and later removed to Pelham Neck on Long Island Sound where in 1643 she, with all of Edward's brothers and sisters, had been massacred by the Weckquaesgecks. Now he, like the rest, had fallen victim to the Indians. Of the entire family only his young niece had escaped this death, by being taken captive, and it will be remembered that, ironically, she had wanted to return to her Indian life when the Dutch in 1645 attempted to restore her to her own race.

When Willard left to ride home into Concord on October 21, a day which he and his troopers always observed afterward as one of thanksgiving, Brookfield simply ceased to exist. It was the first of twelve New England towns that were to be totally destroyed in the course of the war (forty more would suffer attack and partial destruction yet manage to survive). The story of Brookfield, however, is fascinating as being the first appearance of an American classic of the frontier: the ambuscade, the attack on the town, the valiant defense, the heroic effort to go for help, the arrival of the rescuing troops in the nick of time — the story has followed the frontier clear across the continent, but seldom in fiction or fact have the rescuing cavalry been led by a gentleman over seventy.

After Brookfield there was a lull in hostilities; then toward the end of August the fighting shifted to the upper Connecticut Valley where seven settlements were spaced out along the river for more than forty miles northward from Springfield to Northfield or Squakeag, as it was then called. Relations with the Indian tribes neighboring these towns had always been friendly but the news of Brookfield made the white settlers regard them with a warier eye. Overall military command was in the hands of John Pynchon whose father, William, had built his first storehouse across the river from the Agawam Indians on the site of what had become Springfield and whose trading enterprises, fed by grain and cattle from surrounding farms and furs from the Indians, extended down the Connecticut to the West Indies and to England. Pynchon had requested troops from Connecticut to bolster his own small force in protecting the northern settlements, and the General Court at Hartford had responded generously and sent up a strong force under Major Robert Treat. Two companies of Massachusetts soldiers had come in from Boston, the first under Captains Lathrop and Beers, the second under Captain Samuel Mosely, already a veteran of the Swansea campaign and of the second mission to the Narragansetts. He had also lately harassed the Pennacooks of the Merrimac Valley, burning villages even when their chief, Wannalancet, resolutely maintaining his neutrality, refused to fight and withdrew with his people into the wilderness. Thus there was at hand a force of some strength, commanded by an able group of officers, with a band of Mohegans to serve as scouts. The trouble began with a small tribe of Indians near Hatfield whom the Mohegans suspected of treachery. When the English demanded that they surrender their guns, they prevaricated and during the night melted out of their village. Next day the Massachusetts company of Lathrop and Beers went after them, cornered them in a swamp, and had a hot little fight before both sides decided to break off.

It now became evident that the once peaceable tribes had caught the war fever. A week later, on September 1, Deerfield and Hadley suffered simultaneous attacks; two days later Beers and thirty-six soldiers escorting a couple of farm carts were ambushed on the way to Northfield, half the men and Beers himself killed, and the rest just managing to make it back to Hadley, thirty miles to the south. Beers had been sent to help in the evacuation of Northfield. On September 6 Major Treat and his company executed the mission without loss. Through the next weeks the Indians continually attacked, now here, now there. Northfield had been evacuated; then Deerfield, which had been attacked a second time, was also abandoned.

The worst blow fell on October 4 at Springfield. All its protecting troops had been sent north to join the army under Pynchon in what was intended to be a great sweep against the Indians; but nobody felt unduly anxious. The neighboring Indian tribe, living in their palisaded town near by, had always been on good terms with the Springfield people; but now a Mohegan reported that a strong force of Philip's warriors had been slipped into the Indian town. On the following morning a small party, sent out to make inquiries, was ambushed as they approached the town and only one, Lieutenant Thomas Cooper, escaped. He was mortally wounded but managed to stay on his horse until he reached the settlement and gave the alarm. The people had all retired to the various garrison houses and the Indians found these too stoutly defended to attack. But the abandoned houses were easy prey and over thirty were burned, together with outbuildings and barns, which meant that a large part of the summer's harvest had also been destroyed.

The burning of Springfield brought into focus fundamentally opposed theories over how the troops should be used. The General Court at Hartford wanted the troops they had sent north used offensively against the Indians, instead of which they spent a large part of their time in garrison duty at isolated settlements. In Boston the commissioners of the New England Confederation were in emphatic agreement with Connecticut. But matters looked very different to men and women in the frontier settlements. Pynchon himself had experienced grave doubts over stripping Springfield of its garrison, and when he returned to its still smoking ruins, where only a dozen houses were left standing, he was deeply shaken. It was with relief that he soon afterward turned over his command to Captain Samuel Appleton.

The autumn, which had been one of unrelieved gloom, was to end, however, on a more hopeful note. The English, getting wind of a projected attack on Hatfield, were able to concentrate their forces and inflict a savage defeat on the Indians. It had a sobering effect; hitherto the Indians had come off best in nearly every encounter; now, for the rest of the year, they made no more attacks in force in the upper Connecticut.

In Boston and the surrounding towns the disastrous fall, during which for nearly ten weeks the Commissioners of the United Colonies met almost daily, was producing near hysteria. People tried to find a reasonable explanation for the woeful trials that had come upon the colonies. To the most rigid Puritans there could be but one explanation: it was God's wrath wreaked on them for faltering in their efforts to cleanse themselves of heretics. They turned once more against the Quakers, who were forbidden, under the most stringent penalties, to hold meetings. But the principal sufferers of the swelling tide of fear and hate were the Christian Indians.

Though a few had left their mission villages to join the enemy, the vast majority remained loyal. This made no difference to those who saw in them a potential fifth column. Besides, they were ready at hand; they were weak; and those Englishmen who stood up for them — Captain Daniel Gookin, their superintendent; John Eliot, the missionary preacher; and Captain Daniel Henchman, whose dilatory tactics had made possible Philip's escape but who was to prove himself effective in patrolling the Groton-Lancaster-Marlborough frontier — did not have enough persuasive force to convince the Indian-haters of the loyalty of their protégés. Ugly incidents began to multiply, and in the fall of 1675 there were several cases of unprovoked attacks on unarmed Indians. Some were killed, others seized in their villages and led to Boston for trial. A lady with the appropriate name of Mrs. Pray put in writing her recommendation that the Indians be totally exterminated, Christian and heathen alike.

In Concord were living, early in 1676, a group of Nashoba Indians. They had always been peaceable and had been brought in under orders of the council and put under the protection of Mr. John Hoar. Near his own house he had had built for them what he called their "work house" in which during the day they could work at basket making or dressing skins and at night sleep behind locked doors to protect them from the violent white element in the town. Seeing that they could not get at "Hoar's Indians" these people got in touch with Captain Mosely, who had gained a reputation as a harasser of Praying Indians. On a Sabbath morning in February, with some of his troopers, Mosely rode into Concord. Divine service was still in progress, so they joined in worship, but after the service ended the captain addressed the congregation, saying "that he understood, there were some heathen in the town committed to one Hoar, which he was informed were a trouble and disquiet to them; therefore if they desired it he would take them to Boston."

Only a few people spoke up against the Indians; most remained silent; but Mosely affected to take this silence for assent and with his soldiers went to John Hoar's house. Hoar refused to surrender his charges, though he allowed Mosely to look into the workshop to assure himself that the Indians were mostly women and children, only twelve of the fifty-eight being men, and locked the door again when the captain had seen his fill. Mosely would have to show an order from the council if he was going to take away the Indians.

There the matter stood all through the Sabbath, but on Monday morning Mosely and his men appeared again, determined not to be diverted from their purpose. When Hoar reiterated his demand for an order from the council, Mosely showed him his commission "to kill and destroy the enemy," and without further ado ordered his men to break down the workhouse doors and seize the Indians.

They were marched to Boston and from there taken to Deer Island in the harbor, where they were left with scanty shelter and inadequate provisions. Over four hundred more were to join "Hoar's Indians" on Deer Island, which became in effect our first concentration camp. Food was often short and life almost always miserable; but these Indians not only remained loyal, they responded to calls for scouts and spies and served the colony ably and well. In fact even Mosely came round to asking for fifty of these Praying Indian scouts.

More and more through the late summer and fall of 1675 the problem of the Narragansetts came to preoccupy the thoughts of the commissioners of the confederation. The Narragansetts were the most formidable in numbers and probably the best armed of all the hostile tribes. As the summer and early fall months went by, it became increasingly obvious that they had no intention of living up to the clause of the peace treaty engineered by Hutchinson in July that called for their surrender to the English of any members of the enemy tribes who should come into their territory. The presence among them of the entire Pocasset tribe was common knowledge. The one faint ray of hope was the rising uneasiness of the

Niantics over the matter of harboring fugitives and their chief Ninigret's repeated avowals of friendship. He was known as a wily bird and few people had ever put much trust in his word, but now the commissioners were inclined in sheer desperation to listen to him and it was largely because of him that the Narragansetts agreed to reaffirm the July treaty.

In October, at Boston, the new treaty was signed by Ninigret's deputy, a chief named Cornman, for the Niantics, and for the Narragansetts by the youngest of their leading sachems, Canonchet, the son of Miantonomo. The treaty only differed from that of July by Canonchet's guarantee to turn over the Wampanoag and other refugees within ten days. Subsequent events showed that he had no intention of doing so, and one may surmise the scorn and vengeful thoughts that passed through his mind as he put his mark upon the paper and reflected, as indeed he must have, that thirty-two years earlier his father had stood before this same body of men and by them been condemned and turned over to his bitter enemy for execution somewhere beyond English territory. October 28, the date for delivering up the Wampanoag fugitives, came and went. From the Narragansett country there was no sign — except the rumor, brought by an Indian who had passed through at October's end, that Canonchet was planning to commit his people to war in the following year. There were enough other indications to convince the grim commissioners in Boston of the inevitability of a Narragansett onslaught, an inevitability limited only by time.

The minds of the commissioners now turned to the possibility of handling the Narragansett problem by a preventive war. The idea was not new. Connecticut had suggested it in 1642 when the Narragansetts began making hostile gestures, but at the time Massachusetts, which had not recently suffered from attacks as had the Connecticut towns in the Pequot war, refused to go along. Now, her own losses had changed Massachusetts' attitude. Plymouth also was ready to attack. It remained to approach Rhode Island, which had not been permitted to join the confederation and which could field few men, but which could furnish boats for ferrying troops and supplies in the area of Narragansett Bay. When the Rhode Island governor, William Coddington, promised that his colony would cooperate, they went ahead with plans for the expedition.

These called for an army of a thousand men, and the force that actually marched against the Narragansett stronghold numbered 985. Of these Massachusetts mustered 527, Plymouth 158, and Connecticut 300. Overall command was given to Josiah Winslow. Major Samuel Appleton led the Massachusetts contingent, Major William Bradford the men from Plymouth, and Major Robert Treat those from Connecticut. Besides these officers were many who had distinguished themselves in the previous months of fighting, including Benjamin Church, who acted as aide to Governor Winslow.

The operation was for those days a complicated one and called for two rendezvous: the first that of the Massachusetts and Plymouth forces at Rehoboth; the second when these combined troops joined those from Connecticut at Pettaquamscutt, about nine miles south of Wickford. This spot had been chosen because of a large stone garrison house about half a mile east of the Pettaquamscutt River which a man named Jireh Bull used as a trading post and which it was thought would make a good, fortified base from which to start the final leg of the march into the Narragansett country. Heavy supplies were to be sent by boat around Cape Cod; Connecticut would move hers also by boat from Saybrook, while the men marched along the old Pequot trail as Mason's men had done in 1637. The boats promised by Rhode Island were to meet the Plymouth–Massachusetts troops at Rehoboth.

A winter campaign of this sort carried serious risk. Heavy snow could pin the little army down for days. Worse still, if it had not yet concentrated, the separate groups would be vulnerable. Snow could also stop the movement of supplies. Deep cold could slow the movement of troops and supplies almost as badly. But there were compensating factors. If the snow held off, the frost would let the men move freely into the great swamp where the Narragansetts were supposed to have holed up for the winter. And it was easier to find Indians in the leafless winter woods.

For men who were still pretty much amateurs, the movement of the little army went surprisingly well. The Massachusetts troops mustered at Dedham on December 9, under the eye of Winslow. The Plymouth companies joined them at Rehoboth on schedule. The advance guard of mounted troopers crossed the Seekonk at once and made on for Wickford; the rest of the army were ferried over next day to Providence and started down the west side of Narragansett Bay. On the march there was some skirmishing by detached units, so it was obvious that the army would not achieve surprise as Mason had against the Pequots. Winslow spent several days of anxious waiting at Wickford, but then word came that the Connecticut companies were waiting at Pettaquamscutt, and on the eighteenth the army came together, a union made grim by the blackened ruins of Bull's garrison house which the Narragansetts had attacked a few days before, killing most of the people.

The commissioners had issued what they had described as a declaration of war before the army departed from Dedham. According to this document the purpose of the army was to intimidate the Narragansetts into living up to the terms of the October treaty; it was to attack only if the sachems did not come to heel. But once the army marched, there is no reason to suppose that any man in it considered his duty as anything but to kill and to destroy.

Certainly at Pettaquamscutt this was Winslow's attitude. Though the next day was the Sabbath he decided without hesitation to attack, and the troops bivouacked that night in chilling expectation. They had no blankets, only a "fleece of snow"; it was miserable, cold, and wet when at five o'clock on Sunday morning they roused themselves, formed companies, and set out in a long file that wandered in slow segments of dingy brown across the snow. The going was heavy, but the men were not allowed to stop to rest or eat; the piercing cold would only have made the new start more difficult. In a crow's flight the great swamp in which the Narragansett fort was supposed to be was seven miles away; but the course they followed made almost twice that distance and it was not until early afternoon that they came in sight of its tangled waste of underbrush and cedar trees.

At the verge the Massachusetts troops, who formed the van, were fired on by a small band of Indians. The men did not stop for orders but as the Indians retreated pursued pell-mell across the frozen swamp and so in the dim grey winter light came upon the Narragansett town.

It had been built upon a piece of land that stood above the swamp, and the triple palisade of logs twelve feet high looked even higher. It was made more formidable by small blockhouses at intervals above the palisade. Inside was the main village of the Narragansetts, at this time housing perhaps three thousand men, women, and children. To the Indians it seemed impregnable.

The Massachusetts troops had arrived at the strongest section of the palisade where, however, there was a gap for which no gate had yet been built. But across it the Indians had placed a tree trunk at breast height, a barrier which was bound to check any charge, and just above it was one of the blockhouses. Without waiting for the Plymouth and Connecticut companies to come up, the Massachusetts soldiers charged the opening and swarmed over the horizontal tree trunk in the face of a murderous fire. Five company commanders were killed in the charge, but for a while the troops managed to keep a foothold inside the fort. However, this was no Pequot replay: the Narragansetts were well supplied with guns and, concentrating their fire, they presently by sheer weight of numbers forced the English back into the swamp.

While the Massachusetts men, now joined by those of Plymouth, gathered themselves for a second charge, Major Treat led his Connecticut troops round to the back of the fort. They found a somewhat steeper bank, but the palisade at the top had not been wholly finished. Here and there the posts were spaced apart and protected partially by a tangled mass of limbs and brush. The men charged the bank under heavy fire, swarmed up it, and forced their way over or through the palisade. As they gained a foothold inside, the second charge at the gap also forced an entrance and the battle now raged through the massed huts and wigwams. It was a murderous fight, without quarter on either side, and it was still rag-

[383]

ing late in the afternoon when Winslow, over the protests of Captain Church, ordered the wigwams fired.

The sun had set and snow again began gently falling, the inferno of the Pequot town and the equally awful burning of the Indian town by Underhill near Stamford were repeated, though here perhaps a thousand Indians did succeed in breaking out with Canonchet and escaping into the snowstorm. The exhausted victors could now pause and consider their handiwork and their own situation. Both were grim.

They had about twenty men killed and two hundred wounded. They had almost no provisions, and they had burned with the village the great caches of food put down by the Narragansetts to carry them through the winter. There was a chance, however remote, that Canonchet might rally the Narragansetts for a new battle. Winslow decided that he had to get his army out. No shelter existed at Pettaquamscutt; Wickford was the only place that offered any and, hopefully, some of the ships which had been delayed by stormy weather might have arrived with rations. So in the dark the battered army took up its second march of the day, carrying the worst wounded on horses. It was not till two in the morning that the leading units stumbled into Wickford. Some, losing their way, did not get in till daylight. In the days that followed more than eighty of the wounded were to die.

If the Narragansetts were not as completely crushed as the Pequots had been in 1637, they were much weakened, and there can be no question that the Great Swamp fight was the turning point in King Philip's War, in spite of attacks and burnings that followed in the next few months. If the tribe had been able to join the Wampanoags at full strength in the spring, the war would have been far uglier and lasted much longer than it did. The Narragansetts, besides their loss of tribesmen, had also lost almost all their winter food. They had been forced to leave their land and were dependent on the generosity of other tribes. Canonchet, it is true, would have one triumph over the English. In March he ambushed a company of fifty Plymouth men under Captain Michael Pierce, accompanied by twenty friendly Indians, and killed all except one Englishman and nine of the Indians, who were then tortured to death. And he burned Rehoboth and Providence; but in April he was himself ambushed and captured. Brought into Stonington, he refused to accept the terms of submission offered by the English; so, as they had done with his father, they turned him over to some of their Indian allies for execution. When he heard the sentence Canonchet said he liked it well that he should die before his heart was soft. After he was dead his executioners cut off his head and sent it to Hartford as a mark of their good will.

Though the turning point of the war was the Narragansett campaign, the succeeding February, March, April, and May were months of grievous tribulation, especially for the towns of Plymouth and eastern Massachusetts. The first hint of renewed violence came out of the Nipmuck country at the end of January. Two Praying Indians, James Quannapohit and Job Kattenanit, who had volunteered to serve as spies, had made their way to the Nipmuck town of Menameset and mingling with the braves and sachems heard boasts of a coming raid on Lancaster. James Quannapohit came back at once with this preliminary information, adding that several other towns were to be attacked later. No one seemed to be much disturbed. Massachusetts was perhaps still suffering some reaction from the Narragansett campaign. In any case no precautionary moves were made, and January gave way to February without further alarms. But on February 9 Job Kattenanit appeared at the door of Major Gookin's house in Cambridge at ten o'clock at night. Four hundred Indians had already left Menameset and were on their way to Lancaster which they intended to attack next day. Job's sixty-mile run over the winter trails had given Lancaster barely eight hours' grace. It was one of the great runs of American history.

Gookin immediately sent messengers to alert Lancaster and to summon troops from Marlborough and Concord. At daybreak forty troopers rode out of Marlborough under Captain Samuel Wadsworth. When they reached Lancaster the Indian attack had hit full stride and the troopers saw the smoke of burning buildings and heard the musket fire and uproar before they came out of the woods. Their charge across a partly burned bridge and into the town put an end to the fighting, or possibly the Indians had enough loot and prisoners to satisfy them.

The prisoners were almost wholly from the one garrison house they had successfully stormed. There were six garrison houses in the village when the raid began and five of them stood off the Indians; the sixth, the house of Reverend Joseph Rowlandson, was burned, and twelve of the more than forty people who had taken refuge in it were killed. Only one of the rest escaped. The others were all taken prisoners and thus began the famous captivity of Mary Rowlandson.

She herself had been grazed by a bullet as she emerged from the blazing house. Her baby Sarah in her arms was shot "through the bowels" and would die eight days later. She saw her nephew's brains dashed out by a war club as he stood beside her, and her eldest sister shot dead. She herself was separated from her older children and dragged away. In the three months she spent with the wandering tribe she saw her son Joseph just once and briefly. The tribe joined forces north of Massachusetts with King Philip and a band of Wampanoags, and while they were together she made a hat and shirt for Philip's little boy, for which he gave her a shilling and invited her to supper. Finally on the first of May, John Hoar of Concord turned up in the Indian camp with twenty pounds and ransomed her.

Mr. Rowlandson had been in Boston at the time of the raid to plead for more troops as a garrison. He had returned to find the village entirely burned except for the five surviving garrison houses and to receive the dreadful tidings about his wife and children. During her months of captivity Mary had learned that her husband believed her dead, yet she never lost her courage or her faith, and at the end of her remarkable account of her experience she could write:

> . . . The portion of some is to have their afflictions by drops, now one drop and then another; but the dregs of the Cup, the Wine of astonishment, like a sweeping rain that leaveth no food, did the Lord prepare to be my portion. . . . yet I see when God calls a Person to any thing, and through never so many difficulties, yet He is fully able to carry them through and make them see, and say they have been gainers thereby. And I hope I can say in some measure, as David did, *It is good for me that I have been afflicted* . . .

Lancaster was soon abandoned and Mary, passing through it on her return from captivity, was shocked to find it utterly deserted, not a house left standing. Ten days later Medfield became the next victim. Their nearness — twenty miles — to Boston had lulled the inhabitants into a false sense of security and they rose on February 20 at sunrise to come out of their doors still drowsy into the musket fire of Indians who had taken their stations in the dark and waited the last hour to daylight motionless and silent.

The Confederation commissioners sought to counter this wildfire warfare by the formation of a regiment of six hundred mounted troopers to range the Nipmuck country and drive the Indians from their towns. Plymouth could not or would not contribute her share, but Massachusetts mustered three hundred under Major Savage at Brookfield where they were joined by the Connecticut troops and together the combined force moved north toward Menameset. The Indians naturally evacuated before so strong a force and fled north into what was to be Vermont. The troops let them go; they were running low on rations by then, and Major Savage decided to head for Hadley and divided his men among the river towns. They were in time to defend Northampton from an attack by Philip and drove him back in what was near rout.

Though Savage's operation had little to show in results, the idea behind it was sound — to keep the Indians moving, with no time to plant and raise their crops. But the colonies were not quite ready yet to carry out this kind of harassment systematically, and in the east the raids continued. On March 13, Groton was almost entirely destroyed. Though the people had defended themselves successfully, they were too disheartened to go on living there and the town was abandoned. Thirteen days later the Indians burned the greater part of Marlborough, and its people, too, joined the rising number of refugees, but because of the strategic location of the town its garrison was maintained. Mendon and Wrentham were the next to be vacated, and it seemed that the whole frontier was going to collapse.

Besides these major attacks, there were the continual minor incidents of Indian warfare: a man shot in his field, a girl taken captive, a mutilated body found lying by the trail. At times the lesser dread begotten by these single episodes picked at the mind as acutely as fear of wholesale attack upon one's town.

On April 21 more than five hundred Indians who had been encamped near Mount Wachusett made an onslaught on Sudbury. The alarm went out and men or troops rode from Marlborough, Watertown, Concord, and even Charlestown. These parties arrived piecemeal to mix into what had turned into a wild and messy battle fought stubbornly by both whites and Indians. In the end the English were forced to retreat from the field, but their fight had saved the greater part of Sudbury from destruction, and in the hour of their victory the Indians also inexplicably withdrew.

A lull in the fighting followed Sudbury. When hostilities began again in mid-May, it began to be evident that the balance had changed and the English were gradually getting the better of the struggle. On the seventeenth, Captain William Turner of the Hatfield garrison learned that a large party of Indians had camped at the falls of the Connecticut north of Deerfield to fish. Reinforcing troops could not be brought up from Hartford immediately; so, rather than lose the chance of striking a blow, he organized a motley force of his own troops and volunteer farmers, amounting to one hundred and fifty, many of whom were mere boys, and marched out of Hatfield as dusk was falling on the eighteenth. Riding through the night, they came up to the falls a little before dawn, dismounted, and leaving their horses with a few guards, stole into the camp and positioned themselves in little groups before each wigwam. It was the Indians' own game.

The first crashing volley turned the sleeping camp into bedlam. The Indians were sure they were being attacked by Mohawks, and in their demoralization many rushed naked out of the cabins and raced for the river while the English shot them down. More than a hundred were killed in the surprise, and still others were drowned in the flooding water.

But there were other fishing camps and from them strong parties of braves sallied in an effort to cut off Turner's little band. They drove off a portion of the horses and then began stalking the retiring English. The flush of victory turned in an instant to blind panic, the retreat became a rout. Some of the wounded were abandoned on the way in the frenzy of their comrades to escape. Among these was Captain Turner. Slightly over one hundred men got back to Hatfield; the dead were something over forty; but the Indians had suffered far more, and in spite of the rout that ended it, the action had been a severe defeat for the Indians and they failed in an attempt at the end of May to take Hatfield in retaliation.

The colonies now decided to mount another combined operation, this time of real strength. Five hundred Connecticut troops were to march up the Connecticut Valley under Major Talcott and wait at Hadley while five hundred Massachusetts troopers under Major Henchman made a sweep across central Massachusetts to join Talcott. Then the combined force would march north to clear the upper Connecticut of Indians for good and all. Henchman was characteristically slow in reaching the rendezvous and while waiting for him Talcott and his troops easily beat off another attack on Hadley.

Henchman finally reached Hadley in mid-June, but when the combined force in their upriver march came to the falls, the Indians had vanished. With no prospect of action in the upper valley, Talcott returned to Hartford and Henchman marched back across the Nipmuck country to Marlborough. Not much had been achieved by the combined operation, but it must have had a psychological effect upon the Indians. The marching back and forth through their country could not have gone unobserved and the Indians must have been impressed by the number of these armed and mounted troops.

Meanwhile, though it had not contributed men to the Connecticut–Massachusetts effort, Plymouth Colony had organized a company of one hundred and fifty English and fifty friendly Indians to patrol its western boundary. Reports were coming in with increasing frequency of small bands of Indians moving south. At the same time Benjamin Church, who had been out of action since the Narragansett campaign, offered to raise and lead a mixed company of English and Indian volunteers from settlers and refugees on Aquidneck Island. On his return trip he came upon some Sakonnet Indians fishing and learned from them that the tribe had returned to their own country, completely disillusioned about Philip. On a subsequent parley with their female sachem, Awashonks, Church learned that the tribe was not only disillusioned about Philip, they were willing to fight him if the English allowed them to reoccupy their old territory without reprisals.

About this time the Plymouth company under Major William Bradford had reached the Pocasset. More signs of the return of local Indians cropped up: fires on the shore of Mount Hope Bay; Indians seen clamming. There were rumors, too, that Philip himself would soon come back. Bradford, however, did not investigate these scattered bits of information but contented himself with marching his company the length of Mount Hope to Swansea and then on to Rehoboth.

Meanwhile Connecticut's army had been mopping up the Narragansett country, killing more than one hundred and seventy on one successful afternoon, and surprising another smaller group that were waiting patiently on Narragansett Bay for an answer to their overtures for peace. In both these encounters the Connecticut troops killed women and children without discrimination along with the men. Such butchery, however, was effective in shaking the Indians' enthusiasm for Philip's war, and in an increasing tide the tribes or individual small parties came in to the authorities to make what peace they could.

Among them were the Sakonnets whose submission the Plymouth authorities had formally accepted. Church's request that they be allowed to fight under his command was also agreed to. In July, therefore, he was able to form his company of Indians and English volunteers, chosen for their ability in forest fighting, with whom he intended to track Philip down.

At the end of July indications that Philip really had returned began to appear. In a skirmish at Bridgewater, his uncle was found among the Indians killed. A little later Church and his company went in search of a band reported to have crossed the Taunton River, and as they came close they had a glimpse of Philip himself, but before a gun could be fired he had vanished. By the time the frustrated Church and his men had got across, Philip was beyond reach. But they did round up some of his followers, including his wife and son.

So bitter was English feeling against Philip that the little boy's execution was seriously debated. In the end, however, it was decided to sell him and his mother as slaves in the West Indies, the common fate of Indians taken prisoner who were not killed outright, and in effect a death sentence too, for the North American Indian could survive neither the hot and humid climate nor the restrictions of slavery.

Church continued his hunt for Philip and barely missed catching him on August 3. But in his driving search his company caught up with and killed large numbers of Indians: old and young, women and children as well as men, it made no difference as long as their skin was red. And now that the Indians could no longer organize any resistance, the people of the outlying settlements began getting their own back by falling on small migrating groups wherever they found them.

Church's almost feral obsession left him and his company with scarcely a day to rest. When they did return to Plymouth or visit a settlement, a new rumor would call them immediately back to the hunt. He was on Aquidneck Island on August 11, both to visit his wife and rest his men, when news came that one of Philip's braves had deserted and was ready to lead the English to the capture of his former chief. In a matter of minutes Church had said good-bye to his wife and with his host, Major Sanford, and Captain Goulding, who had brought the news, was galloping up the island to see the deserter and then get his company on the road.

In a quick interview Church convinced himself of the Indian's sincerity. His reason for hating Philip was that the latter had had one of his relatives killed. Philip, he told Church, was hiding with only a small party in a swamp on the slope of Mount Hood. He promised to guide Church to the spot, and Church, seized by a sense of his destiny, did not feel an instant's hesitation.

Night had fallen when he and his men, accompanied by the Indian and Sanford and Goulding, pushed off their boats and started rowing for the shore of the Mount Hope peninsula. A little past midnight they were standing at the edge of the swamp. Church saw at once that he did not have men enough to circle the swamp, so he spaced most of them out along the edge as far as they would reach and sent the small remaining party under Captain Goulding to the far side with orders to creep up as close to the Indian camp as they could while it was still dark and then, making all the noise they could, to attack at dawn. The assignments were perfectly carried out. Philip and his Indians slept in peace until the break of day. They were just beginning to rouse themselves when Goulding and his men opened fire.

The Indians broke and raced into the swamp away from the firing. Most escaped but one of the few that did not was a tall man who was spotted running at full speed by a pair of Church's men, an Englishman and an Indian. The Indian's fire dropped him in full stride and he crashed forward in the mud and water with his gun under him. When they turned the body over, they found that it was Philip. In that instant Church had become the hero of New England, a role he certainly did not disrelish, and Philip's head, in what had become established tradition, was cut off and taken to Plymouth and there mounted on a pole on the village green where people on their way to worship could gaze upon it in grateful security.

There still remained a good deal of mopping-up to do. Church finally ran down and captured Philip's war chief, Annawon, but though war still went on in Maine, where the Abenaki had been infected by all the killing of the whites down south of them, in the rest of New England it was over. Indians either made submission or drifted north out of their old haunts forever, joining the Abenaki or heading northwest into Canada or west to the Iroquois country.

The ordeal had ended but the cost was staggering. New England had lost, proportionately, more men than it was to lose in any other war in its history. Thirteen of its towns had been totally destroyed and abandoned. Others had been partially burned. The cost in money was estimated at 100,000 pounds. It was no wonder that people asked why they had been visited with such afflictions.

New England's resentment over the behavior of New York under Governor Andros during King Philip's War did not subside with the end of fighting. Connecticut regarded his attempt to seize Fort Saybrook, even though unsuccessful, as a stab in the back, which indeed it was, and Andros's determination to keep New York out of the war merely underlined it. His only activities against the New England tribes were to keep an armed sloop on duty in Long Island Sound to intercept any possible hostile ventures against Long Island and in 1677 to send an armed force to build a fort at Pemaquid as a check against the Abenaki. In doing so he gained further resentment by refusing to allow Massachusetts fishermen to cure their fish there as they had in the past.

Now that the war was ended, the New England colonies continued making charges against him both in America and London. Not only, these ran, did he send no material aid to them in their desperate hours, he had refused to turn the Mohawks loose on the Massachusetts tribes that were their traditional enemies, he had refused to allow representatives from Hartford to treat directly with the Mohawks, and — the most serious charge of all — he had winked at the sale of guns and ammunition to Philip's Indians. There were some grounds for these complaints, but except for Andros's keeping his colony out of the war, they were not completely valid.

Andros had consistently prohibited the sale of powder to all Indians except Mohawks "on penalty of ten pounds for each quarter pound of powder, or Corporall punishment extending to life," and when the commissioners of the United Colonies reiterated the charges made by Connecticut, he sent his own commissioners to Boston with an indignant demand that the charges be made good by naming names "or false informer punished." Of course there were men who would take any risk, the Dutch traders at Albany foremost among them, to make a dollar by selling guns to Indians, but there is no reason to question Andros's sincerity. As for using the Mohawks against New England's enemies, they had attacked Philip's Indians in November and December 1675 when the latter had appeared east of the Berkshires in two parties of five hundred each (figures that must have included women and children) and come within forty miles of Albany.

Such a trespass on their own land was enough to bring the Mohawk warriors boiling from their towns without any prompting from Andros or anyone else, and they had thrown Philip and his Indians back into Connecticut. When Andros, before learning of this episode, asked for permission to launch a Mohawk attack, both Hartford and Boston, who wanted nothing less than the return of Philip's army, had said no. If the Mohawks were going to make war inside New England, the commissioners wanted them under their control, and this Andros naturally refused to permit. (In any case, at that time controlling the headlong, willful, and bloody-minded Mohawks was pretty much an academic question.) But Andros had grasped the vital importance of having the Iroquois look to Albany and New York for supplies and support and had already been at pains to impress himself on them as the chief deputy in America of the King of England, an image that direct negotiations with Hartford commissioners would certainly diminish.

Moreover, in 1675 the Iroquois were becoming restless, in part because of greatly increased Jesuit activity, reports of which reached New York together with rumors of disturbingly large numbers of converts being induced to migrate to Canada, where they were settled in missions around Montreal. The Iroquois were still shaken by a French expedition which had wiped out five Mohawk towns in 1666 and were much more inclined to listen to the Jesuit message and accept peaceful living under the Cross.

Neither Nicolls nor Lovelace had shown any understanding of the crucial need of keeping the Iroquois in league with the English, nor had James, who seemed willing to turn them over to the French to be converted into proper Catholics. It was only when the effects of Jesuit proselytizing began to deflect the fur trade away from Albany and consequently to bite into his own tax receipts that he changed his tune and urged on Andros the absolute necessity of tying the Iroquois to English interests, "inasmuch as the enmity of the Mohawks would be ruinous to the whole Province."

Not leaving time for the receipt of a countermanding letter from his master, Andros started up the Hudson in August, stopping briefly at Esopus and again at Albany before marching overland to Schenectady. From there with a retinue and Mohawk guides he struck west into Iroquois country, to hold a conference with "the most warrlike Indyans neare a hundred miles beyound Albany, which Indyans (and Associates to about four hundred miles further applyed) declaring there former Allyance, and now submitted in an Extraordinary manner."

The ritual and oratory of an Iroquois conference in the center of a palisaded town deep in the wilderness must indeed have seemed extraordinary to a blunt, tactless, forthright, and impatient English officer of dragoons. He was expected to initiate the ceremonies by lighting and drawing on the ancient and elaborately carved calumet and passing it to the sachem by his side. All the five tribes were represented: Mohawks, Oneidas, Onondagas, Cayugas, and Senecas — a few of them from as far away as Lake Erie. The exchange of presents, the presentation of wampum to emphasize each speech, sometimes to underline each point in a speech, went on for days during which Andros was compelled to sit and listen and, through his interpreter, make appropriate replies. He bore himself so well that the sachems addressed him as "Corlaer," their pronunciation of the surname of Arendt Van Curler who, as representative of Kiliaen Van Rensselaer, had been chief among the white men with whom they dealt, and in calling Andros by the Dutchman's name they honored his memory.

In 1661 Van Curler had founded the little outpost town of Schenectady as a means of tapping some of the fur trade for the Van Rensselaer interests before it reached Albany and there he had been in constant contact with the Mohawks. In 1667 while on his way to Canada to treat for peace in their behalf, crossing Lake Champlain he had met his death lamentably from disregarding an Indian superstition.

The canoe route led close to a cove on the western shore in which there was a rock against which the water would lash furiously in any wind; and the Indians believed an ancient man lived in the water under it with the power to send or dispel the wind; so in passing they always bribed him with tobacco or some other small gift. As Cadwallader Colden heard the story from them, Van Curler considered this a ridiculous superstition.

... Your great Countryman Corlaer (say they) as he passed by this Rock, jested at our Fathers making presents to this *Old Indian*, and in Derision turned up his Backside, but this Affront Cost him his life.

For apparently the old Indian called down a celestial counterblast, the waves grew steep, Van Curler's canoe capsized, and he was drowned.

But in spite of his levity they still remembered him with gratitude and respect and in brightening the friendship chain with Andros it was fitting to call him Corlaer, as they would call all succeeding English governors of New York from that time on.

Some early histories name the Oneidas' castle as the conference site, but this would have been considerably more than the hundred miles Andros reported traveling from Albany, and in early wilderness travel no one ever underestimated how far he had gone. More likely the site was the westernmost of the four Mohawk towns, Tionontogen, a little over forty miles above Schenectady. It served as the Mohawk capital and Andros and his followers were impressed with the strength of the palisades on which two swivel guns were mounted. They also had evidence of Jesuit activity in the bark chapel of St. Mary's Mission in which Father Bruyas conducted mass. Before the chapel stood a fifty-foot pole which the Indians explained had been raised some years before by a Father Frémin after he had first attached to its tip a strip of wampum, now weathered away, which he said showed how high any Mohawk would be hanged if he took the life of a single Frenchman. It was high time that the road to the English should again be "made clear and smooth."

It was indeed a crucial turning point in English–Iroquois relations for with only occasional wavering the Iroquois kept faith thereafter with the English king until the Revolutionary War, when the Oneidas and Tuscaroras (who by then had been added to the Long House) chose sides with the Patriots. But on his return trip Andros took another step of equal importance in Iroquois relations by appointing a Board of Commissioners of Indian Affairs with headquarters in Albany, which thus became one of the strategic towns in colonial America.

To this board of commissioners the Iroquois could come with their needs, their wants, their complaints, and through it they could deal with governors of the other colonies. For secretary to the commissioners, Andros chose an ambitious young Scotchman who, though he had come to Albany only the winter before, was secretary to Rensselaerswyck and town clerk of Albany. In addition to holding these offices, Robert Livingston spoke Dutch fluently and within a year had learned a remarkable lot about the Indians and the Indian trade. He was soon to exhibit a rapacity for acquiring land and a ruthlessness in exploiting his tenants outstanding even for his time. (In later years there was a report that he had said that "he had rather be called knave Livingston, than poor Livingston.") But in public service he was conscientious and proved able and imaginative as Secretary for Indian Affairs. In 1700 after attending a conference at Onondaga castle he pointed out that instead of building a fort there as had been suggested, the English should build it on the south shore of Ontario at the mouth of the Oswego River. Though the suggestion was not acted on for nearly thirty years, Livingston was right in his judgment that this was the strategic point from which to control or at least inhibit French activities in the west.

He was perhaps the first to realize the futility of employing on the frontier troops disciplined in the rigid formations and formal maneuvers of European warfare. Instead he advocated using such troops for brief tours of garrison duty among the outposts and then settling them as farmers, a superior militia that would be halfway between the Canadian habitant and the *coureur de bois*.

He was to hold his position as secretary for forty-six years, except for a nine-year intermission after being suspended in 1696 by Governor Fletcher for political reasons and because of personal animosity. He continued to serve, however, without pay at the request of Fletcher's successor, the Earl of Bellomont. When he attended his last conference at Onondaga in 1721, he was sixty-seven years old.

He did as much as any man during the fourteen years before the outbreak of King William's War, and through that war and Queen Anne's, to hold the Iroquois in line and, as they phrased it, "keep bright the friendship chain." They remained faithful to their commitments to the government of New York in spite of all efforts the French made to woo them away, and though sorely tempted, they refused to sell land to William Penn, a proposal which both Governor Dongan and Livingston considered as full of dangerous implications as a change of Iroquois allegiance to the French.

Penn's colony came to him in return for a debt of sixteen thousand pounds owed his father by the Crown, a magnificent manifestation of the Stuart reluctance ever to part with hard money. But to Penn it came not as something owed him and for his profit but as the setting in which to implement a "holy experiment" that he felt under obligation to God to attempt. His charter called for a proprietary colony, though withholding from the proprietor the absolute powers that had been granted the Calverts in Maryland. In Pennsylvania laws had to win the approval of the Crown before they became valid, and the right of Parliament to levy taxes on the colony was specifically upheld. Within this charter Penn framed his government of a deputy governor, appointed by the proprietor, a council of seventy-two members with power to make laws and establish courts, and an assembly with power to approve or reject bills of the governor and council. In 1701 the legislative powers were passed to the assembly, more in line with his stated belief that "any government is free to the people under it (whatever be the frame) where the laws rule, and the people are a party to those laws, and more than this is tyranny, oligarchy, and confusion."

Penn's character was essentially humane. He believed in reforming criminals rather than executing them. In Pennsylvania only two crimes — murder and high treason — called for the death penalty: a contrast indeed to Massachusetts where fifteen crimes were punishable by death. Being a Quaker he believed that one's religious conviction was nobody's business but one's own; here, for the first time after Rhode Island's granting of it, complete freedom of conscience was guaranteed; but unlike Rhode Island, which was a small colony and dealing almost entirely with Protestant English, Pennsylvania became a colony of greatly diversified nationalities and sects.

For the educated William Penn brought a vision to America curiously like the one that had come to Pierre Esprit Radisson while exploring through the Illinois country a hundred and twenty years before. Penn wanted to create a sanctuary in the New World not only for Quakers but for all people, of whatever nationality or religious sect or liberal cast of thoughts, in which they could enjoy a free government exercised by themselves. The young, untutored *coureur de bois*, awed by a land "so delicious . . . so temperate . . . so plentiful of all things," had suddenly grasped what it would mean to the poor and oppressed of Europe. "What conquest would that be at little cost!" he had thought. Well, it would cost something, and Penn, who had money and did not seek to profit unduly himself, was willing to spend it. (To gain access to the sea he persuaded the Duke of York to lease to him for ten thousand years the three "lower counties" of Delaware, which then became a part of Pennsylvania, much to the Calverts' disgust, and remained so, though with its own legislature after 1704, until the Revolution.)

If he had his visions, Penn was also extremely practical in bringing them to reality, and he was especially effective in his promotion of his colony. Unlike Cecilius Calvert who ran his operation from London, Penn was on the ground in 1682, busying himself with laying out the city of Philadelphia and dealing personally with the Indians, toward whom he was always impeccably just. He had the gift of making himself popular with them and like Frontenac, who had been recalled to France in the spring of that year after ten years as governor of Canada, he was not above joining in their dances. His honest methods of treating with the Indians were not, however, followed by his successors.

In 1682 he published "An Account of the Province of Pennsylvania," a much less highly colored prospectus than was usual, and saw that it was circulated both in England and on the continent. He himself on a tour through Germany had invited people of all kinds and conditions to settle in Pennsylvania, and a wave of immigrants crossed the Atlantic greater than any to reach any other colony. Liberal terms for land-taking, the richness of the soil itself, the colony's mineral wealth, together shaped from the first a varied and rounded society; no other colony matured so rapidly. Within three years the population had climbed to well over seven thousand persons, only half of whom were from Great Britain. In 1683 the first Mennonites arrived, a full congregation. The mass migration of Palatine Germans would come after the turn of the century, most of them settling in the center of the colony; and still later a Scotch-Irish migration took up land beyond them. These were rough and hardy people from the north of Ireland where they had already had a taste of clearing land and fighting wild tribesmen not too far removed from the frontier experience which would presently befall them. They provided garrisons for the Pennsylvania outposts during the final French and Indian wars and from among them came the fur traders who began the penetration of the Ohio country and helped precipitate the final war.

Meanwhile Penn had become interested in developing the Susquehanna Valley and had begun to consider ways of diverting the fur trade from Albany and New York to a second Pennsylvania city he proposed to build somewhere on the river. By the terms of his charter his grant extended from the 40th parallel of latitude to the 43rd. The southern boundary brought him into instant argument with the Calverts, who were doubly incensed by the loss of Delaware which also lay within the geographic boundaries of *their* grant. But giving Penn land to the 43rd parallel was an even more egregious disregard of previous grants and patents, since it violated the terms of the royal grants to Connecticut and especially New York. For the 43rd parallel extended Penn's claim to include all of the Mohawk Valley and the Finger Lakes. Every one of the major Iroquois castles except Oneida fell within this territory.

Penn, however, did not try for his full claim but confined himself to the whole watershed of the Susquehanna, which was no mean bite of land after all. He appointed two men to treat with the Iroquois and authorized the expenditure of four hundred pounds in trade goods, a prize calculated to dazzle the haughtiest tribes, and as an extra precaution he bought the secretary of the New York Council. A great deal hinged on the attitude of New York's new governor, Thomas Dongan, who arrived late in August, 1683.

Dongan quickly grasped the ramifications and as quickly made up his mind that Penn must be forestalled. More than the previous Albany fur trade might hang in the balance, for the Iroquois were in the full tide of their war against the western tribes and the French outposts there: if they won, the whole North American fur trade, except for that to Hudson Bay, might be brought into New York or Pennsylvania, depending on whether Penn succeeded. Moreover, to a soldier like Dongan, seeing the developing frame of war to come, the idea of the Five Nations under the domination of the peace-loving Quakers was dismaying.

In their first approaches to the Iroquois, made in the Mohawk towns, Penn's two emissaries found the sachems highly receptive to the idea of shifting their trade to Pennsylvania. Especially for the western tribes it would be much easier to carry their furs down the Susquehanna, whose tributaries probed deep all through their territory, than via the long and roundabout portages to the Mohawk. The Albany traders were appalled when they heard this. They rushed messages of the direst warning to Dongan and meanwhile, acting on their own, halted all negotiation between Penn's agents and the sachems. The latter they appeased handsomely with gifts, and the Iroquois, old hands at trading between French and English interests, scented greater profits to come in this new rivalry between two English parties.

In September Dongan traveled to Albany, where he met a delegation of sachems for whom the Onondagas and Cayugas spoke. After long thought, they said, they had decided that they could not sell to Penn what they had already deeded to the Duke of York. It was a remarkable exhibition of integrity, but they did not go unrewarded since in his gratitude and relief Dongan saw to it that they were given lavish presents, which, combined with the bribes from the Albany magistrates and the much larger ones from Penn's agents, probably came near what would have been the purchase price.

Confining Iroquois–English relations to New York was vital to the successful defense of the English colonies. In the last and crucial war it would greatly simplify the problems confronting the Indian Commissioner, Sir William Johnson. The boundary between New York and Pennsylvania, however, remained unsettled till 1789, when it was fixed at the 42nd parallel.

The founding of Pennsylvania completed the chain of colonies from Virginia to New Hampshire that confronted the French when war began — New Hampshire had become a royal colony in 1679 and so at last safe from efforts by Massachusetts to annex it — but the brunt of the first war would be borne by New York, New Hampshire, and the Massachusetts outpost settlements in Maine. None of the colonies were in any sense ready for a war, and Massachusetts and New York were in political upheaval, the latter especially.

In 1681 Andros had been recalled to England to answer charges arising from his highhanded treatment of the Carterets in New Jersey as well as his permitting Massachusetts merchants to trade for furs on the Hudson. Still more unfortunate was his failure to renew the Duke of York's customs laws, whose three-year period expired in November 1680. The acting governor did not feel empowered to renew them, so the New York merchants happily declined to pay duties; whereupon the customs collector began impounding their goods. This led to a fine blow-up, with wild and indiscriminate charges and renewed demands for a representative assembly which would have power to levy taxes. Both New Jersey and Pennsylvania had assemblies; Connecticut and Massachusetts their General Courts; why should New York alone be discriminated against? Quite unexpectedly the Duke of York gave in. He appointed Colonel Dongan governor to succeed Andros and instructed him to issue writs for an election of representatives for an assembly. Dongan acted promptly after his arrival. Within two months, on October 17, the assembly sat for the first time, and it seemed that at last New York was on the threshold of representative government.

One of the assembly's first tasks was to draw up its own charter, which was sent to England for James's approval. What with regular business of lawmaking, a good many months had been consumed, and before James got round to signing the charter, Charles II died and James, Duke of York, became James II of England. He had previously indicated to Dongan that he would approve the Charter of Liberties and Privileges, as it was titled, and that if any alterations were made, "they will be such as shall be equally or more advantageous to the people there and better adjusted to the laws of England." But now rereading it through a monarch's eyes, he found it entirely too liberal and "did not think to confirm it," a traumatic decision for the people of New York.

It was not unreasonable, however, from James's point of view. He had received information of French plans to hem his English colonies in against the seaboard and greatly to expand operations in the west, and it seemed to him expedient to consolidate the New England colonies with those of New York and New Jersey in a Dominion of New England under a single governor. This post he assigned to Andros, who had been knighted during his stay in England.

Besides the obvious advantage of securing coordinated military action there were other benefits in this scheme. Charles II shortly before his death had at last succeeded in having the charter of contentious Massachusetts annulled. New York's milder Charter of Liberties and Privileges had also just been revoked. Plymouth had never had a charter. And it now seemed like an auspicious moment to take away the charters of Connecticut and Rhode Island as well by forcible seizure, thus getting the whole proposed Dominion on a sound basis of government — James had never seen the point of representative government in any case.

James could hardly have made a more unfortunate choice than Andros as Dominion governor, or viceroy as he was titled. Andros was honorable enough, but had proved himself overbearing in New Jersey and New York, where his only endearing side was furnished by a gentle, lovely wife. He had also managed to antagonize Connecticut by his attempt to seize Fort Saybrook, and Massachusetts by his actions against its fishermen at Pemaquid. Always blunt and usually tactless, his knighthood seemed to have made him even more highhanded, and from his arrival he thoroughly played up to his role of viceroy.

He imposed taxes arbitrarily, abolished the General Court, suspended habeas corpus, and ordered all Massachusetts records to be brought to Boston, which added to his convenience but put intolerable burdens on officials in small and remote towns. All land titles were declared invalid until a new search could be made, at a stiff fee. Quitrents were revived. All his measures seemed specifically designed to gall the New England character. Only in one instance was he frustrated.

In October of 1687 he journeyed to Hartford to seize Connecticut's charter under a writ of quo warranto. During an evening's discussion marked by considerable acrimony, the candles in the room in which the meeting was being held all simultaneously went out. When after some delay a light was secured the charter, which had been lying on a table, had mysteriously disappeared. Supposedly it was hidden in a large hollow oak tree, always afterward called the Charter Oak. But Andros got in the last word, anyway, by simply dissolving the General Court.

His next excursion was by frigate to Penobscot Bay in the spring of 1688. Here a venturesome Frenchman, Baron de St. Castin, had built a strong trading post. He had come to Canada as a captain in the Carignan regiment and drifted via Port Royal to the Penobscot country where he had obtained a huge tract of land. Having married the daughter of one of the Abenaki sachems, he was reputed to have much influence among them, and was said at this time to be offering two pounds of lead and one of powder to any Indian who would take the warpath against the English.

Andros did not destroy the post as he might justifiably have done, since it was on territory claimed by the English; nor did he make Castin a prisoner. But the stocks of trade goods were too much to resist and he appropriated them for later sale in Boston. Afterward he sailed back up the coast to Pemaquid where, at Fort James, he held a conference with the Abenaki, warning their sachems of the dangers of their connection with the French. In an effort to gain their good will and hoping that his example would lead them to release some of their English captives, he turned over several Abenaki being held prisoners at the fort. The Indians, however, reacted differently: they accepted their fellow tribesmen readily enough but once they had retired to their own villages they tortured several English and killed others. In August, Andros went to New York where he spent two months dealing with public affairs and installing a lieutenant governor. This was Colonel Francis Nicholson, whose fingers were going to be in all kinds of colonial pies during the next thirty years and who would also serve as lieutenant governor of Virginia and governor of Maryland and South Carolina. An arrogant man, though with considerable ability to charm others, he was almost as energetic as Andros, who now wedged a trip to Albany into his New York stay.

However he may have gone about some of his public business, Andros sometimes showed imagination in his administration, particularly in the town of New York. Besides putting the militia on a good footing, strengthening the fort, and building the first public market, he did much to beautify the town, among other things instituting systematic street cleaning. At the same time he had the tanneries moved beyond the municipal limits. Like Nicolls, he foresaw New York's future importance as an Atlantic port and did much to improve the harbor, particularly by building a new and substantial wharf. His first years in New York were probably his happiest in America.

In October he had returned to Boston. There news awaited him of Indian war in Maine. At first he made light of it and criticized the authorities in Boston for having sent troops, but as more news arrived their action was seen to have been entirely justified, and the picture became sinister. This was not merely a series of spontaneous Indian raids but war deliberately stirred up by the French. Ensign Pipon reported from Fort James at Pemaquid that "the French stand mightily upon the Penobscotts being in their precincts." Convinced at last that he had been wrong, Andros moved decisively and in midwinter sailed east with seven hundred men.

But as might have been expected, he was too late. The Indians had vanished into the wilderness, leaving behind them a desolated area along the

Kennebec after having killed or taken prisoners between one hundred and forty and two hundrd people. There was little Andros could do except to strengthen the garrisons remaining. He left five hundred men and officers and headed back for Boston.

Meanwhile in England James was running out his time. The barbarous series of executions after the failure of Monmouth's rebellion in 1685 had cast a pall over England. The people had become weary of the Stuart methods of ruling, of their subservience to Louis XIV, their Catholicism, their bland assumption of their divine right, and when on June 10, 1688, the birth of a son was announced, they gagged at the prospect of yet another generation of the same and invited Mary, James's Protestant daughter, and her husband, William of Orange, to share the throne and save England from further Catholic tyranny. William accepted largely for the purpose of bringing England into war against Louis XIV who in September 1688 had declared war on Austria. In November he landed in England with fourteen thousand soldiers. There was no opposition. James, unable to rally support, fled across the Channel. William and Mary were crowned in January 1689 and duly acknowledged the authority of Parliament, burying forever (as far as England was concerned) the Stuart bugaboo of divine right.

Word of these stirring events did not cross the Atlantic till spring. On April 4, 1689, a ship bearing the news put into Boston Harbor. For two weeks the town remained quiet; then on the eighteenth the townspeople rose, militia poured in from the country, Andros was seized and with some of his councilors put in jail. At a general meeting, presided over by Simon Bradstreet, the governor Andros had displaced, they reestablished the General Court and declared their old charter once more in force. The Dominion of New England was finished.

When word of events in Boston reached New York, Lieutenant Governor Nicholson summoned an informal council made up of city officials, militia officers, and the only three members of the council under the Dominion then on Manhattan — Frederick Philipse, Nicholas Bayard, and Stephen Van Cortlandt. The others were all out of the city, some in Maine, some upriver. Nicholson did not know just what his standing was, with Andros in jail and out of reach. So he sought advice from his informal council in charting New York's immediate course.

The great majority of citizens wanted to proclaim the new monarchs at once, but the three councilors demurred, advising Nicholson to uphold James II. The town was in a ferment. In addition news had come of a French declaration of war against England, disturbing news especially for the Huguenots who had been settling in increasing numbers and who felt that their presence would make New York a prime object for Louis XIV's attack. Nicholson mustered the militia to man the fort and sent a detachment to Coney Island to watch for French ships.

At this point a ship did arrive with a cargo of wine for a wine merchant named Jacob Leisler. Leisler, who was a strong supporter of William and Mary, refused to pay duty on his cargo, amounting to nearly one hundred pounds, because he said that since James II's flight from England no duly constituted government had existed in the port to receive it.

Leisler was of simple origin, but in thirty years he had become one of the most prosperous merchants in New York and through his marriage connected with the very highest society, most of whose members resented him. His impulses were generally good, though he sometimes seemed not to understand them himself. But he was not afraid of responsibility and when the opportunity came he took over command of the fort from Nicholson.

This was made possible by Nicholson's silly threat, while drunk, to burn New York. The threat became public news and the streets were suddenly in a turmoil. Leisler commanded a company of militia who, under their sergeant, marched on the fort. A disgruntled officer opened the gates to them, and shortly afterward Leisler appeared to take command of his men and consequently the fort they occupied. He then issued a declaration announcing an emergency, the lack of any legitimate government, and the need of proper defense, and proposed himself to hold the fort until King William should make his wishes known.

Nicholson left for England. Two weeks later a proclamation from William and Mary reached New York which enjoined all their subjects in each colony to continue under the officials appointed by James until further notice. The lieutenant governor was therefore to continue in office or, in his absence, whoever was for the time being in power was to take over the provincial government. Nicholson was nowhere mentioned by name. Logically the members of the council should therefore have been considered the persons in power, but obviously for the moment they were not and Leisler was. Relying on the ambiguous phrasing of the king's declaration, Leisler summoned a convention of delegates from New York and New Jersey who met at Fort James on June 22, proclaimed William King and Mary Queen of England, and appointed Jacob Leisler acting lieutenant governor and military commander of New York.

The run of citizens hailed these proceedings with enthusiasm; but the members of the council and the great patroons were furious over an upstart's usurpation of powers they considered rightfully their own. It was hardly an auspicious atmosphere in which to face the opening of war.

PART IV

The Marquis de Tracy's expedition against the Iroquois | Intendant Talon's services to Canada | St. Lusson's proclamation of French sovereignty at Sault Ste. Marie | The exploration of the Hudson Bay region by Albanel and St. Simon | The alternating French and English domination of the area | The importance of control of the Mississippi | The discovery of the Mississippi by Marquette and Joliet | Their exploration of the river to the mouth of the Arkansas | The return trip | Joliet's further career | Marquette's death | Duluth, the supreme coureur de bois *| La Salle's exploration of the Ohio River | Governor Frontenac's confrontation with the Iroquois sachems at Cataraqui | His measures to control the* coureurs de bois *| La Salle's seigneury | His royal license to "discover the Western part of New France" | Henri de Tonty | The succession of disasters to La Salle on his first expedition | His discovery of the mouth of the Mississippi on his second expedition | The difficult journey back | Governor La Barre's confiscation of La Salle's last property | The colonizing expedition to the mouth of the Mississippi | The sad history of the Metagorda Bay colony | The murder of La Salle | The friction between Frontenac and Duchesneau and their recall | La Barre's ineffectiveness in dealing with the Iroquois menace | Governor Denonville's exchanges with Governor Dongan over English encroachment on the Great Lakes | The unprofitable attack on the Senecas | Dongan's spurring of the Iroquois to side with the English | The Iroquois massacre of the French at Lachine | Frontenac's return to Canada with instructions to capture New York*

TRACY, Louis XIV's viceroy and lieutenant general in New France, was sixty-three when he set out from Quebec on September 14, 1666, for the rendezvous at Fort Ste. Anne at which his army would muster for the march against the Iroquois. All Quebec gathered to see him leave, fervent with admiration. It was "the day of the Exaltation and triumph of the Cross, for the glory of which," according to Father Le Mercier, "the expedition was undertaken." Others, less religious, must have prayed for a successful outcome from less lofty motives. But for even the lowest the spectacle of the tall and portly old officer leading some four hundred habitants and gentleman volunteers to the waterside was one of profound emotion.

The muster date at Fort Ste. Anne had been set for September 28. Six hundred picked officers and men from the Carignan regiment, six hundred habitants of whom slightly more than one hundred were woodsmen from Montreal, and one hundred Algonquins and Hurons made up the army of thirteen hundred. With them they carried full military equipment, including two small cannon to batter down the gates of the Mohawk palisades and all twenty of the regimental drums. To take them across the water sections of the route they had three hundred boats, "a part of which were very light boats, and the rest canoes of bark, each of which carried at most, five or six persons." Collecting this flotilla, as well as assembling the military stores and rations, had been the work of the intendant, Talon, an extraordinary feat in that poor country and a mark of his quiet and devoted efficiency which all of Canada soon began to take for granted.

The expedition did not start out in a single body as had been Tracy's plan. Some of the troops were late in reaching the rendezvous, and after a day or two Courcelles, compulsively impatient as always, persuaded Tracy to let him go ahead with four hundred men as an advance guard. Tracy himself with the main body launched his boats on October 3, and four days later the rear guard followed under Captain de Chambly of the Carignan regiment and the Sieur de Barthier.

So, in three parts, the long procession, oars and paddles stitching seams across the water, made its way southward to that point which is properly the head of Champlain and was to be called Ticonderoga. Autumn was at its peak, and nowhere in America do the woods become more spectacularly vivid than along the western shore of Lake Champlain. Then as now the beginnings of the Adirondacks, rising steeply, in some places almost from the water's edge, were covered by a mixed forest of oak and maple, birch and beech and ash, in all their shades of scarlet, crimson, yellow, orange, russet, rusty brown, and winy purple, interspersed with dark and towering pines and hemlock, while along the shore ranks of sumac lifted their candles like the blood-tipped spears of marching men. In the late afternoon, just before the sun passed the mountains and its rays conformed to the slope of the hills, the color was intensified to the point of flame and on a day of stillness the passing boats and canoes floated on a carpet of incredible reflections. The old marquis must have looked on this with wonder — such beauty amounted to an omen; but if he did not, it was because fate had chosen this moment to afflict him with the gout.

Ticonderoga comes from a Mohawk word meaning "noisy," no doubt in reference to the small cataract that ends the rapids in the outlet of Lake George. Here the French disembarked and set about carrying their canoes and boats over the portage path which cut straight across the curve of the rapids on the eastern side. A mile and a half ahead it rejoined the outlet at open water. The woods were dense, the trail uphill, but in spite of his pain, Tracy stumped manfully along and in due course saw his flotilla assembled at the upper landing. A mile of rowing up the outlet and thirty-six more on Lake George brought them to its southern end. From there about a hundred miles remained to be traversed before they would come out at the Mohawk towns.

Every man, including the officers, carried his full share of arms and provisions. It was an arduous march, made more so by the problems presented by the two cannon and the two commanders. Small as the cannon were, wrestling them along a hundred miles of Indian trails, over logs and rocks, across streams and bogs, took tremendous effort, and shortly the work was assigned to alternating teams of men. And for a way, and across all streams, it was necessary to carry Courcelles as well as Tracy, for he had been seized by what Talon afterward described as "a contraction of the nerves" that for a time made him quite helpless.

Yet they made surprisingly good time. They followed the same route as Courcelles had on his bitter expedition the previous winter, nearly due south from Lake George to the Hudson at Glens Falls, then west of south, passing Saratoga Lake on the west and then Ballston Lake, to the fork at Fish Creek. Here it was that without guides Courcelles had chosen the left and wrong branch that brought him out at Schenectady and almost certainly saved his life and the lives of his company who survived with him the march home through the snow and cold; but now the French with Indians guiding them took the right-hand trail and so, late on October 14, found themselves in the valley of the Mohawks near the site of present Amsterdam. They had eight or ten miles yet to go to reach the first of the

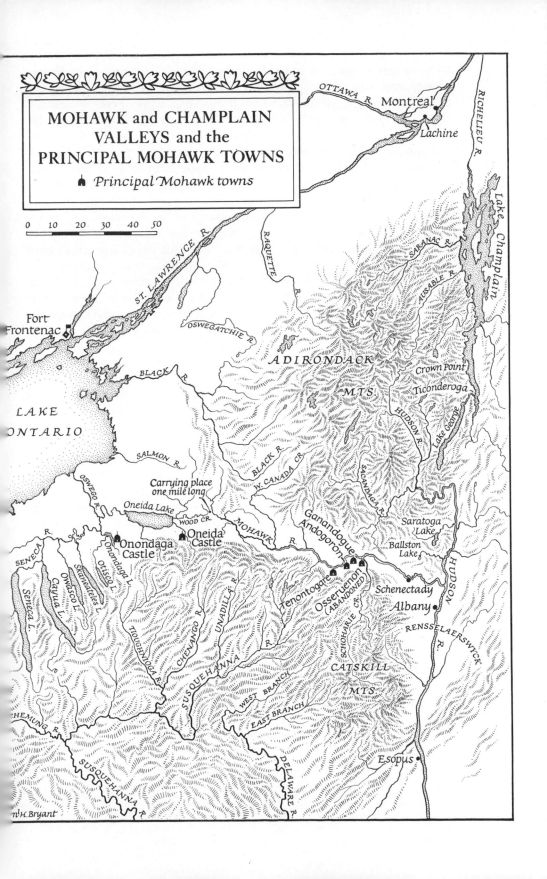

MOHAWK and CHAMPLAIN
VALLEYS and the
PRINCIPAL MOHAWK TOWNS

♦ Principal Mohawk towns

0   10   20   30   40   50

OTTAWA R. Montreal
Lachine
RICHELIEU R.

ST. LAWRENCE R.
RAQUETTE R.
SARANAC R.
AUSABLE R.
Lake Champlain

Fort Frontenac
OSWEGATCHIE R.
ADIRONDACK
MTS.
Crown Point
Ticonderoga

BLACK R.
HUDSON R.
Lake George

LAKE ONTARIO

SALMON R.
W. CANADA CR.
BLACK R.
SACANDAGA R.
Saratoga Lake

OSWEGO R.
Carrying place one mile long
Oneida Lake
WOOD CR.
MOHAWK R.
Ganandogue Andogoron
Ballston Lake

SENECA R.
Onondaga L.
Oneida Castle
Onondaga Castle
Otisco L.
Skaneatles L.
Owasco L.
Cayua L.
Seneca L.

TIOUGHNIOGA R.
CHENANGO R.
UNADILLA R.
Tenontogare
Osseruenon (ABANDONED)
SCHOHARIE CR.
Schenectady
Albany
HUDSON R.
RENSSELAERSWICK

CHEMUNG R.
SUSQUEHANNA R.
WEST BRANCH
EAST BRANCH
CATSKILL
MTS.

DELAWARE R.
Esopus

n¹H. Bryant

Mohawk towns; the river had to be forded; they were short of rations, exhausted, and soaked through from a rainstorm that had begun during the afternoon; but no one hesitated or complained when Tracy ordered a night march. By moving up at night he hoped to take the Mohawks by surprise at daybreak.

The only ford was six miles upstream; the march to it through the howling storm and darkness was nightmarish, maddening, and infinitely slow; fording the river was even more difficult. How they got their cannon over is a mystery — carrying the massive Tracy over would seem problem enough — but Le Mercier testifies that they did, in his *Relation* of 1665–1666, for the cannon were "taken to the very last villages of the Iroquois, in order the more easily to reduce their fortifications." Ironically, they never fired a shot.

Tracy's guides had done well for his army. They brought them to the far edge of the strip of woodland west of the Auries Kill at dawn, and as the French stepped from the trees they saw through the river mists the dim shape of the palisade before them, standing well up the slope of a low hill with the cornfields at its feet. After the long, merciless days of marching and the stealthy approach through the last woods their nerves were at an impossible stretch. The two cannon they knew to be laboring far behind with the rear guard, but they could no longer wait for them. Perhaps a stick tapped a drumhead and set the other drummers afire, for suddenly all twenty roared the charge and the army broke pell-mell from the edge of the woods and raced across the open as though to batter down the palisade by sheer fury. But no musket fire came from the firing platforms, no war whoop sounded; the town was empty, as silent as death.

The French should have realized that it was impossible to move an army of that size into Indian territory without its being seen. Mohawk scouts had picked it up before it was well away from Lake George; and during the days of marching, relays of scouts kept coming into the three main castles with reports of its size, of the fact that it was led by the two principal French chiefs, of the cannon. The impact of these details, and the army's relentless approach together with the fact that so large a force had never entered their country before, increasingly daunted the waiting warriors. Two days before, they had evacuated the women, children, and the old people; they had stayed behind upon the palisades through the stormy night with mounting apprehension. When in the first gray mists of daybreak they heard the thunder of the drums below, panic clutched them and, as the French charged up the sloping ground in front, they fled from the rear gate to disappear in the woods on the path to the next castle.

The town now entered by the French was not Osseruenon, where Isaac Jogues had met his martyrdom and Francesco Bressani undergone the greater part of his six weeks of unremitting torture. Osseruenon had been abandoned several years before, following an epidemic of smallpox, and the people had built this new one, called Gandawague, on the other side of the Auries Kill. But it was not an empty town that the French wanted. Like Courcelles and Tracy, the men were hot to pursue the vanished warriors and took up the march to the next town, Andagoron, three miles to the west.

But Andagoron, like Gandawague, had been evacuated, and the French again resumed their march up the valley. They found two very much smaller villages which like the two castles had been deserted, but like them overflowing with corn and all kinds of dried fruits and vegetables against the winter. At the second village at which the troops stopped to eat a meal from the plundered caches, Tracy supposed that there was nothing more for him to do beyond putting all four towns to the torch. But an Algonquin woman, who like some others had followed her husband to the war, came forward to tell Tracy that she had been a captive of the Mohawks and knew from having been in it that their third and principal castle lay still farther up the valley. It was, she told the marquis, named Tenontogare and had by far the heaviest fortifications.

Her news reheated the old man's blood; he cast off the fact that he and his men had now been uninterruptedly marching for over thirty-six hours; he had come to kill Mohawks and he would. The army marched again as the sun began to set, and it was dark when they prepared to attack the town. They could see the light of a great fire burning inside and they felt confident that at last they would find the Mohawks there in force to defend it, so the officers took care to martial their troops "in regular form," and with the drums beating they began a slow advance.

As they came close enough to see the town clearly, the French were impressed by its solidity. The triple palisade was square in form, with a bastion at each corner, and twenty feet high. It had none of the ragged haphazardness of the older Iroquois and Huron palisades. This looked as though it had been laid out by an engineer and built by artisans. But once again the Mohawk warriors had retired, and the French entered entirely unopposed.

It was obvious, however, that the Mohawks had planned to fight. There were large bark kettles filled with water on the firing platforms and an enormous stock of provisions. There were also the mutilated bodies of Indian captives whom they had been torturing through the day to appease Areskoui, the war god, and nerve themselves to battle. The only living people were a few women too old to be evacuated and an ancient man so terrified that he had hidden himself under a canoe. From these, the French learned that the warriors had indeed resolved on making a stand, but as had happened in the other castles, the waiting hours, even though spiced with torture, and the final terrifying roll of the regimental drums had been too much. At the last moment they had gone after their women and children.

The houses in Tenontogare were superior to those in the other towns. The French were surprised to find many of them solid frame buildings with stout plank walls, though they kept to the plan of the old bark long house. Some were over one hundred feet long, with places for eight family fires.

Since the Mohawks were not there, nothing remained for the troops to do except to burn it. But first they gathered provisions from the Indian stocks to see them through their return journey and "after erecting the Cross, saying Mass, and chanting the *Te Deum* on that spot," they formed on parade while an officer, sword in hand, came forward and proclaimed that he took possession of Tenontogare and "all the country of the Mohawks in the name of the King." Then they set it afire and watched it burn.

The Mohawks from their hiding places watched it, too, knowing that all their winter's food was being destroyed, but they made no effort to attack. They were seized by the same despair that had sometimes made the Hurons helpless before an Iroquois onslaught. In the morning nothing but ashes remained of Tenontogare and the French marched down the valley, burning the other towns as they came to them and leaving, when they had gone, the entire Mohawk nation confronting a winter without shelter and destitute of food.

> . . . As a result [wrote Father Le Mercier], those familiar with these Barbarians' mode of life have not a doubt that almost as many will die of hunger as would have perished by the weapons of our soldiers, had they dared await the latter's approach; and that all who remain will be forced by fear to accept such conditions of peace, and observe such a demeanor, as would have been secured from them with greater difficulty by more sanguinary victories.

The return journey presented difficulties, for the storms had raised the rivers, some by as much as eight feet, and Lake Champlain was stormy too, and they lost two canoes with eight or nine men. But by the fifth of November Tracy was safe home, disappointed by not having been able to do battle, but confident, like Le Mercier, that a lot of Mohawks were going to die. Talon was filled with admiration for the old nobleman's performance: "Mr. de Tracy's advanced age must greatly enhance the merit of the service he has rendered the King, by undertaking, in a broken frame like his, a fatigue of which no correct idea can be formed. I am assured that throughout the entire march . . . including the return, he suffered himself to be carried only two days; and then he was forced to do so by gout." Talon admired him further because, like himself, Tracy was a modest man.

He remained in Canada only nine months more, and after he sailed for France in August 1667 a little of the glitter that had lifted the spirits of the people of Quebec went with him. As Le Mercier recorded, "he went away from us bearing the universal regret of all these peoples," but everyone knew that Tracy had accomplished the task which the king had specifically sent him to do. Though he had killed no Mohawks, if we except the chief, Agariata, who had boasted over the wine of killing the young Sieur de Chasy, he had thoroughly cowed the Iroquois, and Canada would enjoy a peace that, except for minor incidents, would endure for the next twenty years. "The people saw that they could spread abroad, and could till their lands in perfect quiet and great safety."

The colony was left under the supervision of three men: of course the bishop, Laval; Courcelles, the governor; and the intendant, Talon. Of the three it was Talon who made the greatest material impression on Canada and gave it a base so firm that even after the English conquest the Province of Quebec would remain more solidly French than France itself.

"The first thoughts of Monsieur Talon . . . were to exert himself with tireless activity to seek out the means for rendering this country prosperous." Again it is Le Mercier, and he goes on to list some of the areas in which the intendant spent his energies. He had a remarkable mind, able to cut at once to the heart of a problem, yet capable of dealing with it in the most minute detail, and through his five years of service between 1665 and 1672 (from 1668 to 1670 he was in France), while he labored to find ways of increasing the prosperity of Canada as he found it, he worked toward a vision of New France embracing the continental west and northwest.

From the beginning he saw that the key to both was population, and hardly a report to Louis XIV or Colbert left his desk without some reference to it. He wanted men, artisans, and engineers; he wanted women; he wanted people of superior quality, not necessarily gentility, but able people whether they were farmers or of a profession. He wanted the young women sent out to make wives for the colonists, the *filles du roi*, to be healthy and good-looking, familiar with outdoor work and not afraid to undertake it, or at least, as he said, able to cook for themselves and their husbands. To a surprising degree, Talon got what he was after, as far as quality was concerned — the *filles du roi* fell under a category of colonial supply Louis would naturally interest himself in — but he never got them in the numbers he wanted: men enough to force the English out of strategic New York and to hold and develop the great land west of the Appalachian Mountains. He did make some impression, however, for in April 1672 Louis directed that an annual census be taken. That was just four months before Talon left Canada for the last time. Immigrants continued to enter Canada, but at a very slow rate, for the king begrudged sending men on a colonial venture when they might be put to better use in his European armies.

If Talon could not materially increase the number of immigrants from France, he was heartened at home by the decision of more than four hundred men of the Carignan regiment to remain in Canada when the regiment was mustered out. These men were a fiber of strength in the uncertain colony and did much to ease Talon's efforts to infuse energy and hope into the life of the colony. Even the four companies left in garrison on the Richelieu did much to open up that valley by clearing the forest around the forts and planting fields and gardens.

In his campaign to make the people more self-sufficient and prosperous Talon focused his and their attention equally on agriculture and manufactures. The years of constriction caused by the Iroquois menace had left Canadians with a certain listlessness which needed stirring up. Good farming practices, he believed, could be more easily made popular by example than by any amount of persuasion, so he bought himself a tract of land near Quebec of which only two arpents had been cleared; and by November 1670 he was able to report to Colbert, with some of the complacence of a typical gentleman farmer, "I have had it cultivated and improved in such a manner that I can say it is the most considerable in the country."

He introduced the culture of hemp. He encouraged farmers to raise more sheep and noted for Colbert's benefit how the climate of Canada seemed to promote fecundity in sheep as it did in women. "Even French ewes commonly bear two lambs after their first year's growth in this country." He hoped in a few years to have the habitants produce their own cloth. Another agricultural project was the building of three model villages, somewhat resembling those of New England, with the houses close together for defense, and the fields surrounding them.

He built a ship to show people that one could be built in Canada, and then he used it in an attempt to open trade with the West Indies, loading it with salt salmon and dried codfish, and fish oils, eels, peas — "both green and white" — staves, and boards. He built flour mills and a brewery, which even the Jesuits approved of in the belief that it would cut down drunkenness. Talon hoped it would also cut down the importation of wines, which were far too expensive for Canada's poor society; he calculated that a hundred thousand livres a year was being spent on brandy and wine. In addition to these government-initiated industries he encouraged individuals to start manufactures of their own for the making of items such as soap and hats and shoes.

In all these activities he displayed a sensitive and personal interest in the people themselves. His commission had instructed him on the value, in maintaining the people's allegiance to the king, of personal visits to all the settlements. He spent much time in a literal performance of "entering into the details of the households and of all their little affairs," as Louis had phrased it. The Sulpician priest, Dollier de Casson, wrote that Talon, on a visit to Montreal, "made the entire circuit of the island, house by house, in order to see if all, down to the very poorest, were being treated with justice and equity, and to discover for himself whether there were not some whose necessities demanded a share of his alms and liberality." In all these interests and visits he became quickly aware of the injurious effect of the colony's subjection to the Company of the West Indies monopoly. In 1666 he persuaded the king to compel the Company to relinquish the fur monopoly, receiving in exchange a duty on all furs sold by the habitants. But still more damaging was the over-all monopoly controlling prices on all imports. He had ceased to be intendant when the proprietorship of the Company was finally revoked in 1674 and Canada became a colony under the Crown, but it was principally due to his representations that the change took place.

Besides these duties he also had the responsibility of supplying the forts and military outposts. In his first year he procured the building of one hundred and fifty-two bateaux, each capable of carrying fifteen soldiers and their equipment plus a load of supplies. Three or four of these together represented firepower enough to make hostile Indians hesitant about attacking. Supplying the forts alone was a heavy undertaking, costing more than twelve thousand livres a year.

Another of his responsibilities was the discovery of mineral resources. He sent engineers to investigate reports of iron at Baie St. Paul and St. Maurice. The iron was found, though it was some years before it could be profitably mined. Elaborate stories were also circulating about a great deposit of copper on the northwestern shore of Lake Superior. Supposedly the lode was open to the air so that the far Indian tribes periodically went there to hack off bits for their copper ornaments. It was all made to sound so circumstantial that Talon decided this too should be investigated. Casting about for a reliable man to send, he lighted on a twenty-four-year-old graduate of the Jesuit college in Quebec named Louis Joliet. From college Joliet had gone on to the seminary in preparation for the priesthood, but in 1667 he abandoned these plans and never returned to the ecclesiastical life. His education, combined with his love of the wilderness, recommended him to Talon and in 1669, under the intendant's orders, he and another Frenchman, Jean Péré, with Ottawa paddlers left Montreal.

They found no copper, but the Iroquois peace lured Joliet into returning by Huron and Erie, instead of taking the old route down the Ottawa which they had ascended on their way out. He was presumably, therefore, the first white man to pass through the Strait of Detroit. As they neared the eastern end of Erie the old visceral fear of the Iroquois assailed his Indian guides. The Niagara carry would take them right into Seneca territory, and they balked at going further in that direction. Instead, they took Joliet and Péré up the Grand River, from which another carry led down to the head of Lake Ontario. On the carry they encountered another party of Frenchmen: two Sulpician priests from Montreal, Dollier de Casson and René de Galinée, and a young man two years older than Joliet, Robert Cavelier, Sieur de La Salle.

It was a strange and fortuitous meeting of two of the greatest French explorers of the continent at the outset of their careers. How much they came to know of each other is not known. Joliet was Canadian by birth; La Salle had been born in Rouen, but he, too, had for a while studied with the Jesuits before breaking away and coming to New France. It is a bright, firm moment in La Salle's start as an explorer for, after the meeting, his movements for the next year are hidden in a haze of speculation. But it is not necessary to attempt to follow him here, only to let Joliet finish his journey and report its failure to Talon.

In September 1668, Talon had returned to France, confident that he would not see Canada again. He had begged Colbert to limit his service to two years for, to a civil servant such as an intendant, service abroad meant loss of place on the ladder of promotion, and both Louis and Colbert had assured him that they would ask no more of him. But after he had been little more than a year in France, it became apparent that his services were indispensable to Canada and he was assigned for another term.

He was himself partly to blame. His enthusiasm for Canada and his exposition of the monstrous debilitation produced by the monopoly induced Colbert to believe that the time had come to end the proprietary and bring Canada directly into France's colonial empire, the first step toward which would be claiming the vast interior continent for France and then endeavoring to make the claim stick. But one could not lay claim to something wholly undefined. From the Indians the French knew that a great river (the Mississippi) flowed through the country beyond the Great Lakes, but the notion persisted that it must flow into the Vermilion Sea (the Gulf of California) which would mean a water route to the Pacific; and once the Pacific had been reached it was thought that "not more than fifteen hundred leagues of Navigation" remained to reach the shore of China. The course of the Mississippi was the great question that must be answered before the French would have a clue to the land they were reaching out to grasp. Radisson and Groseilliers had been on its upper waters, but that established nothing except that a great river did exist.

After Talon's return, which involved near shipwreck in the St. Lawrence — his ship was stranded on a rock from which, according to Le Mercier, "it could not be taken off except through an extraordinary succor from Heaven, procured for it by Ste. Anne" — he began making his moves to secure and explore the heart of the continent. In 1670 he sent the Sieur de St. Lusson to proclaim the sovereignty of Louis XIV over all the west and northwest of America and the tribes that lived therein. St. Lusson's party was a small one (Talon was always economical in mounting expeditions of exploration, and St. Lusson was supposed to finance his by some trading) but he had the services of Nicholas Perrot than whom no *voyageur* had greater influence with the Indians. In addition, St. Lusson was to make another search for the copper mine on Lake Superior which Joliet had failed to find. But the proclamation of French sovereignty was the essential function of his mission.

The site chosen for the ceremony was the Mission of Ste. Marie, beside the Sault, the gigantic flume through which pours the overflow from Lake Superior. St. Lusson moved leisurely and spent the winter on Manitoulin Island in Lake Huron. Early in May he covered the relatively short remaining distance to Sault Ste. Marie and set about gathering the tribes. This was the work of Perrot. Fourteen nations responded and some which did not attend were represented by another nation as their proxy. Some came from as far as three hundred miles, and the areas they ranged in hunting and war reached even farther: besides the near-by tribes like the Ottawas and of course the Saulteurs, whose bark lodges stood near the foot of the roaring Sault, there were Chippewas from south of Lake Superior, Assiniboins from Winnipeg, Crees who ranged north from Lake Superior to the shores of Hudson Bay, Illinois from the country Radisson had fallen in love with, Nipissings, Pottawatomies from above Green Bay who acted also as proxy for the Miamis, and from beyond them representatives of the Fox Nation, Mascoutens, and remnants of the Hurons. By the fourth of June all those who agreed to come had assembled at the Sault.

To impress them St. Lusson had to compete with the great facts of geography and nature which make the Sault one of the awesome corners of the globe. The vast and boiling flume of the Sault itself (then delivering the full discharge of Superior instead of, as now, when it is impressive enough, one quarter that amount), the illimitable wilderness, the close presence of the three Great Lakes, articulated here before them, reduced the lodges of the Saulteurs and the mission — house and chapel surrounded by a palisade — to insignificance, ephemeral as the cold air perpetually stirred by the rush of water.

Near the Saulteur village and overlooking it and the mission together was a low hill on top of which St. Lusson had elected to hold his ceremony, and on the morning of the fourth the thronging Indians gathered at the foot of it. Their curiosity had been captured, they were intent, excited, and, inevitably, awed and frightened, for this was not a conference as they knew it but an assertion of French power, which only recently had crushed the Mohawks and cowed all the Iroquois.

As they waited, crouching, standing, or moving restlessly about in little groups, the gate of the mission palisade swung open and the French came through, marching in a thin procession behind the white and gold flag of France. They came slowly, St. Lusson in his courtier's clothes, his fourteen

[415]

followers all fully armed; Claude Dablon, the Superior of the Lakes Missions, and three of the four Jesuits who served them, Gabriel Druillettes, Louis André, and Claude Allouez — only Jacques Marquette was absent — in their black habits; perhaps a dozen *coureurs de bois*. Chanting, they came toward the Indians, who parted to give them passage, and walked slowly up the hill. Near the top a large cross lay, and after Dablon had blessed it with all the ceremonies of the church, it was raised and planted in a hole previously made to receive it, while the French bared their heads and, led by the four Fathers, sang the "Vexilla Regis."

Then a cedar pole, on which was fastened a metal plate bearing the royal arms, was raised just behind and slightly higher than the cross, and the French sang the "Exaudiat," and a prayer was said for the person of the king. In the pause that followed, St. Lusson stepped forward, sword drawn, and in his free hand holding a clod of soil, proclaimed this place and all regions surrounding to belong to France:

> "In the name of the Most High, Mighty, and Redoubted Monarch, Louis the Fourteenth of that name, Most Christian King of France and Navarre, I take possession of this place, Ste. Marie of the Sault, as also of Lakes Huron and Superior, the Island of Manitoulin, and all countries, rivers, lakes, and streams contiguous and adjacent thereunto: both those which have been discovered and those which may be discovered hereafter, in all their length and breadth, bounded on the one side by the seas of the North and of the West, and on the other by the South Sea: Declaring to the nations thereof that from this time forth they are vassals of his Majesty, bound to obey his laws and follow his customs: promising them on his part all succor and protection against the incursions and invasions of their enemies . . ."

And warning off all other possible trespassers, from potentates to republics, on "pain of incurring his resentment and the effort of his arms," he raised his sword in peroration and in a high-pitched voice shouted, "*Vive le Roi!*" At which the other Frenchmen echoed, "*Vive le Roi!*" and fired a volley from their muskets.

To all this high-flown rhetoric the Indians had been listening, as Perrot interpreted for them St. Lusson's words, with occasional sibilant murmurs that might or might not have been approval; but now with the musket fire, and excited by they knew not what, they joined their wild yells to the celebration. Without doubt they considered this French performance a success, but now it was thought necessary to drive home to them some conception of the glory of this Monarch of France who had assumed responsibility for them and accepted their allegiance, and for this task they had chosen Allouez.

Claude Allouez needed no interpreter. He had labored among the Ottawas, Pottawatomies, Illinois, Miamis, Mascoutens, and the Nipissings who had retired to Lake Nipigon, and was freely conversant with all their languages and those of other tribes with whom he had journeyed or visited. Like many other Jesuit missionaries, he totally disregarded his body in the demands he put on it. He would paddle for fifteen hours a day, day after day, to reach a distant tribe. But unlike many of the others, he had a body that seemed corded of iron. He had come to the western tribes in 1665, so he had now, at the age of forty-nine, been six years in the country, and his mission labors there would continue without interruption for eighteen years more until his death in 1689. At that date it was said he had instructed more than a hundred thousand Indians and baptized ten thousand. He was a man of extraordinary force, heedless of danger, one might almost say an adventurer of the Cross; and there are times when his conversions seem almost like conquests, which would not be far wrong for, as a man, he had captured the affection of many Indians.

Now he addressed the throng at the Sault, looking down at them from where he stood beside the cross, and asking them to look at it: "Cast your eyes upon the Cross raised so high above your heads: there it was that JESUS CHRIST, the Son of God, making himself man for the love of men, was pleased to be fastened and to die, in atonement to his Eternal Father for our sins. He is the master of our lives, of Heaven, of Earth, and of Hell. Of him I have always spoken to you . . .

"But," he continued, "look likewise at that other post, to which are affixed the armorial bearings of the great captain of France whom we call King." All captains were as nothing compared to him. He had not his equal in the world. He was like a great tree, and others "like little plants that we tread under foot in walking." He reminded them of Onontio in Quebec who had the power to bring down the Iroquois. In France the king had ten thousand others like him, who are no more than soldiers to him:

. . . When he says, "I am going to war" all obey him; and those ten thousand Captains raise Companies of a hundred soldiers each on sea and on land. Some embark in ships, one or two hundred in number, like those that you have seen at Quebec. Your canoes hold only four or five men — or, at very most, ten or twelve. Our ships in France hold four or five hundred, and even as many as a thousand. Other men make war by land, but in such vast numbers that, if drawn up in a double file, they would extend farther than from here to Mississaquenk, although the distance exceeds twenty leagues. When he attacks, he is more terrible than the thunder: the earth trembles, the air and sea are set on fire by the discharge of his Cannon; while he has been seen amid his squadrons, all covered with the blood of his foes, of whom he had slain so many with his sword that he does not count their scalps, but the rivers of blood which he sets flowing . . .

From this description of casual Armageddon, Allouez passed to catalogue the riches of the king. He had more towns than all the Indians —

men, women, and children — in a radius of five hundred leagues from the Sault; and in each town he had warehouses each of which held enough hatchets to cut down all their forests and enough kettles to cook all their moose. "The Father added much more of this sort," Dablon recorded with admiration, "which was received with wonder by those people, who were all astonished to hear that there was any man on earth so great, rich and powerful."

Astonished they no doubt were, but there must have been a lurking bit of skepticism in their Algonquin minds as they reflected that what Allouez said might possibly be true, but of all these hosts all they could see here at Ste. Marie was a force of barely thirty Frenchmen, four of whom were priests. They were too polite, at a ceremony of this sort, to raise embarrassing questions and when at the close of Allouez's harangue St. Lusson requested their chiefs to bear witness by signing a document, they were quite willing to oblige and laboriously and gravely made their hieroglyphs or simple marks upon the paper. It had after all been a stimulating and exciting interruption of the routine of fishing, hunting, and planting corn; and that evening it was concluded by a splendid bonfire round which they joined the French in singing the "Te Deum" — "to thank God, on behalf of those poor peoples, that they were now the subjects of so great and powerful a monarch."

Whatever they thought, those who had attended remembered the day as a novel and impressive event, and it unquestionably was a factor in aiding Perrot, Duluth, and La Salle in forming the alliance of the far tribes that would hold off the Iroquois and play an important role in the French struggle with the English. Yet the night after St. Lusson resumed his journey the armorial bearings disappeared from their cedar pole, so though the French might now possess the midland of the continent and its still vaster northwest, the Indians had the coat of arms of the king.

The sea to the North of us is the famous bay to which Hutson gave his name; it had long been stirring our Frenchmen's curiosity to discover it by land, and learn its situation with reference to ourselves, its distance, and what tribes dwell on its shores. The wish to gain a knowledge of this sea had increased since we learned through our Savages that very recently some ships made their appearance there, and even opened a trade with those Nations, who have always been represented to us as populous, and rich in peltries.

Thus Claude Dablon, recently appointed Superior of the Jesuits' Canadian Mission, introduced the account Charles Albanel wrote of the journey he made with Paul Denis St. Simon, an officer of Talon's, overland to Hudson Bay in 1671–1672.

The news brought by the Indians was indeed disturbing, for it indicated that the English might be about to do to the French the very thing that Colbert and Talon planned to do to the English colonies: encircle them on the north, northwest, and west. Nothing was known of the country that intervened between the St. Lawrence and Hudson Bay except the nebulous tales related by Montagnais hunters when they brought their furs to Tadoussac every spring. To Talon and New France it had become vitally important to know what the country was really like and above all to learn if there was a feasible land route over which the French could send forces strong enough to fend off the trading English. Therefore he appointed St. Simon to lead the expedition and asked the Jesuits to name one of their Order to make the trip with him, for it was unthinkable to make any exploration without the Cross.

The Jesuits chose Albanel because, since his arrival in Canada in 1649, he had served mainly with the Tadoussac mission, from where he had made numerous trips inland with the Montagnais, spending at least four winters among them in the woods. The journey he and St. Simon now undertook proved to be one of the most strenuous and in some ways frustrating in the annals of French exploration in America. Albanel himself left Quebec on the sixth of August for Tadoussac in order to find a guide. St. Simon was to meet him there with one *coureur de bois*, unnamed, in a few days.

At Tadoussac, Albanel found that the chief of the Montagnais, on whom he had been counting to be their guide, had recently died. The tribe was upset and became even more so when he spoke of his coming journey: they were vehement in opposing the idea, possibly from genuine apprehension for his safety, for the Montagnais were extremely superstitious, but more likely from fears that the French, tapping the northern tribes directly, would undercut their own role as middlemen. Albanel could make no impression till the dead chief's uncle, now chief himself, came to his aid, declaring that his young men had no sense and that it was an honor to accompany a missionary. Since he could not go in person, because of his new responsibility, he appointed three relatives to guide the French: two brothers-in-law and a nephew. So there was no delay when St. Simon and the *coureur de bois* paddled in from Quebec.

Their route took them up the Saguenay on which, after fifty miles, they met two Indian canoes coming down. In one of them was a man who said he had been over the land route to Hudson Bay, and after much persuasion he reluctantly agreed to join the expedition. All this took time, as persuasion always did when Indian fear of the country had to be overcome; and his reluctance seemed to be borne out when a powerful head wind joined the Saguenay's fierce current in preventing headway except by the most laborious paddling. But on the twenty-sixth they reached Chicoutimi, where there was a Montagnais town and they were welcomed warmly for Albanel's sake.

They had to stay two days in order that Albanel might hear the confessions of his former converts and administer Communion, but to make up for it the Indians carried their canoes and packs for them over a portage of more than four miles, crossing a small mountain and a valley, to get to navigable water on the Chicoutimi River, the lower reaches of which, falling to the Saguenay, were totally impassable. This was the traditional route: by paddling up the Chicoutimi, they came to a portage that brought them to a lake the Indians called Kinougami (now Little Lake), and easy paddling over it took them to the Belle Rivière, which emptied into Lake St. John, on whose sandy beach they camped on the night of September 2.

From the mouth of the Belle Rivière to the western end of the lake, where the Chamouchouan River enters, it is roughly thirty miles — following the shoreline almost forty. For some reason they spent five days covering it. But they began their journey up the Chamouchouan with high hearts, for its course was gentle and interspersed with islands, and prairies broke the woods along the shores. They were enchanted, but after some hours the roar of falling water disillusioned them. The first of a series of falls forced them to land.

Claude Dablon, making the same journey to its halfway point with Gabriel Druillettes in 1661, described them as "nothing but foam falling upon rocks which block the channel, and are placed one above another — now in the form of steps, which seem to be very ingeniously fashioned; and now like a collection of little Mountains piled one upon another, with peaks projecting above the water only to menace the voyager with shipwreck."

Yet above this violence the river became tranquil again for perhaps seven miles; then they heard again the warning rumble of more falls. So it went, portage following portage, like climbing a gigantic, relentless stairway. They were still on the river when on September 17 they met five canoes with a mixed passenger list of Attikamegues (or Poissons Blancs) and Mistassirinins who brought news from Hudson Bay. Two ships had anchored there and started trading with the tribes along the shore. They did not know this of their own experience but had the word from a Papinachois, and they showed the Frenchmen an English hatchet they had got from the Papinachois, who said he had received it in trade from the ship merchants. But it was not safe on Hudson Bay any more. Violence had flared and people been killed. At the news the Montagnais guides became terrified; but their reluctance at the thought of going farther made no difference, for winter was at hand and ice already forming in the upper rivers.

Albanel and St. Simon knew they must go into winter quarters; but Al-

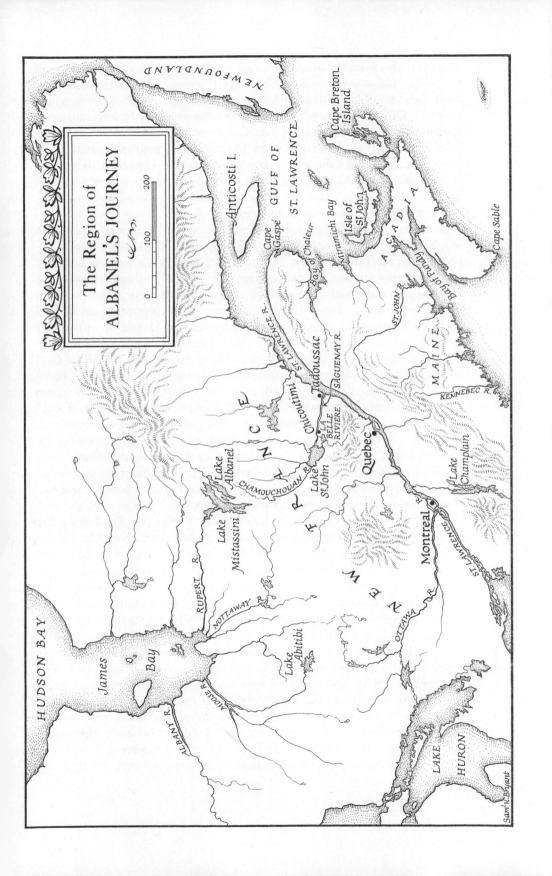

banel was also troubled because he had no passport, so he decided to send to Quebec for one. He and St. Simon both wrote reports of the journey to date and asked for further instructions in the light of the news they had received. On the nineteenth of September the *coureur de bois* with two Indians started back downriver for Tadoussac and Quebec, and Albanel, St. Simon, and their Montagnais, the five canoes of their new friends following them, resumed the slow journey upstream, looking for a likely spot for wintering. They knew time was short, and on the last day of October, ice decided for them. "Our Savages chose that place for passing the Winter, on account of its excellent hunting."

No better commentary on the bleak loneliness of this northern region is needed than the eagerness with which these wild Indians joined their fortunes to the French or the readiness with which the French accepted them. Meeting anyone, except an Iroquois, in that endless wilderness of jumbled hills and rocks and hostile rivers made the hour or the day a shining one, and now at the beginning of winter with their camp established Father Albanel could exercise at leisure his true profession of instructing heathen minds and converting souls. He expressed it simply. Pending the return of their courier, "I engaged in teaching that little band whom God so seasonably had sent me." While the hunters ranged the woods, Albanel spent his days in the smoke-filled, crowded lodges, searching the hearts and minds of his congregation and telling them the story of Christ. An old man who heard, in the mysterious way news permeated the wilderness, of the camp with the priest in it made a long winter journey, bringing his family of nine to accept the Christian faith if Albanel should think them worthy. This family group proved one of the joys of Albanel's months of winter; they were bright, eager, and sincere, and after a month's instruction he had no hesitation about baptizing them.

There was also a chief of the Mataouirious, a tribe that lived along the shore of Hudson Bay, who came to the Jesuit for instruction. He wanted ardently to become a Christian, but his soul was so entoiled in the superstitions and dark fears of his bleak world that he never could nerve his spiritual feet to make the leap to Albanel's side of the chasm that separated their minds. His failure caused Albanel as much pain as the old man's family had brought joy. Conversion of a chief would have augured a wider harvest of souls in his tribe.

The winter, however, was long and the most trying Albanel had ever experienced. The snow was very heavy, but they did not lack food. The hunters brought in moose and caribou occasionally, and there were great quantities of beaver, for the region had not been trapped for many years, and especially of porcupines. What made the winter unpleasant for Albanel was the behavior of their Montagnais guides, who were determined to go no farther in the direction of Hudson Bay. They were rude, abusive, and at times even cruel in their attempts to dissuade Albanel, for they did not dare abandon a missionary so far in the woods for fear of being badly treated in Quebec. St. Simon could go on or not as he chose; he was a soldier. They kept up their contention all winter, and as spring approached the Mataouiriou chief joined forces with them. He described the difficulties of the route, the portages, rapids, and waterfalls, in elaborate detail; then one morning he and the Montagnais guides all declared that they had forgotten the way!

Neither Albanel nor St. Simon was persuaded. Just before deep winter set in, the courier had returned from Quebec with letters patent from Bishop Laval, passports from Courcelles and Talon, and advice from all three. Albanel solved the problem by ignoring the Montagnais and, with a generous gift and the promise of all the tobacco he and his son could smoke during the summer, persuaded an elderly Mistassirinin to serve as guide. And when the die was cast the Montagnais went along.

They broke their winter camp on the first of June, 1672, numbering sixteen Indians and three Frenchmen in three canoes. The river was still at flood force from the melting snow, paddling against the current was nearly impossible, and most of the time they had to pole their canoes or else portage. The portages were indescribable. The country was a jumble of boulders and stones, with occasional little bogs in which the caribou moss was thigh deep.

> . . . Very often we had to land and walk through the woods, — climbing over rocks, leaping into ditches, and again scrambling up steep heights through clumps of trees whose branches tore our clothes; while with all that we were heavily burdened.

The canoes could not be carried in the ordinary way on the men's shoulders. They had to be manhandled over the rocks, from one man to another. Torrential rain pinned them to the ground for two days. On June 9 they had to make the worst carry they had yet faced — fourteen miles of the same incredible footing. They crossed streams by wading — there was no point in loading a canoe and paddling — because now they were going somewhat south of west and the streams ran north and south. But it was worth it. The plateau turned out to be part of the watershed divide and on the tenth they came to a spot the Indians called Paslistakau which was the actual height of land. Here two small lakes lay close together, each giving rise to a river. One ran southeast, joining its water to other streams to empty at last into Lake St. John. The other ran northwest.

A little farther on they met three Mistassirinins in a fine new canoe who told Albanel that the French could not proceed until the chief of the tribe had been notified and had given his permission. This was not unexpected. As Albanel himself pointed out, the Indians were cautious about granting passage to people of distant tribes. "The rivers are to them what fields are to the French, their sole source of subsistence, — whether in

[423]

form of fish or game, or in that of traffic." Nevertheless Albanel decided to be somewhat haughty.

" 'Is it thou that bidst me halt?' 'No, it is not I.' 'Who then?' 'The Old man Sesibaourat.' 'Where is he?' 'Far from here,' was his answer."

Tell him, said Albanel, that the French were in a hurry. They would rest for one whole day and if he had not come they would push on. The chief did not make it but sent four canoes to say he would next day. It was a matter of parrying against each other, so no one lost dignity, and sure enough, on June 13 the old chief arrived at the head of eighteen canoes.

Albanel gave him presents, but not to pay for their passage. The French had defeated the Iroquois and made the country safe, and should therefore have the right of passage as they chose. He intended not only to be friends with Sesibaourat in this mortal world but to maintain their relationship in heaven, and to that end Sesibaourat should "abandon the plan of carrying on commerce with the Europeans who are trading towards the North sea, among whom prayer is not offered to God; and resume your old route to Lake St. John, where you will always find some black gown to instruct and baptize you."

Sesibaourat, finding himself elevated by the prospect of celestial friendship and eying the fine gifts placed just in front of him, was entirely agreeable to everything. There were two days of feasting and speeches and at last, on June 16, they set out with called farewells from the Mistassirinins on the shore. They had another fearful portage to cross to reach a spot well named Pikousitesinacut — "the place where shoes are worn out" — which they reached on the seventeenth, and the next day came out on Great Mistassini Lake, one hundred miles long, from whose western shore the Nemiskau (Rupert) River flowed west into James Bay.

They paddled over the lake in awe of its evident size, the number of islands, the wealth of game upon its shores: bear, moose, caribou, and every kind of wild fowl. In one shallow stretch where fish abounded they found a veritable legislature of bears. In another, a piece of rising ground aroused their curiosity, but the Indians told them in whispers to be quiet. "Do not look at it, unless you wish to die." All this region, according to their myths, was a land of evil, and it behooved men who journeyed over it to refrain from curious inspection of the route they followed. One must take care especially not to examine closely any part of a landing place; coming ashore, particularly on Lake Mistassini, was always fraught with danger. And indeed the enormous size of the lake, lying as it did only a little way below the watershed divide where lakes are expected to be small, was strange and brought one to the edge of menace. It was a relief to enter the river, though according to the Mistassirinins it would provide some of the toughest stretches of their journey.

Their first full day on the river they found so many falls and rapids that they made a long, roundabout portage, leading from one small lake to another, during which their guide went astray, and by the time they got back to the Nemiskau they had had to make seventeen carries. But then for two days they found themselves in open, almost savanna country, with fine grass and obviously rich soil. Such gentle country, after the rough land they had traveled over, was almost disturbing. They populated it in their minds, and thought of the St. Lawrence farms.

It ended in a widening of the river to form Lake Nemiskau which they reached on the twenty-fifth of June. Eight or nine years earlier a very populous tribe had made it their home for, besides being in the middle of a fine region for game, the lake had always teemed with fish. But nothing was left now except the ruins of their village and, on an island, the cause of their departure, a fort built of stout logs that were beginning to rot. A great war party of the Iroquois had built it, according to the Mistassirinins, and sortied from it in frequent raiding expeditions until all the people had moved away. Before the coming of the Iroquois it had been the great trading center for the tribes around Hudson Bay.

They left the lake and on the twenty-seventh made their last portage, but they had to pay for it, for they found themselves assailed by black flies and gnats in swarms that made their surrounding smudges wholly ineffectual. Next day they had ominous evidence of the English presence. In a small tributary stream a hoy of 10 or 12 tons, lateen-rigged and carrying the English flag, was at anchor. No one was visible about it.

They spent that night in two abandoned Indian houses, occasionally firing musket shots in hope of luring the Indians back. Albanel sent a canoe ahead to scout the shore of James Bay next morning to find out where the Indians had moved to, and on July 1 he and St. Simon followed with the rest. About two o'clock in the afternoon a canoe approached, sent to escort them to the Indian town. As they drew near, all the people came out of their lodges to welcome them, led by their chief, Kiaskou. The young men waded into the water to lift the French from their canoes and carry them ashore. Kiaskou (Seagull) welcomed them and led them into his lodge, explaining that he already had people at work on a brand-new cabin for them but until it was finished his must be their home. He was an old man, open and friendly in manner, and sincerely interested in turning Christian. He kept pleading so earnestly that after two days Albanel relented and baptized him, giving him the name Ignace. Whereupon Kiaskou assembled his tribe and said:

"My nephews, you all know the blessing that befell me this morning. I have been baptized; I pray to God now, and I am a Christian . . . I am no longer what I used to be; I disown all the evil I have done, I love with my whole heart the maker of all things, in him alone will I believe, and in him alone will I put my trust. That is my declaration. Every man is his own master, and thus each may think for himself what he has to do."

Though this, of course, was Albanel's translation of the old man's speech and possibly slightly embellished, it must have stirred him. The whole tribe now pleaded to be instructed, and he might have baptized them all had there been time. But on the next day, July 5, they had to start back. It was a cause of keen regret to Albanel, though he promised to return. All came down to the waterside to say good-by and, according to Albanel, "they followed our canoe for a long time with their gaze."

There is no need to trace the return trip in detail, except for two halts they made. The first, on July 9, was at Lake Nemiskau. Here at the outlet, "where the river drinks the lake," with permission granted by Kiaskou, they took renewed possession of all the territories surrounding Hudson Bay and all lands north of the great watershed divide including Labrador.

It was "renewed" possession in Talon's careful phrasing because in 1670 at the mouth of the Nelson River, to which Radisson had brought them, the English had claimed for the Hudson's Bay Company rights granted by Charles II to the whole vast drainage basin that was Hudson Bay. Talon therefore had to claim a prior claim; though just what he based it on is not made clear. Jean Bourdon, the surveyor and council member at Quebec, supposedly had made an overland journey in 1656 to claim Hudson Bay for the Crown of France. But there is no real evidence that he did so, only later and brief references to it. He did set out on a voyage to Hudson Bay in 1667, but pack ice forced him to turn round. Maybe he did claim Labrador and Hudson Bay from there. But words flung to the wind from a ship's deck far from shore were hardly the same thing as nailing an escutcheon to a tree. Or Talon may have relied on the report of Radisson and Groseilliers that they had reached James Bay in 1662; there is more reason to believe their claim to be valid. In any case, whatever justification for it there might or might not have been, "renewed" was a word needed to offset the English claim.

As he had for St. Lusson, Talon had prepared forms for the procès-verbal St. Simon was to draw up and outlined a program for the ceremony of setting up the arms of France, "after having turned up a sod of earth, pulled up some grass, planted some shrubs, and performed other necessary ceremonies." What the Indians may have thought of these antics is anybody's guess, but they helped to make the proceedings strictly legal.

After crossing the divide and the toilsome plateau of jumbled boulders, where the soil was so dry and barren that the Indians of the region had to live "as simply as birds" on what prey they could kill or fish they might catch, St. Simon and Albanel came to Lake Nekouba, which like Lake Nemiskau had been a rendezvous for the tribes inhabiting the southern side of the divide. Here again they set up the escutcheon of France,

[426]

claiming all the territory from the dividing ridge to Lake St. John, into which nearly all of the southward streams ultimately drained.

This second ceremony was the final duty of their assignment, and from there the return went much more rapidly than had the outward journey. They reached Lake St. John on July 23, were at Tadoussac by August 1, and so came back to Quebec a year almost to the day after their setting out.

Their journey is significant mainly for the fact that they made it. Other facts were mostly negative from Talon's point of view. White men could reach Hudson Bay by traveling overland from Lake St. John, but it was not a practicable military route. France, it is true, had now made her claim upon the upper country, but at the moment it was the English who were in possession. Only for a moment, as it turned out, for France was not yet ready to concede her trade rights to the region.

In 1682 Radisson, returned temporarily to the French interest, established French trading posts along James Bay, and came back to Quebec from a summer's trading with a shipload of rich furs. In 1684, however, once more on the English side, he sailed into Hudson Bay with five ships, destroyed the posts he himself had established two years earlier, and plundered the French of sixty thousandweight of the best beaver in the world. Then in 1686 the Chevalier de la Troye led a band of one hundred Canadians on snowshoes to capture the three English posts on James Bay, surprising two with night attacks and also capturing an armed ship anchored near by with its crew, including the English governor. The third fort was now alerted and surprise impossible; but by this time the French had made themselves infinitely more formidable by the ten cannon they had taken from the ship and the first two forts. Planting them on a low hill above the fort, they brought it under heavy fire which in a short time almost demolished the palisades and blockhouse. The English did not even dare attempt to surrender but huddled in a cellar until the firing stopped.

With de la Troye on this expedition were the Sieurs d'Iberville, de St. Hélène, and de Maricourt, three of the seven sons of Charles Le Moyne, all of whom were to fight the English savagely and well. Iberville had already distinguished himself by accompanying Isaac Jogues on a mission to the Iroquois; the other two were making their first notable appearance on the Canadian scene. The astonishing march they made with de la Troye over the heavy snows of early spring did not repeat Albanel's and St. Simon's, but followed the traditional route up the Ottawa; they then worked their way across the still frozen north by lake and river.

The loss of the three forts so stunned the English that they agreed to a treaty of neutrality; both sides were to refrain from acts of aggression during the deliberations of the commissioners, and the two monarchs instructed their respective colonial governors to that effect.

In the war that broke out in 1689, however, affairs on Hudson Bay quickly reverted to their normal ebb and flow. In 1693 an English squadron captured all the bay forts; then in 1694 Iberville retook them. The English rallied and in 1696 captured the most important post, the richest in furs, Fort Nelson, at the mouth of the Nelson River. Iberville again sailed north in 1697, this time with a squadron of five ships. Pack ice in the straits crushed his supply ship and separated him from the other three, but he managed to extricate his own ship and win through to the mouth of Hudson Bay.

As he neared Fort Nelson he sighted three ships of the Hudson's Bay Company bearing down on him, carrying, as he found later, fifty-two, thirty-six, and thirty-two guns, respectively, against his own *Pelican*'s forty-four. He had his choice to fight them or abandon all thought of taking the fort, and he elected to close with the English ships. In an action of the greatest brilliance he sank the largest, forced the second to strike her colors, and was content to let the third scuttle off down the bay. After weathering a gale in his badly damaged ship, he put his crew ashore and, with the timely arrival of his three missing ships, battered the fort into submission. It was a tremendous performance, but it went for nothing, as the Treaty of Ryswick, which had already been signed in Europe, restored Hudson Bay to the English for good.

Albanel's further connection with Hudson Bay was brief. True to his word he returned to Kiaskou's tribe in 1674; but the English, learning of his presence, took him prisoner and shipped him off to England. Finally gaining his freedom, he returned to Canada in 1676 and was sent straight to the Ottawa missions. He worked first at St. Francis Xavier on Green Bay. In 1677–1678 he was Superior of the mission at Ste. Marie beside the Sault and after his term as Superior continued to serve there. He died at Ste. Marie in 1696 at the age of eighty, still in the harness of God.

There was the Mississippi. At the Ottawa missions, by 1669, visiting Indians had made that name familiar; indubitably the river existed. "This, coming from the regions of the North," Dablon wrote in the *Relation* of 1669–1670, "flows towards the South, — and to such a distance that the Savages who have navigated it, in going to seek for enemies to fight with, after a good many days' journey have not found its mouth, which can only be toward the Sea of Florida or that of California." If it emptied into the Gulf of Mexico, it would frame the English colonies; if into the Gulf of California, both the English and the Spanish; and it was becoming evident that whoever controlled the valley would in the end control the continent, as would be demonstrated two centuries later.

Talon's understanding of its importance was greater than Colbert's.

Distance, of course, accounted for this in part. Bits and pieces of fact or rumor were constantly coming Talon's way to stimulate his imagination. For him only a little less vividly than for the missionaries on the Great Lakes the river was beginning to make itself a presence. The missionaries felt that it was nearer than they had at first supposed. Neither Colbert nor Louis was ever really able to appreciate the size of their great dominion beyond the sea — three hundred times bigger than France — for to them France was the first factor of existence, unless in Louis's case it was his right to be king. Talon tried to make them see it as he did. "I am no Courtier," he wrote Colbert in 1671, "and assert, not through mere desire to please the King nor without just reason, that this portion of the French Monarchy will become something grand."

One had to have one's feet on Canadian soil to comprehend. Frontenac did at once when he looked up from the river at Quebec on its great rock: "It could not be better situated as the future capital of a great empire." Yet in 1674, when hard information about interior America, its size and wealth, had begun to flow even into Paris, Colbert could write Frontenac, "His Majesty considers it more consistent with the good of his service that you apply yourself to clearing and settling the most fertile places that are nearest the sea coast and communications with France, than to think afar of discoveries in the interior of the country, so distant that they can never be inhabited by Frenchmen."

September 12, 1672, was the day Frontenac saw Quebec the first time and stepped ashore to replace Courcelles as governor of New France and to become the greatest the country was to have. Before then Talon had decided that exploration of the Mississippi must be undertaken by the government. This was essential for implementing France's imperial motives and also because till then the only authority in the vast region had been the religious one exerted by the Jesuits. The impetus behind the expedition must be secular, but that did not mean that the Cross should be left out of it.

The man Talon chose to lead it was Louis Joliet, still young at twenty-eight, but of long experience now in wilderness travel and familiar with many of the western Algonquin languages. He was something of a mathematician, too, and intelligent and even-tempered. Dablon said of him that the authorities "could not have selected a person with better qualities," and this seems to have been true.

The Jesuit selected to go with him was Jacques Marquette, and again the choice seems to have been a particularly happy one. Born in Laon, France, he had come to Quebec as a missionary in 1666. For two years he studied Algonquin, then came to the Ottawa missions and replaced Allouez at St. Esprit at Chequamegon in 1669. There he quickly proved himself an unusual linguist, for he was soon fluent in the languages of six different tribes. There, too, his qualities as a missionary quickly developed.

He belonged with the early Jesuit Fathers whose souls were dedicated to the conversion of their savage flock. He was entirely unself-seeking and unambitious. A true conversion was to him a true delight, not another mark on the roster of his success. He found it appealing that a time came when "some young women do not blush to declare themselves Christians." To many he became a beloved missionary, and the Illinois began making the thirty-day overland trip from their river in ever increasing numbers.

They made the arduous land trip because they could never bring themselves to use canoes, but they told Marquette about their country where the corn grew tall and they raised squash as large as those of France. The land was rich in all kinds of game: buffalo, bear, deer, turkeys, pigeons, ducks, geese, cranes. They had one peculiarity almost nonexistent in all other North American Indian tribes, the practice of homosexuality, and like the ancient Athenians even trained handsome boys to be male prostitutes. But they also had qualities Marquette valued. They could be both kind and thoughtful and gave him a young man to teach him their language. Above all they told him about the Mississippi as well as another great river just south of their country which could only have been the Ohio. His imagination was so fired by their accounts that he resolved, if a canoe promised him by the Kiskakons was really finished, to find the Mississippi and make a journey down it.

Whether he was given the canoe is of no consequence. The Sioux in one of their cantankerous periods drove him out of St. Esprit. It took someone with reckless boldness like Allouez to keep them civil. Marquette retired to Ste. Marie, and then in 1671 founded the Mission of St. Ignace on the north side of the Strait of Michilimackinac at the entrance to Lake Michigan. There or at Ste. Marie he began to see something of young Joliet and evidently the Mississippi was often in the thoughts of both, for Dablon says that Marquette "had long premeditated the undertaking [of the voyage]" and that they had "frequently agreed upon it together."

Talon returned to France before Joliet received his orders. They were given him by Frontenac who, though he found himself at odds with Talon from the start and would have fought with him as bitterly as he did with Talon's successor, Duchesneau, approved completely the exploration and development of the interior, and apparently he was favorably impressed by Joliet, who started up the St. Lawrence late in November.

> The feast of THE IMMACULATE CONCEPTION OF THE BLESSED VIRGIN — whom I have always invoked since I have been in this country of the outaouacs, to obtain from God the grace of being able to visit the Nations who dwell down the Mississippi River — was precisely the Day on which Monsieur Jollyet arrived with orders from Monsieur le Comte de frontenac, Our Governor, and Monsieur Talon, our Intendant, to accomplish This discovery with me.

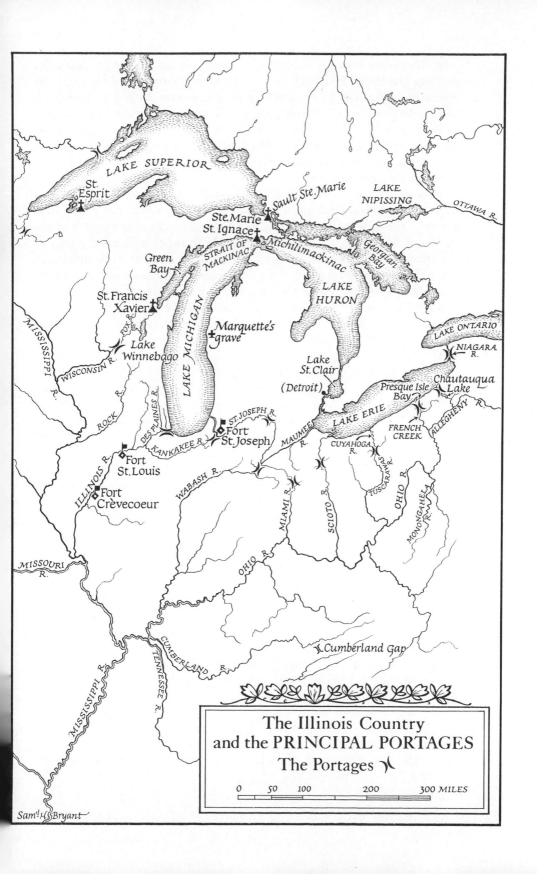

LAKE SUPERIOR

St. Esprit

Sault Ste. Marie

LAKE NIPISSING

OTTAWA R.

Ste. Marie
St. Ignace

Michilimackinac

Georgian Bay

Green Bay

STRAIT OF MACKINAC

LAKE HURON

St. Francis Xavier

LAKE ONTARIO

NIAGARA R.

MISSISSIPPI R.

FOX R.

WISCONSIN R.

Lake Winnebago

Marquette's grave

Lake St. Clair (Detroit)

Presque Isle Bay

Chautauqua Lake

ROCK R.

DES PLAINES R.

LAKE MICHIGAN

ST. JOSEPH R.

Fort St. Joseph

KANKAKEE R.

MAUMEE R.

LAKE ERIE

FRENCH CREEK

ALLEGHENY R.

CUYAHOGA R.

ILLINOIS R.

Fort St. Louis

WABASH R.

SCIOTO R.

TUSCARAWAS R.

OHIO R.

MONONGAHELA R.

Fort Crèvecoeur

MIAMI R.

OHIO R.

MISSOURI R.

CUMBERLAND R.

Cumberland Gap

MISSISSIPPI R.

TENNESSEE R.

The Illinois Country
and the PRINCIPAL PORTAGES
The Portages)(

0   50   100   200   300 MILES

Sam'l H. Bryant

So Marquette began his account of their voyage. On the calendar, the day was December 8. That it was the feast day above all of St. Mary, of whom he was a votary, accounts for his exaltation: he saw a blessing on their enterprise; and remembering his disapproving comment that the Ottawas were "superstitious to an extraordinary degree in their feasts and their juggleries," one is inclined to smile a little. However, theirs were pagan superstitions, and he was remarking a coincidence that seemed to indicate divine approval.

They spent the winter months collecting every scrap of information they could from Indians and Frenchmen. From this material Joliet drew a map of the new country, tracing as nearly as he could the course of the Mississippi and the other rivers they would follow, as well as the names of the tribes living near them. Preparing their equipment took much less time. "Indian corn, with some smoked meat, constituted our provisions; with these we embarked — Monsieur Jollyet and myself, with 5 men — in 2 Bark Canoes, fully resolved to do and suffer everything for so glorious an Undertaking." The romance and the high heart were purely Gallic. The date was May 17, 1673.

They passed through the straits into Lake Michigan, followed its northern shore to Green Bay, and paddled up that till they came to the Menomini village. The Menominies received them with éclat, but when they were told the purpose of the *voyageurs*, they immediately tried to dissuade them, inventing savage tribes that inhabited the Mississippi's lower shores, an all-devouring demon, monsters beneath its waters, and finally swore that the heat was so excessive in those lower countries that Marquette and his friends would surely die of it. They may have been afraid that the French wanted to cut into their game as middlemen to the downriver tribes; they may have been jealous of losing Marquette to other nations (quite a few of the Menominies were now Christian, and to an even partly converted tribe a Black Robe was a status symbol), or they may have genuinely believed at least part of what they told him (the half-known is always more demonic than the unknown). Probably their behavior was actuated by all three. Marquette, however, brushed aside all their persuasions by saying that he could not follow their advice because the salvation of souls was at stake, a statement not to be argued with.

Leaving the Menominies they reached the head of the bay, where the Mission of St. Francis Xavier was, and entered the Fox River. It was placid at first and teeming with duck and geese, but after a short space the rapids began. They mounted them by wading and dragging their canoes. It was not until June 8 that they reached their next Indian town.

This was the home of the Mascoutens who had lately been joined by the Miamis and the Kickapoos. Marquette was delighted with it. The town had been built on a low hill overlooking natural meadows, some with cornfields, and the woods beyond. As there was no bark suitable for building houses, the lodges were made of plaited reeds, picturesque but not impervious to wind and rain. Best of all in Marquette's eyes was a large cross erected in the center of the place, all hung with deerskins, bows, arrows, red belts, and other gifts as the Indians had been wont to do in appeasing their older pagan gods. This did not trouble Marquette. It was their way of worship and in his dealings with all his converts he never insisted on a total change of life. "I keep a little of their usage," he had reported to Dablon from Chequamegon, "and take from it what is bad."

He was especially attracted to the Miamis, who were civil, liberal, and shapely beyond all other Indians he had seen, and wore their hair in two long braids beside their ears. Compared with them the Mascoutens and Kickapoos "seem peasants."

They spent two days in council and feasting. On the tenth of June they reembarked with two Miamis as guides. As the town and the Indians crowding the shore passed finally from sight they knew that this was the real beginning of their journey, for no Frenchman had yet gone any farther.

The river took them southwest, as Joliet had drawn it on his speculative map, but its channel was so winding, choked with wild rice, and in places divided by islands that without their guides they would probably never have found the mile-and-a-half portage that brought them to the Wisconsin. There the two guides said good-by and turned back.

The Wisconsin flowed southwest, a gentle, wide, and shallow river with frequent islands and sand bars which often compelled them to get out and wade. The banks were beautiful, with many natural meadows breaking the woods. They saw buffalo and deer. Their passage became almost dreamlike in its tranquility, with the repeated ritual of making camp while two or three went off to hunt, the campfire supper of fresh-killed game, the voyage renewed at dawn. So it was that they came "with a Joy that I cannot Express" out on the Mississippi on the seventeenth of June.

They pointed their canoes south with the current and felt themselves in the grip of indefinable forces, as though they and their canoes were still and the continent had begun to move. Marquette's canoe was bumped by a vast catfish; for an instant he thought it would be broken or capsized. They saw a strange animal "with the head of a tiger," the head gray, the neck black, almost certainly a panther, in spite of the color. And then buffalo, not in little groups as they had seen them along the Wisconsin, but vast herds moving over the prairie like the shadows of clouds. They were in awe and governed themselves carefully. They made the smallest possible fire at dusk, just enough to cook their meal, extinguished it, and reembarked, to paddle several miles and then anchor their canoes and bed down well out from shore; and even so, one man kept a lookout throughout the night.

For eight days they saw no signs of men; then on the twenty-fifth there were footprints on the west shore and a fairly well used path leading inland. Marquette and Joliet resolved to follow it up and after about seven miles found themselves in an Indian town overlooking a smaller river and two other towns on a hill about a mile away. The river was undoubtedly the Des Moines; the Indians proved to be a tribe of the Illinois. Though only two, the Frenchmen were treated well. These Illinois had heard of Black Robes, so felt no fear. "How beautiful the sun is, O Frenchmen, when you come to visit us!" exclaimed the chief and led them to his lodge where, surrounded by the old men, they smoked a calumet together. Then they were escorted to another town, the seat of the principal chief of this branch of the Illinois.

He greeted them in the same hospitable way. He feasted them on hominy, fish, dog, and buffalo, served in separate courses, and picked out the choicest morsels and placed them in their mouths as though they had been children. But like the Menominies, he did his best to get them to turn back, and probably for the same reasons, hoping that his Illinois might act as middlemen to the southern tribes if the French advanced no further. But he showed no resentment when Marquette insisted that they would proceed, and next morning with six hundred of his people he escorted them back to their landing place on the Mississippi and saw them off.

Again their canoes were taken by the vast current and a while later they came to the rock cliffs on the east shore, a little above the site of Alton, Illinois, with the appalling paintings of two demons, earlier described, which filled them with misgivings, for they were unable to believe that mere Indians could have painted anything so dreadful and seemingly alive. They were still discussing the Satanic implications of the pictures when, drifting "quietly in clear and calm water, we heard the noise of a rapid, into which we were about to run." They were caught in the tumultuous discharge of the Missouri (the Indians called it the Pekistanoui, the Big Muddy, though Marquette and Joliet did not learn that till later) which none of their Indian hosts had thought of mentioning to them.

Muddy it was, yellowish, thick; churning branches, entire trees. Their canoes were tossed and spun on the chaotic water almost beyond control, but they managed to get past and, badly shaken, continue down the now augmented and more powerful current of the combined rivers. That was on the twenty-sixth of June. They were the first white men to see it.

A few days later they were again the first white men to see the mouth of the Ohio. They kept on, and the country slowly changed. There were canebrakes, very high, and so thick that buffalo had a hard time forcing their way through. They shot a Carolina parakeet and admired its plumage: "one half of the head was red, The other half and The Neck yellow, and the whole body green." They met a tribe of strange Indians, at first as frightened of the French as the French were of them, who wore their hair long and tattooed their bodies. They had guns and carried their powder in flasks of heavy glass which they said came from Europeans some of whom looked like Marquette (and were very likely Spanish from Florida); and they told the French that though they themselves did not visit the sea they understood it to be only ten days' journey farther south.

Well down the Mississippi, at the mouth of the St. Francis River in Arkansas, they saw an Indian village whose people thronged the shore in what seemed a very warlike mood. One young man hurled his war club at them, others swarmed into the water to seize the canoes, but when Marquette held up a calumet, which the Illinois chief had given them as talisman to see them past the southern tribes, their hostility evaporated and they welcomed the French. These Indians were probably of Siouan stock. When asked about the lower river they refused any information and said the French should go on to the next village about forty miles below, but they did assign a man to go with the party as an escort.

Next day at the lower town, which was on the east shore, not far above the mouth of the Arkansas River, they were welcomed and feasted. These Indians were a rough-looking crew, the men naked and the women clad in wretched worn-out skins and wearing their hair in knots behind their ears. Usually they hunted buffalo and used the hides in trade, but lately they had been hemmed in by their enemies and depended for food almost entirely on corn and watermelons. And to the question so often asked they replied that their village was only ten days' journey from the sea, but they had never been there because enemies who had guns and were extremely hostile to any strangers traveling the river prevented them.

This time Joliet and Marquette believed what they were told and decided that they had come far enough. If they had not seen the discharge of the great river, they had learned that it was not near Virginia — they were too far south — nor was it into the Gulf of California, for the same reason. It could only be into the Gulf of Mexico. With this certainty they considered that they had fulfilled their mission, and on July 17 they began the long, laborious return against the current.

There were no incidents during their ascent of the Mississippi. One day followed another with the same heat, the same unceasing toil at the paddles. The evening mists, rank from the swamps, more often than not drove them to anchor their canoes well out in the river for cramped and restless sleep. Mosquitoes tormented them and Marquette, who had always been frail, became feverish and developed dysentery which, though he did not then suspect it, marked the beginning of a failure of health that in less than two years would run a terminal course.

They passed once more the mouth of the Ohio, which, confusing it with a tributary, they called the Ouaboukigou, an Indian name later corrupted by the French to Ouabacke or Wabash, thus as it were mistaking the parent for the child. At length they reached the mouth of the Illinois, into which they turned, grateful for its gentle current and the wooded shade of its banks. The river ran smooth and almost free of rapids for its entire length. Marquette reported that in spring and part of the summer only one portage had to be made, and that of half a league. The landscape on either side was rich and tranquil, the same that had enraptured young Radisson, with deer and buffalo everywhere. Finally they came to a large town of the Illinois Indians, called Kaskaskia (a name later transferred to a spot on the east bank of the Mississippi).

The Illinois received them with the greatest kindness and Marquette was so moved that he promised to return to instruct them in the Faith. But now they could not stay, and they went on escorted by one of the chiefs with his young warriors to show them to Lake Michigan. So they reached the mouth of the Des Plaines River and proceeding up it came to a portage. This was the carry between the Des Plaines and the Chicago; it varied according to the season of the year from four to nine miles. Joliet, noting the flat character of the land they walked over, thought it would be feasible to dig a canal linking the two rivers and later suggested it to both Dablon and Frontenac. Indeed the chief assured him that in a spring of heavy rain the carry might be less than a mile; and when the rivers had really flooded their banks, canoes had been known to paddle straight on through.

The French learned later that the Indians used this portage customarily when coming south on Lake Michigan, following the west shore. When going down the lake to the north they always followed the east shore, for here a current flowed north, sometimes as much as ten miles in a day. The easiest way to reach the east shore from the Illinois was to enter the Kankakee River from the Des Plaines and then portage to the St. Joseph, the carry being about where South Bend now is, and so come down the St. Joseph to the southeastern corner of the lake.

These things remained to be learned and they paddled down the western shore and came to Green Bay at last at the end of September.

Aside from the length of their journey, more than twenty-five hundred miles since May 17, theirs had been a great accomplishment. They had been the first white men to travel on the Mississippi with full knowledge of what it was: "in fact, the most important of all the rivers in this country," to use Dablon's words. They had come to within two hundred miles of its mouth and dispelled forever the notion that it might lead to the Pacific — that it did not was to be regretted, but it was a fact in a world where till now facts had been few and hard to come by. And it was possible that one of its tributaries might lead to striking distance of a westward-flowing river that would lead to the Pacific — and here Marquette's eyes fastened on the Missouri. On their return, too, they had opened to the white man's knowledge a new and simpler access to the Mississippi watershed, and Joliet's suggestion of a canal to link Michigan with the Des Plaines was fulfilled two centuries later.

Marquette's dysentery had become a bloody flux by the time they reached Green Bay and the simple wooden buildings of the mission. It was unthinkable, even had it been possible, to move him farther, so there, at St. Francis Xavier, the two explorers parted. Joliet went first to Ste. Marie at the Sault, as it was now too late in the year to attempt returning to Quebec. He spent the winter at the mission, making copies of his maps and journal, which he gave for safekeeping to the Superior, Father Druillettes. In the spring, as soon as the ice broke in the rivers, he left with two Frenchmen and a little Indian boy who had been given them by the chief of the Illinois tribe they had visited on the Des Moines River. It was a wild, swift trip, made on the crest of the spring floods, but with the good fortune that had marked all the prodigious journey of the year before, they passed every obstacle. Then at the tail end of the Lachine Rapids, almost in sight of Montreal, his canoe capsized, his two paddlers and the little Indian boy were drowned and all his papers were lost, while he himself was barely able to get ashore.

He made his report to Frontenac, of course, still shaken by his loss, but neither he nor the governor was too upset about the papers. As the latter wrote to Colbert in the fall of 1674, it was too bad that they would have to wait till another spring to get the copies down from Sault Ste. Marie. But these papers never appeared again. At Ste. Marie there had been a fire; church, mission house, everything had been destroyed. Instead of Joliet's circumstantial journal the only record was that of Marquette, produced by Claude Dablon, the Superior at Quebec, together with his map.

In some scholarly quarters it has been adduced that Dablon must somehow have obtained the copy of Joliet's journal and incorporated it and Marquette's into one which he released as Marquette's work. The argument for this hypothesis is that the journal is so specific about places and dates that it must have been the work of a layman, with a few pious passages thrown in that might have been either Marquette's or Dablon's. This all seems beside the point. No doubt Dablon edited the journal after he received it, and it is quite possible that he interpolated passages from the long interview he had had with Joliet after the latter had seen Frontenac. But Marquette nevertheless was himself a trained observer. The journey for him naturally had religious overtones which are reflected in his account, but it was undertaken specifically for exploration and Marquette would have been as interested in the geographic features of the trip as Joliet was. The tone of the journal Dablon produced as his seems perfectly in key, but the suggestion that Dablon suppressed Joliet's work after stealing portions of it (presumably for the greater glory of his Order) seems utterly gratuitous.

Whatever the opinions of later scholars about the journal, there was never anything but good will between the explorers themselves. They are two of the most engaging figures in American history and their great journey was made in an aura almost miraculous, as though a celestial spotlight traced their course down the map of the continent. No one in their day spoke ill of either.

Joliet married a Quebec girl, Clair Brissot, two years after his return and became the father of seven children. In 1680 he was appointed hydrographer to the king and, "as a reward for having discovered the country of the Illinois . . . and for a voyage made to Hudsons bay in the public interests," granted the whole of Anticosti Island at the mouth of the St. Lawrence. This, because of the extensive fisheries connected with it and the Indian trade, was one of the most valuable seigneuries in Canada. Joliet built a trading post and visited the island every summer. The voyage to Hudson Bay occurred in 1679 and the English there tried to buy him over to their side. They did not succeed, but in King William's War they did succeed in destroying his establishment on Anticosti, as well as capturing his family. The latter were returned in due course, but Joliet never recovered from the loss of his trading post and when he died in 1700 he was reputedly a poor man.

Marquette's dysentery kept him practically immobilized at Green Bay all the rest of the winter and through the summer of 1674, but in September it suddenly cleared up and he turned his mind to the fulfillment of his promise to the Illinois Indians of Kaskaskia. He had already communicated to Dablon his desire to return to them, not only for their sake, but because of a promise he had made to the Virgin, that if she saw them safely through the Mississippi voyage he would found an Illinois mission named La Conception in her honor. While he waited for his instructions for wintering to come from Quebec, he complied with another promise, made to Dablon, making copies of his journal.

The autumn canoes at length arrived, bringing him permission to winter with the Illinois and on October 25, his simple preparations completed, he set out from St. Francis Xavier with two Frenchmen, Pierre Porteret and a man named simply Jacque, to paddle him. At the mouth of the river they found a band of Indians also setting out for Kaskaskia, five canoes of Pottawatomies and four of Illinois, and decided to join forces with them. Wind held them at the river mouth through that first night. It was the season when great winds blow from the north and flights of geese and duck fly like driven bees under the cold gray breakers of clouds. The wind dropped at dawn but rain held them pinned till noon. Then all at once it was calm and bright and in the afternoon they paddled down the east shore to the narrow inlet of Sturgeon Bay, from the head of which they had a short portage to Lake Michigan. They slept on the beach. Again it stormed: "after the rain and thunder, snow fell."

From then on they were continually held up by wind and rough water; and merely reading Marquette's account wears on the nerves with recurring phrases of frustration. "We are unable to go out, on account of the waves . . . We are delayed . . . We had considerable difficulty in getting out of the River at noon . . . We are detained there for 5 days, on account of the great agitation of the lake . . . We sleep near the bluffs, and are very poorly sheltered . . . Being detained by the wind . . . here I had an attack of diarrhoeia . . . and were compelled to make for a point of account of floating masses of ice . . . delayed there by wind from the land, by heavy waves from the lake, and by cold . . ."

The game seemed to have vanished. They found nothing but two wildcats, which "are almost nothing but fat," until on November 27 the Indians killed some buffalo. All the fall color had vanished from the woods or faded into brown. Day after day the lake, like the sky, was a dull and menacing gray. They snatched every opportunity, however brief, to move ahead, but it was not till December 4, nearly six weeks after leaving Green Bay, that they reached the Chicago River, which they found closed with six inches of ice.

After spending eight days at the river mouth in uncertainty, they started packing their canoe and goods over the portage and made their first camp seven miles up the river. Here the severity of his diarrhea forced Marquette to tell the other two that he could not go on, and the two men immediately set about building a cabin for the winter. It was high time. Next day Marquette's bloody flux reappeared.

The last of the Illinois contingent stopped at the cabin on their way to Kaskaskia and, for a cubit of tobacco, sold three buffalo robes, which were of great comfort through the winter. Jacque and Pierre found game: deer, buffalo, turkey, and ruffed grouse; two French traders encamped sixty miles away came to visit, bearing gifts of blueberries and corn. In January Marquette sent Jacque to Kaskaskia with a message that he would come if he could in the spring; he was too weak to move now. Jacque brought back a sack of corn and later the older chiefs sent additional corn, dried meat and pumpkins, and twelve beaver skins to make Marquette a mat. They wanted gunpowder, which he would not give them for fear it would spark their old war against the Miamis into flame again. But he sent them other gifts and promised that even if he was still ill, he would get to their town somehow in the spring, though it would not be possible for him to stay for long. This the Indians contradicted gravely, saying that they had been informed that he would stay in their country for a long, long time.

Through the months of cold and snow Jacque and Pierre cared for him devotedly. The former was, apparently, chiefly the hunter for their little party; Pierre, the nurse. But then in February Marquette appeared to be mending. He ascribed his improvement entirely to a novena to the Blessed Virgin which he had begun on the first of the month and in which, through all the nine days, his companions had shared. Suddenly a hopeful spirit invested the cabin. A band of the Illinois appeared from Kaskaskia on their way north to join the Pottawatomies; they camped close by for a week and then went on to wait on the lake shore for the water to open. Flocks of pigeons settled round them and all at once there was more game. On the twenty-fifth of March the spring thaw set in, on the twenty-eighth the ice broke in the river, and on the twenty-ninth the river overflowed. They had barely time to get their packs out of the cabin and hung in trees before the water entered the door, and they themselves spent a cold and miserable night on a hillock near by. But in the morning, after retrieving their packs, they at last resumed their journey to Kaskaskia.

Rafts of ice on the Des Plaines held them onshore for five days. High winds and freezing cold delayed them further. At this point of hardship and frustration, Marquette's journal breaks off. But he did reach Kaskaskia after eleven days and the Indians came to greet him, in Dablon's phrase, "as an angel from Heaven," which may not be as hyperbolic as it sounds. For the Illinois had been keenly aware of his near-presence through the winter in the woods above the carry. Some, as we know, had seen him in his rude cabin, obviously in the shadow of death. Yet here, suddenly, he came in his canoe down the flooding river, mysteriously, even miraculously manifest. It supplied the kind of drama that appealed most strongly to their superstitious minds.

In any case Marquette was welcomed everywhere as he went from cabin to cabin, telling hushed packed audiences about the Saviour and his Virgin Mother, invoking images of heaven and hell, sowing "in their minds the first seeds of the gospel." Successful and satisfying as this was, he was able to preach to only a limited number at a time, and he was increasingly aware that for him time was borrowed and beginning to run short. So he resolved on speaking to all the people in the town in one grand meeting and arranged with the senior chiefs to hold it on the eve of Good Friday.

On that day an open meadow was prepared for the council by spreading mats upon the ground. On the lines stretched between posts around its perimeter Marquette hung pieces of Chinese taffeta with large pictures of the Virgin pinned to them. He took his place in the middle of the field, surrounded by his congregation. Five hundred old men and chiefs sat in a ring around him. Behind them stood fifteen hundred men and warriors and behind them the women and the children. Frail and haggard in the brilliant sunlight, he spoke to them of the mysteries of the Christian religion and explained the significance of this day, the eve of the greatest sacrifice ever made: the Saviour Jesus Christ hung upon the Cross for them

[440]

as for all men. And then with what pomp he could muster he celebrated mass.

On Easter Sunday the service was repeated. The Indians had experienced nothing like it, and the whole tribe was deeply moved if not en masse converted. And now when Marquette, realizing that little time was left to him, told them he must go, they did not try to keep him but asked him to come back to them when he was well again, and many of the young men escorted him all the way to Lake Michigan.

His strength was ebbing rapidly when, leaving the massed Indians, they put out from shore and started circling the southern curve of the lake. The Illinois had told them about the currents down the eastern shore, and as they were heading for St. Ignace at Michilimackinac, in the end this would be the shortest course. The two paddlers knew as well as Marquette that time was of the essence. He could no longer stand alone but had to be lifted in and out of the canoe whenever they went ashore. His eyesight failed; he could no longer read. He knew his life was now numbered in days, and he tried to prepare the two *voyageurs* for its end in order that they should not worry over what to do. On May 10 he prepared holy water to be used in his final illness and for his burial and gave instructions as to how they should use it. Through all of the seventeenth he was occupied with telling them how and in what kind of place to bury him, how to arrange his hands, his feet, his face; a cross must be erected over the grave; and when he had been put in his grave he wanted one to ring the little hand bell he used in his chapel while the other filled the grave.

On the eighteenth of May as they approached the mouth of a small river with a hill beside it, he told them to make a landing there, for this was the place where he would die. Accordingly, they carried him ashore, started a fire, and built him a tiny lean-to of bark under which they made him as comfortable as possible. When they had unloaded the canoe they rejoined him and found him more concerned for them than for himself. He thanked them for all their faithful service to him and tried to comfort them and even administered the sacrament of penance to them. Then, knowing how tired they were, he sent them off to rest under the canoes, promising to call them before he died.

Two or three hours later they heard his voice faintly and came to the lean-to to find him on the point of death. His one fear had been of dying with his mind unclear, and he had asked them to repeat the names of Jesus and Mary in case he should be unable to do so for himself. One of them now did, on which, in a quite clear voice, he echoed the names several times, and then gently and quietly died.

They buried him as he had directed, on the side of the hill, with a cross at the head of the grave, and rang the chapel bell as they covered him with earth. Then, loading their canoes, they reembarked and resumed their sad return.

In the spring of 1677 a party of Kiskakons (Ottawas of the Bear Clan), who had done their winter hunting east of Lake Michigan and some of whom had been converted by Marquette at Chequamegon, came upon his grave and, knowing from the cross that it must be his, decided to disinter the body and take it back for burial at his own mission of St. Ignace. They found the body intact, completely dried, the skin uninjured. But swayed by the forces of their inherited emotions for the dead, they dissected it according to their immemorial custom, and scraped and washed the bones carefully one by one and placed them in a birchbark box.

Approaching Michilimackinac they sent one canoe ahead with news of what they had done and as they drew near the mission they formed their thirty canoes in a procession. All the Indians and French at the mission, with the Superior, Henri Nouvel, and his assistant, Philippe Pierçon, leading them, came to the water's edge. Nouvel halted the Ottawa procession until they had answered his questions, to convince him that they really had the body of Marquette. When they had satisfied him the combined parties intoned the "De Profundis"; then the canoes came to shore, the box was lifted out and carried into the little chapel. It remained there on view through all that day, and on the next, with all ceremony, it was buried in a little vault in the middle of the floor.

With the notes of Marquette's chapel bell, small and remote on the shore of Lake Michigan, a period of Jesuit history came to an end. He belonged with that earlier group, pure in spirit and fired solely by their missionary zeal, to which such as Brébeuf and the two Lalemants, Bressani and Jogues, Pierre Biard, who in effect founded the Quebec mission, and Ennemonde Massé, who was called "Father Useful," belonged. Not all of them suffered martyrdom, but all braved the torture platforms of the Iroquois and suffered incredible hardships in the service of the Cross, which was the only service they recognized. Other good members of the Order remained in Canada, but more and more from this point on they lent themselves to the political needs of the often hard-pressed government of Canada and to a degree bound the Cross to the sword.

Radisson and Groseilliers had been the forerunners; Joliet and Marquette by inference and logic had eliminated the river's discharge into any western sea; but eight more years would pass before La Salle put the capstone on their discoveries by reaching the mouth of the Mississippi and claiming all its enormous watershed for France, in the name of Louis XIV, for whom he also named it Louisiana. The achievement was only fitting. No man in Canada had made more journeys of exploration; none in the aggregate had gone as far; and his journeying was done not only in the shadow of the great central forest but under what seemed perpetually a clouded fortune; so it was right that he should have the one moment of supreme triumph.

Others after Joliet and Marquette did much journeying also: Claude Allouez, who traveled with God almost as a Personal Companion and probably knew as much about the west and northwest tribes as any other Frenchman of his time, and counted the tally of souls saved, which at times seemed to be his primary objective; Nicholas Perrot, whose beat was north of the country of the Illinois and who became one of the four principal architects of the confederation of the western tribes, but who was a trader *par excellence;* and Duluth (Americanized, his name became so vivid in the western ethos that the ringing syllables of Daniel Greysolon du Lhut have been virtually forgotten) — Duluth, like La Salle, was driven by an ambition to find a passage to the western sea, but he simply never had time to make the search. His first western journey took him mainly among the Sioux and in 1679 he took possession of their vast range in the name of Louis. Then after 1681 he spent ten years almost without a break in the west, much of the time west of Superior and sometimes north of it, forging treaties of peace between the Sioux and the Assiniboins, the Sioux and the Chippewas, and again the Sioux and their inveterate foes, the Crees — though this last was more in the nature of a truce as insubstantial and difficult to hold in being as marshfire. He also planted posts all through the northwest, most notably at Kaministiquia on the northwest shore of Superior and another at the outlet of Lake Nipigon, both of which were instrumental in siphoning off a proportion of the trade that had been going to the English at Hudson Bay. The trade ran in his blood and he had the hard, practical business sense that La Salle lacked; two governors, Frontenac and La Barre, were reputed to be silent partners in his enterprise. For a period he served as commandant of the northwest, and in 1686 marked the strategic importance of Detroit and built a fort there. He was a wilderness diplomat of the first order, a soldier, and trader, the supreme *coureur de bois.* There was always something on hand to keep him from starting for the Pacific.

These were the outstanding men. There were also the rank and file of the *coureurs de bois* who, following the smaller waters and the incidental Indian trails, began bringing the map to life. Some were licensed by the fur monopoly, but the greater proportion came on their own, most of them with only a small stake in trade goods. The Indians, however, were eager to do business and both sides escaped the middleman, who was still the Huron or the Ottawa. At first they tended to base on the Jesuit missions, much to the displeasure of the Fathers, who found their presence disturbing to their converts, but as they gained in numbers they began to build posts of their own to cover the key portages. From these they issued in small parties, six or four together, sometimes two, or a man alone

[443]

with just an Indian paddler. There is no way of knowing how many came into the wilderness in this way, or how many died, drowned in a rapid or tomahawked in a remote village by a drunken brave; but in following the trade they opened the heart of the continent whose main arteries had been traced by the like of Duluth and Joliet and presently La Salle, not in the English sense of breaking soil and making towns, but by mastering the details of its geography and above all learning the Indians. It was through the combination of their skills that Canada was able to contain the English colonies for so long. But they were not explorers in the true sense; fur, and fur alone, was their compelling motivation.

La Salle was different. He not only provided definition for France's imperial dream, he grasped the strategic importance of the Ohio–Mississippi triangle and realized that the Ohio was the boundary along which the question of French or English domination of the midcontinent would have to be settled. His recognition of this fact is not surprising when one reflects on the geographic spread of his American experience, which in the end extended from Quebec to the Gulf coast of Texas. No other Frenchman's equaled it.

Its evolution fell into three chapters. The first, in which he began to grasp the immensity of the continent, was based primarily on Lachine and Lake Ontario; the second, when he tried to implement his vision of a French empire in the heartland of America, took place on the upper Great Lakes and the Illinois and culminated in his one moment of triumph at the mouth of the Mississippi; and the third, his tragic attempt to plant a colony in Texas, ended in his death, twenty-one years after he first set foot in Canada.

René Robert Cavelier, Sieur de la Salle, to give him his full name, was born of a wealthy Rouen family in 1643. He received a good education, displaying unusual talent for mathematics and the natural sciences. As we learned from Joliet's brief meeting with him on the carry between the head of Lake Ontario and the Grand River, he too had entered the Jesuit Order, but he did not remain long enough to become a priest, in spite of the example of an older brother, Jean, who had qualified as a Sulpician and come to Montreal. Not very much that was good could ever be said about Jean, whose character was weak and self-absorbed, but his example probably was a contributing influence in La Salle's decision, after leaving the Order, to come to Canada himself.

He reached Quebec in the spring of 1666 and was soon in possession of a seigneury near the Lachine Rapids on which he established a trading post and palisaded village for his prospective tenants. He began studying Indian languages and proved himself remarkably adept at mastering them. By 1669 it was said that he had made himself fluent in Iroquois and seven or eight Algonquin tongues. Reserved, almost aloof in his dealings with other men, which made many Frenchmen resent him, he was able to impress Indian visitors and had an affinity for them. One such group, a band of Senecas who, now that there was peace, spent the winter at Lachine, told him about a river that had its rise in their country and flowed into the sea, which was an eight months' journey distant. They called the river the Ohio. (The Iroquois had always considered the Mississippi below its juncture with the Ohio to be properly the latter.) To La Salle the sea must be the western sea and the river running into it the route to China; and it was his preoccupation with this possibility that caused people to call his seigneury sarcastically "La Chine," from which the rapids took their name.

In the spring of 1669 he went to Quebec to win the backing of the governor and intendant for the exploration he now proposed to make beyond the Senecas, and there he received his first taste of the official attitude that was to overshadow almost all his efforts. Courcelles and Talon readily gave him permission to go and were, indeed, enthusiastic about the expedition — so long as it was undertaken at his own cost. But they did suggest that Fathers Dollier de Casson and Galinée combine the expedition they were planning, to convert the northwest tribes, with La Salle's in search of the great river of the Senecas. The Sulpicians agreed, which was how Joliet came to meet them, twenty-four Frenchmen and seven canoes, on the Grand River carry.

La Salle was not altogether happy in this partnership. He was never easy on any expedition unless it was under his sole command. Much depended on the success of their exploration, for to finance his share of the expedition he had had to sell his seigneury back to the Sulpicians. But at the time of the meeting with Joliet the explorers had little to show for their effort. They had stopped at Irondequoit Bay, from which La Salle and Galinée had gone south to the Seneca town of Totiakton to find a guide to the Ohio. The Senecas made them welcome — children brought them continual offerings of pumpkin and fresh corn — and promised them a captive Shawnee about to be brought in. He proved to be a young man, alert and intelligent, but the Senecas decided instead to burn him; and the scene that for so long had made the Iroquois country hideous was renewed for the two Frenchmen. At the touch of a red-hot gun barrel along the tops of his feet the Shawnee uttered a loud cry. "This turned me about, and I saw the Iroquois, with a grave sober countenance, apply the iron slowly along his feet and legs, and some old men who were smoking around the scaffold . . ." And in due course they were offered their choice of him to eat.

They decided to waste no more time with the Senecas, but went on to the head of Ontario and their meeting with Joliet, whose description of the unconverted tribes beyond the farther lakes led the Sulpicians to abandon all thought of visiting the Ohio for the prospect of achieving glory by converting the Pottawatomies, whose state Joliet had described as particularly heathen. La Salle had no intention of accompanying them, but not wanting to hurt their feelings he claimed a sudden illness, a subterfuge instantly penetrated by Galinée, who commented sarcastically that he must have seen three large rattlesnakes climbing a rock. In any case, they parted on the carry; the Sulpicians went on to Lake Erie, now so rough with autumn storms that they spent the winter on its shore. Next spring at Detroit they lost their altar and most of their supplies, and thus deprived of the tools of their spiritual trade had no choice but to continue on to Sault Ste. Marie where the Jesuits provided a guide to take them home via the Ottawa River.

Where La Salle went after parting with the Sulpician priests on September 30 is uncertain. He had picked up a Shawnee guide who had been a captive in the Seneca town of Otinawatawa, at the western tip of Ontario. The Shawnee had promised to take him to the Ohio. He seems to have headed back at first, but again, we do not know whether he went as far as Ontario, though some of his paddlers deserted him and crossed the lake, returning to Lachine. La Salle himself is supposed to have gone to Onondaga for another guide, but he already had the Shawnee. More likely he found his way to the Ohio by the route later taken by Céleron: the carry from Lake Erie to Lake Chautauqua, then down its outlet to the Conewango and down the Alleghany to the Ohio; or by the more western carry from Presque Isle (now Erie, Pennsylvania) to French Creek. It is too late to do more than speculate, and for that matter all La Salle's movements for the next four years are not to be defined. But it seems probable that he explored the Ohio, perhaps as far as what is now the site of Louisville, and he probably explored its upper tributaries. In a memorial to Frontenac in 1677 he asserted that he had done so, mentioning that he had stopped at a falls; and a map of the Great Lakes and Mississippi drawn by Joliet in 1674 shows the Ohio with the statement that it had been explored by La Salle. If he had not done so, it would be hard to explain his early perception of its strategic importance in relation to the Mississippi and the Great Lakes.

Nicholas Perrot claimed to have met him on the Ottawa in the summer of 1670, but from that point on, the same shadowed mystery invests his movements in the wilderness. According to the only account of what he had been doing, supposedly dictated by himself to an anonymous person, he must have entered Lake Michigan and from its head have reached the Illinois. Whether, as the paper claims, he reached the Mississippi is dubious. But it does not matter. What does is that when he finally returned to Quebec he knew more about the heartland of America than any other man and already had an idea of what it would mean in wealth and power. In Quebec he met the newly arrived governor, Frontenac, who listened with eagerness to what La Salle could tell him and agreed with him on the importance of this western country to the wealth of New France.

Louis de Buade, Comte de Frontenac et Palluau, was in his fifty-second year when he arrived at Quebec in September 1672. He was of noble blood; though Tracy's title outranked his, no man of higher lineage served the Canadian government under the French regime except Bishop Laval. He was an aristocrat to his fingertips, a soldier, and a courtier. As a soldier he had distinguished himself in Holland, rising to *maréchal de camp*, and three years before coming to Canada had been sent with a French military force to aid in the defense of Crete against the Turks, an apparently hopeless campaign from which he emerged with personal glory.

For such a man the governorship of Canada, with a salary of eight thousand livres, would seem a demotion, but he accepted it gladly because, though noble, he was impoverished and expected to restore his fortune in the fur trade. It also allowed him to escape from a difficult marriage. In 1648, returning from the Holland wars, he had married a girl of sixteen, Anne de la Grange-Trianon, against the wishes of her father, but the young lady had proved to be as overbearing, headstrong, and vibrating with impatience as her husband, and after the birth of a son they separated. However, though incompatible, they were never completely alienated and while he lived she did what she could to further his interests at court.

Frontenac's character bristled with contradictions. He was as dependent as his wife on the praise and admiration he would never give her and insisted on his place at the center of a scene. Everything he had must be acknowledged the best of its kind whether it was or not. His horses were the best and swiftest when, according to one friend, they were in fact "very indifferent." In the same manner the food served by his servants invariably possessed, in his opinion, that extra one cannot say what that the same food on other tables totally wanted. He was very vain of his person and often designed his own clothes, which when new he would leave in the rooms of female friends for their approval, sometimes to their embarrassment. He was at once arrogant and generous. Extremely jealous of the deference due his rank and the perquisites of office — he wrote Colbert, for instance, that he planned to build a barge with fourteen or sixteen oars to be manned by recalcitrant *coureurs de bois*, "for, I assure you, however accustomed I may already be to a Canoe, tis rather the vehicle of a savage than of a King's Minister" — he was utterly without condescension toward people of lower rank than his. This combination of pomp and naturalness fascinated the Indians, with whose children he delighted in playing and toward whose women he was unfailingly courteous. No other French governor ever dealt as effectively with them. He knew instinctively when to threaten and when to cajole with praise. He never addressed them as "brothers" but always as "children," conveying thereby the responsibility he felt for them as an officer of the great King of France. He joined in their dances with enthusiasm as genuine as theirs and listened to their harangues with a stoic patience he seldom reserved for his compatriots.

To a man of such ardent temperament it is little wonder that the vastness of the land he had come to govern was inordinately stimulating — if it had not been so vast he would soon have had to make it so in his imagination — and it is not surprising that he welcomed instantly La Salle's vision of a great French colony in the interior. The coolness and self-restraint of the younger man impressed him from the start; he lent great weight to his opinions and as long as he was governor supported him as strongly as he could. He enlisted La Salle's services now in the first major project of his governorship: the building of a fort on Lake Ontario.

Talon, it will be remembered, had urged this as a means of controlling the fur trade and keeping the Iroquois in check. Courcelles also had endorsed the plan. But it was at the time thought too costly an undertaking, both to build and to maintain. In the winter of 1672–1673, however, news reached Quebec that the Iroquois had made a treaty with the Ottawas to take over the fur trade from the French; the annual trade rendezvous was to take place on Lake Ontario, which would be considerably easier for the Ottawas to reach than Montreal, to say nothing of the English goods they would receive there in exchange, which were at once cheaper than the French and of superior quality. It was obvious that this direct threat to the fur trade must be met head on. Frontenac determined therefore to build the projected fort, fixing its site at a little mission of the Sulpicians at the head of a bay called Quinté, about a third of the way along the northern shore.

During the winter he sent orders to Three Rivers and Montreal to muster each a designated number of men — with Quebec's contingent the whole force was to be four hundred — and the necessary canoes. In addition he had constructed two barges, large enough to take sixteen rowers and a load of supplies, and on each he mounted a small cannon. He also had them painted in brilliant blue and red, with what might have been hieroglyphs, which he intended should mystify the Iroquois, for they were "in a fashion unlike any seen before in the whole country."

News of Frontenac's expedition was greeted with extreme suspicion by some merchants and traders, in some quarters with open hostility. He tried to disarm critics by letting it be understood that he was making only a tour of inspection of the farther regions of the colony, to acquaint him-

[448]

self with the territory for which he had become responsible, and to gain some knowledge of the Indians who lived in it; and by impressing those Indians with the size of the force he could bring into the heart of their country, to secure a firm peace.

The Jesuits in the Iroquois missions had been reporting that the Iroquois had lately become increasingly hostile in their attitude toward the French, so Frontenac decided that he should send an emissary to persuade them to send their sachems to meet him at the Bay of Quinté, and chose La Salle for the job. La Salle, who was then — at the end of May — in Montreal, agreed to go but before leaving sent Frontenac a map which convinced him that the site of his fort, and therefore of the rendezvous with the Iroquois, should be at a place called Cataraqui (the site of modern Kingston) at the outlet of the lake. A messenger was sent to overtake La Salle and change the place of rendezvous.

On June 3 Frontenac left Quebec and after a leisurely trip, stopping to visit all officers along the river, who vied with each other in furnishing entertainment, reached Montreal on June 15.

The town as he first saw it consisted of a street of low and simple houses running parallel to the shore and broken some way up by the tall buildings of the seminary. To the left the walls of the Fort of Villemarie rose in a formidable square with bastions at the corners; and farthest from the river and dominating all other buildings with its spire was the church. The town major, as the mayor was styled, François Perrot, had lined up all the male inhabitants at the river's edge; at a signal they fired in salute a ragged volley in which, a moment later, the cannon of the fort took part. Frontenac had to stay on the riverbank while the magistrates addressed him in turn, followed by a speech offered by the syndic, and only then at last was escorted to the sanctuary of the church, at the door of which, however, he was obliged to stand for another interminable greeting by one of the priests. Then he entered the church and the "Te Deum" was sung, and finally he was taken to the fort, into which he disappeared, one must assume, not without thankfulness.

During the thirteen days he spent in Montreal pressure again was brought for his abandoning the expedition. The Jesuits as well as the merchants were alarmed at the idea of trading posts being built through the Indian country, foreseeing the return of the brandy question on a scale much larger than before. Dablon had already tried to divert Frontenac by a story of a Dutch fleet which had retaken New York from the English and, it was assumed, would now move against Quebec. He urged the governor to give up his Ontario junket and return posthaste to see to the defenses of Quebec. Frontenac refused to be shaken and replied by giving Dablon instructions for the commandant to have all the gun carriages immediately repaired and sent *him* off with admonitions to make all possible speed. Having got rid of the Superior, he now ordered the canoes and the two barges to be taken overland by wagon to Lachine.

Perrot had even stronger reason to be alarmed, for by virtue of his office he had managed practically to monopolize the whole fur trade coming down the St. Lawrence, first by building a storehouse on the next island above that of Montreal, the commander of which was therefore able to stop the majority of canoes coming down and trade for their furs before they ever reached the town, and also by subsidizing many of the soldiers of the garrison to enter the woods as *coureurs de bois* — or, as one might say, by employing them when they became deserters. It was an open scandal and was to result in a confrontation between him and Frontenac, Perrot's imprisonment, and ultimately his dispatch to France.

The expedition got under way on June 29 and on the next day they had their first day of the rapids. The preferred route was along the south shore, where the carry for the canoes was relatively easy; but getting the two ponderous barges up through the raging water was laborious and dangerous. It took fifty men for each one, working in water to their necks, to wrestle them forward foot by foot. A band of Hurons in twenty canoes who had begged to be allowed to join the expedition proved, to everyone's astonishment, exceptionally eager and skilled at the work, vying with the Canadians for Frontenac's approval. "Those conversant with their humor, acknowledged that they performed without any difficulty, for him, what no one had ever before dared to propose to them." When that night in camp he "regaled" them and the whole fleet with brandy and tobacco, they swore everlasting fealty to him; it was one of the first manifestations of his extraordinary affinity with the Indians.

On the second of July they passed two rapids and entered the wider portion of the river called Lake St. Francis, and now for three days the paddling was easy and a fresh wind from the northeast meant that the barges could move as rapidly as the canoes. The whole force was seized by one of those spells of elevation of the spirit that could turn any French expedition all at once into a pilgrimage to Paradise. The landscape around them was "the most delightful country in the world . . . the entire river was spangled with islands . . . both banks of the river are lined with prairies full of excellent grass, interspersed with an infinity of beautiful flowers." On the night of the fourth they halted at a spot "more delightful than any we had yet seen." It might not look so now, being opposite Massena Point and the mouth of the Grass River, on the approach to Cornwall. But they paid for this beauty on the fifth when they had to tackle the rapids of the Long Sault.

Nothing, however, could dampen their enthusiasm now, not even a downpour of two days' duration. The men who had been wrestling with the cumbersome barges would begin dancing as soon as camp was made or play "Prison base" or similar games. Then on the evening of the ninth two Iroquois canoes came flashing down the river. They had come from Quinté where, they said, two hundred sachems and warriors of their nations were eagerly waiting the coming of Onontio. Apparently Frontenac's follow-up message had not been properly delivered. So the two Sulpician abbés, Fenelon and d'Urfé, who had accompanied the expedition from Montreal were sent ahead to urge the chiefs to come to Cataraqui.

Now it was all smooth journeying. On the tenth, they caught alive a small loon, which the Indians assured them was a happening of the greatest rarity, and they constructed a cage for it with the hope that they could keep it alive, and in due course sent it to the king. Next day, with continuing wonder and delight, they were threading their way among the Thousand Islands and during the day two more loons were caught alive. It was an unheard-of thing, the Indians said, to catch three in so short a space of time; an auspicious aura tinged the sunset as they made camp that evening at the mouth of the Gannannokoui. On the twelfth they broke camp very early, then halted at ten o'clock for three hours to eat and rest. At one in the afternoon Frontenac ordered them to the canoes.

They were now on the threshold of Ontario and Frontenac marshaled his flotilla in line of battle. In the van were four "squadrons" of ten canoes in line abreast. Then came the two barges, with their sixteen oars, their mounted cannon, and their wild and meaningless heraldic symbols. Frontenac himself followed in his personal canoe, with those of his guard, his staff, and the volunteers who had attached themselves to the expedition in close formation. On the right were the canoes from Three Rivers; on the left the contingent of Hurons. Twenty more canoes, again in line abreast, formed the rear guard. Thus they entered the open lake. The day was perfectly still, the water like glass on which the slow strokes of their paddles left gleaming, perfectly spaced rings.

An Iroquois canoe containing the Abbé d'Urfé met them with news that the Iroquois had assembled at the mouth of the Cataraqui River. The Indian paddlers offered to lead the way and Frontenac accepted graciously; it gave them face without detracting in any way from the boding impressiveness of his flotilla. When they turned the point and finally entered the bay, he was "enraptured at finding a spot so well adapted to his design," whose harbor he considered "capable of holding a hundred ships." He landed immediately and spent the next three hours inspecting all the features of the site, not returning to camp till after eight. The Iroquois, who had been waiting impatiently, wanted to hold the council at once in his tent; but he sent word, politely and firmly, that he would not greet them till next morning; it would be easier then for both parties to see and entertain each other.

The council on the following day revealed Frontenac's true genius at impressing the Indian mind. He had given orders the night before for the disposition of the troops so that the Iroquois might be impressed by the discipline of an apparently spontaneous maneuver. At dawn the drums beat the reveille; the reverberation against the silent expanse of lake and forest, always a daunting sound to the Indian soul, echoed and thundered. At seven o'clock the men formed in a double line around Frontenac's tent with two more lines extending all the way to the Indian camp, a rigidly aligned facsimile of the gantlet through which they were wont to make prisoners pass on the way to their torture, but through which they were now escorted with the gravest courtesy. Sails had been spread on the ground before Frontenac's tent, where he stood with all his guard in the full splendor of dress uniform to receive the sixty sachems who had been designated to represent the Five Nations in the council; and as the chiefs drew near they made no attempt to conceal the admiration with which they regarded the proceedings. The five spokesmen, one for each nation, spoke their brief greetings in turn, offering at the end not the usual strings of wampum but a full belt as a mark of their estimation of his greatness. They lapsed into silence, for it was now time to hear his thought.

His speech entered them in a way the words of almost no other white man ever could. "Children! Onnontagues, Mohawks, Oneidas, Cayugas, and Senecas," he began and spoke his pleasure at seeing them and their obedience in coming. And instantly he reassured them, speaking in the name of their great father, the King of France. "Take courage, then, my children; you will hear his word, which is full of tenderness and peace; a word which will fill your cabins with joy and happiness; for think not that war is the object of my voyage. My spirit is full of peace, and she walks in company with me." He spoke as if the morning sunshine on the lake were in his heart; there was only the tiny reference to war to give value to his peaceful message. And now he made gifts: a symbolic musket for each of the Five Nations; brandy and biscuits for the men; prunes and raisins for the women and the children.

While these opening ceremonies were still in progress Frontenac's engineer, the Sieur Rendin, had been tracing the outlines for the fort. Now as the first session of the council broke up, the men went immediately to work on the fort, some digging the trench in which the pickets would be set, some felling trees for the palisade, all according to a prearranged program, with such efficiency that the Iroquois, who had never seen work undertaken in this systematic way, were lost in admiration. The work went forward with amazing rapidity, all, including the officers, putting their hands to it. Meanwhile Frontenac, in an ecstasy of pleasure, explored all the bay and went up the river, where he found a natural prairie "as handsome and level as any in France." At every meal he had two or three of the Iroquois sachems, with their families, as guests; he fondled the children and gave them raisins and bread from his pockets; and in the evenings the Iroquois women, who had never received this kind of consideration, volunteered to dance before his tent.

By the seventeenth the fort had progressed so well that Frontenac considered it time to call the Iroquois for their grand council. His speech on this occasion began much as had the first, on a note of affection, but this time calling them to turn themselves to God. Once he had completed this obligation of a Christian ruler he spoke plainly and simply on the need to keep the peace, first with the French and then with the Algonquins and Hurons, who were the allies of the French and whom he treated exactly as he would Frenchmen. He pointed out the size of the flotilla with which he had ascended the St. Lawrence, purely for the sake of coming to see them. If he could surmount all the rapids and currents with so huge a fleet for peaceful reasons, let them "infer from this what he could effect if he desired to wage war . . ." These plain words, supported by the evidence of the fort being constructed so quickly and efficiently, were sobering indeed. But he hastened to assure them that the work going forward before their eyes was not for military purposes but to provide a strong post at which they might trade their furs at more convenience to themselves than by making the long trip to Montreal or Albany, and he declared it his intention to have a real settlement of Frenchmen there before very long.

During the speech periodic presentations were made of fifteen muskets and a quantity of powder and lead; twenty-five long overcoats; five short overcoats with twenty-five shirts, twenty-five pairs of stockings, and five packages of glass beads. The Iroquois were less impressed by these gifts than they were by the forthright nature of Frontenac's speech and its obvious sincerity. But one chief had his own practical question: what kind of prices were the French going to ask for goods brought all the way to Cataraqui? Except for that single note of skepticism, the Iroquois agreed to everything, including peace with the Hurons and Algonquins, and promised not to molest them even in their own country of the Long House. They did not violate this promise throughout Frontenac's term.

Three days later they broke camp and returned to their country. The palisades were now planted and the buildings were so far along that Frontenac began sending off his men in "squadrons," for they would be badly needed in the fields. On the twenty-fifth, with the work nearly finished, Frontenac named the men and officers who would stay to complete the final details and act as its garrison. He himself left on the twenty-eighth, meeting on the first day the fleet of canoes coming up from Montreal with stores enough to supply the garrison for a full year. Everything had gone like clockwork, and he had every right to satisfaction. He had made the arduous ascent of the St. Lawrence with a large expedition, gained all his ends with the Iroquois, and built a fort in record time, without losing a man or even a canoe.

Frontenac's speech to the Iroquois confirmed the worst suspicions of the fur merchants: the fort at Cataraqui was to be used specifically for trading with the Indians. Perrot, who controlled the trade at Montreal, regarded it as a direct challenge and considered the governor now to be his commercial rival. And Frontenac, in the light of his own plans, had the same opinion of Perrot.

Frontenac had orders from the king to bring the *coureurs de bois* to heel. As most of them were controlled by Perrot or were in league with him, arresting them was something of a problem. The governor had no soldiers he could send on such a mission; the *coureurs de bois* were tough people to deal with in the first place; and in the second, what soldiers there were in Canada were the veterans of Carignan, most of whom were settled round Montreal and were in sympathy with the *coureurs de bois*. His only recourse was to send orders to the judge at Montreal to arrest the *coureurs de bois* wherever he could find them. The judge, hearing that two with particularly riotous reputations were then in the house of a lieutenant named Carion, sent a constable to arrest them; but the lieutenant threw him forcibly out of his house and allowed the two *coureurs de bois* to escape. Perrot then threatened the judge with prison if he ever tried to arrest any of his men again.

Frontenac was incensed and sent on three of his personal guard under a Lieutenant Bizard to arrest Carion. He did so and took him to the house of a merchant named Le Ber. Bizard intended to let Perrot receive notice of the arrest under the governor's orders by letter after he and Carion had started for Quebec, but Perrot got word of the proceedings, arrived with a sergeant and some soldiers, rescued Carion, tore up a letter from Frontenac, and haled Bizard off to jail — and then, to ice his little cake of fury, put Le Ber in prison also. After three or four days of reflecting that these actions had been in opposition to the royal authority, he released Bizard with a quite unapologetic letter for Frontenac.

Meanwhile the priests of St. Sulpice had taken the part of their own governor, and when Frontenac invited Perrot in a letter couched in the blandest terms to come to Quebec so that they might work out their differences, the Abbé Fenelon offered to accompany him in the role of referee. The interview, as might have been predicted, was violent on both sides. It ended with Perrot imprisoned in the château and Fenelon in a state of indignant agitation. He returned to Montreal on the heels of an officer, La Nougère, who was to assume Perrot's office, and a judge whom Frontenac could trust. They had strict orders to pursue the *coureurs de bois* relentlessly. As it chanced, the first two to be arrested were those Carion had helped escape. They were sent to Quebec, where Frontenac ordered one of them hanged, which was done without delay, the gallows being thoughtfully erected outside the window of Perrot's cell.

This had a remarkably sobering effect on the *coureurs de bois*, as well as on Perrot, and it was not long before Frontenac could report that all but five had returned to the settlements. This pacification did not apply to Montreal, where excitement and resentment remained at fever pitch. In the arguments that flowed like rising and falling tides among the houses, La Salle declared himself for Frontenac. The merchant Le Ber, however, switched and became the bitter and lasting opponent of both the governor and La Salle, who had previously been his friend. The priests in the seminary were as overwrought as the rest of the population, and after he returned from Quebec Fenelon preached a violent sermon which, though not mentioning Frontenac by name, was obviously directed at him. La Salle, who had been listening from a bench near the door, was outraged and showed it by rising with a stamp of feet. He gesticulated toward Fenelon to make his disapproval plain and then strode out of the church.

News of this scandalous episode soon came to Frontenac's attention. La Salle's indignation, on top of the good services he had already performed, doubly commended the young man to him, and in the fall of 1674 he rewarded him by sending him to France with letters of the highest recommendation.

These letters, which La Salle presented to Louis, helped win him the royal grant of a seigneury which included Fort Frontenac and the land surrounding it to a depth of fourteen miles. The proposal had been Frontenac's. Louis and Colbert were much disturbed over the spending of ten thousand livres to establish a post so far inland, to say nothing of the continuing cost of supplying it. They had made plain that such extravagance was something the royal exchequer could scarcely afford, so Frontenac had suggested to La Salle that if he offered to pay the ten thousand livres and promised to maintain the fort, he might well get it for his own; and as La Salle would be a principal landholder of Canada if he did get it, Frontenac also suggested that he might at the same time plead successfully for a patent of nobility; and so it turned out. Louis was delighted at the thought of having a sound fort at the mouth of Lake Ontario as long as it would cost him nothing. A magnificent tract of land, which in America meant nothing to him, was something to give away in a fine gesture, without a qualm. And as for the nobility, La Salle's service as an explorer deserved some recognition; it was all pleasantly democratic from Louis's point of view, this elevation of a deserving bourgeois, "together with his wife and children, posterity and issue, both male and female, born and to be born in lawful wedlock," by awarding him a patent of nobility (like an editor of a Social Register entering a new name in return for a modest bit of currency passed under the table). La Salle was a man of the most intense pride, so it may have gratified him, but he was not vain. What counted was his title to Fort Frontenac.

It can be assumed that he had from the beginning regarded its acquisition as a first step toward his ultimate goal. Now that he had it, he conscientiously went to work to carry out his obligations under the grant. He tore down the wooden fort and replaced it by a larger and stronger one with stone bastions and ramparts, with a variety of buildings inside to provide officers' quarters, barracks, a bakery, smithy, and mill, all built solidly of squared timber. Within three years the shore of the bay had begun to look like a real settlement. A cluster of habitant houses had been built along the shore just below the fort; at a distance beyond were the long houses of some Iroquois whom he had persuaded to join his enterprise. He had built four vessels, two of them barks of 40 tons to sail Lake Ontario; he had brought up livestock, and nearly a hundred acres had been cleared and put to crops. It was an astonishing transformation, this thoroughly modern community so far in the wilderness; and it was prospering. La Salle was said to be making as much as twenty-five thousand livres a year. If he had chosen to stay he would have become a man of wealth and power, for at the head of the St. Lawrence, there was no other white man who could dispute him.

There were people who were ready and eager to dispute him down the river, however. They formed, in fact, a league against him and tried in every way to discredit his character: he was inveigled into staying in the house of the king's tax collector in Quebec where the latter's wife tried to seduce him into a compromising position; gossip that he had seduced a young woman was broadcast in Montreal; it was said that he had defied the ordinance forbidding traders to travel in the Indian country, but La Salle was able to demonstrate that with an Iroquois village at his doorstep, the Iroquois were bringing their furs to him. The Jesuits were silent partners in this league. The missionaries told their flocks in the Iroquois towns that he was strengthening Fort Frontenac with stone for the ultimate purpose of using it as a base in carrying war against them. When Frontenac came up to Ontario the Iroquois ascribed these rumors to Fathers Bruyas and Pierron; denials settled nothing, and the suspicion remained. It preyed on La Salle's nerves. He was convinced that an attempt had been made to poison him — by, of all persons, Nicholas Perrot. It is conceivable, but somehow it does not consort with what else we know of Perrot.

The struggle framed itself as one between Canadians and French lately come from Europe, with the Jesuits on the Canadian side, as was also the intendant who succeeded Talon, Jacques Duchesneau. The governor himself was in a partnership with La Salle, La Salle's lieutenant La Forest, and at this time a man named Boisseau. Against them was a group headed by Le Ber and including Charles Le Moyne with the formidable phalanx of his sons, La Chesnaye, and others. The lines would shift, but hatred of La Salle never wavered. By what seemed a *coup de main* he made himself master of one of the finest posts in Canada, which they had intended to develop for themselves when they got round to it. That he survived their efforts to destroy him was due solely to an iron determination not to be deflected from his goal. In the end he was betrayed by people he had taken with him on his final expedition, and that was but ten years away.

Now in 1677, after two years of building and developing his seigneury, he could no longer stay sedentary. The fort was finished; in his eyes it was not just a post for trading with the Indians, it was the base from which to launch his project for establishing a great French colony in the west. But to accomplish this he would need financial backing far beyond his own ability to provide and also royal confirmation of his title to Fort Frontenac and to such posts as he would establish west and southwest of the Great Lakes. In the fall, leaving La Forest in charge of the fort, he dropped down the St. Lawrence and at Quebec took ship for France.

His petition to the king was well received. In May 1678, he received a license "to discover the Western part of New France." As he wished, this document confirmed him in his title to Fort Frontenac, commending his accomplishment there, and in his discoveries gave him permission "to construct forts in the places you may think necessary," over which he would enjoy the same seigneurial privileges as at Fort Frontenac (which was another burr to gall the backs of La Salle's Canadian rivals, for only a year earlier Louis had denied a petition by Joliet to build a post on the Mississippi). There was, of course, the proviso "that you perform the whole at your expense and that of your associates," though in return they were to enjoy a monopoly in the trade in buffalo hides. Forbidden was any trading with the Ottawas or tribes of the upper Great Lakes. There was also a stipulation that all must be accomplished within five years or all privileges would be withdrawn, a stipulation that would have daunted any man less visionary and determined than La Salle.

The royal license helped him to find money, but it was not easy. From various sources he raised forty-five thousand livres, though one loan of eleven thousand called for forty percent interest; but his most important source of funds was his own family, who responded handsomely to what they termed "the royal goodness." After he returned to Canada, Frontenac helped him get a second loan of fourteen thousand livres which was secured by a mortgage on Fort Frontenac. Even so, he never had as much as he needed once his bad luck began pursuing him.

While he was still in France, one very fortunate thing did happen to him. The Prince of Conti sent a young Italian to see him, with the strongest recommendations. His name was Henri de Tonty; he was twenty-seven at the time; and he had been trained in and served with valor the French army, rising in ten years from cadet to captain. His service had terminated with the loss of one hand "shot off in Sicily by a grenade." His father was a Neapolitan banker who had gained fame of a sort by inventing a form of insurance that was also a lottery, called after him a "tontine." The character of his son was marked not only by a valorous heart but by an utterly steadfast nature. He was incorruptible. He told La Salle that he would like to join him on his explorations in the west of New France and La Salle, for once correctly assessing another man's character, gladly agreed. From that moment and until La Salle's death Tonty served him fully and loyally in every way, as his lieutenant when they were voyaging together, and as his deputy when La Salle left him with a mere handful of rogues to hold one of his posts in the west.

They sailed from Rochelle in mid-July 1678, together with another, whom La Salle had offered a share in his enterprise, La Motte de Lussière, an association he would regret as deeply as he took comfort in Tonty's companionship, and also thirty men as artisans and soldiers. It was a normal two months' crossing.

After some time spent recruiting in Quebec, both for the expedition and in search of other backers, La Salle was ready to move. La Motte and most of the men set out up the river for Fort Frontenac, which they reached on November 8; he himself with Tonty would not arrive till mid-December. Meanwhile, however, fifteen men were to set out from Fort Frontenac in canoes to spend the winter trading on Lake Michigan and down the Illinois. La Motte himself had orders to move on across Ontario and build winter shelter on the Niagara River. Accordingly on November 18 he embarked with sixteen men and Father Louis Hennepin who, with two other Recollet friars, was stationed at the fort. They hugged the northern shore as closely as possible to find some shelter from a howling northeast wind and on December 6, after a night of beating offshore in boisterous darkness, entered the Niagara River.

Hennepin, whose mind was devoured with curiosity about the wilderness, and who by nature combined more the attributes of a freebooter, braggart, and adventurer than those of a priest (he also had a keenly observing eye and a considerable gift in writing that provided valuable material for historians later), immediately persuaded a few men to join him in a trip up the river. When they could paddle no farther, they landed on the west bank, which soon brought them high above the river and in due course to the awesome falls. Hennepin's description of them was the first ever published. If he estimated their height as five hundred feet instead of their actual one hundred and sixty-seven, he may be forgiven (though perhaps not as easily forgiven for tacking on another hundred feet in the next edition of his book), and his picture of them has accuracies and does convey the overwhelming volume of descending water.

La Motte began promptly the work of building winter quarters: a small stockaded house about five miles from the mouth of the Niagara and under the lee of the great bluffs below what is now the site of Lewiston. It was desperately hard work to plant the stockade; they had to thaw the ground with boiling water. There were other difficulties. Senecas living near by in a small village began to display increasing hostility, so much so that La Motte decided that he should go to the main Seneca town near the Genesee River and make presents to the chiefs and win their approval. Taking Hennepin and several others, he started on the day after Christmas and reached the town on the last day of the year.

Two Jesuits, Pierre Raffeix and Julien Garnier, joined the council and La Motte refused to speak in their presence, knowing the Order to be opposed to any of La Salle's activities. They finally gave in and left the council house, Hennepin accompanying them out of respect, as he said, for the cloth. But even without their ominous presence, La Motte made no headway in persuading the chiefs that a post on the Niagara and a ship on Lake Erie would be good things for the Senecas as well as the French. They listened to him, all forty-two of them, with the gravity of forty-two ceremonial stones; they accepted his gifts of hatchets, beads, and scarlet cloth, but remained coldly noncommittal, though they made a gesture of hospitality by burning a prisoner for his edification. He returned to the Niagara distraught and shaken.

Meanwhile La Salle with Tonty had reached Fort Frontenac, loaded one of the 40-ton barks with supplies and ammunition, and embarked for the Niagara. The winds were still boisterous, the lake very rough, and they were nearly wrecked in the Bay of Quinté, where they spent Christmas Eve. Next day they were at the mouth of the Genesee, and after some delay La Salle, not being aware of La Motte's mission, decided to visit the main Seneca town, which he reached just after La Motte's discomfited departure.

He succeeded where La Motte had failed. The Seneca chiefs were not happy about French activity on the Niagara but, as almost all Indians were, they were impressed by La Salle as a man and gave him permission to use Niagara as a French carrying place and to build his ship on Lake Erie.

It was still storming when he returned to the bark; the wind from the northwest was so heavy that they had to go ashore twenty miles short of the Niagara and finish the trip overland. Leaving their supplies in La Motte's unfinished house, the two men climbed the heights to look for a suitable place to build their ship above the falls.

They found it seven miles beyond, where a small stream now called Cayuga Creek entered the river. Here they could launch their hull and finish rigging it on the quiet water of the creek before towing it out into and up the river. Both men were well satisfied and it was at that moment that a messenger found them with news of the first in the succession of disasters that from that point on was to shroud La Salle's American experience.

This was the loss of his bark, driven ashore by the gale. The crew had managed to save themselves and Tonty said "the things in it" also were saved. By that he must have meant a portion of their provisions (for they were able to survive the winter) but mainly the anchors, gear, and rigging of the ship he was to build and which absorbed him wholly. Hunger was only one of the things to worry over. Dissension had manifested itself among La Salle's men, a crew of different races, often resentful of each other and becoming more and more prone to question his leadership. La Motte had become one of them — in part, La Salle thought, because his enemies had probably got at La Motte on his trip up from Quebec. He may well have been right; but also certain men cannot stand exposure to the wilderness, the lonely places, the lurking presence of strange, dark, and pagan people. La Motte had developed an inflammation of his eyes; he could barely see. If he had been planning to subvert the men, he now became an enemy, as though La Salle were the personification of the wilderness he could not bear. If that was his feeling, he was, in a way, right. No other Frenchman ever joined his soul so closely to the wilderness as La Salle. In due course La Motte returned to Fort Frontenac. All La Salle said of him was that "he served me very ill."

Meanwhile it was essential to get the supplies for the boat builders to the site of the "shipyard" before the fiercest winter storms. The boat which had brought La Motte and Hennepin, with its cargo, was rapelled to the foot of the rapids under the Lewiston bluffs. From there supplies had to be packed up the steep climb and on to Cayuga Creek. Here two Mohican Indians who had joined La Salle's party put up bark lodges for the shipworkers, and Hennepin, who had toiled up the bluff with his portable altar strapped to his shoulders, built a bark chapel near by with the aid of the Indians and some of the French.

With the work well started, La Salle returned to La Motte's house and taking some of the remaining men went down to the mouth of the river. There, on the point where Fort Niagara was later built, he staked out the foundation lines for two blockhouses. This he considered the proper place for a fort and as usual, when dealing with geography and strategy and not with human character, he was right. From that spot the French later were able to control the four upper Great Lakes and supply the thin, scattered web of posts and forts and settlements on their shores and on the Ohio, Illinois, and Mississippi.

Then leaving a crew to build the blockhouses he set out on foot with two men and a dog for Fort Frontenac. It was the first but not the longest of his harsh winter journeys, two hundred and fifty miles along the southern shore and then across the frozen lake in the middle of February. They ran out of food and did the last two days on empty stomachs. At Fort Frontenac he learned that his enemies had spread tales about his having disappeared on an irresponsible and fantastic expedition from which he would never return. Alarmed, his creditors had attached all his property down the St. Lawrence: all he had left was Fort Frontenac.

During the winter and spring Tonty and his crew were occupied in building their ship. The work went rapidly, but there were anxious days when their little camp was infested with sullen and resentful Senecas. But Tonty managed somehow to keep control — perhaps it was here for the first time that he cracked an Indian's head with his false, metal hand, an act invariably inspiring respect — of both the Indians and his own people. As the hull took shape, the Senecas threatened to burn it and from then on, full watches stood through the night. They had her ready to launch when the ice opened.

She was of 45 tons burthen, she carried five small cannon, and she had the figurehead of a griffin, from which she took her name, a carved monster on which the Senecas looked in wonder and dread. The French sang the "Te Deum" as they let her into the water, and once they had her anchored out in the creek they transferred their belongings to her and slept comfortably aboard while they finished her rigging. Sundays Hennepin was able to preach from her deck to the Indians onshore, with her cannon peeping from her ports to underline the word of God.

Later they warped her up the Niagara as far as the site of present Black Rock, and there La Salle found her when he returned from Fort Frontenac. He brought ample stores and more men, including three Recollets, one of whom, Zenobius Membré, would share in his discovery of the Gulf of Mexico. The men now labored to get everything over the steep carry, including the main anchor for the *Griffin* which took four men to pack it up the heights. As soon as they had loaded everything aboard, La Salle's and Tonty's combined groups worked the *Griffin* up the rest of the Niagara until she rested at last on the still water of Lake Erie. As some work still remained to be done, La Salle now asked Tonty to go to Detroit where some of the fifteen men he had sent out the year before were supposed to have been trading.

Tonty, who seemed to be inexhaustible, set out at once in a canoe. He reached Detroit safely but found no Frenchmen. While he was waiting there the *Griffin* sailed into the strait, the first ship to have crossed Lake Erie. La Salle picked up Tonty and resumed his voyage, crossing Lake St. Clair, breasting the current of the St. Clair River, and finally sailing out onto the glittering expanse of Lake Huron. It was an auspicious moment, and for a day they sailed before a fresh breeze with a white curl of foam against their bows.

Then the wind fell, and after some dark and boding hours a storm burst on them and Lake Huron gave vent to the fury which caused some men to call it a cauldron. They came so near to losing the *Griffin* that even La Salle advised his men to make their peace with God, while the shipmaster called down curses on him for bringing him to drown in a sea where the water was not even salt. But the ship weathered through, and in time they reached Michilimackinac, turned into its strait, and anchored in the quiet cove off St. Ignace.

It had grown as a community in the four years since Marquette's death. Besides the palisaded mission buildings, with the Huron village of long houses on the right, and the wigwams of the Ottawas, there was a cluster of square log houses on the left, belonging to French traders and *coureurs de bois*. St. Ignace, whether the Jesuits liked it or not, had become a center of the fur trade.

The arrival of the *Griffin* was a sensation. To the Indians it seemed a floating fort and for days their canoes were clustered thickly round it. La Salle led his followers ashore, himself magnificent in a long scarlet cloak trimmed with gold braid, and entered the Jesuit chapel for the inevitable service of thanksgiving and praise. But around him hatred and fear clouded the atmosphere. The traders and their *coureurs de bois* suspected that he planned to move in on what they considered their territory; even the Ottawas were apprehensive of his motives in coming in this great vessel which made their largest canoes seem puny; and the Jesuits resented his operating in the Illinois country, which they still hoped to turn into another Paraguay.

They had some reason to be suspicious. A number of the fifteen men he had sent ahead the year before to trade for him, presumably among the Pottawatomies and Illinois beyond Lake Michigan, had either sold out to the established traders or gone into the woods on their own, embezzling his goods. He surprised four of them at the mission and put them under arrest and, hearing that others were then at Sault Ste. Marie, sent Tonty there to pick them up. But Tonty found only two to take in charge, along with a few furs.

In Tonty's absence La Salle sailed west across Lake Michigan to an island off Green Bay (now Washington Island) where in a Pottawatomie village he found several of the advance guard who had kept faith with him and were waiting there with a fine stock of furs, valued at twelve thousand livres. Though these represented only a portion of what he had been counting on, they were valuable enough to make it essential, after his losses, to get them to Quebec to satisfy his creditors. Consequently, instead of waiting for Tonty to return and take command of the party which he proposed to have start building on the Illinois, he decided to send the *Griffin* back to Niagara with the furs and to move on at once himself with the expedition to the Illinois.

The ship made sail on September 18 and after firing a parting shot from one of her cannon disappeared over the lake. It was an afternoon of calm and sunshine, but that night a storm of great violence burst over northern Lake Michigan. La Salle, who had set out from Washington Island with his followers in four canoes heavily laden with tools, trade goods, and arms, barely was able to make shore. For five days the storm pinned them there.

Sometime, somewhere during that tempest the *Griffin* disappeared. It was never known whether she survived the storm only to be boarded and burned by Indians. La Salle came to believe that the master and crew had scuttled her after unloading her furs and goods and then joined forces with traders on the upper Great Lakes. But the manner of her disappearance was irrelevant; it was the fact that mattered. Coming that winter, with his growing investment on the Illinois, it was economically a death wound. Yet he managed to survive it.

In the late fall of 1679 La Salle, of course, did not know of the *Griffin's* disappearance. He still expected her to return with a full load of supplies and anchors and rigging for a ship he planned to build on the Illinois, with which to navigate the Mississippi. Following the west shore of the lake, he finally skirted round the head until he reached the mouth of the St. Joseph. Here Tonty was supposed to join him, and while he waited he set his men to building a fort at the river mouth to keep them from mutiny and desertion. They spent some twenty days working at it and had it nearly finished when at last Tonty turned up. La Salle still had no word of the *Griffin*, but though he was now ready to write her off as lost, he nevertheless sent two men back to Michilimackinac to wait for her arrival and then bring her to the mouth of the St. Joseph. He himself with the combined parties, thirty men and three Recollet priests in eight canoes, started up the St. Joseph on December 3. After some difficulty they found the five-mile portage to the Kankakee, a mere thread of dark water in a bog; but they launched their canoes in it, and it brought them to the Illinois.

They paddled down it in the last days of the year, passing Starved Rock, a precipitous sandstone cliff rising sheer from the riverbank. On the opposite shore was the chief town of the Ilinois, which Marquette had called Kaskaskia, and which now, according to Hennepin, numbered four hundred and sixty houses. But it was deserted. In any case, La Salle wanted a base nearer the Mississippi, and they went on, hungry and chilled in the falling snow, with the men very close to mutiny.

On the fifth of January, 1680, they came to a widening of the river into a broad stillwater and at the far end rising smoke. As they approached they saw it came from an Illinois town of eighty houses which stood on both banks of the river. After a first flurry of surprise — the Illinois seeing their canoes coming down the stream in line abreast had taken them for Iroquois — they were made welcome and given some bark lodges just outside the town. Here on the second night, six of his men deserted him. In the morning he brought the rest together and promised that any who feared the wilderness could go back, but for their own sakes as well as his, let them wait till spring.

Three quarters of a mile below the Indian town he found a strong site for a fort on a small square hill whose top was just large enough to accept the banks and palisades, two low blockhouses in the angles to house the men, a third to serve the Recollets and act as a chapel, the fourth for a shop, while he and Tonty set up tents in the open center. He called it Fort Crèvecoeur.

His mind was still on the mouth of the Mississippi. At the end of February he persuaded Hennepin to undertake an exploration of the Illinois and then to ascend the upper Mississippi in search of the Sioux. Hennepin went with two paddlers. He found the Sioux or they found him. They were holding him prisoner along with his companions when Duluth heard about them and came to their rescue, bullying the Sioux into giving them up and then seeing them out of the country as far as Michilimackinac.

Meanwhile La Salle had resolved that the only way in which he could save his enterprise was by going himself back to Fort Frontenac and from there attempting to get some order once more into his tangled and desperate affairs. He proposed to make the journey overland. Tonty was put in command of Fort Crèvecoeur. On March 1, with four Frenchmen and a Mohican hunter who, in a wordless Indian way, seems to have made La Salle's cause his own, he started up the Illinois through drifting ice with two canoes.

At the wide stillwater, now Peoria Lake, they found the ice impassable, so they dragged the canoes ashore, built crude sleds, and hauled them over the snow to the top of the stillwater. There they found the ice on the river too weak to walk on and too heavy to break. They carried their canoes along the bank. Then for a day they were able to break their way laboriously through the ice; and then again they had to carry. The snow was too mushy for their snowshoes and floundering through it with their packs and canoes was agonizingly hard. But a hard frost on the next night allowed them to drag their canoes on the crusted snow.

On the fourth they came again to Marquette's Kaskaskia. The great town was still empty, but they spent several days there during which they met a small band of Illinois under their principal chief. When La Salle explained that he was on his way to fetch guns and ammunition with which to fight the Iroquois, the chief became friendly and promised to send supplies to Fort Crèvecoeur. There were rumors that the Iroquois were coming against them in the summer, and they wanted friends.

Meanwhile the great cliff of Starved Rock had caught his attention as a natural fortress which, crowned by a palisade, would be invulnerable to Indian attack, and when a little later he met two Frenchmen coming down Lake Michigan he sent a message back to Tonty to examine and fortify it.

It would gain nothing to detail minutely the struggles and sufferings of La Salle and his party on their incredible journey. The land was flooding, they waded marshes. They had abandoned their canoes, and now when they met rivers they had to build rafts. They spent a night at Fort St. Joseph and then struck out across southern Michigan. That was on the morning of March 25. Two of the men became ill and unable to walk. Making them as comfortable as possible and leaving them in the care of the others, La Salle scouted ahead through the woods for a stream that would take them to Lake Erie or Detroit.

Before long he came upon a small river whose course promised well. Returning for his companions, he brought them to the river, which was probably the Huron, and while the sick men rested he and the others set about making a canoe. It rained or sleeted almost constantly and to make their work more difficult they had to use elm bark as there was no birch. The canoe was clumsy, like the Iroquois canoes, but it floated all five, and in it they set off down the river.

For a while they had easy paddling; then they came to what appeared to be an unending jam of fallen trees. The river was impassable and since the two sick men were now able to walk La Salle abandoned his canoe and, following the river on foot, came out eventually on the Detroit River.

Here he decided to split his party. Two of the Frenchmen were to stay, build themselves a canoe, and go to Michilimackinac. He himself with the other two and the Mohican built a raft to carry them over the Detroit and then struck southwest for Lake Erie. They came out on it either in Pigeon Bay or on the eastern shore of Point Pelee. But now the Mohican and one of the Frenchmen had come down with the same sickness, so La Salle made another camp and with the other Frenchman built a second canoe. In this, with the two sick men huddled helpless in the middle, they paddled the length of Lake Erie and on the day after Easter entered the Niagara River.

The year before, La Salle had left several men at the site of the "shipyard" where the *Griffin* had been built. They were still waiting there when he put the canoe into Cayuga Creek — among the very few of his followers and employees who faithfully obeyed his orders. They greeted him cordially, but they had news even grimmer than the nonappearance of the *Griffin*. A ship from France with a cargo consigned to him, valued at over twenty-two thousand livres, as well as twenty men who had come to join him, had been wrecked in the St. Lawrence below Quebec. The cargo was a total loss. The men had escaped, but some had been seduced away from him by the intendant, Duchesneau, and the others, except for four, hearing that he was dead, had returned to France.

In the face of this disaster he kept his courage. The second Frenchman had fallen sick, so now all three of his traveling companions were unable to move, and he alone was able to finish the journey. At Niagara he picked up three fresh men and at length on the sixth of May, through driving rain, he came back to Fort Frontenac. He had been sixty-five days on the way from Crèvecoeur to Frontenac, he had covered more than a thousand miles, and he still had to go on to Montreal and possibly Quebec to do whatever could be done to recover his fortunes.

The people of Montreal looked on him as a man returned from the dead. Their very amazement together with the apparent coolness with which he confronted his sequence of disasters ennabled him to collect the supplies he would need both for his return journey and for the posts on the Illinois. Within a week he was back at Fort Frontenac, ready to head west. But almost at the moment of starting he received a message from Tonty. It struck home, after all his other reverses, like the last nail in the coffin.

Tonty wrote that, pursuant to instructions, he had left Fort Crèvecoeur to survey the site proposed by La Salle on Starved Rock. In his absence, the garrison at Crèvecoeur had decided to desert. They had appropriated what stores and ammunition they would need for their return to Montreal. All else they had thrown into the river and had then destroyed the fort itself. Nothing was left for Tonty but three men newly arrived from France and the two Recollet Fathers, hungry, shelterless, and virtually without arms, at the mercy of the Indians. The situation is best summed up by Tonty's laconic sentences. "All that I could do was to send an authentic account of the affair to M. de la Salle. He laid wait for them on Lake Frontenac [Ontario], took some of them and killed others, after which he returned to the Illinois."

It was August 10 when La Salle reached Fort St. Joseph with twelve men. The remaining thirteen of his company under La Forest were to follow from Michilimackinac as soon as they had gathered additional stores, if that was possible, for the post had proved as hostile as before. Now as he looked at the ruins of his fort, which he knew had been burned by the deserters on their way north, his anxiety for Tonty redoubled. From here on speed was essential, for rumors of an Iroquois war against the Illinois had been spreading through the summer. Leaving his heavy stores under guard of five men, he pushed on for the Kankakee portage and paddled hard down it and then the Illinois. They stopped only for three days when they met herd after herd of buffalo; they killed and smoked a dozen of the great beasts and then once more hurried on their way. They came under Starved Rock and looked over the river at the great Illinois town.

It, too, had been burned. There were only the skeletons of the lodges. When they went ashore and walked toward it they found themselves picking their way through hundreds of corpses in all stages of mutilation and decay. A little beyond the town was one of the rude stockades the Iroquois were wont to throw up when operating in enemy country — its palisades were hung with dismembered skulls and bones. The valley was full of the stench of death and corruption and the darker smell of fear.

Below Starved Rock they came on six more abandoned Illinois villages. The town at Lake Peoria had also been wiped out, and below it they came to the ruins of Fort Crèvecoeur. All that remained was the partially built hull of the vessel he had designed for use on the Mississippi, but the Iroquois had managed to pull the nails and spikes from the timbers.

They went on down the Illinois. Along the banks they kept finding camping places where the Iroquois had been. The land was still and bleak and soundless, as if life had been swept forever from it. Then at a distance they saw six people standing in a line to watch them and they went ashore. But as they drew near they saw that the "people" were six Illinois women bound to torture stakes, their bodies half consumed by fire. It had been a camping place for the Iroquois where they had briefly entertained themselves.

They went all the way to the Mississippi before they turned back. They reached the mouth of the Kankakee on Janury 6 — it was now 1681 — and on impulse La Salle turned away and chose the northern route to the Des Plaines. There on its banks they came across a cabin of bark; and then as they searched through it found a piece of board that had been cut off by a saw. It convinced La Salle that Tonty must still be alive.

After the desertion of the garrison Tonty dispatched two men to carry the news to La Salle. This left him with only one man, a Frenchman, and the two Flemish Recollet priests, Membré and Ribourde, the latter in his sixty-fifth year. An odd mixture to find in such a remote fastness of paganism and violence, and all the less capable of real defense when one remembers that Tonty himself had only one usable hand, the other being of iron.

In the summer the Iroquois army reached the Illinois country, five hundred strong, and accompanied by one hundred Miamis, hereditary foes of the Illinois, who had been deluded into believing that they would have something to gain in siding with the Iroquois, when as a matter of fact they had been marked next on the list for destruction.

The first news of them to reach Peoria was brought by a Shawnee who reported that among the advancing horde was a Black Robe. At once this meant to the Illinois mind, inflamed by terror, that the French had instigated the war against them. A crowd rushed down on Fort Crèvecoeur, burst their way in, and accused Tonty of treachery. It was of course a delusion. The "Jesuit" was merely an Iroquois warrior who had somewhere acquired a black hat, soutane, and stockings and elected to wear them into war, but none the less terrible for that. Even if they had known, it would have made no difference to the infuriated Illinois and for a moment the lives of Tonty and his companions hung in the balance. Only when he promised to go to war with them did the Illinois relax, though by that time they had thrown in the river all the tools and anything else they could find in the ruins of the fort.

Tonty was in the forefront when the first skirmish opened and saw at once that the Illinois, who had relatively few muskets, were heavily outgunned. He determined to try to win a peace. Taking a belt of wampum from his pocket, he laid down his musket and advanced toward the Iroquois battle line, accompanied by one of the Frenchmen and a courageous Illinois. When he saw that the Iroquois would not abate their fire he sent the other two back and went on alone, and miraculously entered their lines uninjured. Instantly the wampum was snatched from his hand and a brave stabbed his chest, but the knife was turned on a rib. Then some of them recognized him because of his iron hand, and recalled that he was the friend and officer of Frontenac. They took him back to their camp and held a council, asking his purpose in coming to them.

He told them that the Illinois were the children of the French king and of Onontio and asked them why they wished to rupture their peace with the French. In the midst of the discussion a warrior brought news that their left wing was giving way and their anger against him suddenly flared. The Seneca war chief demanded that he be burned, but the leader of the Onondagas argued for setting him at liberty. For a while Tonty's life depended on the whim of the council. "There was a man behind me with a knife in his hand, who every now and then lifted up my hair." In the end the Onondaga carried his point and Tonty was sent back to the Illinois with a belt and an offer of peace. Bleeding from chest and mouth, Tonty made his way to the Illinois lines and amazingly, for a time, he achieved a truce.

The Iroquois built themselves a fort and after a few days brought Tonty and his party into it with them. They held various councils with the Illinois in which peace was still a word in the air. But it was finally concluded and the Illinois warriors dropped down the river to where they had left their women and children. The Iroquois of course had no idea of keeping their word. But first they wished to get Tonty out of the way, so they held another council and offered him six packs of beaver as gifts to speed his going. When he asked when *they* intended to leave the country, one burst out that they would not leave until they had eaten some Illinois. Tonty then kicked their beaver pelts back at them and said he would deal with them no more. It was a miracle that they allowed him to leave with his companions, in a worn and leaky canoe.

Their journey north was harrowing enough. It began in tragedy when old Father Ribourde wandered off and was murdered by a band of Kickapoos who had come south hoping to pick up a few Iroquois scalps but settled for a tonsure. A few days afterward their canoe became unusable and they went ahead on foot, choosing unfortunately to go along the west coast of Lake Michigan. Their moccasins gave out and they made shoes of a sort from the cloak of Father Ribourde. They lived for days on wild garlic. They became so weak that some days they could barely move. At last on December 4 a party of Ottawas came upon them and took them in their canoes to a friendly Pottawatomie village. There they wintered and in the spring found their way to Michilimackinac.

La Salle had wintered at Fort St. Joseph; his mood as he contemplated his situation, with his enemies triumphant and friends despondent, and with his avalanche of debt, must have been as black as the charred timbers of the fort; yet it was here that he formed his plan of a confederation of the western tribes which, if it did not bring him fortune, was to stand Canada in good stead during the approaching wars with the English. He would build his fort on Starved Rock as he had intended and around it gather the various tribes who must be made to reconcile their old feuds for common survival. There they would learn to live as neighbors, develop their primitive agriculture, receive religious instruction from the Recollet missionaries, and sell their furs, which he would send down the Mississippi to a post he would build at its mouth, instead of transporting them by the tortuous journey through the Great Lakes to Montreal. It was a grand design, and with a little luck he would have made it good. As it was, it provided the outlines for those who came after him.

He began working toward it early in 1681. Near Fort St. Joseph were a cluster of refugees from New England and King Philip's War: Narragansetts, Mohegans, Abenakis. They welcomed his suggestion of an alliance. A Shawnee chief, who could call on one hundred and fifty warriors, came to see him and promised to bring his tribe to the Illinois in the autumn. Then the Miamis, whom the Iroquois had turned on the year before after their only partial success against the Illinois, wanted to negotiate. But this meant that La Salle must first win the Illinois over to the idea; they were by far the most numerous of the tribes, if not the best in war; and it was their land that would provide the setting for his plan.

Early in March he started for the Kankakee portage with sixteen men; they were held up on the way by what seemed an epidemic of blindness; but it had compensations, for one of La Salle's hunters came across a band of Foxes from Green Bay and learned from them that Tonty was safe. La Salle could have had no better tonic. He recovered his sight, the river opened, and they were free to paddle south. Near the site of the great town destroyed by the Iroquois they met a party of Illinois, come back to open caches of corn. To them La Salle unfolded his plan, urging them to make peace with the Miamis, describing the fort he would build on the great rock, and assuring them that he with other Frenchmen would make his permanent home among them. They were intensely interested in his ideas and promised to present them to the rest of the tribe.

La Salle now turned north again. He sent La Forest ahead to Michilimackinac to find Tonty and tell him to wait. He himself then went up the St. Joseph to the main Miami town above the Kankakee portage. He found the Miamis treating with some Iroquois envoys whom in council he was able to outface and humiliate so severely that they melted away during the night, which made a tremendous impression on the Miamis. There were more refugees from the New England tribes here also, who were attracted by his idea of an alliance — perhaps because of having failed in their own attempt to form one. He promised them new lands of their own and protection under the flag of France and urged them to act as intermediaries between the Miamis and the Illinois. Then in a final council with the Miamis he won them over, in part by resuscitating one of their great chiefs who had recently died, himself assuming the dead man's soul, and then in his new being making lavish gifts. The Miamis were completely won over. They promised to make the Illinois their brothers and to listen to the persuasion of those who had come to them from New England for sanctuary. This was the first valid step in forming the confederation of the western tribes.

La Salle now turned his attention to the discovery of the mouth of the Mississippi on which all the rest of his design depended. But first it was necessary to return to Montreal, placate his creditors and collect the supplies and men he would need for the descent of the great river. He stopped first at Michilimackinac for a moving reunion with Tonty and Zenobius Membré; for once, La Salle's face revealed his emotions. They wasted little time in reminiscing, however, and were soon on their way to Fort Frontenac. They reached it safely and pressed on to Montreal. There with the backing of Frontenac and the advice of his secretary, a man of great business sagacity, and with the help of a relation, he made his peace with his creditors and secured fresh loans, though at the cost of some of his monopolies.

Early in September he was on Lake Ontario, this time with a force to reckon with: thirty Frenchmen and the invaluable Tonty as his lieutenant; and about a hundred Indians, Shawnees and refugees from the New England tribes, all of them familiar with the use of firearms. He chose to make the portage from Toronto to Lake Simcoe, a difficult one but sheltered from the lake storms. From Simcoe the passage was comparatively easy down the Severn into Georgian Bay. It was late in the fall when, having crossed Lake Huron and traversed the length of Michigan, they came to Fort St. Joseph, with winter at hand.

On December 21, they finally started on La Salle's most important journey. Circling the head of Michigan they went up the Chicago to the Des Plaines carry — it made little difference as both rivers were solid with ice. The Indians had lagged behind and faded out; but the French made sledges for the canoes and dragged them slowly down the frozen river till at length they found open water at Lake Peoria. From then on the way was swift. On February 6 they floated out on the broad current of the Mississippi, dark from the dark winter sky.

The ninth of April, 1682, was the momentous day. They had been to the very Gulf and now, withdrawn a few miles above, they set up a cross and, "the whole party under arms, chanted the *Te Deum*, the *Exaudiat*, the *Domine salvum fac Regem*." Then they planted a tall pole with the arms of France and La Salle stepped forward and, "with a loud voice," proclaimed in the name of the king and by "virtue of the commission of his Majesty which I hold in my hand, and which may be seen by all whom it may concern," that he was taking possession "in the name of his Majesty and of his successors to the crown . . . of this country of Louisiana." It was the ceremony as we have seen it before, but with a new and vast significance. It framed the continent and, in all the enormous watershed of the Mississippi complex, procured an American empire for France.

The ceremony also had a form of legality missing from those previously described. Jacques de la Metairie, "Notary of Fort Frontenac, in New France, commissioned to exercise the said function of Notary during the voyage of Louisiana," drew up an instrument to which he affixed his signature and seal, and which afterward was witnessed by the signatures of the other members of the expedition.

For a day the sun had shone on Robert Cavelier de la Salle. It did not shine long. On the return journey he was stricken with a disease so acute that he was unable to travel. He went ashore at Chickasaw Bluffs where his men had put up a small stockaded camp on the voyage down. He ordered Tonty on to Michilimackinac to send out news of their success, and then to return to the Illinois. For forty days he lay face to face with death, nursed only by Membré, but at the end of July he resumed his journey by slow stages and finally in September reached Michilimackinac.

He had hoped to continue to Quebec and on to France, for now it seemed vitally important to establish a post at the Mississippi's mouth and use the river for access and commerce to his Illinois country. But he was still too weak to risk the journey in the fall; if winter caught and pinned him to the wilderness he would never survive the kind of food he would have to eat. So he decided to return to Starved Rock with Tonty and the rest of his expedition, where there would always be plenty of game.

During the winter La Salle and Tonty were occupied in building their fort. The top of the great rock was cleared; storehouses and barracks were built and enclosed on three sides by a palisade. The fourth side was the edge of the sheer cliff from which one could look down on giant catfish lying in the shallows, one hundred and twenty-five feet below. He named it Fort St. Louis. From it he could look over the river and far out across the prairie beyond, where another evidence of his work was taking shape and growing continually more impressive: the gradual gathering of assorted Indian tribes who had settled down in towns and camps, often in sight of one another.

Nearest was the great town to which the Illinois had once more returned. Farther out were the lodges and wigwams of perhaps ten more tribes, and scattered through them the camps of the fragments of others, like the Abenaki, and even more obscure people with such names as Piankishaws, Pepikokias, and Ouabonas. The Illinois, largest of these groups, numbered six thousand souls. The tribes together could muster thirty-eight hundred warriors. Some twenty thousand Indians in all had come to live under his eye. There had been nothing like it in America, and the idea spread to the northern tribes, where Duluth was quick to implement it. In 1684, after La Salle had returned to France, Tonty held the confederation firm and fought off an Iroquois invasion. "We repulsed them with loss," Tonty reported briefly. In 1686 the Iroquois finally subdued the Illinois, but this was an isolated victory, without lasting importance. Their great plan of conquest in the west had been broken irretrievably by the alliance of the western tribes.

His accomplishment should have filled La Salle with satisfaction; indeed it must have; but he knew that its permanence would hang on communication with the Mississippi and the depot that must be built there. More and more the men he sent to Montreal, with or without furs, were being tampered with by his enemies. It was impossible to hope to supply the alliance with arms and ammunition, or even the trade goods necessary to win their furs and bind them to the side of the French, by the difficult route through the Great Lakes unless he and his agents were permitted freedom of action in Quebec and Montreal.

Early in 1683 he learned to his dismay that in September 1682 Frontenac, without whose support his situation was hopeless, had been recalled to France, along with the intendant, Duchesneau. His successor was Le Fèbvre de la Barre, the same naval officer whom in 1664 Tracy had installed as governor of Cayenne. At the moment all that needs to be said of this unappetizing gentleman was that his avarice exceeded startlingly his intelligence and courage. From almost the moment of his arrival, scenting the profits in the wind, he had, with a determination of purpose notably lacking in every other phase of his administration, made common cause with the merchants and traders who, with the ecclesiastics, had intrigued for Frontenac's recall and who were, of course, La Salle's enemies of long standing. To the king's minister, Seignelay, who had succeeded his father, the great Colbert, in 1681, La Barre began feeding accusations and stories about La Salle which, whether he himself believed them or not, provided justification for his next move, the confiscation of Fort Frontenac. He sent two of his intimates, Le Ber and La Chesnaye, to take it over, sell its stores, and appropriate any furs — a proceeding all three shared the profits of — in spite of the protests of La Salle's creditors.

La Salle was now deprived of his last property in Canada except Fort St. Louis; he was entirely cut off from his base of supply; he had only a few men left. There was nothing for him to do except to seek justice in France, and in the early fall, leaving Tonty in command, he set out for Quebec. On the way he met an officer of La Barre's, the Chevalier de Baugis, who under orders from the governor was on his way to take possession of Fort St. Louis. La Salle could only add a note to Tonty to accept the situation. It was the last blow.

When he presented his case at court in 1684, it seemed for once that his fortunes had turned. He had a personal interview with Louis which resulted in La Barre's being ordered to restore his forts and seigneuries on Ontario and the Illinois. The king and Seignelay also listened favorably to his proposals to found a colony near the mouth of the Mississippi. It would be a useful threat against the Spanish, now that the two countries were at war. Louisiana had captured their imagination and they saw the importance of allowing it to grow without interference from a hostile Canada. Louis appointed La Salle governor of Louisiana and promised ships, men, and money to support the expedition.

But this was the last ray of brightness in the strangely dark course of La Salle's career. Before preparations for the expedition had been properly begun, other interests were meddling with its purpose, and to save what he could La Salle was forced to compromise. So when the expedition finally sailed, in four ships instead of the one he had originally asked for, and with four hundred persons of whom one hundred and eighty, including a few young women and girls, were to be colonists, its ostensible goal was to establish a base from which to capture the silver mines of northern Mexico; and to reconcile his purpose with his own, La Salle had felt compelled to report the mouth of the Mississippi as being considerably farther west than it actually was.

Sickness, dissension, and a succession of mishaps dogged the sea voyage. The ships passed the mouth of the Mississippi unaware and anchored off the Texas coast four hundred miles to the west. From there they searched unsuccessfully for the Mississippi until the two naval escorts had to return to France. La Salle then turned to the business of establishing his colony, taking his colonists ashore in Matagorda Bay. During the landing one of his ships, which carried all the stores for the colony, was lost with nearly all its cargo. When the second ship, on which La Salle counted for finding the mouth of the Mississippi by sea, was wrecked by its drunken pilot, they lost the last means of communication with France.

From then on the colony would be haunted by a growing sense of helplessness, by hunger, disease, and finally despair. But they began bravely enough under La Salle's urging. They built a crude post beside a little river at the head of Matagorda Bay. Crude as it was, it represented an enormous amount of labor, for they had no horses and its site, the only good one within reach, was two and a half miles away from any timber. Every stick for the palisades and buildings had to be dragged across the intervening marshes.

The future of such a post on a small and desolate Texas river was at best tentative. The keystone of La Salle's entire design was the location of his colony on the Mississippi, which alone could offer it a hope of permanence and the promise of growth, and he saw that now their very survival depended on finding the river. So, as soon as he had his people housed after a fashion, he set out with fifty men to look for it. For months they wandered across the country from one tribe of Indians to another, until they came at last to a large river which La Salle for a time mistook for the Mississippi. He built a small fort on its bank and, leaving a few men as garrison (with his departure these men disappear from history), he returned to Matagorda Bay.

There he learned of the wreck of his second ship and he realized that the fate of the colony now rested not only on finding the Mississippi but ascending it to Fort St. Louis, and from there making his way to Canada for help.

It would have been an incredibly difficult journey for even a well-equipped party, but at the little Texas post, after two years of near destitution, supplies were almost nonexistent. The chests of the dead were ransacked for clothing; the needs of the expedition for gunpowder were painstakingly weighed against those of the garrison; it was even harder to accumulate a store of what was equally essential — gifts for Indians.

La Salle allowed himself a bare three weeks to rest and prepare for the new expedition. On the twenty-second of April he started out again, this time with twenty men. But fever, desertion, and dwindling ammunition forced him once more to return. He brought back with him five horses which he had bought from the Indians, but he had lost twelve men, and he had not reached the Mississippi.

To La Salle it was a dark homecoming. The very joy with which he

[474]

was greeted told him how the garrison's despair had deepened during the eight months of his absence. Their number, too, had shrunk; the crosses in the rude cemetery just outside the palisade now far outnumbered the living souls within. Of the one hundred and eighty men and women who had left France as colonists, fewer than forty-five, even now that they were reunited, remained; and these survivors looked on La Salle as their final hope in life.

It was the Christmas season. On Christmas Eve they celebrated midnight mass in a service in which the vestments of the priests before the altar must have made a bizarre contrast to the ragged garments of the congregation, improvised from buffalo skins and the sails of the wrecked ships; and to some, perhaps, France may for a moment have seemed nearer. But there was no longer time to give way to dreams and longing, and by Twelfth Night La Salle was ready to make his third attempt to reach the Mississippi.

They all came together again for the traditional Twelfth Night feast and tried to recapture some of the cheer of happier times. But it was hard to do. The wine had long since given out and there was only water to fill their cups, and a chill of foreboding shadowed every heart. In the morning they gathered again, while La Salle spoke to the twenty who must be left behind — among them seven women and girls — with a gentle kindness that seldom showed through his habitual reserve. Then with his party he passed through the gates for the last time, while the pathetic garrison watched their figures slowly diminish in the prairie perspective until, at length, they disappeared.

La Salle's course led his company steadily north and northwest through a succession of prairie and forest. They crossed rivers as they came to them in a coracle of buffalo hide which one of the horses carried. Time urged their pace and they kept close together, but their progress was slow and they were not a united party. Besides La Salle they counted sixteen. With him were his older brother, the Sulpician priest Jean Cavelier; two nephews, Moranget and Robert Cavelier, who was only seventeen; his personal servant, Saget; a simple but honest-hearted soldier, Joutel; a Recollet friar, Anastase Douay; and a Shawnee hunter named Nika who, with a devotion La Salle often inspired among Indians, had followed him for years and had even accompanied him on his last voyage to France.

All these had faith in La Salle and his ability to lead them to safety. But among the rest were men who believed that he was solely responsible for every misfortune that had befallen the colonists since leaving France. Two of them, one a man named Duhaut and the other the surgeon of the party, Liotot, violently hated him and had for some time been plotting against his leadership. They were men of some substance at home who had invested heavily in the enterprise. Now, whether they succeeded in getting back to France or not, they were ruined. It meant nothing to them that La Salle was himself far more disastrously in debt than they; they were determined to eliminate him and waited only for an opportunity.

Two months, however, passed before it developed. By then the party had crossed the Brazos River and the Trinity, though they were probably less than two hundred miles in actual distance from their starting point. Rains and their necessarily winding course as they followed the buffalo trails had made progress slow. Their provisions had begun to give out. But on the fifteenth of March they recognized landmarks which told them that they were only a few miles from a spot in which they had left a cache of corn on the preceding expedition.

La Salle made camp where he was and sent seven men to retrieve the grain. They included Liotot and Duhaut; the latter's servant, l'Archevêque; a German ex-buccaneer named Hiens; a pilot from one of the ill-fated ships, Teissier; Saget, and the Indian hunter, Nika. Whether the ringleaders had any intimation that the moment for casting their snare of murder was approaching is uncertain. Probably not; for when they found the cache with its contents spoiled, they started to return without delay. Then circumstances began to play into their hands.

They had gone but a little way before they sighted buffalo, of which Nika managed to kill two. So they made camp on the spot to butcher the carcasses, and Duhaut ordered Saget to return to the main camp for horses to carry in the meat. Saget's departure left Nika the only member of the party loyal to La Salle, but if they thought of this, Duhaut and Liotot took no overt action. The business of cutting up and drying the meat proceeded without incident and the night passed quietly.

Meanwhile Saget had reached the main camp, which by now had attracted, as almost invariably happened, a fringe of curious Indians. He made his report, but as it was already late, La Salle decided to wait till next morning before sending the horses. Then, to accompany Saget, he sent two more men: his nephew Moranget and the Sieur de Marle. It would have been impossible to find two men more unlike. Marle was a colorless individual of little force of character; but Moranget was a thoroughly passionate man, arrogant, overbearing, contentious, and devoted to his uncle. His temperament had already caused serious trouble and he had quarreled with both Duhaut and Liotot, who hated him now as much as they did La Salle. They clashed again almost as soon as he reached the hunting camp.

Most of the buffalo meat was curing on the drying racks over the fires, but Duhaut and the others had put aside some of the finer cuts for their own use. This infuriated Moranget, and after an abusive harangue he took possession of the meat, including the pieces that had been set aside. His highhanded behavior brought to a head all the resentment and hatred that had been festering in the minds of Duhaut and Liotot. Calling the buccaneer Hiens, Teissier, and l'Archevêque to join them, they walked out of the camp.

It did not take them long to decide that they would kill Moranget that night. But to kill him it would be necessary to kill the two others who were loyal to La Salle, and the three together made a formidable assignment. The only safe way seemed to kill them in their sleep. And so it was worked out. As darkness settled, an hourly guard was arranged, and the first three men to serve were Moranget, Saget, and Nika. After they had stood their watch, lain down, and wrapped themselves in their blankets, the conspirators rose. Duhaut and Hiens stood with muskets cocked while Liotot struck each of the three with an ax. Nika and Saget died where they lay, but Moranget, speechless and spouting blood, managed to sit up. To ensure that Marle would stand with them, the murderers forced him to give Moranget the *coup de grâce*.

They were now committed to murdering La Salle. No other course would ensure their future safety. But though they were nearly equal in numbers to the men remaining in the main camp, two of whom were priests, and were better armed, they still were afraid to confront La Salle. As it turned out, however, he came to them alone, or virtually so.

Moranget and his companions had been expected back at the main camp on the evening of the sixteenth. When the whole next day passed and night fell, a premonition of tragedy seized La Salle. He spent that night in great anxiety and next morning decided to go himself in search of his missing people. Not being familiar with the path, he offered one of the visiting Indians a hatchet to guide him. He had intended to take the soldier, Joutel, but at the last minute changed his mind, feeling that Joutel was needed to command the camp. Instead he borrowed the soldier's musket and pistol and started out with only the strange Indian and the unarmed friar, Anastase Douay, for company.

On the way he was suddenly overcome by a wave of melancholy which was as puzzling to him as to the friar, but he soon regained his composure and they went on till they came near the stream on the far side of which was the hunters' camp. It was not visible from La Salle's position, so he fired the musket and then the pistol to attract attention.

The shots were heard in the hunters' camp, where none doubted that the man who fired them was La Salle. Duhaut and Liotot, who had already made their plan, disappeared into the woods with l'Archevêque, crossed the stream to La Salle's side of it, and concealed themselves in the long grass near the crossing La Salle would normally take. Then l'Archevêque stepped into the open to accost him, hold him in parley, and if possible to decoy him closer to the spot where Duhaut and Liotot lay hidden. While La Salle angrily inquired about Moranget, l'Archevêque kept backing away. Suddenly two shots rang out and La Salle fell, shot through the head, beside Douay. With horrified eyes the friar saw the murderers rise from the grass and come forward to exult over the dead man, reviling and mocking him. Then they stripped off his clothes and tumbled his naked corpse into the grass for the buzzards to dispose of, and picking up his firearms began the return march to the main camp.

So La Salle's effort of more than twenty years to lay the foundation of a strong new France in the interior came to an end; but he had drawn the outlines for his compatriots to build to, though when they finally acted it was too late. His forts were a principal factor in containing the Iroquois; later, settlements were made at Cahokia and Vincennes, and New Orleans was founded almost thirty years afterward in the area where all along he had felt his own settlement ought to be. Beset by enemies and envious rivals, with almost no friends except the faithful Tonty, without sustained support from the government except for a few years of Frontenac's first term, the wonder is that he accomplished so much. With a little luck he might have succeeded and the American continent have worn a different mantle, but luck consistently avoided him.

For the murderers also, though they did not know it, luck was running out. At the main camp Duhaut appropriated La Salle's personal possessions. Joutel and La Salle's relatives were disarmed, and though Duhaut assured them that they had nothing to fear, they realized that they would never be allowed to reach civilization with their knowledge of the murderers, and this conviction persisted even after their arms were restored to them.

The murderers now decided to move into the country of the Cenis Indians, a tribe that had treated La Salle with special friendliness on his previous expedition. The Cenis lived in huge circular houses, as much as sixty feet in diameter, with a central fire which the various families inhabiting them shared for cooking, and their young women and girls had accepted the Frenchmen with the greatest cordiality. Their attitude had not changed, and in this parasitic, if not exactly paradisiacal, existence they continued for nearly two months, picking up several of La Salle's followers who had deserted earlier and who had, to all intents, become Indians.

Then suddenly the murderers found themselves at violent odds. Becoming bored with the life, Duhaut decided to return to Matagorda Bay and there build a ship that would carry his party back to France. Joutel and the Caveliers, who had been looking for means to escape with the object of reaching Canada, saw this as their opportunity. Jean Cavelier approached Duhaut with the argument that he was neither young nor strong enough to make the trip back to Matagorda Bay and begged for arms and supplies to support him in the Cenis country. Duhaut willingly agreed but, when Cavelier's real intention was betrayed to him, changed his mind and said he would go with the Caveliers to Canada — a decision which they knew well was their death sentence.

During these negotiations, the buccaneer, Hiens, had been away refreshing himself among the Cenis, but when news of Duhaut's decision reached him he returned at once to the camp with two of the French Indians and a band of Cenis. He said he would never return to France or Canada and bluntly demanded half the arms and supplies for himself. Duhaut refused.

Hiens, who had lightheartedly taken part in the murders of Moranget, Saget, and Nika, had refused to share in La Salle's, though he had not really opposed it. He now made a virtue of this abstention. Drawing a pistol he accused Duhaut of having murdered their leader and shot him dead, while one of the French Indians at the same instant killed Liotot. Hiens's explosive violence struck all the onlookers dumb, most of all the Cenis, who had never seen such a display among friends. The Caveliers and Joutel expected him to turn on them, but he chose instead to ally himself morally with them as a man who had simply meted out justice, and he would have made a clean sweep by executing l'Archevêque if the priests had not dissuaded him. In the end he proved generous in outfitting them for their attempt to reach Canada, though he himself intended to remain among the Cenis.

The Caveliers set forth early in June, taking with them, in addition to Anastase Douay, the ineffectual Marle, Teissier, who had played a neutral role through the bloody course of the murders, and a young man named Barthelemy. Not one of the party had any outstanding qualities of leadership, yet they were to complete their immense journey in a little over a year with the loss of only one of their number, Marle, who drowned while swimming.

It took them two months to reach the Arkansas, which they struck a little way above its confluence with the Mississippi. Here in an Indian town they found two Frenchmen who had come down with Tonty the year before in search of La Salle and who, when Tonty was forced to return to Fort St. Louis, had volunteered to remain among the Arkansas tribes in case La Salle should appear. The account of his death shocked them to the point of tears, but they agreed with the Caveliers that it must be kept secret from the Indians, who had venerated him. This was the beginning of a deception that the older Cavelier was to carry on, with the approval of the others, till they reached France more than a year later.

Now, with canoes, they went down the Arkansas to the Mississippi and began the grinding upward journey against the current. On the third of September they turned into the mouth of the Illinois and eleven days later saw on their right the towering rock crowned with the palisades of Fort St. Louis.

Tonty was away fighting the Iroquois but the small garrison all inquired eagerly for La Salle. Cavelier, whose conscience as a priest was not permitted to interfere with the advantage of representing a living La Salle, replied that his brother had been well when he had last seen him, a reply that satisfied Tonty when he returned in October. As the autumn storms had now begun, the Caveliers accepted Tonty's hospitality for the winter, recounting the sad history of the little settlement and of La Salle's overland journeys in search of the Mississippi, but never giving away the secret of his death. When in March they were able to resume their journey, Cavelier borrowed four thousand livres in furs from the trusting Tonty in his brother's name. At Michilimackinac he disposed of part of the furs for a draft on Montreal; then they continued by the orthodox route through Georgian Bay and down the Ottawa, reached Montreal in mid-July, and now in funds pressed on to Quebec from which they sailed at the end of August. Early in October they landed in France and then, at last, unfolded the whole, true, melancholy story.

It roused little concern in high places. The Caveliers had hoped that a rescue mission might be sent to the settlement on Matagorda Bay; but Louis apparently decided that the lives of the survivors would not be worth the expense and left them to their fate.

As it turned out they were doomed anyway and rescue from France could not have reached them in time. In April 1689 a Spanish expedition, which had long searched for the French interlopers, finally came upon the fort. Its palisades were broken down, the buildings ransacked, and the only relics of the garrison were the bodies, far out on the prairie, of two men and a woman who had evidently been struck down in flight.

While the Spanish party lingered at the scene, two men approached across the prairie. They were dressed in Indian fashion but turned out to be Frenchmen, one of whom was l'Archevêque. They reported that the fort had been overwhelmed by Indians in the preceding February after an epidemic of smallpox had left the garrison too weak to defend themselves. All but two men and some young children, who were saved by the Indian women, died in the massacre.

As for the buccaneer, Hiens, and his companions who had cast their lot among the Cenis, their fate is obscure. Tonty believed they had been murdered by Indians. In September 1688 one of his men had returned from the Arkansas and, of course, informed him of La Salle's death. Though there was nothing he could now do for the leader he had served so well, he determined to try to reach the unfortunate colony on Matagorda Bay.

He left Fort St. Louis in December with a small party of five Frenchmen and three Indians and reached the Red River in March after many difficulties. There he was told that Hiens was in another village about two hundred miles away and he prepared to go there. Before he could start, all his men but one Frenchman and one Indian deserted. This did not stop him, nor was he daunted when in a river crossing a little later he lost nearly all his ammunition. He persisted until he reached the village where Hiens was supposed to be. But there was no sign of the buccaneer or any of his companions, and when he began to make inquiries, the manner of the Indians convinced him that they had killed all the Frenchmen. Moreover, they refused to help him in any way, and without guides he had no hope of finding the Matagorda settlement. He was forced to turn back, bitterly disappointed, not knowing that the little colony was already destroyed and that he himself, with his two companions, was the last vestige in that vast country of what had been La Salle's dream.

Frontenac's recall in 1682 after ten years as governor of New France was due as much to his obsessive dislike and resentment of the intendant, Duchesneau, as to any other factor. His feeling was all the more acute because for the first three years he had been left free to govern the colony without the checks and supervision that an officious intendant could exercise.

Duchesneau (Jacques Duchesneau, Sieur de la Doussinière, to give him his full name, though one never sees him referred to except as Intendant Duchesneau — dignifying the man with the office, whereas Talon's title, "The Great Intendant," reflects the distinction the man brought to it) was an official who liked nothing better than to be lost in a world of paper work. Anything done outside the rigid lines of established procedure frightened and angered him. No one questioned his honesty of intent, except Frontenac on occasion, who saw cabals and intrigues in everything the intendant touched; but his mind was small, unimaginative (except where it conjured up wrongs done himself or his young son), and hard as a turtle's. In reading his reports one finds astonishing how little he grasped the vastness of Canada: he served there with two purposes, to get the fur trade back into the hands of the established Canadian merchants for whom it had been a virtual monopoly until Frontenac's arrival and to pull the governor down by any means possible.

Like most men of his type, when he found himself in a real contest, he liked to do his fighting from behind a screen, and early in his term of office he allied himself with the clergy, in whose cause, as he reported back to France, he was obliged to confront the governor to the latter's displeasure. He found it also convenient to ascribe some of his most outrageous charges to Jesuit sources. On their part, the Jesuits and the regular clergy were more than happy to have such a high official allied to their cause. The old brandy dispute was once more at full blast, and none the less so for the return in 1674 of Laval. This time he came back to Canada the bishop of Quebec, as he had longed to be for fifteen years, instead of apostolic vicar with a merely titular see of Petraea. Even with Laval among them, however, the clergy had found it difficult to stand against the imperious manner and blazing temper of Frontenac.

Duchesneau's opening moves took the form of disputes on matters of precedence. In documents arriving from France both Frontenac and he were addressed or referred to as "President of the Council." Each therefore insisted on presiding every time the council sat. Floods of letters passed back and forth across the ocean about this simple matter until at last, his patience all but gone, Louis decreed that Duchesneau being of third rank should not be president of the council but that as intendant he should preside over its meetings.

At such distance it was difficult to exert much persuasive force. Colbert before he died, and after him his son, wrote letters as if these two top officials of New France were children, scolding Duchesneau for not showing more respect and urging Frontenac to make an effort to arrive at a harmonious relationship with the intendant. It was of little avail with two such temperaments in collision, and it is not surprising that the king should write somewhat plaintively to Frontenac that throughout all his kingdom "I do not hear of so many difficulties on this matter."

In another matter concerning a member of the council, Villeray, whom Frontenac found obnoxious and therefore tried to deprive of his seat, the intendant emerged victorious. Villeray remained, but Frontenac in a letter to Colbert wrote ominously that Villeray was the principal tool of the bishop and Jesuits and was bruited to be actually a Jesuit himself, but in plain clothes. It all sounds nonsensical today, but it is impossible not to conclude that both sides, lacking outside diversions, derived a measure of satisfaction from their diatribes addressed to persons comfortably distant and neutral.

So one finds Frontenac saying pleasant things about the Jesuits in his letter to Colbert, but lapsing into cipher when he had one of his vitriolic accusations to make. His main point was that the Jesuits and the bishop were in a conspiracy to undermine the royal prerogative, of which he of course was the embodiment in Canada. He accused them of engaging surreptitiously in the fur trade, and he also accused them of not being interested in civilizing the Indians.

Frontenac had very much at heart a project of taking each year a certain number of Indian children to be brought up at first by the Jesuits and nuns, and later by lay families, as little French boys and girls. The Jesuits resisted this. They did not want to make Frenchmen of the Indians — it was not possible — they wanted to make them Christians, and keep them primitive but believing (it was still their dream of a Paraguay). Frontenac refused to accept their sincerity; he accused them of refusing to civilize the Indians because they wanted them to remain subservient. "They think more of beaver skins than of souls."

As always, all controversy was peripheral to the fur trade, with both sides jockeying for power, but with Frontenac holding most of the trumps. When the *coureurs de bois* were called in from the wilderness with a promise of amnesty, Frontenac could issue them new licenses to go to the wilderness to "hunt." With the collaboration of men like Duluth and Nicholas Perrot, his faction controlled the bulk of all furs from the *pays en haut*, which were of course the best, as well as those from the Illinois and other streams beyond Lake Michigan which were channeled back through the posts established by La Salle and Tonty. Their success led to wilder and wilder charges by the opposition. Frontenac was even accused of letting his furs be sold in Albany — the ultimate perfidy in the eyes of a Quebec merchant (if not of a Montreal trader).

The amount of correspondence that resulted from this internecine warfare challenges belief. The long days of winter combined with rancor to speed the pen. Frontenac liked to initiate a new dispute after the last fall ship had sailed for France — which left him at best eighteen months and twelve at shortest to pursue his chosen course without criticism from the king or his minister. His reports on procedure and comments on the conduct of the intendant and the clergy were scathing and protracted, but of nothing like the length of the communications from Duchesneau who in addition to his own letters ("God is my witness, my Lord, that nothing afflicts me so truly as the necessity under which I find myself of writing to you of disagreeable things," and then doing so for an inordinate number of pages) attached affidavits and procès-verbaux and other communications as substantiation, not to mention accounts of outrages in the streets of Quebec which according to him were originated wholly by partisans of the governor. The wonder is that this behavior was permitted to continue for so many years. In the end Louis and Seignelay, who had had to endure only a year of it, suffering more from sheer engorgement than conviction of the merits, decided that it was time for a change. Both Frontenac and Duchesneau were summoned back to France.

Yet beneath all the turmoil Canada had been not unprosperous. Population had increased to a little over nine thousand, and though the church and Jesuits and a majority of merchants openly rejoiced at Frontenac's departure, the Franciscans, at least, and the people at large were sorry. No one before him had been able so to overawe the Iroquois. He had stopped their warfare with the St. Lawrence tribes and against the Ottawas. For ten years Canada had been at peace and men could work in their fields without watching over their shoulders. Above all as a person he had left an impression on the Canadians. Arrogant, impatient, sometimes cruel though he was, he could also be considerate and even tender. He had protected them, and they were loath to see him go.

They had more reason than they knew to feel so. The two succeeding governors were unmitigated disasters.

We have already had a small measure of the quality of Le Fèbvre de la Barre in his dealings with La Salle. In his capacity as governor of Cayenne he had had some minor engagements with the English, from which he had emerged victorious and to which he was wont to refer on all possible occasions. His early reports resound with a good deal of drum beating about what he is going to do to keep the Iroquois in their place, but the truth was that confronted with the wilderness and its savage inhabitants he was overcome with dread; and his arrival at Quebec occurred just after one of the most dreadful of its fires. Fifty-five buildings along the waterfront had been reduced to ashes, many of them warehouses, including that of the Jesuits, filled with the season's accumulation of furs waiting to be sent out on the autumn ships. The loss in buildings and goods was staggering and said to be greater in value than all the property remaining in the colony. People from the burned houses had had to crowd into those on the heights, and though the governor had the château to move into, the new intendant, Jacques de Meulles, was hard put to it to find quarters. It cast a shadow on La Barre's assumption of his duties, and the specter of an Iroquois war immediately began to haunt him.

On October 10, 1682, about a month after his arrival, he summoned a conference to discuss "the state of affairs with the Iroquois." In attendance were the governor, intendant, bishop, the Superior of the Sulpicians, the Superior of the Jesuits, and various missionaries and seigneurs, among them men like Le Moyne and Duluth. Together they formed a comprehensive group that covered the whole of Canada, including the *pays en haut*, and the picture they presented to La Barre, as he reported it, obviously left him full of apprehensions, and not without reason.

Letters from the Iroquois missions reported the three western nations were in ferment. The English had been selling goods, especially muskets and gunpowder, cheaply and in great quantities and at the same time using every possible means to induce the Iroquois to make war on the French. This was mainly at the instigation of the new governor of New York, Thomas Dongan, and the fact that he was himself a Catholic lent a peculiar ghastliness to the possible outcome. The missionaries reported that two or three times already the Iroquois had been on the point of taking up the hatchet against Quebec; all that deterred them was their unfinished business in the west. They feared that if they sent their armies down the St. Lawrence, the western tribes would rally and attack their undefended towns.

So in 1681 they had sent a large army into the Illinois country where they claimed to have killed three hundred or so of the enemy and brought back nine hundred prisoners — no doubt that was their own figure — to be burned or become recruits in their own war parties. This year — 1681 and 1682 were the years La Salle and Tonty were preparing for and making their journey to the Gulf of Mexico — the Iroquois were supposed to have sent an army of twelve hundred west with the object of wiping out the Illinois, the Kiskakon Ottawas, and the Miamis; if they succeeded, they would control all the west below Superior.

It was agreed that destruction of the Senecas would be the first objective and La Barre felt that this called for an army of a thousand men. He hoped the king could be induced to send over two or three hundred soldiers to garrison Fort Frontenac and the new post at La Galette on the St. Lawrence just below the mouth of the Oswegatchie. Removing so many men from the farms posed a threat of crop failure, but La Barre counted on a rapid stroke. He would embark five hundred men in three or four vessels at Fort Frontenac, while five hundred more in canoes would "post themselves on the Seneca shore," and they would "fall on the Senecas in forty hours." Of course if the king would add one hundred and fifty hired men to the soldiers as help for the farms, it would be a blessing. But it was essential to use every bit of force they could muster. The war, he said, was one "which is not to be left unfinished, because . . . if it were to be undertaken without completing it, there was no hope left of preserving the Colony, as the Iroquois were not the people to be appeased." That was sound policy; unfortunately he did not heed it.

It all sounded efficient and martial and he was soon writing Seignelay that though the Iroquois had twenty-six hundred fighting men he would attack them with twelve hundred, but added that "the failure of all aid from France" had begun to "create contempt for us among the said Iroquois," and if aid were only sent he believed that the Iroquois would "come to heel and make peace." Such hints and messages were little more than whistling down the wind, for all the results they gained, and it must have become evident to La Barre, as it was becoming to others, that he did not want to take an army to Lake Ontario at all.

During the winter and spring of 1683 La Barre concerned himself with all sorts of ostentatious preparations for war, building two vessels on Ontario which were to act in defense of Fort Frontenac but which, according to the intendant, Meulles, were never available for transporting supplies to the fort because they were used by the governor for trading along the shores of the lake. Similarly lines of canoes dispatched up the St. Lawrence were only half laden with military stores, the rest of their cargoes being trade goods belonging to the governor or his allies. It was a fine racket for all concerned, having their goods transported at the king's expense, as Meulles pointed out. His reports contain none of the animus or flights of near hysterical hyperbole that distinguished those of Duchesneau; he was merely reporting, drily, with as it were a sad shaking of the head. In his opinion La Barre's military preparations were mere gestures and as late as July 1684, when La Barre mounted his expedition to Lake Ontario, Meulles wrote Seignelay, "I do not perceive any disposition in the Governor to make war on these Savages. I believe he will content himself with paddling as far as Cataracouy or Fort Frontenac, and then send for the Senecas to negotiate peace with them, and make a fool of the people, of the Intendant, and of His Majesty (were it allowable so to speak with all due respect)." He had La Barre's measure to the inch, as it turned out. The expedition resulted in grim farce, a parody of Frontenac's electric performance, that reaped only humiliation for the French.

Events in 1683 had led inexorably to the necessity of curbing the western Iroquois. All during the later winter months and those of early spring La Barre had waited for a deputation to arrive from the Iroquois so that the new Onontio might greet his "children." When they failed to appear he sent Charles Le Moyne, whom they had always held in respect, to Onondaga, and as a result of his persuasion forty-three chiefs finally showed up at Montreal.

At the council held in the church lavish presents were given and La Barre pleaded for them to show restraint toward the Lake tribes, especially the Ottawas, and toward French traders who carried his license — which meant that any of La Salle's men were fair game. The chiefs somewhat scornfully agreed, but when the governor asked why they attacked the Illinois, one of the chiefs burst out that "the entire Iroquois nation reserved to itself the power of waging war against the Illinois, as long as a single one of them should remain on earth." La Barre listened meekly to this fiery threat and when the Iroquois went on to accuse La Salle of selling firearms to the Illinois, he not only promised to punish La Salle on his return but assured the chiefs that as far as he was concerned they were free to attack his posts or kill him, as they chose. Thus for the sake of his own profit he lifted the last bar to warfare on the Illinois, and left the Illinois Indians to their fate, allied only with La Salle and Tonty and their handful of followers.

Meanwhile word had come of an army of five hundred Iroquois about to march against Michilimackinac, and for once (perhaps because its preservation was vital to his interests) La Barre acted with promptness and decision, sending off thirty "good men" in six canoes as reinforcements. Even more fortunate was the fact that Duluth was at the post when they arrived with their news. He immediately assumed command and strengthened the defenses so effectively that the Iroquois dared not attack it.

After this episode La Barre was hopeful of maintaining the precarious peace at least through one more year, but then late in the season of 1683 he sent out seven canoes to trade at Fort St. Louis, where the Chevalier

[486]

de Baugis had taken over command from Tonty. But before they reached the fort they were intercepted by a war party of Senecas to whom French canoes were French canoes, irrespective of whom they belonged to. They took the men prisoners and confiscated all La Barre's goods. This was in February 1684. When in the spring the news got back to La Barre, he was enraged and immediately set about assembling the expedition to Ontario.

The force he took with him amounted to twelve hundred men, three hundred of them Indians, more than three times the number Frontenac had taken to face down the Iroquois eleven years before. But in addition to his own army, La Barre had called on the western posts to send a force to meet his. Duluth, Perrot, and the newly appointed commandant at Michilimackinac, Olivier Morel de la Durantaye, another of the Carignan regiment officers and a thorough soldier, succeeded in persuading four hundred Indians, mainly Hurons and Ottawas, but with contingents from the Menominies, Sauks, and Foxes and a scattering from other tribes, to accompany them into the dread land of the Iroquois. With the Frenchmen available their army came to almost six hundred men. The idea was an innovation, and a portent of things to come; but in this instance, like all the rest of La Barre's campaign, it turned into a fiasco. For at the crucial moment this veteran gasconader simply lost his nerve.

He had no real idea of how to handle an army in a situation such as the ascent of the St. Lawrence, but later he tried to shift the blame to Meulles by saying that the intendant had not provided enough food. Meulles, however, could prove that he had filled every requisition, and the fact of the matter was that La Barre delayed inordinately wherever there was an opportunity: ten or twelve days wasted at Montreal on the journey up, two weeks at Fort Frontenac, and as many again at La Famine, the site he finally chose for the council.

At Frontenac sickness swept his men, apparently malaria, which Meulles ascribed to the swampy nature of the ground La Barre chose to camp in. So many were incapacitated that La Barre dared not hold the council at the fort. Instead he decided to move on to La Famine, or Hungry Bay, at the mouth of the Salmon River, and there await the arrival of the Iroquois dignitaries.

La Barre had come ostensibly to exterminate the Senecas. He did not dare now even summon them to a council. Instead he sent Le Moyne to the Onondagas inviting them to meet him, for they were reported by their missionary, Lamberville, to be less hostile toward the French. Thirteen chiefs agreed to return with Le Moyne and duly arrived at La Famine.

There, malaria was making further inroads among the French, and La Barre piled all sick indiscriminately into canoes to be returned to the fort, pretending when the Onondagas came that he had left his big army behind at Fort Frontenac and come to their country only with a small escort. They were not deceived. They knew as well as anyone else what had happened at Fort Frontenac. They knew his force was hopelessly weak and they saw at a glance that he himself was terrified. But he made them a bombastic speech, bearing down with special heaviness on the Iroquois sin of robbing French traders in the Illinois country. If they were amused, as indeed they must have been, they gave no sign but heard him out in stately silence, even when he said that the Illinois were the children of the French king, even as the Iroquois, and that if the Iroquois attacked them he had been ordered to declare war. If they did not heed his words, their villages would be burned and their people exterminated.

It was not the kind of speech to make from a weak hand. The Onondaga deputies, whatever they felt, gave no sign but waited for their spokesman to reply. He was a singular character named Hotreouaté, who was known among the French as La Grande Gueule, or Big Mouth, which Lahontan contracted into Grangula, and Colden later to the more ringing version, Garangula, the name by which he has come down in history. Why he was called Big Mouth has never been satisfactorily explained — some said he was noisy, others that he liked his food, all of which is by the way. He was a politician to the bone, who liked to play two sides off against each other, who talked rough in public and came round privately with soft words.

Now he arose and walked five times slowly round the circle formed by La Barre and his officers and the seated chiefs, and finally, facing La Barre, he replied with a quiet sarcasm and mounting indignation that left the governor speechless and infuriated.

Garangula first greeted Onontio with the customary phrases of welcome and then remarked that he must have come thinking that all the Iroquois forests had burned down with all the Indians in them, intimating that otherwise he would have feared to come at all. But Garangula assured him that all Five Nations were yet alive and that "it was happy for you that you left the Hatchet, that has been so often dyed in the blood of the *French*," behind. La Barre, he went on, might be "a great Captain at the head of a Company of soldiers," but he spoke like a man who is dreaming. The Iroquois were well aware that if sickness had not weakened his army his purpose in coming to see them "was to knock us on the Head." "We are born free, we neither depend on Onontio or Corlaer. We may go where we please, and carry with us whom we please, and buy and sell what we please. If your Allies be your Slaves, use them as such."

Such belittlement and contempt made it impossible for La Barre to reply with any effect. One version of the remainder of the council describes it as a scolding match. All La Barre got out of it was an assurance by the Onondagas that they had no present intention of attacking French Canada, and with that he had to content himself, although he tried to blow it up into a diplomatic victory. But the moment the Onondaga canoes had moved out of sight he himself vamoosed.

I consider it also my duty to inform your Lordship that the General left La Famine the moment peace was concluded, without taking the least care of the troops, abandoning them altogether to their own guidance, forbidding them on pain of death to leave the place until a long time after him, fearing to be surprised by the Iroquois, and having (so to say) lost his wits . . .

He did have wits enough to send a courier to Niagara to tell Duluth, Perrott, and Durantaye they were not needed after all and could go home. The effect was stunning. All through the long canoe trip down from Michilimackinac only the continual persuasion of the three officers and their *coureurs de bois* had kept the Indians in line. This was to be a final war against the Iroquois. Now they realized that this new Onontio, the captain of the great French king, did not dare invade the Seneca country, and they had learned too that he had abandoned them and all the western tribes La Salle and Frontenac had promised the French would protect. They turned back, repeating in reverse their fruitless journey, and when they got back to Michilimackinac they found a flotilla of canoes from Albany, loaded with Dutch and British goods at those alluringly low prices, waiting to do business. It further underlined the ineffectiveness of the French. For a time it looked as if the confederation of the western tribes would fall apart, and except for the strength and skill of men like Duluth and Durantaye it would have.

La Barre, safe back in Quebec, did nothing. Except for his abortive foray into Ontario he had spent all his time and energy in projects for his own enrichment. Canada had stagnated. Louis was especially displeased by his "abandonment of the Illinois." In September 1685, he was recalled, leaving the prestige of France in America, especially in the west, at a new low.

He was succeeded by Jacques René de Brisay, Marquis de Denonville, a former colonel of dragoons and a genuinely pious man. He brought his wife with him and part of his family. Also on the ship was Jean Baptiste de Saint Vallier, whom Laval while in France had chosen as his successor to the bishopric. Their passage was a grisly one. Of five hundred soldiers aboard, one hundred and fifty died of scurvy, and so many of the rest were sick when the ship docked at Quebec on July 30, 1685, that the nuns of the Hôtel-Dieu found their hospital overflowed and had to place their patients wherever they could find room — in the church, the granary, even in the henyard.

Denonville's instructions called for a reversal of all the harmful measures of La Barre: he was to bring to an end the factional strife that had begun under Frontenac over the fur trade; he was to restore French prestige among the Indians and once more take the part of the western tribes against the Iroquois and to halt English pretensions to all the west south of the Great Lakes which were being pushed more and more forcefully by Governor Dongan. This was a large order of accomplishment to ask of a new governor when the means at hand were as slender as they were. But the king justly had confidence in Denonville, who was a man of the Court and of thirty years' experience in the army, where he had been noted for his enterprise and courage if not for humor, of which he had not a vestige.

One objective, however, was easily achieved. Denonville's feeling for Laval was one of reverence, and Laval, who had received glowing accounts from Saint Vallier of the new governor's piety during the voyage, showed an instant readiness to accept Denonville's proffered support and friendship. When Meulles was succeeded by a new intendant in the following summer, harmony at last reigned once more between the church and government on every level, for Jean de Champigny was as devout as Denonville.

Denonville's early impressions of the Canadian people were unfavorable. "The *noblesse* of Canada is of the most rascally description and to increase their body is to multiply the number of loafers . . . Canadian youth are for the most part wholly demoralized; that there are married men who, in addition to their own wives, keep Squaws whom they publicly deceive; and that the most frightful crimes are perpetrated by the Young men and French who resort to the woods." The poor he found overwhelmingly miserable; they had no clothing to speak of; the consequences of such poverty were melancholy; "the children being obliged to lie together, frightful irregularities result." He was enormously serious and wholly sincere in his concern. He did what was possible, which was not a great deal. And he never got over his horror of the *coureurs de bois* and the immorality of their way of life. But he was quite ready to use them in war, and it was to war that he now turned his undivided attention, as well as the problem of circumventing Governor Dongan's growing encroachment on the Great Lakes.

He first attempted to dissuade Dongan from these activities by a reasonable correspondence, for which Dongan complimented him, comparing his letters favorably with the haughty outbursts in writing of his predecessor. When this produced no result he accused Dongan of inciting the Iroquois to make war on the French, which he did not consider neighborly. English rum was destroying all chances of religion in the

[490]

Iroquois lodges, which instead were turned into "counterparts of Hell."

Dongan replied that "our Rum does as little hurt as your Brandy, and in the opinion of Christians, is much more wholesome," though he cites no particular Christian authority for this interesting statement, and he did not cease promoting trading activities on the Great Lakes. In the fall of 1686 an Albany trader named Johannes Roseboom set out with twenty canoes to winter with the Senecas. In the spring an officer stationed at Albany, Major McGregory, would leave Albany with fifty soldiers and woodsmen to join him, and the combined parties, heavily armed, were to move on to Michilimackinac. Denonville was rendered frantic when this news reached him; but his expostulations met only with good-humored argument that there was room in America for both English and French traders. In the growing heat of their exchanges Denonville accused his English counterpart of using fine words to cover bad faith. Yet the amenities were not neglected. In a postscript on June 20, 1687, Dongan said that he was sending some oranges, "hearing they are a rarity in your part," and Denonville in his reply thanked him, and added, "It was a great pity they should have been rotten."

Meanwhile he went on with plans for his projected attack on the Senecas, without allowing himself to be seriously diverted by the actions then taking place around Hudson Bay, which have been previously outlined. He was encouraged at the increased forces which were being made available. Eight hundred regular troops were now stationed in Canada, and eight hundred would arrive in early summer. He made his preparations with all possible secrecy. He would not even allow the Jesuit missionary at Onondaga, Jean de Lamberville, to be warned, for fear his coming away would reveal the French intentions. "I am sorry to see him exposed to danger," he wrote; but there it was. In a holy cause such as this, there had to be some sacrifices; at least so it seemed to a military mind. Yet Lamberville was the greatest protection Canada had against Dongan's machinations among the Iroquois.

Denonville did, however, inform Durantaye of his intentions for, taking a leaf from La Barre's book, he wanted to bring in the western tribes against the Senecas. There would be no better propaganda than letting them see, if they did not take part in, a Seneca defeat. He and Duluth and Tonty were to recruit as many Indians as possible and proceed with their *coureurs de bois* to Niagara early in July and wait there until he sent for them to join his army at Irondequoit Bay.

Now as the spring lengthened he began mustering the militia. It was not easy, for the habitants, remembering the fiasco of La Barre, were reluctant to leave their fields for what might be just another wild goose chase. But here the church came to his aid. Laval issued a pastoral mandate; sermons about the subjugation of the heathen Iroquois were preached through all the churches, prayers for victory were said, and gradually the tide of opinion turned. If there was not the magic sense of Tracy's great crusade against the Mohawks, the men began to muster with what Denonville considered "an extraordinary animation."

At this point, almost on the eve of his campaign, Denonville perpetrated an act of perfidy that was difficult to account for even in those heated times, and one that within a year he was harrowingly to regret. The king had suggested — as he had previously suggested to La Barre — that, with a view to lowering the number of fighting men among the Iroquois, all men taken prisoners should be sent to France to serve as galley slaves in the royal navy. Denonville had been informed that it was virtually impossible to take Iroquois prisoners in any quantity, so he resolved to please his royal master by using other means. Knowing that there were two small communities of Iroquois on the north shore of Ontario, one in the Bay of Quinté and one just beyond, Denonville sent the intendant, Champigny, on with the advance troops to Fort Frontenac with instructions to round up the men of both Iroquois groups and ship them back down the St. Lawrence to Quebec.

Accordingly, when he reached the fort, Champigny sent an invitation to the tribe at Quinté to come to join him in a feast. They accepted readily enough. There was no reason why they should not have. They were on the best of terms with the garrison, fished and hunted for them, and jointed them in games. They came with their women and children but, once inside the walls, were surrounded; the men were tied to a line of stakes down the middle of the parade and the women and children turned away. Then Champigny sent out a strong party to round up the men in the second village. The officer in command, one Perré, completed his mission with address, bringing in eighteen more men, while some sixty puzzled women and children trailed along in his wake. More stakes were planted, and after the captives were tied to them, the warriors from the mission villages who had come up with the soldiers, finding a pleasant game at hand, began amusing themselves by applying minor tortures. About the same time a new detachment of troops ascending the St. Lawrence surprised a group of Onondagas harmlessly fishing with their women and children among the Thousand Islands, and the men of this party also were taken prisoners. Among them were the son and brother of Garangula, but because of his previous friendship toward the French they were at length set free.

Meanwhile, however, one of the prisoners broke out of his bonds and escaped. He brought the news straight to Onondaga Castle, not only of the capture of their relatives but of the French intention of carrying war to the Senecas. The fury of the Onondagas knew no bounds; the whole town in minutes was buzzing like a hive; Lamberville was haled before the council, where for the first time he heard the news and realized that the governor had used him as a cat's-paw. He prepared himself mentally for the death he felt inevitable. But the chiefs, reading his astonishment in his face, told him that they had known him too long to think he would take any part in such a betrayal. To save his life from the more violent, younger men, they gave him an escort out of their country, and he met Denonville, who was greatly relieved to see him, just below Fort Frontenac.

By the end of June Denonville had his full force mustered there. On July 4 they embarked in 400 bateaux and canoes and started around the end of Ontario in bright and windy weather, then followed the southern shore toward Irondequoit, over 2,000 strong — 1,762 French of whom 832 were regular troops and 930 militia, and 300 Indians. The roughness of the lake slowed their progress; it took them six days to reach Irondequoit; but as they approached from the east they saw far across the glittering water the dark shapes of canoes and paddlers driving toward them from the west. Luck and efficient management had brought the brigade from the western posts to simultaneous rendezvous.

It had not been an easy thing to organize, and luck played a large part in getting it started at all. Throughout the winter Perrot on the upper Mississippi, Durantaye at Michilimackinac, Tonty at Fort St. Louis, and Duluth at Detroit had been working on the western Indians to join them on another expedition against the Senecas. But the Indians were reluctant or skittish. Their hearts still rankled from La Barre's behavior toward them. The name *Onontio* was rancid in their mouths.

Perrot brought in a few Foxes as well as the Pottawatomies and Menominies. His Indians were still highly temperamental about the expedition, but they reached Michilimackinac at the most auspicious possible moment. Johannes Roseboom's brigade of canoes from Albany and the Seneca country had appeared in the strait not long before, and Durantaye with all his *coureurs de bois* had leaped into canoes and, followed by the large gathering of Indians already assembled — who were at the moment intending to favor the English — had gone boiling out to meet them. The Dutch and English naturally assumed that the Indians were as thirsty for their blood as the French appeared to be and meekly surrendered. With an infallible eye for effect, Durantaye forced the Iroquois paddlers to stand in their canoes and sing their death songs as the Dutch and English slowly paddled them to shore. There the precious trade goods were given to the Indians who, delighted at such loot, instantly changed their attitude toward making war on the Senecas, and most of them enthusiastically paddled off behind Durantaye down Lake Huron to Detroit.

There at Duluth's fort they waited till Tonty arrived after an overland march from the head of Lake Michigan with twelve *coureurs de bois* and two hundred Illinois and Miamis. Altogether their force amounted to five hundred and eighty, four hundred of them Indians, who included even a band of the hesitant Ottawas. On their way across Lake Erie they encountered Major McGregory's flotilla of canoes and captured the lot. Again there was a jubilant division of the spoils, which included an even more exciting supply of rum. It helped beguile away the time they had to wait at Niagara till a courier arrived from Denonville directing them to start at once to the rendezvous.

There was, of course, no surprise. Seneca scouts watched them land and called to the French Indians asking why they were there. "To break your heads," a Christian Mohawk shouted back.

It was the eleventh of July. Denonville wasted not a minute in starting to build a fort. "We cut 2000 palisades the planting of which we completed on the forenoon of the 12th." He put the Sieur Doruilliers in command with a garrison of four hundred and forty men; "for the loss of this post would be the assured loss of the entire country." He then ordered all men and officers to pack rations for fifteen days, and at three o'clock in the afternoon gave the order to march. The weather was hot and dry and they made only seven miles, though the woods were open and the going easy.

Next morning it was still hotter. "About 4 o'clock in the afternoon, having passed through two dangerous defiles, we arrived at a third where we were very vigorously attacked" — by eight hundred Senecas, according to Denonville, but the Senecas themselves said they numbered four hundred to four hundred and fifty, which is probably the more accurate figure. Even so, the ambush very nearly succeeded in panicking the Indians of the western brigade who were leading on the right and nearest the Seneca fire. The Ottawas fled at the first shot, but Tonty, Perrot, Duluth, and Durantaye rallied the rest and they held firm till Denonville, hurrying up with the main army, ambushed the ambuscade from the rear.

The Senecas had mistaken the vanguard for the whole French army; when they swept in to attack its rear they were themselves trapped. The battle in the heavy woods became confused, but suddenly the Senecas broke it off and, carrying their wounded, left the field. The French were so exhausted that they made camp on the battle site, watching their allies cutting up the bodies of dead Senecas to cook, and drinking their blood, a practice at which the Ottawas, who had returned to the field when the firing ceased, proved particularly savage.

Next day they moved on to the town, which they found burned, so Denonville ordered all the corn destroyed, both that standing in the fields and whatever they could find in caches. Then they moved on to the other three Seneca towns, repeating their destruction of the corn at each. They were ten days at the work and during that time they saw not a Seneca. The land, shimmering with heat waves, seemed empty of all life but themselves. At the end of their devastation, they took possession of the country formally for the king.

Denonville had no idea of hunting down the Senecas. His troops, gorging on green corn, were beginning to sicken, and on the twenty-fourth he withdrew the army to the lake. Once more entering their canoes and bateaux, they moved up the lake to the mouth of the Niagara, and here in the cool stir of air from the great river, on the point where the later version still stands, near the site of La Salle's two blockhouses, they built the first Fort Niagara. It was laborious work, for they had to float their logs along the shore from the east or over the river from the west and then work them up the steep bank, but in three days they had finished "a pretty good fort of four bastions, where we put two great guns and some pattareras, and built some cabins on the four sides of the square in the middle of it."

Their numbers were already thinning as they worked, for as soon as their wounded were well enough Tonty, Duluth, Durantaye, and Perrot started back to their posts with their increasingly nervous and impatient Indian allies. Denonville gave command of the fort to the Sieur de Troyes and left him one hundred men to garrison it, promising to send a shipload of supplies before winter. He himself then left for Montreal, from which he wrote the king's minister a full, but modest, account of his expedition on August 25. He left no doubt in Seignelay's mind, or his own, that it had been a successful one. But he was wrong, infinitely more wrong than he could guess.

His capture of the friendly Iroquois on Lake Ontario was bad enough; dispatching them to France to be slaves on the king's ships seemed to the Iroquois as immoral as hanging. The Onondagas were almost equally incensed at the way he had left Lamberville's life to their mercy. As for the Senecas, he had hurt but not destroyed them. Their towns could be rebuilt, they might go hungry but they would not starve because their Iroquois brothers would come to their assistance, but they were totally enraged against the French. As one Christian Mohawk said to Denonville: he had knocked down the wasp nests, but he had not killed the wasps.

Not only the Iroquois were stirred up: the English were furious over the capture of their trading flotillas, and Dongan angrily demanded the return of the captives. Denonville, still vibrant with what he believed to be the successful outcome of his campaign, replied that he would not release them since the English had interfered with the Iroquois whom he claimed as French subjects. Dongan's answer was to summon the Iroquois to a council at Albany, where he urged them to stop making war on the western tribes and instead form an alliance with them so that together they could drive all the French out of the west. The Iroquois were dubious, but when it came to the French in Canada they swore to fight them while they had but one man left. As for France's claim to the Iroquois country, Dongan asked Denonville why the French did not claim the Kingdom of China.

His hand had lately been strengthened by an order from King James which acknowledged the Iroquois as his subjects and took them under his protection. Dongan therefore sent four hundred and fifty infantry to Albany with a company of fifty horse, and himself spent the winter in the fort. There had been rumors that Denonville would attack Albany, and Dongan, his Irish up, was spoiling for a fight. From there he dispatched further messages to Quebec demanding payment for the trade goods seized on the Great Lakes and also the return of the Iroquois taken prisoners on Lake Ontario and condemned to the French galleys. When Denonville sent a Jesuit, François Vaillant, to negotiate these matters, Dongan informed him that there would never be peace with the Iroquois till Fort Niagara was abandoned.

The pressure on Denonville was becoming excessive. He did not know where to turn next. But suddenly word came from Versailles that he must keep on good terms with his vis-à-vis in New York, who in any case was about to be recalled, because the two monarchs were going to settle all these problems between themselves. From then on his correspondence with Dongan was correct, if stiffly formal. But when Dongan was superseded by Sir Edmund Andros in the summer of 1688, Denonville found little relief. By then, too, the Iroquois had launched on Canada the most dreadful single blow in her history.

Everything seemed to turn sour for Denonville in the spring of 1688. The garrison he had left at Fort Niagara the summer before had received their winter's provisions just before the freezing of the lake. The captain of the vessel, agitated by fear of being caught in the ice, merely dumped them on the shore and set sail straight back for Fort Frontenac. When the soldiers got their provisions into the fort, they found all of them uneatable. The tale of their winter is one of the grimmest in this book. They slowly starved; many died of the cold, for they ran out of firewood, and by then the Senecas were prowling like wolves at the edge of the woods. Scurvy attacked them. Their commandant died. When at last a war party of friendly Miamis showed up outside the palisade, and broke in when they got no reply to their yells, they found ten men, barely alive, too weak to leave their beds. About the same time, a spring supply ship arrived with reinforcements, but there seemed no point in staying. After some days of nursing, the sick were taken aboard and Fort Niagara was abandoned. The Senecas were getting their way, but they had not yet got their blood.

On August 5, 1689, they finally did. The night before had been a wild one of wind and rain and hail. Under cover of the storm fifteen hundred warriors paddled over Lake St. Louis and landed near the settlement of

Lachine, just above Montreal. Moving as silently as cats, they stationed themselves around the houses and at the break of day with a united war whoop began a massacre so ghastly that it left Canada stunned. Men, women, and children were killed without mercy. Two hundred were killed in a few minutes of insensate butchery and a hundred and twenty taken prisoner. Two hundred regular troops had camped about three miles away, but their commander was in Montreal six miles farther south to see Denonville, who with his wife had arrived from Quebec. By the time he returned to his command the slaughtering was over and the Iroquois had retired to some woods a mile and a half from the town, herding their prisoners before them and carrying their loot, which included a large supply of brandy. When the troops entered the town they found it littered with mutilated bodies and the tracks of the huge war party plainly leading toward the woods. The officer, Daniel d'Augier de Subercase, whose company had now been reinforced by some one hundred habitants and a few more soldiers from the garrisons of three small forts in the vicinity, resolved to follow and attack them. If he had been allowed to do so, he would undoubtedly have slaughtered a large number of the Iroquois, for by then most of them were drunk. But as he gave the command to march, a courier brought stringent orders from Denonville for him to fall back on Montreal with all his men to strengthen its garrison.

Denonville's nerve had broken. He was not to recover it in the next two months, and his last action before leaving Canada was to order the destruction of Fort Frontenac because he felt that its garrison was needed to strengthen the defenses of Montreal. Obviously he was ashamed to give the order, for he sent an officer secretly to its commandant. That officer, Philippe Clement Duvault, Sieur de Vallerenne, reported that he had followed his orders completely, throwing the cannon in the lake, scuttling the three barks belonging to the fort, setting fire to what would burn, and leaving a slow match burning in the magazine, which he had heard explode when he and his men had traversed eleven of the miles to Montreal. But either he had been too anxious to get away or his ears had deceived him into mistaking the pounding of his own heart for the explosion of the magazine, for when the Iroquois entered the fort a little afterward, they found a huge quantity of munitions and stores waiting for their taking.

In the low case to which Canada had fallen only one man seemed capable of putting it back on its feet. Frontenac was summoned to Versailles and ordered to proceed to Canada forthwith. He went with the comforting assurance that Louis had decided not to give credence to the charges that had been made against him. If he served the king as well as he had done previously, nothing more would be asked of him. Two ships of the royal navy at Rochelle were under orders to convey him at once to Quebec, for France and England were now at war, and Frontenac carried with him orders for the invasion and capture of the colony and city of New York.

The two navy ships and the forces then in Canada were considered strong enough if he struck at once. With a thousand regular troops and six hundred militia he would cross Lake Champlain and Lake George, march down the Hudson and take Albany by surprise, after which he would continue down the Hudson to New York where the two ships were to join him in the attack. The whole campaign should be concluded within a month. Boldness and speed were of the essence. The plan was not new. Avaugour had first suggested something like it. This time it had been presented to Louis by Denonville's second-in-command, Louis Hector de Callières. The king accepted it, largely because it was cheap and also because the capture of New York particularly appealed to him; and he added instructions of his own devising as to what should be done to its inhabitants.

All Catholics were to be allowed to retain their property and continue their lives undisturbed. Mechanics and artisans who might be useful in furthering public works should be retained as prisoners. All French Huguenot refugees were to be returned to France for justice. All other foreigners, men, women, and children, were to be sent to other colonies of the English. Officers and important persons capable of paying ransom must be kept in prison until they had paid up. New York, like Quebec, was to become an oasis of pure French Catholicism.

The cold war was a thing of the past. From now on France and England would come to grips in the struggle for the continent. Frontenac was, of course, entirely powerless in the shaken state of Canada to muster a force capable of carrying out Louis's plan, but he would devise his own means of making war. The plan, however, was sound in its use of the Champlain–Hudson Valley route as the strategic path to the conquest of the English colonies. In reverse, it was the historic route of Iroquois attack, and it would be the route used by the English, with Amherst's elaborations, to accomplish the fall of Canada.

Author's Note

THIS book is intended as a narrative of our early Colonial experience; it makes no pretension to formal scholarship, and for that reason I have not included a bibliography or notes. My debt to the *Jesuit Relations*, the *Documents Relating to the Colonial History of New York*, and the first five volumes of Parkman will be everywhere evident. I have relied on the same sources Parkman used; but I have made no attempt to uncover new material, though I have tried to read the old with a fresh eye; and I have reread the standard classic historians from the erratic Charlevoix through Fiske to Morison with renewed interest.

But I should like to acknowledge indebtedness to a handful of modern and relatively modern books. In the French scene, to Arthur T. Adams's *The Explorations of Pierre Esprit Radisson;* Bernard De Voto's *The Course of Empire;* Francis Xavier Talbot's *Saint among the Hurons;* Harold A. Innis's *The Fur Trade in Canada;* George T. Hunt's *The Wars of the Iroquois;* Grace Lee Nute's *Caesars of the Wilderness;* and to a book of essays by C. W. Colby, *Canadian Types of the Old Regime.*

On the English-Dutch stage I owe particular debts to Oscar Handlin's *The Americans;* Alden T. Vaughan's *New England Frontier;* Robert Greenhalgh Albion's *The Rise of New York Port;* Henry Christman's *Tin Horns and Calico;* David Maldwyn Ellis's *Landlords and Farmers in the Hudson Mohawk Region;* and Douglas E. Leach's stirring history of King Philip's War, *Flintlock and Tomahawk.*

INDEX

[505]

Manhattan, 11, 154, 159, 163, 164–165, 170, 172, 255, 275, 290. *See also* New Amsterdam; New York
Manitoulin Island, 415
Manning, Capt. John, 334
Marechkawieck tribe, 282
Maricourt, Paul Lemoine, Sieur de, 148, 427
Marlborough, Mass., 370, 374, 376, 377, 385–389
Marle, Sieur de, 476–477, 479
Marquette, Jacques (Père Marquette), 65, 107, 429–442
Martha's Vineyard, 145, 323
Martin, John, 229, 257
Maryland, 197, 276, 306, 335–336, 338–343, 347, 355
Mascouten tribe, 15, 415–418, 432, 433
Mason, Col. George, 356
Mason, Capt. John, 199–200, 204, 216, 219–221, 223, 319
Massachusett tribe, 209, 268
Massachusetts, 144, 160–170, 206, 218, 314, 381, 388, 391, 398; Council of, 143; General Court, 170, 201–203, 223, 271–272, 313, 316, 318–319, 401; population, 196; treatment of Quakers, 301; claim to Maine and New Hampshire, 319–320; commercial life, 322; march on Narragansetts, 381–384
Massasoit, 202, 209, 210, 364
Massé, Ennemond, 442
Matagorda Bay, 474–475, 478, 480
Mataouiriou tribe, 422
Mather, Cotton, 209, 224
Matsepe, N.Y., 288
Mattopoisett, 371
Maverick, Samuel, 312–313, 315–321, 326
May, Capt. Cornelius, 154, 157, 160, 162, 304
Mayflower (ship), 159, 209
Mayflower Compact, 159
Mayhew, Thomas, 145, 146
Mazarin, Cardinal, 43
McGregory, Maj., 491, 498
Medfield, Mass., 386
Megalopensis, Johannes, 146, 151
Melyn, Cornelius, 275–276, 282, 293–295, 297
Membré, Zenobius, 461, 467, 470, 471
Memecho, George, 374
Menameset, 385, 386
Ménard, René, 24, 98–99, 100, 105–107
Mendon, Mass., 370, 372, 386
Mennonites, 276, 396
Menominie tribe, 432, 487, 493
Meulles, Jacques de, 484, 486, 487, 490

Mézy, Augustin de Soffray, Chevalier de, 89, 93, 95, 112–115
Miami tribe, 415–418, 432–433, 439, 467, 469, 485, 493, 496
Mianotomo, 210–214, 217–220, 267–269, 381
Michaelius, Jonas, 168, 171, 172
Michigan, Lake, 32, 432, 439, 458, 471
Michilimackinac, 441–442, 460ff, 480, 486ff, 491, 493
Michilimackinac, Strait of, 430
Middleborough, Mass., 369
Milet (Jesuit missionary), 109
Milford, Conn., 276
Minqua (Mingo), tribe, 338
Minuit, Peter, 164, 166, 168, 171–173, 191, 198, 304, 306
Mississippi River, 33–34, 414, 428–429, 433, 471, 479
Missouri River, 434, 437
Mistassirinin tribe, 420, 423, 425
Mohawk tribe, 11, 12, 17–21, 24–25, 70, 132, 133, 136, 138, 143, 146, 147, 156, 183, 197–198, 327, 338, 354–355, 391–393, 405, 410, 415–418
Mohawk River, 6, 132
Mohegan tribe, 146, 212, 218, 220–223, 267–273, 378, 469
Mohican tribe, 10–12, 144, 156, 161, 165, 194, 197, 198, 204–205, 220, 290, 354–355
Monacan tribe, 240
Monk, William, Duke of Albemarle, 328
Monotto, 217, 223
Montagnais tribe, 7, 15, 67, 419–423
Montreal, 7, 47, 109–111, 405, 448–449, 466, 470
Moody, Lady Deborah, 276, 282
Moore, Henry, 186
Moranget, 475–477
Moravians, 146
Morrice, Sir William, 318
Morris, William, 161
Mosely, Capt. Samuel, 378, 380
Mount Hope, R.I., 365, 368, 370–380
Munsey tribe, 308
Murray, Brig. James, 5, 6

Nadorth, Samuel, 318
Nahawatkse, 102
Nansemond River, 343
Nantucket, 145, 323
Narragansett tribe, 146, 209–220, 267–273, 316–317, 365, 368–373, 380–384, 469
Nashoba tribe, 379
Nassau, Fort, 11, 154, 155, 156, 160, 162, 304, 307
Natick, Mass., 369

Villeray, Rouer de, 94–95, 97, 112, 114, 482
Vimont (Jesuit missionary), 12, 156; on brandy traffic, 72
Vincennes, La., 478
Virginia, 196, 224, 338; Charter of 1606, 196; export products, 251; Great Charter, 257–259; House of Burgesses, 257–258, 264, 347, 350, 356–357, 359; growth, 260; Good Friday massacre, 262–263; becomes Crown colony, 264; corruption, 348–350; life described, 350–352; taxes, 350–351; types of colonists, 352–353; Indian trouble, 354–357
Virginia Company, 337
Vriesendael, 275, 281, 282

Wabash River, 436
Wachusett, Mount, 387
Wadsworth, Capt. Samuel, 385
Wahunsonacock. *See* Powhatan
Wallabout Bay, 159–160, 167
Walloons, 158–160, 168, 197
Wampanoag tribe, 146, 202, 208–209, 364–366, 369, 373–374, 381, 385
Wampum Maker Indians, 133
Wamsutta. *See* Alexander
Wappineck tribe, 290
Wappinger tribe, 283
Washington, Col. John, 356
Washington Island, 462
Watertown, Mass., 200, 201, 206, 343, 387
Webster, Daniel, 189
Weckquaesgeck tribe, 278–280, 283, 290, 297
Wells, Me., 319
Werrowocomoco, 229, 232–234, 238
Westchester tribe, 281
Westchester, N.Y., 165, 170
West India Company. *See* Company of the West Indies (Dutch); Company of the West Indies (French)
Wessells, Maj., 183

Westminster, Treaty of, 324, 332
Weston, Thomas, 209–210
Wethersfield, Conn., 200, 206, 217
Weymouth, Mass., 210
Whalley, Edward, 322
Wheeler, Capt. Thomas, 374
Whitaker, Alexander, 343
Whitbourne, Capt. Richard, 336
White, John, 225–226
Wickford, R.I., 370, 372, 382
Willard, Maj. Simon, 376, 377
Willett, Marinus, 285
Willett, Thomas, 285
William II of Holland, 331
William of Orange, 332; and Mary, 401, 402
William (ship), 193, 194–195
William and Mary, College of, 204, 264
William & Nicholas (ship), 311
Williams, Roger, 196, 202, 216–217, 220, 268, 270, 287, 370
Williamsburg, Va., 362
Willis, Samuel, 143
Wilmington, Del., 191, 304
Wilson, John, 202, 203
Windsor, Conn., 198, 200, 204–206, 218, 272
Wingfield, Edward Maria, 229, 231, 235, 246
Winnipeg, 415
Winnipeg, Lake, 40
Winslow, Josiah, 369, 374, 381, 382–383
Winthrop, John, 143, 149–150, 167, 196, 198–199, 203, 267, 333, 372
Winthrop, John (the younger), 199, 314, 316
Winthrop, Capt. Waite, 372
Wisconsin River, 433
Wrentham, Mass., 386

Yeardley, Sir George, 256–257, 261
Yonkers, N.Y., 165, 297
York, Me., 319
Young, Henry, 376

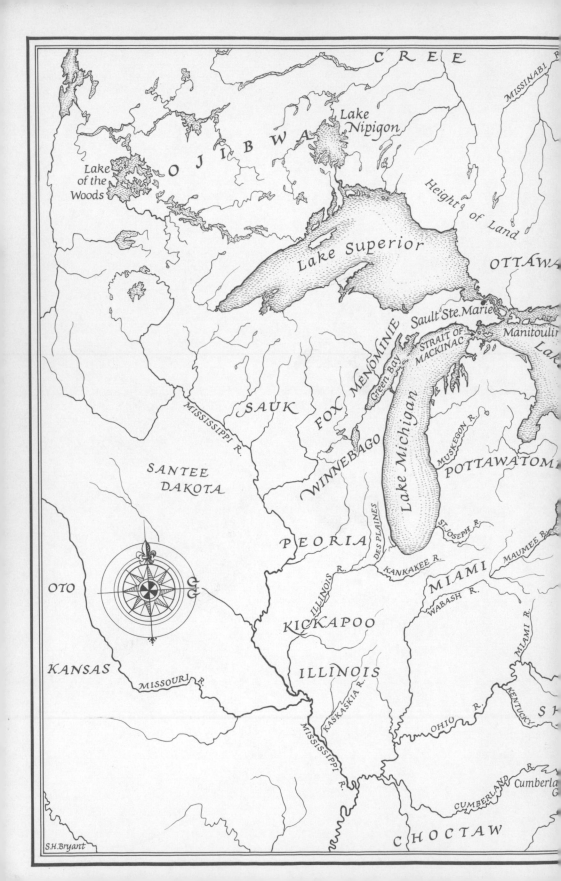